EMERGING PERSPECTIVES
ON
BUCHI EMECHETA

EDITED BY MARIE UMEH

Africa World Press, Inc.

P. O. Box 1892   P. O. Box 48
Trenton, New Jersey 08607   Asmara, ERITREA

Africa World Press, Inc.

P. O. Box 1892
Trenton, New Jersey 08607

P. O. Box 48
Asmara, ERITREA

Copyright © 1996 Marie Umeh

First Printing 1996

Book Design: Jonathan Gullery
Cover design: Carles J. Juzang

Library of Congress Cataloging-in-Publication Data

Emerging perspectives on Buchi Emecheta / edited by Marie Umeh.
   p. cm.
  Includes bibliographical references and index.
  ISBN 0-86543-454-9 (cloth : alk. paper). -- ISBN 0-86543-455-7
(paper : alk. paper)
    1. Emecheta, Buchi-Criticism and interpretation. 2. Women and
literature--Nigeria--History--20th century. 3.Nigeria--In
literature. I. Umeh, Marie.
    PR9387.9.E36Z66 1995
    823--dc20   95-10357
                                         CIP

DEDICATION

IN MEMORIAM

MARY ELIZABETH WILLIAMS-HINDS
(1900-1972)

AND

FLORA NWANZURUAHU NWAPA-NWAKUCHE
(1931-1993)

CONTENTS

NIGERIA

Produced by Laboratory for RS & GIS UNILAG Nigeria (1993)

Ibuza - Buchi Emecheta's ancestral home

Lagos State - Buchi Emecheta's place of birth

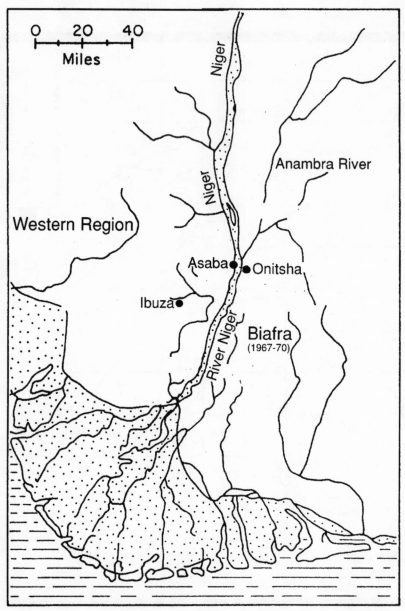

Mapping Buchi Emecheta's Nigerian World

FOREWORD

Margaret Busby

Women in Africa and in the African diaspora have a recognized preeminence in the oral tradition—orature: unscripted stories told by grandmothers have shaped the lives of countless generations. Nevertheless, acknowledgement in terms of the written word is not always forthcoming.

However, what is now regarded as "African Literature" (usually written in European languages) has more recent origins, dating from the 1950s when works such as Chinua Achebe's *Things Fall Apart* were published. But whereas male writers initially concentrated on the struggle against colonization by Western powers, women have in addition had to struggle against colonization by their own men and by those traditional attitudes that reserved formal education for males. The absence of women from most early anthologies of African writing speaks for itself. Only in the last two and a half decades have Black women writers based in Africa begun to receive recognition at all, let alone rightful acclaim and wide audiences in their lifetime.

One who deserved a far better fate is South African-born novelist and short-story writer Bessie Head (1937—86), who found neither peace of mind nor much acceptance before her untimely death.

In a personal letter dated June 1980, written to Professor Charles Sarvan of the University of Bahrain, she wrote: "My novels and I never came in from the cold. They remained in the village building up pathetic little rural industries and cooperatives in the hope that they would expand the world and open new doors. The books stayed with the people who were in the cold."[1] Another who was denied a hallowed career was Senegalese Mariama Bâ, whose brilliant first novel *Une si longue Lettre* (1980, translated as *So Long a Letter*) was the only book she saw published in her lifetime. Her only other novel, *Le Chante écarlate* 1983, (translated as *Scarlet Song*) appeared posthumously. But the honor of being the first Black African novelist to gain international reputation goes to Nigeria's late Flora Nwapa, whose unexpected death in 1993 we all still mourn. It was Nwapa who inspired Buchi Emecheta to follow in her footsteps as a writer. This is how Adah, Buchi's *alter ego* in *Second-Class Citizen* (1974), tells her husband about the manuscript of her first novel:

> She told Francis about *The Bride Price* in the evening. (178)
>
> Francis laughed, "Whatever was he going to hear next? A woman writer in his own house, in a white man's country?"
>
> "Well, Flora Nwapa is black and she writes," Adah challenged. "I have seen her books in all the libraries where I worked."
>
> Francis did not reply to this. He was not going to read Adah's rubbish and that was that. Adah was hurt badly, but she said nothing.(179) Her books might not be published until she was forty, but her first story had been completed. She could not go back now.[2]

That Buchi Emecheta herself did go on, and now inspires this varied collection of essays is no slight achievement, for the first step towards ensuring that our future writers receive the lifeblood of critical attention while they are still creating depends precisely on such serious consideration.

"Why is there no recognized female equivalent of Chinua Achebe, Wole Soyinka or Ngugi wa Thiong'o?" asks Adeola James in her 1990 collection of interviews with African women writers, *In Their Own Voices.*[3]

"Every artist thrives on controversy; so you are killing the writer if you don't even talk about her. Being ignored is worse than when you are writing trash about her," said Flora Nwapa, taking up a theme expounded on earlier by Ghanian writer Ama Ata Aidoo.[4] That Buchi Emecheta's work has been more successful than that of her foresisters is a phenomenon that must be placed in context. The better to appreciate the significance of Marie Umeh's tribute to Emecheta, we must consider the context in which other writers have struggled for recognition.

Ama Ata Aidoo—another pioneer who deserves wider celebration— believes that the question of the woman writer's voice being muted has to do with the position of women in society generally, that women writers are just receiving the writer's version of the general neglect and disregard that women in the larger society receive:

> [T]he assessment of a writer's work is in the hands
> of critics and it is the critics who put people on
> pedestals or sweep them under the carpet, or put
> them in a cupboard, lock the door and throw the key
> away. I feel that, wittingly or unwittingly, people
> may be doing this to African women writers. . . .
> Bessie Head died of neglect. So how is she going to
> be an Achebe? When nobody gives recognition to
> her as Bessie Head, as woman in her own right writing something relevant and meaningful?[5]

The role of critics in the fortunes of African women writers deserves fuller exploration elsewhere. But it is significant that, according to Florence Stratton, "Buchi Emecheta's literary upward mobility has been due largely to the attentions she has received from feminist critics,"[6] for male critics are frequently patronizing and legislative about women's writing, feels Nigerian poet and academic Molara Ogundipe-Leslie:

> Many feel the concerns of women are not serious
> enough since they are about the area of emotions
> and the private life. I wonder how we got the idea
> in colonized societies that only political themes are
> respectable. A cultural lag from colonial times perhaps. Great literature has always been about human
> emotions and the actions which spring from them.
> *Anna Karenina* is first and foremost a love story;

> *Crime and Punishment* is about the psychology of a
> young man in a specific situation. But no; these are
> not respectable themes in Africa.[7]

But is the African woman writer different from her counterparts
elsewhere in the world? Because of patriarchal arrangements of
African societies, publicly and privately, most women have even
less time and leisure than their Western counterparts to write, since
their time is often spent waiting on others and managing other people—their husbands, their children, older relatives and visitors—
in addition to managing their own lives. Where a man can withdraw
into his study to write, a woman usually cannot. Ogundipe-Leslie
maintains:

> African society may welcome women writers, but
> it would certainly be shocked if they handled cer-
> tain subjects on which Western writers have now
> gained the freedom to be vocal. A woman will prob-
> ably be expected to write mainly for children or to
> be edifying in general, since the male-folk seem to
> feel the responsibility for the nation's morals rests
> solely on her shoulders. She is falsely grandified
> with this task while all around she is discriminated
> against, excluded from real power, exploited at all
> levels and derided most of the time in the society.[8]

Expanding on questions she posed in her 1980s article, "The
Female Writer and Her Commitment," Ogundipe-Leslie asks: "Is
there anything that recommends the female writer more particularly to this socially educative role? Does the female writer have
any moral prerogative to point the way to others and educate the
spirit? And why?" She adds: "We are closer to human suffering
through the experiences of motherhood and womanhood. We gain
more compassionate hearts thereby and history has shown that
women demonstrate more probity and commitment in situations
of responsibility."[9]

This resonates with statements that Buchi Emecheta, too, has
made on several occasions. Indeed, at a Rwanda benefit evening
hosted by Black writers in London, in September 1994, at which I
was a participant, Emecheta herself suggested that the way to
address the ailments of many African nations would be to put
women in positions of power.

Any evaluation of women's contribution to African literature must take into consideration the proportionate number of women historically given the opportunity to contribute or to function in such circles. There is nothing inherently male about literary creativity, yet constraints of role, status, and financial independence still conspire to keep even the best-educated women from realizing their full potential and reaching prominence equal with that of men. As 'Zulu Sofola, one of Nigeria's few female playwrights, has said: "Whatever a woman achieves in her discipline or profession, she achieves it against plenty of odds because a woman's life is more burdened and confused. . . . So that the woman who finally pulls through is virtually ten men in one."[10]

African writers are now seeking a respect and recognition that is long overdue. Praise is surely due to those who despite the odds have made it into print. "Women have no mouth," goes a traditional proverb from the Beti of Cameroon.[11] But an ever increasing number of women enriching literary history gives the lie to this. Clearly the voicelessness of African women is becoming a thing of the past.

In this context, the outspokenness of Buchi Emecheta's writing has shown the way. She can be seen as "both a disruptive and a cohesive force within the contemporary African literary tradition," firmly situated within a female tradition which she celebrates, from which position she launches an attack on the male tradition.[12] As Lauretta Ngcobo puts it:

> Buchi Emecheta knows the hidden feelings of African women and she voices them as perhaps no one has done before. Where the African woman has made a virtue of silent suffering, Emecheta exposes the conspiracy, insisting that female complacency and the unquestioning acceptance of male domination do not constitute the quintessence of femininity.[13]

When I first happened upon Buchi Emecheta's writing in the early 1970s, I was in no doubt about the importance of making her personal experiences—transmuted into autobiographical literature—known to the British society in which we both found ourselves: they were experiences shared by many Black women who had not had the stamina and signal determination Buchi possesses to speak out. I was able to witness at first hand the dedication and effort she put into combining her role as a single parent in a frequently uncaring society; and as her editor and publisher for over a decade, until the mid 1980s, it became my mission—and a satisfying one—to ensure that her view of the world was disseminated as widely as possible. It was never likely to be easy, for her as an African woman writer and in a different way for me as an African woman publisher—an even rarer breed, whose ranks Buchi herself was to join by her setting up her own press (Ogwugwu Afo), as Flora Nwapa and a few other women such as Asenath Bole Odaga in Kenya and Aminata Sow-Fall in Senegal had also done. This present volume testifies to the fact that her words continue to be heard. A signal triumph.

The final word should go to Buchi Emecheta herself, writing in her autobiography, *Head Above Water* (1986):

> As for my survival for the past twenty years in England, from when I was a little over twenty, dragging four cold and dripping babies with me and pregnant with a fifth one—that is a miracle. And if for any reason you do not believe in miracles, please start believing, because my keeping my head above water in this indifferent society, which is probably succeeding in making me indifferent and private too, is a miracle.[14]

NOTES

1. Published in *Wasafiri* 12 (Autumn 1990).
2. *Second-Class Citizen*. New edition, African Writers Series (Oxford/Portsmouth, N.H.: Heinemann, 1994), pp. 178—9.
3. Adeola James, ed. *In Their Own Voices: African Women Writers Talk*. (London: James Currey, 1990).
4. Flora Nwapa, interviewed in James, *Voices*, p. 114.
5. Ama Ata Aidoo, interviewed in James, *Voices*, pp. 11—12. Aidoo also notes that "criticism becomes a major business, it is the going thing, and not even half the critics are Africans. Whereas African literature can be added to only by Africans, African criticism is like meat out there in the market place, with everybody dragging at it, including people who do not care for Africans or what they are writing" (ibid.).
6. Florence Stratton, *Contemporary African Literature and the Politics of Gender* (London: Routledge, 1994), p. 109.
7. Molara Ogundipe-Leslie, interviewed in James, *Voices*, pp. 72—3.
8. *Ibid.*, p.67
9. *Ibid.*, p. 71
10. 'Zulu Sofola, interviewed in James, *Voices*, pp. 144.
11. Quoted in Mineke Schipper, ed., *Unheard Words: Women and Literature in Africa, the Arab World, Asia, the Caribbean and Latin America*. (London/New York: Allison & Busby, 1985), p.20.

12. Stratton, *Contemporary African Literature*, p. 132.
13. Lauretta Ngcobo, ed., *Let It Be Told: Black Women Writers in Britain* (London: Pluto Press, 1987), p. 10.
14. Buchi Emecheta, *Head Above Water*, African Writers Series, New edition, (Oxford/Portsmouth, N.H.: Heinemann, 1994), p.5.

ACKNOWLEDGEMENTS

Special thanks go to colleagues who read drafts of the introduction to this collection of essays or who read the essays themselves, making suggestions that affected the final product. For their invaluable contributions I would like to thank Tuzyline Jita Allan, Gregory Darling, Sherry A. Gibson, Oladipo Ogundele, Yvonne Purdie, Nancy J. Schmidt, Shirley Schnitzer and Christine Stacco. I am most grateful to my friends Ezenwa-Ohaeto, Tunde Fatunde, and Shivaji Sengupta for writing introductions to various sections of the book.

Among my many advisors and colleagues, the following were of special help in the development and completion of this project: Susan Gubar, coordinator of the 1991 NEH Summer Seminar, Feminist Criticism and Female Literary Traditions in the First Half of the Twentieth Century, in which I was a participant; Edward Davenport, coordinator of the New York Circle for Theory of Literature and Criticism; Chikwenye Okonjo Ogunyemi, who generously shared her expertise in womanist literary theory; and Brenda F. Berrian for her enthusiasm, her sisterhood, and her professionalism. For both emotional and financial support, I wish to thank my husband, Davidson C. Umeh, Azubuike and Ndidi Ezeife, Rebecca Boostrom, Joan Hoffman, Marvie Brooks, Obioma Nnaemeka, and Tess Onwueme.

Finally, I am indebted to my ancestors for their blessings, as well as to Akuaza, Ikechukwu, Uchenna, Chizoba, and Ugochukwu for being marvelous children—a circumstance that allowed me to spend much of my time collecting data and completing research away from home with peace of mind.

INTRODUCTION
(En)Gendering African Womanhood: Locating Sexual Politics in Igbo Society and Across Boundaries

Marie Umeh

> Marriage should be a play not a fight.
> — Chinua Achebe, *Things Fall Apart*

Buchi Emecheta is one of Africa's most acclaimed women writers. Bernth Lindfors, in his empirical survey, "Big Shots and Little Shots of the Anglophone African Literary Canon," places her in a tetrarchy of the most influential of contemporary African women writers.[1] Since 1972 she has been able to support herself and her five children (one of whom died)[2] through writing books, which have been translated into fourteen languages, among them Dutch, French, German, and Swedish. She has published thirteen novels, three autobiographical works, four children's books, and a collection of photographs. Her novels include *The Bride Price* (1976), *The Slave Girl* (1977), *The Joys of Motherhood* (1979), *Destination Biafra* (1982), *Double Yoke* (1982), *Naira Power* (1982), *The Rape of Shavi* (1983), *A Kind of Marriage* (1986), *Gwendolen* (1989) a.k.a. *The Family* (1990), and *Kehinde* (1994). Her autobiographical works consist of *In the Ditch* (1972) and *Second-Class Citizen* (1974), reprinted together in 1983 as *Adah's Story* (1983), and *Head Above Water: An Autobiography* (1986). *Our Own Freedom* (1981) is a book of photographs of Black women. Her children's books are *Titch the Cat* (1979), *Nowhere To Play* (1979), *The Moonlight Bride* (1980), and *The Wrestling Match* (1980). Three plays—*Juju Landlord* (1975), *A Kind of Marriage* (1975), and *Family Bargain* (1986)—and numerous essays published in anthologies, scholarly journals, newspapers, and magazines in Africa, Australia, Europe, and the United States have added to her stature. In 1992, Fairleigh Dickinson University, in Madison, New Jersey, awarded her an honorary Doctor of Literature degree, to name only one of her many distinguished awards.

The novels of Buchi Emecheta reflect what Kate Millet calls "sexual politics," the patriarchal principle by which males dominate females and elders dominate the young (37). According to Emecheta, Igbo society embodies the principle of male dominance and female subordination. Emecheta's women for the most part are sacrificed at the altar of a male-oriented society, and men exploit the sex/gender system to maintain male dominance. In fact, Emecheta's reputation in world letters as a major voice in African woman's liberation rests on her protest against the victimization of women in Ibuza society and, by extension, in all societies. Her poetic rendition of "wives at war," to borrow Flora Nwapa's phrase, has earned her a reputation as Africa's "most sustained and vigorous voice of direct, feminist protest."[3] Femi Ojo-Ade asserts that Emecheta's "war cry" is nothing more than her conversion of personal problems into a public crusade and as such bodes ill for African society (21). But Ojo-Ade's trivialization of an African woman writer's *cri de coeur* is nothing new. His dismissal of the legitimacy of her personal experience betokens the typical male attitude toward women's struggle for self-actualization and recognition outside the domestic sphere. Symbolic clitoridectomy[4] —the effacement of women through cultural norms such as polygamy, son preference, and wife inheritance—occurs daily in African women's lives and is recorded in their oral and written literature. Emecheta's unique contribution to world letters lies in her commitment to the representation of women's life stories in order to draw attention to the inegalitarian gender and class relations that cut across racial and geographical boundaries.

EMECHETA'S LIFE STORY

Buchi Emecheta's struggle to achieve parity with men both for herself and for women the world over began early in her own life, when her parents sent her younger brother Adolphus to school and kept her at home because she was a girl. However, the young daughter of Jeremy and Alice Emecheta would not accept the secondary status her parents tried to force upon her. One afternoon, acting on impulse, she paid a visit to the Methodist School where a Sierra Leonian neighbor, Mr. Cole, taught. This action, which signified her desire for a Western education, made her parents realize that she was unwilling to be treated as a non-entity, to be consigned to marginality. They felt they had no choice but to enroll her in her brother's school.

Unfortunately, as with many of her novelistic characters, Emecheta was separated from her biological parents very early in life. When she was nine years old, her father died following a brief illness; shortly thereafter, her mother was "inherited" (in keeping with African custom) by her dead husband's brother. Consequently, Buchi was sent to live with her mother's cousin in Lagos, where she was treated more like a servant than a relative. Arrangements were made for her younger brother to live with their father's brother in another part of Lagos.

Fatherless, and estranged from her mother, brother, and paternal relatives, Buchi came to the early realization that no one was available to provide for her basic needs for love, protection, direction, and understanding. Finding no earthly beings to guide her through life, she turned inward for sustenance and direction. That force within her, which she refers to as "The Presence," did not fail her. It was this "presence" that prompted her to appropriate two shillings from the family's food money to pay for a scholarship application and entrance examination to high school. This was her first important act toward self-actualization despite all the odds against her. Emecheta won that four-year scholarship to the prestigious Methodist Girls' High School, where she found herself in the company of some of the best students in the nation and studied under Nigeria's finest expatriates and indigenous teachers. It was at Methodist Girls' that her imagination was stirred to entertain desires that were "unnatural" for a girl, such as the dream of going to the University of Ibadan. When her aspiration for further self-improvement was not forthcoming, she took the next best option. She selected a young man, Sylvester Onwordi, whom she had met at school and who appeared to be ambitious, as a marriage partner. His family, however, was in no position to pay the bride price of 500 pounds that her mother and relatives demanded. So, to her family's great disappointment, Emecheta eloped with the man of her choice.

Her early married life was a happy one: she found a good job at the American Embassy in Lagos, and she gave birth to two children. In 1961 her husband went to London to study accounting while she remained behind to work and save her money so that she could join him later.

In London, where three more children were born, bad family planning and estrangement from relatives, among other factors, put a strain on the marriage. The final blow descended when Emecheta's husband burned the manuscript of her first book, *The Bride Price*,[5] because he thought it would shame his family. As soon as she had saved enough money, Emecheta fled from their flat, taking her five children with her.

Sheer defiance against all odds enabled her and the children to survive and succeed. While raising Chiedu, Ikechukwu, Chukwuemeka, Obiajulu, and Chiago alone, Emecheta enrolled in the Department of Sociology at London University. By the time she had earned Bachelor's and Master's degrees, she had published three novels and two plays. The rest is herstory.

CONFRONTING FEMALE SUBJUGATION

Emecheta's treatment of sexual politics in her society is grounded in Igbo women's protest against retrogressive cultural norms, such as clitoridectomy, women as baby-machines, the prioritizing of boys at the expense of girls, and widow inheritance. By focusing on women's issues, Emecheta exposes oppressive relationships that are sanctioned by myths and customs, such as the rigid sex-role socialization practices that are denounced in the following song in Ifi Amadiume's study, *Afrikan Matriarchal Foundations*:

> Is it any shame if we do not marry?
> Is it any shame if we wish to marry a young man?
> Is it any shame if we will not lie with a man? (84)

The rebellion against female oppression in these lyrics mirrors African women's dissatisfaction with cultural prescriptions that bars women from exploring fields, both public and private, outside the domestic realm. Underlying this lament is opposition to the double standard that allows the male sexual freedom while consigning women to socially prescribed roles.

The "pounding song" below, chosen from Margaret Busby's anthology, *Daughters of Africa*, is another example of female resistance against "otherness":

> A shared husband I don't want!
> I want my own
> Who looks on proudly as I pound,
> Not somebody else's
> Who when I pound
> Turns his back on me!
> I want a beautiful child
> Who sleeps on a mattress
> In a house with a wooden door! (8)

The speaker in this traditional song is rebelling against customs in her society that work against individual happiness and fulfillment for a woman. The attitude expressed here is unequivocally anti-polygamous, contrary to the tendency by African male writers to romanticize polygamy. The song also expresses a class consciousness, a desire for material possessions that enhance life and contribute to one's total well-being.

In her autobiographical works, *Adah's Story* and *Head Above Water*, Buchi Emecheta records her own dissatisfactions with marriage, which eventually brought about her permanent separation from her spouse. She observes that her marriage ended in much bitterness primarily because of her husband's disregard for her artistic development, culminating in the burning of her manuscript *The Bride Price*, *In the Ditch* and *Second-Class Citizen*, jointly published as *Adah's Story*, make the point that mutual respect between male and female is an important ingredient for lasting wedlock. The pain and frustration of African women who, like herself, yearn for sensitivity in their relationship with partners but hardly ever get it, is a constant in Emecheta's art.

While Emecheta portrays some of her women, such as Akunna, Nnu Ego, and Ma Blackie, in bondage, many of her characters transcend their "nervous conditions." Whereas Nnu Ego in *The Joys of Motherhood* attains feminist consciousness only after her premature death at the age of forty-five, Kehinde, in the novel of the same name, immediately recognizes her "second-class" status within her polygamous household and takes action. She shares her psychological torture with her friend, Moriammo, who helps to liberate her. Not only does Moriammo send her an air-ticket to return to London to start life anew, but she also gives her the following invaluable advice: "Don't let fear of what people will say stop you from doing what your *chi* wants" (100). So, eventually, Kehinde takes control of her own body and redirects her life outside of the limiting definitions of patriarchally controlled womanhood.

Faithful to the realities of African women in Ibuza society, Emecheta shows how African women make sisterhood work for them when the men fail to live up to their promises. As Ifi Amadiume observes, in her study of matriarchal societies in Igboland, "Men incessantly sought to control women and their services and succeeded more often than not. In Igbo societies where they did not succeed completely, women combined power with autonomous organizations" (84).

African women are well aware that they can fight back if and when they choose to exert their rights. Judith Van Allen describes Igbo women's traditional political institutions, in which women exert control over their lives and men can do nothing about it:

> "Sitting on a man" or a woman, boycotts and strikes were the women's main weapons. To "sit on" or "make war on" a man involved gathering at his compound, sometimes late at night, dancing, singing scurrilous songs which detailed the women's grievances against him . . . . Although this could hardly have been a pleasant experience for the offending man, it was considered legitimate and no man would consider intervening.(45)

When Maria Ubakanma, the heroine of the novel *A Kind of Marriage*, learns of her husband's clandestine second wife and children, she nevertheless decides to stay with him. This situation brings to mind the proverb "It is only one's child that keeps a wife in the house of a wicked husband." Maria remains in Christian, holy wedlock with Charles, but on her own terms. She informs Charles, "I will keep my income separate from now on . . . I will help you look after your new children, but not with my money. Another thing, that woman is not coming to live with us in Lagos.

You met her here, so she is your Ibusa wife" (47). Maria knows how to sit on her man, a stratagem of the women before her, to save face and respect and maintain a shred of dignity for herself under debilitating circumstances.

INFLUENCES ON EMECHETA'S ART

As the two folk songs quoted earlier indicate, Emecheta is not the first African griotte (storyteller) to speak out against male dominance in African society. In fact, Emecheta attributes her first-hand knowledge of African women's struggle for selfhood to the Ibuza tradition of storytelling. In an interview with Oladipo Ogundele, she acknowledges the Ibuza griottes whose stories fed her literary imagination:

> My [writing] style is more like my storytelling . . . Nigeria is a land full of stories. Every time I am there, I always come in contact with something new. I returned a few months ago and I am already digesting my experiences there to see how I can fit them into another story. The way I recount things that happen comes from the way we speak in our part of Nigeria.[6]

To the griottes who exposed her to the tradition of storytelling she showed her gratitude by naming her publishing company "Ogwugwu Afor," i.e., "ancestral staff," in honor of her family's ancestral goddess.[7] Not only Igbo culture but the oral traditions of Yoruba, Hausa, and Itsekiri also figure in Emecheta's work and account for her "capturing the voices of the ancients."

Another influence on Emecheta has been the female grassroots discourse in Africa with which she is so familiar. Daughters' and wives' village organizations often provide opportunities for women to verbally air their grievances and to take action against adverse situations through a united women's front. The Nigerian novelist Elechi Amadi, in his novel *Estrangement*, makes this point. The poet and gender theorist Molara Ogundipe-Leslie, in an interview with Adeola James, also credits the women folk with having power because they use autochthonous survival tactics. Emecheta's women often rebel in similar fashion against oppressive social and cultural practices.

In addition to listening as a child in Ibuza to the stories of her "Big Mother" (her father's big sister, Nwakwaluzo Ogbueyin),

Emecheta also learned to listen as an adult to women in the diaspora. During one of her speaking engagements in New York, Emecheta informed the students in my class: "I gave a lecture at Sussex and a number of girls came to my room afterwards. Eight out of ten had been sexually abused. None of them had ever told. They said, 'How can I tell on my father? It would be too humiliating.'"[8] In line with these disclosures, *Gwendolen*, Emecheta's eleventh novel, is the story of a number of women who as children were sexually abused by their fathers or male guardians.

Of no less importance, Flora Nwapa, Nigeria's first African woman writer of international repute, influenced Buchi Emecheta. Florence Stratton, in her book *Contemporary African Literature and the Politics of Gender,* contends that Emecheta regards Nwapa as "the mother of a female tradition in [Nigerian women's] fiction" (119). Stratton points to the fact that Emecheta uses Nwapa as her role model in *Second-Class Citizen* and makes the heroine of *The Joys of Motherhood*, Nnu Ego, a goddess similar to the lake goddess, Uhamiri, in Nwapa's novels (119).

Apart from acknowledging her literary foremothers and their role in her artistic development, Emecheta admitted, in an interview with Davidson and Marie Umeh at the University of Calabar in Nigeria in 1980, where she was a visiting professor, that her British education has exerted considerable influence on her writing in that both her attitude and her language are very English (21). At the same time, she added, "The Bible has influenced all my work. I like its simplicity. If I feel that I'm losing touch with my style, I always go back to The Bible, the King James edition" (21).

Craig Tapping has noted yet another source for Emecheta's writings: "*In The Ditch* and *Second-Class Citizen* are in the Kate Millet influenced mainstream of feminist European literature—and both Kate Millet and Edna O'Brien are admitted references and inspirations in Emecheta's works" (179).[9] Tapping goes on to say, "I learned that in her final year as a sociology student, Emecheta studied Kate Millet's *Sexual Politics,* an ideological examination of the position of women in a patriarchal capitalist society" (179).

Elsewhere Emecheta informs us that the women's movement in the West has had a great impact on her success as a writer. In an interview with Adeola James, she declared that the feminist movement "has helped in bringing women out of Africa. For example, the feminist movement in England brought Flora Nwapa and Ama Ata Aidoo here recently. At various conferences they always make sure that Black women are well represented" (43).

Yet Emecheta is supremely aware that there are factors other than gender oppression that work against African women's attainment of self-actualization and empowerment nationally and internationally. She understands that sociopolitical differences separate African women cross-culturally from women in other societies despite their shared second-class status.[10] That is what she means when she says, in her widely cited essay, "Feminism with a small 'f'," "I chronicle the little happenings in the lives of African women I know. I did not know that by doing so, I was going to be called a feminist. But if I am now a feminist then I am an African feminist with a small f" (175).

Finally, Emecheta's literary achievements are indebted to her contacts with women the world over. As she states in an interview with Jussawalla and Dasenbrock: "My friends are not just friends from Africa anymore. My friends are those who are going through the same experience. They don't have to be African, and they don't have to be black. I've found that as I get older and I stay longer, I may have something more in common with you . . . than with my sister in Nigeria . . . . I'm just a citizen of the world" (96-97). In short, Emecheta utilizes the voices and life stories not only of African women but also of Afro-Caribbean and European women to scrutinize and record the quotidian experiences of women in male-dominated societies. Emecheta's books and essays, in sum, reflect a unique synthesis of ancestral voices, the life stories of other people, introspection, confrontation with her various environments, and inspiration from feminist writers and theorists. As Carol Boyce Davies, in *Black Women, Writing and Identity: Migrations of the Subject*, asserts:

> For the many Black women writers whom we read in English or French or Portuguese, a variety of boundary crossing must occur. English or French or Portuguese become indispensable for the writer who wants to reach a larger community. And for the women who tell their stories orally and want them told to a world community, boundaries of orality and writing, of geography and space, engender fundamental crossings and re-crossings.(20)

EMECHETA'S PLACE IN CONTEMPORARY NIGERIA

The "Aba Women's War of 1929" was an historical reality that must have fed Emecheta's imagination.[11] Her female militants, Debbie Ogedemgbe and Adah, are good fighters and survivors. Unfortunately, it was after this powerful rebellion by Igbo women against the British taxation of their properties that the colonial administration banned traditional political associations by declaring them illegal. Women's organizations accordingly lost their vitality and their capacity to mobilize and exact retribution when women were abused. Van Allen writes: "The British also weakened women's power by outlawing 'self-help' —the use of force by individuals or groups to protect their own interests by punishing wrongdoers. This action made 'sitting on' anyone illegal, thereby depriving women of one of their best weapons to protect wives from husbands, markets from rowdies, or coco yams from cows" (178).

While the British removed legitimacy from women's traditional political institutions, they did nothing to help Igbo women move into modern official establishments. Passive, Christian wives and mothers, not Amazons, is what they had in mind for African women. Apolitical market women's associations, where market prices and trade were the topics of discussion, replaced women's political influence at general meetings and village assemblies. However, despite the disruption of women's access to female empowerment when the British intruded in African village affairs, all was not lost. The spirit of the ancestors through the power of the word kept women in touch with their foremothers' wit. In fact, women's associations in Nigeria today, such as WIN (Women in Nigeria), formed in 1982, and the Better Life Program for the Rural Women under the leadership of Mrs. Maryam Babangida, the wife of the former President of Nigeria, General Ibrahim Babangida (1985-1993), are extensions of traditional daughters and wives' associations. Both programs aim to protect women from domestic oppression and political "exclusionary practices." Pat Okoye attests to the effectiveness of Nigeria's Better Life Program:

> Traditionally, women have no right to ownership of land. It is culturally believed that the woman has no *locus standi* in matters related to land. . . . However, through public enlightenment mounted by the Better Life Programme [sic], which has created an immense awareness among the rural women of their rights and responsibilities and the need to wake up and make their own contributions to

xxxii

national development, the women are becoming more self-confident and so now have a positive self-image. They now consider it proper and so make bold to ask for large expanses of land from their traditional rulers in particular and the men in general to enable them to make their own contribution to the agricultural development of our dear country.(51)

However, these recent advances in African women's status are largely a form of tokenism. Women's participation in the existing halls of power is yet to become a reality. Thus the violation of women's humanity at most levels of Nigerian society continues to assert itself, making a mockery of the Nigerian constitution's edict that every citizen shall have equality of rights, obligations and opportunities before the law (3). Indeed, Emecheta is right on target in her consistent, impassioned attack on female victimization and deprivation in the face of male self-actualization and attendant abuse of power. The steady mapping of female duress in the media as well as in contemporary African writing demonstrates the need for a counterrevolution not only in words but also at state and national levels of government. Among other things, the formulation and practice of clear and definite government policies in the protection of women is needed to improve the lives of present and future generations of Nigerians. For example, if the Nigerian Government had pursued progressive legislative policies which supported women's issues, as well as working-class and peasant interests, *WIN (Women In Nigeria)* would not have had to prosecute the father and the husband of the thirteen-year-old girl who died after the husband, whom the father had chosen for her against her will, took an axe to her legs for successive attempts to escape from him.[12] Certainly this is Aku-nna's story in *The Bride Price*, the novel that Emecheta's husband burned. In fact, as Pat Okoye rightly points out, if Nigeria had good intentions towards its female kith and kin, Nigerian women would not have had to wait twenty-five years after their country's independence from foreign rule to hear from one of its military administrators that "there is enough space in front. Allow women, who have been selected on their individual merits, to come to the forefront and make their contributions to national development" (108).

There can be no question that the "politics of gender" has to cease in order for the collective struggle against the real enemies—

social injustice and human degradation—to take place around the world. Buchi Emecheta raises the consciousness of many of her readers to move toward genuine power sharing between males and females, so that living and loving together may be fun and empowering rather than cruel and crippling. As Emecheta says in her autobiographical work, *In The Ditch*, "Love is like a living thing. It has to be fed, nurtured and even pampered to weather times" (58). Micere Mugo adds that reciprocity, two entities mutually giving and taking unselfishly, makes all the difference. Her poem, "Look how rich we are together," celebrates that concept:

> Look how rich we are
> together now!
> Hold here feel
> how my heart dances with sheer joy
> listen to that new rhythm you have created
> those thrilling, caressing blood currents
> that flow through my whole being
> bringing home a million messages
> telling me how I truly belong. (38)

Perhaps there is also something to learn from the poetry of Chimalum Nwankwo, an unyielding proponent for embracing the basic pragmatics of Igbo culture for the mediation of our various crises. Nwankwo's poem, "Man to Woman," advocates more sharing, more playfulness, more reciprocity and a reduction of those rigidities which constitute the bane of many relationships. There is a suggestion that meaningful triumph can only emanate from that dualistic base that is capital in Igbo community and its cosmology:

> The sums of love run no totals
> On the great road
> Toward the aerial zone
> Winners spar in padded gloves
> On the great road
> Toward the aerial zone
> Formations change like lightning streaks
> Passions melt like clouds in the rain
> Or grumbling thunder from a spent sky
> No dancers dance for shining gold
> No puppy wrestles for sweet curtain calls
> But for dustgrain on life's palate

The great audience waits at the flowered gate
With no fronded arches no streaming buntings
No blazing colours or fiery anthems
The great audience is at the flowered gate
With showers of stars in black and white
Burning bright at the aerial zone.(68)

Cooperation, honesty and commitment are worthy attributes that should rule our lives rather than competition, power, and status. As the elders say, "if a man sees a snake and a woman kills it, it doesn't matter as long as the snake is killed." This is the attitude that will transform Africa from the status of a pawn to a powerful player in global affairs. This is the essence of Emechetian poetics.

Certainly, the sense of community looms large in Emecheta's *oeuvre* and is reflected in the author's inclusion of a multiplicity of female and male voices in resistance to violence against women and in search of a new world order. In Emechetian feminist discourse, the political is not limited to the personal. She proposes that "what's good for my village is good for the world."[13] As Chandra Mohanty reminds us, "we take ourselves seriously only when we go 'beyond' ourselves, valuing not just the plurality of the difference among us but also the massive presence of the [d]ifference that our recent planetary history has installed" (40).

Having herself suffered "otherness" in both African and European environments, Emecheta depicts the life stories and concerns of women from different classes, regions, and ethnic backgrounds to engender balance between males and females and all people. By advocating global feminism as a powerful form of resistance against sexism and racism, Emecheta constructs a liberating model for female solidarity and cultural transformations across differences in her multivoiced characters.

AN OVERVIEW OF THE ESSAYS

PART ONE, entitled "Igbo Women and Culture," delineates the background and cultural setting of the author and examines her attempt to give the African woman a "voice of her own" in world letters by creating realistic portraits of Igbo women. Theodora Akachi Ezeigbo, in "Tradition and the African Female Writer: The Example of Buchi Emecheta," argues that although Emecheta in her novels points to male oppression and social injustices against women, there is enough evidence, in those same novels, of rich and influential women, such as Ona in *The Joys of Motherhood* and

Ma Palagada in *The Slave Girl*, who exploit and manipulate the existing systems in their society to carve out a secure and healthy place for themselves. Susan Arndt, in "Buchi Emecheta and the Tradition of *Ifo*: Continuation and Writing Back," demonstrates through a study of Igbo folklore the ways in which Emecheta questions and then rewrites Igbo folk tales, which depict Igbo women as ne'er-do-wells and *femme fatales*. Rebecca Boostrom, in "Nigerian Legal Concepts in Buchi Emecheta's *The Bride Price*," argues that Akunna's refusal to submit to a marriage against her will was in line with modern trends and changes in the British law courts of her day. Therefore, it was unnecessary for the author to kill her heroine to show how patriarchal traditions dominate the psyche of Igbo women. Florence Stratton, in "The Shallow Grave: Archetypes of Female Experience in African Fiction," contends that in Emecheta's novels *The Slave Girl* and *The Joys of Motherhood*, the shallow grave, a metaphor for living burials, suicidal impulses, and madness, provides a paradigm for the female experience in Africa. Through her interpretation of these two novels, Stratton demonstrates how female human potential, according to Emecheta, is more often than not buried in a narrow definition of her sex. Tom Spencer-Walters, in "Orality and Patriarchal Dominance in Buchi Emecheta's *The Slave Girl*," examines Emecheta's skillful utilization of elements of oral traditions in order to demonstrate the preeminence of patriarchy in Igbo society. His essay focuses on Emecheta's aesthetic vision of a society rife with contradictions and ambiguities in gender relationships while tenaciously clinging to the very traditions that make these anomalies possible.

In **PART TWO**, "(Re)Visions of Female Empowerment," Nancy Topping Bazin explores the "exclusionary practices" reflected in the thematic preoccupations of Emecheta's novels. In "Venturing into Feminist Consciousness: Two Protagonists from the Fiction of Buchi Emecheta and Bessie Head," Bazin argues that both of Emecheta's protagonists, Nnu Ego and Adaku, in *The Joys of Motherhood* achieve feminist consciousness, an awareness of power asymmetry in a particular community, which allows them to dissolve gender inequities that elide their humanity and right to self-determination. On the other hand, Ezenwa-Ohaeto, in "Replacing Myth With Myth: The Feminist Streak in Buchi Emecheta's *Double Yoke*," is critical of Emecheta's attempts to present a corrected view of the female image in literature. He concludes that a lack of distance between author and subject matter, melodramatic endings, unrealistic characters, incredible events, and implausible situations reflect the prejudices of the author and are artistic flaws in her work. Brenda F. Berrian, in "Her Ancestor's Voice: The Ibéji Transcendence of Duality in Buchi Emecheta's *Kehinde*," states that there is no division between human beings and the spirits in the African cosmic universe. Therefore, a person's true nature is spiritual. According to Berrian, *Kehinde*'s communicating spiritually with her dead twin sister Taiwo empowers her to liberate herself from her husband Albert when he takes a second wife.

PART THREE, "Female Sexuality—The Body As Text," focuses on women's bodies in Emecheta's novels, with particular attention paid to the absence of discourse in African women's literary scholarship concerning female desire, sexuality, and rape. Marie Umeh's essay, "Procreation, Not Recreation: Decoding Mama in Buchi Emecheta's *The Joys of Motherhood*," examines the ways in which Emecheta protests against Igbo patriarchy's sexual blinding of women through various codes. In "Trajectories of Rape in Buchi Emecheta's Novels," Tuzyline Jita Allan explores the problems inherent in Emecheta's effort to insert women into African rape discourse in the face of cultural and literary practices that render the rape act unspeakable or as a trope for registering Africa's economic violation by foreign and local regimes of power. Shivaji Sengupta, in "Desire and the Politics of Control in *The Joys of Motherhood* and *The Family*," discusses the women protagonists of those two novels in terms of their struggle with their own desires and with the control they experience from a male-dominated society.

The essays in **PART FOUR**, "Reading Emecheta—The Poetic Voice(s)," analyze the stylistic and metaphoric qualities in Emecheta's fiction. Ernest Emenyonu, in "Technique and Language in Buchi Emecheta's *The Bride Price, The Slave Girl* and *The Joys of Motherhood*," praises Emecheta's realism and her use of figurative language, especially irony, and contends that her artistry makes her one of the best storytellers in modern Africa. Abioseh M. Porter, in "*Second-Class Citizen*: The Point of Departure for Understanding Buchi Emecheta's Major Fiction," asserts that *Second-Class Citizen* is an excellent example of an African *Bildungsroman* in spite of the narrator's exaggerated characterization of Francis as an unredeemable villain. Porter illuminates how Emecheta uses rhetoric to establish the protagonist's innocence, naivete, and immaturity up to the point of her epiphany. Margaret J. Daymond provides a close analysis of laughter and silence in *The Bride Price, The Slave Girl*, and *The Joys of Motherhood* in her essay, "Buchi Emecheta, Laughter and Silence: Changes in the Concepts of 'Woman,' 'Wife' and 'Mother.'" For Daymond, Emecheta's novels reveal how language may be subverted by the shared laughter of women or by their chosen silence. On the other hand, Obododimma Oha, in "Language and Gender Conflict in Buchi Emecheta's *Second-Class Citizen*," explores the deployment of language to advance the interests of gender in Buchi Emecheta's autobiographical work. According to Oha, the language of narration possesses face-threatening potential which deepens, instead of alleviates, gender conflict.

PART FIVE, "(Re)Constructing Gender Relations," attests to the resilience and ingenuity of women. Abioseh M. Porter, in "They Were There, Too: Women and the Civil War(s) in *Destination Biafra*," says that what makes Emecheta's powerful novel unconventional and compelling is her description of the probable causes of the Nigerian Civil War (1967–70) and the role of women during that war. Although he points to the work's weakness, namely, the author's depiction of the Igbos as victims and their enemies as villains, he maintains that *Destination Biafra*'s major contribution to war literature is its portrayal of women as potential leaders in a new Africa. John C. Hawley, in "Coming To Terms: Buchi Emecheta's *Kehinde* and the Birth of a 'Nation,'" suggests that the novel embodies Emecheta's own struggle throughout her writing career to find a "story" that conveys her "ongoing" birth. Having said this, Hawley concludes that Kehinde's choosing significance in Western culture over acceptance in an African environment symbolizes the author's resolution of the conflict of her dual attraction to both cultures. Ezenwa-Ohaeto, in "Tropes of Survival: Protest and Affirmations in Buchi Emecheta's Autobiography, *Head Above Water*," pays tribute to Emecheta's ability to survive by her turning adversity into affirmation and dreams into reality. Christine W. Sizemore, in "The London Novels of Buchi Emecheta," focuses on the "community of women who make life worth living for the abused child or the battered wife, far away from home." Sizemore contends that from Adah to Kehinde, female bonding across racial, class, and cultural boundaries creates "room in the city of London for the diasporic and postcolonial to achieve both place and space." J. O. J. Nwachukwu-Agbada's "Buchi Emecheta: Politics, War and Feminism in *Destination Biafra*," contends that the novel is Emecheta's boldest attempt to transcend the domestic scenario by dramatizing how women battle to save themselves and their families in a time of national emergency. Whereas John Hawley (see above) commends *Kehinde* for the author's ability to "come to terms" with her dual nationalities, Pauline Ada Uwakweh has reservations about Kehinde's representing the African new woman. In "To Ground the Wandering Muse: A Critique of Buchi Emecheta's Feminism," Uwakweh argues that Kehinde's individualism and cultural alienation jeopardize the African woman's role as nurturer of children and preserver of culture, a role which ensures a sense of ethical and moral stability for a new African nation.

The contributors to **PART SIX**, "African Pedagogy in Emecheta's Fiction for Children and Adolescents," discuss Emecheta's commitment to the development of the African child through her creation of culturally relevant books. Julie Agbasiere, for example, in "Toward A Cultural Symbiosis: Buchi Emecheta's Children's Books," examines the African value system that Buchi Emecheta projects, and the nature of didacticism, in her four books for children. Also in this unit are Jacqueline Brice-Finch's "The Magic of Motherhood: Buchi Emecheta and the Caribbean *Bildungsroman*" and Tunde Fatunde's "Conflicting Social Values in *Naira Power* and *A Kind of Marriage*." Brice-Finch illustrates how Nigeria's rich cultural heritage is revived and rehabilitated by the artistic genius of the author in the novel *Gwendolen*. On the other hand, Tunde Fatunde focuses on the ways in which Emecheta exposes the hypocritical Nigerian elite's systematic destruction of Nigerian youth through their elaborate network of subtle and corrupting industry nebulously called "business," which includes smuggling, stealing, and drug trafficking.

PART SEVEN, "Interview With Buchi Emecheta," presents Oladipo Ogundele's recent conversation with the author following her fiftieth birthday celebration in London, in which Emecheta talked extensively about her latest book, *Kehinde*, her happiness upon hearing of Toni Morrison's receipt of the 1993 Nobel Prize for Literature, and her shock upon learning of the untimely death of her literary sister, Flora Nwapa, Africa's renowned woman of letters.

NOTES

1. The other three are Ama Ata Aidoo, Bessie Head, and Efua Sutherland. Lindfors found Wole Soyinka, Ñgugi wa Thiong'o, Chinua Achebe, and Ayi Kwei Armah to be the leading male authors.
2. Chiedu Florence Onwordi, Emecheta's first daughter, died of anorexia at the age of twenty-three in her sleep while a student at the University of Edinburgh in Scotland. She was on a diet to lose weight for her wedding.
3. See Lloyd W. Brown, *Women Writers in Black Africa*, for a full discussion of Emecheta as Africa's foremost feminist writer.
4. See Gayatri Chakravorty Spivak, "Displacement and the Discourse of

Women," for her definition of symbolic clitoridectomy.

5. It took Emecheta five years to reconstruct the manuscript. In an interview with Feroza Jussawalla and Reed Way Dasenbrock, she discusses the difference in the plots of the two versions, which she attributes to the breakup of her marriage, thus her consequent decision to have her heroine die.

6. See Ogundele's "A Conversation With Dr. Buchi Emecheta" (recorded in London on July 22, 1994), which appears in its entirety in this anthology.

7. In 1982 when Buchi Emecheta returned to London after teaching at the University of Calabar in Nigeria, she established a publishing company in London and in Umuezeokolo, Ibuza, Nigeria, which she named "Ogwugwu Afor." Her novel *Double Yoke* was its first publication, followed by *The Rape of Shavi* and *Destination Biafra*.

8. The occasion was a lecture to my literature class at John Jay College of Criminal Justice of The City University of New York in March, 1991.

9. Donna Jeanne Haraway, in *Simians, Cyborgs, and Women: The Reinvention of Nature*, makes the same point.

10. See Cheryl Johnson-Odim, "Common Themes, Different Contexts: Third World Women and Feminism," in which she contends that the oppression of Third World Women is linked to race and imperialism as well as to gender and class.

11. See Nina Mba's essay, "Heroines of the Women's War," in Bolanle Awe's *Nigerian Women in Historical Perspectives*, for a detailed account of ordinary women fighting against unfair taxation.

12. Ayesha M. Imam, in "The Dynamics of WINning: An Analysis of Women in Nigeria," gives an account of this atrocity, which made national and international headlines in the 80s.

13. Ali A. Mazrui makes this point in his film and book, *The Africans: A Triple Heritage*, Episode Nine. BBC, 1986.

WORKS CITED

Achebe, Chinua. *Things Fall Apart*. London: Heinemann, 1958.

Amadiume, Ifi. *Afrikan Matriarchal Foundations*. London: Karnak House, 1990.

Boyce Davies, Carole. *Black Women, Writing and Identity: Migrations of the Subject*. New York: Routledge, 1994.

Brown, Lloyd W. *Women Writers in Black Africa*. Westport, Conn: Greenwood P, 1981.

Busby, Margaret. *Daughters of Africa: An International Anthology of Words and Writings by Women of African Descent from the Ancient Egyptian to the Present*. New York: Pantheon Books, 1992.

Constitution of the Federal Republic of Nigeria (Promulgation) Decree. 1989.

Emecheta, Buchi. *The Bride Price*. New York: George Braziller, 1976.

—. "Feminism with a small 'f'!" *Criticism and Ideology:Second African Writers Conference, Stockholm*. Ed. Kirsten Holst Petersen. Uppsala, Sweden: Scandinavian Institute of African Studies, 1988. 173–82.

—. *Head Above Water: An Autobiography*. London: Fontana, 1986.

——. *In the Ditch*. London: Allison and Busby, 1972.

——. *Kehinde*. London: Heinemann, 1994.

——. *A Kind of Marriage*. London: Macmillan, 1986.

——. *Second-Class Citizen*. London: Fontana/Collins, 1977.

Imam, Ayesha M. "The Dynamics of WINing: An Analysis of Women in Nigeria." *Women In Nigeria: The First Ten Years*. Ed. Elsbeth Robson. Zaria: WIN, 1993. 20–44.

James, Adeola, ed. "Buchi Emecheta." *In Their Own Voices: African Women Writers Talk*. London: Heinemann, 1990,34–45.

Johnson-Odim, Cheryl. "Common Themes, Different Contexts: Third World Women and Feminism." *Third World Women and The Politics of Feminism*. Eds. Chandra Mohanty, Ann Russo, and Lourdes Torres. Bloomington: Indiana University P, 1991,314–327.

Jussawalla, Feroza, and Reed Way Dasenbrock. "Buchi Emecheta." *Interviews with Writers of the Post-Colonial World*. Eds. Feroza Jussawalla and Reed Way Dasenbrock. Jackson: UP of Mississippi, 1992. 82–99.

Lindfors, Bernth. "Big Shots and Little Shots of the Anglophone African Literature Canon." *Commonwealth: Essays and Studies* 14.2 (Spring, 1992): 89–97.

Mazrui, Ali A. *The Africans: A Triple Heritage*. London: BBC Enterprises, 1986.

Mba, Nina. "Heroines of the Women's War." *Nigerian Women in Historical Perspectives*. Ed. Bolanle Awe. Lagos/Ibadan: Sankore/Bookcraft, 1992. 75–88.

Millet, Kate. *Sexual Politics*. New York: Avon, 1970.

Mohanty, Chandra T. "Feminist Encounters: Locating the Politics of Experience." *Copyright 1: Fin de Siecle 2000*. Cambridge, MA, 1987. 30–44.

Mugo, Micere. *Daughter of my People, Sing!* Nairobi: East African Literature Bureau, 1976.

Nwankwo, Chimalum. *Toward the Aerial Zone*. Lagos: Africa Spearpoint, 1988.

Ogundipe-Leslie, Molara. "Interview." *In Their Own Voices: African Women Writers Talk*. Ed. Adeola James. Portsmouth, N.H: Heinemann, 1991, 64–73.

——. *Re-Creating Ourselves: African Women & Critical Transformations*. Trenton, NJ: Africa World P, 1994.

Ojo-Ade, Femi. "Of Culture, Commitment, and Construction: Reflections on African Literature. *Transition: An International Review*. 53 (1991): 4–24.

Okoye, Pat. *The Better Life Programme: Meteor or Monument*. Onitsha, Nigeria: Africana-Fep Publishers, 1993.

Spivak, Gayatri C. "Displacements and the Discourse of Women." *Displacement: Derrida and After*. Ed. Mark Krupnick. Bloomington: Indiana UP, 1983, 169–195.

Stratton, Florence. *Contemporary African Literature and the Politics of Gender*. New York: Routledge, 1994.

Tapping, Craig. "Irish Feminism and African Tradition: A Reading of Buchi Emecheta's Novels." *Medium and Message. Proceedings of the International Conference on African Literature and the English Language.* General Ed. Ernest N. Emenyonu. 1 (1981): 178—96.

Umeh, Davidson and Marie. "An Interview with Buchi Emecheta." *BaShiru: A Journal of African Languages and Literature.* 12.2 (1985): 19—25.

Van Allen, Judith. "'Sitting on a Man': Colonialism and the Lost Political Institutions of Igbo Women." *Canadian Journal of African Studies.* 6.2 (1972): 165—183.

PART ONE
IGBO WOMEN AND CULTURE

Culture as defined by Molara Ogundipe-Leslie is "the total self-expression of a people in the two relations between generic man and nature and the relations between person and person in that society" (1994, 26). How then does one describe the Igbo woman's position in her society? One has to examine the African woman in her diverse roles as mother, daughter, sister, wife and so forth—in presenting slices of her reality or elucidating the position of the African woman in a culturally specific environment.

Sociocultural attitudes toward women globally are largely negative, positing that woman is basically inferior to man. Exceptions to this belief of the female as the "second-sex" are reserved to those mythical figures such as divinities, earth goddesses, water spirits, priestesses, rain-queens and so forth. The position of the Igbo woman in her society is just as complex. However, Buchi Emecheta in her *oeuvre* argues that Igbo society, like most patriarchal societies, limits a woman's scope and talent by restricting her to male-dominance and domestic spaces. According to her, particularly weighted against the Igbo woman are many entrenched traditional customs that marginalize woman as "other." Igbo men are born with privileges and opportunities while most Igbo women must earn those same rights that men take for granted. Through intelligence, resourcefulness, industry, resilience, talent, wealth or impeccable character, a woman can gain the glory and recognition reserved for the male. Emecheta, giving the female point of view, exposes this double standard and other inequities that exist in Igbo society even today. The relationship between male and female among the Igbo is therefore largely a love-hate relationship in which the woman who is subservient and respectful to her male kith and kin is tolerated. On the other hand, a woman who realizes her status as a minor and fights against it is despised. It is this aspect of female oppression in Igbo society upon which Emecheta reflects in her creative works; hence she writes to bring about feminist consciousness and female transcendence.

Most of the essays in this section of the book discuss the subjugation of Igbo women living in a patriarchal society. However, Theodora Akachi Ezeigbo in "Tradition and the African Female Writer: The Example of Buchi Emecheta" contends that although Igbo women may have many limitations pitted against them, they are still able to challenge the social prejudices that set out to suppress them through their collective power as daughters and wives, or as members of an age-group, as well as through professional activities such as trading, teaching, nursing, or acting as spiritual advisors to the group.

Similarly Susan Arndt in her essay, "Buchi Emecheta and the Tradition of *Ifo*: Continuation and Writing Back," buttresses Emecheta's premise that Igbo society erases women's contributions to nation-building, particularly in the oral narrative traditions. Why *Ifo* deceives its constituents with stereotypical images of women as disobedient daughters but never men as disobedient sons, women as unfaithful wives but never men as unfaithful husbands, women as wicked step-mothers but never men as wicked step-fathers, and hardly ever presents flattering representations of women as wealthy traders, nurturing and helpful partners or independent and capable individuals in order to present authentic renditions of women is the question! The myth of women as *femme fatales*, Arndt concludes, is a misrepresentation, even falsification, of the reality of women's lives, illustrating men's fear and resentment of female empowerment.

In *The Bride Price*, Emecheta departs from her generally iconoclastic attack against Igbo cultural norms if her tragic ending is anything to go by. Rebecca Boostrom in "Nigerian Legal Concepts in Buchi Emecheta's *The Bride Price*" therefore rightly challenges the author's patronizing ending in favor of Igbo cultural traditions. Boostrom writes, "Emecheta's portrayal of Aku-nna needing to die as an exemplar for modern times is in conflict with a law enacted in mid—nineteenth century Nigeria that upheld anyone like Akunna who refused to enter into a relationship with someone she found repulsive." Emecheta's cultural dilemma, her vacillation between traditionalism and feminism is apparent in her contrived ending. However, the promotion of universal human rights, Boostrom insists, is more important than compromising one's principles and condescending to the maintenance of cultural identity and tradition.

While Ezeigbo and Arndt point to the myth of the uncreative and powerless African woman, and Boostrom argues that British law in Nigeria upheld a woman's right to assert her individuality, Florence Stratton in "The Shallow Grave: Archetypes of Female Experience in African Fiction" demonstrates how African women are "living in bondage to men" (147). From her study of Emecheta's *The Slave Girl* and *The Joys of Motherhood*, she posits that most African women are sacrificial victims to tradition, except for the few who through ingenuity and great courage triumph in their struggle out of patriarchy's "shallow grave" (147).

Finally, Tom Spencer-Walters in "Orality and Patriarchal Dominance in Buchi Emecheta's *The Slave Girl*" states that Ibuza oral traditions tend to favor males. There is no equality for women in a society, he says, where traditions demand that women renounce self-pride and dignity in service to indolent and self-indulgent men. Illustrating the ways in which Emecheta reveals through ogbanje Ojebeta female entrapment in a patriarchal culture, he champions African women like author Emecheta who effect change through creating a literature of social transformation.

Marie Umeh

Tradition and the African Female Writer: The Example of Buchi Emecheta

Theodora Akachi Ezeigbo

I. INTRODUCTION

Many critics agree that the most significant achievement of
Emecheta's novels is the broad perspective they have given to the
African novel by presenting the feminine point of view in a way
that challenges the false representation of women and women's
experience in male-authored literature.[1] There is much information in Emecheta's novels about the various aspects of tradition
and culture that at one time oppressed and continue to oppress
women in traditional societies, in modern Nigeria and even in the
British society. The studies carried out both by feminist critics and
by other scholars devote much space to exploring the oppressive
mechanisms, built into Igbo cultural tradition and modern Nigeria
that marginalize and enslave women. This is especially the case

in studies on Emecheta's novels that are set in traditional society, precolonial and colonial Nigeria: *The Slave Girl, The Bride Price* and *The Joys of Motherhood.*

The arguments in these studies explicate Emecheta's thesis in the novels—an unambiguous portrait of male oppression as well as societal injustice against women. Emecheta's central vision in these novels has been described by Katherine Frank as "female bondage" (Frank, 479). The impression one has after reading much of the critical writing on Emecheta's works is that the African woman's condition was one of total submergence and enslavement. But this is not the case in the novels themselves. It is true that in these novels there are severe limitations and inequities in traditional society reinforced and complicated by colonialism; yet the perceptive reader also knows that there are structures and institutions in these societies that empower women and enhance their participation in the sociopolitical, economic and spiritual activities in the community. Even though critics have not emphasized this reality, there is clear evidence that Emecheta commends what is beautiful and affirmative in traditional society and modern Nigeria, as well as exposes what is negative and destructive. Any meaningful and balanced study of Emecheta's fiction must underscore this duality in her vision of women's experience in both traditional and colonial societies. Emecheta is first and foremost an African feminist. According to Carole Boyce Davies, "African feminism examines societies for institutions which are of value to women and rejects those which work to their detriment" (Davies, 9). This is what Emecheta has done in the three novels under discussion in this paper. By showing the way women's experience was in the past, she also depicts the way it is in contemporary society and projects the way it could be and should be. By examining the social, economic and historical realities of African women's lives, she not only destroys myths about women's contentment with the status quo but also gives fresh insights into women's struggle under male domination and women's ability to map out strategies that enabled them to survive the patriarchal society that was structured to dominate and oppress them. Contrary to what many readers of Emecheta's works think, she does not simply condemn our male-dominated society for its oppression of women; more than anything else, she exposes the injustices lined up against women so that society could be restructured in a more equitable manner.

In this paper we intend to examine some of the structures and institutions that empower women in Emecheta's novels and ana-

6

lyze how women have manipulated them to ensure their survival in the patriarchal society. It is our intention also to highlight how these structures and institutions are exploited positively by some individual female characters and how others concede to oppression and domination in the patriarchy, through personal weakness or lack of intellectual maturity, with negative and even disastrous consequences to their lives. Our approach will be textual as well as contextual. The latter presupposes that we would analyze the three novels—*The Slave Girl*, *The Bride Price* and *The Joys of Motherhood*—in the context of the world (traditional Igbo society and colonial Nigeria) with which they have material and spiritual affinities. Our focus primarily would be to explore how women have managed to survive in an environment where they are dominated and marginalized.

II. IGBO TRADITIONAL SOCIETY: BACKGROUND TO EMECHETA'S NOVELS

Igbo traditional society refers to the period of Igbo history before colonization. Uzodinma Nwala identifies the traditional man or woman as one who "has a way of life, a tradition, or a civilization to which he (or she) adheres faithfully and uncritically most of the time" (Nwala, 11). He further states that the traditional individual is distinguished from the modern individual by "this attachment to a way of life with little exercise of independent judgement but rather an almost slave attachment to the ideals of his (her) society" (Nwala, 11).

Tradition as conceived in this study implies the body of principles, beliefs, practices and experiences passed down from the past to the present. We also adopt an aspect of Abiola Irele's definition of tradition as "an abiding permanent, immutable stock of beliefs and symbols" (Irele 1990, 45).

A rigidly and clearly defined code of morals existed in Igbo traditional society, as in every other such society. Any infringement of these laws attracted penalties or punishments that were commensurate with the offence committed. Most Igbo communities did not have kings and so traditional morality was formulated and enforced by elders, priests, priestesses, wealthy and titled men of integrity, articulate and respected members of the society, age-grade groups, association of daughters and association of wives. Some of these, especially the elders, priests and titled men, make up the leadership and intellectual class in traditional society while the age-

7

grade and other associations were empowered to have influence as well as control over their members. Judging by the great power their position as custodians of moral values bequeathed upon them, it was not surprising that sanctions were applied rigorously by them whenever any member of the community broke any of the laws.

The sanctions enforced when laws were infringed, according to Uzodinma Nwala, ranged from "death, selling into slavery, banishment, ostracism, or propitiatory sacrifices, to simply apology and doing some work to appease the anger and assuage the feelings of the man wronged" (Nwala, 147). Traditional society in Igboland was patterned as a communal one; and so it was the responsibility of the society to uphold the moral code and ensure that it was rigidly adhered to by all. The proverbial saying "If a finger touches oil, all the others become soiled" was truly applicable to traditional society because a community could be made to suffer as a result of the misdeed of one of its members. Consequently individuals were answerable to the people and each person's conduct was the responsibility of the entire community. Little wonder, therefore, that Aku-nna's rebellion and elopement with Chike Ofulue drew the anger of the entire community.

Igbo communities are found mainly in the eastern parts of Nigeria as well as a section of the West. In the majority of these Igbo-speaking areas, the code of morals is very similar. This was even more the case in traditional society. The Ibuza people who were the ancestors of Buchi Emecheta migrated from the eastern part of the Niger River to the western part. According to Emecheta's account in *The Slave Girl*, they were led by a young prince called Umejei:

> The prince had come from Isu, an Ibo town in the eastern part of Nigeria, but he had been sent into exile for accidentally killing his opponent in what started as a friendly wrestling match. To the people of Isu it was always a case of a life for a life; it did not matter whether one of the lives was that of a peddlar and the other that of a beloved prince like the gallant Umejei. However, his life was spared on the condition that he left Isu. His father, the Oba of Isu, brokenhearted, sent Umejei away with blessings and a gourd of medicine to guard him. He told his son: 'where this gourd drops to the ground, there shall be your home, and there you shall increase

8

and multiply, and your people, your sons and daughters, shall fill the new town, and that town will grow and will always be yours. I forgive you for what happened; it was a misfortune. But in our clan all souls are equal, none is greater than the other. The law of our land will not permit you to stay in Isu and live, so you must go, and go in peace.'(9)

The Isu people did not hesitate in applying sanctions[2] against a prince who infringed on the community's moral code and expelled him from their town. Emecheta tells us that when Umejei and his followers "reached the spot now known as Omeze, Umejei had a fall, and the town of Ibuza was founded" (10).

From all probability, as the town of Ibuza grew and multiplied, the community's tradition became modified as well as extended. New practices like the cutting of a curl of a girl's hair—*isi mmo*—and the kidnapping of girls as prospective brides,[3] which were not common in Igbo traditional society on the eastern side of the Niger, were introduced. Emecheta highlights some of these customs and traditions that are peculiar to her own people in some of her novels and explores how they oppress and traumatize women in the Ibuza traditional and modern society.

III. Traditional Institutions and Structures that Empower Women in Emecheta's Novels

Having examined the nature of Igbo traditional society and the moral code and sanctions that guided and controlled the life of the individual, we shall explore, in this section, ways in which Igbo women exercised their free will and retained aspects of their individuality in the male-dominated society.

Most historians who studied Igbo traditional society described its political system as 'democratic' and 'egalitarian'.[4] Considering the degree of restriction women suffered and the relative powerlessness of their position and condition, it is difficult to agree with the views of these scholars from the women's point of view. Yet there is some truth in the claim that Igbo traditional society had ingrained in its sociopolitical and economic structures a system of "checks and balances" which enabled women to manipulate situations to their advantage. Clearly this is seen in the way some of Emecheta's women characters wield power and influence in their community. The social and political institutions which women exploit to advantage in these novels are the age-group associations, the association of wives of a particular lineage and the solidarity that daughters, especially those married, enjoy in the natal family or extended family. In all of Emecheta's novels that are set entirely or partly in traditional society, the solidarity enjoyed by women in these groups or associations constitutes the mainstay of their survival, their control of their own affairs, and their influence on the men and on the community as a whole. The importance of the age-group is seen in the manner in which it is used to foster friendship among women and bring together people born about the same period. In *The Slave Girl*, when Ojebeta returned to Ibuza from her long sojourn in Ma Palagada's home as a slave in Onitsha, "she sought out her age-group, *Ogu Aya Okolo*" (188). Her life is transformed by the reception and cooperation she receives from her age-group. She joins them in the palm-oil trade to Onitsha, starts to save money in the cooperative esusu society they have formed to enable them to save in order to invest in future projects:

> She goes with her age group and friends to the big
> market to select the abada material to buy for this
> celebration or that one. (195)

Young women are allowed to move freely with members of their age-group, to trade and use the profit to take care of themselves. They are not inhibited and are allowed to travel to distant villages and towns to trade. In this way they prepare themselves for adult life when they will have to support their families through the earnings from their trading. By that time also most of them become economically independent of their husbands and enjoy a measure of freedom and respect in the community.

Traditional or modern, Igbo women, no matter their age, status or condition, espouse dynamic economic ethics. It is their capacity to start early in life to gain experience in economic matters that distinguished women in Igbo traditional society and set them apart from their counterparts from other ethnic groups in Nigeria. By the time they reached middle-age, most Igbo women had become relatively successful or even quite comfortable, depending on their line of trade. This ability was also exhibited by women who traded during the colonial period. In *The Slave Girl*, Ma Palagada and Ma Mee, another successful "market mammy" (84), control the bulk of the trading activities going on in the big market in Onitsha.

Emecheta's novels show women striving towards economic independence even from childhood. Materialism is not just a masculine ethic in Igbo culture but even more of a feminine one. Rather than curbing it, the colonization of Igboland heightened the materialistic instinct in the women. Whether in Onitsha or Lagos or even in Ibuza, we encounter Emecheta's women striving to hold their own as successful traders. Ma Palagada is very rich and "has built many houses in Otu at Onitsha" (49). In an interview Emecheta gave to this writer, she said, "The strong woman, Ma Palagada, was recreated in the image of the woman my mother served. They called her Ma. My mother always said: 'Oge ayi bi na be Ma' (when we lived in Ma's house). The picture she painted of this woman was so memorable and vibrant that I had her in my imagination all the time until I recreated her in *The Slave Girl*" (11). Emecheta's verdict is that "Igbo women survive in spite of all odds" (16).

The economic structures of traditional Igbo society were favorable to women in spite of other limitations of their position in the community. Men and women were engaged in the same occupation more or less. They were either farmers or traders. But the evidence in *The Slave Girl*, *The Bride Price* and *The Joys of Motherhood* shows that women engage more in trading than men do. In *The Bride Price*, for example, most of the women trade to distant towns and their daughters help them, as Ogugua reminds Aku-nna:

> Have you forgotten that we are meant to go and
> meet our mothers coming back from Abuano and
> help them to carry their market buys? (119)

Ogugua hurries out, "calling to the other girls at the top of her voice to leave their food; the moon was out and their poor mothers were on their way home from Abuano" (119). Women who enjoy enhanced economic status are confident, and influential and they are respected by their families and the entire community. In *The Slave Girl*, Umeadi's praise name "she who is on a mountain of money" (17) suggests her economic standing in the town; and her general comportment conveys the influence she wields over her husband and sons. In *The Joys of Motherhood*, even though she is carrying his baby, Adankwo refuses to come to Lagos with Nnaife who has inherited her after her husband's death. A competent and "very composed woman" (232), she tells the dismayed Nnaife, "I shall look after the family compound here. I don't want to go to that one room of yours" (232). Adankwo is speaking with the confidence of a woman who is sure of her position in the family and whose roots have grown so deep that she cannot easily be uprooted in the Owulum family.

11

The need to support one another and maintain a common front to fight the oppressive structures in the Igbo patriarchal society compelled traditional women to come together and form associations. Apart from the age-group, there were also two separate associations already mentioned in this study to which belonged all the daughters and all the wives in every lineage or clan. The functions of these associations were social as well as political. Through them women managed their own affairs and exerted influence over the men and the community.

Daughters[5] exercise considerable power in their natal homes and often influence decisions on socioeconomic and political issues in the family or extended family. In *The Joys of Motherhood*, Ona is an indulged and respected daughter and her influence both in her natal home and over her lover, Nwokocha Agbadi, is given great prominence by Emecheta. Ona is in perfect control of the situation in which she finds herself in the traditional society and decides, in a very rational manner, to whom her unborn child should belong. To Agbadi she says:

> ... my father wants a son and you have many sons. But you do not have a girl yet. Since my father will not accept any bride price from you, if I have a girl, she will be yours. That is the best I can do for both of you. (32)

Her decision is implemented, for when a baby girl is born, she is called Nnu Ego and becomes Agbadi's first daughter.

Nnu Ego herself enjoys the status of a favorite daughter in the household of Agbadi. When Amatokwu ill-treats her because she has given him no child, she is received with open arms by her people. Years later, after her second marriage to Nnaife, she returns to Ibuza with her children to see her dying father. Again, she is given a hero's welcome by her stepbrothers and her father's wives. During her stay in Ibuza, her position as the daughter of the great chief Agbadi brings her much respect and

> On the day of Agbadi's second burial, Nnu Ego was surrounded by relatives from both families, the Owulums and the Agbadis. A medicine man who had been following them through the whole ceremony said:
>
> 'I can see your father now in the land of the dead, busy boasting to his friends what a good daughter you are.'

12

> There are few women who could feel as honored
> and fulfilled as Nnu Ego did then. So happy did she
> look that people remarked to her jokingly, 'you don't
> seem to miss your husband very much, do you?'
> (195)

In *The Slave Girl*, the same marked honor and consideration are
showered on Ogbanje Ojebeta after she returns to Ibuza after years
of existing as a slave in the Palagada home. It is a joyous crowd that
welcomes her:

> Ute, the senior daughter of Obi Okwuekwu, let go
> her tongue. She sang the praise of all their ances-
> tors right down to Ogbanje Ojebeta, the daughter of
> Okwuekwu Oda.
>
> She had a piece of *nzu*—sacrificial chalk— in her
> hand, and she sprinkled some on each homestead
> god or goddess as they passed; she also left them
> pieces of kolanut. When they came to Umuodafe, a
> village at the extreme edge of Ibuza, she said to their
> god:
>
> 'Afo, have this chalk, and eat this piece of kolanut,
> for my daughter who I thought had died is back. Afo,
> eat kolanut....'(183—4)

It is very clear in these novels that Ibuza women are very proud
of their natal homes and are highly regarded there. Even in the
issue of marriage, women's views are not usually discountenanced.
We learn in *The Slave Girl* that

> ... despite the fact that the final choice of a husband
> for a girl was made by her people she was free to
> protest in private, and if she came from a good fam-
> ily, where money was not the be—all and end—all,
> they would listen to her and make some adjust-
> ments as to the man in question. In most cases you
> knew the man beforehand, especially if he was a
> farmer, and the two of you would have been allowed
> to amuse yourselves together in the evenings and
> on moonlit nights. (193)

In Emecheta's novels set in traditional society it is clearly portrayed
that women's greatest strength lies in their paternal base and they

exploit the privileges it confers on them to the fullest, especially when they have personal problems or when their marriages break down. They are never rejected by their own people.

The association of wives bound together the wives of all the men in one lineage. Women who belonged to this association were also members of the association of daughters in their natal homes. The association of wives is weaker than that of daughters; nevertheless wives wielded considerable influence through the power they derived from their ability to unite and cooperate among themselves. It became difficult to divide them and they were, thus, able to make their views heard and compel their men to satisfy their demands. Their support for one another sometimes extended across family or even village boundaries as Leith-Ross observed in her book, *African Women*, when she wrote, "... among the women, there seems to be something—perhaps merely the bond of sex that links them up over wide areas so that a woman's call to women would echo far beyond the boundaries of her town" (Leith-Ross, 337). Leith-Ross was referring to the uprising against British colonial administration known in history as the Aba Women's War of 1929.

Cooperation amongst women is depicted on several occasions in *The Bride Price*. When Aku-nna and her family return to Ibuza after her father's death, the women go out of their way to give the bereaved family a warm welcome. The fifteen women whom they meet at the market in Asaba promise to help them carry their property home after selling their goods in bulk which would entail their making less profit. The plight of their widowed friend motivates them and draws their sympathy:

> True to their word, in less than an hour the happy
> group were chattering like monkeys as the Odias
> were escorted back to Ibuza. Every suitcase and box
> found a carrier. (78)

The same gesture of support and sympathy is extended to Ma Blackie when Aku-nna is kidnapped by the Obidi family as a bride for Okoboshi. Joined by the women of the lineage, Mgbeke, "the chief wife of the family" (162) raises the alarm to alert the whole village:

> Wake up, all Ibuza, wake up all the dead both in
> heaven and in hell. An insult has been heaped upon
> us....(162)

Women's position in Emecheta's novels is inferior to that of men and they seem to be mostly in a state of powerlessness. However, there is clear evidence that the limited power they have is exploited to the fullest in order to protect their rights when they are threatened and to come to one another's aid. This sense of solidarity also ensures their taking care of each other's children; rallying round a distressed member and providing material and psychological support for bereaved members. In these novels set in traditional society, women's roles as mothers, wives, friends and providers bind them together into one indivisible force. Relevant to Emecheta's novels is Flora Nwapa's claim in a lecture delivered in Oslo, Norway, that in pre-colonial Igbo society, "men and women have always had separate and defined roles and functions. The men use theirs to oppress the women and the women use theirs to survive" (4). Indeed for women in traditional society, survival is the keystone of their life's experience in the patriarchy.

IV. Unmasking an Ancestral Spirit: Women's Experience in the Colonial Period in Emecheta's Novels

From the experience of the women characters in the three novels under discussion, we tend to get the impression that the role and status of women underwent drastic changes from what they were in the traditional society to the subsequent political, cultural, and economic powerlessness that characterized women's lives in the colonial period. The conflict of cultures that the imposition of European civilization and religion brought about was a scourge not to men alone, but even more to the women. Women groaned under the burden of double oppressive structures—the Igbo patriarchal system and the alien patriarchal system introduced by the white man. It was, therefore, almost impossible for the women to remain afloat; and to survive they needed to devise new strategies to confront the new areas of oppression lined up against them.

The colonization of Africa meant the total emasculation of the African male. He tumbled from his highly regarded position to one marked by subservience and impotence.[6] In Igboland, where masculinity is revered and femininity despised, the imposition of an alien culture, which weakened the position of the male, was like publicly unmasking an ancestral spirit[7] in the full view of everyone, especially the uninitiated—women and children. It was an unforgivable act. The result of colonization was the intensification of the conflict between indigenous traditional culture and European culture. The consequence was disastrous for the traditional culture.

The Igbo man, having been symbolically 'unmasked' and 'stripped naked'[8] by the white man, suffered a loss of face with his women. He lost all dignity, having been reduced to a state of impotence and powerlessness by the colonial master. Unable to deal with the source of his pain and humiliation, he turned his anger on the women who, though innocent, nevertheless witnessed his emasculation.[9]

The emasculation men suffered in the colonial period as well as the way it affected women is an important theme in the three novels treated in this study, especially *The Joys of Motherhood*. In the remaining part of this section, we shall analyze Emecheta's exploration of the historical, economic and political processes that affected the fortunes of women in the colonial period—from the rural community to the urban center—and how women responded to them.

Raised in traditional society, Nnu Ego arrives in Lagos to meet her husband, Nnaife, expecting to live with a strong, well-built and healthy man. She comes with set ideas about what men are, what they should look like and the strong position they occupy in the household. Her vision of manhood is shaped by her knowledge of her father, Chief Agbadi, and her first husband, Amatokwu—men whose lifestyle is still largely untouched and uncomplicated by the culture of the colonizer. Predictably, Nnu Ego is rudely shocked by the reality of Nnaife's repulsive physique and unnatural occupation. Her sense of manliness is outraged

> ... when in walked a man with a belly like a pregnant cow, wobbling first to this side and then to that. The belly, coupled with the fact that he was short, made him look like a barrel. His hair, unlike that of men at home in Ibuza, was not closely shaved; he left a lot of it on his head, like that of a woman in mourning for her husband. His skin was pale, the skin of someone who had for a long time worked in the shade and not in the open air. His cheeks were puffy and looked as if he had pieces of hot yam inside them, and they seemed to have pushed his mouth into a smaller size above his weak jaw. And his cloth—Nnu Ego had never seen men dressed like that: khaki shorts with holes and an old, loose, white singlet. If her husband to-be was like this, she thought, she would go back to her father. Why marrying such a jelly of a man would be like living with a middle-aged woman! (54)

Nnu Ego's reaction is neither strange nor isolated, for further on in the narrative we learn that there had been a case of a bride newly brought from Ibuza who ran away at the sight of her future husband but was caught and brought back by the man's friends. Nnu Ego's greatest mistake in the novel is to decide to remain rather than return to Ibuza after her discovery. All through the novel, she pays dearly for her decision.

Nnaife's emasculation is total; he is a servant in the home of the Meers where he is employed as a washerman. Nnu Ego feels the humiliation intensely "every time she saw her husband hanging out the white woman's smalls" (61). It is not possible for the men in white men's employ to keep their dignity. Men in the cities, in general, cannot keep their dignity and the situation is even worse for domestic helps like Nnaife who spends all day washing a woman's smalls and Ubani, the cook, whose occupation is to prepare food for the Meers (in a culture where men do not usually cook).

Cordelia, the cook's wife, captures succinctly the tragedy of these men in the colonial set-up:

> Men here are too busy being white men's servants
> to be men.... Their manhood has been taken away
> from them. The shame of it is that they don't know
> it. All they see is the money, shining white man's
> money. (66)

Yet the money they make is not enough to take care of them and their families, as the experience of the Nnaife family illustrates. They are perpetually overwhelmed by grinding poverty.

The new realities in Lagos create new areas of distress for women. Unlike in the traditional society, husbands and wives in the urban setting become estranged and hardly communicate:

> Now each was in a different world. There was no
> time for petting or talking to each other about love.
> That type of family awareness which the illiterate
> farmer was able to show his wives, his household,
> his compound, had been lost in Lagos, for the job of
> the white man, for the joy of buying expensive lap-
> pas, and for the feel of shiny trinkets. Few men in
> Lagos would have time to sit and admire their wives'
> tattoos, let alone tell them tales of animals nestling
> in the forest, like the village husband who might

> lure a favorite wife into the farm to make love to
> her with only the sky as their shelter, or bathe in
> the same stream with her, scrubbing one another's
> backs. (67)

There is little romance or affection in these marriages and the situation worsens when the man brings a new wife into the crowded one-room apartment shared by all the family, as Nnaife does when he inherits Adaku, his dead brother's third wife. The loss of dignity and freedom suffered by men in the colonial period, especially in the urban areas, makes them treat their wives and children harshly. They become insensitive and uncaring. They feel slighted or affronted if their wives talk back to them or show dissatisfaction with the unnatural condition in which they live. Nnaife disowns his children and blames Nnu Ego for their misbehavior.

How then does the woman break loose from this vicious condition in which she is trapped? How does she recapture some of the female autonomy she enjoyed in traditional society and achieve some measure of fulfillment for herself? In the city she is more or less alone and does not enjoy the security provided by owning her own hut as in the traditional society; she cannot rely on or receive other women's maximum support to do some of the back-breaking chores she is saddled with and she does not enjoy fully the company and friendship of other women in a way that blunts the sharp edge of the monotony of everyday living in a male-dominated society. These privileges that are taken for granted in the rural or traditional environment are denied the woman in the urban colonial set-up.

Nnu Ego does not develop the right frame of mind nor the suitable strategies to overcome her predicament. Her tragedy lies in the fact that she is a victim of two worlds which are in conflict—the traditional and the colonial worlds. Her upbringing in traditional society binds her to the principles and ideals of that society in ways that her mother, Ona, was not. The failure of her first marriage compels her to migrate to the urban environment where traditional values are untenable and where she is like a fish out of water. It is an environment where one has to scrape a living, hardly finding enough to eat. Most of the people portrayed in the novel live in the ghetto; an unhealthy area, far from the rural world where a man

> belonged to the clear sun, the bright moon, to his
> farm and his rest hut, where he could sense a

nestling cobra, a scuttling scorpion, hear a howling
hyena. (55)

Nnu Ego fails to adapt to her new environment nor does she succeed in taking advantage of the positive aspect the new culture
might have. This is where Adaku, her co-wife and foil, surpasses
her in intelligence, resilience, resourcefulness and sheer courage.
Nnu Ego's world tumbles when her husband and sons reject her
and she has nothing to fall back on. Her disorientation and loss of
memory at the end of the novel are a logical development arising
from her state of confusion and her paradoxical experience. Even
the joy and fulfillment of motherhood for which she craved and
for which she has sacrificed so much neither save her nor bring
her security and contentment.[10] Her children's reflexes and reactions are shaped and conditioned by the new culture and the positive as well as the negative developments it throws up.

It is to Adaku that we must turn to really appreciate the new
strategies the woman employs to survive in the new patriarchal
set-up that threatens to stifle her. Adaku has been described by
Eustace Palmer as "a forerunner of women's liberation in Africa"
(49). Katherine Frank has observed that

> Adaku, Nnu Ego's co-wife, actually seems more of a
> descendant of Ona than does Nnu Ego herself, and,
> like Ona, Adaku recalls the courage and cleverness
> of Aku-nna. But she is not crushed in her struggle
> with a hostile environment, though her successful
> accommodation to Westernized Lagos in the forties
> and fifties is attained only at a great cost. (487)

Our view is that it is erroneous to describe Adaku as "a forerunner
of women's liberation in Africa." She is not a feminist either, in the
Western sense of it. The truth is that Adaku is the modern version
of those traditional women of the past who were able to overcome
the limitations of their position in patriarchy through their intelligence, resourcefulness and business acumen; and through the
'checks and balances' in the socio-political and economic system.
She is able to find space to manoeuvre in the urban set-up and
improve her position and condition. Above all, she should be seen
as following the foot steps of her forebears in traditional society
who devised survival strategies to thwart the oppressive structures
of patriarchal institutions so as to carve out a healthy niche for
themselves and their daughters. Contrary to Katherine Frank's

comment, there is no evidence in the novel that Adaku resorts to prostitution even though she threatens before Nnu Ego, "I am going to be a prostitute" (212). Rather we should see her as taking her second stated option, "I want to be a dignified single woman. I shall work to educate my daughters, though I shall not do without male companionship.... They have their uses" (216). Her relations with men will henceforth be on the basis of equality and mutual interest; and that is not necessarily prostitution.

Adaku knows from the tradition of the past how to deal with uncooperative and irresponsible husbands. Her action is validated by Ifi Amadiume's research finding:

> At worst, if lineage men proved stubborn, wives went on strike, in which case they would refuse to cook for or have sexual intercourse with their husbands. In this culture, men did not cook: control of food was therefore a political asset for the women. In sexuality, too, gender realities were such that it was believed that females provided sexual services; hence the political use of the threat of collective withdrawal of sexual services by women.
> (Amadiume 1987, 65)

Left to Adaku, these weapons of denial of food and withdrawal of sexual services towards Nnaife would work as it did in the traditional past and force him to increase their housekeeping money, but without conferring with her, Nnu Ego withdraws from the strike both of them embarked upon; thus allowing Nnaife to get away with his selfish and peevish ways. Adaku later liberates herself from Nnaife's tyranny by moving out of his home and leaving the ghetto for good.

Another survival strategy Adaku adopts is to increase her volume of trade and achieve remarkable success in this area, thereby gaining economic independence as did many women in the traditional society. In this way, Adaku recalls Efuru and Idu, two successful traders whose names provide titles for the two novels by Flora Nwapa in which they are heroines. Idu stresses the significance of economic independence to the traditional Igbo woman by asserting that "a woman who does not know how to trade in our town is a senseless woman. She is not a woman at all" (29). Adaku also calls to mind those women of the past like the merchant queens, Ma Palagada and Ma Mee in The Slave Girl and also the Amazons who triggered off the Aba Women's War of 1929 in order to protest the taxation of women by the British colonial administration.

But, perhaps, Adaku's greatest survival strategy which will benefit her daughters immensely and be a huge investment in their future is her foresight in embracing Western education for the girls. She says to Nnu Ego:

> I will spend the money I have in giving my girls a good start in life. They shall stop going to the market with me. I shall see that they get enrolled in a good school.... Nnaife is not going to send them away to any husband before they are ready. I will see to that! I'm leaving this stuffy room tomorrow, senior wife. (212)

Unlike Adaku, Nnu Ego does not realize fully the value of female education and so does not ensure that her daughters get educated. It is Adaku's three daughters who will be in a position to experience and enjoy Nnu Ego's wish and prayer:

> God, when will you create a woman who will be fulfilled in herself, a full human being, not anybody's appendage? (236)

By exploiting the situation to her advantage, Adaku has taken steps to see that her daughters can become such women. She is thus appropriating to her advantage one of the few positive values of colonization.

Aku-nna in *The Bride Price* exhibits the courage and independence of Ona and Adaku, but she fails because she lacks the psychological and mental frame of mind to face and live up to her conviction. The raw courage that propels Adaku to cry fiercely, "My *chi* be damned!" (212) as she moves out of Nnaife's home also energizes Aku-nna to elope from Ibuza with Chike and marry him in Ughelli with her bride price unpaid, even as the birth of her baby draws near. But where Adaku sustains her resolve and her new position, Aku-nna is weighed down by guilt and allows herself to be crushed by the superstitious belief that says, "if the bride price is not paid, the bride will die at childbirth" (190). Aku-nna has every chance to live happily with Chike far away from Ibuza and its harsh custom. But she dies at childbirth, giving credence to the obnoxious belief and consequently strengthening its "psychological hold over every young girl that would continue to exist, even in the face of every modernization, until the present day" (208).

V. CONCLUSION

Our discussion in this study has affirmed that, though women have many limitations in Emecheta's novels set in traditional society and the colonial environment, they are able to rise above most of the structures imposed upon them by their male-dominated community through exercising collective power as daughters, wives and members of their age-groups, as well as through economic activities like trading, and through the liberating force of Western education. In the case where the woman is crushed by patriarchal structures or by traditional mores, it is often the result of the woman's failure to explore alternative options that can liberate her from the oppressive set-up. This is the fate of Nnu Ego and Akunna. Nnu Ego is so busy having babies and taking care of them that she neither cultivates other women's friendship nor engages in the type of economic activity that could free her from her dependence on Nnaife.

To survive in the environment depicted in Emecheta's novels, a woman has to be courageous, independent, self-determined, ambitious and assertive. Ona, Adaku, Adankwo and Ma Palagada have these qualities and their success or liberation depends on them. On two occasions in *The Joys of Motherhood*, the word "ambition" is used to describe Adaku by Nnu Ego (150) and by Adankwo (200). We are not surprised that Adaku charts her own course of progress and succeeds like many other women before her.

Igbo traditional society was harsh and strongly patriarchal in its structure. Both men and women were forced to face the consequences of their actions when they infringed on the moral code. However, it was also a society where the individual could succeed depending on his or her will. In Emecheta's novels, there are individual women who succeed in challenging repressive customs and traditions. Additionally, in the urban colonial environment, the emasculation men have suffered often makes them violent or callous towards women. In *The Joys of Motherhood*, Adaku, who Nnaife "had been trying to punish had left the family fold to strike out successfully on her own" (218).

In sum, Emecheta does not only explore the negative impact of traditional culture and the imposition of colonialism on women, but she also shows how women have reacted and fought oppression, sometimes succeeding and sometimes failing. What is most important to Emecheta is that women be given the prominent position they deserve in African fiction and that women's experience in the society be given a realistic portrayal. By doing this herself, Emecheta has brought out strongly the women's perspective as never before in the history of the African novel. In the interview she granted this writer, she had this to say about women from her culture and about those male writers who have misrepresented the African woman in their works, "Igbo women survive in spite of all odds. Achebe is an excellent writer, but I feel bad about his women and all those other male writers who are creating colorless women" (Ezeigbo 1993, 16).

NOTES

1. Among the critics are Eustace Palmer, Katherine Frank and Helen Chukwuma. See the reference section for details of their publications.

2. This story reminds us of a similar rigorous application of sanction in Chinua Achebe's *Things Fall Apart*, forcing Okonkwo to go into exile after he accidentally killed a kinsman.

3. This writer interviewed a number of Ibuza people in Lagos who confirmed that the cutting of a curl of hair from a girl's head and the kidnapping of a girl as a bride were practiced in Ibuza in the past and until the early years of the 20th century. One man told me that his sister was almost a victim and it was by a stroke of luck that she escaped losing a lock of her hair to a certain man from their village. He also told me of a cripple in their village who married the unfortunate girl whose lock he had cut in a very dramatic and cunning manner.

4. See the work of scholars like Professor V. C. Uchendu and the late Professor K. O. Dike (listed in accompanying Bibliography).

5. Daughters are referred to as *Umuada* and wives as *Alutaradi* in some parts of Igboland. For more information on the activities of the two groups, see T. A. Ezeigbo's "Traditional Women's Institutions in Igbo Society: Implications for the Igbo Female Writer," *African Languages and Cultures* 3, 2 (1990) and Ifi Amadiume, *Male Daughters, Female Husbands* (London, Zed Books Ltd., 1987).

6. The colonial imposition was strongly resisted everywhere in Africa but the white man violently put down the resistance, using superior arms and ammunition.

7. "Unmasking an ancestral spirit" is viewed symbolically or metaphorically here. But in Achebe's *Things Fall Apart* there is an incident in which new Christian converts unmask a masquerade in public. The people of Umuofia retaliate by burning down the church and beating up the christians. The act of unmasking an ancestral spirit was a taboo in traditional society and it attracted very stiff sanction. The unmasking of the masquerade in *Things Fall Apart* spelt the beginning of the collapse of the traditional Igbo society even as the new and alien culture of the white man took over.

8. The colonized state inflicted upon the Igbo man was comparable to the state of being stripped naked. In Igbo culture it is taboo for a man to be

stripped naked in public and for a child to see his or her father's nakedness. In *The Joys of Motherhood* Nnu Ego desperately tries to hold up Nnaife's "night cloth" which has become undone as he is bundled into the waiting police van: "Please, police man, let me tie his lappa round him more securely. He is the father of all my children, he is my husband," she cried (267).

9. Black slaves and later freed blacks suffered the same loss of dignity in America and the West Indies in the lands of their white owners and fellow countrymen—after they gained their freedom. These black men in the diaspora, like their counterparts at home in Africa, resented the fact that their women saw their humiliation and took it out on the women—punishing them for the knowledge of their emasculation. The conflict that sometimes existed between black men and women as a consequence of the psychological trauma the men might have suffered is implied in some sections of Alice Walker's book of essays titled *In Search of Our Mothers' Gardens*. (See, for instance, pages 290–312 and 320–325.)

10. The tragedy of Nnu Ego is used by Emecheta to highlight the irony in the title of the book—*The Joys of Motherhood*. But as readers, we should neither be deceived nor confused about the importance of motherhood. To be a mother is the most important achievement to the African woman; it is a joy she alone can know and which is denied the other gender. It was so in the past and will continue to be so for a long time to come. However, no true African woman would sacrifice her life to motherhood to the exclusion of other pursuits and achievements, as Nnu Ego has done. Emecheta herself is a happy mother of five children and in the dedication to her novel, *Second-Class Citizen*, the sentence of dedication partially states, "... without whose background noises this book would not have been written"—emphasizing how important her children are to Emecheta. The truth is that the achievement of many black women today came about as a result of their having experienced "the joys of motherhood."

Works Cited

Achebe, Chinua. *Things Fall Apart*. London: Heinemann, 1958.

Amadiume, Ifi. *Male Daughters, Female Husbands*. London: Zed Books Ltd., 1987.

Chukwuma, Helen. "Positivism and the Female Crisis: The Novels of Buchi Emecheta." In *Nigerian Female Writers, A Critical Perspective*. ed. Henrietta Otokunefor & Obiageli Nwodo. Ikeja, Lagos: Malthouse Press, 1989.

Davies, Carole Boyce. "Introduction: Feminist Consciousness and African Literary Criticism." In *Ngambika: Studies of Women in African Literature*, ed. Carole Boyce Davies and Anne Adams Graves. Trenton, New Jersey: Africa World Press, 1986.

Dike, K. O. *Trade and Politics in Niger Delta 1830—1885: An Introduction to the Economic and Political History of Nigeria*. Oxford: Clarendon Press, 1956, 37.

Emecheta, Buchi. *Second-Class Citizen*. London: Allison and Busby, 1974.

——. *The Bride Price.* London: Flamingo, Fontana Paperbacks, 1979.

——. *The Joys of Motherhood.* London: Flamingo, 1979.

——. *The Slave Girl.* London: Flamingo, 1989.

Ezeigbo, Akachi. "Conversation with Buchi Emecheta." *The Independent.* Lagos, Nigeria. (September–October, 1993), 19–25.

——. "Traditional Women's Institutions in Igbo Society: Implications for the Igbo Female Writer." *African Languages and Cultures* 3.2 (1990):149–165.

Frank, Katherine. "The Death of the Slave Girl: African Womanhood in the Novels of Buchi Emecheta." *WLWE* 21.3 (Autumn, 1982):476–496.

Irele, Abiola. *The African Experience.* Bloomington: Indiana University P, 1990.

Leith-Ross, Sylvia. *African Women.* London: Faber and Faber, 1939.

Nwala, T. Uzodinma. *Igbo Philosophy.* Ikeja, Lagos: Lantern Books, 1985.

Nwapa, Flora. *Efuru.* London: Heinemann, 1966.

——. *Idu.* London: Heinemann, 1970.

——. "Sisterhood and Survival: The Nigerian Example." A paper read at the International Feminists Book Fair, Oslo, Norway, 1986.

Palmer, Eustace. "The Feminist Point of View: Buchi Emecheta's *The Joys of Motherhood.*" *African Literature Today* 13 (1983):38–55.

Uchendu, V. C. "Concubinage Among The Ngwa Igbo of Southern Nigeria." In *The Igbo—As Seen by Others,* Col. F.C. Ogbalu. 142–150. Onitsha: University Publishing Company, 1988.

Walker, Alice. *In Search of Our Mothers' Gardens.* London: The Women's Press Limited, 1984.

Buchi Emecheta and the Tradition of *Ifo*: Continuation and "Writing Back"

Susan Arndt

> I was intrigued by the whole way of life (in the Igbo village S.A.)....Some women will be telling stories....I saw it and I used to sit with them. I liked the power these women commanded as story-tellers. *Since then, I thought I would like to be a story-teller myself.*
> — Adeola James, *In Their Own Voices*

> *All I ever wanted was to tell stories from my home, just like my big mother Nwakwaluzo used to tell her stories in her very own compound.*
> — Buchi Emecheta, *Head Above Water*

I. BUCHI EMECHETA'S ORAL POETICS AS INDEBTEDNESS TO *IFO*

As these utterances suggest, Buchi Emecheta's inspiration to become a writer traces back to her being intrigued by *Ifo*.[1] However, she was not only influenced by the Igbo narrative tradition, but also by the western literary tradition. This sets her apart from a narrator of *Ifo*. Emecheta herself recognized this difference claiming: "...instead of using the moonlight and [my] own emotional language as [my] tools, I have to use electricity, a typewriter and a language that belonged to those who once colonized the country of my birth" (*Head Above Water,* 242).

But her distance to *Ifo* is not limited to her making use of electricity, a typewriter and—in order to be read and understood far beyond the Igbo area—her writing in the "colonizer's language." She moreover sets herself apart from *Ifo* by employing the European and North American based-novel genre, which was substantially determined by a Western—although nationally different—tradition.[2]

However, whereas Buchi Emecheta uses both a language and a genre of non-Igbo origin, the world she depicts in her novels is Igbo. In order to minimize this gap between the literary medium (language and genre) and the subject (the world of the Igbos) she decolonizes or *igboizes*[3] both her English and the Western-origin novel, thus paying tribute to *Ifo* which inspired and influenced her becoming and being a writer.

The *igboization* of English in Emecheta's novels is achieved by the transmission of Igbo syntax into English, by the integration of numerous metaphors and similes, rooted in the world of the Igbos, by the inclusion of ideophones, exclamations and untranslated Igbo words that relate to Igbo public and domestic life and, last but not least, by Igbo names that characterize the figures implicitly.[4] These practices make Emecheta's English mirror Igbo, in an impressionistic way.

Emecheta *igboizes* the novel genre by negotiating devices going back to the Igbo oral narrative tradition, such as irony, repetition, dialogues and integrating of genres of Igbo oral literature into her narratives.

As Emecheta herself outlined, "Igbo language is very ironic" (James 30). Thus it does not surprise us that this economical stylistic means is cherished by *Ifo* narrators. On the one hand, irony contributes to amuse the audience and is thus entertaining. By expressing the opposite of what is meant, irony moreover addresses the audience's intellect. Like the oral narrators, Emecheta uses irony in order to suggest meaning without stating it. Thus she increases both the aesthetic pleasure of her novels and the sharpness of her critics. Emecheta makes use of irony mainly to ridicule male sexual desire and men's arrogance. In this respect Emecheta frequently employs images of animals.[5]

As the oral narrator has to complete the story in one go, the audience has to follow attentively as long as the narrator continues. If they miss important information they probably get lost. To make sure that s/he will not lose the attention of his/her audience and in order to stress important passages, to draw attention to special points and to enliven the performance, the narrator repeats certain phrases, sentences or even scenes. As a reader of Emecheta's novels may return to any part of the text as often as s/he likes, repetition has lost the mnemonic function which it holds in oral narratives. However, both its aesthetic component and its ability to stress an important statement is nevertheless continued in her novels.

The performer of *Ifo* often uses the dialogue form while narrating and moreover finds him/herself in a permanent dialogue with his or her audience. In her novels, Emecheta adopts the oral form's oral-aural nature by making use of dialogue. This often replaces or at least qualifies the necessity of the omniscient narrator's presence. This narrative mode is especially relevant in her Macmillan Pacesetter novels, *Naira Power* and *A Kind of Marriage*. The anonymous omniscient narrator is replaced there by Amina, who tells her sister-in-law, Auntie Bintu, stories she experienced and participated in as the protagonist's lover or neighbor respectively. Like the audience of a storytelling session, Auntie Bintu interrupts, scrutinizes and comments on Amina's narration (See *Naira Power* 3, 62; *A Kind of Marriage* 40, 51, 59, 104—105, 118—119). It is the former listener, Auntie Bintu, who finally writes down what was unfolded to her. She does not simply retell Amina's stories but additionally gives an account of the atmosphere, of both women's discussions and commentaries which framed Amina's utterances. Both novels catch the atmosphere of an oral storytelling event. Thus the reader becomes more of a listener.

Narrators of *Ifo* make use of riddles, praises, proverbs and songs to open or structure a story, to enliven the narrative, to increase its tension, to characterize a figure, to underline the very concern of the story itself, to add important commentary which otherwise would have to be added more ponderously, and, last but not least, to offer a welcome and entertaining distraction for the audience. Like oral storytellers, Emecheta integrates proverbs,[6] songs,[7] praise names[8] and, moreover, *Ifo*[9] in her novels, which sometimes advance the plot[10] or even carry the basic message of Emecheta's narrative.[11] As a novel about the world of the Igbos would appear unauthentic, if it failed to integrate the genres of oral literature so important in the everyday lives of that people, the inclusion of oral genres in Emecheta's narratives, however, mainly serves as an aesthetic element—to create the atmosphere and to catch the Igbo flair which her texts depict.[12]

A writer who has been inspired and intrigued by the Igbo narrative tradition, Emecheta employs narrative modes which originate from the oral narrative tradition and which make her novels often remind the reader of an oral narrative performance. A committed African woman writer, Emecheta is, at the same time, one of the most serious critics of *Ifo*, which induced her to write back to them. Why *Ifo* provoked Emecheta's poetics of writing back and how it is manifested in her novels shall be discussed in this study.

II. Buchi Emecheta's poetics of "writing back" to *Ifo*

Many European novels on Africa underscored the colonialist notion that Africa lacked culture, history and literature and that Africans were inferior to Europeans.[13] This Eurocentric and discriminating view provoked African writers to start an intertextual dialogue with these texts in order to project a just and truer picture of African cultures and peoples. Salman Rushdie described this process thus "the Empire writes back to the imperial center" (Quoted from Ashcroft, Griffths, and Tiffin, 33). This term—writing back—has since then often been used to describe this intertextual dialogue.[14]

While African male writers challenged novels by European writers as far as their presentation of Africa was concerned, they supported the views on African women.[15] Both silenced African women in their texts; they depicted them stereotypically, and thus excluded them not only from literature but also from history. This discrimination against women is aggravated in so far as African literatures for a long time lacked women writers and as women writers still are "the other"[16] (See Ogunyemi, 60–61, Brown, 4). That this insensitive negotiation of and discrimination against women in African literature is rooted in the oral narrative tradition shall be outlined on the following pages.

III. *IFO* AS MIRRORS OF PATRIARCHAL IGBO SOCIETY'S WISHES AND FEARS

In one of the most famous novels by an author of Igbo origin—Chinua Achebe's *Things Fall Apart*—the novel's protagonist Okonkwo rebukes his juvenile son Nwoye, because he enjoys listening to the tales of his mother. Okonkwo declares this to be effeminate:

> Okonkwo encouraged the boys to sit with him in his obi, and he told them stories of the land—masculine stories of violence and bloodshed. Nwoye knew that it was his right to be masculine and violent, but somehow he still preferred the stories that his mother used to tell, and which she no doubt still told her younger children—stories of the tortoise and his wily ways, and of the bird eneke-nti-oba... Whenever Nwoye's mother sang this song he felt carried away...That was the kind of story that Nwoye loved. But he now knew that they were for foolish women and children, and he knew that his father wanted him to be a man. And so he feigned that he no longer cared for women's stories. And when he did this he saw that his father was pleased, and no longer rebuked him or beat him. So Nwoye and Ikemefuna would listen to Okonkwo's stories about tribal wars, or how, years ago, he had stalked his victim, overpowered him and obtained his first human head. (Achebe, 46)

This quote suggests that the Igbo clearly differentiate between tales of male and female narrators.[17]

Ifo figure large in the noninstitutional education of children. As female relatives are predominantly responsible for this education, mainly women are the narrators of this literature. However, the attitude that *Ifo* are effeminate, as expressed in *Things Fall Apart,* has to be qualified. Men may narrate *Ifo* and join the listeners. However, as this is rather seldom and only happens sporadically, it can be argued that *Ifo* are primarily the domain of women.[18]

Both as narrators and recipients, men on the other hand are said to be neatly associated with creation myths, migration legends, heroic legends, war legends, epics, stories about travels and adventures, allegorical and fabulous tales, and tales about certain causes of famine, the existence of different soils, the cause of animal and human diseases, and helpful medicine. To find access to these narratives both as performers and audience proves to be difficult for women.

To define both the heroic and the more recent ancestral history as a world of men, to declare such public issues as famine, diseases, farming and medicine and the discussion of them as an exclusive concern of men, and to depict adventures and travelling as the province of men alone, means to claim public issues and their responsibility within Igbo society and life in general as the domain of men. Although it is likely to happen unconsciously, the patriarchally informed narratives suggest that men make history as warriors or elders, that men are the heads of families and leaders of society, and that men have higher responsibility and mobility. This means that men occupy the central cornerstones of power.

In their article on *izibongo*, Elizabeth Gunner and Mafika Gwala define the dichotomy of "official" and "inofficial" culture in relation to power. The literary genres

> of those with, or close to, power have come to be seen as part of official culture while...[those] of ordinary people, which are outside the circle of power have tended to become marginalized, almost invisible. They are close to what can be seen as 'inofficial culture' (Bakhtin, 1984), to use Bakhtin's phrase. The dominant forms seem to be the only forms. Yet the other forms exist with their own robust inofficial vitality, enjoying often a sort of 'extra territoriality' (Bakhtin, 1984) alongside and unmarked by these dominant forms. (Gunner & Gwala, 34)

In patriarchal Igbo society, women are "the Other." As women are claimed to be inferior to men as far as political power and official social recognition are concerned, the literature that is associated with them is reputed to be the inferior, "inofficial" counterpart to men's literature. There is a dialectical relationship because *Ifo* are associated with women and not because of their supposed more banal content or their less demanding form, they are deemed the "inofficial" literature as opposed to the "male" genre. The gender—oriented differentiation of genres of Igbo oral literature does not only mirror the patriarchal nature of Igbo society and the social position of men in it but it also serves to reproduce it.

The literary texts themselves—including *Ifo*—both stabilize the patriarchal society and justify its norms. As *Ifo* harmonize with the male discourse, they have to be labelled "male authored," although mainly women are their powerful and skilled narrators.

A discussion of the female images that are shaped in *Ifo* may verify this evolved thesis. In this context it is of interest in what respect and why female images do rather harmonize with the patriarchal society's social ideas and norms of behavior than with the material reality of Igbo women.

Female images are shaped in nearly all *Ifo*. These figures are stereotypes in so far as they are flat and one-dimensional. They can be termed so because it is only a single idea or characteristic that motivates the nature and the actions of the figure. They symbolize a certain type which lacks any traces of individuality.[19] They hardly ever act as independent individuals. In *Ifo*, women are either presented in their social relation to men, as daughters to be married or as wives, and/or in their "biological function" as mothers or non-mothers.[20] This stereotyping harmonizes with the Igbo's patriarchal notion that women move from their father's guardianship to their husband's and that wifehood and motherhood define womanhood (See Boyce Davies, 8).

Within these categories, good and evil women are paired and juxtaposed, while these extremes of rating are never relativized. Characterizing female figures as good or bad is frequently associated with juxtaposed characterizations such as good and bad, active and passive, patient and scheming, despised and beloved, barren and fertile, caring for and maltreating children, and lazy and industrious (see Emenjano, xvii). All of these diametrically opposed characteristics can be reduced to obedience or disobedience shown towards patriarchal Igbo society.

As disobedience and its consequences are generally central in *Ifo*,[21] their most frequently recurring stereotypes are evil women—i.e., daughters who marry the "complete gentleman" without the consent of their fathers, adulterous women, evil co-wives, stepmothers, barren women and some old women, who have mystic powers at their disposal. The protagonist's disobedience and punishment is the actual subject of *Ifo*. Form, source and consequence of the female figures' disobedience is to be outlined briefly.

In *Ifo*, the female characters are generally negotiated as daughters. They are protagonists, stereotyped as beautiful girls who are soon to be married to husbands of their parents' choice (see "Owuelo and the Fish," in Umeasiegbu, 93; "The Proud Girl's

Punishment" in ibid., 93; "Onumara and the Spirit," in ibid., 100, "Onwuero and the Three Fishes," in Ekwensi, 1; "The Proud Girl and The Devil," in Bordinat & Thomas, 88). Daughterly obedience is manifested in a marriage with the man chosen by her father. The daughter's claim to choose her husband herself is interpreted as disobedience. Her misguided behavior is rooted in her pride, which is due to both her beauty and her having been spoiled by her parents. However, the handsome stranger, who has been chosen by her, retransforms into an evil skull, a fish or a spirit, who will kill her or keep her captured. Whether she survives this or not, the daughter has learned her lesson: decisions of her father have to be accepted; disobedience will be punished. The category of stereotyped daughters is very fixed, as the cause of the daughter's disobedience and the fact of her being punished for it are omnipresent in these *Ifo*. Although the existence of an arranged marriage is therefore a recurring theme in oral tales, *Ifo* do neither deal with the reason for arranged marriage or do they refer to the girl's thoughts about it. In this sense *Ifo* hold that women do not have much power to influence their future actively.

Many *Ifo* on the topic of girls who are to be married stress that the bride has to leave her parents to stay with her husband's extended family and thereby harmonize with the patrilocal and exogamous nature of Igbo society.[22] Moreover, the future husband has to discharge a bride price. This only casually mentioned fact elucidates that the parents' material compensation nowise depends on the individual wishes of the bride's parents or the husband.

The *Ifo*, "Tortoise Gets a Wife With a Grain of Wheat," (Umeasiegbu, 27-28) underlines this assumption. The king announced that he would divide his property with any young man who succeeded in finding a wife in return for a grain of maize. He only risked this because he was convinced that it was out of the question to marry a woman without an appropriate bride price. And it is indeed impossible. It is only the tortoise's witty cleverness that enables him to exchange the grain of maize repeatedly for different items of higher value until he exchanges it for a wife.

Another recurring stereotype of daughters found in *Ifo*, is the jealous co-wife or evil stepmother who instructs her stepdaughter to fetch water or wood from the evil spirits' river or forest, believing that the girl will be killed there (see "The Pot from the River," in Ekwensi, 22-26; "Two Wives," in Umeasiegbu, 61-62; "A Husband, His Two Wives and Their Children," in ibid., 62). But because of the girl's good heartedness, selflessness, helpfulness and modesty, she manages to win over the evil forces. Her good character not only saves her life, but also enables her to return wealthy. Now the co-wife sends her own daughter to try her luck, hoping that she will return rich. But the girl, who embodies the characteristics of her mother and represents her stepsister's negative anti-image, is selfish and greedy, and so she is punished. The evil spirits do not spare her and cause her to return dying or sick.

These *Ifo* teach people that girls should behave modestly, selflessly, helpfully, and obediently. This realization is especially important in so far as boys who are in danger of being killed by their evil stepmothers save their lives with the help of their intelligence and farsightedness. This reflects subtly but importantly the socialization of male and female behavior.

Since infidelity is one of the most serious crimes an Igbo woman can commit, the image of the adulteress is frequent in *Ifo*. The woman's beauty is responsible for her being admired by men. According to the *Ifo* moral code it is her pride, which causes her to commit adultery. *Ifo* suggest that without exception women are responsible for adultery, whereas men are the innocent victims of seduction and treason. Therefore only women are punished for adultery, whereas the men involved are not even censured. The basic *Ifo* morality is that female infidelity is both reprehensible and pointless, as it will be detected and severely punished in any case. In this sense this category is inflexible.

In "An Unfaithful Wife and Her Lovers" (Umeasiegbu, 59—60) the woman is happily married, but nevertheless longs for other men. As she is the most beautiful woman in the village, a number of men desire her. When her husband is told of her adultery, he at first does not believe it. Finally, he agrees to test her and he pretends to go on a trip. The adulterous woman immediately invites three of her lovers. As her ill luck would have it, they arrive one after the other. When the first hears the voice of the second lover, he hides under the bed, as does the second upon hearing the third. When the husband enters the hut, the third lover hides under the bed, too. In the first place the husband is happy to find his wife alone. He admits his suspicion against her and apologizes for his lack of trust. Now the lovers indicate their presence. This suggests that they have nothing to fear. The woman, however, will be divorced and thus become a social outcast.

As we see from the images of adulterous wives and proud daughters, in *Ifo* beauty is often interpreted as the cause of a woman's disobedience. But at the same time, *Ifo* often reflect upon the fact that a woman's beauty constitutes her father's and husband's pride and even wealth.[23]

The ambivalence of beauty in being both desired and feared by men becomes obvious in the *Ifo* "The Woman With a Hunchback" (Egudu, 119-121). A man marries a woman with a hunchback. Although he pretends to love inner beauty more than anything, he requests a dibia to take the hunchback away. The dibia warns him that it will come back, if the wife carries heavy things. Trusting his wife's industry, the husband decides to tell her that if she carried a heavy weight, he would die. The woman's beauty makes her so proud that she wants to get rid of her husband. To kill him, she carries water. Consequently she is punished with the return of her hunchback, which symbolizes the loss of her beauty.

On the one hand this *Ifo* reflects the notion that every man wants his wife to be beautiful, as this prospect is a delight for him. This is why the husband asks the dibia to help him. On the other hand, it is argued that a beautiful woman is a danger to her husband's authority. She may even jeopardize his life. In this sense the *Ifo* moral that ugly women make the best wives is juxtaposed with men's longing for beauty.

As polygyny is both an established institution and a tradition that provokes conflicts, the image of jealous, scheming co-wives is frequently negotiated in *Ifo*. Some of these narratives depict a woman who is obsessed by jealousy and envy and therefore schemes against her co-wife. Although this tormented wife is often also ignored by her husband, she remains silent and passive. In many cases this is symbolized by a pathological muteness. But she does not need to become active, as eventually the two women's husband unmasks the evil co-wife's intrigues. Whereas this woman is punished by divorce or even death, the passive patience of the formerly suffering woman is rewarded with his love and favor. Both women are paired antithetically.[24] Envy and jealousy are punished; patience and obedience are lauded.

In "The Two Wives of the King" (Umeasiegbu, 68—69), the evil co-wife conspires against her dumb sister. The evil woman slaughters a pregnant goat and accuses the mute woman of it. Shocked by the king's anger the betrayed woman started to sing to herself the true version of the story. When others hear this, the king asks both women to profess their innocence to the river goddess, who punishes the evil woman with death. The voiceless one is rewarded by the now monogamous husband.

In other *Ifo* a woman's jealousy makes her attack her co-wife's children. This very frequently used motif of a woman who sends her stepchild to do a job which will very likely kill it has already been mentioned. The evil co-wife, who is here juxtaposed with her good stepdaughter, is punished twice. Not only does her own daughter return sick or dying, but also the scheming woman herself loses her life or social status.

In other stories the co-wife intends to poison or stab the other wife's child—mainly her son—to death. Again her evil deeds are not only punished by her own child's death but by her own death or downfall.

Having killed her co-wife, the woman in "A Husband, His Two Wives and Their Children" (Umeasiegbu, 62), intends to kill her stepson because he is more prosperous than her own child. But he is aware of the danger and exchanges his sleeping place with that of his stepbrother. The evil co-wife thus stabs her own child to death and is additionally punished by being divorced.

Ifo which narrate of jealous women do not challenge the myth of polygyny's necessity and practicability. They do not condemn men whose polygynous practice often causes distress, but rather the women, who oppose this male privilege. Thus *Ifo* admonish women to accept polygyny, without, however, suggesting that it means happiness. They rather argue that there is nothing women can do against it without becoming outcasts in the society.

Although there are many versions in which the image of the evil co-wife is negotiated, this category of female figures is hardly flexible. The narratives always move between jealousy, intrigues and punishment. For one thing, jealousy is without exception associated with violence. This is a subtle but an effective way of condemning this passion as criminal. Also, jealousy is always connected with motherhood. The scheming murderess is barren, a mother of daughters or of good-for-nothing children, whereas the good wife is a mother, has sons or prosperous children. The scheming woman is jealous of her co-wife because she is a more successful mother and she, therefore, considers the latter's children a greater menace than the woman herself. In this context it is not surprising that the co-wife's malignity is often symbolized by her ill-treatment of children. However, her spitefulness is actually not directed towards the children themselves, but to their mothers. In this respect the image of the evil co-wife often coincides with the image of the evil stepmother.

Even in tales where the evil stepmother is not simultaneously a jealous, scheming co-wife—e.g., when the child's mother has already died—this figure, like the evil co-wife, appears to maltreat her stepchild. The *Ifo* image of the malicious stepmother symbolizes all mothers, who don't do justice to their so-called social responsibility—to their maternal duties. Her behavior is rooted in her selfishness and her irresponsibility towards the child who depends on her love, which is often due to her own inability to become a successful mother. Although the textual presentation of this subject may vary, this category is inflexible as the maltreated children are always saved and the stepmother never escapes her punishment.

A recurrent version is to be found in "The Maltreated Child and His Mother" (Umeasiegbu, 76–7). The stepmother refuses to cook for her stepchild. The ill-treated child cries at the grave of his or her mother so that her dead mother's spirit cooks her a meal. Finally, the dead mother even returns to life and punishes the evil stepmother by death and by starving her child to death. This maltreatment is justified in the *Ifo* as it is understood as a double punishment for the evil woman.

Ifo which deal with barren women argue that womanhood is defined by motherhood. Barren women are disobedient in so far as they don't meet their so-called "social responsibility" of motherhood. Their lot is one of everlasting misery.

In "The Origin of Day and Night," the other wives torment the barren women by saying "you are an evil woman..., that is why you are cursed with barrenness" (Egudu, 19). Here barrenness is understood as an ancestor's or god's punishment for nonconformist social behavior. Because of her distress the childless woman went to a dibia, who advises her to wait. The unhappy woman does not want to be patient any longer and thus urges him to help her to have a child. The son she has, however, is obsessed by evil spirits and soon starts to kill all villagers, including his parents.

In "The Spirit Child," the barren woman is introduced as a "most unhappy woman" (Umeasiegbu, 119). One day a young woman asked her to look after her child and then disappeared. Delighted, she did not realize that it was a spirit child, who would return to the cemetery, leaving the sad woman even more sorrowful.

Although the two stories approach the image of barren women in different ways, their message is identical. They suggest that although barren women are regarded as evil or are most lonely and unhappy people, they should wait patiently. A child born at the wrong time and against nature will cause mischief.[25] This notion seems to imply that barren women can never find happiness in their lives, that non-mothers are condemned to suffer all their lives.

While the hitherto discussed *Ifo* treat barren women very badly, there are others whose attitude are more benevolent. "The Woman Who Boasted of Her Children" (Umeasiegbu, 73), is about two women. One is the mother of many children; the other is reputed to be barren. In contrast to the women in the previous *Ifo*, the mother acts in a way that calls for censure. She refuses the barren, lonely woman a share in caring for the children. As children are considered part of the extended family and as, consequently, all female relatives are entitled to take part in the children's education, the mother's selfishness is severely punished. Her children soon leave her. The disobliging woman stays behind childless and lonely. The supposedly barren woman, however, is blessed with several children. Now she bars the lonely woman from associating with her children. The villagers, however, sympathize with her deportment, as it is understood as a punishment to the woman who formerly refused solidarity to the barren woman.

Like other *Ifo*, this one does not doubt that barrenness is a tragedy. A happy end is inconceivable without the woman finally becoming a prosperous mother. What is more, the disobliging woman is punished by loneliness, manifested in childlessness—an equivalent to barrenness. As this *Ifo* not only sympathizes with barren women but even demands solidarity with them. It represents an internal scrutinizing of other *Ifo* that negotiate other images of barren women.

The category of barren women is therefore flexible, open and even ambivalent, as the *Ifo* assign very different causes for and advocate different social reactions to barrenness. Whereas some *Ifo* refer to maliciousness as a reason for barrenness, others simply consider a malign *chi*[26] to be responsible. Whereas some *Ifo* argue that childless women will never enjoy social acknowledgement, others make no mention of this and call for solidarity with these women.

This wide range of approaches reflects a sensitive understanding of the gap between what is regarded as social norms and what is experienced in reality. Although the social value structure is hard on barren women and denies a barren woman the right to consider herself a woman, childlessness remains a social fact. While co-wife stories without exception condemn jealousy and do not sympathize with jealous women (although jealousy relating to polygyny doubtlessly exists), stories about barren women show a higher degree of sensitivity for a childless woman's emotions.

The stereotype of old women represents another open and variable category of *Ifo* women images. In *Ifo* old women hold magical power, which can be understood as a metaphor for wisdom and which gives them strength and power over their fellow beings. But their age helps them not only to acquire wisdom, but also to achieve a certain degree of social independence. Because of their age these women are relieved of the "social duties" of motherhood and wifehood. With the loss of their fertility they are no longer considered women. Thus access to social power becomes easier for them and old women move outside direct male control and influence. Though wisdom demands social respect, the independence of old "non-women" frightens patriarchal Igbo society. *Ifo* reflect these fears by stressing that old women often employ their magical power for evil deeds and cause harm.

In "The Crocodile Woman" (Ekwensi, 27), the old woman pretends to use her magical power for a good cause. But actually she causes the protagonist's death. The old woman lives in the shape of a crocodile. When a man finds her crocodile skin, he restores it to her, even though it is quite precious. Grateful, she provides him with the gift to speak and understand animal language on condition that he will not tell anybody about it. His wife's nagging curiosity finally makes him break his promise and he dies. This *Ifo* suggests that it is better to keep away from old women, who hold mystic powers.

Female images show that *Ifo* in presenting "appropriate female behavior" argue that activities by women always lead to violations of social norms. The disobedient daughter chooses her husband herself, the adulterous woman is unfaithful to her husband, the co-wife refuses to accept polygyny and—as an evil stepmother—disregards her duty to care for and feed her (step)children and the old woman ignores the authority of men. The images of *Ifo* suggest that when women act it is always with malicious and scheming intent and fatal consequences. Their "crimes," however, are severely punished.[27]

The anti-images of these spiteful women, however, are those who adapt to the norms of patriarchal society. They avoid activity; they are passive and voiceless. They do not refuse to marry the man their parents' have chosen; they do not commit adultery; they do not scheme against their co-wives, they do not ill-treat or kill their (step)children, and they do not defy the patriarchal authority. In *Ifo* obedience is associated with passivity and voicelessness, which are rewarded.

An understanding of womanliness is not restricted to the social forms of women's existence; it also gains substance from the imagination. Imaginative fiction, on the other hand, does not necessarily mirror material reality but provides subjective reflections about the latter. This subjective presentation makes specific ideological interests serve their purpose—a situation which may exercise an influence on life styles and the development of society. Experience, ideas and concepts which contradict this myth are—consciously or unconsciously—ignored (see Bovenschen, 41). In respect of the female images negotiated in *Ifo* this ideologically informed selection is a product of the Igbo's patriarchally molded way of thinking. Starting from this thesis, it can thus be questioned whether *Ifo* notions of ideal womanhood and censurable female behavior correspond to Igbo material reality.

In her influential book, *Male Daughters, Female Husbands*, the Igbo ethnologist Ifi Amadiume drew a clear picture of the real eyes and lives of traditional Igbo women that widely differ from *Ifo* notions. Igbo women's real reputation is actually based not only on their motherhood and wifehood, but also on their industry and self-determined activity in daily family and public life, which is the precondition for wealth. Frequently they are the chief providers of their families' wealth and well-being—a situation which allows them to influence family decisions. By buying political titles they are also able to influence the politics of their communities. The different riots in the 1920s, the climax of which were the Aba Riots in 1929, proved that Igbo women made and influenced history. Such active women, however, cannot be considered unacceptable.

Abstracting from the fact that neither the moral essence of *Ifo* nor women's reality are homogenous, the female images proliferated by *Ifo* misinterpret, even falsify, the reality of women's lives. The myth of womanliness as proliferated by *Ifo* rather reflects the fears and the wishful thinking of patriarchal society and of those who are privileged by it—men.[28]

This wishful thinking, which is manifested in the *Ifo's* ideal women, may be defined as the patriarchal notion that womanhood is nothing but wifehood and motherhood. Lack of activity, obedience, and dependence on and inferiority to men characterize these female figures.

Men's fears are mirrored in women depicted as evil, but rarely self-confident and powerful. These women defy patriarchal notions and are thus beyond direct male control. The tales depict these active women with disobedience, which lends them a certain superiority to men.

Ifo's highly functional claim makes it improbable that its corpus of female images is accidental. Thus the glaring fact that *Ifo* primarily deal with disobedient women suggests that there are such women. However, the question is whether the *Ifo* interpretation of this disobedience does justice to the material reality or whether they rather harmonize with the interests of patriarchal Igbo society. By portraying nonconformist behavior as dangerous maliciousness, they keep the (artificially created) myth of woman as source of all evil alive. Thus not only is the fear of (such) women—characteristic of patriarchal Igbo society—reproduced and reestablished, but also, men's alleged superiority is also justified: if women have so many imperfections and faults their inferiority to men cannot be questioned. Men are the "legitimate privileged" because they are morally superior to women.

The dialectics of patriarchal Igbo society's fears and wishful thinking, which are responsible for the dichotomy of *Ifo* female images, throw light upon Igbo men's ambivalent attitude towards women. They esteem them as their children's mothers, as reproducers of life and their families. Their daughters or wives enjoy social recognition because of their beauty, cooperativeness, industry and economic power. These qualities call for the men's respect, too. But they simultaneously fear these attributes because they may pave woman's way to power over and independence from man—a situation which may put her out of their reach. Women's social dependence on men could turn into its opposite.

As it is mainly women who keep the *Ifo* narrative tradition alive, it could be inferred that the image of women which is spread by this literature also embodies the female narrator's individual notions of womanhood. The conclusion that every single narrator individually agrees with the *Ifo* moral stance, however, cannot be sustained. The German literary critic M. Hoffmann argues:

> Ideology stands for the social involvement of the statement, not necessarily of the person who expresses it. Thus even those who are victims of an ideology may become its proliferators, if their consciousness has been sufficiently deformed. Ideologies are expressions of the interests of those members of society, who hold power. They actually promote the stabilization of the existing rules. (Quoted from Honsza, 22, my translation)

Although *Ifo* narrators reproduce a misogynistic ideology, an individual misogynous attitude cannot automatically be made responsible for this. That women narrators keep alive what discriminates against their own existence and equal status is rooted in their narrow individual margins. On the one hand, they fail to develop a critical distance towards the *Ifo* moral stance; on the other hand, they are subjected to a kind of social censorship.

The potential *Ifo* narrators have been socialized by Igbo patriarchal society and its institutions, including the century-old tradition of "male-authored" *Ifo*. Even before girls are able to reflect upon the patriarchal norms and values which underlie *Ifo*, they have already (unconsciously) internalized their dogmas as normality. As a result of their socialization *Ifo* narrators neither had the opportunity nor were strongly inclined to consider these patriarchal norms worth transgressing. But it is not only their socialization that "forces" women to spread moral notions concerning women's appropriate behavior which might be alien to themselves. Even if an Igbo woman should choose literature as a sociocritical mouthpiece, *Ifo* would be ineligible. As other African oral literatures, *Ifo* are in their innermost nature, a socially conformist literature. On pain of being doomed, they not only hand down concepts of social norms, they moreover function as the ruling ideology's instance of control. It is true that the decision of which of the *Ifo's* stock of themes, motives and figures are chosen and combined is incumbent on the respective narrator. The moral message has by necessity to move within the socially fixed norms. A narrator, who violates this rule could not meet the responsibility she has as an artist and would thus risk the loss of social recognition.

The implication of this emotional-intellectual harmony between the artist and his audience is that there is no point at which the artist may be seen to be contravening or rebelling against the outlook of his society of which the audience is a random sample. The success of a performance is judged fundamentally by the degree to which the artist mirrors the outlook and expectations of this society and the audience of the performance seems obliged primarily to aid the artist in his task of mirroring (Okphewo, 161).

Ifo narrators move within a vicious circle, which most of them might not be aware of. As narrators of *Ifo* they justify and reproduce those patriarchal norms and values, which ignore their individuality and reduce their freedom. As long as they do not liberate themselves from the chains of patriarchy, however, they will uncritically reproduce the roots of their oppression through *Ifo*.

IV. NARRATING WOMEN'S REALITY
RATHER THAN MYTH

Only the social changes brought about by industrialization offered women a way out of this dilemma. After Igbo women in particular and African women in general gained access to institutionalized education, independent from traditional patriarchal ideology, a new literature emerged: the feminine committed literature by African women writers. The main concern of this new generation of women writers was and is to criticize patriarchal society and to challenge women's social status. Speaking on behalf of other African writers, Mariama Bâ declared in 1982:

> The woman writer in Africa has a special task. She has to present the position of women in Africa in all its aspects. There is still so much injustice...In the family, in the institutions, in society, in the street, in political organizations, discrimination reigns supreme... As women, we must work for our own future, we must overthrow the status quo which harms us and we must no longer submit to it. Like men, we must use literature as a non-violent but effective weapon. We no longer accept the nostalgic praise to the African Mother who, in his anxiety, man confuses with Mother Africa. Within African literature, room must be made for women..., room we will fight for with all our might. (Quoted from Stratton, 1991, 111)

To improve women's situation in a patriarchal society always means correcting the female literary images that have been created and nourished by it. As literature is a major reproducer of notions of womanliness that discriminate against women, it was imperative for committed African women authors to challenge the patriarchally informed female images in "male authored" oral literatures.

With their novels, short stories and dramas committed female authors such as, Buchi Emecheta, Flora Nwapa, Ama Ata Aidoo, Sindiwe Magonna, Miriam Tlali and Mariama Bâ present a more adequate picture of African women's material reality and history than that proliferated by African oral literatures. They correct the images of African women in oral narratives, in order to lead women out of the corner into which African oral literatures have relegated them. This intertextual dialogue with African oral narratives can be described as a writing back to the patriarchal center—to the "male authored" African literature, which is to be depatriarchalized.[29]

In order to write women's reality rather than myth, the new generation of women writers on the one hand, claimed that African women are neither voiceless nor powerless and thus challenged the images that are based on men's wishful thinking. The South African writer Miriam Tlali stressed the difficulty of this task:

> It is a problem when men...put you on a pedestal, because then they want you to stay there forever without asking your opinion—and unhappy you if you want to come down as an equal human being.
> (Quoted from Schipper, 49)

Although they know that "it is far more difficult to murder a phantom than a reality" (Wolf, 7), they took up this challenge. Committed African women writers wish to belie the oral literary images of women which are the outcome of men's fears. They stress the fact that African women have dignity, power, self-respect and an identity beyond passivity, voicelessness, motherhood and wifehood and that they are, nevertheless, far from being the source of all evil.

For correcting the patriarchally informed female images, African women writers made use of the perspective of women upon social life. Introducing the women's voice into African literature was then a novelty. As we have seen in the discussion of *Ifo*, African oral narratives throw light upon "male thinking," whereas the female point of view is passed over in silence. Neither the obedient nor the disobedient women in oral tales ever get the opportunity to reflect upon motivations of their activities or their emotions that result from these actions. Moreover, the depicted contradiction between the negotiation of womanhood as it appears in this literature and the material reality of Igbo women makes it impossible for many Igbo women to identify with *Ifo* protagonists and to find themselves in this literature. It alienates the female recipients of tales from their own reality. *Ifo's* criminalization of active women as well as the discrepancy between idealized and real women, coerced female listeners to identify with incompatible images. As contemporary male writers continued this literary negotiation of women, it was only the new generation of women narrators, who created a literature that offered African women both the opportunity to articulate themselves in literature and to accept their presentation there. Therewith, African women writers claimed that women are entitled to a place in historiography and literature. The Dutch literary critic Elleke Boehmer states:

> In writing, women express their own reality....To write is not only to speak for one's place in the world. It is also to make one's own place or narrative, to tell the story of oneself, to create an identity. (Boehmer, 10)

Buchi Emecheta is a powerful representative of this poetics of "writing back." Her feminine commitment leads consequently to a revision or reinterpretation of *Ifo* and their underlying assumptions. Her revisioning dialogue with *Ifo* is manifest in the renegotiation of their conventional categories of female images, such as daughters, mothers, stepmothers, co-wives, barren, adulterous, and old women. Emecheta continues the *Ifo* antithetical or oppositional pairing within these categories. But she rewrites rather than adopts, questions rather than continues, revises rather than reproduces the connotations that are associated with and underlie the female images in oral tales. Whereas *Ifo* criticize not the rules of the society but those who violate them, to challenge the ruling ideology means that Emecheta must reverse the characterization of a woman as good or evil. Whereas the oral narrator dissociates him/herself from the disobedient daughter, from the jealous, rebellious co-wife, from the barren and the mystic old woman, these figures enjoy Emecheta's sympathy and understanding, which she tries to express by giving some insight into the woman's own thoughts and motivations. While the patient and abused co-wife and the woman who does not seek an identity beyond motherhood are both advocated by *Ifo*, Emecheta dissociates herself from these notions, often by using tragedy. Here, the concept of evil is embodied by the very advocates of patriarchal society. The women's enforced inferiority complex, selflessness and lack of activity are presented as behavior to be changed. The more or less limited but active transgression of patriarchal dogma, defined as disobedience in the oral narratives, reflects the wishful thinking of the author. To illustrate Emecheta's poetics of "writing back" two of her novels shall be discussed.

The Bride Price (1976) adapts the *Ifo* about the girl who chooses her own husband and ignores the objections of her father. The alleged complete gentleman, whom the girl chooses as her husband, however, will turn into an evil skull, spirit or fish, who will kill her or keep her imprisoned. This *Ifo* moreover promotes the superstition that a woman will die in childbirth if her bride price is not paid.

Emecheta does not change the story outline crucially. Aku-nna, the protagonist in Emecheta's narrative, refuses to marry the man, chosen for her by her uncle. She opts for the man of her heart and runs away with him. Her uncle, however, refuses to accept the bride price for Aku-nna and thus provokes her death.

But consistent with her poetics of "writing back" Emecheta does reinterpret this *Ifo*. In her version of the story, Aku-nna does not fall victim as a punishment for rebellious daughters. She rather dies because she is too young and weak to give birth to a child. Repeatedly Emecheta makes her characters comment on Aku-nna's physical immaturity and weakness, which cause her death in childbirth. When she becomes pregnant, her doctor tells her husband Chike:

> Your wife is so young, and so small. She has been undernourished for a long while, so you should have given her time to recuperate after you married before deciding on a baby. Is she sixteen yet?...You must both be careful. She has hardly enough blood for herself, let alone for a baby. (160)[30]

By demystifying the death of her heroine, Emecheta replaces the mythical superstition with a realistic explanation and thus "writes back" to it.

However, Emecheta does not completely deny, but reinterprets the influence of Igbo superstition. Since Aku-nna believes in the curse, it undermines her health. In this sense, it is Aku-nna's belief in the myth rather than the curse itself that contributes to her death. While the death of the *Ifo* heroine embodies the warning not to be rebellious against social conventions, Aku-nna's death symbolizes Emecheta's notion that it is dangerous to emancipate, if it is done only half-heartedly.

Emecheta ends her novel by demonstrating how the emancipatory motive of Aku-nna's and Chike's story is finally turned into its opposite and used to prove the validity of the myth that they wanted to overcome:

> So it was that Chike and Aku-nna substantiated the traditional superstition they had unknowingly set

> out to eradicate. Every girl born in Ibuza after Aku-
> nna's death was told her story, to reinforce the old
> taboos of the land. If a girl wished to live long and
> see her children's children, she must accept the hus-
> band chosen for her by her people, and the bride
> price must be paid. If the bride price is not paid, she
> would never survive the birth of her first child. (168)

As Emecheta thereby outlines how—in order to justify and reproduce patriarchal Igbo norms—oral tales contrive reality by applying myth, the end of the novel constitutes the climax of her poetics
of "writing back" to *Ifo*.

The Joys of Motherhood (1979), the story of Nnu Ego, also offers
some insight into Emecheta's poetics of "writing back." In her first
marriage, Nnu Ego is abandoned by her husband, who marries
another woman. While the evil co-wife in *Ifo* schemes against the
other wife and abuses or even seeks to kill the other woman's children, Nnu Ego accepts polygyny and cares for her co-wife's child.
Ironically, her husband interprets this behavior, however, as jealousy and sends her away. In Nnu Ego's second marriage, both
wives have to live in one room. This forces the protagonist to "participate" in her husband's and her co-wife's sexual interaction with
each other:

> She tried to block her ears, yet could still hear
> Adaku's exaggerated carrying on. Nnu Ego tossed in
> agony and anger all night, going through in her
> imagination what was taking place behind the cur-
> tained bed....(124)

Thus humiliated, she shows her jealousy this time. While oral tales
argue that jealousy always results in criminal actions, and must
therefore be censured, Nnu Ego's suffering under polygyny does
not lead to viciousness. As Emecheta's narrative gives room to the
protagonist's thoughts these sufferings are rather explored. Thus
Nnu Ego's jealousy is justified or, rather, polygyny itself is challenged.

As implied in the novel's ironic title, the major theme of *The
Joys of Motherhood* is the revision and rewriting of the myth that
only motherhood makes a woman a woman and gives her joy—a
myth that is spread by *Ifo*. As Nnu Ego dedicates herself to motherhood, her life exemplifies the novel's essence as expressed in the
proverb: "If you don't have children the longing for them will kill

you, and if you do, the worrying for them will kill you" (212).

When, at first, Nnu Ego does not become pregnant, she suffers because she is considered to be—and regards herself as—a failure, a non-woman. When her first son dies, she wants to commit suicide, arguing: "I am not a woman any more" (62). Thus Emecheta reproduces the oral narrative notion that barren women cannot find happiness. Yet she does not pity barren women generally, but rather those who suffer because they accept their reduction to the mother function. By stressing Nnu Ego's tragedy Emecheta dissociates herself from such thinking. Moreover she challenges tales that argue that barrenness is a punishment for women who violated the norms. Apart from her barrenness Nnu Ego is an ideal woman. She is obedient, patient, and voiceless. Emecheta demonstrates that the afflictions of barren women are not "natural" but the result of patriarchal conventions. She accuses the society that denies such women any positive and self-chosen identity.

In her second marriage, however, Nnu Ego becomes a successful mother. But her sorrows nevertheless continue. The daily struggle for survival in a town like Lagos preclude the mother of five children from experiencing "the joys of motherhood." After she spent all her energy and money on feeding and educating her children, her sons refuse her the traditionally guaranteed support in old-age. Challenging the myth of "the joys of motherhood," the "feminist with a small f" (Emecheta, 1988a, 175), as she describes herself, is not criticizing motherhood itself. A woman should have children if she so wishes, but she should not limit herself to being a mother. Emecheta's biography exemplifies this attitude. As a single mother of five children she achieves self-realization as a student, a social worker and a writer.

In so far as Nnu Ego's life as mother and co-wife adapts to the norms of patriarchal Igbo society, Emecheta's heroine harmonizes with the notion of an ideal mother and co-wife as spread by the *Ifo*. But Emecheta's moral reinterpretation of the protagonist's behavior sets her novel apart from these narratives. In her version of the story, Emecheta argues that although Nnu Ego behaves like the *Ifo's* patient, obedient, voiceless, selfless and passive co-wife and mother, she does not find happiness, but rather becomes the victim of her obedience. Thus *The Joys of Motherhood* "writes back" to the patriarchally informed assumptions, which are at the bottom of *Ifo's* female images.

Again, her poetics of "writing back" finds its climax at the end of the novel, which differs drastically from the moral essence of the oral tale. Nnu Ego, dying and lonely, becomes aware of the disturbing power of a myth which reduces a woman's existence to selfless motherhood. After her death, a holy shrine dedicated to this "ideal mother" is to enable infertile women to have children. But in death Nnu Ego behaves according to the lesson that life taught her. She refuses to give barren women children. Therefore, she is condemned again by her society. The omniscient narrator concludes:

> Poor Nnu Ego, even in death she had no peace....Stories afterwards, however, said that Nnu Ego was a wicked woman even in death because, however many people appealed to her to make women fertile, she never did. (224)

Obviously these "stories afterwards" pay tribute neither to Nnu Ego's selfless suffering as a mother, nor to her changed viewpoint on motherhood at the end of her life. The tales about Nnu Ego not only ignore, but even manipulate the truth of her life. As in *The Bride Price*, Emecheta obviously intends to reveal the manipulative nature of *Ifo*. She sets her own view of society against the myths of oral narratives.

V. *IFO* DON'T LIE?

Buchi Emecheta erected a monument to the oral literature that inspired her to become a writer, by igboizing both her novels and the English language. Due to her commitment as an African woman writer, she simultaneously "writes back" to this literature. Unlike *Ifo*, she presents women's lives from a woman's point of view in her novels, using the literary voices of women. Thus, her dream, to become as powerful as the oral narrators of her village, came true. However, since this power Buchi Emecheta commands as narrator, enables her to question the Igbo women's status in her society and thus to challenge Igbo patriarchal society, the *Ifo* notion that powerful women are a menace to a patriarchally informed society has proved to be true.

NOTES

1. *Ifo* denotes the Igbo oral genre, whose distant English equivalent is folk tales. *Ifo* are only remotely an equivalent for the English term of folk tale because their social function has very little in common with modern "bedtime tales" in the UK and other European countries. Moreover, the fact that *Ifo* are improvised and dramatized in the course of the perfor-

mance distances *Ifo* from folk tales, which are nowadays nearly always in writing and therefore fixed.

Various Igbo scholars called this Igbo oral genre differently, e.g., *Akuko-Iro* (Chukwuma, 23-24), *Akuko Ifo* (Acholonu, 53-54), *Nkiti* (Ezikeojiaku, 72), *Ifo* or *Iro* (Emenanjo, quoted from Okoh 75; Uba-Mgbemena, 53), or *Inu Ita* (Okoh, 76—78). To denote this genre, which is related to the English genre folk tale, however, I rely on Emenanjo, who argued: "Although (the terms) *ilu* and *Ifo* are by no means universally known and used in Igboland, they are now sufficiently well-known as proverbs and folk tales respectively" (quoted from *Categories of Igbo Oral Literature*, 80).

2. Chinweizu and Ngugi wa Thiong'o see the origins of the African novel in both the Western and the African tradition: "...even though it might be demonstrated that the novel, a written bourgeois form, did not exist in Africa before the European invasion, its oral antecedents and proto-types did. And since African novelists have utilized and modeled them-selves upon these prototypes, the African novel cannot rightly be regarded as a purely borrowed form without African antecedents." (Chinweizu, Jemie and Madubuike, 31-32; See also Ngugi wa Thiong'o, 69). Following this assumption, it can be argued that Emecheta's usage of the novel genre is rooted in the African narrative tradition. However, in so far as the novel genre itself is concerned, I see an even more sub-stantial indebtedness to the Western tradition of realistic novel writing, in as much as Emecheta, for example, tries to describe reality as authen-tically as possible, without the magic realism of the oral narratives, but employing an omniscient narrator who appears as just another fictitious character, and dividing the text into chapters.

3. I use the term *igboizing* of contemporary literature by analogy with Chinweizu, Madubuike and Jemie, who said that African literature has to be Africanized to be decolonized. (See Chinweizu, Jemie and Madubuike, 242).

4. The figures in Emecheta's novels carry, for example, figurative Igbo names. In *The Joys of Motherhood* the figures are named: Ona ("priceless jewel"), Nnu Ego ("twenty bags of cowries"), and Oshiaju ("the bush that refused it").

5. In *Double Yoke* the protagonist's father, who rules his anyway subservient wife, is ironically referred to as tiger: "He heard his mother's voice, that silly woman was laughing quietly in a sickly sort of way, and wait a minute, she was calling his father. What? Calling him her tiger? Tiger! Good lord!" (*Double Yoke*, 60). When Adah, the protagonist in *Second-Class Citizen*, denies her husband Francis his "right" of sex, he looks "like an enraged bull" (85). In a similar situation it is stated that "all that Francis needed to be a gorilla was simply to bend his knees" (74). By applying this ironical description Emecheta manages to symbolize the ambiva-lence of Francis' brutality and ridiculousness.

Another ironical description of a protagonist's husband is to be found in *The Joys of Motherhood*: Nnaife is introduced with the ironical sub-heading "A man is never ugly" (*The Joys of Motherhood*, 63). Actually he is not only depicted as ugly, but ridiculous: his hands are softened by washing the slips of his white female employer. This irony stresses the contradiction between Nnaife's arrogant and macho-like behavior, and his inability to meet all requirements of a husband and father.

6. In *The Bride Price* she uses four (18, 44, 80, 142), in *The Joys of Motherhood* four (131, 135, 198, 212), in *Naira Power* five (20, 28, 40, 58, 60) and in *A Kind of Marriage* ten (5, 20, 22, 27, 46, 51, 56, 64, 112, 114) proverbs. In Emecheta's novels proverbs are either cited by a figure who is characterized by the kind of proverb s/he uses, or by the narrator of the story, with the sayings serving to catch the atmosphere of the world they describe.

7. In correspondence with their appearance in oral literature, Emecheta includes songs to create an atmosphere, to characterize a figure or to carry the story forward. Generally speaking, both the proverbs and songs in Emecheta's novels refer to the domain of women, i.e., cooking and caring for children. For the treatment of songs see *The Bride Price* (22—27, 135).

8. In both oral and written narratives praise names are a welcomed means to characterize a literary figure. In *The Bride Price* there are four (7, 112, 152, 184), in *The Joys of Motherhood* three (18, 29, 201), and in *Naira Power* two (21, 47) praise names.

9. In *The Bride Price* a story is included which tells the heroine of her father's death (22—27).

10. In *The Bride Price* Emecheta includes a song, in which Chike tells his lover that he is around and ready to run away with her (135).

11. In her novels *The Joys of Motherhood* and *Naira Power* the cited proverbs— "they said... that if you don't have children, the longing for them will kill you, and if you do, the worrying over them will kill you" (*The Joys of Motherhood*, 212) or "...our people say a thief steals daily, the owner only needs to catch him once" (*Naira Power* 59, 108) sum up the moral essence of the novels. In *A Kind of Marriage* the name of the communal hero— the family of Ubakanma—implies the moral of the novel: "Because his name was Ubakanma—a large family is better—I think he wanted to live up to his name, he ended up having no children at all"(119).

12. Chinweizu, Onwuchekwu Jemie and Madubuike, who are the earliest and most important theoretical representatives of decolonization of African literature, stressed that "novels about contemporary Africa need to capture the flavor of contemporary African life" (240). Although Emecheta and other women writers such as, Flora Nwapa and Ama Ata Aidoo, applied this mode of decolonization even before Chinweizu, Jemie, Madubuike and Ngugi wa Thiong'o wrote their theoretical essays, they are hardly mentioned much less appreciated by them.

13. For example, Joyce Cary's *Mr. Johnson*, Tania Blixen's *Out of Africa*, Joseph Conrad's *Heart of Darkness*, Rider Haggard's *King Solomon's Mines*.

14. See, for example, Ashcroft, Griffths, and Tiffin *The Empire Writes Back*. Sol T. Plaatjes novel, *Mhudi*, is the first and Chinua Achebe's, *Things Fall Apart*, the most famous representative of the poetics of writing back.

15. Achebe's novel *Things Fall Apart*, Senghor's poetry and Okot p'Bitek's

Song of Lawino belong to this category.

16. The term "the Other" originates from Simone de Beauvoir. In her influential book *The Second Sex* she uses this term to refer to the socially discriminated groups of blacks and women.

17. However, this is not evident lexically in Igbo language.

18. I refer to scholars or writers respectively, such as Amadiume (84–85), Nwapa (105) and Okoh (36).

19. For a discussion of what qualifies a figure as being a stereotype see Chinweizu, Jemie and Madubuike, 114, Forster, 103–104, 118; Emenanjo, xvii.

20. This social or biological assignment is revealed in *Ifo* first sentences which introduce women as property of men and/or as mothers respectively: See "A man had two wives. Both women had one child each."(Umeasiegbu, 76); "A king had two wives, one wife had two children while the other had none" (ibid., 86); "A king had a wife....This woman had four sons for him"; (ibid., 103).

    On the other hand, men are not only presented as sons, fathers and husbands, but frequently as belonging to a certain people or professional or social group.

21. The Igbo Reverend Augustine Ihedinma pointed out that as every Igbo is expected to behave properly, the tales are about how you should not behave. Whereas any deviation from appropriate behavior is commented on, people are rarely praised for appropriate behavior (interview with Reverend Augustine Ihedinma, in London, December 12th, 1991).

22. See, for example: "A few days afterwards, the unknown suitor came back to the palace to pay the dowry. As soon as this was done, he took his wife away" (Umeasiegbu, 94); "She there and then said she was going with the young bridegroom" (ibid.); "The devil paid the bride price...and amid all festivity the bridegroom expressed a wish to lead his bride away" (Bordinat & Thomas, 20); or "The girls all got married and followed their husbands. The boys got married and took their wives at distant places" (Umeasiegbu, 74).

23. There is, for example, "Egoyibi and Her Husband" (Umeasiegbu, 60–61), the story of the woman who is so beautiful that her husband wants to have her all to himself and therefore does not allow her to go out.

24. This contradiction is underlined by sentences such as: "Though they were the wives of one husband, one was the incarnation of jealousy and malice, while the other was gentle as a lamb, unrevengeful and peace-loving" (Bordinat & Thomas, 94).

25. This imagery of spirit children presumably embodies the Igbo notion of the *ogbanje*-child, the dead-living child. S/he torments his/her mother all her life: after his/her death s/he only returns to the mother in order to die again.

26. The term *chi* describes a kind of personal destiny that influences Igbo persons' lives tremendously.

27. *Ifo* also negotiate powerful and influential women, who are not characterized as spiteful. However, such female images are rather rare.

28. This tendency is found in many African oral narratives.

29. Simultaneously, the committed African women writers practice an intertextual dialogue of writing back with African male writers such as Chinua Achebe, Elechi Amadi, Okot p'Bitek and Leopold Senghor. (See "The Shallow Grave," "Periodic Embodiments," *Manichean Aesthetics Reconsidered.*)

30. Moreover Aku-nna is introduced as an *ogbanje*, a "living-dead," who is "much too thin and weak and is likely to catch any disease" (9). So her mother stresses, "I am not allowing you out of my sight until you are seventeen, or you are bound to die of childbirth" (111). People repeatedly recognize her weakness, so they gossip: "Can you see her bearing children, that one? Her hips are so narrow..."(78).

WORKS CITED

Achebe, Chinua. *Things Fall Apart.* London: Heinemann, 1958.

Acholonu, Catherine Obianuju. *Western and Indigenous Traditions in Modern Igbo Literature.* Ph.D. University of Düsseldorf, 1985.

Amadiume, Ifi. *Male Daughters, Female Husbands: Gender and Sex in an African Society.* London and New Jersey: Zed Books Ltd, 1987.

Andrade, Susan. "Rewriting History, Motherhood, and Rebellion: Naming an African Women's Literary Tradition." *Research in African Literatures* 21.2 (1990): 91–110.

Ashcroft, Bill, Gareth Griffths, and Helen Tiffin. *The Empire Writes Back.* London: Routledge, 1989.

Bakhtin, Mikhail. *Rabelais and His World.* Bloomington: Indiana UP, 1984.

de Beauvoir, Simone. *Das Andere Geschlecht. Sitte und Sexus der Frau.* Hamburg: Rowohlt Taschenbuch Verlag, 1988.

Blixen, Tania. *Jenseits von Afrika.* München/Zürich: Heyne Allgemeine Reihe, 1986.

Boehmer, Elleke. "Stories of Women and Mothers: Gender and Nationalism in the Early Fiction of Flora Nwapa." *Motherlands: Black Women's Writing from Africa, the Caribbean and South Asia.* Ed. Susheila Nasta. London: The Women's Press,1991, 3–23.

Bordinat, Phillip, and Thomas, Peter. *Revealer of Secrets.* Lagos: African UP, 1975.

Bovenschen, Silvia. *Die Imaginierte Weiblichkeit.* Frankfurt am Main: Suhrkamp, 1979.

Brown, Lloyd W. *Women Writers in Black Africa.* Westport, Connecticut: Greenwood Press, 1981.

Cary, Joyce. *Mister Johnson.* London: Penguin Books, 1985.

Chinweizu, Onwuchekwa Jemie, and Ihechukwu Madubuike. *Toward the Decolonization of African Literature: African Fiction and Poetry and Their Critics.* London: KPI Limited, 1980.

Chukwuma, Helen. *The Oral Tradition of the Ibos.* Ph.D. University of Birmingham, 1974.

Conrad, Joseph. *Heart of Darkness.* London: Penguin Books, 1989.

Davies, Carole Boyce. "Introduction: Feminist Consciousness and African Literary Criticism." *Ngambika: Studies of Women in African Literature.* Eds. Carole Boyce Davies and Anne Adams Graves. Trenton, NJ: Africa World

Press, 1986. 1—24.

Egudu, Romanus. *The Calabash of Wisdom and Other Igbo Stories.* Lagos, Enugu: NOK Publishers Ltd, 1973.

Ekwensi, Cyprian. *Ikolo the Wrestler and Other Ibo Tales.* London, New York: Thomas Nelson, 1954.

Emecheta, Buchi. *The Bride Price.* New York: George Braziller, 1976.

—. *Double Yoke.* New York: George Braziller, 1982.

—. *Head Above Water.* London: Fontana Paperbacks, 1986.

—. *Second-Class Citizen.* London: Flamingo Press, 1987.

—. "Feminism with a small 'f'!" *Criticism and Ideology. Second African Writer's Conference.* Ed. Kirsten Holst-Petersen. Uppsala: Scandinavian Institute of African Studies, 1988 (a). 173—185.

—. *The Joys of Motherhood.* New York: George Braziller, 1988.

—. *Naira Power.* London: Macmillan Education Ltd, 1991.

—. *A Kind of Marriage.* London: Macmillan Education Ltd, 1991.

Emenanjo, E. "Introduction." *Omalinze, A Book of Igbo Folktales.* Ed. E. Nolue Emenanjo. Ibadan: Oxford UP, 1977, pp. vii—xx.

Ezikeojiaku, Iche. "Classification of Igbo 'Orature'." *Nigeria Magazine* 53.2 (1985): 66—83.

Forster, E. M. *Aspects of the Novel.* New York: Harcourt, Brace, 1927.

Gunner, Liz, Mafika Gwala. *Musho! Zulu Popular Praises.* East Lansing, MI: Michigan State UP, 1991.

Haggard, Rider. *King Solomon's Mines.* Leipzig: Bernhard Tauchnitz, 1886.

Honsza, Norbert. *Moderne Unterhaltungsliteratur: Bestandsauf-nahmen, Thesen, Analysen.* Wroclaw: Wydawnictwa Universytetu Wroclawskiego, 1978.

James, Adeola. *In Their Own Voices: African Women Writers Talk.* London: James Currey/Portsmouth, NH: Heinemann, 1991.

Nwapa, Flora. *Efuru.* London: Heinemann, 1966.

Ngugi wa Thiong'o. *Decolonizing the Mind. The Politics of Language in African Literature.* London: James Currey, 1986.

Ogunyemi, Chikwenye Okonjo. "Women and Nigerian Literature." *Perspectives on Nigerian Literature: 1700 to the Present.* Vol. I, Ed. Y. Ogunbiyi. Lagos: Guardian Books, 1988. 60—67.

Okoh, Nkem. *Traditional and Individual Creativity in Enuani Igbo Tales.* PhD Thesis: London School of Oriental and African Studies, 1984.

—. "Categories of Igbo Oral Literature: the Enuani Example." *Journal of Asian and African Studies.* 35(1988): 73—83.

Okphewo, Isidore. "The Oral Performer and His Audience: A Case Study in the Ozidi Saga." *The Oral Performance in Africa.* Ibadan: Spectrum Books Limited, 1990: 160—184.

p'Bitek. Okot. *Song of Lawino, Song of Ocol.* London: Heinemann, 1984.

Plaatje, Sol T. *Mhudi.* London: Heinemann, 1978.

Schipper, Mineke. "Mother Africa on a Pedestal: The Male Heritage in African Literature and Criticism." *Women in African Literature Today* 15 (1987): 35—54.

Shelton, Austin. "The Articulation of Traditional and Modern in Igbo Literature." *The Conch* 1.1 (1969): 30—49.

Stratton, Florence. "The Shallow Grave: Archetype of Female Experience in

African Fiction." *Research in African Literatures* 19.2 (1988): 143—169.

—. "Periodic Embodiments. An Ubiquitous Trope in African Men's Writing." *Research in African Literatures* 21.2. (1990): 111—126.

—. *Manichean Aesthetics Reconsidered: Contemporary African Literature and the Politics of Gender.* PhD. Thesis. London: School Of Oriental and African Studies, 1991.

Uba-Mgbemena, A. "*Ifo* Prose Narratives as Bearers of Beliefs in Traditional Igbo Society." *Nigeria Magazine* 54.3 (1986): 70—76.

Umeasiegbu, Rems Nna. *Words are Sweet: Igbo Stories and Storytelling.* Leiden: E.J. Brill, 1977.

Wolf, Naomi. *The Beauty Myth: How Images of Beauty are Used Against Women.* London: Vintage, 1991.

Nigerian Legal Concepts in Buchi Emecheta's *The Bride Price*

Rebecca Boostrom

Court cases occur at or near the structural climaxes of many of Buchi Emecheta's novels, including *The Joys of Motherhood*, *Naira Power*, *Second-Class Citizen*, and *Gwendolen*. This study will consider the law depicted in Buchi Emecheta's *The Bride Price* applicable to the families and circumstances surrounding the fictional court case which occurs in Ibuza, Nigeria in the early 1950s, after Akunna Odia elopes with the descendant of a slave. This interdisciplinary study will show that *The Bride Price*, by depicting many realities of lived traditional customary law of the Ibo people, reveals the need for social changes which were already in the process of being enacted in modern law, whether customary law or received British law. Buchi Emecheta's didactic conclusion of having Akunna die as an exemplar to modern young Ibo women will be examined in light of the law at the time of the novel's setting in the early 1950s and subsequent modern Nigerian law in the 1950s and 1960s.

Despite the authorial intention (168) to show that Aku-nna should not have opposed the tradition of the Ibo people by eloping with a son of the Ofulue family without the consent of her patriarchal stepfather, the Ofulue family to which Aku-nna joins herself is representative of social changes in Nigerian society at a time in history when those changes were ready to be translated into new laws made in the mid- and late-1950s by the political leaders, legislators, and judges. Aku-nna's forbidden union with the descendant of a slave occurs just prior to important legislation that could have helped protect her choice—if she had not died in childbirth. Therefore, the novelist's stated purpose in having her die appears quite unnecessary except to belie the novelist's sympathetic portrayal of her tragic heroine, which in turn causes the reader to be sympathetic to the need for social change.

The Bride Price is not an exotic story of modern folk lore, despite its simple folk-tale style. Emecheta is primarily true to her stated purpose in her fiction: "Every good novel must depict a society. The society is the bone of the story."[1] Economical and geographical sources, in addition to law, support many details of Emecheta's cultural milieu in Iboland at an important time in Nigerian history in the early 1950s, near the apex of British colonialism in Nigeria just prior to national independence in 1960.

In Nigeria in the early fifties, there were two legal systems, the British judicial system and the customary judicial system.[2] The dual system of courts seen in Emecheta's story had been evolving all during the colonial period and evolved even further into a converted dual system after nationalism:

> Law was central to colonialism in Africa as conceived and implemented by Europeans and as understood, experienced, and used by Africans. Laws and courts, police and prisons formed essential elements in European efforts to establish and maintain political domination. They were instrumental as well in reshaping local economies to promote the production of exports for European markets and the mobilization of labor for African and European enterprises....Finally, Europeans believed that they were in Africa for the local peoples' own good. The idea of rule of law seemed to them to provide evidence of this fact, and it powerfully legitimized colonial rule.

...Law not only affected nor was it only affected by
engagements between Africans and Europeans.
Struggles among Africans were central as well....It
reminds us, however, that in the colonial period
Africans met one another on the legal battlefield far
more often than they did Europeans. The legal discourses and debates, disputes and conflicts among
Africans were as important as those between
Africans and Europeans in shaping the colonial
social order. (Roberts and Mann, 3–4)

By the time Emecheta's story takes place, the judge and the lawyers
in the British law court in Ibuza and other similar cities would have
been Nigerians trained in law in Great Britain. Emecheta correctly portrays the village, Ibuza, historically as having a British law
court there in the 1950s. Knowing more about the historical Ibuza
can help the reader follow and understand better some factors in
Emecheta's portrayal of the Ofulues vs. Obidis trial and its aftermath. Geography shows that Ibuza was in a fertile rain forest agricultural area[3] good for growing both domestic and export crops,
was on a westward land transport route to Lagos,[4] and was near
enough to the Niger River at Asaba for good transportation to the
coast. Therefore, the British were commercially interested in Ibuza.
By 1962, a Federal Survey's map showed more schools (eight) and
more courts (two) in Ibuza than in nearby Asaba, although Asaba
was a river port and the provincial seat of Benin province. The two
courts of Benin province were located in Ibuza.[5] Although Ibuza
had only a town population of 12,851 in 1952 (1952 census), it was
twice as large in population as Asaba, the provincial seat and a
British commercial river station since the nineteenth century.[6]
Ibuza also was relatively large for an interior rural town's population in comparison with Lagos with a population of only 90,193 in
1952, although Lagos was a major port and a capital city with one
of four major administrative divisions of the British government.[7]
Moreover, in 1928, the oldest teacher training college in southern
Nigeria[8] was opened at Ibuza.

The actual historical and political background of Ibuza helps
explain why Buchi Emecheta portrays that "the whole town" of
Ibuza turned out against the alien[9] and slave Ofulue family in the
British-law court. Various factors generated pride in indigenous tra-
dition in Ibuza. Ibo culture in Ibuza begins around 1580, during the
Nri and Isu movements. Oral tradition has kept a complicated and

a seemingly complete genealogy[10] of the clans in the town since its settlement. The Ibuza native political government is based on patrilineal and matrilineal ties between the original indigenes of Ibuza.[11] Historically, Ibuza's town population was estimated at 40,000 in 1910 and was the highest in the Western Igbo area.[12] When natives of Ibuza moved elsewhere for employment in the 1920s and 1930s, they still kept political ties with Ibuza through the Ibuza "unions" formed in the major cities, such as, Lagos, Enugu, Ibadan, Port Harcourt, Zaria, Jos, and Kano.[13] On July 31, 1942, all the Ibuza unions throughout Nigeria were unified. Some monies collected from union members helped renovate the Ibuza Customary Court in 1953,[14] around the time of Emecheta's court case in the British-based court. Therefore, the town's pride in the native customary court (as contrasted to the British-law court) would have been high at the time the slave-background family chose to use the British-law court in Ibusa.

The love triangle background behind the court case begins when Chike Ofulue and Aku-nna fall in love when Chike is Aku-nna's teacher. Chike is called the descendant of a slave behind his back by the Ibuza people, although he attended St. Thomas' Teacher Training College in Ibuza, Nigeria (*supra*), in the late 1940s (146). Four years after his graduation (146), he is a young, unmarried middle school instructor teaching Aku-nna.

Aku-nna falls in love with Chike after moving from Lagos, a modern big city, to Ibuza,[15] a rural village, where she feels lonely. Her ignorance of Ibuza marriage customs is made clear by her surprise to learn that they had moved because her mother had been "inherited" (64) in marriage by her father's brother, according to the customary law of "widow inheritance."[16] When she moves with her mother and brother from Lagos to Ibuza, upon the death of her father, Aku-nna experiences the group mind's control:

> What she still had to learn was the fact that her people, the people of Ibuza, have what psychologists would call the group mind. They all help each other when in trouble or in need, and the extended family system still applied even in a town like Lagos, hundreds of miles from Ibuza. They are a people who think alike, whose ways are alike, so much so that it would not occur to any one of them to behave and act differently. (16)

Emecheta's emphasis on the "group mind" is a preface to her somewhat oversimplified authorial thesis that Aku-nna's independent decision to marry a descendant of a slave brings an unbearable "guilt" that causes her death: "guilt for going against her mother and her uncle killed her. . . ."[17]

Against a background of Aku-nna's naivete of Ibuza marriage customs, she begins to attend the Christian Missionary Society (CMS) school (*supra*) where young Chike Ofulue, the head teacher, age 24, is her handsome teacher. Though Chike has been sexually promiscuous with various married women, he falls in love for the first time with Aku-nna.

When Aku-nna's stepbrothers, Iloba and Osenekwu, hear the teacher might be interested in their new stepsister, they feel concerned about her:

> "The son of Ofulue? You mean Chike, the school teacher? But he is the son of slaves, Mother, and he knows his place. Chike is only Aku-nna's teacher. He can't help talking to her, because she is in his class. She couldn't be interested in him to that extent!" Iloba cried, his mouth tasting salty. If this was true, it was the greatest insult that could befall a family like theirs, which had never been tainted with the blood of a foreigner, to say nothing of that of the descendants of slaves.
>
> "I will kill her if this is true," Osenekwu swore to himself. (79)

The stepbrothers' comments portray a social stigma also found in a mid-twentieth century legal study by a distinguished Nigerian lawyer, a study written after the Act of Emancipation of the Abolition of Osu Law of 1956 (which made it illegal to call anyone "slave" (*oru/osu*) who descended from a slave):

> For, though socially there are still numerous oru (*ohu*) [species of slaves] in Iboland in spite of the Act of Emancipation and the Abolition of Osu Law, these can now own land as freely as anybody else. The social stigma remains, but as far as land rights are concerned partially every trace of legal disability is gone. An oru may not marry a free-born, but he can purchase, lease or take a pledge of land from anyone within the village or town....

> Today [1963] the position [of descendants of the *osu*
> species of slaves] is quite different. There are no first
> generation *osu* of the buy-and-delicate type any
> more. And though their descendants are still called
> by that dreadful name, though inter-marriage
> between *osu* and freeborn is still anathema, an *osu*
> of this class can and does own land individually.
> (Obi, 80–81)[18]

Emecheta allows Chike the advantage of a secret time of courtship
in which he could overcome his disadvantage of being a social *osu*[19]
(slave) to win Aku-nna's heart as her suitor in marriage. As a rich
man's son, he uses his advantage of having extra spending money
to meet her on market days and to buy all the plantain she was carrying to market, so she would have time to sit alone with him.
Chike also buys and gives food gifts to Aku-nna's mother, which
she accepts because there is a shortage of food. The malnourishment of Aku-nna and her family during the time of courtship foreshadows malnourishment as being a factor in her later death during
childbirth. During the courtship kept secret even from Aku-nna's
mother, her mother chooses to view the gifts of food as signs of
friendship.

According to Ibo customs, Aku-nna is eligible for a legal customary marriage when she begins to menstruate around age 15.
By customary law, puberty must be reached before marriage
(Kasunmu & Salacuse, 76). By received British common law (as
interpreted by Nigerian lawyers for its relevancy in Nigeria), the
minimum marriage age for a monogamous marriage for boys was
age 14 and for girls age 12, because the Nigerian jurists viewed the
age of 21 for marriage in modern England as legally irrelevant for
use in Nigeria (Kasunmu & Salacuse, 13). Emecheta follows Ibo
tradition in portraying that most Ibo girls were betrothed and
entered an arranged customary marriage soon after their first menstruation. However, modern Nigerian jurists recommended that
the minimal marriage age should be higher, 16, due to poor nutri-
tion to give the girls more physical development before child-
bearing. The jurists also desired that more girls get more education
(Kasunmu & Salacuse, 77).

On Chike's first visit to Aku-nna's patrilineal home after she
had become secretly eligible for marriage, his family's slave background dominates the scene. Throughout the novel, the only
description of the interior of the hut is in this passage (97).

Emecheta simply describes a mat on a mud couch on which the lovers sat. The wealth of symbolism simply reflected in the woven mat arises from the mat's origins and history. It was made in Sierra Leone and bought in Lagos, Nigeria. Lagos had a history[20] of many former slaves who settled there. Perhaps half the population of Lagos in 1850 were slaves (Mann, 86), many of whom became rich and powerful, similar to the Ofulues in Ibuza.

More slavery symbolism is contained in the detail that the mat was made in Sierra Leone. Ties between Sierra Leone and Nigeria were based on Sierra Leone being the geographically closest British colony to Nigeria, from which slaves and ex-slaves had come to Nigeria and to which British colony many repatriated slaves were sent. Lagos, as a British colony in 1862, was administered as part of Sierra Leone after 1866 and then as part of the Gold Coast from 1874 to 1886, at which time Lagos was separated from the Gold Coast and began a self-governing British colony.[21]

The mat also hints at family history because her father had moved from Ibuza to Lagos where Aku-nna had been born. Her mother had bought the Sierra Leone mat in Lagos before Aku-nna's father had died there. Then, her mother had brought the mat to Ibuza (97). Now, by customary law, her paternal uncle, her step-father, would have to give his consent to any marriage she entered.

Chike knows his slave background might cause Aku-nna's step-father to reject him as a suitor. While alone until Aku-nna's mother returns home, Chike inquired: "Had she not heard that his ancestors were slaves[22] and had never been born in this land? Did she think it was a joke...?"(98) While sitting and petting on this Sierra Leone-Lagos mat, Aku-nna tells Chike to have his father ask to arrange their marriage with her paternal uncle. Although this request of Aku-nna's at age 15 may seem bold to the Western reader, her request to Chike is timely and necessary, because, now that she has begun menstruation, she can be promised in marriage by her stepfather. Historically, at that time, the Ibo girl had no legal right to choose her partner in marriage. Aku-nna's request is important because her request shows that if she could choose her marriage mate, she herself would choose to marry an *oshu* (descendant of a slave). Her request significantly follows Chike's admission that he is not only a descendant of a slave, but also a foreigner.[23]

In December after her exams are over, Aku-nna can no longer hide her menstrual period, and the news of her new status of being eligible for marriage spreads quickly. Aku-nna's stepfather immediately has a patriarchal talk with her:

"Aku-nna, Chike Ofulue is only a friend... Now that you have grown, that friendship must gradually die. But die it must!"

...But the way he had spoken just now was the voice of authority, that authority which was a kind of legalized power. He was telling her, not in so many words, that she could never escape. She was trapped in the intricate web of Ibuza tradition. She must either obey or bring shame and destruction on her people. (116)

In this passage, Buchi Emecheta states the authorial theme of her novel in which Aku-nna becomes a tragic heroine because she does not obey.[24]

Any society is in a state of change, however. Aku-nna and Chike are pitted against "Ibuza tradition" at a historical time when changes within the country appear to make their future married life together possible, at least to Chike's *oshu* family. Although Chike's grandmother had been a slave, his father was educated at a missionary school in Ibuza and later returned to Ibuza as a well-educated and rich man. Chike's older brothers and sisters were well-educated and rich and able to marry mates from other towns. Chike's father, who has lived through much social change and has known deep love with Chike's mother, sympathetically counsels him:

"There is one thing I beg of you. Whatever you do, don't spoil that girl—don't disvirgin her before you are sure she will be your wife. There is no worse fate for any woman in this town than that of one who arrives at her husband's couch polluted."

"No one is having her but me," Chike insisted.

"And you are not stealing her, either. We may be descended from an *osu* woman, but I like to do things in the proper manner. Tell me when she becomes a woman, then we shall go and speak to her people."

"But, Father, if they refuse, what are we going to do?"

"You are dancing yourself tired before the music has even begun. Wait until it starts. If the tune changes,

we too will change with the tune. But we cannot do
anything until the music starts. Keep your ear to the
ground and be watchful, so that you will not be the
second to ask for her when she becomes a woman.
Be very careful." (106)

True to his word, Chike's father, along with male relatives, begin
talks with Okonkwo, Aku-una's stepfather. Old Mr. Ofulue financially can offer a very high bride price for Aku-nna, and Okonkwo
needs money to obtain a higher political position of "*Obi*" or chief
(75). Therefore, Okonkwo does not reject talks with the Ofulue
men (128).

The normal course of events for a young Ibo woman drastically
changes when Aku-nna is kidnapped one night while she, her
cousin, and a group of girlfriends are practicing with their instructor for an "outing dance." The girls' public performance and singing
aja songs at this "outing dance" is a happy community event preceding marriage, and is usually done before being betrothed. After
her abduction, her forced marriage with Okoboshi is celebrated
with gun shots, fertility rituals, singing, dancing, and feasting at
the Obidi family's *obi* or compound.[25]

According to Emecheta, kidnapping the bride is a custom that
does not invalidate a customary marriage if the bride's paternal
family shows acquiescence and subsequently accepts the bride
price (154). But according to Ibo lawyers, who mainly began record-
ing customary law in the mid-twentieth century, kidnapping the
bride made the purported marriage void:

GIVING AWAY THE BRIDE

Our fourth and final essential for a valid customary
marriage is what may be called the "giving away" of
the bride, for want of a better term...

...In a number of societies, including the Ibo and
some Yoruba, this "giving away" takes place at the
home of the bride or some other place of her family's choice, the bridegroom and/or his representative going there to receive her....

VOID, VOIDABLE AND INCHOATE MARRIAGES[72]

...A purported marriage which lacks one or more of
these essentials is either void, voidable or merely
inchoate....

(a) Void marriages

A purported customary marriage is void *ab initio* in five sets of circumstances.

...(i) If the consent of the bride's parents or guardian to the transaction was not obtained, there could be no marriage, since in the nature of things, there would be no agreement on the payment or waiver of the bride price; neither could the bride be properly given away in marriage.

... (v) Finally, a customary marriage is void if it is not supported by the payment or express waiver by the bride's family of a bride price (dowry). It should be remembered, though, that payment may be postponed in whole or in part either for a fixed period or indefinitely....

[[72]In strict logic, a "void marriage" is a contradiction in terms, for what is void is no marriage. Nevertheless, we use "marriage," "husband," "bride," etc., in such cases as shorthand for "purported marriage," etc.] (Obi 1966, 181–182)

Because Aku-nna was kidnapped, not "given away" by her family, the marriage ceremony at the Obidi *obi* resulted in a *void ab initio* (void from commencement) marriage, by law.

In 1966, a family law professor from the University of Ife, Alfred B. Kasunmu, LL.M., also wrote that a common essential legal element of customary marriage throughout Nigeria is a physical or symbolic delivery of the girl by the girl's family to the boy's family, separate from the payment of the bride price (Kasunmu & Salacuse, 81–83). Aku-nna is kidnapped, not delivered by her family; accordingly, the purported marriage between Aku-nna and Okoboshi is a void marriage.[26]

Moreover, a valid marriage was also voidable by customary law if not consummated (Kasunmu & Salacuse, 155—159). As a simple Ibo girl, she merely acts on her instincts when afraid after the kidnapping and when Chike offers her security. The evening she is kidnapped, after ritual ceremonies are performed to bless her marriage to Okoboshi with fertility, she is left alone awhile before Okoboshi first comes alone to her. Guarded by Okoboshi's sister, Aku-nna goes outside the compound to the *owele* (toilet). Upon hearing Chike whistle a song to her in the dark, she makes her own decision:

> There was a comforting feeling of security in her knowledge that she was also being watched by Chike, and that moment clinched her determination. If ever she got out of this alive, there was no man for her but Chike, slave or no slave. (136)

Soon thereafter in the bridal room when Okoboshi comes to her in his handsome bridegroom's robe, he disrobes and begins wrestling with her to take her by force. Based on the situation, Aku-nna is legally[27] justified in angrily accusing Okoboshi's family of "stealing" (136) her. To repulse him, she fabricates a story that Chike had disvirgined her that afternoon and mocks Okoboshi in bitter laughter:

> "Look at you, and shame on you. Okoboshi the son of Obidi! You say your father is a chief—dog chief, that is what he is, if the best he can manage to steal for his son is a girl who has been taught what men taste like by a slave."

> "Even if you do sleep with me tonight, how are you ever going to be sure that the child I might bear would be your own? I may already be expecting his child, and then you would have to father a slave child. What a come-down for the great and mighty Obidi family! For I should never stop telling my son whose child he was."

> "But you were unclean until two days ago. My mother said so."...

> "Oh, yes, that is true. But today I passed my examination. We celebrated my success together," she snarled....(138)

Okoboshi believes her, spits on her, curses her, and knocks her out of his bed into unconsciousness for that night. Aku-nna sacrifices her pride and her reputation of being a virgin, highly valued in the Ibo culture at that time, and thereby succeeds in keeping the purported marriage from being consummated the marriage night.

Emecheta narrates that the kidnapping of a bride was permissible by Ibo customs (132), but an "insult" to her stepfather.

Okonkwo begins drinking to adjust psychologically. Aku-nna's mother follows ancient custom to beat a gong to seek information about her kidnapped daughter. Late that night, after their marriage celebration is over, the Obidi male relatives approach Okonkwo. Without being concerned enough about Aku-nna to wait until the next morning to know if she was peaceful or not, they falsely tell Okonkwo: "his stepdaughter Aku-nna was lying peaceably on the mud couch specially prepared for her and her husband, Okoboshi" (132—133). Then, "they brought more gin to dull his senses and a minimal amount was agreed upon as the bride price for Aku-nna" (133). If her stepfather had known Aku-nna had not lost her virginity yet, he would have demanded a higher bride price, especially because Aku-nna was somewhat educated.

The Obidis obtain acceptance of a low bride price and her stepfather's acquiescence in their possession of Aku-nna by "false pretense," which is a form of stealing:

> It is the offense of Cheating for anyone to obtain, by any fraudulent trick or device, from another anything capable of being stolen, or to induce another to deliver such a thing to any other person or to pay or deliver money or goods or any greater sum of money or greater quantity of goods than he would have paid or delivered but for such trick or device. (Elias, "Criminal Law," *Groundwork of Nigerian Law*, 1954, 197)

Her paternal stepfather's consent is all the consent needed for her marriage to Okoboshi; Aku-nna's own consent in marriage is not necessary by traditional customary law at that time (Kasunmu & Salacuse, 75). A few years later, however, between 1955 and 1965, the Native Authority Declaration of Native Law and Custom in Biu Federation, Borgu, Idoma and Tiv and the customary law practices in Igo, Igbomina, Igbirra and Birom changed to provide that the woman must consent to the marriage (Kasunmu & Salacuse, 76).

On the second night of the purported marriage, because the girl's father has acquiesced to the kidnapping by accepting the bride price, if Okoboshi had succeeded in his plan to take Aku-nna by force[28] (then allowable for a husband to consummate a lawful marriage), thereafter any spokesman for Aku-nna would not have been able to disprove that a purported marriage existed in a customary court. But when Aku-nna goes outside the compound on the second night to the *owele* (toilet hut), Chike is waiting for her and they run away to Ughelli, where an international oil company is located, both in the novel and historically. Old Mr. Ofulue had told his son: "If the tune changes, we too will change with the tune" (106). Upon learning his friend's daughter has been kidnapped, he boldly approves of his son's plan to take Aku-nna to Ughelli and provides him money (148). Because old Mr. Ofulue and his family have suffered the stigma of their grandmother having been kidnapped as a slave, Mr. Ofulue feels the courage of heart to approve of Chike's plan to rescue Aku-nna from her kidnapping, with foresight that hostility against himself would most likely follow.

Settled in Ughelli, Chike explains to Aku-nna that "his father would pay the bride price in good time. His family would pay double whatever Okonkwo asked" (149). If the stepfather would accept a bride price from Mr. Ofulue, then he would be obligated by customary law to return the bride price to the Obidi family. Such transfers of the bride price were the local customs for obtaining a divorce[29] without any judicial proceedings and remarriage under customary law (Kasunmu & Salacuse, 172). The Obidi people were obligated to return the bride price because Aku-nna had refused to live with Okoboshi and because Okoboshi had not had sexual relations with Aku-nna, contrary to his family's belief.

To control indirectly Aku-nna's life, Okoboshi, in arrogance, hurt pride and cruel revenge, lies about his first night with Aku-nna: he "told his parents not only that he had slept with the girl the night before and found her empty but that he had cut a lock of her hair...and so, according to their laws and customs, she could not get away from her husband" (154). If Okoboshi had not lied to his parents, the "elders" (154) in Ibuza would have considered the matter of lack of consummation of the marriage in their opinions on the problem. Okoboshi's false boasting is legally arguable as *jactitation* of the marriage by falsely pretending to be the husband (Kasunmu & Salacuse, 195).

The prevailing motive for kidnapping Aku-nna had not been to obtain a bride for Okoboshi, but to revenge old Mr. Ofulue. Okoboshi disdainfully explains he had wanted another girl as his choice:

> "I was not too keen on you anyway. My father wanted you simply to get even with his old enemy Ofulue, your slave lover's father. So you are not a virgin! That will be the greatest fun of it all. You will remain my wife in name, but in a few months I shall

> marry the girl of my choice and you will have to
> fetch and carry for her and for my subsequent
> wives. (139)

Her escape with Chike from this frightening and demeaning situation should not have been so morally culpable as Emecheta authorially decided it was by having Aku-nna later die in childbirth, for having defied tradition for not submitting to Okoboshi deflowering her against her will and for not obeying her stepfather. Mid-century law commentaries reveal that the refusal of a young woman to live with the husband of her parents' choice appears to have been a commonplace occurrence treated casually by Nigerian lawyers. "If after being led to the man's house the girl refuses to stay or the marriage is broken up for whatsoever cause, the dowry is refundable" (Begho, 32). Barrister Obi wrote that "...desertion by a wife is a common feature of domestic life under customary law.[30] ...Customary law has nothing corresponding to the English action for restitution of conjugal rights. In other words, neither the customary courts nor the superior courts applying customary law have power to compel a deserting spouse to return to the matrimonial home against his or her will" (Obi, 1966, 227). "...Occasionally [a girl] will refuse to follow the intended husband in spite of entreaty or applied persuasion. In such a case any expenses incurred by the man must be refunded by the guardian of the girl" (Basden, 69).

The Ofulues' abetting Aku-nna's escape from the Obidi compound and flight to Ughelli with Chike is soon revenged by an act of criminal mischief[31] in cutting down the Ofulue's plantation:

> He [old Mr. Ofulue] accepted that he was of slave
> ancestry and would antagonize the people on that
> score; but he did not mind. Ibuza was the only town
> in which he had roots. He planted cocoa beans and
> palm trees and coconut palms on the piece of land
> that he bought, and this caused a great deal of jeal-
> ousy as the people could see that he began to reap
> the fruit of his labors. This plantation was a sensi-
> tive spot with Ofulue, and it was exactly here that he
> was hit. He simply woke up one morning to find all
> his plants hewed to the ground. (155)

This vengeful destruction of the Ofulue plantation is unlawful by customary law. By Ibo law, Mr. Ofulue can legally purchase land and therefore has legal rights attached to his land (Obi 1963, 80—

81). One reason why Ofulue has come back to Ibuza is to purchase land[32] there. Moreover, although at that time there were problems in customary law with the right of succession[33] to land, there were more protective[34] customary laws protecting the right of ownership of trees than of land in Iboland in the fifties. Food-producing trees or "economic trees" were usually owned by whoever planted them or their heirs. Food-producing trees were highly valued[35] because there was an inadequate food supply at that time. Due to the inadequate food supply of the average person, the Ofulue's plantation of abundant food for export was a clear sign of their wealth.

By Ibo customary law, Ofulue's trees are his property and he has a right as a non-native or foreigner, by law, to use a customary court. However, the whole Ofulue family would have been considered under a legal disability[36] as *oshu* and as non-natives and thereby would have been without equal rights. According to Obi,[37] a customary law court had the following procedure:

> If the parties belong to different families, the head of the complainant's family communicates the complaint to the head of the offender's family. In each case, if a private settlement is not reached, a day is fixed by the two family heads for a trial of the issue. ...On the day fixed for the hearing each party is invited by the *okpala or isi nze* (who acts as chairman) to state their case. After the complainant has done so, the "arbitrators" may have to decide whether this is purely a case of moral (or social) obligation, in which case the parties would be asked to go back and have it settled "at home" (that is privately), with words like *'o buro ife a ga-akpolu okwu'* (Lit. "This is no case for legal proceedings"). If, however, the case is allowed to go on, witnesses are called, or are allowed to volunteer evidence, after the parties have each stated their case. Everyone present is then free to give an opinion on the merits of each party's case. Finally, a smaller, inner court is selected from those present. These go into a final secret session—*igba izu*. The decision of this secret session is the final decision on the case, and is usually announced by the senior *ozo* title-holder or *ofo* holder (okpala).

> There is always a right of appeal to another arbitral
> court.... (Obi 1963, 27—28)

In a customary law court, the Obidi family and their allies would have outnumbered the Ofulue family. The customary law was not written or fixed[38] at that time. With the Ofulue family suffering a legal disability as slaves and as foreigners, the Obidi men would all have had rights to speak first. The Ofulue men could only have spoken when addressed, due to their disability. The court elders deciding the matter were inter-related in blood ties with the Obidi family and the other families who took their side, and so the elders would not have been neutral. Also, previously, "some elders ...pointed out that as long as Okonkwo did not accept any bride price from the slave, the girl still belonged to Okoboshi...."(154). The elders would not have regarded factors that made the purported marriage void or voidable, and might have sympathized with the motive of revenge. In addition, Emecheta's narrator stated that "no one in his senses would use the same standards to judge the deeds of a slave and those of the son of a free man" (154). These Ibo elders would apply two different standards, putting the Ofulues men in the same category as women and children with legal disabilities, without much voice in the elders' group decisions controlling their lives.

Mr. Ofulue's decision to take the petition for damages to the Ofulue plantation to the British law court in Ibuza indicates the value of the plantation was high because the Ofulue family is willing to pay the high cost to obtain Nigerian lawyers trained in England in British law and in received British law in Nigeria. Even Mr. Ofulue does not have the cash resources to pay for the lawyers, and his children have to pool their wealth for the legal retainer. Customary law applied mainly to indigenes (Kasunmu & Salacuse, 85). Therefore, the Obidi family did not need to submit themselves voluntarily to a customary court, although there was a tendency to make the application of customary law territorial, rather than personal (Kasunmu & Salacuse, 85–86). Throughout Africa, it was not until during the 1950s and 1960s that lawyers and lawyer-administrators seriously began to try to comprehensively record customary law.[39] Thus, the Ofulue family in a customary Ibo court would have had to go by the unfixed, primarily oral tradition that could vary from court to court.

At the time of this case, British-law courts upheld customary law, and customary law upheld the rights of descendants of slaves owning plantations. The British court could have felt it had jurisdiction because export crops and non-natives were involved.

When the Ofulue family takes the Obidi family to court, the prominence of old Mr. Ofulue, now in his late sixties or seventies, should not be overlooked. His high status is known because he is "a member of the Native Administration" (84), a historical politico-legal system[40] of indirect rule[41] by the British. Also, only his slave background has prevented him from becoming a chief in Ibuza[42] (84). Ironically, his slave background has helped him to become an educated and important man:

> In the olden days, slaves used to be sent there [to missionary schools] simply to appease the disapproval of the white missionaries; but later events were to show that it was these same educated slaves who ended up commanding key positions. (*The Bride Price*, 74)

Also, the Ofulues were somewhat socially integrated into the Ibuza society, with one Ofulue a former headmaster, one a gynecologist, and Chike a middle school teacher.

The whole village turning out to the trial is not atypical of Ibo people: "Or, a whole village, with the right of all present to participate in the settlement of disputes, might turn out at a market-place for the same purpose as often as occasion arose" (Elias, 9). The legal authorities cited in this study do not allude to any parallel situation to the one Emechetas presents of the "whole of Ibuza" (155), which would include the elders, testifying against one foreign, slave family in a dispute. Buchi Emecheta narrates the court story simply, only telling the essence of the court justice involved:

> The whole of Ibuza came forward as witnesses against the Ofulues. But the law was based in British justice which did not make allowance for slaves, so the Ibuza people lost the case and were ordered to compensate the Ofulue family in kind. The free men had to plant new cocoa for the slave and the heavy fines were fully paid. (155)

In the British colonial court, the Ofulue family are considered foreigners[43] domiciled in Nigeria. The Nigerian law stating that children born in Nigeria of second and third generation descendants of a foreign-born ancestor are still non-natives in Nigeria was an exceptional[44] law in Africa.

The narrator is ambiguous in stating, "British justice...did not make allowance for slaves, so the Ibuza people lost the case" (155). The narrator implies that prejudice against descendants of slaves would have caused the Ofulues to lose all or a major part of their claim in a customary court. Emecheta as author might not have known that in the early 1950s Ibo customary law protected property rights of so-called "slaves" (Obi 1963, 80—81, 90). Otherwise, if Emecheta had known that so-called "slaves" had property rights in Iboland, then she would or should have mentioned that a key to winning in a British law court was the British-law court's disregard of slave ancestry in considering any Obi clan's counter-claim, set-off claim or defense argument based on their loss of possession of an intended bride to a foreign family of slave ancestry.

Certainly recorded customary law, albeit subsequently recorded, and British law protected the property rights of owners of "economic trees" producing food: the oil palm (*nkwu*), the raffia or wine palm (*ngwo*), the bread-fruit (*ukwa*), the coconut (*aku oyibo, aku bekee*), the pear (*ube*), the banana (*une, ogede, unele*), the plantain (*jioko, ojoko*), and the *oha* (*ora*) economic trees. By customary law, persons with a legal disability, including women, children, and former slaves, could own economic trees. Such trees were "all individually owned by the person who planted them and his heir or heirs" (Obi 1963, 91—92).

In British-law courts, "English law is imported into Nigeria by means of reception statutes" (Kasunmu & Salacuse, 8).[45] Also, British-based courts prior to the independence of Nigeria enforced much of the known customary law, when not in conflict with received British law or the repugnancy doctrine. The famous repugnancy doctrine was stated originally by Lord Lugard, who was also well-known as the articulator of indirect rule. The repugnancy doctrine eventually spread throughout all of Africa and continued to be used after independence by various African legal systems:

> The British courts shall in all cases affecting natives (and even non-natives in their contractual relations with natives) recognize native law and custom *when not repugnant to natural justice, and humanity or* incompatible with any ordinance, especially in matters relating to marriage, land, and inheritance. (*Political Memoranda*, 1913–1918, 84) (Kasunmu & Salacuse, 17; emphasis added)

In the Ofulues vs. Obidis case, the repugnancy doctrine would have operated to disallow a defense that kidnapping Aku-nna made her a bride. As far back as the nineteenth century in colonial courts in Nigeria, the British-based courts in general were sympathetic to women who argued that they had been coerced[46] into marriage. The Ibuza British-law court would not have upheld any counterclaim or set-off claim of loss of the value of a bride or a defense argument by the Obidi family that the Ofulue family interfered with Okoboshi's marriage to Aku-nna, which they revenged by cutting down the plantation. If known, Okoboshi's stated plan to sexually take Aku-nna as his wife merely to make her a servant or a kind of slave to other wives would also have been found repugnant. Also, a Magistrate's court of a British-law trained judge and lawyers would have found "repugnant" the Obidi family's claim that Aku-nna was the wife of Okoboshi because he claimed he had cut off a lock of her hair (154)—an act that legally bound a customary marriage.[47]

Apparently the British-law court gave no opinion with regard to Aku-nna's forced purported marriage to Okoboshi because Emecheta never states that a counterclaim for loss of a bride was entered. However, "when the whole of Ibuza came forward as witnesses against the Ofulues," the story of the forced marriage of Aku-nna would have been brought forth. They were present in the court to try to justify the destruction of the plantation to counteract the Ofulues' obtaining of Aku-nna. Discrimination against descendants of slaves would have subtly influenced their statements. In a British-law court, because slavery had been abolished in Nigeria by written law of the Act of Emancipation, any custom or customary law to prohibit marriage between the descendent of a slave and a freeborn person would have been considered contrary to the intent of the written law abolishing slavery, as well as repugnant to "natural justice, equity and good conscience." For many years, colonial courts had upheld customary law, with two exceptions:

> The various courts' laws of the regions and the Federal Territory of Lagos specifically direct the judiciary to observe and enforce every native law and custom so long as (i) it is not inconsistent with any written law, and (ii) it is not repugnant to "natural justice, equity, and good conscience."[48] (Kasunmu & Salacuse, 18)

The British-law court would have been more sympathetic to the Ofulue family for the destruction of their plantation of cocoa, palm, and coconut trees than a customary law court would have been, because in actuality the British had encouraged and promoted the growth of agricultural products, particularly the cocoa and palm tree products found on the Ofulue plantation, as desired exports to England[49] and British markets. At this time, the British were economically interested in Nigeria for its agricultural exports. More than half of the world's exports at that time were being produced in West Africa.

This Ofulue plantation was representative of a new phenomenon of large-scale farming used for the wealth of the cash crops of cocoa and palm oil which were exported to England or British markets. In contrast, sociological-geographical studies record that the average Nigerian farmer by this time had a modest plot of land on which he also grew some marginal cash crops, but only enough to pay colonial taxes, to buy a few goods, and to support meagerly his family, not for the development of the resource of the cash wealth of the Ofulues. A historical antagonism against the British can be realized by the contrast between the British sending foodstuffs from Nigeria to British markets abroad and the indigenous people represented by Aku-nna and her family being malnourished.

Mr. Ofulue could have petitioned the British-law court to nullify the claimed marriage between Aku-nna and Okoboshi because Aku-nna was kidnapped, but Chike's father planned to use tribal customs of the bride price to solve that problem.[50] The Ofulue family probably considered that such matters were very difficult and embarrassing to try to prove in court and could be handled more easily through the local customs of the bride price. Mr. Ofulue knew that his family, as educated people[51] elsewhere in the world, might overcome social stigmas and live in happiness. Buchi Emecheta's novel does not mention that in many areas in Iboland, some families had little or no objection to their children marrying an elite, educated, wealthy descendant of a slave.[52] Therefore, old Mr. Ofulue's thinking is in accord with customary law that is oral, dynamic and based on the consent of the governed, unlike British law that is set once it is written:

> Customary law is unwritten, indigenous law, the law which existed in the land now known as Nigeria before the coming of the British. It is 'a mirror of accepted usage,' a reflection of the habits and social attitudes of the various ethnic groups, and it derives

> its validity from the consent of the community
> which it governs. Because it has this basis, custom-
> ary law is not a static but a flexible body of rules and
> principles, changing and developing to meet new
> conditions. (Kasunmu & Salacuse, 17)

When the Ofulues win the court case in the British law court, the
Obidi family is shamed because "the free men had to plant new
cocoa for the slave and the heavy fines were fully paid" (155). The
prideful anger over this outcome of the court trial causes the Obidi
family to place "curses" on the family of Aku-nna's paternal uncle,
Okonkwo. Therefore, some of the curses may have been to use presumably evil powers to prevent Okonkwo from accepting a bride
price from the Ofulues, due to the prideful anger of the Obidi family in losing Aku-nna to a slave family. Also, the Obidi family may
have felt angry that Okonkwo might accept a large, £50 bride price
(155) from the Ofulues. They may have interpreted this offer as
being a transfer of actual and incoming money, in part, from the
hard labor and the heavy fines they had just had to pay the Ofulues.
Since the Obidis had to suffer, they retaliate by cursing Okonkwo,
the patriarchal head of "the family that had started it all" (155). The
stepfather becomes ill and "forgets his ambition for the Eze title,
and fought for his life and the life of his immediate family" (155).
Emecheta's authorial portrayal of the Obidi family's evil curses as
having power over life, makes understandable Okonkwo's subsequent refusal of a £50 offer of a bride price.[53] Also, "the oracles"
(155) that Okonkwo consults blame Okonkwo for Aku-nna's actions.

Up until then, Okonkwo has sided with the Obidi family against
the Ofulue family, and continues to do so, even against his own
family inherited from his deceased brother, Aku-nna's father. This
study does not purport to explain Okonkwo's cruel reactions
against Ma Blackie and Aku-nna, but Okonkwo appears to try to
appease the evil powers coming against him by sacrificing Aku-
nna's life to them, and to try to regain his social standing by divorcing Ma Blackie. Okonkwo's oral repudiation of Aku-nna's mother
to divorce her (155) is referred to in recorded tribal law.[54] Okonkwo
puts a "hex" or curse on Aku-nna, sticking needles to kill her in a
doll effigy resembling her on the altar of his chi or "personal god"
(156). The narrator describes such a curse as effective in causing
a slow and painful death to its victim (156). Aku-nna tells her new
father-in-law: "I know my uncle does not want ever to accept the
bride price. He calls me back in the wind.... I don't want to die,

Father" (163). By British law in Nigeria, such a noxious curse was legally punishable,[55] but this study found no customary law showing it was punishable in a customary law court. Emecheta's portrayal appears probably correct that this religious rite was condoned by the Ibuza people.

Emecheta presents the nervousness and exhaustion from the curse (158—163), the malnutrition of many years (160), and the young age and slight frame (160) of Aku-nna as physical factors causing her death at childbirth. The author ends her novel by making Aku-nna's story an exemplar:

> Every girl born in Ibuza after Aku-nna's death was told her story, to reinforce the old taboos of the land. If a girl wished to live long and see her children's children, she must accept the husband chosen for her by her people, and the bride price must be paid. If the bride price was not paid, she would never survive the birth of her first child. It was a psychological hold over every young girl that would continue to exist, even in the face of every modernization, until the present day. (168)

Emecheta's ending may depict some old taboos, but it does not depict the law of the 1950s. Because Aku-nna and Chike's story occurred at a pivotal time in Nigerian history, they would have had a chance at happiness had she lived longer. Law and changing law in Nigeria existed then to uphold Aku-nna's rights.

In Ughelli, the narrator tersely describes Chike and Aku-nna's ordinance marriage: "their marriage at the local registry office, Chike and his bride..."(156). Their ordinance marriage was received by British law for monogamous marriages had to be performed back then at the marriage registry office, then based on the Marriage Act, 1914, with amendments.[56]

The dissolution decree of an Ibo couple's marriage by the Supreme Court at Enugu in 1947 in *Agbo v. Udo* based on the Marriage Ordinance (XIX *Nigeria Law Reports Marriage* 152) illustrates the operation of the Marriage Ordinance in Emecheta's Iboland. Under this ordinance, Aku-nna would have been asked if she was lawfully married to another party under customary law, when she signed a form for publication of notice for the intended marriage. Aku-nna's answer would have had to have been "no." When the Ofulue family hired British-trained lawyers to sue for the cutting down of the plantation, undoubtedly the Ofulue family had been legally advised then by these lawyers that received British law would not recognize the purported marriage with Okoboshi as a marriage. At least by independence in 1960, national Nigerian courts also began applying the repugnancy test to customary law (Allott, 159—175). If the Obidi family claimed a marriage existed, then during the three-month waiting period after the notice of marriage was published, the Obidi family needed to enter a caveat against the proposed marriage (Obi, 1966, 191; Kasunmu & Salacuse, 63—64). Within the three-month waiting period after the banns were published, because no caveat was entered either by Aku-nna's stepfather about his need for consent (Obi 1966, 190–191) or by Okoboshi claiming that Aku-nna was his claimed lawfully married wife, Aku-nna and Chike were lawfully married in the registry office and issued a marriage certificate (Obi 1966, 192). Later, if Okoboshi would have wanted to contest her marriage to Chike, if he could have proven in a British-law court that she had been lawfully married to him by customary law at the time of her marriage to Chike, then she would have been liable for imprisonment for five years (*Ibid.*, 197).

For an ordinance marriage, the consent of the parent or guardian had to be documented by an affidavit (Obi 1966, 190) if the girl was under 21. If over 21, the parents' consent was not needed (Kasunmu & Salacuse, 52–66; Elias, 290–294, 303). So Aku-nna must have lied about being age 21 to obtain[57] an ordinance marriage certificate. Such a defect in her ordinance marriage to Chike, however, was not a *fatal defect* so as to void the marriage: "Thus a marriage one or both parties to which are minors but which was celebrated without the necessary parental consent (or its statutory equivalent) is a valid marriage nonetheless" (Obi 1966, 194–195).

Emecheta's portrayal of Aku-nna needing to die as an exemplar for modern times conflicts with a law enacted in 1958 in Nigeria that would have upheld historically anyone like Aku-nna refusing to consummate a marriage. The Marriage Divorce and Custody of Children Adoptive By-Laws Order, 1958, Section 7, allowed a divorce in a British-law court for "(b) refusal of either party to consummate the marriage" and also "(f) ill-treatment, cruelty or neglect of either party by the other" (Ekundare, 31).[58] Also, Section 5 of the said law stated:

> When any parent or guardian of a bride refuses his
> or her consent to a marriage or refuses to accept his
> or her share of the dowry, the bride, if she is eigh-

teen years of age or above, and the bridegroom jointly may institute legal proceedings in a competent
court against the parent or guardian to show cause
why he or she should refuse consent or to accept
his or her share of the dowry; and if the court is of
the opinion that no sufficient cause has been shown,
it shall order that the marriage may proceed without the consent of such parent.[59]

An Ibo barrister, Chinwuba Obi, discusses how this law "deals a
serious blow to the principle of family solidarity and representation in civil litigation" because the bride and her new husband in
a customary marriage may go to the court if the girl's parents are
uncooperative" (Obi 1966, 163). After independence, this law was
adapted and used in customary courts. An Ibo Judge of the High
Court of Midwestern Nigeria, Benin City, Mason A. Begho, LL.B.
(London) of Gray's Inn, wrote in 1971:

> These days, a husband who is unwilling to release
> the wife or who is unwilling to accept back his
> dowry can be sued by the wife to the customary
> court. The whole situation having been fully con-
> sidered, the court may grant the divorce despite any
> objection from the husband. If he refuses to take
> back his dowry, this may be ordered to be paid into
> Court. (Begho, 50)

Although Emecheta has Aku-nna die because the bride-price was
not paid and accepted by her stepfather for her ordinance marriage
to Chike, these soon-enacted modern laws show that she did not
deserve to die; these laws show that the court might find a parent
at fault for not accepting a bride price.

Also, in 1956, a statute titled "Abolition of Osu System Law" [60]
was enacted by the Eastern House of Assembly which forbade Ibo
people from inflicting social disabilities on descendants of slaves
because all forms of slavery were previously abolished. Section 6
of that law particularly forbade prejudice with regard to marriage:
"The significance of section 6 for our present purposes is that it
would be a punishable offence for a parent to refuse to give his son
or daughter in marriage to a suitor (or female applicant) on the
grounds that the said suitor or applicant is a person of slave
descent" (Obi 1966, 172). The Obidi family's social pressure and
curses against Aku-nna's stepfather to prevent him from accepting

the bride price from Chike's father would have been punishable by 1956, under this law enacted by Ibo legislators. It must be noted, however, that this opinion of 1966 is a change in Obi's earlier opinion of 1963, found in *The Ibo Law of Property* where he stated that descendants of slaves could not marry indigenes (quoted *supra*). His diametric views indicate the *osu* law had never been enforced as punishment for discrimination against former *osus* in arranging marriages.

Modernization shows that although in the early 1950s Aku-nna's consent was not necessary for a customary marriage (Kasunmu & Salacuse, 75), before or by 1965 "an investigation of Ibo, Igbomina (Northern Yoruba), Igbirra and Biron customary law indicates that at present a valid customary marriage cannot take place where the intended spouses have not given their consent" (Kasunmu & Salacuse, 76).[61] Aku-nna's refusal to submit to a marriage against her will is actually in line with modern trends and changes in the law of her day.

Emecheta's authorial comments about her heroine do not correspond with mid-century law:

> "Aku-nna had to die because at sixteen she chose someone other than the one her family wanted her to marry. Instead of accepting the husband chosen for her by her family she chose someone who had a history in the family of slavery. So she died because she went against her people by marrying the person she chose. I feel that at sixteen she didn't know what the world was about. She was too young to choose her own husband. Although she knew the man, she was going against her tradition so she had to die. Igbo culture helps here in that if you're that young, your parents know the families and can advise you. If you're young and you want to marry, you should rely on your parents' judgement. On the other hand, if you're old enough then you can judge for yourself and ask, 'Is this the type of person I can share my life with?' If people know how to take the best from each culture [Western and African] and apply it so that things complement each other, different cultural mores can co-exist. They can clash but they don't have to." (Umeh & Umeh, 24)

Buchi Emecheta made these statements in 1980 in an interview at the University of Calabar, years after she had written *The Bride Price* and at a time when her own children were at or approaching marriageable ages. Emecheta's comments in Calabar, in *Head Above Water*, and within *Second-Class Citizen*,[62] suggest she may have been over-reacting to others' criticism and to self-criticism. As a gifted young writer, she used *The Bride Price* to project some of her own feelings into her heroine in creating a marvelous work of art. Based on the laws of the early 1950s, however, there was no need for Aku-nna to die for marrying Chike without her parents' consent. Ms. Emecheta was trying to uphold what she considers to be the better side of the Ibo tradition: that parents should approve of whom their children married, while showing the worse side: that some parents, as Aku-nna's stepfather, would approve of a cruel husband. Her statements that indicate her purpose for writing this work belie her authorial sympathy for her heroine, Aku-nna, whom she portrays as never planning or intending to defy her family, but trapped into doing so. Despite Buchi Emecheta's statements in 1980 in Calabar and in 1986 in *Head Above Water*, her artistic work can be interpreted within itself. Most readers who read *The Bride Price*'s ending will think Emecheta is being ambivalent in saying that all good little girls will be told Aku-nna's story to help them obey their parents' wishes in marriage. Emecheta's delineated "moral" ending to her story, *The Bride Price*, is a notable exception to the many parallels between her story and the laws of mid-century Nigeria. To the foreign reader, Emecheta's portrayal of the love relationship between Aku-nna and Chike appears to be useful in developing both social sympathy for and social acceptance of Ibo girls who choose lawfully to marry the man of their choice, "slave or no slave."

NOTES

1. Umeh and Umeh, 25.
2. "Except for the Federal Territory of Lagos, Nigeria has a dual system of courts. On the one hand, there are the native and customary courts which in civil matters administer primarily customary law. On the other hand, there are the High Courts, Magistrates' Courts and (In the North) District Courts, which are patterned after the English models and in civil matters administer essentially English and non-customary Nigerian law." (Kasunmu and Salacuse, *Nigerian Family Law* 1966, 28).
3. Cf. climatic chart, p. 3, vegetation chart, p.4, and soil chart, p. 12, in *African Environments and Resources*, by Lewis and Berry.
4. *The National Atlas of the Federal Republic of Nigeria*, 99.
5. Asaba, a port city and the seat of Benin province, had one school in town

and four more schools near an outlying hospital area in 1962. There were no courts in Asaba in 1962. *Nigerian Sheet History* (topographic map) of Nigeria, First Edition, Sheet 300 S.W.

6. Asaba's population in 1952 was 5,474. Asaba was an agricultural trade center opposite Onitsha on the Niger River. Cf. Seltzer, Leon E., ed. *The Columbia Lippincott Gazetteer of the World* (1952).

7. Leon Seltzer, ed. *The Columbia Lippincott Gazetteer of the World* (1952).

8. Onwuejeogwu, 5.

9. Cf. Okogwu's *The Legal Status of The Aliens in Nigeria*.

10. Cf. M.A. Onwuejeogwu, 3, 6-13.

11. Cf. M.A. Onwuejeogwu, "The Traditional Political Organization of Ibusa" and "Government of Ibusa," 14-31.

12. The 1910 figure is from M.A. Onwuejeogwu, *The Traditional Political System of Ibusa*, 4, which he bases, without further reference, on "Northcorte Thomas, 1912."

13. M.A. Onwuejeogwu, 32.

14. M.A. Onwuejeogwu, 35.

15. "Ibusa" is the spelling in the governmental publication of a topical map of 1962, after independence, by the Government of Canada for the Government of Nigeria. "Ibuza" is the spelling Buchi Emecheta uses.

16. Although Aku-nna's mother had the right of "first option" to marry her husband's brother or a "second option" to marry another patrilineal male "heir," she did not have the legal right to remarry someone of her own choice outside her husband's patrilineal family. Emecheta portrays Aku-nna's mother as being subject to patrilineal "inheritance" rights in marriage as a background for Aku-nna coming to the age of womanhood and needing to know that, by the dominant Ibuza customs, or customary law, women and children did not have full legal status as men did, and their rights to marry were defined in customary law and were primarily controlled by decisions of the men in their patrilineal clan. Cf. Obi, *The Ibo Law of Property*, "Widow Inheritance," 185-188.

17. *Head Above Water*, 165.

18. A legal authority on property law was interested in marriage laws because of how the laws on ownership of property were tied to the laws of marriage and divorce, and the law of succession.

19. Emecheta's use of the word *osu* for the Ofulue family, whose members were professionally accepted in Ibuza as a gynecologist, a high school teacher, and a former head master, appears to be in line with the usage of the word *osu* as an all-comprehensive term used in the Eastern House Assembly's *Abolition of the Osu System Law*, 1955:

    Mr. E.O. Eyo: "Mr. Chairman, I rise to move in clause 2 to leave out the definition of *Osu* and insert the following 'Osu' means an *Oru* or *Ohu* or *Ume* or *Omoni*, and also includes the descendant of an *Osu*, an *Oru*, an *Ume*, and an *Omoni* and any person subject to a legal or social disability or social stigma which is similar to and nearly similar to that borne by an *Osu*, an *Oru*, an *Ohu*, or *Ume* or an *Omoni*" [Added as Amendment] (Okeke, 142-158).

20. "In the early nineteenth century Great Britain abolished her own slave

trade and began pressuring other nations to end theirs. Reformers believed that abolishing the slave trade in Africa required creating new opportunities for local peoples to sell agricultural products to Europe....

The introduction first of British consular authority [in Lagos] and then of colonial rule stimulated the development of the new international trade [in agricultural products for export] and attracted to Lagos Brazilian and *Sierra Leonean repatriated slaves* and European merchants and missionaries" (Mann, 86; brackets and emphasis added).

21. Cf. "Lagos" in *The Columbia Lippincott Gazetteer of the World* (1952).

22. *The Bride Price* never names the foreign country from which Chike's slave grandmother had come to Nigeria. Also, the kind of slave that the Ofulue's grandmother was is not made clear just by Emecheta's use of the words "*osu*" (107) and "*oshu*"(106,107) without any description anywhere in the novel of whether the grandmother was a work slave or a slave dedicated to a juju god.

As some members of the Eastern House of Assembly had stated in their debates on The Abolition of the Osu System Law in 1956, many descendants of ordinary work slaves (*oru*) had inter-married with the ordinary Ibo people, as Chike's family had. Note also that during the legislative debates, the speakers brought out that there were various words for "slave" and that there was some confusion among the Ibo-speaking people over the meaning of the word *osu* (Okehe 142–158).

Technically, an *osu* slave is one captured or bought and then dedicated to a juju god (Obi, 79-80).

But Emecheta appears to use the broad term *osu* to include both work slaves (*oru/ohu*) and slaves dedicated to a juju god. The lack of information and ambiguity pointed out above prevents a definitive answer as to what kind of slave the Ofulue grandmother was.

23. By Nigerian law defined in the 1960s, a marriage between Aku-nna and Chike would not have been necessarily subject to the Ibo customary laws because Chike was legally a non-native or foreigner domiciled in Nigeria (Kasunmu & Salacuse, 83-87).

24. Emecheta stated her authorial intent for *The Bride Price* in *Head Above Water*:

"During the next few weeks, I wrote five pages a day of *The Bride Price*. The concept behind this book is tradition. Although I was then approaching thirty, whenever I failed in anything I always remembered what I considered my greatest failure—the inability to make my marriage work....I decided that people like me who go against tradition must die.

"In *The Bride Price* I created a girl, Aku-nna, who had an almost identical upbringing to mine, and who deliberately chose her own husband because she was "modern" but was not quite strong enough to shake off all the tradition and taboos that had gone into making her the type of girl she was. Guilt for going against her mother and her uncle killed her when she was about to give birth to her first baby.

"Aku-nna died the death I ought to have died. In real life, due to malnutrition and anaemia, I had a very bad time with my first daughter, Chiedu...a staff nurse took charge..., and I think her quick thinking saved Chiedu and me.

"In *The Bride Price* Aku-nna did not recover. She died because she had gone against our tradition. The original story ended with husband and wife going home and living happily ever after, disregarding their people. But I had grown wiser since that first manuscript. I had realized that what makes all of us human is belonging to a group. And if one belongs to a group, one should try and abide by its laws. If one could not abide by the group's law, then one was an outsider, a radical, someone different who had found a way of living and being happy outside the group. Aku-nna was too young to do that. She had to die" (Ibid. 165-166).

25. The word "obi" means either "chief" or "compound" according to the context. Cf. Obi, *The Ibo Law of Property*, p. 11, for *Obi* meaning "compound" and p.13 for *Obi* meaning "political head."

26. Cf. See also Begho's terminology on the girl being "led" to the man after all marriage arrangements had been made (Begho, 32).

27. In legally considering all the various types of customary law in Nigeria, Kasunmu and Salacuse found essential elements exist for all customary marriages, and one such requirement is the payment of the bride price:

"One of the most distinctive features of Nigerian customary marriage is the requirement that a payment of some sort be made by the boy or his family to the girl's family in order to establish a valid marriage. The authors are unaware of any system of Nigerian customary law which does not have such a requirement. This payment, which must be distinguished from gifts made by the prospective groom, has been given various names such as "bride price," "dowry," "marriage payment," and "marriage consideration."

"The amount of the bride price to be paid varies. In some places, it is arrived at through negotiations by the families; in other places it is established by custom. The factors relevant in determining the amount payable include the education of the girl and her social status. For example, in Eastern Nigeria, the more educated the girl is, the higher the bride-price one has to pay. Another relevant factor is whether the girl has been married before. There is a tendency for the amount payable to be higher on the first marriage than on a second one....

"...The Eastern Nigeria Limitation of Dowry Law [No. 23 of 1956] provides that no more than thirty pounds may be paid. The Western Nigeria Marriage Divorce and Custody of Children Adoptive Bye-Laws Order 1958 [W.R.L.N. 456 of 1958] and the various Northern Nigeria declarations of native law and custom also establish maximum amounts. In practice, however, it is difficult to enforce such regulation of bride-price. It is common knowledge that no one observes the statutory limits on dowry....

"One thing is however clear, something, no matter how small its value, must be paid before a valid marriage can come into existence...It is a simple debt and the parents may take judicial action to enforce it, or in some places, request their daughter to return to their house until they have been paid" (Kasunmu & Salacuse, 78-79).

28. "In the past, customary law gave a husband the right to attain his legal right to sexual connection by using (perhaps reasonable) force. This was probably because a man would normally find it difficult to determine whether his wife's refusal (especially when young) was genuine and intended to be final, or merely inspired by modesty, or else just a preliminary to extracting a favor from him. Cases of this nature seldom ever reach the law courts. And so it would be difficult to say how far, if at all, the traditional customary law stated here still holds good. Under the general law, too, a husband no longer has a legal right to compel his wife by physical force to have connection with him. If he did, he would be guilty of common assault,[10] but not, in our view of indecent assault." [[10] *R. v. Miller* [1954] 2 Q.B. 282, following *R.v. Jackson, ante.*] (Obi, 225).

29. Customary law did not distinguish between annulling a marriage and granting a divorce (Kasunmu & Salacuse, 155).

30. Obi was writing in 1966 about Southern Nigeria, where there are many Ibo areas. S.N. Chinwuba Obi, B.Sc. Econ. (Hons), LL.M., Ph.D. (London) of Lincoln's Inn, Barrister-at-Law, in 1966 was a Solicitor and Advocate of the Supreme Court of Nigeria, and former Research Officer in African Law at the School of Oriental and African Studies, University of London.

31. "Criminal mischief" is a legal term for an act of malicious destruction of property. A case based on criminal mischief can be heard in either a civil court to obtain financial retribution or in a criminal court to seek imprisonment of the offender.

32. Cf. "Individualizing Rights in Land," in *Law in Colonial Africa,* 69-74.

33. One example of such a problem can be found in Meeks, p. 172, in which he states if any man leaves his village, he "may lose his rights over his land, but he does not lose his rights over his trees" (Obi, 92). Also, a woman could own land during her lifetime, but there were complications in the right of succession to her land after her death (Obi, chapters 8 and 9). If such complications existed for land owned by women, surely there were complications when the land was owned by *osus.*

34. Cf. Obi, "Economic Trees Planted by Man," 91-92.

35. When a child was born, sometimes a gift of a food-producing tree was made to the child, and then the child owned that tree. Likewise, husbands might give gifts of food-producing trees to their wives, which were then owned by their wives, who had a responsibility to help provide food for their children (Obi, *The Ibo Law of Property,* 94-97).

36. Cf. Obi, *The Ibo Law of Property,* 68, 79-85.

37. S.N. Chinwuba Obi in 1963 was of Lincoln's Inn and Research Officer in African Law, School of Oriental and African Studies, University of London.

38. Finally, in Iboland, with the exception of comparatively advanced areas like Onitsha, law and custom had not at the time of the British advent become sufficiently institutionalized. While there was a form of chieftaincy system in places like Onitsha, with some kind of traditional courts

which that institution often implies, the greater part of the Ibo areas had no centralized political authority capable of laying down binding rules or enforcing them....A council of elders, sometimes set up *ad hoc*, sometimes permanently empaneled, fulfilled most of the elemental necessities of a legal order in Ibo polity (Elias, *Groundwork of Nigerian Law,* 9). T. Olawale Elias, LL.M., Ph.D.(London) at the time of his writing in 1954 was a Barrister and Solicitor of the Supreme Court of Nigeria and sometimes research fellow of the United Nations Economic and Social Council.

39. Roberts and Mann, *Law in Colonial Africa,* 6.

40. Cf. "Indirect Rule," "Native Authority System," and "Modifications to the Native Authority System," pp.3-7, in *Local Government in Nigeria,* by Philip J. Harris of Cambridge and Nigerian Colleges of Arts, Science and Technology.

41. Igboland, Nigeria, where *The Bride Price* is set, historically did not have the centralized native government needed for the British to use the "native administration" of government to incorporate the native government into the British colonial government. Cf. Kristin Mann's "Indirect Rule, Native Administration, and Customary Law," in *Law in Colonial Africa,* 19-23.

   "In some places the kinds of authorities sought by the British did not exist. Where administrators could not find local rules, they invented them, as among the Igbo of Southeastern Nigeria. British officials constructed Native Administration in Igboland around Macdonald's and Moor's warrant chiefs, reaffirming their executive as well as judicial authority. Conjoining these responsibilities and vesting them in single individuals departed fundamentally from precolonial Igbo political systems (Afigbo, 1972; Adewoye, 1977 a: 40-42 ff). For this reason, Native Authorities in Igboland lacked the legitimacy of their counterparts in Northern Nigeria. Charles Meek, an anthropologist sent to investigate the origins of the Aba women's war, blamed the disturbances in part on the implementation of precolonial village-councils. The women "used their judicial and executive authority to personal advantage, generating widespread hostility. When the chiefs at first supported and then began to collect new taxes, Igbo women rose in protest." (Meek, [1937] 1949: x; Van Allen, 1972; Mba, 1982: 68-97; Mann, 1991).

42. A true account of a famous former slave, Taiwo Olowo, in Nigeria in the nineteenth century who was made an olofin, or king, in his native hometown, Iseri, after he became a wealthy and powerful man in Lagos, is found in "The Rise of Taiwo Olowo," *Law in Colonial Africa,* pp.85-107. He was the second-most politically powerful African man in Lagos by the end of the nineteenth century (Mann, 99). "When delegations visited the colony from Ibadan and Ijebu, Taiwo alone enjoyed the privilege of presenting them to the British authorities." (Cole, 1975: 63, 170, 199; Mann, 99).

43. "(i) Customary law applies mainly to natives....The term native is defined to include a non-native. In both the East and the West, the expression 'Nigerian' is used as against the term 'native.' A Nigerian is a person whose parents were members of any tribe or tribes indigenous to

Nigeria, and the descendants of such persons, and includes a person one of whose parents was a member of such a tribe.

"(ii) Where *both* parties to any dispute or transaction are non-natives or non-Nigerians, the presumption is that customary law could not apply to them or to the transaction. This presumption appears to be indisputable.

"[Footnote 18: This principle should be distinguished from the voluntary submission to the jurisdiction of a customary court by a person not normally subject to that jurisdiction.]" (Kasunmu & Salacuse, 86).

44. Cf. Allott, *New Essays in African Law*, 184.

45. The reception statute may be worded so as to eliminate a transfer of the English law into a completely identical Nigerian law. Cf. Kasunmu, 8. "These reception statutes do not re-enact English laws; they simply state that the English law as of a particular date or on a particular subject shall apply in Nigeria. This technique of incorporation by reference can cause uncertainty with regard to the extent and scope of English law in force in Nigeria." (Kasunmu & Salacuse, 8).

46. Cf. two cases filed by Taiwo Olowo in the Lagos Supreme Court in the nineteenth century: "Taiwo lost his suits against both Oduntan and Okilu, demonstrating that he did not always get what he wanted by going to the supreme court. In the first case, the judge ruled that Taiwo had made his own decision to take the matter before a Yoruba tribunal at Abeokuta and that the colonial court could not now interfere with the ruling of the local authorities. Somewhat contradictorily, the judge then stated that Taiwo's claim was very old, his books were very badly kept, and his eyewitnesses were all illiterate. On the basis of the facts, the court could not sustain Taiwo's claim for 486 pounds" (*Taiwo v. Oduntan*, 1896, LSCR). If Taiwo was to collect any money from Oduntan, he would have to rely on the Egba authorities at Abeokuta. In the second case, the judge simply found for the defendants, without giving reasons. *In general, the court was sympathetic to women who argued that they had been coerced into marriage* (Emphasis added; Mann, *Law in Colonial Africa* 98).

47. The strength of tradition in Ibuza in keeping customary marriage traditions described in *The Bride Price* can be deduced from the activity of the Ibuza student unions, under Ibuza Youth Association, founded in 1956, which had a national youth headquarters in Lagos in 1960 and "agitated for the abolition of the isi mmuo (a system of traditional forced marriage done by cutting off a lock of hair from the head of a woman), and initiated the fixing of a maximum bride gift of £30," without successfully changing at that time the tradition (Onewuejeogwu, 34-35).

The Ofulue family in the early 1950s were up against a very strong marriage tradition that still honored sanctioning a marriage by Okoboshi Obidi's alleged "rape of the lock" of Aku-nna: "he had cut a lock of her hair—some stray curls were produced as evidence—and so, according to their laws and customs, she could not get away from her husband." (*The Bride Price*, 154).

48. E.g., s. 27, High Court of Lagos Act (Cap.80); s. 20, Northern Nigeria Native Courts Law (Cap. 78); s. 19, Western Nigeria Customary Courts

Law (Cap. 31).

49. "...Both the French and British tried to introduce plantations in West
Africa. By and large, most of these projects failed for two reasons. First,
the high mortality of European personnel prevented a large permanent
managerial class from becoming established. Second, it was found to be
more economical to obtain African products through trade. Although the
French were more in favor of plantations than the British, peasant production was dominant everywhere. In West Africa, as a whole peasant
agriculture was the safest way to meet the needs of colonial powers, both
from a political and an economic perspective. European investment, was
largely limited to government, roads, railroads and ports, all of which
were orientated towards export growth. Prior to 1945, little effort was
expended on improving the agriculture of the African peasant farmer.
Subsistence crops, such as yams and cassava, were of little interest to
the colonial powers, with the possible exception of the Germans in Togo
and the Cameroon. Yet revenues from export crops increased dramati-
cally during this period with minimal technological help and investment
from the colonial country.

"From an agricultural perspective, the major impact during this period was the change over from subsistence economies oriented toward
local areas to cash-crop and subsistence economies where a small per-
centage of crops were grown for cash or bartered foreign goods. The
change to a partial cash economy results from a diverse set of events due
to colonial actions. Some of these actions were the reduction of tribal
warfare and the introduction of health services. These changes lowered
death rates and population growth occurred. With the limited introduction of new agricultural technologies, land shortages began to appear in
West Africa. Two responses to this emerging land pressure were: the
African farmer began to grow cash crops to help purchase some of his
needs, and the beginning of wage labor. Other stimuli resulting in the
increase of lands under cash crops were the need of Africans to raise
their incomes to pay colonial taxes and the desire of the people to purchase European goods or services.

"...Dalton described some effects of these changes in agriculture that
in the colonial period resulted in most West African farmers having a
cash component or income as "growth without development." As the bulk
of the farmers' time and labor was used for their subsistence crops, often
they could only cultivate enough cash crops to pay their taxes and to purchase the most basic goods. Nevertheless, in total, West African peasant
agriculture produced large quantities of export crops during this period
much to the advantage of the colonial powers.

"The major export crops of West Africa were peanuts, gum, cocoa,
palm oil, and rubber....

"Cocoa, like peanuts, was an American crop in origin....The largest
area of cocoa cultivation was in Ghana (Gold Coast), Nigeria, and Ivory
Coast. As cocoa requires large labor inputs, population dynamics of growth
and seasonal migration were set into motion by this cash crop. The introduction of cocoa into West Africa encouraged population growth—large-

ly through migration—into the forest country....From zero exports in the 1890s, West Africa accounted for about two-thirds of the world's exports by the end of the colonial period." (L.A. Lewis and L. Berry, *African Environments and Resources*, 80-82).

50. Dissolution of customary marriages was done by returning the bride price without any judicial proceedings (Kasunmu & Salacuse, 172). Judicial proceedings usually occurred when one party held that all or part of the bride price need not be returned due to a fault of the other party or due to other benefits, as work of the wife, that the other party received (Kasunmu & Salacuse, 175-178).

51. Cf., for example, the speech of the Premier in the "Debates in the Eastern House of Assembly on Abolition of the Osu System Law, 1956" (Okeke, 142–158).

52. The debates in the Eastern House of Assembly of 1956 contained arguments referring to marriageable-aged children from well-educated and well-positioned *osu* families, comparable to the Ofulue family (Okeke 142–158).

    The Eastern Province's Abolition of the Osu System Law passed in 1956 would have strongly effected Ibusa and Iboland just west of the Niger River. In Nigeria, the Niger river divides the western and eastern provinces, but Iboland is both in the mid-western and eastern provinces. Ibusa is in the heart of Iboland a few kilometers west of the Niger River.

53. Cf. Begho's discussion of the history of the bride price in Nigeria as compared to other cultures' use of the dowry or gifts before marriage (Begho, 27-38).

54. Cf. "Non-Judicial Dissolution" of customary marriages by a unilateral act of oral repudiation of the wife in front of adult male witnesses (Kasunmu & Salacuse, 172-173).

55. See this reference: "In the early 1880s, he [Taiwo Olowo of Lagos] told his people to seize the goods of some of Ajasa's supporters and prevent them from trading at Iro market. When several of the victims sued for damages in the [British] supreme court [in Lagos], Albert Owolabi Taiwo, eldest son of Taiwo Olowo put a curse on one of them. In this instance the court found Taiwo guilty, and the judge sternly warned him not to engage in any more illegal activities. The Crown subsequently convicted A.O. Taiwo of administering poison or a 'noxious thing.'" (Kristin Mann,"The Rise of Taiwo Olowo," *Law in Colonial Africa*, 99).

56. The Marriage Act, 1914, was for Lagos Colony originally, but extended when British power and law was extended in 1906, when the Colony of Lagos became the Colony of Southern Nigeria, and then in 1914 the two administrations of Northern and Southern Nigeria were amalgamated to become the Colony and Protectorate of Nigeria, with additional practical extension of power and law when colonial registry offices were opened in various important cities. Cf. the "Chronological Table of Ordinances," *The Laws of the Federation of Nigeria and Lagos* (1958), Vol. I, xxxii; and Chapter 115, "Marriage," with sidenotes citing legal references for the history of *The Marriage Ordinance*, Vol. 4, 2349. Also, cf. Obi, *Modern Family Law in Southern Nigeria*, 188-220. Also, see Elias,

Groundwork of Nigerian Law 290–294, 65–106, 122–162.

57. Subsequently, after the time of Chike and Aku-nna's marriage, a governor could dispense with the necessary parental consent (Kingdon, Vol. 4, 2352; Chapter 15, "Marriage," section 13).

58. See also *Western Nigeria Law Reports* of 1958–1966.

59. Quoted by Obi, *Modern Family Law in Southern Nigeria*, 163.

60. Cf. Appendix A, Okeke 142–158.

61. See Salacuse, *A Selective Survey of Nigerian Family Law*, 1965.

62. Cf. her autobiographical novel, *Second-Class Citizen.* The young writer's husband burned the first edition of *The Bride Price* because his patriarchal family would not have approved of the novel. Francis Eze states, "I have read it [*The Bride Price*], and my family would never be happy if a wife of mine was permitted to write a book like that" (*Second-Class Citizen*, 170).

WORKS CITED

Adesanya, S. Abiodun. *Laws of Matrimonial Causes.* Ibadan: Ibadan University Press, 1973.

Aguda, T. Akinnola, ed. *The Marriage Laws of Nigeria.* n.p. The Nigerian Institute of Advanced Legal Studies, 1981.

Allott, Antony. *New Essays in African Law.* Butterworth's African Law Series, No. 13. London: Butterworths, 1970.

Basden, George. *Among the Ibos of Nigeria.* London: Seeley, Service & Co., Ltd. 1921.

Begho, Mason A. *Law and Culture in the Nigerian and Roman World.* Benin City, Nigeria: Commercial Printing Department of Midwest Newspapers Corp., 1971.

Bryde, Brun-Otto. *The Politics and Sociology of African Legal Development.* Institut für Internationale Angelegenheiten der Universitat Hamburg. Frankfurt am Main: Alfred Metzner Verlag GmbH., 1976.

Chanock, Martin. "Paradigms, Policies, and Property: A Review of the Customary Law of Land Tenure." *Law in Colonial Africa.* ed. Kristin Mann. London: James Currey, 1991, 61–85.

Ekundare, R.O. *Marriage and Divorce Under Yoruba Customary Law.* Ile-Ife: University of Ife Press, 1969.

Elias, T. Olawale. *Groundwork of Nigerian Law.* London: Routledge & Kegan Paul, 1954.

——. *The Nigerian Legal System.* London: Routledge & Kegan Paul, 1954.

Emecheta, Buchi. *Adah's Story.* Originally published in Great Britain by Allison & Busby, n.d. New York: George Braziller, 1976.

——. *The Bride Price.* London: Allison & Busby, 1983.

——. *Double Yoke.* Originally published in Great Britain by Ogwugwu Afo, n.d. New York: George Braziller, 1983.

——. *Gwendolen.* London: William Collins Sons & Co., Ltd., 1989.

——. *A Kind of Marriage.* London: MacMillan, 1986.

——. *The Joys of Motherhood.* Originally published in Great Britain by Allison & Busby, n.d. New York: George Braziller, 1979.

——. *Naira Power*. London: Macmillan, 1982.

——. *Second-Class Citizen*. Originally published in Great Britain by Allison & Busby, n.d. New York: George Braziller, 1975.

——. *The Slave Girl*. Originally published in Great Britain by Allison & Busby, n.d. New York: George Braziller, 1977.

Government of Canada for the Government of Nigeria. Sheet History. Vancouver: Pathfinder Engineering, 1962. [Nigerian topographic map.]

Harris, Philip J. Local Government in Southern Nigeria. *A Manual of Law and Procedure Under the Eastern Region Local Government Law, 1955, and the Western Region Local Government Law,* 1952. London: Cambridge University Press, 1957.

Kasunmu, Alfred B. and Jeswald W. Salacuse. *Nigerian Family Law*. Butterworth's African Law Series, No. 12. London: Butterworths, 1966.

Kingdon, Q.C., Sir Donald. *The Laws of the Federation of Nigeria and Lagos*. Twelve volumes. London: Eyre and Spottiswoode Ltd., 1958.

The Law Faculty, University of Ife, editors. *Integration of Customary and Modern Legal Systems in Africa*. University of Ife, Institute of African Studies. New York: Africana Publishing Corporation, 1971.

Lewis, Lawrence, and L. Berry. *African Environments and Resources*. Boston: Unwin Hyman, 1988.

Mann, Kristin and Richard Roberts, eds. *Law in Colonial Africa*. Social History of Africa Series. London: James Currey, 1991.

——. "The Rise of Taiwo Olowo: Law, Accumulation, and Mobility in Early Colonial Lagos." *Law in Colonial Africa*. ed. Kristin Mann. London: James Currey, 1991, 85-108.

Miers, Suzanne. "The Abolition of Slavery in British Africa." Staff Seminar Paper No. 3 (1990-1991), University of Nairobi, Department of History. n.p.

National Atlas of the Federal Republic of Nigeria. Lagos: Federal Surveys, 1978.

Nigeria Law Reports. Vols I-XXI. Lagos: Government Printer, 1938.

Obenson, Gabriel. *Land Registration in Nigeria*. n.p. 1977.

Obi, S.N. Chinwuba. *The Ibo Law of Property*. Butterworth's African Law Series, No. 6. London: Butterworths, 1963.

Obi, S.N. Chinwuba. *Modern Family Law in Southern Nigeria*. London: Sweet and Maxwell, 1966.

Okeke, Igwebuike Romeo. The "Osu" Concept in Igboland. *A Study of the Types of Slavery in Igbo-Speaking Areas of Nigeria*. Enugu: Dona Prints (Nigeria), 1986.

Onewuejeogwu, M.A. *The Traditional Political System of Ibusa*. No. 1. Publication of Odinani Museum, Nri. Institute of African Studies' Project. University of Ibadan, 1972.

Public General Acts and Church Assembly Measures 1965. London: Her Majesty's Stationery Office, 1966.

Public General Acts and Church Assembly Measures 1969. London: Council of Law Reporting, 1969.

Roberts, Richard and Kristin Mann. "Law in Colonial Africa." *Law in Colonial Africa*. Ed. Kristin Mann. London: James Currey, 1991, 3-61.

Sagay, Itsejuwa Esanjumi. *Case Law Under the Matrimonial Causes Decree*. Ife:

n.p., 1974.

Salacuse, Jeswald W. *Selective Survey of Family Law in Northern Nigeria*. Zaria, Northern Nigeria: Pittsburgh: University of Pittsburgh, 1965.

Seltzer, Leon E., ed. *The Columbia Lippincott Gazetteer of the World.* Geographical Research Staff of Columbia University Press with the Cooperation of The American Geographical Society. New York: Columbia University Press, 1952.

Umeh, Davidson and Marie Umeh. "An Interview with Buchi Emecheta." *Ba Shiru: A Journal of African Languages and Literature* 12.2 (1985): 19-25.

Western Nigeria Law Reports. *Law Reports of Cases Decided in the Federal Supreme Court:* 1956-1966. Edited by Committee for Law Reporting, Western Region, Nigeria. Lagos, Nigeria: Sweet & Maxwell, 1982.

Yahaya, A.D. *The Native Authority System in Northern Nigeria 1950-1970: A Study in Political Relations.* Zaira: Ahmadu Bello University Press, 1980.

Buchi Emecheta at her desk in her North London home, 1994

The Shallow Grave: Archetypes of Female Experience in African Fiction

Florence Stratton

I

In their preface to *The Madwoman in the Attic*, an extensive study of Victorian women writers, Sandra Gilbert and Susan Gubar recount their discovery of recurrent literary patterns as they prepared themselves for their task by examining the works of nine-teenth—and twentieth—century English and American women writers:

> Reading the writing of women from Jane Austen and Charlotte Brontë to Emily Dickinson, Virginia Woolf, and Sylvia Plath, we were surprised by the coherence of theme and imagery that we encoun-tered in the works of writers who were often geo-graphically, historically, and psychologically distant from each other. Indeed, even when we studied women's achievements in radically different gen-

> res, we found what began to seem a distinctively
> female literary tradition, a tradition that had been
> approached and appreciated by many women read-
> ers and writers but which no one had yet defined in
> its entirety. Images of enclosure and escape, fan-
> tasies in which maddened doubles functioned as
> asocial surrogates for docile selves, metaphors of
> physical discomfort manifested in frozen landscapes
> and fiery interiors—such patterns recurred through-
> out this tradition, along with obsessive depictions of
> diseases like anorexia, agoraphobia, and claustro-
> phobia. (Gilbert & Gubar 1979,ix)

That patterns similar to those that Gilbert and Gubar bring to light, such as images of living burial and homicidal and suicidal impulses, should occur in the works of women at an even greater geographical, historical, and psychological distance—contemporary African women—is much less to be expected. That such is the case in the fiction of such writers as Mariama Bâ, Buchi Emecheta, Bessie Head, Rebeka Njau, Flora Nwapa, and Grace Ogot is one of my main theses. As the nature of the similarity makes it evident that it is highly unlikely that this is an instance of literary influence, what can be said to link these two groups of women living in distinctly dissimilar cultural milieus? The most likely hypothesis is similarity of female psychological and artistic response to what, despite cultural specificity in its manifestations, is a cultural constant: patriarchy. A social institution, patriarchy functions according to the two principles that "male shall dominate female" and "elder male shall dominate younger" (Millet 25), its purpose being to regulate the sexual life of the dominated to the advantage of the dominator. That every woman would respond to her lifelong subjugation and powerlessness with anxiety over the limitation, and that this would find its literary correlative in such forms as images of enclosure and escape, is an intuitively satisfying hypothesis. As all historical societies are patriarchal, the explanatory adequacy of this hypothesis can be assessed through the study of literary works created by women in all cultures.

In approaching this task, however, it is essential that a critic be neither indifferent to the culturally specific manifestations of patriarchy or any other cultural elements that a writer has incorporated into her text, nor ignorant of their form and function in the cultural milieu outside the text on which the artist has drawn. For in the works of Emecheta, Nwapa, and others, it is frequently within the writer's adaptive integration into her text of such cultural elements as myth, rites, and social practices that the defining features of a distinctively female literary tradition lie.[1]

In a study of fiction by African women, attention should also be paid to the strong historical sense that explicitly marks their work, as it does that of their African male colleagues. As well as infusing into the works a reflection of and a perspective on a historical period, the historical elements are functionally integrated with the theme of female experience. Integration occurs on two levels. One is the sociological in that the writers seek an explanation in history for the thralldom of the women portrayed. This they find not solely in the cultural dynamics of the societies portrayed. Culture contact brought about by intrusions into Africa by patriarchal cultures from both the East in the form of Islam and the West from the time of the slave trade up to the neocolonial present, they indicate, resulted in a deterioration in the condition of women and, some suggest, in the suppression of once-powerful feminine values.

The other level of integration is symbolic in that a symbolizing analogy is frequently created between the condition of women and that of the state. While there is a degree of reciprocity between the two images which provides the works with a dual focus, the figure of woman in the analogy functions predominantly as the subject of description or tenor that is embodied in the image of the state.[2]

One of the aims of the analysis of texts that follows is to suggest the possibility of there being a female literary tradition that transcends all cultural boundaries. At the same time, despite a marked increase in critical attention, writing by African women has been generally undervalued by critics and sometimes grossly maligned. The demonstrated literary quality of the three texts selected for study (Buchi Emecheta's *The Slave Girl* and *The Joys of Motherhood* and Mariama Bâ's *So Long a Letter*) implies that the analytical tools previously employed have not been sensitive enough to intrinsic literary quality. A major part of the problem has been the narrow range of critical methodologies used, related to which is a slighting of cultural elements a writer has incorporated into her text or a misapprehension of creative adaptation. Thus aesthetic evaluation or reevaluation is also an aim from which may possibly emerge a prototypical approach to the writing produced by at least some African women.

As Katherine Frank states in her useful discussion of Western feminist critical methodologies and their relevance to African fiction, the stereotypical approach has dominated feminist criticism of African fiction thus far.[3] The aim of this type of analysis is to elicit the images of woman—girlfriend, mother, prostitute, and so forth—that a writer produces. In his recent *Female Novelists of Modern Africa*, Oladele Taiwo, when he rises above plot summary and facile sociologism, indulges in a condescending variety of criticism of feminine stereotypes to which he adds a masculine variety of the same mode as well. Criticism of masculine stereotypes is the mainstay of Femi Ojo-Ade's discussion of Bâ's *So Long a Letter*: "Man, the unfaithful husband; Man, the womanizer; Man, the victimizer," he writes incredulously (Ojo-Ade 1982,73).

While some studies, such as Lloyd Brown's and Abioseh Porter's, are perceptive sociologically, the stereotypical approach is severely limited in that, as Frank states, "Judgement is passed in accordance with sociological and moral rather than aesthetic criteria" (Frank 1984,36).

While not eschewing the stereotypical approach altogether, several critics of works by African women have combined it with other modes. One is Eustace Palmer, whose intervention on the side of aestheticism in the wider debate over the most appropriate critical approach to African literature in general marked one of the turning points (Palmer 1979,1–10). Palmer's article "The Feminine Point of View: Buchi Emecheta's *The Joys of Motherhood*" is marred by his apparent ignorance of the distinctive meaning of each of the terms "female," "feminine," and "feminist." He uses the first two interchangeably, and while he avoids the third altogether, he seems a trifle disconcerted by the obvious feminist thrust of the novel, Emecheta's advocacy of "total emancipation for women, for example" (Palmer 1979,45). Nonetheless, Palmer does combine with some success a moderately sensitive sociologism with the principles of new criticism. Another study is Lloyd Brown's *Women Writers in Black Africa*, the first and to date the only consequential book-length treatment of African women writers. In his introduction Brown anticipates Frank's assessment of stereotypical criticism:

> The critics have treated the [women] writers as if the novels, plays, short stories, and poems are simply political tracts, or anthropological studies. In so doing they ignore the extent to which such works should be approached as committed works of art in

which theme, or social vision, is integrated with an effective sense of design and language. (Brown 1981,12)

Although Brown does not always fully appreciate the structure of values in which the female characters are enmeshed and on occasion he comes dangerously close to equating an undefined standard of realism with literary quality, in the main both his textual interpretation and literary evaluation are insightful. However, the book's main strength lies in the generic analysis. Through his careful study of the writers' integration of Western and traditional African literary forms, Brown shows the distinctive contribution African women have made to the genres in which they work.

Regarding the application to writing by African women of the modes of analysis employed by Western feminists, Frank recommends the archetypal, affirming that it provides insight not only into an "author's vision of what it means to be a woman in a particular environment" but also into "a writer's artistic gifts—the way in which she transforms experience into art by creating telling and effective symbols, images, and metaphors for her vision" (Frank 1984,39). While a judicious blend of critical modes is essential to reach and elucidate the nature of the fiction produced by African women, the archetypal mode has proved to be a most rewarding approach, and it is central to the analyses that follow.

On occasion an archetype is also sufficiently rich and resonant to be employed intertextually as an enabling strategy for illuminating the vision of a group of writers. As Gilbert and Gubar show, such is the case with the figure of Rochester's mad wife in Charlotte Brontë's *Jane Eyre*, with reference to which their work takes its title. In the context of fiction by African women, such, it seems to me, is also the case with Emecheta's nameless slave woman whose story she narrates in both *The Slave Girl* (62) and *The Joys of Motherhood* (23). Thus in this attempt to establish an effective critical framework for the study of fiction by African women, it seems appropriate to begin, before branching out into other works, with a close examination of the novels in which this story appears.

Most of the details in the two versions of the slave woman's story are identical.[4] Ordained by tradition to be buried alive with her deceased mistress in order to serve her in the afterlife, the slave woman rebels. She wants to live! She entreats the chief, her owner and the husband of the deceased, to spare her and then, to the amusement or annoyance of the male mourners, fights for her survival, struggling out of "the shallow grave" into which she has been pushed. Not even a crushing blow to the head administered by the dead woman's son who, in the version told in *The Joys of Motherhood*, admonishes her to "go down like a good slave" entirely subdues her. She thanks the chief who has rebuked his son for his brutality, promising to show her gratitude by being reborn as a member of his family. Then, in *The Joys of Motherhood* "a final blow" sends her "into the grave silenced forever," while in *The Slave Girl* "her voice was [only] completely silenced by the damp earth that was piled on her and the dead woman."

This harrowing story of living burial encompasses many of the attitudes and anxieties expressed by African women in their fiction. "The shallow grave," with reference to which my study takes its title, in itself provides a paradigmatic image of the novelists' reflection of female experience. Their female characters are enclosed in the restricted spheres of behavior of the stereotypes of male tradition, their human potential buried in shallow definitions of their sex. Silenced, like the slave woman, by blows—either to their bodies or their psyches—they are forced to submit to the necessity of conforming to the externally imposed requirements of their masculine societies. Living in bondage to men, but desiring to live freely and fully, they are bewildered by or seethe with inner rage at their servitude to a structure of values matched to the needs of others. Some, like the slave woman's dead mistress, in an attempt to enlarge their lives, become active agents of patriarchy, perpetuating female enslavement—possibly into eternity. Others resist, but in so doing, like the slave woman in her expression of gratitude to the chief for the most hypocritical of kindnesses, respond to their oppressors with ambivalence. They are schizophrenic, their personalities fragmented by their desire both to accept and to reject their condition. With the exception of the few who through ingenuity and great courage triumph in their struggle out of patriarchy's "shallow grave," all are sacrificial victims. Denied both personal identity and self-determination, they are metaphorically buried alive in the patriarchal polity of their societies.

II

Emecheta's interest in the story of the slave woman dates at least from the time she was writing *The Bride Price* (1976), as passing reference is made in that novel to a similar incident (83). However, it was not until *The Joys of Motherhood* (1979) that Emecheta discovered the possibility of fully integrating the story into the larger narrative, for although the story is told in detail in *The Slave Girl* (1977), the incident itself is only a minor character's recollection of a brutal event that she witnessed in her youth. Nonetheless, the slave woman's story is not extraneous to the meaning of *The Slave Girl*. The image of woman as slave pervades the novel, and it is the struggle of its heroine, Ojebeta, to come to terms with her bondage, to accommodate herself to the fact that "all her life a woman always belonged to some male" (112), that provides much of the biting irony that is so characteristic of all Emecheta's work. In addition, as will be shown, the slave woman's story does serve as a paradigm for much of the female experience in the novel, although this seems to occur at the level of subconscious artistry.

This practice of experimenting with an idea before fully developing it appears to be one that Emecheta has adopted as part of her creative strategy. In *The Bride Price*, with the same kind of casualness with which she inserts the slave woman's story into *The Slave Girl*, she introduces the *ogbanje* myth of the Igbo into her text. This she seizes on in *The Slave Girl*, making it the novel's single most important source of energy. However, even with *The Bride Price* a careful consideration of the function of this myth in its creative adaptation is essential to an understanding and appreciation of the work.[5] The heroines of both novels are identified as *ogbanje*, the Igbo term for spirit-children, children believed to be destined to die and be reborn repeatedly to the same mother unless a means can be found to break the cycle. In its cultural form the *ogbanje* myth is a "myth of infant mortality" common to many Western African societies.[6] In *The Bride Price* Emecheta translates *ogbanje* to mean "a 'living dead'" (9), and in both novels she uses the ambiguous status of such children to represent the state of her sex in a society that denies the female any measure of self-determination.

In *The Slave Girl*, with evident conscious intent, Emecheta employs this image as her archetype of female experience. In addition, the *ogbanje* myth determines the form of the novel, the subgenre to which it belongs. *The Slave Girl* is a *Bildungsroman,* but one of a peculiarly female type: a story of entrapment. Ojebeta's journey through life is a journey from autonomy and self-assertion into dependency and abnegation, from the freedom and fullness of girlhood into the slavery and self-denial of womanhood. On the figurative level of meaning, it is an *ogbanje*, "a 'living dead,'" that Ojebeta is to become.

Like so many of Emecheta's heroines, Ojebeta has her roots in the Igbo village of Ibuza, where in the early 1900s her story begins. As a result of her identification at birth as an ogbanje, Ojebeta is accorded for the first seven years of her life the extraordinary license of full vitality. Although "girl children were not normally particularly prized creatures" (19), as the only surviving daughter of middle-aged parents, Ojebeta is a much-cherished child. "Encouraged to trust everybody, to say what she felt like saying, to shout when she felt like doing so" (87), Ojebeta passes her initial years in an idyllic world of personhood and freedom which makes her initiation into the reality of the anonymity and silent servitude of her sex all the more painful. To protect her from the spirits of "the other world, which they believe have claimed her on previous incarnations" (18), Ojebeta's parents enact the rites of the *ogbanje* myth, bedecking Ojebeta with rare charms that serve figuratively as an external sign of her individuality. But as Emecheta makes clear, what a girl-child needs are "charms" to protect her from the life-denying "spirits" of this world: the values of the male-dominated society she inhabits. There are none.

In Ojebeta's mother, Umeadi, Emecheta creates a repository of the feminine values of nurturing, love, and sharing which stand in opposition to, or complement, the masculine values of power and status. Umeadi literally nurtures her daughter at her breast for the first six years of her life and when news of an influenza epidemic reaches Ibuza, she murmurs a prayer over Ojebeta: "I hope my *chi* preserves me for you" (23) — an indication that she is aware that it is only she, not her husband, the family breadwinner, who can provide protection for her daughter. While neither of Ojebeta's parents are spared, the circumstances surrounding the death of Umeadi are especially significant. Succumbing shortly after her husband, Umeadi becomes a victim not only of the disease but also of Igbo patriarchal tradition. Dying while "confined to her hut" during the period of mourning prescribed for widows (29), Umeadi is, as custom required, denied burial, "her body" instead being "thrown into the 'bad bush'" which no one can visit (82). At the same time, through the provenance of the flu epidemic, Emecheta, as she does repeatedly in this novel, points symbolically to the deleterious effects of the West's intrusion on the delicate balance of values in her society. With the death of Umeadi from this virus that has been carried to Nigeria by the British, all traces of feminine harmony vanish from the world of the novel. Ojebeta's change in status is immediate: transformed from a much loved child into a commodity item, the motherless Ojebeta is reborn as the slave girl of the story's title. The first of Ojebeta's owners is her indolent and self-serving brother. Bent on gaining prestige at his coming of age dance through a display of costly adornments, he takes Ojebeta to the Onitsha market where he sells her as a domestic slave for "eight [significantly] English pounds" (65).

Ojebeta's passage from girlhood to womanhood is marked by the journey she makes with her brother from Ibuza to Onitsha. That this is a ritual journey is indicated quite clearly by the chapter's title, "A Short Journey," and the symbolism with which the chapter is charged. It is indeed "a short journey" and one, so Emecheta implies, that sooner or later every girl must make. Setting off before daybreak, Ojebeta and her brother travel through a dark forest:

> As they padded through the bush tracks, they seemed to be entering the very belly of the earth. It was as if they were being gradually but nonetheless determinedly swallowed by dark, mysterious, all-green world, the walls of which were enveloping them, fencing them in, closing them up. Overhead hung the tangled branches of huge tropical trees, on both sides of them were large leaves, creeping plants and enormous tree-trunks, all entwined together to form this impenetrable dark green grove. (31)

The imagery of enclosure and entrapment in this excerpt is almost obsessive. It is also the case that such images are present only in this chapter, where they occur in several other passages as well (33, 36). Coming at this turning point in Ojebeta's life, their uniqueness endows them with special emphasis and meaning. Ojebeta is being initiated into the "dark, mysterious ... world" of patriarchy. Her fate from this point on is to live in its "impenetrable dark green grove" which will envelop her, fence her in, and close her up. Later in their journey when they stop to bathe, a reluctant Ojebeta is forcibly scrubbed by her brother. When he goes "deep into the dark belly of the forest" to take his own bath, Ojebeta wonders "what it would be like to go into the men's bathing place," and she longs for "a glimpse of what it [is] that the men [keep] there in such a secret place" (33). Although the secret of male power is still kept from Ojebeta, her rites of passage have now been performed. She arrives at Onitsha shortly after noon, and from this point on her personal development is a matter of diminishment. Just as her mother literally died in confinement, so Ojebeta will figuratively die in the confines of patriarchy.

Ojebeta's next owner is a wealthy market woman, Ma Palagada. As Ojebeta's second "mother," she is as false as Umeadi was true. Like the slave woman's mistress, Ma Palagada is an agent of patriarchy, a custodian of the values of her male-dominated society. Having acquired great wealth by serving the patriarchal institutions of slavery and colonialism, she has become so influential that even her husband has taken her name. But rather than using her power to liberate herself and others of her sex, she employs it to further entrench female enslavement. While her first act on receiving Ojebeta is the nurturing one of providing food, her motivation is based solely on self-interest. Slavery has been declared illegal, and she wishes to allay the child's growing fears and thus avoid the exposure a public scene would occasion. Her first order is that Ojebeta's protective charms be removed. However, as Emecheta shows, agents are bound by the same chains as slaves. When Ma Palagada dies several years later, her devoted service does earn her a grave, and one of her own with an "expensive tombstone." But her vast business empire, passing into the inept hands of her husband and son, soon crumbles, and all that is left of her name are church wall inscriptions and the tombstone engraving (174). Like the nameless slave woman before her, Ma Palagada will ultimately meet her female destiny: she too will pass into anonymity.

Under Ma Palagada, Ojebeta acquires a suitably feminine temperament. Her loss of her individuality is signified by the removal of her distinctive charms, and she quickly learns the lesson of her sex: that physical welfare is dependent upon "being docile and trouble-free" (63). Now, almost prepared for her final female vocation, Ojebeta soon passes on to the last of her owners, her husband Jacob. That her period of domestic slavery at the Palagadas is both an apprenticeship for and a presentiment of this final vocation as Jacob's wife, his domestic slave, is indicated by Ojebeta's automaton-like response to Jacob's demands in the closing chapter of the novel and by her ready acquiescence to her wifely role: "In her own way, Ojebeta was content and did not want more of life; she was happy in her husband, happy to be submissive, even to accept an occasional beating"(173-74). And several years later, following the official transferal of her ownership to Jacob from the Palagadas, in a speech reminiscent of the slave woman's expression of gratitude to her owner just before she is killed, the thirty-five-year-old Ojebeta offers a heartfelt vote of thanks to Jacob:

"Thank you, my new owner. Now I am free in your house. I could not wish for a better master" (179). Ojebeta has now inherited her birthright: she has become "a 'living dead.'" Thus Emecheta indicates how destructive it is for women to inhabit a culture created by and for men. The constraints placed on her sex cause female emotional and cognitive development to be a process of regression. Female maturity is indistinguishable from simpleminded, almost imbecilic, acquiescence to the requirements of others those of the male.

However, Ojebeta does not "go down like a good slave." Before accepting her fate of being mastered, she makes several bids for freedom. In the first instance, the seven-year-old Ojebeta, not yet stripped of the signs of her individuality and becoming conscious of the meaning of her abandonment in the Palagada's market stall, dashes into the marketplace "festooned with bells and cowries" crying out repeatedly to the market women and to her own mother to save her, for "Oh, my mother, I am lost" (59). That Ojebeta should, in the first moment of real crisis in her life, instinctively seek sanctuary in "mothers" and not "fathers" (though she felt the death of her own very deeply) is a very significant aspect of this story. It is an expression of the deep-seated female knowledge that only mothers, only an assertion of the feminine principle, can save daughters from bondage in patriarchy.

But, indeed, Ojebeta is "lost." Feminine values are, like her mother, dead, and in this first attempt to reclaim her freedom, Ojebeta is literally cornered in an adjacent market stall by one of Ma Palagada's colleagues. Ten years later, as yet unaware of the nature of her plight, she makes her second attempt. Sensing an opportunity in the upheaval caused in the Palagada family by Ma Palagada's death, Ojebeta, her eyes shining "with the first joys of freedom," announces "I'm going home" (144). But as Ojebeta is soon made to realize, a woman is never free, and she has no home of her own but only a temporary lease on whatever space patriarchy consigns to her. Her uncle with whom she takes up residence in Ibuza, seeing like her brother an opportunity to make a capital gain, promises Ojebeta in marriage to a complete stranger in return for her bride price. Cornered once again, Ojebeta makes her final move. Having at last understood the secret of male power and thus realizing that she is fated to "be a slave all her life," she determines at least "to be a slave to a master of [her own] choice," and she elopes with Jacob (168).

Through Ojebeta's musings just prior to this decision, Emecheta explicitly indicates that in choosing to write of female development in Igbo society of the period, this story of humiliation and defeat is almost the only story she could tell: "[No] woman or girl in Ibuza was free, except those who had committed the abominable sin of prostitution or those who had been completely cast off or rejected by their people for offending one custom or another" (157). Molded from birth by the male social order, most women recoil with horror from such avenues of escape and instead renounce themselves to the categories of their culture. Her novel is, Emecheta implies, an archetypal female *Bildungsroman*.

III

The Joys of Motherhood, published two years later, is wider in scope than *The Slave Girl*. Though it is set mainly in Lagos between the mid 1930s and late 1950s, it spans the lives of three successive generations of women inhabiting both Westernized urban and traditional rural environments. Emecheta's thematic focus in this novel is on the implications for women of patriliny in the context of which "a woman without a child for her husband [is] a failed woman," her primary role in life being to render her husband immortal by producing and nurturing a number of sons (62). The central irony arises from the anticipation of the novel's heroine, Nnu Ego, that if she executes this function, the "joys of motherhood"—fulfillment in reflected glory and the assurance of security in her old age—will be hers. As both verbal and plot echoes indicate, the novel is in part a response to Flora Nwapa's *Efuru*, in which the plight of the barren woman in traditional society is the central concern. Emecheta initially replicates this theme and then by shifting settings and circumstances provides the ironic twist. Although what causes Nnu Ego's greatest anguish is the incompatibility of traditional values with a Westernized urban environment, Emecheta, like Nwapa, makes clear that for a woman rural life is no paradise either.

As in *The Slave Girl*, the slave analogy is pervasive, but it is used to define not only the condition of women in patriarchy but also of men under colonial rule. And the anticipation of a politically independent Nigeria near the end of the novel serves as an image of the possibility of freedom for women. That it was in this work Emecheta's conscious intention that the slave woman's story should function as a paradigm for the larger narrative is made abundantly clear, in part by the position of prominence she accords it in the first few pages of the novel, but more so by the intimate relationship she creates between the slave woman's destiny and that of Nnu Ego. The commencement of life for Nnu Ego sounds the death knell for the slave woman, and as Nnu Ego's father is the slave woman's owner and because Nnu Ego is born with a lump on her head on precisely the spot where the slave woman was hit, she is declared to be the slave woman reborn, a fulfillment of the promised reincarnation. At the same time, the slave woman is identified as Nnu Ego's *chi*. As defined by Achebe, in "*Chi* in Igbo Cosmology," "a person's *chi* [is] his other identity in spiritland—his *spirit being* [which complements] his terrestrial *human being*" (93) and which has almost complete control over the "person's fortunes in life"(98). In providing an explanation for the disparity between a person's expectations and actual lot in life, the *chi* myth furnishes the Igbo writer with a store of ironic possibilities that Emecheta utilizes fully. While as yet financially secure, the apparently barren Nnu Ego dreams of her *chi* taunting her by holding out a beautiful baby boy and then vanishing (45). Shortly afterward, Nnu Ego gives birth to a son who dies in infancy. Some time later when she and her husband are experiencing privation, Nnu Ego has a similar dream. On this occasion the baby is extremely dirty, and her *chi*, mocking Nnu Ego with laughter, tells her she can have as many babies of this kind as she wants (77—78). Soon Nnu Ego, who has repeatedly implored her *chi* to allow her to conceive, is encumbered with a bevy of children that she cannot afford to feed or clothe. Nnu Ego clearly has a "bad *chi*."

However, it is in her linking of the *chi* myth with the Igbo myth of reincarnation that Emecheta effects her master stroke, finding in this combination a perfect vehicle to express female schizophrenic response to male oppression.[7] As Nnu Ego's *chi*, the slave woman gives vent to her anger, taking her vengeance on the chief and his family by disgracing the family name through Nnu Ego and by making her life a culmination of miseries; while in her reincarnation as Nnu Ego, she provides the chief with his most-cherished child, thus expressing her gratitude to him for his small show of mercy just before she is killed. As Nnu Ego's story reveals, Nnu Ego is, indeed, both in her psychological makeup and in the sacrifice of her human potential to the patriarchal order, the slave woman reborn—as are all women who do not defy that order and attempt to establish an alternative mode of being.

As with Ojebeta, life for Nnu Ego begins at Ibuza in circumstances that are to find their parallels repeatedly in her later life.

Nnu Ego is the only child of the great chief Agbadi and the grand passion of his life, his much-loved mistress, Ona. Ona's father, having had no sons, has decreed that Ona "must never marry," though "she was free to have men" and that "if she bore a son, he would take her father's name, thereby rectifying the omission nature had made" (12). Nnu Ego is conceived in Agbadi's courtyard, the passionate cries of the two lovers sounding within full hearing of Agbadi's wives. As a result of the frustration and humiliation the joy of the two lovers had caused her to suffer, Agbadi's senior wife soon sickens unto death, and it is in her honor that the slave woman is killed. A few years later, feeling that her life has been wasted and realizing that she is dying, Ona makes Agbadi promise to allow Nnu Ego "to be a woman," "to have a life of her own, a husband if she wants one" (28).

Never having married herself, Ona is unaware that being a wife, just as being her father's daughter, precludes having "a life of *her* own." Paradoxically, the only acceptable forms of female self-definition are by means of the sexual roles of marriage and motherhood, the discovery of this male trick of entrapment being the legacy Ona leaves to her daughter. Married twice, on each occasion as required by tradition to a man of her father's choice, Nnu Ego, dreaming of "her own home" (30), enthusiastically embraces her fate until its contradictions overwhelm her. In contrast to Ojebeta, Nnu Ego never rebels—at least not in her lifetime. As she herself eventually realizes, she has been too thoroughly conditioned by her ultraconservative upbringing as a chief's daughter ever to defy openly the strictures of patriarchy. Conforming outwardly, but inwardly seething with anger over the injustice of male power, Nnu Ego, like so many women of her type, finds an outlet for her frustration in acts of subversion that are ultimately self-defeating. Divided against herself, she remains helplessly trapped in her assigned role of sacrificial victim.

In her first husband, a young and virile local farmer, Nnu Ego finds a suitable partner for her blossoming sexuality, their passionate lovemaking becoming for many years afterward an excruciating memory of an avenue of personal fulfillment that she is subsequently denied. However, he proves to be a false lover, though true to the egotism of his sex. When Nnu Ego fails to conceive during the first year of marriage, he bluntly tells her he has "no time to waste [his] precious male seed on a woman who is infertile," ejects her from his hut—the dreamed—of home of her own—and promptly replaces her with a new wife (32). Heartbroken and humiliated by her nebulous status as "a failed woman," nine months later when her co-wife, right on cue, gives birth to a baby boy, Nnu Ego commits her first act of subversion. Lacking her grandfather's authority, she nonetheless seeks to rectify "the omission nature had made." She longs to kidnap the baby and "run miles and miles from anywhere" (34), but this is too radical a course for her reactionary self. Instead, she takes advantage of her husband's desire to spend nights of uninterrupted bliss with the woman who has made him immortal and begins secretly to suckle the baby, her breasts eventually producing milk under the stimulation. Caught in the act as she was bound to be, she receives from her husband "a double blow from behind" and, as she will again near the end of the novel, returns to Ibuza in disgrace (35).

Her second husband, Nnaife, a Lagos laborer, is an older man whose bulging belly and crude lovemaking repulse Nnu Ego until he gains her respect by making her pregnant. Her attempted suicide following the death of this baby is on one hand an act of despair, the result of a crisis of self-confidence. But it can also be seen as a subversive act, an attempt to free herself forever from the impossible demands of her male society. Nnu Ego is, however, "saved," and she goes on to bear eight more children, seven of whom survive. Given her inflexible adherence to traditional values the children, nurtured in the urban environment of Lagos, rather than bringing her the anticipated "joys," become her "chains of slavery," binding her to the feckless Nnaife and to the backbreaking drudgery of abject poverty (186). Even with the arrival of Nnaife's second wife, Adaku, Nnu Ego is unable, despite her jealousy and her concern over the further sharing of scarce resources, to raise an effective protest, schooling herself instead to play the traditional role of "the mature senior wife" (124), a role stripped of its meaning by the exigencies of Lagos life. And even though, when Nnaife is unemployed and when he is abducted into the British army, she is for years the family's sole provider, she never ceases to see her earnings from petty trading as merely supplementing the main—though often nonexistent—income of Nnaife. The notion that she might become financially independent if she only stopped having babies never enters her mind.

Unable to effect her own escape and having herself sought marriage and motherhood, she is overwhelmed by feelings of powerlessness and entrapment imaged by the literally claustrophobic atmosphere of Nnaife's one-room apartment in which the family lives. Even before the ever-increasing number of occupants causes the room to become "choked with sleeping mats and utensils" (130), Nnu Ego is presented nursing her third pregnancy and fretting over the condition of her malnourished son in "the one room that served as bedroom, playroom and sitting-room" (101). Frequently "tied down at home" by young children (161), she has neither the time nor the energy "to cultivate those women who [offer] her hands of friendship ... what with worrying over this child, this pregnancy, and the lack of money" (219). Unable to leave Lagos to visit her ailing father because of her "duty" to Nnaife, her son's schooling, and financial constraints, her personal life is severely circumscribed, the "choked" room reflecting its suffocating quality. With the coming of Adaku, her personal space, both physical and emotional, is further reduced. Ousted on the evening of the arrival from the only bed in the room, she spends the night on the floor listening to Adaku's love cries and biting "her teeth into her baby's night clothes to prevent herself from screaming" (125), thus arriving at full knowledge of the killing effort (as it literally was for her father's senior wife on the night of her conception) required to stifle a woman's innermost distress. When a second bed is acquired, the "space" between the two is so "minimal" that there is no "living" room at all (130), and Nnu Ego's "haven," reminiscent in its physical details of a coffin, becomes "her curtained wooden bed" (131), even in the privacy of which she dare not weep her tears of sorrow and vexation for fear of betraying her position as "mature senior wife." Confined in her stereotypical view of her role, she lies on her curtained bed wondering why motherhood is "supposed" to make her "happy in her poverty, in her nail-biting agony, in her churning stomach, in her rags, in her cramped room" (167); or she anxiously paces "up and down the narrow gap between the beds in the room" (163). And because Nnu Ego believes that only Nnaife can get her out of that "cramped room," the move when it does finally come is meaningless in terms of enlarging her personal life.

As Emecheta indicates, Nnu Ego's response to the female situation is inadequate—destructive of self and potentially of others of her sex. Increasingly fragmented, she buttresses the very institution that oppresses her. Through her child-rearing practices, she conspires to consign her daughters to the same restricted existence she so desperately needs to escape, admonishing them when they protest against the sacrifice of their talents for the advancement of their brothers: "But you are girls! They are boys. You have to sell to put them in a good position in life, so that they will be able to look after the family. When your husbands are nasty to you, they will defend you" (176). And she rebuffs Adaku's proffered alliance in sisterhood, taunting her instead with the same deficiencies the male order indicts her with. At the same time, Nnu Ego takes the slave's covert pleasure in maligning the master behind his back—in exclusively female company or from the privacy of her bed in the appeals she makes to her god. In the case of the latter, the impassioned plea she makes after Nnaife has registered his disgust at her delivery of a second set of twin girls constitutes the strongest feminist statement in the novel:

> "God, when will you create a woman who will be fulfilled in herself, a full human being, not anybody's appendage? ... After all, I was born alone, and I shall die alone. What have I gained from all this? Yes, I have many children, but what do I have to feed them on? On my life. I have to work myself to the bone to look after them, I have to give them my all. And if I am lucky enough to die in peace, I even have to give them my soul. They will worship my dead spirit to provide for them: it will be hailed as a good spirit so long as there are plenty of yams and children in the family, but if anything should go wrong, if a young wife does not conceive or there is a famine, my dead spirit will be blamed. When will I be free?"

> But even in her confusion she knew the answer: "Never, not even in death. I am a prisoner of my own flesh and blood. Is it such an enviable position? The men make it look as if we must aspire for children or die. That's why when I lost my first son I wanted to die, because I failed to live up to the standard expected of me by the males in my life, my father and my husband—and now I have to include my sons. But who made the law that we should not hope in our daughters? We women subscribe to that law more than anyone. Until we change all this, it is still a man's world, which women will always help to build." (186—87)

But despite her insight she is incapable of liberating herself, and she remains to the end of her life both victim and collaborator.

111

It is in Adaku that Emecheta resurrects the rebellious spirit of the slave woman. Functioning as Nnu Ego's double, Adaku, waiting for neither man nor god, actualizes Nnu Ego's faint dream by recreating herself as a woman who is "not anybody's appendage." An outsider in patriarchy in any case, for although she has daughters she has no son, she initially sustains her humiliation with fortitude, living with the hope that her relations with Nnaife will produce the issue that will confirm her worth. But when her reproductive shortcomings are invoked to place her in the wrong in a quarrel Nnu Ego has initiated, she revolts. Warned by the men who are called to settle the dispute that if Nnaife had been married only to her he "would have ended his life on this round of his visiting earth" and admonished for making unhappy "the only woman who is immortalizing [her] husband" (166), Adaku tells Nnu Ego, in words full of symbolic import, that she is "not prepared to stay ... and be turned into a madwoman," that she is going to "leave" the "stuffy" and "stinking room" and "be a prostitute" (168–69).[8]

In discussing the double as a literary device, Gilbert and Gubar, quoting another source, state: "'[T]he novelist who consciously or unconsciously exploits psychological Doubles' frequently juxtaposes 'two characters, the one representing the socially acceptable or conventional personality, the other externalizing the free, uninhibited, often criminal self'" (360).[9] They also note that the woman writer of nineteenth-century England usually identified "not only with her model heroines, but also with less obvious, nastier, more resilient female characters who enact her rebellious dissent from her culture" (169). Emecheta's exploitation of this device is quite conscious, and while she presents the plight of Nnu Ego with full sympathy and understanding, it is Adaku who emerges as the role model. Adaku enacts what Nnu Ego can only wish for, not only becoming a woman "fulfilled in herself" but one who has "hope in our daughters." Determining to become "a dignified single woman," she reinvests her profits from prostitution in the more socially acceptable cloth trade (170); taking male lovers—she wryly notes that men "do have their uses" (171)—but remaining unmarried, and educating her daughters at the best schools, she in effect establishes a countercommunity—a matriarchal family. While denouncing the social institution that makes prostitution the only economically viable means by which an uneducated woman can liberate herself from bondage, Emecheta applauds Adaku's resoluteness, making clear that although Adaku sells her body, she redeems her soul. Choosing prostitution over marriage may seem mad, but remaining within the confines of the relationship is madness. Having walked out the door of that "stuffy room," she enters "a separate room of her own, much bigger than the one they had all shared before" (171): Adaku clambers out of patriarchy's "shallow grave."

Nnu Ego does go mad. Having been sustained in all her travails by the thought "that one day her boys would be men" (161), their repudiation of the traditional communal values for which she has sacrificed herself in favor of the Western-style individualism they have imbibed in Lagos is the "final blow." Rejected by Nnaife, who blames her for the children's defection, she returns once again in disgrace to Ibuza; and realizing that her sacrifice has not been worth the making, she cracks and one night dies quietly by the roadside "with no child to hold her hand and no friend to talk to her" (224).

Nnu Ego's madness is both a response to and a metaphor for the absurd contradictions of her life. It can also be seen as representing her last subversive act—a subversion of normality—and the final stage of her fragmentation—a psychic dislocation. Ironically, it is only in death that Nnu Ego acquires psychic integration and that her explosive anger finds a revolutionary course. Reminiscent of the decision taken by Nwapa's Efuru to dedicate herself to the Woman of the Lake, a goddess who "gave women beauty and wealth" but who "had never experienced the joy of motherhood" (221), Nnu Ego refuses to "answer prayers for children" (224). Thus, now literally in the grave in which she has figuratively been buried all her life, she strikes at the roots of patriarchy. The symbolic role of Igbo cosmology in the novel makes Nnu Ego's posthumous transformation highly significant. Unlike the slave woman through whom Nnu Ego traces her spiritual genealogy, Nnu Ego does ultimately find spiritual wholeness. Thus Emecheta provides an affirmation of and a metaphor for her belief that the female psychic conflict can be resolved. Woman will be reborn, not as the slave woman, but "as a full human being."

IV

While in *The Joys of Motherhood* Nigeria's political independence is anticipated, in *So Long a Letter* Mariama Bâ looks retrospectively at this same historical event in Senegal. Setting her novel in Dakar about twenty years after Senegal's independence from France, Bâ evaluates from a contemporary perspective the outcome of the nationalist and feminist movements of the late 1950s. The world of the novel is that of Dakar's established professional class, the members of which in their student days were in the vanguard of these progressive movements. What she reveals is the betrayal by this same privileged elite of the hopes and aspirations of both. While Bâ's focal concern is the female experience, the national fate that provides the backdrop enlarges the scope of the novel, and the undermining by bourgeois materialism of the nationalist ideals of liberty and equality serves as a vehicle to illuminate the compromising by women as well as men of the feminist ideal of a marriage contract based on parity between the sexes. As with Nnu Ego, the unhappiness of Ramatoulaye, the work's central character, is a result not only of her victimization by the male social order but also of her continuing complicity in the process.

Crucial to an understanding and assessment of this novel is an appreciation of the narrative framework Bâ has so carefully and skillfully elaborated. The story is told in the first person by Ramatoulaye in the form of a letter-diary that she addresses to her friend Aissatou and writes following the death of her husband Modou. Working within the genre of pseudo-autobiography, Bâ has her heroine tell her story, not directly, but with subconscious evasion and revelation. While Bâ's exploitation of the ironic possibilities of her narrative mode provides the novel with much of its meaning and flavor, it is in the narrative setting created for the telling that the informing force of the novel lies. Ramatoulaye writes her letter during the four months and ten days of secluded mourning prescribed by Islam for widows. In this Islamic practice, Bâ found her archetypal image of female experience. As will be shown, Ramatoulaye's physical confinement during this period of mourning in the house she once shared with Modou replicates her psychological confinement in a debilitating stereotypical view of a woman's role.[10]

As Ramatoulaye's narrative reveals, the crisis in her life came, not with the death of Modou, but with his acquisition five years earlier, after twenty-five years of marriage to Ramatoulaye, of a second wife, a teenage friend of the eldest of their twelve children. It is on this moment that Ramatoulaye ruminates during her confinement, endeavoring to come to terms with the choice she herself made, "a choice that [her] reason rejected" and one made against the wishes of her children: to remain within the marriage and "live according to the precepts of Islam concerning polygamic life"(45-46).

For Ramatoulaye, Aissatou serves not as a correspondent—she already knows the story and in any case the letter is never sent—but as an alter ego. Ramatoulaye writes to herself in an attempt to locate the source of her disequilibrium. Although comprehension eludes Ramatoulaye, she unwittingly lays bare for the reader the mainsprings of her personality. What materializes from the reader's interaction with the text is a psychological case study of a contemporary, middle-aged and middle-class Senegalese woman.

The picture that emerges is of a kind of latter-day—a neocolonial—Nnu Ego. A college graduate, Ramatoulaye's Western education has liberated her from the "frustrating taboos" of her own society's patriarchal practices (16). She is genuinely opposed to any Islamic tradition, including polygyny, that denies dignity to women. But the prohibitions and prescriptions of one patriarchal culture have merely been replaced by those of another, and these have been so completely assimilated that living her life in terms of them has become Ramatoulaye's prerequisite for happiness.

The reason Ramatoulaye advances for not choosing "the right" and "dignified solution" of obtaining a divorce is "the immense tenderness I felt towards Modou Fall" (45). The story she tells reveals otherwise. Considering herself "one of those who can realize themselves fully and bloom only when they form part of a couple" (55-56), Ramatoulaye contemplates the fate of divorced women of her generation:

> I knew a few whose remaining beauty had been able
> to capture a worthy man, a man who added fine
> bearing to a good situation and who was considered
> "better, a hundred times better than his predeces-
> sor." ... I knew others who had lost all hope of renew-
> al and whom loneliness had very quickly laid
> underground. (40)

She then examines herself in the mirror: "I had lost my slim figure, as well as ease and quickness of movement. My stomach protruded from beneath the wrapper.... Suckling had robbed my breasts of their round firmness. I could not delude myself: youth was deserting my body" (41).

Ramatoulaye is unable to face the possible consequence of divorcing Modou: the dreadful prospect of being a single woman. When, by severing all ties with her and the children, Modou in effect thrusts this fate upon her, Ramatoulaye is plunged into emotional turmoil. Believing, on the one hand, that her heart remains "faithful to the love of [her] youth" (56), she at the same time calls out "eagerly to 'another man' to replace Modou" (53). After Modou's death, a number of men answer this call, but though she is lonely and craves male attention, Ramatoulaye rejects every proposal. In a fashion Ramatoulaye does remain "faithful to the love of [her] youth." A romantic in the classical mode, she clings to her youthful fantasy of living happily-ever-after with the man of her dreams. Reliving that thrilling moment of thirty years past when she first saw the "tall and athletically built" Modou, full of "virility" and with fine features "harmoniously blended," Ramatoulaye bursts forth in ecstatic apostrophe: "Modou Fall, the very moment you bowed before me, asking me to dance, I knew you were the one I was waiting for" (13). When her true-story romance deviates from its fictional origins, she is emotionally and sexually paralyzed.

Although she is a professional woman, Ramatoulaye skips with barely a glance over that aspect of her life, focusing instead almost exclusively on the domestic domain. It is in her housewifely role that she finds her primary identity, and she expends most of her human energy on executing that role to perfection. With a satisfaction that borders on the masochistic, she bears witness to her limitless devotion:

> I loved my house. You can testify to the fact that I made it a haven of peace where everything had its place, that I created a harmonious symphony of colors. You know how softhearted I am, how much I loved Modou. You can testify to the fact that, mobilized day and night in his service, I anticipated his slightest desire. (56)

With her romanticization of the monogamous union and her role in it as the tractable, serviceable, selfless wife, there is little to distinguish her from her counterparts in the West's middle class: Ramatoulaye seems to have sprung full-blown from the pages of studies such as Betty Friedan's *The Feminine Mystique*. She makes a cult of domesticity and mounts (to borrow a phrase from Friedan) what sounds like "a propaganda campaign to give women 'prestige' as housewives" by transforming the drudgery of daily domestic tasks into exalted professions (255):

> Those women we call "house"-wives deserve praise. The domestic work they carry out, and which is not paid in hard cash, is essential to the home. Their

116

compensation remains the pile of well ironed, sweet-smelling washing, the shining tiled floor on which the foot glides, the gay kitchen filled with the smell of stews. Their silent action is felt in the least useful detail: over there, a flower in bloom placed in a vase, elsewhere a painting with appropriate colors, hung up in the right place. (63)

Dietitian, economist, and interior designer rolled into one! When Modou dies, she is, it would seem, as much disconcerted by the state of the house following the inundation of mourners as she is over his death: "Cola nuts spat out here and there have left red stains: my tiles, kept with such painstaking care, are blackened. Oil stains on the walls, balls of crumpled paper. What a balance sheet for a day!" she groans (7). The order in which Ramatoulaye names the objects of her affection—"I loved my house ....I loved Modou"—is apparently not entirely arbitrary. She is, first and foremost, a house-proud housewife.

As she begins her period of confinement, Ramatoulaye makes the following diary entry: "The walls that limit my horizon for four months and ten days do not bother me. I have enough memories in me to ruminate upon. And these are what I am afraid of, for they smack of bitterness" (8). The walls do not bother her because the commodious house with its modern conveniences is essential to the image of female fulfillment that directs her life. The house is also all that remains of her romantic dream. As wife, abandoned wife, and widow, she dwells in that house, and unlike Modou, who comes and goes—"He never came again," she says sadly after his second marriage (46)—it is a permanent feature. But it is precisely those walls and not her bitter memories that Ramatoulaye should fear. By obstructing her view of life's other and larger possibilities, they in effect become her prison. Unable to conceive of a life beyond those walls, Ramatoulaye remains trapped in her dead-end romance and her domestic enclosure.

In narrating her story, Ramatoulaye also relates the stories of other women, in the telling of which she unconsciously reveals more of her own—her fears, her inner tensions, and her knowledge that the choice she has made is a debasing and self-destructive one. In one, the story of a Frenchwoman who is hospitalized because of a sore throat, Ramatoulaye projects her fears for herself in her now functionally unmarried state into her imaginings about this woman, her dread of being single taking on a psychoneurotic character. Observing that the woman is "old, for her unmarried status," Ramatoulaye hypothesizes that in "her loneliness all her frustrated dreams, all her disappointed hopes, all her crushed revolt [must have] connived to attack her throat" (44). Watching this woman tapping her throat, Ramatoulaye surely mentally taps her own.

In the telling of her friend Jacqueline's story, Ramatoulaye comes as close as she will get to acquiring an understanding of her own. Having interjected this tale into her own just prior to its climax, Ramatoulaye wonders why she has done so. While her narrative tactics indicate an embarrassed reluctance to admit her choice openly, the substance of Jacqueline's story is even more revealing. Jacqueline, herself a victim of marital neglect and deceit, has had a nervous breakdown. What the narrative sequence implies is that it is Ramatoulaye's fear of this that determines her choice — her fear of being afflicted by the same disorder if after twenty-five years of personal nonentity she leaves the security of wifehood in Modou's tidy and immaculate house and enters the anomalous world as an autonomous person. As a result of psychiatric treatment, Jacqueline finds for herself "a reason for living" (45). If Ramatoulaye's story is also to have a happy ending, a breakdown, at least in the figurative sense, is precisely what she requires in order to break out of her confinement in her debilitating image of woman and be reconstituted in wholeness. She too needs to find an independent "reason for living."

Aissatou, to whom Ramatoulaye addresses her letter, is in a literal sense her alter ego—her other self or double. When her husband Mawdo Bâ takes a second wife, she does what Ramatoulaye knows she ought to have done. "And you left," Ramatoulaye writes. "You had the surprising courage to take life into your own hands. You rented a house and set up home there" (32). Like Adaku, Aissatou both literally and figuratively storms the walls that confine her. Having "rented a house" and "set up home there" for herself and her children, in this case boys, she proceeds, again like Adaku, to find a means of becoming economically independent and, though warned that "boys cannot succeed without a father" (31), to raise her sons successfully, "contrary to all predictions," in the absence of a patriarchal figure (34). Aissatou is fortunate enough to be able to obtain her independence without a devastating loss of social standing, though she too is reviled for her choice. She upgrades her qualifications and eventually acquires an international job. And from her salary, Aissatou is able to supply

Ramatoulaye with precisely what Ramatoulaye knows she ought to be able to provide for herself: she replaces with a brand-new model the car Modou has deprived Ramatoulaye of by handing it over to his second family. But in so doing, in becoming so directly a monetary image, Aissatou also becomes Ramatoulaye's nemesis, and Ramatoulaye's feelings toward her friend become increasingly ambivalent. While praising Aissatou's courage, she belittles her choice, wondering snidely, for example, whether when they next meet Aissatou will be wearing "a tailored suit or a long dress" (89); and while extolling the virtues of friendship— Friendship has splendors that love knows not. It grows stronger when crossed, whereas obstacles kill love" (54)—she betrays her friend by retaining Mawdo as a confidant and as the family doctor.

In employing the device of psychological doubles, Bâ dramatizes, even more explicitly than Emecheta does through her co-wives Adaku and Nnu Ego, the psychic split so common to women. The lives of Aissatou and Ramatoulaye run in perfect parallel—up to a point. Friends from childhood, they attend the same schools, graduate from the same college, choose the same profession, and even marry essentially the same man, for there is in the final (painful) analysis little or nothing to distinguish doctor Mawdo from his lawyer friend Modou. But confronted with the same dilemma, they opt for different solutions. One seeks to assert herself in the world; the other retreats even further into the home.

As both Bâ and Emecheta show, a woman's acceptance of the female condition is an acceptance of confinement in the restricted roles of femininity prescribed for her by men. Aissatou and Adaku represent all women who seek freedom in personhood and find it. Through these female figures, Bâ and Emecheta challenge the basic assumptions of the status quo. Asking the question "Is marriage a necessary part of life for a woman?" both unequivocally answer no. Indeed, as they show through their submissive heroines, patriarchal marriage—the only currently available form of the institution—stifles a woman's human potential. Nor, so Bâ and Emecheta imply, is a father figure necessary to the well-being of children. What women do need is access to remunerative and undemeaning work; their children, a nurturing mother with a viable means of support.

In her co-wife Binetou, who is prevailed upon by her mother to leave school and marry the affluent Modou, Ramatoulaye acquires a double of a somewhat different sort: an identical, though unrecognized, twin sister. While Ramatoulaye realizes that Binetou is "a victim" (39), "a lamb slaughtered on the altar of affluence" (48), that with her marriage to Modou she became "dead inside" (71), what she fails to see is a mirror image of herself, another sacrificial victim, "a 'living-dead,'" to use Emecheta's metaphor.

The story of Aissatou's mother-in-law Aunty Nabou is the most cautionary tale of all for women like Ramatoulaye. A widow, she has come into power by virtue of having outlived the males who could exercise it over her. And this she wields with a fury on her offspring, manipulating their lives with no view to their happiness but with the utmost determination to have her own way. A product of patriarchy and its ally, class, she has become an aggressively assertive agent on their behalf. Having seen her daughters "well married," she is enraged when Mawdo, "her 'one and only,'" marries Aissatou without her consent; Aissatou is a mere goldsmith's daughter who will "tarnish her noble descent." Scheming and wheedling, whining that "shame kills faster than disease," she knows no rest until, it must be admitted, a not entirely reluctant Mawdo, has agreed to take a second wife, a young girl of his mother's class and choice (26–30).

A thoroughly obnoxious character, Aunty Nabou is, if not Ramatoulaye's actual twin double, her potential one, for Ramatoulaye, who has already joined Aunty Nabou in widowhood, displays some of her suspect traits. A telling sign is her shock and dismay when she, "who wanted to control everything," catches her teenage daughters smoking (77). Another is her chiding of her son-in-law for spoiling his wife by sharing with her the household tasks. She also exposes a class bias in her remark about Aissatou, that "Mawdo raised you up to his level, he the son of a princess and you a child from the forges" (19). And her antipathy to Binetou's mother, whom she spitefully refers to as "Lady Mother-in-Law," seems to arise more from outrage at the fact that this lower-class woman has acquired the very amenities that she so cherishes—"delicious jets of hot water [to] massage her back," "ice cubes [to] cool the water in her glass"—than at the means she has employed to do so (49). Aunty Nabou is a grim parody of Ramatoulaye. Nurturing mother metamorphosed into destructive demon, she is an image of what not only Ramatoulaye but every women is in danger of becoming if she does not seek the power to liberate herself.

Ramatoulaye's final diary entry is filled with optimism:

> I have not given up wanting to refashion my life.
> Despite everything—disappointments and humilia-

tions—hope still lives on within me....The word "happiness" does indeed have meaning, doesn't it? I shall go out in search of it. (89)

But she also reveals that she has "obtained an extension of [her] widow's leave" (88). Ramatoulaye has been on "wife's" leave from full participation in human affairs throughout her adult life. As one of her suitors following Modou's death justifiably retorts when she complains that there are too few women in the National Assembly: "You who are protesting; you preferred your husband, your class, your children to public life"(62). While her period of confinement figuratively represents her psychological condition, it is also literally little more than an extension of her prior mode of existence. This second "extension" contains the unhappy suggestion that Ramatoulaye has now become permanently housebound, that her fear of entering life as an autonomous person has been translated into the agoraphobic's fear of open spaces. As it is only in those open spaces beyond the wall of her domestic enclosure that Ramatoulaye can "refashion" her "life," it is unlikely that her "search" for "happiness" will be a rewarding one.

With the exception of Aissatou, Ramatoulaye is, as a professional woman, the only female figure in the three books discussed for whom the road to freedom is clearly marked. But in making Ramatoulaye's confinement in this sense self-imposed, Bâ, though she treats her creation with a gentle irony, neither trivializes nor mocks her anguish and bewilderment. The highly personal narrative mode conveys with poignancy the depth and substantiality of Ramatoulaye's feelings; and Ramatoulaye's ideal of romantic love and selfless devotion is far more appealing than the philandering and indolent egotism of the men in this text, its dysfuntionality originating not entirely in itself but in part from a mismatch with the masculine world it inhabits.

Like Emecheta, what Bâ demonstrates is the power of patriarchal socialization to render a woman powerless. This is the state of being that Ramatoulaye perhaps dimly recognizes as being her own when, in an attempt to console herself, she compares her plight to that of "the blind people the world over, moving in darkness," "the paralysed ... dragging themselves about," "the lepers ... wasted by their disease" (11). As Bâ indicates, Ramatoulaye has been blinded, paralyzed, wasted— disabled—by her conditioning. And by having her heroine tell her story while literally confined in a house of death, Bâ tells the story of the living death of every woman who is unable to break out of that conditioning. In effect, Ramatoulaye mourns her own demise.

V

In the light of the findings of Gilbert and Gubar, the discussion of the three texts written by African women points to the possibility of the existence of a widespread female literary tradition. Of more immediate interest is the textual richness elucidated by the analysis. Indeed, as I worked with these texts and others by African women, I found that they yielded more and more insights, both sociological and artistic, with each interpretive and evaluative effort. This indicates that the analytic tools previously employed were in some sense lacking. Particularly detrimental has been the narrow range of critical methodologies employed and the slighting of elements of cultural milieu that an author has incorporated into her text in order to portray her vision of female experience. While Bu-Buakei Jabbi's prescription of "a relatively eclectic holism" in critical orientation is appropriate to the fiction produced by African women, allowing the archetypal mode ample scope has proved most effective as a means of raising the fiction produced by African women from "the shallow grave" of facile commentary and insensitive criticism in which it has lain half buried.

NOTES

1. For a comprehensive examination of the relationship between a literary text and its wider milieu, see the excellent article by Bu-Buakei Jabbi, "Milieu and the Criticism of African Literature." While he proposes "a relatively eclectic holism," he concludes that "the basic desideratum all the time is for the criticism to maintain sufficient apprehension of the artistic integrity of the work of literature under review."

2. A number of African men writers including Mongo Beti, Nuruddin Farah, Ngugi wa Thiong'o, and Ousmane Sembène have also described the female situation. In their works a similar symbolizing analogy frequently occurs, but in it the figure of woman functions predominantly as illuminating vehicle. For example, in Ngugi's *Petals of Blood* Wanja's engagement in prostitution images the condition of the masses in a neocolonial state, and her pregnancy after years of barrenness signals the possibility of new life for the nation. This raises the question as to whether the interest of these writers always lies in the female situation itself. In at least some instances it would seem that it is the metaphorical potential of that situation that has attracted their attention.

3. For examples of the stereotypical approach, see Brown ("African Woman as Writer"), Little, Taiwo, Ojo-Ade, McCaffrey, and Porter. The stereotypical approach, it would seem, is not always conducive to critical equa-

nimity. While Taiwo exhibits signs of stress, this is most evident in the testiness displayed by Ojo-Ade throughout his discussion of *Une si longue lettre*. It reaches its pitch when he observes in his concluding paragraph that, should another such letter be written, there is every possibility that he and his brothers will "tear it up and throw it into the dustbin"(Ojo-Ade 1982,86). Ojo-Ade says of the novel's heroine, Ramatoulaye, "Bitterness engenders bias" (Ojo-Ade 1982,83). Could the same be said of Ojo-Ade?

4. Of the critics who mention this story—Brown (1981,56); Palmer (1983,54-55); and Frank (1984,39)—all refer to the figure whom Emecheta consistently designates in both versions as the slave *woman* as the slave *girl*, thus unwittingly exposing through their "misreading" the power of patriarchal socialization to perpetuate reductive images of women.

5. In their discussion of *The Bride Price* and *The Slave Girl*, neither Brown in *Women Writers* nor Taiwo makes mention of the *ogbanje* myth. Nor does Taiwo make even the slightest reference to the story of the slave women in his presentations of *The Slave Girl* and *The Joys of Motherhood*.

6. I am indebted to Bu-Buakei Jabbi (*O-Level African Poems* [N.p. (Njala, Sierra Leone): privately printed, 1985] for the locution "myth of infant mortality" (11). It is the same myth, known by other names in different parts of West Africa, on which John Pepper Clark and Wole Soyinka base their abiku poems. It continues to provide a rich source of material for the creative imagination.

7. Palmer finds this combination a product of "some confusion of thought," and he wonders whether Emecheta's presentation will "stand up to sociological scrutiny" (Palmer 1983,55). Regarding the latter, while Achebe's discussion does not provide an answer to this question, he does pose two questions which at least suggest the possibility of somewhat open interpretation: "What happens to a person's *chi* when the person dies?" and "What happens at the man's reincarnation?" (Achebe 1975,93). In any case, as Palmer states, "*The Joys of Motherhood* is an imaginative and not a scientific work," and it "must be judged as a work of art." As I try to show, the combination is a product of deliberate artistry from which the novel derives much of its meaning.

8. Interestingly, Palmer, despite textual evidence to the contrary, refuses to believe that Adaku becomes a prostitute, thus indicating an inability or refusal to recognize that the stigma of prostitution is preferable to the ignominy of remaining within the marriage (Palmer 1983,49).

9. Claire Rosenfeld (1967,314), as quoted in Gilbert and Gubar (1979,360).

10. Ojo-Ade overlooks Bâ's use of this Muslim practice. In addition, he confuses autobiography with pseudo-autobiography or fiction and many of the inadequacies with which he charges *So Long a Letter* are a result of this lapse in his own critical methodology. Identifying the novel's narrator with its creator, he accuses Bâ of being inconsistent and ambivalent. Bâ did specify the character with whose stance she identified: in addition to making Aissatou a divorced woman, as she herself was, she gave Aissatou her own last name.

WORKS CITED

Achebe, Chinua. "*Chi* in Igbo Cosmology." *Morning Yet on Creation Day: Essays.* London: Heinemann, 1975

Bâ, Mariama. *So Long a Letter.* Trans. Modupé Bodé-Thomas. London: Virago, 1982.

Brown, Lloyd. "The African Woman as Writer." *Canadian Journal of African Studies* 9.3 (1975): 493-501.

——. *Women Writers in Black Africa.* Westport, CT: Greenwood, 1981.

Emecheta, Buchi. *The Bride Price.* New York: George Braziller, 1976.

——. *The Joys of Motherhood.* London: Heinemann, 1980.

——. *The Slave Girl.* New York: George Braziller, 1977.

Frank Katherine. "Feminist Criticism and the African Novel." *African Literature Today* 14 (1984): 34-48.

Friedan, Betty. *The Feminine Mystique.* London: Victor Grollancz, 1971.

Gilbert, Sandra, and Susan Gubar. *The Madwoman in the Attic: The Woman Writer and the Nineteenth-Century Literary Imagination.* New Haven: Yale UP, 1979.

Jabbi, Bu-Buakei. "Milieu and the Criticism of African Literature." NJALA 7 (1985): 34-50.

——. *O-Level African Poems.* n.p. [Njala University College]: Privately printed, 1985.

Little, Kenneth. "The Sociology of Urban Woman's Image in African Literature." *West Africa* September 3,10,17, 1979.

McCaffrey, Kathleen M. "Images of Women in West African Literature and Film: A Struggle against Dual Colonization." *International Journal of Women's Studies* 3.1 (1980): 76-88.

Millet, Kate. *Sexual Politics.* London: Hart-Davies, 1971.

Nwapa, Flora. *Efuru.* London: Heinemann, 1978.

Ojo-Ade, Femi. "Still a Victim? Mariama Bâ's *Une si longue lettre.*" *African Literature Today* 12 (1982): 71-87.

Palmer, Eustace. "The Feminine Point of View: Buchi Emecheta's *The Joys of Motherhood.*" *African Literature Today* 13 (1983): 38-55.

——. *The Growth of the African Novel.* London: Heinemann, 1979.

Porter, Abioseh. "Ideology and the Image of Women: Kenyan Women in Njau and Ñgugi." *Ariel: A Review of International English Literature.* 12.3 (1981): 61-74.

Rosenfeld, Claire. "The Shadow Within: The Conscious and Unconscious Use of the Double." *Stories of the Double.* Ed. Albert Guérard. Philadelphia: Lippincott, 1967.

Taiwo, Oladele. *Female Novelists of Modern Africa.* London: Macmillan, 1984.

Orality and Patriarchal Dominance in Buchi Emecheta's *The Slave Girl*

Tom Spencer-Walters

Mohamadou Kane in his "Sur les formes traditionelles du roman africain" (an article published in 1974 in *Revue de Litterature Comparee*) asserts that we cannot discuss the originality of the African novel without appropriately looking at its symbiotic relationships with various forms of oral literature (537). It is a viewpoint shared by a number of African writers and critics alike. In an interview with Cosmo Pieterse and Dennis Duerden, Ama Ata Aidoo, for example, disagreed "with people who feel that oral literature is one stage in the development of man's artistic genius. [For her] it is an end in itself" (23-24). Scheub's submission that oral and literary traditions in Africa have never been discontinuous or conflictual, complements Aidoo's viewpoints on this issue. And Chris Wanjala, writing on the emergence of the literary tradition in East Africa, instructively cautions that it is impossible for the contemporary writer "to reveal the creative ethos of his community unless he integrates his activities into the creative dynamism of his community" (67).

This is precisely Buchi Emecheta's contribution to this debate. She draws copiously from her community's oral traditions and myths and her own experiences in that community in order to construct social contexts that would illuminate her aesthetic. She does not view written literature and oral traditions as belonging to mutually exclusive communities of discourse: one western and objective, the other African and primordial. Rather, through key works of art, notably *The Bride Price*, *The Slave Girl*, and *The Joys of Motherhood*, she unobtrusively utilizes oral narratives through the storytelling art form to pinpoint her social and ideological vision: giving voice to women who have suffered under neglect and marginalization not only from male writers but from the very cultural traditions such writers evoke and valorize so freely.

Using *The Slave Girl*, this essay examines Emecheta's aesthetic vision in relation to her references to orality in the novel. I grant that the term "orality" has been used sometimes simultaneously with "orature" and "oral literature," to name only two, raising questions about definitional accuracy. I do not wish to add to this confusion by purporting a clear distinction among these terms. Having said that, I would like to offer a working definition of orality: it is the promulgation of the aesthetic, social, and ideological vision of the author through the conscious and skillful adaptations of oral traditions (riddles, proverbs, legends, myths, and folktales) into a work of art. Necessarily, the mere infusion of riddles, tales, proverbs, and other oral forms into a novel does not constitute orality. Eileen Julien calls such infusions "topographical" because they lack the necessary "rules and processes by which a work has been constructed" (46). Orality should add novelty not only to the traditional oral genres but to criticisms about such genres.

In Kirsten Petersen's *Criticism and Ideology*, Buchi Emecheta reminisces about a cultural tradition that has guided a great deal of her writing: the art of storytelling among the Igbos:

> ...the Igbo story teller was always one's mother. My Big Mother was my aunt. A child belonged to many mothers. Not just one's biological mother. We would sit for hours at her feet mesmerized by her trance like voice. Through such stories she could tell the

> heroic deeds of her ancestors, all our mores and cus-
> toms. She used to tell them in such a... sing-song
> way...that I used to think that these women were
> inspired by some spirits.... I was determined when
> I grew older that I was going to be a story teller like
> my Big Mother. (173–4)

Storytelling is not a cultural or artistic novelty in traditional societies, certainly not in traditional African communities, where the
activity is widely utilized for its didactic, entertaining, and arguably
moralizing functions. Equally common is the preeminence of
women as accomplished story tellers in many African societies,
notable among which are the Igbo of Southeastern Nigeria, the
Xhosa, and the Zulu of Southern Africa. Emecheta's reverent testimony above to the artistry of women story tellers in Igbo culture
helps to shape our understanding of her approach to literary creativity.

Like Flora Nwapa and Ama Ata Aidoo, Emecheta views story
telling by women enervating, liberating, and empowering. It recognizes the power of women as preservers and disseminators of
oral traditions, especially in patriarchal societies. Equally important, it engenders solidarity among women and firmly situates
women as significant socializing agents in the community. That
Emecheta should create literary correlatives of storytelling in her
novels is a manifestation of her efforts to utilize orality as a stylistic devise from which she can examine social and gender inequalities in Igbo society and mythology. Her fourth novel, *The Slave
Girl* (1977), exemplifies this effort. Using creation myths of origins,
legends, mythical journeys, traditional rituals, and oral historical
narratives, Emecheta tells the story of a young Igbo girl, Ojebeta,
who lost her parents to a fatal outbreak of influenza. This girl is
later sold to wealthy and distant relatives in Onitsha, the Palagadas,
by her brother, Okolie, whose only motive for this desperate act is
to secure funds to enhance his stature in his coming-of-age dance.
It is Ojebeta's lingering experiences in serfdom that provide for the
reader a sustained and symbolic context for the critical examination of oral traditions and the African woman in the novel.

Let us briefly consider the Prologue, a cleverly constructed
prefatory material that highlights Emecheta's skillful utilization of
oral noetics and the attendant historical and sociocultural contradictions rife in such traditions.

In the Prologue, Emecheta is committed to the storytelling art form right from the start. Her narrator, the raconteur, commenced her story with details of the grandeur and significance of the Eke Market only to quickly put in juxtaposition with the village of Omeze, the area where the exiled Prince founded Ibuza. This seemingly innocent and straightforwardly factual opening is well-known to a listening audience. What is not so obvious to that audience is how the raconteur intends to proceed with such mundane details. Such an approach, an important one in storytelling techniques, is designed to heighten expectancy and, at the same time, hold the attention of the audience. It is important to remember, as I have argued elsewhere, that oral literature is a performing art; one that constantly demands ingenuity, drama, and acuity from the performer.[1] A new tale is only new when it is told again. Therefore the ability of the artist to combine imagery, legend, drama, and everyday experiences is an ability to create new dimensions of African oral literature.

In order to characterize the legendary beginnings of Ibuza, the narrator engages in elaborate spatial descriptions mainly to establish geographical boundaries (locus of markets to homesteads, streams to rivers, villages to towns, bush paths to roads, and center to periphery), and more importantly, to invoke the audience's creative visualization of the setting where the drama is about to unfold.

Furthermore, as she tells her story, the raconteur engages in useful diversions that reinforce the audience's knowledge about the Igbo worldview. The intent is most certainly anticipatory, as will be evident in the main tale itself:

> To the people of Isu it was always a case of a life for
> a life; it did not matter whether one of the lives was
> that of a peddlar and the other that of a beloved
> prince like the gallant Umejei. (9)

In Igbo ontology, as in many African ontologies, life is perceived as the ultimate "leveller"; that metaphysical reality that exemplifies our spirituality. Status, power, wealth, even regality cannot accord one life preferential consideration while denigrating another because of the absence of these attributes. Thus, the Oba of Isu, even with his regal grandeur and opulence, the narrator tells us, cannot save his son, Umejei, from imminent banishment for inadvertently taking the life of a clansman, anymore than Obierika could help Okonkwo in *Things Fall Apart*, to avoid banishment for the accidental killing of Ezeudu's son. Both Umejei and Okonkwo must submit to the will of the community, the collective custodians of the will of the gods, in spite of their eminently powerful positions in their respective communities. To spill the blood of a kinsman is to desecrate the earth which would bring collective suffering to the community. Thus, the imperative need for catharsis.

Some critics may find the preeminence of the community in Igbo society ponderous given the Igbo's commitment to individual achievement and initiative. But as Achebe explains,

> ...the Igbo are unlikely to concede to the individual
> an absolutism they deny even the *chi*. The obvious
> curtailment of a man's power to walk alone and do
> as he will is provided by...the will of his communi-
> ty...No man however great can win judgement
> against all the people. (99)

In other words, Igbo individualism is rooted in group solidarity. A man who has supporters will always be protected from danger and from the wrath of the gods.

The perceptive reader/listener will begin to see Emecheta's artistry as she looks more closely into the thematic subtleties of the Prologue. The affirmation of equanimity so ably championed by Oba Isu himself and sanctioned by traditional laws and custom is a solemn testimony to the rigid adherence to social order in Igbo society:

> But in our clan all souls are equal, none is greater
> than the other. The law of the land will not permit
> you to stay in Isu and live....(9)

However, and herein lies Emecheta's characteristic irony, how rigidly *and fairly* are these tenets applied to women? The women of Umuisagba, fiercely independent, proud, fashionable, and doggedly loyal to their culture are shunned, ostracized, and negatively labeled when they dare to demand respect and practice self-actualization:

> They never forgot that they came from the center,
> and they never let you forget either. When they drop
> something...they would call upon the goddess of the
> market to help them out. So if you do not wish your
> hut to be brought to shame...steer clear of the girls
> from Umuisagba. (11)

Furthermore, girls as young as seven are treated no better than common commodities, chattels, and playthings for the rich. Progressively then, the proclamation of equality in the Prologue becomes antithetical to the realities of subjugation and oppression against women in the novel. We can therefore assert that equality is not evident in traditions that demand that the woman renounce self-pride and/or dignity in service to indolent and self-indulgent male characters.

Emecheta's approach to these contradictions in Igbo culture is deliberate. She does not accept "mythological charters" that tend to enshrine gender inequalities in her society. Man, the divine representation of the social order, shall rule and woman, the voiceless, functional subordinate, shall follow. One is reminded of what Schipper calls "the mythological pre-phase" through which religious edicts and creation myths have reinforced this hierarchical relationship between man and woman.

Conversely, Emecheta does not dismiss traditional culture as irrelevant to her artistic vision. In an interview with Adeola James, Emecheta explains how the ordinary activities of traditional life in the village (peeling melon seed, storytelling among women, etc.) intrigued her and accelerated an interest in storytelling as an art form (37). What Emecheta attempts to do with a great deal of success in *The Slave Girl* (and later in *The Joys of Motherhood*) is to use the conventional narrative structure of traditional folktales to tell stories, describe rituals, and explain world views. But she does so with a different ideological, social, and historical emphasis. The resultant dichotomy between her interpretation of myth, for example, and male writers' interpretation of the same has served to highlight perspectives of female discourse as it relates to artistic merit.

While tradition demands silent submission from women, Emecheta on the contrary, creates female characters who are vocal, sensitive, and realistic. She then puts them in meaningful dialogic relationships simultaneously with self and with others of the same ilk. The hopes, fears, and aspirations of women are articulated by women whose discourse communities are now shared by empathic and like-minded participants. Mae Gwendolyn Henderson, in her erudite discussion of the discursive dilemma of black woman writers, reinforces this assertion when she writes:

> What is at once characteristic and suggestive about black women's writing is its interlocutory, or dialogic, character, reflecting not only a relationship with the "other(s)," but an internal dialogue with the

plural aspects of self that constitute the matrix of
black female subjectivity. (118)

Take Ojebeta and Amanna, "comrades in mat-wetting," for example, who develop a very special friendship in captivity. As children
who have been deprived of the normalcy of childhood, they have
common fears and apprehensions about themselves and about
their future. Even in captivity, they manifest the spontaneous
frivolity of children. It was during one of these episodes of childhood remembrance that they ran into trouble with Pa Palagada:

> "What do you think you two are doing, making so
> much noise that we cannot talk in the house?...Come
> up to the parlor—and you go and get me the whip. I
> will teach you two to laugh properly next time." (97)

Pa Palagada epitomizes terror in the eyes of the children. He is a
man to be feared, to be loathed, for his relationship with the
enslaved females is putative and sexually abusive. His sadistic
desire to see Amanna and Ojebeta physically destroy each other
is symptomatic of his contemptuous disregard for women. Perhaps
it is a recognition of this trait in Pa Palagada and a realization that
they are both hapless victims of one man's terror that Amanna and
Ojebeta deny him the pleasure of seeing them continue the fight.
Later, Ojebeta, with her characteristic sensitivity, nudges Amanna
into reconciling their differences:

> She sat by Amanna, and they both swore that they
> would always be friends, that they would never
> again betray one another just to amuse Pa. (100)

Ojebeta's conciliatory move here can be seen as a valiant attempt
to transcend physical and psychological pain in order to create vis-
tas of lasting friendship with an empathic partner. Two women,
from such diverse backgrounds; Ojebeta, an *ogbanje* child but wanted and cherished by parents; the other, Amanna, a discarded twin,
abandoned for fear of male-initiated sanctions. Here they are bonding in captivity.

A similar nurturing relationship seems to have developed
between Nwayinuzo and Chiago. Both have come to understand
and anticipate the violence, be it physical or psychosexual, that
characterize their lives as women slaves. When Chiago chooses to
confide in Nwayinuzo about sexual molestation from Pa and his
son Clifford, she finds in her a patient and sympathetic listener, a

devoted friend, and a trusted confidant. Both wrestle with the unmitigating sexual persecution and dehumanizing treatment they must endure on a daily basis. And, both appear resigned to the seeming futility of their condition:

> "...But if both father and son want you, there'll be trouble in this household."

> "Yes. I certainly don't want the father to feel that I like his son better than him. I don't like either of them. But what can I do..."

> "Yes," drawled Nwayinuzo sleepily, "but what can we do?" (94)

What we see in these dialogues is a special kind of freedom for women to vocalize their concerns about the stranglehold of patriarchal culture: an opportunity to challenge the hegemonic discourses of that culture and, at the same time, strive to (en)gender the self. In short, we come face to face with the structures of black female discourse within the context of orality in the contemporary African novel written by and about black women.

Emecheta presents other variations of this discourse in her narrative structure, notably the symbiotic relationships between oral traditions and history which accounts in large measure for the legitimation of patriarchal dominance in traditional cultures. Centuries of socialization have seen legends, epics, rituals, tales, etc. reinforce the notion that power, leadership, and the acquisition of wealth, are the exclusive domain of males, and procreation and domestication that of the females. Thus, an "appropriate" praise name for Okweukwu, Ojebeta's father, is: *"Your father's wealth is the greatest."* However, his response to Umeadi, Ojebeta's mother, is not so complimentary:

> *"She who is on a mountain of money."* (16)

Even in situations where the male characters are indolent, inept, greedy, and clearly irresponsible, such characters use tradition and history to secure political, social, and economic domination. Okolie chooses to sell his sister for a few pounds of adornments in preparation for his coming-of-age dance; Pa Palagada, whose actual economic contribution to the Palagada household is zero, insists on, and is given, unlimited powers over everyone, especially the female members of the household. Chiago rationalizes that power from the need for domestic order such as controlling "giant slaves like Jienuaka" (96) is a task suitably befitting males only! The narrator is less condescending when she summarily announces that "The man was crazy with power" (95). While reflecting on Ma Palagada's ailing health, the raconteur virulently criticizes a traditional system that seems to favor an indigent father over a hardworking mother:

> She might be just a woman like every other mother, but what a woman! It would be true to say that in fact it was she who owned all the family's wealth, but who would dare voice such an opinion when his drunkard of a father with his bulging stomach was there telling everyone, "Palagada is my wife, don't you forget that." (116)

The last comment ascribed to Pa Palagada in the above excerpt clearly illustrates the subordinating nature of traditional relationships sanctioned by history. In a sense, it does not matter how industrious or how wealthy a woman becomes. Tradition has it willed that as long as she is "classified" as wife, she must submit to every whim of the husband. Like Pa Palagada, Clifford and Okolie are miserable failures too. The former in maintaining the business empire his mother had built and the latter in farming. However, because they are males and are *expected* to lead and to dominate, they do not take responsibility for their failures and their shortcomings.

Another variation in Emecheta's narrative discourse is her use of intertextuality primarily to exemplify the vitality and centrality of certain folk beliefs in Igbo culture. Among these are the *ogbanje* myth and the story of the slave woman buried alive with her mistress. Both myths are important thematically. But I will focus on the *ogbanje* myth for my discussion here.

Julien has defined intertextuality as "the continuous dialogue of works of literature among themselves." Such "texts comment and expand upon their predecessors, or break with them entirely, as their situation in specific social and historical contexts shape them" (26). Stratton aptly interprets the *ogbanje* as "children believed to be destined to die and reborn repeatedly to the same mother unless a means can be found to break the cycle" (148). This has been utilized by a number of African male writers like Achebe, Soyinka, and Clark. Emecheta first introduced it in *The Bride Price* to demonstrate the resilience of tradition in the face of the indomitable will of the individual: in this case, Aku-nna, the protagonist of the novel. With the precariousness of her birth and the weight of the *ogbanje* myth hanging over her head, Aku-nna plods through life learning the intricacies of community control through traditional rituals and values, while developing a sense of self, individual initiative, and a better understanding of the nature of birth, death, and rebirth. The latter can be viewed as somewhat cathartic for Aku-nna as she herself had gone through that cycle a number of times.

In *The Slave Girl*, the *ogbanje* myth is expanded and transformed to symbolize birth and renewal, freedom and enslavement, power and powerlessness. When Ojebeta is born, her father, Okwuekwu, is finally happy because he now has the daughter he always wanted. But in order to break the *ogbanje* child's cycle of life and death, he must undertake what amounts to an epic journey to the mythological country of Idu to secure the charms necessary to keep Ojebeta from going back to the land of the dead. It is a journey fraught with all kinds of danger and one requiring "Sundiatan" courage to be successful:

> To get to Idu, it was believed you would have to pass seven lands and swim or row your canoe through seven seas. It was a long way to Idu. Idu was said to be situated at that point where the blue sky touched the earth, sealing it up in a neat compact. The people of Idu were the last humans you would see before you come to the end of the world. (19-20)

Of essence here are references to modalities of epic or mythological journeys. There is numerological symbolism (seven lands and seven seas) designed, on one hand, to dramatize the scope of the journey, and on the other, to highlight the balance and the struggle between good and evil, universe and man, and judgement and consequence. There is also metaphysical imagery, such as the convergence of earth and the firmament to depict infinitesimal distance; and finally, ontological imagery designed to locate the Idu in this whole metaphysical schemata.

The magnification of the journey that Okwuekwu must take, just as the dramatic digging up of Ezinma's "iyu-iwa" in Achebe's *Things Fall Apart*, signifies the pricelessness of the *ogbanje* child and the unbridled eagerness of her parents to break the *ogbanje* cycle. In short, the father has to learn to appreciate the girl right from the start in order to convince her to stay in the land of the living. Indirectly, these rituals tend to celebrate the nascent power of women to determine their own destiny; a power that will be snuffed by the rigidities of a male-dominated culture, once a way has been found to break the mystique of the *ogbanje*.

In addition to the protection the charms from Idu offer Ojebeta, they are loaded with symbolisms worth looking at. First of all, the charms symbolize love: a manifestation of parental love. Even friends of Umeadi recognize this:

> They all laughed briefly, and Ojebeta covered her face as she ran...her waist beads jingling with her safety charms. Those watching knew that she was a loved child, over-decorated with trinkets and expensive tattoos. (25)

Maternal love is also exemplified by Umeadi's willingness to allow six-year old Ojebeta to continue sucking on her "milkless breasts." As a child, Ojebeta was encouraged to think independently and to articulate her ideas without fear. This was unusual for women in patriarchal societies. Thus, this is a period in her life when the charms become synonymous with positive self-identification; a period when love, freedom, and dignity are given not from the practiced dicta of traditional culture but from the loving hearts of parents.

Conversely, the charms and Ojebeta's elaborately tattooed face signify the loss of innocence and freedom. The "short journey" that she takes with her brother to the Onitsha market to be sold, exemplifies that transcendence. At this point in the narrative, Emecheta employs contrastive imagery to show the dichotomous relationship between past and present realities in Ojebeta's life. In Ibuza, her charms are "trinkets" and face-markings are "expensive tattoos." In Onitsha, the charms are "pagan" and "junk," and the face-marks are tribalistic and backward. Ibuza people are simple, honest, and warm and Onitsha people seem "to be made of mechanical wood, working without feeling at their work and not daring to look at her..." (56). It is also significant that the market, which in Ibuza provides for important cultural and legitimate economic functions, is in Onitsha a place that easily accommodates the traffic in human beings.

The filing off of Ojebeta's charms by the blacksmith in the market takes on an even more significant meaning. It symbolizes the deflation of the protective cocoon provided by her parents and her village, leaving her exposed to the exigencies of a hostile environment, and therefore prompting instinctual self-preservation. In Ibuza the filing would have meant the dawning of a new life free from intemperate spirits trying to reclaim Ojebeta for the land of the dead. But in Onitsha, the filing is like a funeral dirge:

> Ojebeta could cry no more. She saw the charms
> which had been tied on her by her loving parents,
> to guide her from the bad spirits of the other world,
> filed painfully away. The cowries, too, which hung
> on banana strings were cut off with a big curved
> knife. She now cried in her heart which was throb-
> bing up and down as though it would burst, as the
> hard lesson made itself clear to her that from this
> moment on she was alone. (71)

All Ojebeta has now are the dishevelled pieces of the charms: frag-mentary thoughts of unlimited love, freedom, and individual dig-nity. This new and strange experience is not only her first introduction to slavery but it is a revealing exposure to female entrapment in a patriarchal culture.

Images of the *ogbanje*, which Stratton, quoting Claire Rosen-field, calls the "living-dead," continue to haunt Ojebeta right through her enslavement in the Palagada household. All attempts to shake them off are unsuccessful until the death of Ma Palagada. When she succeeds in negotiating her release from that household, she jubilantly proclaims, "I am going to my people. I am going home," thinking that she has gained her freedom (144).

Emecheta is quick to point out however, that Ojebeta has not escaped the vicious stranglehold of enslavement. She is only exchanging economic enslavement with traditional and domestic enslavement. For how else, the narrator seems to be saying, can you explain a tradition that allows a man to own a woman once he cuts a lock of her hair; or how can Ojebeta's relatives, Uteh and Eze, haggle and quarrel over bride price and suitors for Ojebeta without even acknowledging her say in the matter? She, Eme-cheta's narrator, a collective voice for all women, equivocates in irritation:

> Would she ever be free? Must she be a slave all her
> life, never being allowed to do what she liked? Was
> it the fate of all Ibuza women or just her own? Still
> it would have been better to be a slave to a master
> of your choice, than to one who did not care or even
> know who you were. (168)

The realization of her condition finally dawned on Ojebeta: it is the futility of female self-expression and independence in a patriarchal society. Without the much needed revolutionary changes to the traditions of a society that give authority to men to denigrate women, to make them "second-class citizens," women will continue to thank "new owners" like Jacob for being "better masters."

Emecheta's message in *The Slave Girl* is ensconced in her belief that patriarchal culture is intransigent, oppressive, and stifling. And since patriarchal authority is derived largely from oral traditions that tend to favor males, those traditions must be changed, amended, or discarded. Change itself is an inevitable outcome of life. Therefore, women must take responsibility to see that such changes are possible.

NOTES

1. This issue was discussed in "Orality and the African/Caribbean Novel." I presented this paper at the National Council for Black Studies International Conference in Accra, Ghana, July, 1993.

WORKS CITED

Achebe, Chinua. "Chi in Igbo Cosmology." *Morning Yet on Creation Day: Essays*. London: Heinemann. 1975. 85-110.

Emecheta, Buchi, *The Slave Girl*. New York: George Brazillier, 1977.

Henderson, Mae Gwendolyn. "Speaking in Tongues: Dialogics, Dialectics, and the Black Woman Writer's Literary Tradition." *Reading Black, Reading Feminist*. Henry Louis Gates. New York: Meridian, 1990. 97-126.

James, Adeola. *In Their Own Voices: African Women Writers Talk*. London: James Currey, 1990. 29-43.

Julien, Eileen. *African Novels and the Quest for Orality*. Bloomington: Indiana University Press, 1992.

Kane, Mohamadou. "Sur les formes traditionelle du roman africaine." *Revue de Litterature Comparee*, 48 (1974): 530-549.

Petersen, Kirsten. *Criticism and Ideology*. Uppsala, Sweden: The Scandinavian Institute of African Studies, 1986.

Stratton, Florence. "The Shallow Grave: Archetypes of Female Experience in African Fiction." *Research in African Literatures*. 19.2 (1988).143-169.

Wanjala Chris. "The Growth of a Literary Tradition." *African Literature Today*. 18 (1992): 60-83.

*Jeremy and Alice Ogbanje Emecheta, Emecheta's parents
at their wedding, Lagos, Nigeria in 1938.*

PART TWO
(RE)VISIONS OF FEMALE EMPOWERMENT

The continuous interrogation and (re)vision of female empowerment in African literature is part of the reality of recent creative
works by not only Buchi Emecheta but also by other African female
writers. However, in this (re)visioning of female empowerment it
should be expected that the reactions are neither uniform nor
unanimous. Emecheta like other significant female writers generates both contentious and positive appraisals, but those appraisals
coalesce to highlight the essence of the radical perspectives inherent in her works. In this particular case that appraisal is related to
the issue of feminist consciousness often projected in varied ways.
The papers in this section are part of that juxtaposition, conflicting or harmonious critical appraisals, for analysis of female empowerment.

Nancy Topping Bazin in "Venturing into Feminist Consciousness:
Two Protagonists from the Fiction of Buchi Emecheta and Bessie
Head" discusses the growth of Nnu Ego in *The Joys of Motherhood* as
daughter, wife and mother. Bazin emphasizes the awakening feelings of female empowerment in Nnu Ego because she "has ventured
into feminist consciousness, but it is not until after her death that

she is free to take action by denying fertility to the young women who worship her. She knows that the continuous pressure to bear sons that drives them to her shrine will enslave them as it did her. Freedom for them must begin with rejecting the patriarchal glorification of motherhood." Contrastively Elizabeth, in *A Question of Power* by Bessie Head, arrives at the same destination through a bout of madness. However, Elizabeth like Nnu Ego, rejects the patriarchal model of thinking and behaving. The conclusion is that the two protagonists in Emecheta's and Head's novels portray the social and spiritual consequences of a power structure based upon a philosophy of domination and that "as the protagonists explore [this domain], they venture into feminist consciousness and thereby gain confidence in the rightness of their own vision." This view is challenged in the next essay by Ezenwa-Ohaeto entitled "Replacing Myth With Myth: The Feminist Streak in Buchi Emecheta's *Double Yoke*."

Ezenwa-Ohaeto uses *Double Yoke* to demonstrate that in the process of Buchi Emecheta's female empowerment, she replaces the current unpleasant patriarchal myths with contentious matriarchal myths. Thus he insists that the creation of unrealistic characters, incredible events and implausible situations do not advance the vision of female empowerment. The critic identifies instances of confusion in Emecheta's vision, especially in the conclusion that there is the need for artistry and analysis of "the social bases on which the liberation of women is conceived." Nevertheless, Brenda F. Berrian's "Her Ancestor's Voice: The Ibéji Transcendence of Duality in Buchi Emecheta's *Kehinde*" contrasts Ezenwa-Ohaeto's study and extends the critical discussion of Bazin. Berrian argues persuasively that the myth of twins enables Emecheta to introduce a character that contributes to Kehinde's empowerment. In the process Kehinde fulfills herself first as a woman before considering the social roles of mother and wife. Berrian comments that "very much in tune with her spirituality *via* her twin, Kehinde transcends the duality that lies within her conscious and subconscious states of mind." Significantly that comment by Berrian confirms the transformational creative focus in Emecheta's fiction, and it indicates not only a growth that informs Ezenwa-Ohaeto's critical observations but also extends the notion of female empowerment illustrated by Bazin.

Ezenwa-Ohaeto

Venturing into Feminist Consciousness: Two Protagonists from the Fiction of Buchi Emecheta and Bessie Head

Nancy Topping Bazin

Media reports about international women's meetings and even sessions at the National Women's Studies Association conferences too often perpetuate the myth that Third World women hold women's issues in low priority. It is important, therefore, to note that two of the best novels by contemporary Black African women writers focus upon the growing feminist consciousness of their protagonists. Nnu Ego in Buchi Emecheta's *The Joys of Motherhood* (1979) and Elizabeth in Bessie Head's *A Question of Power* (1974) both move away from innocence into an understanding of the patriarchal culture in which they live. They gain this understanding through experiences so overwhelming and horrifying that each woman barely survives. However, the two protagonists emerge from their ventures with strength, wisdom, and clarity of vision they did not previously possess.

Buchi Emecheta's *The Joys of Motherhood* illuminates brilliantly the meaning of Adrienne Rich's concept "the institution of motherhood" (20). Although the general public rarely perceives the distinction, feminists are not against biological motherhood but they are against what Rich describes as the patriarchal use of motherhood to keep women relatively powerless. Buchi Emecheta's novel begins with Nnu Ego, in a state of despair, running blindly towards the river to drown herself. Nnu Ego has already lost one husband because she did not become pregnant, and the son she had born for her second husband has just died. At this point Nnu Ego attempts suicide because, when pain and anger rose inside of her, "sometimes anger came to the fore, but the emotional pain always won" (9). By the end of the book, her consciousness allows the anger to dominate the pain, thereby giving her the power to act and to choose rather than simply to suffer. Like Elizabeth in Bessie Head's *A Question of Power*, Nnu Ego never achieves much freedom. However, anger has forced her to analyze the situation of women, thus giving her the basis for wiser decisions.

Buchi Emecheta frequently uses African belief systems to provide the framework for her story. In *The Joys of Motherhood*, Nnu Ego's initial infertility is said to be the revengeful work of her father's slave girl who became understandably angry when she was told she must accept the custom of being buried alive with her dead mistress. Although "a good slave was supposed to jump into the grave willingly," even happily, this slave had to be killed to make her lie still (23). To free Nnu Ego from the young slave woman's curse, the father frees all his slaves (35). Longing so for the baby required by the community, Nnu Ego dreams that a baby boy is offered to her; as she wades across a stream to get it, the slave woman laughs mockingly at her and the water rises so she cannot reach the baby. Ironically, she is glorified after her death by a shrine, and she herself has become the woman in the other world who denies fertility to young wives: "however many people appealed to her to make women fertile, she never did!" (224). She denies them fertility, however, not, like the slave woman, to be vengeful, but rather to save them from the fate she had known. The change from weeping because she is childless, to anger because she spent the rest of her life bearing nine children and caring for the seven who lived, is the consequence of the feminist consciousness she has acquired through her experiences.

Nnu Ego has long been aware of the cruel treatment women receive from many men. In her flight towards suicide, she recalls the tales of her father's polygamous behavior. He had at his disposal seven wives and two mistresses. He flaunted his favoritism for one of the two mistresses, Nnu Ego's mother, by noisily making love to her in the courtyard so all his neglected wives could hear. To dominate even this favorite, the father tried to reduce her "to longing and craving for him," to humiliate her "in her burning desire" (20). This courtyard behavior caused his first wife to have a seizure and die (22).

Nnu Ego has also learned about patriarchal attitudes through her experiences with her first husband. When she does not become pregnant, she masochistically takes the blame: "I am sure the fault is on my side. You do everything right" (31). But he feels free to make this cruel statement: "I have no time to waste my precious male seed on a woman who is infertile" (32). Soon he takes a second wife who becomes pregnant the first month. The husband tells Nnu Ego: "I will do my duty by you. I will come to your hut when my wife starts nursing her child. But now, if you can't produce sons, at least you can help harvest yams" (33). Such male behavior was usual; therefore, although Nnu Ego suffers, she continues to blame only herself for her pain.

Nnu Ego's education in the ways of the patriarchy continues as her father buys her back from her first husband and sells her to another family. In each case, the bride price changes hands between the males. Although Nnu Ego finds herself in Lagos with an ugly, fat husband whom neither she nor her father had met, she feels she must accept the situation because the chief concern of her family back in Ibuza is that she get pregnant. She knows they will not tolerate any rebellion on her part. When she receives a message from home, it is, "Your big mother said I should tell your husband to hurry up and do his work because her arms are itching for a baby to rock" (76). Given this kind of pressure from the family, her reaction to pregnancy is not surprising: "He has made me into a real woman—all I want to be, a woman and a mother" (53). Although that first baby dies, she goes on to have two sons, Oshia and Adim. At times she is extremely miserable in the marriage, for example, when her husband inherits his dead brother's three wives and brings one home to live with them. But still she cannot protest, for her father would say:

> Why do you want to stand in your husband's way?
> Please don't disgrace the name of the family again.
> What greater honor is there for a woman than to be
> a mother, and now you are a mother—not of daugh-
> ters who will marry and go, but of good-looking
> healthy sons, and they are the first sons of your hus-
> band and you are his first and senior wife. Why do
> you wish to behave like a woman brought up in a
> poor household? (119)

Even when she goes back for her father's funeral, she knows that people will soon send her home, saying, "You have already proved you are a good daughter, but a good daughter must also be a good wife" (155). Her roles of daughter, wife, and mother are rigidly defined and she is expected to fulfill them according to custom for, in her husband's words, "What else does a woman want?" (49).

In fulfilling her roles, which include almost constant pregnan-cy, Nnu Ego suffers from the practices of polygamy and son prefer-ence. Her husband Nnaife's attitude was: "If a woman cared for him, very good; if not, there would always be another who would care" (95). When the second wife, Adaku, comes into their home, Nnu Ego observes: "Strange how in less than five hours Nnaife had become a rare commodity" (121). She has to prepare her bed for Nnaife and Adaku and at night has to listen to their love-making: "She tried to block her ears, yet could still hear Adaku's exaggerated carrying on. Nnu Ego tossed in agony and anger all night, going through in her imagination what was taking place behind the curtained bed (124). On Nnaife's first night home after the war, Nnu Ego endures his pub-lic declaration that he must go to Ibuza to see another wife, Adankwo, inherited from his dead brother. He makes all the male visitors laugh by saying, "She must be longing for a man. For a woman to be with-out a man for five years! My brother will never forgive me" (182). Although Nnu Ego becomes pregnant once again, he still visits Adankwo and gives her "last menopausal baby" (183). However, she will not go back to Lagos with him, so he pays the exceptionally high price of thirty pounds to bring home a sixteen-year-old bride (184). Nnu Ego, who is expecting twins, screams at him, "We only have one room to share with my five children, and I'm expecting another two; yet you have brought another person. Have you been commissioned by the white people you fought for to replace all those that died dur-ing the war?" (184). Yet a neighbor quiets her by saying, "Your father would not be happy to see you behave this way." She does not think for herself, for "even in death Nwokocha Agbadi ruled his daughter. She belonged to both men, her father and her husband, and lastly to her sons. Yes, she would have to be careful if she did not want her sons' future wives to say, 'But your mother was always jealous whenever her husband brought home a young wife'" (185).

Nnu Ego accepts for a long time the patriarchal attitude that sons are much more valuable than daughters. When she bears twin girls, she feels ashamed. Her worst fears are realized when their father looks at them and says, "Nnu Ego, what are these? Could you not have done better? Where will we all sleep, eh? What will they eat?" (127). Her co-wife Adaku consoles her by saying: "It's a man's world this. Still, senior wife, these girls when they grow up will be great helpers to you in looking after the boys. Their bride prices will be used in paying their school fees as well" (127). Adaku herself is not respected because she has no male children. But ironically, the female loses either way; for even the mother of sons is trapped. Simply because Nnu Ego was "the mother of three sons, she was supposed to be happy in her poverty, in her nail-biting agony, in her churning stomach, in her rags, in her cramped room...Oh, it was a confusing world" (167). When Adaku loses a baby boy, she goes into deep depression. As Nnu Ego's son Oshia tries to console her by saying she still has her daughter Dumbi, Adaku snaps back, "You are worth more than ten Dumbis." From then on, Oshia realizes his superior status; he refuses to fetch water or help cook because "That's a woman's job." This behavior is excused by the community as being "just like a boy" (128).

Nnu Ego follows the custom of expecting boys to get much more education than girls. Her daughters go to school for only a couple of years and, even at that, they must do petty trading after school; "the boys, on the other hand, were encouraged to put more time into their school work" (180). Nnu Ego tells her girls that they must do this work to raise money to educate the boys and "put them in a good position in life, so that they will be able to look after the family." The mother cites the reward for the girls: "When your husbands are nasty to you, they will defend you" (176).

As Nnu Ego participates in the patriarchal system both as victim and as perpetrator of it, she is angry more and more frequently. She realizes more and more clearly that the institution of motherhood has greatly limited her freedom and power. When Nnaife gives his wives too little money for food, Nnu Ego finds that, because her children might starve if he becomes angry, her power to struggle against him is minimal:

She was a prisoner, imprisoned by her love for her children, imprisoned in her role as the senior wife. She was not even expected to demand more money for her family; that was considered below the standard expected of a woman in her position. It was not fair, she felt, the way men cleverly used a woman's sense of responsibility to actually enslave her. (137)

Growing more and more rebellious, she asks, "God, when will you create a woman who will be fulfilled in herself, a full human being, not anybody's appendage?" She laments: "What have I gained from all this? Yes, I have many children, but what do I feed them on? On my life. I have to work myself to the bone to look after them" (186). Even after her death, they will worship her dead spirit, and if things do not go well, they will blame her. In desperation she asks, "When will I be free?" (187).

Finally, through her experiences with her father, husbands, and sons, she has come to understand the patriarchal nature of her culture and her own role in perpetuating it:

> The men make it look as if we must aspire for children or die. That's why when I lost my first son I wanted to die, because I failed to live up to the standard expected of me by the males in my life, my father and my husband—and now I have to include my sons. But who made the law that we should not hope in our daughters? We women subscribe to that law more than anyone. Until we change all this, it is still a man's world, which women will always help to build. (187)

Moreover, when Nnaife is proud of his sons, they are his children; but when they fail to meet his expectations, they are her children. Nnu Ego became fed up with "this two-way standard" (206).

But Nnu Ego has awakened too late; she says at the end of the book, "I don't know how to be anything else but a mother" (222). She has also recognized too late a fact that is evident to the reader all through the book—male and female perspectives are very far apart. Her drunken husband, Nnaife, tried to kill a potential son-in-law because he was from the wrong tribe, so he is put in jail. Her sons whom she expected to care for her in her old age are university students who neither write nor send money. The reality of her life is contrasted with the views of a man who is driving her back to her home village:

146

"This life is very unfair for us men. We do all the work, you women take all the glory. You even live longer to reap the rewards. A son in America? You must be very rich, and I'm sure your husband is dead long ago...."

She did not think it worth her while to reply to this driver, who preferred to live in his world of dreams rather than face reality. What a shock he would have if she told him that her husband was in prison, or that the so-called son in America had never written to her directly, to say nothing of sending her money. If she should tell him that, he would look down on her and say, "But you're above all that, madam." (223)

Nnu Ego's experiences have made her realize that women must work together to "change all this" (187). Nnu Ego has ventured into feminist consciousness, but it is not until after her death that she is free to take action by denying fertility to the young women. She knows that the continuous pressure to bear sons that drives them to her shrine will enslave them as it did her. Freedom for them must begin with rejecting the patriarchal glorification of mother-hood.

Nnu Ego's journey into feminist consciousness is through marriage and motherhood. Bessie Head's protagonist in *A Question of Power* arrives at the same destination through a bout of madness. In her mad, nightmare world, Elizabeth struggles against and survives patriarchal efforts to manipulate her spiritual and sexual being. She is able to regain her sanity only by recognizing that she must not respond passively to those who wish to dominate her. But Bessie Head's protagonist goes beyond the rejection of domination as a principle that determines attitudes and behavior to the articulation of an egalitarian philosophy. Whereas Buchi Emecheta's focus is upon personal experiences and social customs in a patriarchal African culture, Bessie Head's concern is with the spiritual or philosophical significance of patriarchal behavior.

The title *A Question of Power* clarifies further what this novel is about.[1] To Bessie Head whose daily life was shaped by the racist practices of South Africa and the sexist attitudes of the men she lived with, the question of who has the power is indeed important. Like Virginia Woolf, Zora Neale Hurston, and Doris Lessing, Bessie Head views the need of the male to see himself twice as big as he really is as one of the chief causes of unjust, undemocratic, and unkind behavior. In *A Question of Power* the male need to dominate and feel superior to others is represented by two men, Sello and Dan. They come to life and into power through the mad imaginings of Elizabeth. They are so real to her that she talks with them and feels her life literally threatened by them. It is because Sello and Dan use every power they have to try to destroy Elizabeth psychologically that she is mad. To regain her sanity, she must defeat them.

Elizabeth learns that Sello has already "killed several women," and he has molested his own child (28, 144). Moreover, he is the creator of the powerful Medusa, who inhabits Elizabeth's mad world. His Medusa is really "the direct and tangible form of his own evils, his power lusts, his greed, his self importance" (40). Medusa, manipulated by Sello, tortures Elizabeth until she almost obliterates her: "It wasn't Elizabeth's body she was thrusting into extinction. It was the soul; the bolts were aimed at her soul. It seemed to make death that much slower, that much more piecemeal. The narrow, mean eyes of Sello in the brown suit stared at her over Medusa's shoulder" (87).

Sello and Dan try to kill Elizabeth's spirit. They do this primarily through manipulating her feelings about sexuality and through using sexuality to degrade her. To undermine Elizabeth's sense of herself as a woman, Sello uses Medusa, and Dan uses his "seventy-one nice-time girls" (173). Medusa with a smile offers Elizabeth some secret information:

> It was about her vagina. Without any bother for decencies she sprawled her long black legs in the air, and the most exquisite sensation travelled out of her towards Elizabeth. It enveloped her from head to toe like a slow, deep, sensuous bomb. It was like falling into deep, warm waters, lazily raising one hand and resting in a heaven of bliss. Then she looked at Elizabeth and smiled, a mocking superior smile:
>
> "You haven't got anything near that, have you? (44).

Sello displays before Elizabeth his own attraction to Medusa. He "issued a low moan of anguish. He seemed to be desperately attached to that thing Medusa had which no other woman had. And even this was a mockery. It was abnormally constructed, like seven thousand vaginas in one, turned on and operating at white heat" (64).

Elizabeth is attracted to Dan's overwhelming masculinity: "He made a woman feel like an ancient and knowledgeable queen of love" (106). But Dan displays his power not just over her but over all women. He sadistically parades his many women before her and his message to her is that she should be jealous: "I go with all these women because you are inferior. You cannot make it up to my level." But, of course, just at the moment when she decides she dislikes him and wants "to pull her mind out of the chaos," he says: "If you leave me I'll die, because I have nothing else" (147).

One of the key images in Elizabeth's madness is Dan "standing in front of her, his pants down, as usual, flaying his powerful penis in the air and saying: "Look, I'm going to show you how I sleep with B...She has a womb I can't forget. When I go with a woman I go for one hour. You can't do that" (12-13). His women include Miss Wriggly-Bottom, who "had small round breasts and a neat, nipped-in waist. She walked in time to a silent jazz tune she was humming and wriggled and wriggled her bottom" (129). There was also Miss Sewing Machine who "liked her penny-button tickled" (127). He added to the display "Miss Pelican-Beak, Miss Chopper, Miss Pink Sugar-Icing, whom he was on the point of marrying, Madame Make-Love-On-The-Floor where anything goes, The Sugar-Plum Fairy, more of Body Beautiful, more of The Womb, a demonstration of sexual stamina with five local women, this time with the lights on, Madame Squelch Squelch, Madame Loose-Bottom—the list of them was endless" (148). Elizabeth took heavy doses of sleeping tablets to block out all his night activities with these "nice-time girls." For Dan sometimes tumbled these women into bed right beside Elizabeth ("They kept on bumping her awake"), and he encouraged them to use her personal possessions to clean up: "He was abnormally obsessed with dirt on his women. They washed and washed in her bathroom; they put on Elizabeth's dresses and underwear and made use of her perfumes" (127-28).

Of course, if Dan finds that any of his seventy-one "nice-time girls" are *too* sexual, then he panics and turns against them. He views women as dirty if they are more sexually potent than he. He could not stand the sexual potency of Madame Loose-Bottom or the hysterical, feverish orgasm of Body Beautiful. Because the pelvis of Madame Squelch Squelch was like "molten lava," going with her made him throw up (164-65). One night he decided Miss Pelican-Beak with her long, tough vagina was "too pushy," so he broke her legs and elbows and redesigned her pelvis to make it more passive (167-68). Then he left her for Miss Chopper. Thus, his hatred for women was not all directed at Elizabeth. But she takes his behavior personally: "Why, why, why? What have I done?" Indeed it drives her further into madness; she becomes dysfunctional and must be hospitalized (173, 176).

Both Sello and Dan use male homosexuality to make Elizabeth feel excluded. Dan tells Elizabeth it is a "universal phenomenon" (138). He makes Sello appear before her with his boyfriend (148), and he says, "They do it all the time" (139). The displays of homosexuality, like the displays of heterosexuality, are meant to degrade her. These nightmares are extensions of her experiences with her husband: "Women were always complaining of being molested by her husband. Then there was also a white man who was his boyfriend. After a year she picked up the small boy and walked out of the house, never to return" (19).

Elizabeth's recognition of the similarity between racist and sexist attitudes is clear. She knew that white people "went out of their way to hate you or loathe you" (19); similarly, Dan hits her with a "torrent of hatred" every day (168). She finds the misogyny of many African males to be untempered by "love and tenderness and personal romantic treasuring of women" (137). She calls both racists and sexists power-maniacs. "What did they gain, the power people, while they lived off other people's souls like vultures?" (19). Medusa serves as an image for domination; she represents these attitudes: "Who's running the show around here? I am. Who knows everything around here? I do. Who's wearing the pants in this house? I am" (43).

On a philosophical level, Elizabeth is saved from permanent madness by her faith in a value system different from Dan's and Sello's and by a different concept of God. In practice, she is saved by working in a garden with a woman friend Kenosi, who admires and respects her. Her work relationship with this woman provides her with a feminist model. Ultimately, Elizabeth rejects the patriarchal model of thinking and behaving in favor of a feminist mode of thinking and behaving. This rejection of a philosophy of domination in favor of an egalitarian philosophy is reflected in her comments about God.

Elizabeth rejects a god in the sky, because "God in heaven is too important to be decent" (197). Her ideal is to bring holiness down to earth. The gods are, in fact, those "killed and killed and killed again in one cause after another for the liberation of mankind." She saw the gods as "ordinary, practical, sane people, seemingly their own distinction being that they had consciously concentrated on spiritual earnings. All the push and direction was towards the equality of man in his soul, as though, if it were not fixed up there, it would never be anywhere else." She concludes that "there are several hundred thousand people who are God" (31). Her prayer is "Oh God. . . . May I never contribute to creating dead worlds, only new worlds" (100).

Elizabeth concludes that this can occur only through a struggle against greed and arrogance and an excessive concern for self (134). Sello admits, "I thought too much of myself. I am the root cause of human suffering" (36). At one point Elizabeth and Sello "perfected together the ideal of sharing everything and then perfectly shared everything with all mankind" (202). But it is through the horrors of her contract with Dan in her hallucinations that she has learned the most:

> He had deepened and intensified all her qualities. . . . he taught by default—he taught iron and steel self-control through sheer, wild, abandoned debauchery; he taught the extremes of love and tenderness through the extremes of hate; he taught an alertness for falsehoods within, because he had used any means at his disposal to destroy Sello. And from the degradation and destruction of her life had arisen a still, lofty serenity of soul nothing could shake. (202)

The aim must be to tap into one's powers, and she places her emphasis on the soul: "If it's basically right there, then other things fall into place. That's my struggle; and that's black power, but it's a power that belongs to all mankind and in which all mankind can share" (135).

Although her language is sometimes sexist, Bessie Head's philosophy and ethics parallel those of feminist philosopher/theologians such as Rosemary Ruether, Naomi Goldenberg, and Elizabeth Dodson Gray. They too reject the hierarchy in traditional religions and cry out for a more egalitarian world view. Feminist theologians speak out against the male God in the sky and the lingering Christian view that the world was created specifically for Man and that he has the right to use nature and women as he pleases.[2] Nor is it surprising that the political philosophy in feminist utopian fiction is most akin to anarchism, for women are tired of being ruled, manipulated, and exploited by authoritarian figures. So, too, is Bessie Head's protagonist.

Throughout Elizabeth's madness, there existed the possibility of being healed and made sane by working in a vegetable garden with Kenosi. Kenosi had about her a quiet strength and purposefulness that appealed to Elizabeth. As they worked together, "Elizabeth clung to the woman. There seemed to be no other justification for her continued existence, so near to death was she" (89). She found in the uneducated, hardworking Kenosi a "knowingness and grasp of life" that made her beautiful (90). Most important of all, Kenosi needs her. Kenosi tells her, "you must never leave the garden. . . . I cannot work without you" (142). Her relationship with this woman keeps in sight the possibility of something quite different from the patriarchal relationships she has in the nightmare world: their "work-relationship had been established on the solid respect of one partner for another" (160). Kenosi enables Elizabeth to maintain her belief that egalitarian relationships are possible. Sello's comment to Elizabeth about her relationship with Dan also helps to save her: "Elizabeth, love isn't like that. Love is two people mutually feeding each other, not one living on the soul of the other like a ghoul!" (197).

Elizabeth withstands the cruelty and torture of Medusa and the two men who inhabit her madness through not giving in to their view of her as nothing. At one point she tells Sello that he is making a mistake, for she is God too (38). Although they almost totally annihilate her sense of self, their misogynist behavior only serves to confirm her faith in the opposite of everything they represent. Throughout her struggle against these symbols of the patriarchal power system which people her hallucinations, she continues to articulate her faith in goodness, love, equality, and inner strength.

The movement toward mysticism found in feminist philosophy is obviously present in Elizabeth's as well. Elizabeth has been tested by the nightmare of madness created by Sello in his role as spiritual mentor. Once she has passed through this hell, her knowledge of evil helps her to rediscover an impersonal, mystical love. She is transported into a state in which there are "no private hungers to be kissed, loved, adored. And yet there was a feeling of being kissed by everything; by the air, the soft flow of life, people's smiles and friendships." This "vast and universal love" equalizes all things and all people. Elizabeth emerges from her hell with a confirmed belief in such love and a "lofty serenity of soul nothing could shake" (202). At the end of the book she recognizes that humankind's fundamental error is the "relegation of all things holy to some unseen Being in the sky. Since man was not holy to man, he could be tortured for his complexion, he could be misused, degraded and killed" (205).

Bessie Head chooses to focus on sexism rather than racism in *A Question of Power*. This forces her African readers, more familiar with racism, to see the similarities between the two and their common root in the philosophy of domination. Men degrade, manipulate, and abuse women in Elizabeth's nightmare, basically because they fail to perceive sacredness in them. Elizabeth advocates a philosophy that insists upon the sacredness of all life because of her subjection to this patriarchal behavior. This is typical of the evolution of feminist thought. That is why feminists speak of ecological and peace issues as well as equal rights; and that is why they speak of equal rights not only for women but also for the poor, the handicapped, and the racially oppressed.

Buchi Emecheta and Bessie Head[3] speak for millions of Black African women through their novels, for they describe what it is like to be female in patriarchal African cultures. In *The Joys of Motherhood*, Nigerian Buchi Emecheta focuses upon the patriarchal beliefs and practices that must be eradicated—son preference, polygamy, double standards, rigid sex roles, and above all, the glorification of motherhood in order to render women powerless. In *A Question of Power*, set in Botswana, Bessie Head portrays even more abusive patriarchal behavior, relates it to all forms of oppression, and presents a philosophy for living quite differently.

The two novels describe the spiritual growth of their protagonists, Nnu Ego and Elizabeth. Both "female heroes" rise above their suffering by resisting the training for submission that they have had within the patriarchal culture. Both finally are able to release themselves from dependency, because they have acknowledged at least inwardly the patriarchal cause of their suffering. Through very personal experiences, the two protagonists show us the social and spiritual consequences of a power structure based upon a philosophy of domination. Buchi Emecheta focuses upon the social and Bessie Head upon the spiritual consequences. As the protagonists explore these domains, they venture into feminist consciousness and thereby gain confidence in the rightness of their own vision.

NOTES

1. Bessie Head (1937-1986) published two other novels—*When Rain Clouds Gather* (1969) and *Maru* (1971). She has two collections of stories, *The Collector of Treasures* (1977) and *Tales of Tenderness and Power* (published

posthumously in 1989). She wrote *Serowe: Village of the Rain Wind* (1981), a history as told by its people, and *A Bewitched Crossroad* (1984), a history of Africa which focuses on the Bamangwato tribe and its chieftain Khama III, who had lived in Serowe. A collection of her autobiographical writings is entitled *A Woman Alone* (1990). She also composed plays for television, children's stories, articles, and poetry. Born of a white mother and black father in South Africa, Bessie Head left there in 1964 to live the rest of her life in Botswana.

2. See, for example, Rosemary Ruether's *New Woman New Earth: Sexist Ideologies and Human Liberation* (New York: Seabury P, 1975), Naomi Goldenberg's *Changing of the Gods: Feminism and the End of Traditional Religions* (Boston: Beacon P, 1979), and Elizabeth Dodson Gray's *Green Paradise Lost* (Wellesley: Roundtable P, 1981).

3. For further information about Bessie Head, see an interview with her in *Conversations with African Writers: Interviews with Twenty-six African Authors*, ed. Lee Nichols (Washington, D.C.: Voice of America, 1981), 49-57 and her statement about her life which precedes her short story "Witchcraft" in *Ms* 5 (Nov. 1975): 72-73. See also Charlotte Bruner, "Bessie Head: Restless in a Distant Land" in *When the Drumbeat Changes*, ed. Carolyn Parker et al., 261-77, the chapter on her work in Lloyd W. Brown's *Women Writers in Black Africa*, 158-79, and Craig MacKenzie's monograph *Bessie Head: An Introduction*. Her papers are located in the Khama III Memorial Museum, Serowe, Botswana.

WORKS CITED

Emecheta Buchi. *The Joys of Motherhood*. African Writers Series, 227. London: Heinemann, 1980.

Head, Bessie. *A Question of Power*. African Writers Series, 149. London: Heinemann, 1974.

Rich, Adrienne. *Of Woman Born: Motherhood as Experience and Institution*. New York: Bantam, 1977.

Replacing Myth with Myth: The Feminist Streak in Buchi Emecheta's *Double Yoke*

Ezenwa-Ohaeto

This paper posits that Buchi Emecheta, in order to counter the myth of male chauvinism in African literature, fashions her own myths of female superiority. Through a structural and thematic study of the novel *Double Yoke*, we will demonstrate a lack of distance between author and subject matter, melodramatic endings, and weaknesses in character delineation. We will also reveal the creation of unrealistic characters, incredible events, and implausible situations. The conclusion is that a novelist who uses the material of the subject matter to substantiate personal prejudice creates flawed works of literature, and that Emecheta's attempts to present a "corrected" view of the female image in literature amount to a replacement of myth with myth.

It seems that African female writers and critics are beginning to awaken from a creativity stupor. Their minimal contribution to the growth of African literature had been stupendously shocking. However, in their recent awakening, it also seems that the prejudices of the much vaunted women's liberation movement have found outlets in modern African fiction and its criticism. Perhaps the time is now appropriate, with the successful incursions into previous male-dominated disciplines like Engineering. [What is left after castigating colonialism, condemning the indigenous successors to leadership positions and fictionally recreating the past?] The time is therefore also appropriate for an intellectual sex war, since the ingredients are ready.

African writers and critics of African literature have assumed different postures in their analysis and perception of this trend. There are calls and requests that women should commence portraying the true picture of women in their novels. Kenneth Little for instance wonders why it is difficult to find as a central character a female doctor, lawyer, high-ranking civil servant and director of a public service since such persons exist in real life. He insists:

> Surely it is time for this fact to be signalized in the literature of the novelist in particular?

> Until it is done the charge of male chauvinism may be difficult effectively to rebut. Here, then is a challenge. It is a challenge that needs to be faced by female authors especially. They need to come forward in greater numbers and they need to take up the gauntlet.[1]

A similar opinion has also been offered by one of Africa's erudite female scholars, Molara Ogundipe-Leslie. She feels that "it is up to women to combat their social disabilities; to fight for their own fundamental and democratic rights, without waiting for the happy day when men will willingly share power and privilege with them—a day that will never come."[2] The pessimism in Ogundipe-Leslie's view is due to her belief that colonialism swept off previous female political structures in the society, and the modern society inherited the new male-dominated structures.

The revival of female consciousness is therefore one of the most significant trends in the development of the African novel. Eldred Jones identifies it when he confirms "the emergence of a very powerful feminist streak—the rise into prominence of a number of highly accomplished and articulate women novelists like Buchi

Emecheta, Mariama Bâ and Rebeka Njau."[3] It is heart warming that these female novelists have emerged and that they are likely to threaten the position of some established male and even female writers. However, despite this pleasant development, some female African writers complain of isolation. The Ghanaian writer, Ama Ata Aidoo, feels that while female writers have the same sense of ridiculous responsibility with their male counterparts, they also suffer from peculiar female frustrations. Aidoo, however, erroneously attributes the lack of rave reviews for her novel *Our Sister Killjoy* to the fact that it is written by a woman when she insists that she is "convinced that if *Killjoy or anything* like it had been written by a man, as we say in these parts, no one would have been able to sleep a wink these couple of years [That is for all the noise that would have been made about it]."[4] Aidoo's reasoning appears faulty for there are definitely other reasons why critics may neglect a creative work. It is therefore unfortunate that Femi Ojo-Ade adopts an apologetic stance that is unacceptable. He feels that "the male writers, like the male social animals is more fortunate than the female. His presence is taken for granted."[5] The publisher seeks him out, unlike the woman "whose silence is also taken for granted." The female writer's silence could be related to some other causes and should not be placed entirely at the feet of the publisher. The fact that few women have written does not mean that they should be placed on exotic pedestals in the realm of literary criticism. It is the product that will justify whichever position the writer will occupy on the ladder of international acclaim.

Moreover, the nature of feminism itself compounds the problem of a female writer creating with female consciousness. The brand of feminism which Emecheta dwells upon is not the feminism of the self-seeking radical proposed by Aidoo and it is not the temperate feminism or womanism of Flora Nwapa,[6] but the feminism which is put thus: "I am a feminist with a small 'f'." I love men and good men are the salt of the earth ... Personally, I'd like to see the ideal, happy marriage. But if it doesn't work for goodness sake, call it off." Moreover Emecheta's view[7] confirms one of the fundamental aspects of feminism, which is that a "subordinated group has inadequate redress through existing political institutions, and is deterred thereby from organizing into conventional political struggle and opposition."[8] The result is that women often develop group characteristics common to those who suffer minority status and a marginal existence. Sheila Rowbotham puts it succinctly when she reveals that feminism has given expression to a new consciousness among women and that the "cultural and economic liberation of women is inseparable from the creation of a society in which all people no longer have their lives stolen from them, and in which the conditions of their production and reproduction will no longer be distorted or held back by the subordination of sex, race and class."[9] We shall examine Emecheta's attempts in *Double Yoke* to champion a feminist cause through a structural and thematic study in order to determine whether her attempts to present a "corrected" view of the female image in literature amounts to a replacement of myth with myth.

It is noteworthy that the ponderous nature of Emecheta's early novels have given way to the much improved *Joys of Motherhood* and *Double Yoke*. The vestiges of autobiographical characteristics still remain but Ebeogu confirms that she "is fast out-living the passions and sentiments forced on her by unpleasant personal experiences and which have characterized the mood of her earlier novels."[10] The implication is that the propaganda prejudices that any male is a devil have diminished considerably too. The result is that a notable critic like Eustace Palmer indicates that Emecheta "shows great psychological insight in the penetration of her characters' thoughts. She is particularly good at the presentation of the feminine psyche. Scarcely any other African novelist has succeeded in probing the female mind and displaying the female personality with such precision."[11] It is in this presentation of the female personality that the danger emerges, the danger which prompts a closer scrutiny of the structure of *Double Yoke*.[12] The clear scrutiny is in confirmation of Smith's belief that "for books to be understood they must be examined in such a way that the basic intentions of the writers are at least considered."[13] The basic intention of Emecheta is to recreate the image of women, through feminism.

One of the myths which Emecheta debunks in *Double Yoke* is the myth of (male) masculinity. She uses the new African females who are encumbered by tradition and at the same time are expected to carry the burden of acquiring suitable education. Nko, the heroine of *Double Yoke* is faced with that problem. It is clear that the story which Ete Kamba is purportedly narrating is the story of Nko. The author conveniently shifts to the third-person point of view which enables her to debunk the myth of (male) masculinity. The female lecturer who gives Ete Kamba the assignment that elicits the story is presented by the author as having "entered with her masculine brief case and quiet tread" (p.3). The introduction of the word masculine is not accidental but a deliberate attempt to show "the strong silent woman," a counter myth to the "strong silent man." The female lecturer, Miss Bulewao, according to the author, enters a classroom of thirty raucous male students discussing campus girls in "uncouth language, punctuated by derisive uneasy laughter."(3) With these introductory commentaries the author sets the stage for the demythologization of the male through a feminist exposition of his weaknesses. The myth which Emecheta has created is that the male is uncouth and primitive.

This image of primitivity in the male is graphically illustrated through the author's presentation of the thoughts in the mind of Ete Kamba. The young man would like to be a writer like the lecturer, Miss Bulewao, but when he considers reality through his thoughts, the author writes: "He was wishing to be as successful as a woman: he was wishing to adopt the method being adopted by an ordinary woman in the field of Arts! How low could one sink!"(9) The impression this passage gives is that it is a male prerogative to excel and shameful for a man to imitate a successful woman. Emecheta replaces the myth of male superiority with the myth of female superiority through the creation of a male character who strives to imitate a woman.

Emecheta seems in agreement with females who show a sense of competition and boldness in the acquisition of whatever they desire. At the party to celebrate Arit's success and qualification as a hairdresser, she boldly asks Ete Kamba for a dance. Arit's action is the type that would have cowed most girls—a girl asking a boy for a dance. It is equally significant that most of the adults started clapping;

> "You see, women know what they want these days, they just go and get them. Not these old ones pretending, pretending ..." Ete Kamba heard Arit's father saying loudly. (24)

The myth which Emecheta is seeking to replace here is the myth that a woman has to wait until the man makes the advances. However, the behavior of Nko later in the same scene contradicts the replacement of that myth. The contradiction manifests through the differences between Arit and Nko, for where Arit is bold Nko is timid. Although Emecheta seems to support brashness, she equally advocates individuality for women. She relates it to a supposedly male syndrome of overbearing behavior.

The author describes the actions of Ete Kamba with profuse details of overbearing behavior. When Ete asks Nko for a dance and she accepts, Emecheta portrays him unflatteringly as a man who:

> tried to lead her rather proudly like a fisherman
> would lead a big catch, but Nko's arm though warm
> and soft, had a tinge of stiffness. (24)

There is a conscious attempt to create the impression that the myth of the softness of women is obsolete, for women may be soft and warm but they are tigers beneath that facade. To buttress the replacement of this myth there are juxtapositions of male savagery and female gentility in the novel. The man is degenerate while the woman is a quintessence of angelic virtues even when she is erring. The fault in this structure shows Emecheta as artistically unreliable because as Lloyd Brown observes, "even more self-defeatingly, her criticisms of African men are often marred by generalizations that are too shrill and transparently overstated to be altogether convincing."[14] The scene where Ete and Nko have their first sexual encounter is noteworthy. The author writes:

> He bore on her, unceremoniously half pushed and
> half dragged her towards the walls of this unfinished
> house, then right to a corner inside. He was deter-
> mined. He had squared his shoulders ready to com-
> bat any protest, but none came. (51)

The connotation is that the sexual encounter is nothing short of rape though with Nko's consent. On the other hand Nko is

> a bundle of soft tender, warm flesh, very young,
> very moist, not very difficult. They stayed there for
> a long time, until she started to wilt. Her legs
> became weak. (52)

This is an implausible situation, for the author converts it into a brutish male-dominated and male-oriented affair. It seems that Emecheta's heroine, moreover, has a stifled sense of individuality for she does not make the move but responds passively to the man. This exaggerated description of sexual encounter mars Emecheta's creativity and makes the incident unconvincing.

Furthermore Emecheta makes Ete Kamba who gains admission to the University ungrateful and callous in order to justify the myth that men are insensitive. She replaces this myth with the myth of a sensitive woman by depicting Nko as presenting with sincerity her most prized possession of virginity. Ete regards her as a loose girl but he needs reassurance. It is not quite clear why the author makes Nko tongue-tied at the crucial moment when she ought to confide in Ete. The incident however enables Emecheta to demonstrate her feminist convictions. Nko reasons that since she is perceived as a prostitute then Ete is automatically a prostitute too. The subsequent debate degenerates into an altercation and inexorably leads to a fight or as the author presents it a "beating-up" because Ete does not like girls who exhibit tendencies for

> the blatant, the loud and the obvious. He lost his cool, and he reacted the way his father would have reacted, like an ordinary village man, who cared for his woman and had little patience in talking her out of her evil ways. He resorted to the method he knew was the quickest and the most effective—the brutal near animal method. He started to beat her up. (59)

The fallacy here is that village life is synonymous with crude behavior and the reference to Ete Kamba's father seems unjustified. It is incredible because there is hardly an instance of aggression generated by the father in the novel. Moreover bestiality is not more pronounced in rural areas than in urban centers. It also appears that Emecheta is gradually losing touch with authentic African experience, for Africa has changed considerably.

Double Yoke has been perceived as a novel with the satiric sting of a *roman a clef*, but which lacks the telltale pointillism of that subgenre. Ikonne therefore informs us that "in an attempt to transform recognizable living persons into fictitious ones, Emecheta has so distorted her models that they are just a little more than two-dimensional caricatures. Even Miss Bulewao, the author's attempt at self-portraiture, is not more rounded. Many of the characters either lack motivations or their motivations are not adequately fused into their actions. Ete Kamba and Nko the main characters are not exceptions."[15] Nko, for instance, gains admission into the University and it marks a turning point in her life. It also serves as an avenue for the author to compare Nko with her mother who at her age, "thought only of how to go to the fattening room" (94). Nevertheless Nko discovers the isolationist female tendency like the inability to confide in other women, for they rarely discuss male-female relationships. Nko thereby finds it difficult to respond emotionally to her female friends and room-mates. It is ironical that the individualistic attitude Emecheta is championing reveals its weakness here. Nko puts it succinctly when she ruminates:

> Yes, just like menstruation, a thing all of us have to
> endure each month, some with more pain and dis-
> comfort than the others. Yet is it considered bad
> manners or downright dirty to talk about it. (97)

It is this isolationism that actually makes Nko unprepared for her
subsequent experience. But that reason cannot be accepted as a
justification for her failure to show courage in the course of her
temptations.

A myth which Nko's moral failure substantiates is the myth
that all males in positions of authority normally take advantage of
the women under them. Emecheta is obviously using this myth to
ameliorate the unfortunate transformation of Nko, who succumbs
to temptations and decides to apply the age-old tactic of using what
she has to get what she wants. She threatens the Dean, Professor
Ikot, to award her high grades after her seduction because:

> Most girls here come to read for their degrees. If
> they become what you think, which is "prostitutes
> Nigerian style," it is because people like you made
> them so. But with me Sir, you are not going to be let
> off lightly.(14)

Emecheta tries to prove the point that often female students are
turned into prostitutes due to pressures from the leaders in academic institutions but in the process Nko emerges as an unrealistic character. Her resolution to blackmail the Professor is weak and
escapist. Acholonu agrees that Emecheta's "solution to the woman's
problem is avant-garde and in itself brutal. . ."[16] The consequence
is that the author lets her significant female character gain emancipation through promiscuity.

The major issue, however, is that the right path for the women
is not quite clear as Mrs. Nwaizu puts it:

> We are still a long way from that yet. Here feminism
> means everything that society says is bad in women.
> Independence, outspokenness, immorality, all the
> ills you can think of. (104)

Nwaizu's view seems to generate a consensus when the ladies get
to know of Nko's predicament through the vengeance of a jilted
Ete on a lecherous Professor Ikot. Their discussion encapsulates
the author's artistic demolition of the remnant myths related to

the role of sex in acquiring certificates and the marriage institution. The role of Mrs. Nwaizu who is married with four children appears hypocritical. She sympathizes with Nko but at the same time she feels that women like Dr. (Mrs.) Edet are "pioneers; you must not forget that. They worked hard to achieve their academic positions and they still would like to be seen as the pillars of tradition" (102). Moreover the mischievous manner through which Nwaizu informs Ete Kamba that Nko went to the Water Falls with Ikot is replete with signs of dishonesty. She sarcastically says: "She probably forgot to mention that to you, when she told you she was going to the Falls. That is rather strange, because Nko is always a direct and straightforward girl, with no nonsense about her..." (129). Nwaizu's attitude is to humiliate Ete Kamba and it illustrates the myth that a man can also be made to look stupid and foolish contrary to the masculine image of invincibility.

One of the female characters in the novel tackles another aspect of the myth related to the marriage institution. Julia questions: "Must you marry him anyway? Must you marry at all if you don't particularly want to?" (155). The error in the reasoning is that marriage is not a male preserve for it involves a man and a woman. The myth which the author is demolishing is the myth that a woman must be in want of a husband. Emecheta hints at this myth when she makes Ete Kamba say that "a woman who is not married is better off dead" (63). Emecheta replaces this myth with the myth that a woman is free to raise her own children outside marriage.

There are weaknesses in character delineation in *Double Yoke* because the author fails to create the necessary distance between herself and the subject matter. Akpan is presented as a timid, unappealing, illogical, conservative young man. He does not want a girlfriend and he believes in going home to take a wife when the need arises. It is obvious that the author derides this view and she makes Akpan say:

> "...can you imagine me mooning about like you are
> doing now? I'd go mad. When I want a girl, I'll get
> one on campus, or if she becomes difficult, I'll go
> into town and pay some money, get all I can for my
> money, see, no strings attached. When I am ready
> to have children in order to please my parents, I'll
> get them to bring me a bride, again no strings
> attached." (130)

The weakness in the delineation of Akpan is that Emecheta fails to illustrate that characters are not merely embodiments of fixed values but persons with discernible history and psychology. The flaw here is that the author unintentionally draws attention to her self-conscious narration and to her limits as a detached observer. If it is true, according to Taiwo, that Emecheta "supports the feminist movement because of her belief in the individuality of everybody, man or woman. All citizens must be able to act in freedom and dignity,"[17] then *Double Yoke* fails to give the same sympathetic presentation of the female characters to the male characters.

The author quite often intrudes through authorial comments. The presentation of the women discussing in Nko's room elicits this authorial comment to the questioner who seeks to know if women must be made love to in order to be sane: "But what those young women in that room in Malabor did not know was that society would like them to think that the answer was yes. And few women bother to question it" (105). Moreover at the end of the presentation of Akpan as a man who is so conservative that he would want a village girl as a wife, the author comments: "Poor Akpans of this world!" (163). Authorial comments can aid the illumination of ideas, but they do not always deepen the creative insight.

The irony in *Double Yoke* is that Emecheta in treating this issue of feminism succeeds in elevating masculinity. It is Ete Kamba who shows remorse, courage, and understanding in taking back Nko. The presentation of Nko is faulty for she is incapable of taking a courageous decision to stand up to the Professor.[18] Emecheta however uses her to attack certain masculine "preserves" like having children out of wedlock and expectations of humility from women especially in the traditional sense. The author makes Ete say, "Madam, you seem to be forgetting that I am a man. I can do what I like. A man can raise his own bastard, women are not allowed to do that" (162). Miss Bulewao, a character obviously speaking the mind of the author insists that Nko can look after her own bastard too and with an irritated tone asks Ete, "Are you strong enough to be a modern African man? Nko is already a modern African lady, but you are lagging... Oh so far, far behind" (162). The impression one gets from Emecheta's "modern African lady" is unsatisfactory because it seems that she is confusing moral laxity with modernism. To encourage women to acquire bastards because men also have them in an aspiration for negativism. Furthermore, the manner in which Nko submits to Ikot or even to Ete Kamba does not show frailty but rather the action of an individual with eyes wide open.

There is definitely a lapse in the creation of emotional convictions in *Double Yoke*. Although it is possible to say that what seems clear is "that the modern African woman in the future is not going to accept much longer a position ascribed to her by her male counterpart," the author does not set about it in an artistic manner. Emecheta rather allows her ideological and social prejudices to mar her creativity. She is a committed writer (committed to feminism) whose sympathies lie with a literature that outlines a plan of action for the liberation of the African woman. She is correspondingly hard on those characters, no matter how inappropriate their embodiment of masculine views or how vibrant their personalities, who fail to demonstrate a consciousness for the liberation of the African woman.

On the other hand, the deprivations women suffer are also suffered by man. Feminism could then be seen as a luxury in African literature. Flora Nwapa who prefers the label "womanist" to the term "feminist" confirms that "in some ways Nigerian women are better-off than Western women. Traditionally women have been economically independent and it has long been accepted, for instance, that men and women go out with their own groups of friends. The social structure of the extended family tends to place less pressure on the husband and wife."[19] In other words the aims of the feminists appear far-fetched for the needs of the society. It is even a contradiction because as Katherine Frank points out, "feminism, by definition, is a profoundly individualistic philosophy: it values personal growth and individual fulfillment over any larger communal needs or good. African society, of course, even in its most westernized modern forms, places the values of the group over those of the individual with the result that the notion of an African feminist almost seems a contradiction in terms."[20] There is therefore an inherent paradox generated by feminism.

The structural lapses in Emecheta's *Double Yoke* show this inherent contradiction. In a situation where survival depends on the ability to exploit others, it means that decorum is discarded by both men and women in the effort to survive. But Emecheta never questions the social bases on which the liberation of women is conceived. She therefore fails to express her views with tact and restraint which often introduces inordinate posturing through authorial commentaries and a replacement of myth with myth.

The lack of distance between author and subject matter, melodramatic endings, unrealistic characters, incredible events and implausible situations substantiate the prejudices of the author which are artistic flaws. Ngugi has shown that the best way to counter a supposedly male-oriented portrayal of the negative female is not through the creation of a superhuman female. He successfully uses Wanja in *Petals of Blood* and Wariinga in *Devil on the Cross* to teach the lesson that art could be subtly manipulated. This is necessary because propaganda calls for counter-propaganda, lest we forget the substance and chase the shadow to our detriment. It can only blind us to the reality of our exploitation and nurture destructive rivalries. The masses would then be confused into chasing the shadow and not the substance of their daily deprivations. Moreover, the sexes in Africa are not even sure of surviving the atomic upheavals of the eighties and nineties threatened by the "civilised" continents of the world. It is for this reason that Emecheta's replacement of myth with myth is unacceptable.

NOTES

1. Kenneth Little, *The Sociology of Urban Women's Image in African Literature* (London: Macmillan,1980), p. 27.
2. Molara Ogundipe-Leslie, "African Women, Culture and Another Development," *Journal of African Marxists* 5 (February, 1984): 89.
3. Eldred Jones, "Editorial," *African Literature Today* 13 *Recent Trends in the Novel* (1983): vii.
4. Ama Ata Aidoo, "Unwelcome Pals and Decorative Slaves," *Afa: Journal of Creative Writing* 1 (November 1982): 8.
5. Femi Ojo-Ade, "Female Writers: Male Critics," *African Literature Today* 13 (1982): 159.
6. Davidson and Marie Umeh, "Interview with Buchi Emecheta," *Ba Shiru* 12.2 (1985): 13.
7. See Buchi Emecheta "African Women Step Out" *New African* 218 (November, 1985): 7-8.
8. Kate Millet, *Sexual Politics*. New York: Avon, 1970, p. 24.
9. Sheila Rowbotham, *Woman's Consciousness, Man's World*. Harmondsworth, Middlesex: Penguin Books, 1973, p. xvi.
10. Afram Ebeogu, "Enter the Iconoclast: Buchi Emecheta and the Igbo Culture," presented at the Conference of Literary Society of Nigeria, University of Benin, Nigeria (February 22–25, 1984), p.1.
11. Eustace Palmer, "The Feminine Point of View: Buchi Emecheta's *The Joys of Motherhood*," African Literature Today 13 (1982): 53.
12. Buchi Emecheta, *Double Yoke* (London and Nigeria: Ogwugwu Afo, 1982). All subsequent references are indicated with only the page numbers in the body of the essay.
13. Barbara Smith, *Toward A Black Feminist Criticism*. New York: Out and Out Books, 1977, p.2.
14. Lloyd Brown, "Buchi Emecheta." *Woman Writers in Black Africa*. Westport, Connecticut: Greenwood Press, 1981, p.36.

15. Chidi Ikonne, "Biography into Fiction: Review of *Double Yoke*," *The Guardian* (January 9, 1985): 9.
16. Catherine Acholonu, "Buchi Emecheta," *The Guardian* [Literary Series], January 15, 1986: 13.
17. Oladele Taiwo, "Buchi Emecheta," *Female Novelists of Modern Africa* (London: Macmillan, 1984), p.102.
18. I am aware of a different interpretation by Marie Umeh who feels that Emecheta is saying that men should understand the problems of women in terms of getting children outside marriage in contradiction to societal norms.
19. Alison Perry, "Meeting with Flora Nwapa," *West Africa* 3487 (18 June, 1984): 1262.
20. Katherine Frank, "Feminist Criticism and the African Novel," *African Literature Today* 14 [*Insiders and Outsiders*] (1984): 45.

Buchi Emecheta with her five children: Obiajulu, Chiedu, Chiago (seated on lap), Ikechukwu, and Chukwuemeka.

Her Ancestor's Voice:
The Ibéji Transcendence of
Duality in
Buchi Emecheta's *Kehinde*

Brenda F. Berrian

> Listen more to things
> Than to words that are said.
> The water's voice sings
> And the flame cries
> And the wind that brings
> The words to sighs
> Is the breathing of the dead.
> —Birago Diop, *"Souffles"*

Buchi Emecheta has written three novels about the Nigerian woman's emigrant experiences in London, England. In *In the Ditch* (1972), *Second-Class Citizen* (1975) and *Kehinde* (1994) the female protagonist is either already residing in England or planning to move there. The reasons are either to accompany a husband so that he can complete his studies at a British university or to look for gainful employment. The aim is always to return to Nigeria armed with the diploma(s) and anxious to participate in a newly independent Nigeria. In the first two novels, the aim and the dream are never realized for the protagonist and her family remain living in their adopted motherland—England. However, Emecheta's third and most recent novel *Kehinde* departs from the other two in that Kehinde, the protagonist who bears the same name as the book's title, moves back to Nigeria and then decides to return to England after some major personal disappointments.

As in all of Emecheta's novels, there is a deep psychological insight into a woman's behavior. Shifting between the third and first person narratives, the reader enters the characters' thoughts and empathizes with Kehinde while she connects with other female Nigerians who migrated to London, England during the 1960s. Like Adah from *Second-Class Citizen* and *In the Ditch*, Kehinde's worth is reduced to the economic level because her husband Albert and their two children are dependent upon her income for partial subsistence and the payment of school fees. Although the themes of economic exploitation for the benefit of the male and his eventual betrayal are dominant in *Kehinde*, more emphasis is placed on the notion of pairing, duality and the Yoruba ibéji-orisa myth about twins. This mythology about twins aligned with its spirituality provides the essence of the novel.

The incorporation of the ibéji myth permits Buchi Emecheta to make Kehinde aware of that "intrusive inner voice, the voice of her dead twin, Taiwo"(45). In an interview appropriately titled "A Writer Who Seeks To Reconcile 2 Worlds" Emecheta explains that in her novels she is telling "the West how we [Nigerians] live and letting our people know about the world." Her plan is reconfirmed in *Kehinde* when she utilizes both the Yoruba1 and Igbo concepts of twins. Formerly, Igbo abhorred the birth of twins and eliminated them and sometimes the mother, whereas the Yoruba have always revered twins. With the intervention of Christian missionaries and changing value systems, twins are presently cherished by the Yoruba and tolerated by the Igbo. According to Kofi Asare Opoku, "The souls of the twins are believed to be inseparable and when one of the twins dies, a little ibéji statuette is carved to serve as the abode of the dead twin" (106-107). By capitalizing on this myth about twin-goddesses Emecheta provides the spiritual core of *Kehinde*.

The introduction of a spirit (or deity) is not limited to this novel for in *Second-Class Citizen* the protagonist, Adah, is visited by her

Presence, and Nnu Ego calls upon her *chi* in *The Joys of Motherhood* (1979). Now, in the novel, *Kehinde*, Emecheta brings Taiwo, the former still-born twin, into the narrative to help the protagonist whenever she breaks a taboo deeply rooted in a woman's biological function as a mother. This implies that *Kehinde* is a quasi-mystical novel of human identity, a search for self, and a transcendence of the Igbo limitations of traits which constitute a good mother and wife. By recalling and inserting the present day reverence for twins, Emecheta uses her skills to create a protagonist who possesses the courage to confront her goals without compromise. Neither defeated by indigenous Igbo gender definitions nor constrained by Western gender definitions, Kehinde conjures up her own self-definition with the aid of her spirit twin Taiwo and embraces only those values which are the most beneficial for her lifestyle.

According to Donatus Nwoga, Emecheta uses the *chi* in *The Joys of Motherhood* as it is conceptualized among the western Igbo to refer to not only an individual's personal god but also to the person who has reincarnated the individual (65). In *Kehinde*, Taiwo functions as her sister's *chi* because as Nwoga notes,

> The deceased who is believed to be reborn in the new child is generally called the child's *chi*. The woman's *chi* is the alter ego of the person concerned, whose present life must be supervised and guided by circumstances (65).

Since Taiwo, as Kehinde's *chi*, dies in Ibusa in their mother's womb, Kehinde is forbidden to stay there. Hence, the spirit Taiwo returns to the physical/worldly realm as a result of Kehinde's two difficult moral decisions: an abortion and a tubal ligation.

During the process of reading this novel the reader is transported into Kehinde Okolo's daily struggles to abide by her cultural expectations of a good wife and mother. She finds that listening to the spirit of her twin Taiwo aids her in discovering what a Lagos-born woman in London needs to do to find happiness. In the early 1960s, Albert and Kehinde Okolo arrive in London when it is relatively easy for emigrants to obtain employment. Kehinde finds a job with a bank in Couch End, and Albert locates one as a shop-keeper. Considering themselves to be temporary emigrants, they assume that "they would return eventually and build their own house in Ibusa, their home village"(41). Living in London provides Kehinde with the opportunity to talk to Albert "less formally than women like her sister, Ifeyinwa, who were in more traditional marriages"(6). In addition, she relates to her husband "as a friend, a compatriot, a confidant" (6). However, she is completely oblivious to the fact that Albert is not satisfied with his role of the Igbo man in London. He feels restricted, longs for home, and, after much persuasion by his two sisters, he decides to return to Nigeria "alive and strong, awaiting an opportunity to reclaim his birthright" (35). However, Kehinde's unexpected third pregnancy sets him back.

After eighteen years of living in London, feeling like an outsider and enduring racial slurs, Albert's dream about a new life of ease is to be realized at all costs, therefore, Kehinde's happiness about being pregnant with a third child must take second place to his dream. The solution is for Kehinde to have an abortion so that money will not be diverted away from the accumulated savings designated for the Nigerian trip. There is no way Albert can save "for their home-coming on his income alone, to say nothing of feeding another mouth" (22). Against her best wishes, her Igbo ingrained cultural beliefs and inclination, Kehinde reluctantly agrees to the abortion because no other option exists.

Unbeknown to Kehinde, the abortion foreshadows the end of her marriage to Albert. In Nigeria, many children are a sign of wealth and a necessity. Children function as the retirement fund for aging parents; and male children assure the family's lineage. Being an Igbo man, Albert knows that abortion is wrong, but he convinces himself and Kehinde that they are living in a strange land (England) where emigrants do things that are contrary to their own culture. Kehinde is spiritually wounded by the abortion and, as a consequence, Taiwo returns to the land of the living to chastise and warn her about the future. To hurt Albert for his insistence on the abortion, Kehinde tells him "My father's *chi* was coming back to be with us. He was coming as my child to look after me. I even saw my Taiwo and my mother" (32-33).

For the first time in their marriage Albert neither comforts Kehinde immediately after the abortion nor after her revelation about the three spirits' visits and voices. Inserting the three spirits—the deceased mother and father and the stillborn twin—into the narrative permits Emecheta to discuss a mixture of Yoruba and Igbo traditional cultures and religions and the ways in which they influence both the individual and the collective group. Each child is born with a *chi* to guide her, and the naming of a child is not taken lightly. Kehinde's name implies that she is the second twin to be born. During the birth process Taiwo, the first twin, and her mother both die, but Kehinde, the second twin who follows behind, survives. Nobody wanted Kehinde in her Igbo village of Ibusa because the fear among the villagers is that twins bring bad luck. Fortunately, Aunt Nnebogo takes Kehinde to Lagos where the Yoruba believe that twins bring good luck and bestow the special names: Taiwo and Kehinde. This belief becomes the truth for Aunt Nnebogo's fish business flourishes.

During her childhood Kehinde sensed that something was missing from her life. With the exception of Aunt Nnebogo, she knew no other family members and suffered from an acute loneliness. Each time she asked a question about her birth she was ignored. Also, not fully understanding a yearning for an essential part of herself, she automatically begins to speak to her Taiwo, sharing her food and a space in her bed for her. Since they have the same genes, Kehinde even develops a private communication system with her Taiwo. As the literature on twins suggests, there is an uncanny affinity between them which is part of their mystery. Finally, around age ten, Kehinde's feelings about having a twin are confirmed, to her delight, by her eldest sister Ifeyinwa when she goes to meet her and their father.

In the Yoruba's eyes, the first born Taiwo has seniority and is given the greater respect. In *Kehinde* the deity Taiwo is sent into the world as Kehinde's confidant who reports back with the news of the world's welcome or its threat. As her sister's *chi* and/or spiritual double, Taiwo is also fully respected but not fully defined. She is connected to Kehinde's pride, fortune and fate and sets limits on her sister's conduct so that she can avoid humiliating situations. Representative of the ibéji myth, Taiwo, most importantly, specifies a paradigm of transcendence for Kehinde.

Even though Albert and Kehinde are native born Nigerians, Kehinde is more in tune with the spiritual world due to her special relationship with her twin's spirit (who is more often with her during her adult years in England). According to Kehinde, the spiritual world for Albert is limited to his registering the children in a Catholic church, inferring that he sees things on a more literal level. While Albert busily prepares for his return trip to Nigeria, an uneasiness creeps into the marriage until Kehinde feels "like a boat adrift on a stormy night" and, in spite of what people say about a marriage being two people in one, she feels all alone because Albert "had nothing to offer her" (33) and was "slipping through her fingers like melting ice" (41). The two of them never discuss the lack of closeness that enters into their marriage, but Kehinde's sixth sense is verified. Before his departure to his homeland Albert tells his office mate: "Here, I am nobody, just a shopkeeper. I'm fed up with just listening to my wife and indulging her" (35).

Leaving Kehinde behind in London to sell their house, Albert asks for the children to join him a year later. At first, without Albert and her children, Kehinde feels like a half-person and suffers from being shunned by other Nigerians. To her surprise, her best friend Moriammo is forbidden to associate with her because her husband Tunde calls her a disobedient wife. Then her Taiwo rouses her suspicions by urging her to go to Nigeria lest Albert gets a girlfriend. Frustrated by the inability to sell the house, Kehinde finally joins her family in Nigeria despite Albert's heated disapproval. To her utter shock, Kehinde's hopes about returning home in triumph as the respected "been-to madam" are quickly destroyed for Albert has another son and a second wife who is pregnant. Her only genuine welcome comes from her sister Ifeyinwa.

As she recoils from the pain and the shock, Kehinde remembers her Taiwo's warning that "in Nigeria it's considered manly for men to be unfaithful" (46). She also bitterly remembers how Albert persuaded her to abort their second man child. Yet he meets and marries the pregnant Rike who gives birth to a son in Lagos. Overwhelmed by the news, she gives thanks to her culture for her sister's support, but her faith in Albert is dashed into pieces. At the Lagos airport she noticed that Albert "had acquired a new layer of self-control and detachment" (67), but he looked at her like "someone he had just met" (67). Her wonderment about Albert's strange behavior is answered and causes her to have a troubled dream during which "her spirit was seeking solace in its own beginnings" (75).

Kehinde's troubled dream reminds her how insignificant she felt when she met her father for the first time. At their meeting her father had been surrounded by his many wives, leaving her at a loss and outside of the circle of love. Luckily, her older sister Ifeyinwa's boundless love touched her, and she hears the entire story about her birth and the deaths of her mother and twin. Kehinde's interpretation of this dream is that Albert, who had been a very responsible husband, has evolved into another "father" figure who is encircled by his second wife and two sisters, relegating her to the margins.

Feelings of hopelessness, anger and despair about Albert's deceit ensnare her. She cannot believe that Albert deliberately kept Rike's existence a secret. In order to deal with the shock, Kehinde's subconscious in the form of Taiwo intervenes, soothes her and causes her to question if it is possible for her to continue to live with a man who betrayed her trust. Admittedly, enough advanced hints were provided: Albert's distance after the abortion; Albert's rare letters from Nigeria; Albert's angry phone call when he asks her not to come back to Nigeria; and Albert's detached reception at the airport. However, with twenty years of marriage shared between them, Kehinde expected her husband to be "man enough" to tell her of important decisions that affect her and their children. Obviously, her initial conclusion that Albert has nothing to offer her in London comes back to haunt her in Lagos for it is, indeed, the absolute truth.

During her one-year stay in Lagos Kehinde finds herself psychologically rooted within a space from which she is unable to move forward or backward. After many years of living abroad she is unfamiliar with the ways of Igbo women. She does not understand the relevance of her sister's constant reminders about Igbo customs that favor the man but demote her status as a woman. Thinking about her children's future and totally dependent upon Albert because she cannot find a job, Kehinde gradually slips into a depression. Because Lagos and her citizens are undergoing a rapid change, she receives none of the rewards conferred upon a senior wife from either her co-wife or Albert's sisters. Even her physical space has shrunk with an assignment to a small room with a twin bed. The double bed that she once shared with Albert is located in the largest bedroom reserved for him. Suffocating from such a confinement, a desperate Kehinde writes her friend Moriammo, describing how cheated and undervalued she feels. With luck, her cries for help and her sanity are answered with Moriammo's renewed friendship, sympathy and money for a plane ticket. With gratefulness, Kehinde counts her riches because she has her biological sister (Ifeyinwa), her spirit twin (Taiwo), and an adopted sister (Moriammo) who all provide her with support and understanding.

A previously used technique in Emecheta's novels is this convention of pairing female characters, who serve as Florence Stratton states, as an "antithesis of each other in their response to their patriarchal society" (117). Coming from different social backgrounds, Rike and Ifeyinwa choose to conform to patriarchal role definitions of gender and marriage. On the other hand, Kehinde and her countrywoman, Mary Elikwu (who she had known in London), revolt against these definitions which stifle their potential to prosper. An element marking the difference in Rike and Kehinde's respective abilities to adapt to a polygynous household is their individual characters. Facing some similar circumstances—the same husband and the mother of his children— and dissimilar ones—different class backgrounds and levels of education—the two attempt to adapt with differing degrees of ease. This is due to the traits found in their personalities which helps Rike and hinders Kehinde in their pursuit of happiness. The fact is that Rike knew about Kehinde's existence when she met the polished Albert whose sophisticated speech "used to take her breath away" (117). In spite of this knowledge she enters into an affair with him with the intent of luring him into a marriage once she becomes pregnant. Additional encouragement comes from the seven wolis (prophets) attached to Rike's church who urge her to entice Albert. No compassion for Kehinde's plight is given, just a coolness and an attempt to make her as uncomfortable as possible.

In spite of Rike's education and independent state, she disrupts Kehinde's life in her desire to marry a man who has lived abroad. By doing so, she maintains the status quo by offering no resistance to a system that favors men. Angry about the unhappiness that Rike has caused her sister and too traditional to confront Albert, Ifeyinwa takes much pleasure in destroying Rike's confidence in her marriage, informing her that Albert has a third wife. Following the same pattern of non-confrontation with his first wife, Albert marries an even younger woman from the northern part of Nigeria without telling Rike. Highly worried and shaken, Rike realizes that she and Kehinde are on equal footing; Albert is not "her own," too.

During a 1986 interview Emecheta spoke about her disappointment in some Nigerian women who do not practice sisterhood in the same manner as some foreign women, "...half of the problem rests with the women. They are so busy bitching about one another, the men say the women are acting just as expected" (36). This is definitely a lesson that Kehinde learns at the going-away party held for Albert in London when she rejected and labeled a countrywoman, Mary Elikwu, "a fallen woman who had no sense of decorum" (38). Unexpectedly, Kehinde finds herself in a similar situation and "The world was suddenly much more complicated than it had seemed hitherto" (61). Mary Elikwu, a married woman with six children, had summoned up the courage to leave her abusive husband and to start afresh. After having been betrayed and ignored by Albert and humiliated by Albert's sisters and second wife, Kehinde currently admires Mary Elikwu's spirit and determination to start a new life despite other Nigerians' negative remarks about her being the guilty party. Most importantly,

Kehinde realizes that women "in their ignorance pass judgment on their sisters" (132). She and Mary Elikwu have not committed a crime, and they need not acquiesce in any ridiculous plan that their husbands devise.

Demonstrating a lack of concern about sisterhood, Rike prefers to place her future in the Church's hands and those of Albert. Upon analyzing her future with Albert, Kehinde rejects him, assumes responsibility for the direction of her future, and makes appropriate changes to achieve personal happiness. Even though her decision is not looked upon with favor by Albert's family, Kehinde has no misgivings about a separation from Albert. After all, Albert's family did not come to her aid; they conspired to aggravate her and also regarded her as a nonperson.

When traditional rural Igbo values meet Western urbanized ones, the result is often confusion and conflict within a person who must try to reconcile the different ways of life mandated by the two belief systems. Understandably, Emecheta does not create Kehinde as a madwoman like her counterpart, Nnu Ego, in *The Joys of Motherhood* who devoted her entire life to her children to be found dead alongside a road without one child beside her.[2] She recognizes that her children are on the verge of adulthood. Their silence about Rike, encouraged by Aunt Ifeyinwa to avoid unbearable pain for their mother far away in London, makes them co-conspirators with Albert. Intuitively understanding their torn devotion to the near-by father in Lagos and the absent mother in London, Kehinde maintains ties with them, sends money and exchanges letters. Thus, she does not forsake her role as a mother. She establishes the fact that she is a woman who has other needs such as male companionship.

Since Albert, a Nigerian man, has proven to be a disappointment, Kehinde develops a relationship with Michael Gibson, a sympathetic Caribbean tenant. Here, female sexuality is not reduced to an expression of male dominance for as an educated woman she is no longer willing to share a man in a relationship. The Western notion of romantic love has impacted her to believe in monogamy. As far as Kehinde is concerned, Albert is unfaithful according to the western concept about monogamy, but he is faithful to Igbo notions of polygyny. Since Albert pulls at will from the dual value systems to affirm his manhood, Kehinde, the woman, has the freedom to do likewise.

Michael is appreciated as someone who sparks the dormant romantic flame that is almost extinguished in Kehinde. Rather than

177

rush Kehinde into an affair he slowly builds up a friendship and a mutual trust. Her stubbornness and work ethic are attractive to Michael, and her hesitant response to a dinner invitation increases his interest in her. Through exposure to Michael, Kehinde confronts her prejudices about Caribbean people, changes her attitude, and admits that she enjoys the attention that is bestowed upon her by Michael. On her behalf, with caution and some timidity, Kehinde reaches out to him with five years of unspent affection and tenderness.

Ironically, the battleground between Kehinde and Albert is their London terrace home rather than her love affair. Not satisfied with having a rented home in Lagos with Rike and maintaining another home in northern Nigeria with his third wife, Albert sends their son Joshua to be his emissary to regain the London home when he becomes unemployed. Recognizing that Albert wants to strip her of everything, Kehinde declares "This house is not for sale...This house is mine" (108). One of her first acts of liberation to claim her new identity as a permanent emigrant in London had been to tear down the "For Sale" sign in front of the home. For a second time the tables are reversed; this time in Kehinde's favor. While on Albert's "home" turf in Nigeria, Kehinde had been the insignificant other. Now, Albert (indirectly) and their son (directly) are jolted awake when they confront a wife/mother who lays claim to *her* property and rights on her *turf*.

The symbolic reference to the London home in connection with Kehinde's self-actualization goes full circle. At the beginning of the novel Kehinde remarked to her husband "Now you earn enough money, own a house" to which he replied, "*We* own a house" (4)

Albert was not, and still is not unaware, of the legal status of a wife in England. Her independence within her family is in defiance of the Nigerian traditions that govern female behavior. Traditionally, the home belongs to the husband and is inherited by the oldest son after his death. Since Kehinde left him and is "dead" in his memory, Albert, true to form, again draws from Igbo traditions in an effort to regain and sell the home. What Albert does not take into consideration, however, is the reformed Kehinde who has more space in which to maneuver (reflecting the duality of bi-cultural identity and the convention of using the rules of one or the other as the situation or need warrants).

Kehinde creates a new life with her Caribbean lover, her new job as a social worker and merges as a complete woman/person with her twin Taiwo, a merger that occurs when Kehinde re-entered her London home:

> ...the smell of the London terrace house welcomed her like a lost child. Before she could suppress it, a voice inside her sang out, 'Home, sweet home!' Taiwo, who had not spoken to her since she had gone to Nigeria was back. Kehinde rebuked the voice: 'This is not my home. Nigeria is my home.' As she said it, she knew she was deceiving herself, and Taiwo would not let her get away with it. 'We make our own choices as we go along,' came the voice. 'This is yours. There's nothing to be ashamed of in that' (108).

Consciously and deliberately unashamed, Kehinde is a flexible, adaptable person in her effort to redefine her identity in London. She moves beyond the concept that her existence is inseparable from her socio-historical background. Therefore, in response to her son's angry accusation "I thought you were supposed to live for your children," she says "Mothers are people too, you know" (139).

At this stage in Kehinde's life, children are neither a binding force nor the only goal. She is not inclined to be exploited by an estranged husband or a son who both see her as a commodity. In addition, Kehinde no longer defers to a man simply because of his gender. Her adolescent son is to abide by her rules and to show her respect if he wants to continue to live in her home. If not, he has a choice to move. Her conclusion is "A man-child did not need to kill his parents to establish manhood" (137). In this vein, Kehinde's comments to Joshua confirm Nikki Giovanni's observations about a woman's change and empowerment: "We've got to live in the real world. If we don't like the world we are living, change it. And if we can't change it, we change ourselves. We can do something" (68).

Very much in tune with her spirituality via her twin, Kehinde transcends the duality that lies within her conscious and subconscious states of mind. The lesson is that something good can be gained from something bad. Out of pain and betrayal, Kehinde grows with age and experience. Her growth began with Albert's duplicity which prepares her for a later encounter with a wealthy Arab sheik at a hotel where she worked (when she first returned to London after studying to be a social worker). Displaying a condescending behavior, ingrained racial and class prejudices about

Black women and an unwanted sexually oriented demand, the sheik orders Kehinde to disrobe in front of him. Frightened and disgusted, Kehinde knows that her Taiwo will never allow her to accept humiliation. With strength and dignity, she leaves the hotel and washes the sheik's pollution off of her. After several days she finally finds a part-time job in the field for which she earned a university degree due, in part, to a sympathetic female human resources person.

Kehinde's decisions to educate herself, to reaffirm her sexuality, and to keep the house also permit her to escape the confining image of the long-suffering wife. She does not want to be a victim but a rebellious survivor. Her insightful analysis of the need for autonomy and self-reliance submerges the former assumption that her needs hold second place to those of her children and husband. Having her own house and a job empowers her to appreciate herself more before she opens up to the possibility of taking a lover. When she needed sympathy and lost her dream of being a pampered been-to wife and mother, her sister gives her moral support. When she made up her mind to leave Nigeria, Moriammo comes to her rescue. When she is propositioned by the sheik, Taiwo's silence causes her to sort things out herself.

The lines "Those who are dead have never gone away...The dead are never dead" (44) from Birago Diop's poem "Souffles" reveals that there is no division in the African cosmic universe. Every person is an incarnation; a spirit who takes on a bodily flesh. Therefore, a person's true nature is spiritual as supported by Emecheta's introduction of Taiwo, who as both Kehinde's twin and *chi,* is the carrier of wisdom by which Kehinde is to live. Not having any flesh also makes Taiwo more useful because she can move into Kehinde's dreams and reality. As a result, Taiwo's intervention confirms that contact with the ancestors is transformational for Kehinde.

The ibéji myth infers that no split exists between the material and the spiritual; thereby creating a close connection between thought and reality. Kehinde's call upon her childhood memories and strong focus upon her twin are natural processes since the supernatural is an integral part of the natural world of a human being's everyday life. Consequently, the invoking of the spirit Taiwo is an integration of an established religious world view and a reaffirmation of reincarnation as supported by Malidoma Patrice Somé with the statement,

> In many non-Western cultures, the ancestors have
> an intimate and absolutely vital connection with the
> world of the living. They are always available to
> guide, to teach, and to nurture. They represent one
> of the pathways between the knowledge of this
> world and the next. Most importantly—and para-
> doxically—they embody the guidelines for success-
> ful living—all that is most valuable about life. Unless
> the relationship between the living and the dead is
> in balance, chaos result (9).

Functioning as the unborn child who comes from the place where
the living are going to, Taiwo reappears, as a source of illumination, whenever Kehinde needs enlightenment regarding her
female plight to avoid a chaotic life.

With her twin, Kehinde achieves a victory over the forces that
oppressed her. She avoids conducting her life like Nnu Ego who
blindly lived according to the patterns laid down by Ibusa patriarchy. Instead she negotiates her freedom through rebellion and,
at the same time, manages not to be alienated from Ibusa society
whose laws she transgresses. Neither defeated by the Igbo world
nor totally assimilated into the Western world, Kehinde embraces
those values which are the most beneficial for her lifestyle.

Emecheta gives ample consideration to the social forces that
impact the success or failure of male-female emotional relationships. After the destruction of her marriage Kehinde returns to
London in a state of some disillusionment, feeling the emotional
tugs of a person born in one country who settles in another one.
During her search for romantic love Kehinde learns that her world
is shaped by five sometimes conflicting forces: African religion,
Western education, Christianity, Igbo values and British racism.
These forces create a split in her marriage with a confusion of values, leaving her with guilty feelings (like her creator Emecheta)
because she does not identify more with Nigeria.

"When I write," Emecheta says, "I look for a problem in a certain society and I write about that problem strictly from a woman's
point of view" (37). Later, in 1992, she expands on her position, "I
think my writing isn't English or African as much as more international, more universal...I try to write for the world" (85). By combining and synthesizing aspects of Igbo, Yoruba and British culture
in *Kehinde* Emecheta creates a protagonist who supports her preference for dual citizenship, requiring a coming to terms with her-

self and reaching a level of comfort with multiple assimilations and exposures. The natural ambivalence is the allegiance to one's emotional language and birth country in connection with Kehinde's original sense of loss within the core of her childhood years for a part of herself—her Taiwo.

Emecheta writes about a society and people who are in transition and conflict. Kehinde and Albert Okolo are caught within a marginalized space. Since "the Igbo culture lays a great deal of emphasis on differences, on dualities, on otherness" (771), according to Chinua Achebe, Emecheta, as a novelist and sociologist, creates an Albert who moves in and out of more than one culture: Igbo and British. His resolution is to return to his homeland where a man has more privileges and choices and is respected as somebody. Not neglecting Kehinde, Emecheta constructs a woman who observed with a keen eye that she has more opportunities in England. Here lies the conflict within the couple for there are more advantages and a higher status for each one within a different culture and society. At the same time, neither one is single minded; each one pulls from or discards something from the same culture or another at will.

Another major difference between Kehinde and Albert happens to be their belief or non-committal belief in the ancestral world. Due to Kehinde's birth as a twin and her family's history, she inherits the ibéji legacy, an affinity from which she can never escape. Only a minimal amount of information is available about Albert's family background. Most of what is told is filtered through Kehinde's perceptions and the narrator's. In spite of these limitations, it is surmised that Albert used religion to his advantage in marrying Rike. In an effort to cover up his blunder for not telling Kehinde about Rike in advance, he conveniently hides behind the seven wolis' prediction that his and Rike's unborn child is the lucky star that will bring him a good-paying job. He also feels that Rike and her mother "were praying enough for the two of them" (118). Thus, religion fulfills a specific need for the Okolos with each one responding from a different indigenous point of view.

Kehinde is a complex novel with Emecheta employing a variety of devices, such as the first and third person narratives, flashbacks, letters, an alternating dialogue in Pidgin English and Standard English and the ibéji myth to provide an insider's view of Igbo society and an emigrant's ambivalent position in England. This dualistic view of traditional Igbo society and adopted western values are presented by Emecheta to intensify the two fundamental tensions that reside within Nigerian emigrants. In her earlier work, *Second-Class Citizen*, Emecheta's Adah calls upon the Presence, "It had been active in Nigeria. Was that because in Nigeria she was nearer to Mother Nature? She only wished somebody would tell her where she had gone wrong" (55). The reverse occurs in *Kehinde* for the protagonist is visited more often in England by her twin, who directly advises her. Kehinde also picks up where Adah ends up with a determination to create a new life without her husband. She also decides not to follow a *chi*, like Nnu Ego did, that causes an immeasurable amount of mental anguish. Looked upon as being a rebel by her son, Kehinde only smiles and announces: "Claiming my right does make me less of a mother, not less of a woman. If anything it makes me more human" (141).

Emecheta exhibits a sensitivity to societal ills and triumphs. Her novels reflect that marriage and one's native country are not the only places for the contemporary Igbo woman. And that through merging traditional and contemporary beliefs/patterns, the duality of a bi-cultural existence can be transcended. In London, Kehinde handles a home, an education, a new career, motherhood and a lover. All of her decisions are not made alone; she has started to accept her Nigerian self and "Taiwo's voice as a permanent part of her consciousness" (135). Consequently, her movement alongside her twin's spirit and voice is an area of reality like any other, and it provides her with the means to transcend her duality while remaining faithful to some of her Igbo traditions and adopted Western ones.

NOTES

1. Begley, Sharon "All About Twins," *Newsweek* 23 Nov. 1987. 58-69. In this featured article on twins, the author notes that there is a high proportion of multiple births among the Yoruba attributed to the eating of yams. One of the twins from a different ethnic background who was interviewed, Laura Techeggen, stated "You have a best friend...If you can't relate to something half of yourself, you can't relate to anything."
2. Emecheta, Buchi. *The Joys of Motherhood*. New York: George Braziller, 1979.

WORKS CITED

Diop, Birago. "Souffles" (Translated as "Breaths"), *Poems of Black Africa*. Ed. Wole Soyinka. New York: Hill and Wang, 1975. 44-46.

Emecheta, Buchi. *Second-Class Citizen*. New York: George Braziller, 1975.

——. *Kehinde*. London: Heinemann, 1994. All further references will be cited within the text from this edition.

Fraser, C. Gerald. "A Writer Who Seeks to Reconcile 2 Worlds." *The New York Times.* 9 June 1990.

James, Adeola. "Buchi Emecheta." *In Their Own Voices: African Women Writers Talk.* London: Heinemann, 1990. 34-45.

Jussawalla, Feroza. "Buchi Emecheta." *Interviews with Writers of the Post-Colonial World.* Ed. Feroza Jussawalla and Reed Way Dasenbrock. London and Jackson: University Press of Mississippi, 1992. 82-99.

Nwoga, Donatus. "Ritual Evidence and the Igbo Pantheon." *The Supreme God As Stranger In Igbo Religious Thought.* Ahiazu Mbaise, Imo State, Nigeria: Hawk, 1984. 61-67.

Ogbaa, Kalu. "An Interview with Chinua Achebe." *Research in African Literatures* 12. 1 (1981): 1-13. For more information about the *chi,* read Chinua Achebe. *Morning Yet On Creation Day* (Garden City, NY: Doubleday Anchor, 1976. 131-45).

Opoku, Kofi Asara. *West African Traditional Religion.* Accra: FEP International, 1978.

Somé, Malidoma Patrice. "Introduction." *Of Water and the Spirit.* New York: Putnam, 1994. Read also: T.J.H. Chappel. "The Yoruba Cult of Twins in Historical Perspective," *Africa* [44. 3 (1974): 250-65] and Oruene To, "Cultic Powers of Yoruba Twins: Manifestation of Traditional and Religious Beliefs of the Yoruba," *Acta Genet Med Gemellol* [(Roma) 32. 3/4 (1983): 221-28].

Stratton, Florence, "Their New Sister: Buchi Emecheta and the Contemporary Literary Tradition." *Contemporary African Literature and the Politics of Gender.* London: Routledge, 1994. 108-32.

Tate, Claudia. "Nikki Giovanni." *Black Women Writers at Work.* New York: Continuum, 1983. 60-78.

Uyoh, Susan B. "Review of *Second-Class Citizen.*" *The Gong* (Calabar) May 1981. 34.

PART THREE:
FEMALE SEXUALITY —
THE BODY AS TEXT

It happened in Washington, D. C. I was going in a taxi from Union Station to one of those massive buildings, housing the U.S Department of Education, when I realized that my taxi driver was a Nigerian. As I have been spending a disproportionate amount of my time reading Nigerian novels, I asked the cab driver if he had heard of Chinua Achebe. "Yes," he broke into the glorious laughter of a proud Nigerian. He went on to praise him as a national hero, internationally renowned award winner and the ultimate *tour de force.* "He comes from my own village," he said with a satisfied smile, cap accentuating a good-natured face.

"And how about Buchi Emecheta?" I asked, though a suspicion lurked inside me that my taxi-driver friend would not have heard of her. I was wrong. In a trice, the jovial happy look was gone. Nostrils flared in anger. Eyes showed disgust. "Ah, shame, man!" he shouted, suddenly with an exaggerated American accent. "Buchi Emecheta is no writer! The woman is a troublemaker!" Upon further interrogation, he declared that the only thing Emecheta wants is to "turn all the women against men." He reclined his huge frame on the back rest of the driver's seat so that I could see his full face in the rear view mirror. With a booming voice, he proclaimed, "We turned her out of Nigeria! She writes nothing but sex, sex, sex."

Sex, said the French anthropologist Claude Levi-Strauss, is good for thinking. Most people, he goes on to explain, are not philosophers and do not enjoy abstractions. In order to realize abstract thoughts such as freedom, integrity, enjoyment they need to make concrete references: the Nazis, Martin Luther King, Jr., and a good bottle of wine.

The subtitle for this section of the book, The Body As Text, serves the same purpose. Emecheta's texts serve as discussion points on the female body and its sexuality. It is perhaps not a coincidence that Buchi Emecheta's novels are all reflections of hard concrete realities. The plots are unidirectional, moving energetically headlong toward the denouement. But they also denude, uncovering the female body, baring men's lust for power. Little wonder that most Nigerian men do not like Emecheta! To them, she is too vivid, too appealing and ultimately, too controversial.

The three essays in this section discuss Emecheta's position regarding women's sexuality, especially Nigerian women's. Marie Umeh leads off with a clear observation that to Emecheta, sex should not simply be a means to motherhood. It should be enjoyed by women as well as men. Thus Umeh's title, "Procreation, Not Recreation: Decoding Mama in Buchi Emecheta's *The Joys of Motherhood*," serves to deconstruct ironically the ideal motherhood through a reading of *The Joys of Motherhood*. Casting Emecheta's well-known novel against the backdrop of African nationalism, Umeh's question is as follows: "How can Africa be worrying so much about nationalism when it stifles female potential through a sex/gender system that makes a fetish of the female anatomy, clothing it with hypocritical ideals of motherhood?" This comes as a sharp reminder to men all over the world who want to be heroes and yet treat women as mere instruments for their success. Motherhood, Emecheta suggests, is a male institution, forged by seduction, rape, and brutal power.

Tuzyline Jita Allan's essay, "Trajectories of Rape in Buchi Emecheta's Novels," surveys nearly all of Emecheta's novels to observe the "trajectory of rape" in the narratives. Since rape is the *modus operandi* of men throughout the world, women deal with the violation of their bodies through a spectrum of different attitudes and behaviors. The women in Emecheta's novels are no exception. What Allan has been able to show, however, is that rape in Emecheta takes on symbolic meaning, from being the signifier of alterity (other) to the developing idiom of overcoming Father. Allan shows how different women in Emecheta's novels expose themselves differently to their own rapes. The violating act becomes the violation of a gigantic metaphor: rape, a metonymy for an entire continent, the ultimate symbol of the destruction of desire and brute control.

But what is women's desire? Is it different from men's? Given the basic struggle for survival in Third World countries, desire is *not* the same as the Western concept of desire. For Nigerian women, and other women of color, desire could be simply the longing for a life with ordinary dignity. In Emecheta's novels women are denied even that. Their revolution is not a Madam Bovary's, provoked out of boredom and dissatisfaction with life's ordinariness. Emecheta's women want ordinariness. Being no more than pawns in the politics of control exerted by men, Emecheta's women, while coveting the ordinary, try to make this internal desire external. They try to wrest away the control over their lives from men who dominate them, to control the center of their own lives instead, to steer their own destiny. This is what Shivaji Sengupta argues in his essay, "Desire and the Politics of Control in Buchi Emecheta's Novels." He does so through a detailed textual reading of two novels, *The Joys of Motherhood* and *The Family*.

Susan Sontag once write, "Every era has to reinvent the project of spirituality for itself." She explained, "Spirituality is an idea of deportment aimed at resolving the painful structural contradiction inherent in the human situation." The structural contradictions in Emecheta's novels put women at the edge of their bodies: sexuality, on the one hand; control, on the other. To resolve this contradiction is the spirituality that Emecheta aims for.

Shivaji Sengupta

Procreation Not Recreation: Decoding Mama in Buchi Emecheta's *The Joys of Motherhood*

Marie Umeh

A feminism that does not speak of sexual pleasure has little to offer women in the here and now.
— Amber Hollibaugh

Like gender, sexuality is political.
— Gayle Rubin

. . . It is a permanent task of feminist literary criticism and scholarship to contest and delegitimize the "under-textualization" of women and "women's affairs" in the mostly male-authored writings which claim to speak on behalf of the "nation," the continent, the Black World."
— Biodun Jeyifo

All sexuality is constructed.

— Michel Foucault

Many Africanist and feminist scholars have written essays on the theme of motherhood and its foil, barrenness in Buchi Emecheta's *magnum opus*, *The Joys of Motherhood*. For example, Carole Boyce Davies contends that although there is no single view of motherhood in the works of male and female Igbo writers, motherhood is crucial to a woman's status in African society. It is through motherhood that a woman is esteemed (243). Eustace Palmer, in another essay extolls the novel as a first in African literature to present the female point of view in registering its disgust at male chauvinism and patriarchy's unfair and oppressive system towards mothers (39). For Eustace Palmer, Nnu Ego's famous lament, "God, when will you create a woman who will be fulfilled in herself, a full human being, not anybody's appendage?" contradicts the "phallocratic" images of happy, cheerful mothers in African literature (46).

Besides the novel's preoccupation with Igbo society's making the female body a fetish for begetting sons, it is my contention that the book is also about female sexuality among the Ibuza/Delta Igbo and by extension African women generally. Female sexual expressivity is taboo in Igbo society. Hence, the author cloaks issues of female erotic and hedonistic experiences, and their attendant sexual deprivation, in a number of semiotic codes. *Joys*, as a result, is laced with cultural codes and feminist messages protesting the culture's outer oppression of women which results in their inner repressions and denial of female sexual desire, passion, and fulfillment.

The Joys of Motherhood is the story of Nnu Ego, the daughter of Chief Nwokocha Agbadi and his concubine Ona. Nnu Ego is the reincarnation of a slave girl who was killed by Chief Agbadi and his sons. According to the oracle, the revenge of the slave girl is heaped on Nnu Ego. So, Nnu Ego is barren in her first marriage to Amatokwu and loses his love and affection. On the brink of a nervous breakdown, Nnu Ego returns to her father's compound where he makes sacrifices to the oracle so that Nnu Ego's *chi* will have a change of heart. Nnu Ego is lucky in her second marriage, to Nnaife Owulum: although she finds him repulsive, she stays with him because he impregnates her and together they have healthy children: three boys and four girls. By the end of the novel, Nnu Ego realizes that while nurturing children brought her status in Igbo society, it does not bring her personal fulfillment. Her life was marked with loneliness, poverty, and strife. Nnu Ego dies a premature death at the age of forty-five, all alone, separated from Nnaife and abandoned by her sons who went abroad to further their education. Her sons, disappointed that she died before they were in a position to provide their mother with a life of comfort and joy, give her the costliest second burial ceremony the Ibuza people have ever witnessed. They even erect a shrine in her honor so that childless women can appeal to her for children. Ironically however, Nnu Ego never answered prayers for children.

Between Ona, Agbadi's glorious woman, and Nnu Ego, the offspring of their love, there was a great schism: of character; of pleasure and its consequences; of will to power, and of mother and daughter. The story of Ona and Agbadi was the great drama; Nnu Ego was its tragedy. The cruelest irony of *The Joys of Motherhood* is that Nnu Ego became what Ona dreaded: the forgotten, unfulfilled wife. When Nnu Ego did not conceive children for her first husband, she was denied his companionship. After having seven children with her second spouse, including three sons, she died after loosing her mind, alone again, by the roadside. In her *magnum opus*, Emecheta makes her strongest indictment against the powerful paternal presence, where the bride's father receives the bride price and the bride gets nothing in return for even her children belong to their father. As Ifeyinwa Iweriebor quotes from Robert Magabe on the ironies of the patrilineal system: "The child born of a woman despite the nine months spent in her womb, was never hers by customary right of ownership, and remained her child only as long as the marriage between her and her husband was good" (176).

Igbo society, according to *Joys*, effaces female sexual desire and expressivity by subconsciously programming its female kith and kin to carry a "moral albatross" around their necks.[1] To prevent female rebellion, which would lead to a complete disregard for tradition and the ways of the ancestors, various methods have been devised by patriarchy to control Igbo women's sexuality: clitoridectomy, rape, incest, sexual deprivation, ostracization, fear, humiliation, and the psychological sexual blinding of women. Generally speaking, the only time a woman is regarded as being chaste and pure is when the sex act is performed by her husband for his recreation, and for her procreation. The wife's joy does not figure in the equation.

The idea that chastity and fertility are jewels possessed by good daughters is delineated early in *Joys*, when Nnu Ego's in-laws "came to thank Chief Nwokocha Agbadi, the great elephant hunter, for giving them his precious daughter. They did so with six full kegs of palm wine because Nnu Ego has been found to be an unspoiled virgin" (31). This education of young girls only promotes the moral ethic that for women *plaisir*, to borrow Julia Kristeva's term, is achieved only through happiness in marriage and motherhood. The sexual codes by which the lives of Igbo women are governed are listed in order of importance: the glory of a woman is a man; a woman without a son is a failure; marriage is for the production of male heirs to continue the husband's lineage; and a complete woman is a mother of healthy sons. These codes give voice to the historical repression of female sexuality in an African society. By inscribing the inner repressions Igbo women live by, and by giving voice to the inarticulate, covert codes controlling the emotions of women, Emecheta exposes how female sexuality is denied, camouflaged and replaced with euphemisms that enable the male to restrict female sexuality.

The argument advanced by Africanists that more critical problems such as, AIDS, hunger, cultural genocide, war and imperialism, warrant our attention, as usual marginalizes women's concerns. It may be recalled that similar criticism by modern critics was aimed at another female novelist, Jane Austen. How could she be so involved only in the private lives of insignificant women when the French Revolution was dominating European history? The truth of the matter is that women's dignity was important to Jane Austen. Similarly, female sexuality and its exploitation is important to contemporary Black women writers like Buchi Emecheta. In fact, one would not be remiss in stating that a more equitable and humane attitude toward female sexuality would positively influence many of our social ills. Sexual fulfillment is at the core of our lives touching every human being from adolescence to old age. And woman is the logos and the topos of sexuality. Obioma Nnaemeka argues that the African woman writer's awareness of the male gaze compels her to compromise her actual rage through ambivalent fictional characters (142). On the contrary, Emecheta's women, from Adah to Kehinde, become pariahs in their communities for their protests against retrogressive cultural norms. Emecheta scrutinizes the denial of female sexual desire and fulfillment in the novel, *Joys*, with the same zeal and emotion with which she describes the victimization of mothers by Igbo society's double standards for women and primacy of sons. Who says mothers don't need *plaisir*? Who says sons, not *jouissance*, make women complete? Who says children, not loving partners, bring happiness to women? And who says the glory of a woman is a callous, insensitive partner? More African writers need to delineate the pain and suffering of our women. If they do not or worse, if they are not allowed to, we will continue to live in a society where the odds are stacked against women, where one group will be allowed to explore life to the fullest and the "other" forced to pretend that sexual fulfillment is unimportant and sinful. In short, there would be more "madwomen in the attic." It is therefore significant that madness, sickness, and premature death are the metaphors for Emecheta's mothers.[2]

Emecheta protests against the sexual blinding of women in a number of ways. First, she delineates the right to female sexuality and *jouissance* in her characters, Nnu Ego and Nnu Ego's mother, Ona and Adaku. Then she protests against the sexual deprivation of wives, mothers and barren women in Agunwa, Nwokocha Agbadi's senior wife, Adaku, and Nnu Ego in her first marriage to Amatokwu. Emecheta's focus on female sexuality is evident in a number of episodes in *Joys*. It is clearly stated in Nnu Ego's sexual desire and pleasure with her first husband, Amatokwu. The author writes, "Nnu Ego and her husband Amatokwu were very happy" (31). So satisfying and powerful was Nnu Ego's sexual pleasure that when Amatokwu stopped loving her and transferred his affection to his second wife, Nnu Ego pleads with him at first, to come to her bed. When he fails to come, she becomes "thin and juiceless" (33). Upon recognizing Nnu Ego's "nervous conditions" and psychological imbalance, Nwokocha Agbadi takes his daughter back to his compound to appease her *chi*[3], in hope of restoring her mental health. When Nnu Ego recovers and shows signs that she needs male companionship, Nwokocha Agbadi finds his daughter a second husband. He makes it a point of searching for one "who could spare time to think. The art of loving, he knew required deeper men. Men who did not have to spend every moment of their time working and worrying about food and the farm" (36). However, what Nnu Ego got was Nnaife.

The normality of the female sexual experience in a community that accentuates "the joys of motherhood," all the while undermining the "joy of sex" for women, is also evident in the characterization of Ona, Nnu Ego's mother, and Adaku, Nnu Ego's co-wife. Ona, for example, enjoyed "it," "it" meaning the "joy of sex" (15). Ona confesses to Nwokocha Agbadi at one point in the book that he is the "greatest joy of [her] life" (24). And during that famous erotic scene in African literature between Ona and Agbadi, Ona is burning with desire for Agbadi, and she is not too timid to express her passion. In response to Agbadi's foreplay and sexual arousal, she implores him to take her sexually. She cries, "please, I am in pain" (20). When he complies with her demands the author says that Ona "was grateful when at last she felt him inside her" (20). So happy is she with her lover that she is determined to be his "favorite." So, to keep his attention, Ona plays the game of constant seduction by refusing to give Agbadi sex when he desires her and by refusing to marry him. Emecheta writes, "she suspected that her fate would be the same as his other women, should she consent to be one of his wives . . . . Maybe the best way to keep his love was not to let that happen" (15). She decided not to let him know how much she cared for him. She saw how he treated his wives, who sank into motherhood, domesticity, and oblivion. They were forgotten as he gave attention to his latest woman. In fact, Agbadi was notorious for the neglect of his senior wives and concubines, so much so that the women often showed signs of sexual neglect. The author says, "He would be reminded to do his duty by them, then when they became pregnant he would not be seen in their huts until the time came for him to mate them again" (12-13). With Emecheta's forthright characterization of Ona's and Nnu Ego's sexuality, it becomes clear that women, not only men, experience the "joy of sex," and they also pursue it.

There is also the idea that motherhood devours *jouissance.* There is certainly the assertion that a woman without a husband (Adaku), one without children (Ona) can be happy. Indeed, it is the novel's competing discourses of the "joys of motherhood" and the "joy of sex" that prompt the critic Ketu Katrak to surmise that there is ambivalence about motherhood alone, bringing contentment to women in *Joys.*[4] Although the book maintains the Igbo social mores of the importance of children to a successful marriage, there is a constant undercurrent of doubt about a woman's happiness with children in the absence of a supportive companion, a loyal, industrious, sensitive, and sexually satisfying partner. Emecheta here is protesting against the society's contention that wives and mothers don't need healthy sex lives. Legitimate wives rarely achieve sexual gratification because of the culture's moral code: chastity and sexual demure is the measure of a good woman's moral character. This code does not apply to men. Ona's dialogism is comprised of her weakness and her need for Agbadi's *plaisir,* as well as her manipulation of him, and her air of independence and chilliness, to make sure his attentions never waver. Repeatedly, *Joys* offers advice on how to keep a man. Nnaife Owulum, Nnu Ego's second husband loved her most out of all his wives because she was the most difficult to please. Indeed, *Joys* is a radical novel, intended to subvert the idea that a woman cannot be complete without children.[5] The depiction of good-time girls abounds in African literature. African writers such as Cyprian Ekwensi (*Jagua Nana*), Ngugi wa Thiong'o (*Petals of Blood*), and Ousmane Sembène (*God's Bits of Wood*) describe these women as pleasure seekers and cash madams who are denied commitment from men and "the joys of motherhood" because of their wantonness. However, it takes an African woman writer to conflate female sexuality with decency and normality, without the taint of looseness. Ona, for example, controls her sexuality; she has *plaisir* when she is so inclined. She also chooses Agbadi to be her lifetime lover because he is sexually satisfying to her. Together they maintained a healthy erotic relationship because Ona was allowed to express her sexual desires without any fear of being thought by him to be a loose or wanton woman. The author states:

> Nwokocha Agbadi would not have minded sending all his wives away just to live with this one woman. But that was not to be. People said she had him bewitched, that she had a kind of power over him; what person in his right mind would leave his big spacious household and women who were willing to worship and serve him in all things to go after a rude, egocentric woman who had been spoilt by her father? (12)

It is therefore apparent that Agbadi was attracted to her unrepressed sexuality. The relationship that they had was for the joy of making one another sexually and emotionally happy. No child was anticipated at all. However, when Nnu Ego arrived, the couple was overjoyed. Nnu Ego was her father's joy and the only daughter that he had. Ona dies and leaves this child with Agbadi with one wish: "however much you love our daughter Nnu Ego, allow her to have a life of her own. Allow her to be a woman. . ."(28). Agbadi lives to fulfill Ona's death wish. Charmed by her ability to please her man, Ona remains his heart's desire, even after her death.

Emecheta suggests that most Igbo women want a fulfilling sex life as much as they want sons. This is certainly the case of Agunwa, Agbadi's senior wife, who suffers from the stress of pretending to be a complete woman, a happy mother of sons. But, in actuality, she is miserable; suffering in silence from sexual deprivation, the longing for her husband according to Igbo law and custom, who gives away generously what belongs to her, to younger, seductive concubines. Emecheta's criticism of the limited (or non-

195

existent) sexuality of mothers in polygamous households is manifested at the beginning of the novel. Her diatribe against the all-
too-common abuse of women through sexual neglect, public
humiliation and disrespect, is depicted through the characterization of Agunwa, as well as that of Nnu Ego. Agunwa's private suffering is put forth by Chief Nwokocha Agbadi's best friend, Chief
Idayi, who tells Agbadi that his lovemaking with Ona on the night
that Agunwa becomes ill "woke the very dead." But worse still was
the statement that Agunwa was watching "from the corner of the
courtyard . . . last night" (22). As Agunwa's illness progresses and
she dies soon afterward, the villagers say that "it was bad for her
morale to hear her husband giving pleasure to another woman in
the same courtyard where she slept" (21). Agunwa's humility and
security turns into humiliation and heartbreak as Agbadi flaunts
his sexual prowess before her and his junior wives, their children,
as well as his kith and kin. Ona too takes responsibility for
Agunwa's predicament. The author reports:

> She knew that the people blamed her for Agunwa's
> death though no one had the courage to say so open-
> ly. That night after she had given Agbadi his meal
> and helped the men to rub life into his stiff side and
> shoulder, she curled up to him and asked: 'Would
> you like me to go now? My father will be worrying,
> wondering what the people are saying.' (22)

In response to everyone's feelings about Agunwa's sudden death,
Agbadi denies Agunwa's sexuality by claiming that Agunwa was
happy because he took her to Udo, the day he became an Obi (chief).
He rationalizes that "she is the mother of my grown sons. You are
wrong to suggest that she might be bitter just because last night with
Ona I amused myself a little" (22). He goes on to pacify Agunwa's
sons by telling them that their mother was a good woman: "So unob-
trusive, so quiet. I don't know who else will help me keep an eye on
those young wives of mine, and see to the smooth running of my
household" (22). Agunwa, like most women, has never been told that
desire and pleasure in sexual intercourse was natural and meant for
both women and men to enjoy. It was said to be important only in
producing children to ensure her husband's lineage. Voicing her
needs rather than accepting that her sexuality was taboo, was a radical notion. So naturally, when she hears Ona actually accepting
Agbadi's pleasure as if it were as natural as drinking water, her world
falls apart, to say the least. It is shocking to realize that you have

been duped. It's the knowledge that she has been weeping in silence, deprived for years, the reality that she's been exploited that brings on an illness which culminates in her death and curse on the family. It is Nnu Ego, Chief Nwokocha Agbadi's only daughter, the daughter of Ona, who spends a lifetime, over forty years, paying for the callousness of her father. In her marriages to both Amatokwu, who loses interest in her sexuality because she is barren, and Nnaife, who is incapable of being a loving and caring companion, Nnu Ego lives a lonely, unfulfilling life. According to Emecheta, adhering to indigenous Igbo codes, wearing a mask of contentment in a loveless marriage and repressing one's passion for sexual fulfillment is psychologically devastating. Nnu Ego discovers this early enough when she is married to Amatokwu. So traumatic is her pretense of happiness as Amatokwu's senior wife that, when his people find him a second wife her body rejects the lie and she experiences her first nervous breakdown. Adaku, Nnu Ego's co-wife in her second marriage to Nnaife Owulum, is also stigmatized as a barren woman because she has two daughters. At one point in the novel when Adaku lodges a legitimate complaint against her co-wife, Nnu Ego, who has three sons and four daughters by Nnaife, the court of elders denies her a fair trial because she gave birth to girls and no son(s). Nwakusor, the spokesperson for the group, scolds her: "Don't you know that you are committing an unforgivable sin?" He continues:

> ". . . our life starts from immortality and ends in immortality. If Nnaife had been married to only you, you would have ended his life on this round of his visiting earth. I know you have children, but they are girls, who in a few years' time will go and help build another man's immortality. The only woman who is immortalizing your husband you make unhappy with your fine clothes and lucrative business. If I were in your shoes, I should go home and consult my *chi* to find out why male offspring have been denied me." (166)

Adaku, realizing that she is worse than a "second-class citizen" in the Owulum family decides to leave her loveless marriage. She confesses to Nnu Ego that Nnaife comes to her bed reluctantly for he favors Nnu Ego (168). So, in saving herself from madness and premature death, she leaves Nnaife. This is her way of protesting against a society that disregards women. As Adaku says, "The way they go on one would think I know where sons are made and have been neglectful about taking one for my husband" (169). She decides to move out with her daughters and build a more fulfilling life. By taking control of her body and choosing to live a better life with "some of our men who returned from the fighting," she fights back.

As Eustace Palmer rightly points out, Adaku is the "forerunner of women's liberation in African literature"(49). As far as Adaku is concerned, the so-called love and happiness that married life supposedly brings is a sham. Financial support, companionship, mutual respect and sharing were strangers in the one-room flat Nnaife provided for his family. What a wife needs whether she's a mother or not is affection, understanding, compassion, care, and a partner who senses one's joys and suffering. Nnaife was nobody's sweetheart. Adaku's self-worth and sanity are more important than the bogus respect she imagines she receives by being the wife of somebody. Indeed, she fights back in her decision to leave Nnaife. In a similar way Amaka, Flora Nwapa's dauntless heroine in the novel, *One Is Enough*, becomes a prosperous, wealthy woman upon leaving the climate of entropy her marriage degenerates into because she had no child. With Adaku taking responsibility for her life rather than leaving it in the hands of an uncaring spouse, Emecheta drives home the point that women are their own worst enemies by passively letting others control their destinies. Adaku loses nothing by being honest with herself and refusing to be a slave to a selfish and insensitive spouse. Certainly with Emecheta's deconstruction of African women in *Joys*, one can agree that gone is the "anxiety of authorship" found in the works of African women writers, such as Ifeoma Okoye and Mabel Segun, who shun female sexuality in their creative works (Gilbert & Gubar 1979, 49).

Outside of the Nigerian literary canon, other contemporary African authors write about liberating both men and women from cultural/sexual inhibitions by subverting and by undermining the sexual codes and conventions that have become so ingrained in the psyches of the people that women and even some men don't notice them. As Robert Scholes contends, the modus vivendi we live by and accept as natural is in fact cultural (127). According to the law of the Fathers, in Igbo society and by extension most African societies, decent and virtuous women are incapable of erotic feelings. This is particularly true when it comes to mothers. Women, as a result, attempt to live up to the expectations of the status quo and repress their desires not knowing that they have become the "living dead," to use a metaphor Florence Stratton has created to describe Emecheta's imprisoned heroines (143). Men and women complete each other. And as the graceful, soothing lyrics of the Nigerian popular singer Sade remind her listeners, "Nothing [should] come, nothing [should] come, nothing [should] come between [them]."[6]

This revisionist code, found in the literature of contemporary African writers, counters the sexual bias that for women, children alone bring fulfillment. According to Ousmane Sembène, a Senegalese writer, women, especially mothers, want to feel the male "presence." In Sembène's short story, "Her Three Days," Noumbe, the third wife of Mustapha, anticipates "her three days" when she would have her husband all to herself. According to Muslim tradition, a husband must spend three days with each one of his wives. Sembène writes, "It was a long time since Noumbe had felt such emotion. To have Mustapha! The thought comforted her" (38). Noumbe prepares a "delicious dish so that Mustapha will forget the cooking of his other wives, including the fourth wife he had taken four months ago and he will come to her and wreck her bed" (39-40). It is reported that Noumbe has a heart condition brought on by bearing five children in quick succession, in one pregnancy after the other, which caused her to age before her time. One can also surmise that the stress of competing with her co-wives, fighting to maintain satisfying erotic experiences with Mustapha, and caring for her five children alone without Mustapha's support or companionship, brings on her illness. Nevertheless, as she imagines what "her three days" would be like, she forgets her illness and is quite happy in cooking a succulent dish "which cost him nothing" (42).

Two days pass and Mustapha has not come. In the meantime, Noumbe's health degenerates and her anger rises. She finally sends her son to Mustapha's fourth wife with the message: "Tell him I must see him at once . . . I am not well" (49). She borrows one thousand francs from her neighbor Aida and prepares another tasty meal for her husband whom she thinks "would stay in bed" (50). When he appears at the end of her third day, Noumbe is so upset that she breaks the three plates that were neatly placed on the table for him. Then suddenly a sharp pain stabs at her heart and she bent double falls to the floor (52). Mustapha, unconcerned about the part he plays in his wife's ill health, casually walks out of her house complaining that "one of these days her jealously will suffocate her" (52). The author skillfully makes his point, women the Muslim ones included look forward to sexual pleasures their husbands are sanctioned to perform in the name of Allah. When denied their natural desires, sickness, madness or even death is a possible outcome. Mustapha does not escape the author's criticism. Male dominance in sexuality is seriously out of control because of the amount of exploitation and abuse inflicted on women. Affection, care, and *jouissance*, as a woman's right, is not a priority for men. Rather, it is the thrill of control and women's subordination that give men excitement and pleasure (West, 127).

In Reginald McKnight's novel, *I Get on The Bus*, Aita Gueye takes a lover to satisfy her sexual craving. Her husband, Old Gueye, is unable to fulfill her sexually because he spends months away from her marital bed with his younger wife in The Gambia. So she takes matters into her own hands by having an affair with a man she fancies. Aita is described by Mamadou Ford, an African-American man living in Senegal, as a sex-starved wife who uses supernatural powers to entice him to her bed. Ford tells Evan "she was in love with me . . . so that one-eyed bastard killed her. Her own husband . . . he wants me dead too" (258). Ford escapes the wishes of his enemy for a long time, by protecting himself through magical charms and amulets, before he too is eventually murdered.

The magical, medicinal powers of the male "presence" is also at the center of the Kenyan writer Muthoni Likimani's book, *What Does A Man Want?* In the Bakhtinian tradition of a plurality of independent and merged discourses, heteroglossia, the prose poem opens with a distressed daughter of Africa's *cri de coeur*: "What does a man want?/ I demand to be told!/ What do men look for/ In a woman I mean:/ Is it beauty?/ . . . Let me know,/ Let me read,/ Let me see,/ And let me compare" (1). An atmosphere of the community of women is created from the conglomeration of different cultures the women come from Asian, Black, Caucasian, as well as different classes, the privileged and underprivileged. More importantly, Muthoni dexterously makes the point that the problem of male dominance and female subordination is universal, cutting across geophysical spaces and thus bonding women together. Honestly and openly one woman after another attempts to shed light on the problem of female sexual deprivation. One woman's strategy is as follows:

> Bluff him,
> Shut your mouth,
> And be shy.
> Never answer back
> Walk like a cat.
> Let him not

Hear your footsteps.
He will boast among his friends:
He is the head,
He is the spokesman,
You are under him,
He controls you. (10-11)

The advice is of no use. All the women agree that "all these sto-
ries/ I have heard before./ None of them work" (12). The experiences are similar to those of Nnu Ego, Agunwa and Adaku. The
women do their level best to please their men. Many cannot sleep
from worrying. Some arrive at the point of madness. Others pretend to be happy, knowing full well that they are living a life of
lies. In each and every case, however, the woman is sexually
abused. Another woman laments:

I had a sleepless night
On the wrong side I had slept
. . . I look like an old woman
Suffering from trachoma,
All this caused
By sleepless nights
Worrying about my husband
Where did he spend the night? (13)
A third woman confesses:
The thought of him
Brought tears to run,
I bit my lips
I hated myself,
I must do something
Why should I deserve this?
I am not ugly,
I am not old,
I am . . . .
All by myself
With my misery. (16)

The sadness of the situation is that Likimani's women are not
alone. Gloria Naylor's victims in *Linden Hills* are also at their wits
end. It is the same scenario: Willa Prescott Nedeed, the wife of
Luther Nedeed, III, is disturbed about "her lonely nights in that
half empty bed" (174). Gradually the reader learns that four generations of Nedeed wives led "twisted lives" because they have been

relegated to the backwaters of sexual deprivation once they gave their husbands a son. No intimate play, no conversation, no sharing, no life, period. This saga ends tragically as Willa Nedeed goes mad upon discovering through family records that they've all been married to sexual perverts (175).

The oppression of women through the denial of female desire and sexual pleasure is just as traumatic for Ruth Foster, the protagonist's mother in Toni Morrison's novel, *Song of Solomon*. Ruth Foster is married to a wealthy business man, Macon Dead, who punishes his wife for years by denying her sexual gratification. She survives his cruelty by nursing their son, Macon, Jr., way past his weaning period, which points to the perversity which can arise when one is denied the elixir of love (Rigney, 102).

It is time for African men to pay heed to the popular adage, "What's good for the goose is good for the gander." Transformation from the patriarchal gaze which is a devourer of hedonic experiences of women is at the bottom of the protest one identifies in the literature of Buchi Emecheta and contemporary Black writers generally. Susan Andrade has rightly defined the Nigerian female literary tradition as a tradition of rebellion, with African women writers becoming more militant than their foremothers and forefathers. And this tradition is rooted in Nigerian women's grassroots associations and networking channels in every village, township and city which has been a great force in enacting change. Judith Van Allen, in her essay, "'Sitting on a Man': Colonialism and the Lost Political Institutions of Igbo Women," points to the strength of indigenous African feminism:

> "Sitting on a man" or a woman, boycotts, and strikes were the women's main weapons against abuse. To "sit on" or "make war on" a man involved gathering at his compound, sometimes late at night, dancing, singing scurrilous songs which detailed the women's grievances against him and often called his manhood into question, banging on his hut with the pestles women used for pounding yams, and perhaps demolishing his hut or plastering it with mud and roughing him up a bit. A man might be sanctioned in this way for mistreating his wife. . . . Although this could hardly have been a pleasant experience for the offending man, it was considered legitimate and no man would consider intervening. (170)

Elechi Amadi, in his novel *Estrangement*, illustrates possibilities for sexual fulfillment and happiness in marriage through the women's association, *omirinya*, which is similar to that which Van Allen describes.[7] For example, Oyia, the second wife of Ibekwe didn't have much trouble getting him to come to her bed during her four days. With the help of the *omirinya*, Ibekwe was reminded that he was going against tradition. And in the end he complies, for as his mother bluntly puts it, "can you bury me alone when I die?" (92) I disagree with Patricia Williams when she contends that "one of the things that has always impressed me most about the law of contract is a certain deadening power it exercises by reducing the parties to the passive" (28). But a marriage does not have to be disempowering for the female and empowering only for the male. While Nnu Ego internalizes her subjectivity to her father, husbands, and sons, Adaku refuses to play second fiddle to her capricious husband and his kinsmen. The playwright, Tess Onwueme, in her dramatic epic, *Go Tell It To Women*, similar to Elechi Amadi, attests to avenues of female empowerment within Nigerian society. She goes a step further to address the issue of western radical feminism, suggesting that African women create a "world without men."[8] Onwueme, in reflecting upon the philosophical, spiritual concepts in African societies, writes:

> THE GODS OF OUR LAND FORBID! . . . .
> Women sleeping with women . . .
> men sleeping with men? Ugh! That is no
> subject in our world. Let it remain in
> their world where it is now . . . .(321)

African women are a group whose rights are constantly "appropriated," to borrow Catherine MacKinnon's term, by the mere fact of the dismissal of our needs for hedonic and sexual experiences. For example, many of us are deprived of claiming our children, controlling our sexuality, owning the land we cultivate and farm, and directing our destinies outside the domestic realm (Aluko & Alfa, 163). By exploring the role of love, sexuality, and male companionship within African women's lives in a variety of contexts, constructive and destructive, African women writers are redefining African women's sexuality and showing possibilities for happiness within the African world. Buchi Emecheta courageously challenges the status quo in exposing the painful atrocities against the female body. It is these truths that will loosen the cage-like matrix that continues to suppress sexual healing and set us all free. It is, therefore, through the recognition of our positionality and the (re)construction of societies that heed the needs of *all* members of the family that African women can (re)shape their worlds to save their lives. It is through communicating with our men to transform rigid sex-roles that will make our erotic fantasies a reality and create:

> . . . midnight licorice nights . . .
> arms, legs, breasts, chests wet in the waves of love's
> spicy sauces,
> swallowing rounds of bursting orange on the sheets
> of the universe,
> marinating in the liquids of our joys . . .
> eternally in you and you in me. . . . [9]

NOTES

1. This term was suggested by Professor Tuzyline Allan in a conversation at Baruch College, CUNY.

2. See Florence Stratton's article, "The Shallow Grave: Archetypes of Female Experience in African Fiction," *Research in African Literatures* 19 (1988): 143-169, in which she contends that Emecheta's women are paradigms of a shallow grave, the living dead.

3. According to Chinua Achebe in his book, *Morning Yet On Creation Day*, the word *chi* in Igbo cosmology means a personal spirit, one's guardian angel. For the Igbo, everyone has a *chi*. Therefore a person's success or failure in life is said to be determined by his/her *chi's* kindness or animosity. Nnu Ego's *chi* is callous and cruel because she is the reincarnation of the sacrificed slave girl. Nnu Ego's brothers were most insensitive in not granting the slave girl her wish to live. So they killed her to accompany their dead mother to the world of the spirits. The slave girl takes out her revenge on Nnu Ego. Hence, happiness eludes Nnu Ego.

4. See Ketu Katrak's article, "Womanhood/Motherhood: Variations on a Theme in Selected Novels of Buchi Emecheta," *Journal of Commonwealth Literature* 22 (1987): 159-170.

5. Flora Nwapa also subverts this idea in her novel, *Idu* (London: Heinemann, 1971). When Idu's husband dies, she too wills to die and that she does, leaving behind their infant son.

6. This comes from a line in the song, "Nothing Can Come Between Us" in Sade's album *Stronger Than Pride*.

7. *Omirinya* is an Igbo word meaning "daughters of the clan or village."

8. See Katherine Frank's essay, "Women Without Men: The Feminist Novel in Africa," *African Literature Today* 15 (1987): 14-34. She reports that Africa's female writers' solution to sexism is repudiation of patriarchy and acceptance of a world without men.

9. See P. J. Gibson's poem, *"Midnight Licorice Nights,"* in the book, *Erotique Noire*, Eds. M. DeCosta-Willis et al. (New York: Doubleday, 1992), p. 18.

Works Cited

Abrams. M. H. *A Glossary of Literary Terms.* 6th ed. New York: Harcourt, 1993.

Allen, Dennis. *Sexuality in Victorian Fiction.* Norman: U of Oklahoma P, 1993.

Aluko, Grace and Mary Alfa. "Marriage and Family." *Women in Nigeria Today.* London: Zed, 1985, 163–173.

Amadi, Elechi. *Estrangement.* London: Heinemann, 1986.

Andrade, Susan Z. "Rewriting History, Motherhood and Rebellion: Naming an African Women's Literary Tradition." *Research in African Literatures* 21 (1990): 91–110.

Bakhtin, Mikhail. *The Dialogic Imagination: Four Essays.* Ed. Michael Holquist. Trans. Caryl Emerson and Holquist. Austin: U of Texas P, 1981.

Boyce Davies, Carole. "Motherhood in the Works of Male and Female Igbo Writers: Achebe, Emecheta, Nwapa and Nzekwu." *Ngambika: Studies of Women in African Literature.* Eds. Carole Boyce Davies and Anne Adams Graves, Trenton: Africa World P, 1986, 25–39.

Demetrakopoulos, Stephanie. "Maternal Bonds as Devourers of Women's Individuation in Toni Morrison's *Beloved.*" *African American Review* 26 (1992): 51–59.

Egwuonwu, Ani. *Marriage Problems in Africa.* New York: Continental, 1986.

Emecheta, Buchi. *The Joys of Motherhood.* New York: George Braziller, 1979.

Frank, Katherine. "Women Without Men: The Feminist Novel in Africa." *African Literature Today* 15 (1987): 14 –34.

Gibson, P. J. "Midnight Licorice Nights." *Erotique Noire.* Eds. Miriam DeCosta-Willis, Reginald Martin and Roseann Bell. New York: Doubleday, 1992, 18.

Gubar, Susan and Sandra Gilbert. *The Madwoman in the Attic.* New Haven: Yale UP, 1979.

—. *No Man's Land: The Place of the Woman Writer in the Twentieth Century.* Volume I. New Haven: Yale UP, 1988.

Hollibaugh, Amber. "Desire for the Future: Radical Hope in Passion and Pleasure." *Pleasure and Danger: Exploring Female Sexuality.* Ed. Carole S. Vance. Boston: Routledge & Kegan Paul, 1984. 401–410.

Iweriebor, Ifeyinwa. "Shugaba-ing Rawlings: An Appraisal of the Marriage Institution (A woman's point of view)." *Women in Nigeria Today.* London: Zed, 1985. 174–177.

Jeyifo, Biodun. "Okonkwo and His Mother: *Things Fall Apart* and Issues of Gender in the Constitution of African Postcolonial Discourse." *Callaloo.* 16 (1993): 847–858.

Katrak, Ketu. "Womanhood/Motherhood: Variation on a Theme in Selected Novels of Buchi Emecheta." *The Journal of Commonwealth Literature.* 22 (1987): 159–170.

Kristeva, Julia. *Desire in Language. A Semiotic Approach to Literature and Art.* New York: Columbia UP, 1980.

Likimani, Muthoni. *What Does a Man Want?* Nairobi: East African Literature Bureau, 1974.

Mba, Nina. "Heroines of the Women's War." *Nigerian Women in Historical Perspective.* Ed. Bolanle Awe. Lagos/Ibadan: Sankore/Bookcraft, 1992,

73–88.

McDowell, Deborah. "That Nameless...Shameful Impulse": Sexuality in Nella Larson's *Quicksand and Passing." Studies in Black American Literature.* Volume III, Eds. Joe Weixlmann and Houston A. Baker, Jr. Greenwood, Florida: Penkevill. 1988, 139–166.

McKnight, Reginald. *I Get on the Bus.* Boston: Little, Brown, 1990.

Morrison, Toni. *Song of Solomon.* New York: Penguin, 1977.

Naylor, Gloria. *Linden Hills.* New York: Ticknor & Fields, 1985.

—. "Love and Sex in the Afro-American Novel." *Yale Review* 78 (1989): 19–31.

Nnaemeka, Obioma. "From Orality to Writing: African Women Writers and the (Re)Inscription of Womanhood." *Research in African Literatures.* 25.4 (1994): 137–157.

Nwapa, Flora. *Idu.* London: Heinemann, 1971.

—. *One Is Enough.* Trenton: Africa World P, 1991.

Ogbalu, F. C. *Igbo Proverbs on Sex.* Onitsha, Nigeria: University Publishing, 1980.

Onwueme, Tess. *Go Tell It To Women.* Newark: African Heritage P, 1992.

Palmer, Eustace. "The Feminine Point of View: Buchi Emecheta's *The Joys of Motherhood." African Literature Today* 13 (1983): 38–55.

Rigney, Barbara. *The Voices of Toni Morrison.* Columbus: Ohio State UP, 1991.

Robinson, Patricia. "The Historical Repression of Women's Sexuality." *Pleasure and Danger: Exploring Female Sexuality.* Ed. Carole S. Vance. Boston: Routledge and Kegan Paul, 1984, 251–266.

Rubin, Gayle. "Thinking Sex: Notes of a Radical Theory of the Politics of Sexuality." *Pleasure and Danger: Exploring Female Sexuality.* Ed. Carole S. Vance. Boston: Routledge & Kegan Paul, 1984, 267–82.

Scholes, Robert. *Semiotics and Interpretation.* New Haven: Yale UP, 1992.

Schipper, Mineke. *Source of All Evil: African Proverbs and Sayings on Women.* Chicago: Ivan R. Dee, 1991.

Sembène, Ousmane. "Her Three Days." *Tribal Scars and Other Stories.* Ibadan: Heinemann, 1987, 35–55.

Snitow, Ann et. al. *Powers of Desire: The Politics of Sexuality.* New York: Monthly Review P, 1983.

Stratton, Florence. "The Shallow Grave: Archetypes of Female Experience in African Fiction." *Research in African Literature* 19 (1988): 143–169.

Uchendu, Victor. *The Igbo of Southeast Nigeria.* New York: Holt, Rinehart and Winston, 1965.

Van Allen, Judith. " 'Sitting on a Man': Colonialism and the Lost Political Institutions of Igbo Women." *Canadian Journal of African Studies* 4, (1972): 165–181.

West, Robin. "The Difference in Women's Hedonic Lives: A Phenomenological Critique of Feminist Legal Theory." *At the Boundaries of Law: Feminism and Legal Theory.* Eds. Martha Fineman and Nancy Thomadsen. New York: Routledge, 1991, 115–134.

Williams, Patricia. "On Being the Object of Property." *At the Boundaries of Law: Feminism and Legal Theory.* Eds. Martha Fineman and Nancy Thomadsen. New York: Routledge, 1991, 22–39.

Trajectories of Rape in Buchi Emecheta's Novels

Tuzyline Jita Allan

Ah, this land
This black whore
This manacled bitch
Tied to a post and raped
By every passing white dog...
Listen! Listen to the pack
Of scavenger dogs from white heartlands
Snarling in their gang rape of Africa

— Chinweizu, *Admonition to the Black World*

'Now listen to me. You make any noise and your
body will be found in the dam after the dam has
dried. You are my wife and I will sleep with you
now....' So I sit here alone with the wounds.... Blood
flowing all the time, hurting my inside....

— Chenjerai Hove, *Bones*

Of the many subjects that have been played out in the theater of Buchi Emecheta's mind, rape provides the most significant index into the author's problems and promise. Her incursion into this dangerous patriarchal space demonstrates at once her rejection of silence in the face of gender oppression and the attendant difficulty of fashioning a strong voice of protest. The conflict is grounded in a socio-literary nexus of beliefs and practices that organizes the idea of rape in the African social order. "Sexual intercourse performed without the consent of the woman involved" *(Women and Values* 189), the commonly accepted definition of rape, is an act that mirrors and supports gender inequity. Men commit rape and women keep silent mainly because the rape act, as Ama Ata Aidoo points out in *Changes,* is literally unspeakable. Following her rape by her husband, Esi Sekyi, Aidoo's heroine, searches in vain for "an indigenous word or phrase" (12) to articulate her experience. Esi comes to the painful understanding that her mother tongue fails her at the critical moment of her violation because it is a patriarchal instrument designed to protect male sexual privilege. "Sex," Esi muses, "is something a husband claims from his wife as his right. Any time. And at his convenience" (12). Taking into account the corollary to this patriarchal logic, namely, that a woman is by definition a wife, female rape is tantamount to marital rape and is, therefore, incommunicable. Chenjerai Hove, in his prose-poem *Bones,* provides a telling example of the cultural threads that bind woman to wifehood and rape. Chisaga, the rapist, configures his young victim through a thought process that first transforms the girl-child into a woman on the grounds that she was left with "the things of womanhood" (86)—pots, plates, and spoons—then renders her husband-ready and, finally, rapable. As the epigraph reveals, Chisaga, furious for not having his way with the girl's benefactor, deals his victim a savage sexual blow. The woman-equals-wife idea thus works with the inexpressibility of marital rape to ground the rape act in a conspiracy of silence.

Here, language has an easy ally in literature. Africa's quintessential rape narrative tells the story of the economic and cultural ravishment of the continent by foreign prowlers and native sons. The feminization (and idealization) of Africa finds its finest expression in the trope of rape which carries a potent threat of displacing "real" women in rape discourse. Although it is not gender-restrictive, this trope is tellingly pervasive in men's writing. Male authors find it a particularly irresistible tool for capturing the crippling trauma of Africa's invasive experience. Its coercive impact, illustrated above in Chinweizu's "Admonition to the Black World," is generally distilled through the imperative force of poetry but, as Ayi Kwei Armah's *The Beautyful Ones Are Not Yet Born* demonstrates, it can also unpack the latent meanings of fiction. Manifest or latent, the figure of Mother Africa as rape victim has long dominated the imagination of male authors, all but obliterating women from considerations of rape. In this regard, Hazel Carby's statement about the status of female rape in African-American discourse is illuminating: "[T]he institutionalized rape of black women has never been as powerful a symbol of black oppression as the spectacle of lynching" (*Reconstructing Womanhood* 39). In the African context the spectacle of Africa's rape evokes in male writers strong nationalistic feelings that are simply not replicated in the representation of female rape.[1]

Turning the discourse of rape from the embodied figure of Africa to the bodies of women constitutes an urgent and mammoth challenge for African women writers given their dual sense of loyalty to woman and nation. Most of these writers are committed to reimagining what Molara Ogundipe-Leslie calls "the reality of the African woman" which, she argues, is either distorted in or deleted from the African literary canon (8). Emecheta, for example, aims to "reconstruct her [mother's] life" (*In Their Own Voices* 44) and the lives of women of her mother's generation. Asenath Odaga of Kenya sees "a need to focus on women" because they "do quite a lot in the family and society as a whole" (*In Their Own Words* 129). The sentiment is shared by her fellow Kenyan Rebecca Njau: "I've been thinking about women's situation. Whatever they do, it is not appreciated, they are not fulfilled. That is why I have decided to look at woman of the past and ask, how did they make it?" (*In Their Own Voices* 105). Finally, Aidoo's remarks about her own practice underscore the importance of women's experience in the African female literary tradition: "I hope that being a woman writer, I have been faithful to the image of women as I see them around, strong women, who are viable in their own right" (*In Their Own Voices* 12).

The resonant links between women's issues and what Flora Nwapa calls "the problems of nation-building" (*In Their Own Voices* 113) in African women's writing suggest a keen and revisionist political sensibility. Women authors share the partisan view of colonial and postcolonial misrule in Africa but their refusal to evacuate the female subject from the site of restoration sets them apart significantly from most of their male counterparts. They aim, instead, to locate the postcolonial project at the intersection of gender and nation in order to adjudicate the rival claims of these competing categories. The repressed culture of rape offers a glimpse at the difficulties facing these writers as they negotiate their dual loyalties to woman and nation, and Emecheta's canon, in particular, provides a fascinating case study in light of her expansive treatment of rape. My aim in this essay is to examine Emecheta's inventories of rape and the path charted in her fiction toward voicing uninhibited opposition to the sexual violation of women.

There is ample evidence in Emecheta's early and middle novels of her desire to break the cultural code of silence governing female rape and of the concomitant difficulty in doing so within the protracted marriage plot that frames much of her fiction. Emecheta accommodates this dialectic by constructing a rhetoric of evasion (as opposed to silence) that encodes both resistance and acquiescence. In *Second-Class Citizen*, for example, following an acrimonious reunion in London between Adah and her husband, Francis, both are said to have "made ... up that night "(40). The point is later elaborated in less euphemistic tones:

> Adah did remember in the confusion that her nickname at home was "Touch Not." But how could she protest to a man who was past reasoning? The whole process was an attack, as savage as that of any animal.

> At the end of it all, Francis gasped and said, "Tomorrow you are going to see a doctor. I want them to see to this frigidity. I am not going to have it." (40)

The disjunction evident here between manifest and thwarted desire to achieve voice works through direct locution and euphemism, respectively. The passage begins with the euphemistic phrase "[t]hey made up that night," which by connoting reconciliation, harmony, and amicability, deflects attention entirely away from rape. But the euphemism is, in turn, undercut by its description: "an attack as savage as that of any animal." This language clearly denotes violence and it also provides counterpoint to the romantic idea inscribed by the euphemism. More important, it points to rape without naming it, creating at most the strong suspicion of sexual abuse and at least the impression of male sexual potency. The word "frigidity" reinforces the ambiguity by suggesting simultaneously resistance on the part of the victim and the unresponsiveness of a sexual partner. Interestingly, both meanings find support in the text. First, Adah's rape symbolizes her objectification as the goose that laid the golden eggs (39), a reference to her culturally sanctioned fecundity. In Francis's eyes, she is a baby-machine and therefore well suited for the wear and tear of sex, including rape. Support for the use of frigidity to register Francis's dissatisfaction with his sexually unexcitable wife comes, not surprisingly, from the author narrator:

> When, days later Adah discovered what frigidity meant, she realized that Francis had become sophisticated in many things. She kept all this to herself, though. He was as remote as the English people Adah had seen at Liverpool. (40)

But the narrative view expressed here is located at a tangent from the message of protest carried by the phrase "an attack as savage as that of any animal." The latter sentiment is undermined, if not invalidated, by Adah's discovery of the meaning of frigidity. The term's evocation of female sexual dysfunction recasts Adah in the role of emasculator rather than rape victim. If, as Louise Kaplan observes, frigidity is an imperious strategy for diminishing the worthiness and significance of the penis (Female Perversions 176), Francis's violent sexual performance becomes a justifiable act of self-defense, proof of this perennial law student's acculturation to the "sophisticated" ways of the British. The narrative silencing of the rape plot corresponds with Adah's self-imposed silence, and one can easily assume that included in the unspecified all that "[s]he kept...to herself" is her "rape," an experience neither she nor Emecheta can name or articulate.

In *The Bride Price* this rhetorical duel between voice and silence is played out on a larger rape plot, with narrative twists and turns that underscore the author's dilemma. Emecheta attempts to broker a ceasefire by giving her heroine full voice, but the textual irony is inescapable: there is no rape in this rape plot. The resulting questions, therefore, are edged with feminist concern: Does Aku-nna speak out because rape is a threat, not an act? Is her speech empowering and liberating? Can the real rape victim speak? The second and third questions take on a greater resonance in *The Rape of Shavi* but they are also germane to an understanding of the problematic trajectory outlined in *The Bride Price.* The novel captures in unforgettable close-ups the shattering impact of gender oppression on a young girl. Of these the near-rape event provides perhaps the strongest evidence of the heroine's tortured existence under an implacable male regime of power. Barely sixteen, Aku-nna, confined and indelibly defined by gender, becomes ensnared in a vicious game of competing masculinities, culminating in her kidnapping and emotional torment by the hubristic Okoboshi. The coherence of rape ideology allows for full play on the psychology of the victim and her attacker. For the latter, rape, as Sue Lees notes, "is the expression of power and the desire to humiliate" ("Judicial Rape" 11). Judging from the pair of eyes ... scanning her very being, Aku-nna realizes that Okoboshi "hates her" and "[is] going to be wicked" (136), if he wants to recover (as in fact he does) his manly pride which has suffered defeat at the hands of Chike, a man he considers an inferior and she the better choice for a husband. Unfortunately, Okoboshi is armed with more than sadistic desire. He is backed by a cannonade of cultural signs that give men wide latitude in the relations with women. Marriage, for example, even the type he commandeers, is enlisted to render Aku-nna power-less and rapable.

As the web of support for her rape tightens around her, Aku-nna, revolted as much by the female collaborators in this mascu-line game of oppression as by her tormentor, breaks her silence in a preemptive move that betrays her revolutionary potential:

> Look at you, and shame on you. Okoboshi the son of Obidi! You say your father is a chief [. . .] dog chief, that is what he is, if the best he can manage to steal for his son is a girl who has been taught what men taste like by a slave. (138)

The story about her defloration by Chike is intended to puncture Okoboshi's masculine pride, to mock and humiliate him. Spewing the "facts" about the couple's sexual encounters and the possibili-ty that she could be pregnant, Aku-nna rankles her oppressor enough to effect a turnabout in her situation from that of a defense-less young woman facing aggravated rape to a clever architect of her sexual destiny.

Is Aku-nna's self-empowering act plausible? Can she speak to real rape as she does to its threat? The questions return us to Emecheta's own (in)ability to speak/write about rape, an issue that, I believe, can be illuminated by the extent to which Aku-nna's fic-tive achievement bears up under scrutiny. One might begin with the fact that Aku-nna's speech-act throws into sharp focus the chaos of silence that rules over her life. Of "the dos and don'ts of wom-anhood in [this] culture" (115), silence exacts the greatest influence. Aku-nna, a practiced self-effacer, owes the habit to the belief "that a good woman did not repeat everything she experienced" (130). Estranged from her mother and her new family, "[s]he took refuge in tears" (90), not words. This configuration is consistent in all but one significant detail with the image of Aku-nna captured under male eyes:

> Azuka, the son of Nwanze of Umuidi, was watching her rather closely. He enquired if she has a headache but she denied it. The others stopped talking for a while, sensing that she was unhappy.... What appealed to all of them, though they did not realize it then, was the gentle helplessness about her; she would sooner have died than hit her husband back with an ozo handle if he beat her. *She always spoke her mind only when necessary, not before.* (emphasis added, 119)

In a deliciously ironic way, the last sentence leavens the image of Aku-nna as the paragon of female passivity with a dash of expressive resistance. Aku-nna can and does speak, in spite of the cultural strictures against female voice. When it comes to rape, however, words fail her. She realizes that the euphemistic phrase "agree[ing] to be Okoboshi's wife" (150) is jarringly at odds with the act of sexual violence but she works with it in her verbal battle for freedom. Rendering herself unfit to be wived due to an active premarital libido, Aku-nna unwittingly participates in her own subjugation and simultaneously engenders her escape. The textual paradox of accommodation and subversion speaks to Emecheta's own difficulty with the cultural narrative of rape.

The next time Emecheta evokes the specter of rape, it reappears in the now familiar context of marriage and, not surprisingly, in disguise. This time, however, there is an unexpected development: the term rape makes its debut in Emecheta's fiction in the following scene from *The Joys of Motherhood:*

> He demanded his marital right as if determined not to give her a chance to change her mind. She thought she would be allowed to rest at least the first night after her arrival before being pounded upon by this hungry man, her new husband. After such an experience, Nnu Ego knew why horrible-looking men *raped* women, because they were aware of their inadequacy. This one worked himself into an

213

> animal passion.... She bore it, and relaxed as she had
> been told, pretending that the person lying on her
> was Amatokwu, her first husband. This man's
> appetite was insatiable, and by morning she was so
> weary that she cried with relief.... (emphasis added,
> 44)

The episode, reminiscent of the sexual encounter between Adah
and Francis in *Second-Class Citizen,* bears all the marks of forced
coitus concealed behind the veil of matrimony and therefore enacts
the by-now familiar struggle between speech and silence that characterizes Emecheta's attempt to write rape. Narrative stammering
is evident in the very first sentence, with its mixed messages of
consent and force. The former, implicit in the end phrase "to
change her mind," is weakened by the imperative tone of the preceding terms, such as, "marital right," "demanded" and "determined." Indeed, the line dividing marital right and marital rape is
blurred by the narrative shifts between consensual sex and sexual
assault. If a resolute note is sounded by the term "raped," it is, upon
close inspection, a false alarm. The long-awaited locution makes
an entry into Emecheta's rape discourse not directly, but oblique-
ly: "After such an experience, Nnu Ego knew why horrible-looking
men raped women." While the statement analogically links Nnu
Ego's experience with female rape, it also undermines the idea that
her experience is a rape. The subversive opportunity embodied in
"raped" is thus lost and with it the voice of protest against sexual
violence.

The subsequent novels in Emecheta's rape canon chart a different path and confront new challenges. In *Destination Biafra* and
The Rape of Shavi the author struggles with the nationalistic
impulse to appropriate rape and in *The Family* she ventures into
the psychically wrenching terrain of incest. These texts mark a significant turning point in Emecheta's engagement with rape, not
only because the discourse is elevated to national and transnational
levels, but also because she seems to have been released from the
anxiety of naming rape. The word echoes chillingly amid the war-
driven malevolence portrayed in *Destination Biafra* and in *The Rape
of Shavi.* It leaps onto the title page in a gesture of defiance. *The
Family,* on the other hand, enunciates a language of feeling that
evinces a strong sense of authorial self-confidence and maturity
regarding rape and its representation. The author's wilful cultivation of voice in these texts signals both the difficult nature of the

214

project to articulate rape and her deep commitment to it.

"In *Destination Biafra* is my dream woman, Debbie Ogedemgbe," Emecheta proclaims in her autobiography, *Head Above Water* (1). The reason for this vote of confidence lies in Debbie's valiant attempt to connect the prose of nationhood with the passion of feminism. With her feet planted solidly in both camps, Debbie sets out to investigate the relation between women and nation to determine whether it is reciprocal, as she thinks it ought to be, or hostile, according to patriarchal practice. To this end, she throws off the straitjacket of gender convention for a soldier's uniform and plunges into the nightmare of the Biafran War. The textual enactment of one of the bloodiest civil wars in contemporary African history posits the bodies of both women and the nation as sites of plunder and rape. In other words, *Destination Biafra* inaugurates Emecheta's attempt to put women into African rape discourse next to the symbolically ravished body of Africa. The act challenges but fails to unsettle the standard practice of rape representation in the African literary establishment, forcing a compromise that undercuts the centrality of women's rape experience in the novel.

The characterization of Debbie as a "dream woman" captures something of the problem facing Emecheta in her effort to write women into the discourse of rape. Debbie embodies the author's feminine ideal: the educated, sturdily independent woman who strikes a path of freedom from society's encroachments. Emecheta's heroine is over-endowed with brains, wealth, and class privilege. Oxford-educated and-accented, Debbie is a veritable "been-to," whose foreign acculturation gives birth to her exotic aberrations at home in Nigeria. Of these, her English lover and her "overfed black cat" (91) pale in comparison to a series of unwomanly acts, ranging from scoffing at marriage to playing soldier. Debbie also incarnates Emecheta's ideal of nationhood. Her determinedly non-tribalistic nation-idea drives the novel's anti-war engine. Amid the waters of ethnic balkanization overrunning the land, Debbie alone stands firm in the belief that "she is neither Ibo nor Yoruba, nor ... Hausa, but a Nigerian" (126). Debbie's significance transcends her role as "peace ambassador" (95). She is the truest embodiment of what she hopes will be "a new clean Nigeria" (160), a decolonized, degendered, and detribalized society rife with possibility for all its members.

This imagined community befits the idealism of Emecheta's "dream woman" and both merge under her linked nationalist and feminist agendas. But, as Benedict Anderson cautions, nationalistic "imaginings" are often sites of "colossal sacrifices" (16) both in the literal and imaginative realms. In *Destination Biafra* the merger between New Nation and New Woman is wrought at a tremendous cost to the latter. Imagined commensurately with the nation-state, Debbie ultimately suffers from role overload, a condition clearly manifested in the text's inscription of rape as a tactic of political terror that is tame compared to the heroine's messianic sense of mission. As a symbol of regeneration, Debbie obeys the authorial demand for her self-sacrifice. Her descent from the paternal lap of luxury into the murderous swamps of war signals a self-denial suited to the shocks of battle, including sexual violence. Thus, the seductive spirit of heroism robs Debbie of the opportunity to respond persuasively to her sexual violation.

Debbie blunts the impact of an especially brutal gang rape with the inspired confidence of an icon. First, she slips into a state of un(self)consciousness:

> She could make out the leader referred to as Bale on top of her, then she knew it was somebody else, then another person.... She felt herself bleeding, though her head was still clear. Pain shot all over her body like arrows. She felt her legs pulled this way and that, and at times she could hear her mother's protesting cries. But eventually, amid all the degradation that was being inflicted on her, Debbie lost consciousness. (134)

The passage provides an excellent example of Emecheta's telegraphic narrative style that allows her in this case to distance Debbie (and the reader) from the fury of rape. This exceptionally violent act of sexual abuse lacks an emotional correlative. Indeed, when Debbie regains consciousness, we are told that "she was not crying; she was even trying to smile" (134). The emotional blank widens with the shift from Debbie's victimization to her guilt over her inability, despite all her education (134), to protect her mother from their attackers. Silence establishes Debbie's final cut-off from her sentient self: "She was not going to talk about it ... no one was going to hear her tell all that had happened" (136). Debbie's stoicism in the face of gang rape is a by-product of her representation as an ideal and, as the author-narrator seems to suggest, ideals do not die: "Debbie was alive, and that was everything" (136).

But Emecheta's dream woman exists in tandem with the reality of gender-based inferiorization of women in general and of the raped woman in particular. Debbie's multiple army rape experience threatens to push her beyond the pale of social and sexual commerce into pariahdom, thereby rupturing her iconic self-image. Narrative damage control involves the deployment of the problematic strategy used in *The Bride Price* to rescue the heroine from rape. Like Aku-nna, Debbie appeals to the conventions of female sexuality in order to thwart her attacker during the second rape experience. Both women hit at the heart of masculine pride by mocking the rapist's desire for a "tainted" woman, an act that betrays their complicity in the oppressive operations of gender. For Emecheta, however, the latter outcome is insignificant considering the subversive effect of the former. She mines its full value in *Destination Biafra* in an attempt to halt further slippage by her heroine. Playing the tainted woman, Debbie puts her violator on the moral and cultural defensive and recaptures the initiative in the "war for her womanhood" (174) and her nation:

> Allah will never forgive you now because you tried to violate a woman who has been raped by so many soldiers, a woman who may now be carrying some disease, a woman who has been raped by black Nigerian soldiers. You thought you were going to use a white man's plaything, as you called me, only to realize that you held in your arms a woman who has slept with soldiers. (176)

This verbal punch knocks Debbie's attacker out cold and simultaneously revives our sense of her symbolic importance with majestic equanimity. She reaffirms "her mission ... to talk to that other silly man Abosi into giving in now and betting his people live" (176) and, by inference, her apostolic role in the war against the rape of Nigeria. As Debbie walks off the battlefield of female rape to take on the "rapists" of the nation, she leaves behind a nervous concern that women have once more been robbed of the opportunity for equal representation in the discourse of rape.

This feeling abates in *The Rape of Shavi*, which both chronologically and, in the province of rape, appropriately succeeds *Destination Biafra*. *The Rape of Shavi* marks a radical shift in Emecheta's rape trajectory from the near-muzzling caution exhibited in the early novels to controlled defiance. This attitude is manifest in the title, which centralizes rape as the rape of nation. The distinction, however, becomes clear only after one reads the text, failing which the noun "Shavi" in the title might easily suggest a woman's name. The ambiguity is deliberate, given the novel's dual subject of state and female rape and Emecheta's refusal to relinquish the latter to the periphery. In *The Rape of Shavi* the difficulty intrinsic to the project to write rape is still evident but the author seems to have disencumbered herself of the anxiety that aborted her earlier speech-acts on the subject. At work is a new feminist imperative allied to but not dominated by the nationalistic impulse that is on full display in *Destination Biafra* and is no less tenacious in this novel. The idealized feminism of the previous text gives way to a subversive performance that takes aim at hegemonic forms of dominance, including gendered practices in the African literary establishment. The novel's theme of European incursion into a politico-cultural African idyll shows the influence of Achebe's *Things Fall Apart,* the ur-text of African coloniality. *The Rape of Shavi,* however, elides the tragic vision, the exhaustive sociological apparatus, and, most significantly, the enhanced male perspective of Achebe's novel. Emecheta finds in the conventions of feminist utopian fiction a textual strategy that fits her two-fold purpose: to revise the patriarchal narrative of pre-colonial African life in order to account for female agency and to satirize (rather than lament) colonial Europe's encounter with Africa.

The novel evokes a utopian world governed by a hard-won democratic tradition under which even "a child was free to tell the king where it was that he had gone wrong" (3). In this patriarchal cradle of freedom women are agents of the social order, not oppressed outsiders: "For is it not known that if one's women are contented, life will offer one contentment?" (5) The posited social prestige of women is poignantly dramatized in the opening scene where the Queen Mother's displeasure with her husband, King Patayon, for failing to inform her of his plan to marry his ninth wife becomes an issue of national security. While gender remains a demarcated terrain, as evidenced in the king's repressed anger at his wife's intransigence and the need for the Queen Mother to have a spokes*man,* female integrity is not compromised. On the contrary, the scene ends with prima facie evidence of the impending collapse of Shavian society unless Queen Shoshovi's demands are met. To analogize from the markedly androcentric opening scene in *Things Fall Apart* to this woman-centered view is to recognize Emecheta's subversive intent.[2] The displacement of Okonkwo, Achebe's supermasculine hero, as custodian of pre-colonial African life is a counter-hegemonic move that assumes heretical dimensions given his cult-status in the African literary tradition.

Emecheta, however, is interested in more than simply a game of substitution. She hopes to shatter the master text's founding stereotype of female marginality by suffusing women's roles with political and emotional significance. Under the leadership of the Queen Mother, women in *The Rape of Shavi* give a command performance in self-asserted authority that enables their retributive response to rape.

In the text's economy of subversion, Shavi's economic and cultural rape is conflated with Ayoko's sexual assault: "Ronje fell on her and, in less than ten minutes, took from the future Queen of Shavi what the whole of Shavi stood for" (94). This story of the colonial violation obviously follows a different script from the one enacted in *Things Fall Apart*, where the comprehending view of colonialism is unflinchingly male. By locking in the fate of Shavi with Ayoko's sexual fate, Emecheta underscores the interdependence of colonial and patriarchal economies, a fact that is evident but not conceded in Achebe's novel. Implicit in Emecheta's fusion of national and individual rape is the assumption that the buried subtext of women's psychological rape by African patriarchs in *Things Fall Apart* needs to be rewritten to fully comprehend that text's engagement with colonialism. Her own attempt to do so in *The Rape of Shavi* posits the violation of female sexual sovereignty rather than the humiliation of a patriarchal dynasty as the de facto colonial event.

Emecheta takes her subversive agenda two steps further. First, she reverses the paradigm of racial and cultural otherness, ascribing the disadvantage of difference to the colonial rather than the native. This bold new position is staked out at the outset with the crash-landing of the Newark, the aircraft carrying a small group of European professionals fleeing the threat of nuclear war in the West. The crash engenders a clash-of-cultures theme that communicates a different message from the one inscribed in *Things Fall Apart*. The wrecked plane (appropriately called the "bird of fire") stands in sharp contrast to the "iron horse" that transports the "white man" to Abame, setting the stage for the breakup and destruction of the clan (*Things Fall Apart* 128). The small but powerful invading force that wreaks havoc in Achebe's novel is reconfigured in Emecheta's text as a pitiful mass of "burning flesh" out of which slither "strange. . . creatures . . . with the color of lepers," whose cries resemble "wild things when provoked" (11). Brought down both literally and symbolically from the (culturally?) dominant position depicted in *Things Fall Apart*, the European is relocated in Emecheta's text in the vengeful region of the Other where the self in invalidated in a devastating collision between differing identities.

As Other, the European contingent represents the antithesis of Shavian culture and humanity, their pronounced alterity engendering both comic and tragic results. Take, for example, the mock-heroic battle between King Patayon and his power-hungry son, Asogba, over the issue of whether or not the Europeans are human and therefore deserving of Shavian hospitality. While it is a foreboding occurrence that contains the seeds of the deadly power play depicted at the end of the novel, it is suffused with comic significance gained at the expense not only of the King but also of the foreign crew. The King's face-saving antics are laughable but the joke is on the seven survivors, whose evolutionary progress from "leper creatures" (12) to "badly washed albinos" (13) bespeaks the deficiency of status suffered by the Europeans in this text. Their cultural alterity is also treated satirically. They are objects of ridicule, for example, as they advance towards the Shavians, "carrying their bundles not on their heads like any sensible person would do, but in their hands" (33). Andria's rank display of individualism is also subject to scorn in Shavi's communal culture, "[f]or why should one human wish to monopolize her sorrow, or even her child?" (34)

This wounding of European dignity is an intertextual act aimed at the glorified self-image of the colonial invader in *Things Fall Apart*. In the psychic economy of Emecheta's text the Europeans are enculturated into Shavian society and, by implication, humanized. Once their humanity is established they are made to partake of a cornucopia of citizenship rights and privileges in true utopian fashion, prompting Emecheta to declare that "[i]n *The Rape of Shavi* is my hope for us all that not only will the nuclear war be a non-starter, but that the white European woman from the North will regard the black woman from the South as her sister and that both of us together will hold hands and try to salvage what is left of our world from the mess the sons we have brought into it have made" (*Head Above Water* 1).

Ironically, the male-generated "mess" Emecheta speaks of contaminates the ideal world she tries to fashion in this text. Ronje's rape of Ayo sets in motion a series of male-directed acts of aggression that eventuate in the transformation of Shavi's utopian community into a dystopia. These acts range from economic rape to genocidal war, the former pointing to the novel's competing visions of rape. However, Emecheta seems intent on projecting Ayoko's violation and ending the uneven contest between women and nation in the arena of rape. The corrective gesture begins with speech, the victim's and, by implication, the author's. The silence attending rape in Emecheta's fictional universe breaks with Ayoko's reporting of the crime to her mother, ending a charade unrelieved even by the nightmarish presence of rape in *Destination Biafra*. Unlike Adah, Aku-nna, or Nnu Ego, Ayoko refuses to cooperate with her own oppression or to sacrifice her body, like Debbie, to the body politic, even though as future queen of Shavi she embodies fully the nation-idea. Freed from her predecessor's crisis of confidence, Ayoko shuns paternal authority and seeks instead a female-directed solution to the crime perpetrated against her. The ensuing "women's war" is waged verbally and literally. "[T]ransformed into a warrior," Siegbo takes verbal aim at her daughter's attacker: "You have not been violated. The creature, Ronje, is an animal, for what human would destroy a beautiful person like you?" Then she rips open the rape act to reveal its sinister intent: "Rape ages and humiliates any woman, young or old" (98). This is the prelude to swift action, once "the women of Shavi" (106) determine that Ronje is both guilty and unrepentant. Their "pact" calls for "silence" to protect Ayoko's public image and themselves from the charge of murder, but their act reverberates resoundingly beyond Shavian borders into the discursive space of Emecheta's narrative of rape. The text's determination to speak against and resist female rape is strong enough to withstand Ayoko's problematic rescue of the trapped and dying Ronje to ease her fear of retribution.

This spirit of resistance is carried over into *The Family*, where Emecheta ventures into the forbidden terrain of familial rape. The author's testing of this subject's perilous waters from distant cultural shores (perhaps because incest in the African societies is the absolute unsayable) makes it difficult for me to amplify the text's terrifying message of incestuous desire and rape, given this essay's focus on the problematics of writing about female rape with the rubric of African feminist and literary traditions. The fact that Emecheta's treatment of rape takes on a new importance in this text, however, warrants attention, even if only cursory.

In *The Family* Emecheta presents the traditional motors of female rape: the injunction to silence, the victim's guilt, self-blame and self-devaluation. To these Emecheta adds the props of familial rape the deceptively innocuous family environment and a trusting, vulnerable victim, for example to give us a compelling narrative of betrayal and sexual violation. However, while the text accents the young heroine's absorption in her family and the shattering effect of her double rape, it also protects her autonomy. Emecheta goes to the greatest length yet to provide an emotional context for the rape victim and to confront the dilemma of speech and silence buried in women's experience with rape and in her own effort to articulate that experience. Emecheta feels new possibilities in this text, resulting in a renewed determination to break the bonds of silence, isolation, and fear that trap women in the ugly fact of rape.

According to the text, a palpable symptom of Gwendolen's entrapment within the patriarchal culture that legitimates her rape is the parental gift of grand deception embodied in her name. The text opens with the lie that all but erases Gwendolen's identity, rendering her an easy target of patriarchal reconstruction: "She was christened Gwendolen. But her Mommy could not pronounce it, neither could her Daddy or his people" (9). To Uncle Johnny, her first rapist, she is "Juney-Juney," an abandoned girl whom he transforms into a "big 'oman" with a "big, big bed" (20) to herself to which he stakes a claim. With an "iron grip over her mouth the same Uncle Johnny who used to bring her ... sweets and lemonade drinks at Christmas" (22) rapes her, leaving her with the injunction to keep silent "because they'll say you're a bad girl" (22). Having renamed Gwendolen, Uncle Johnny reimagines her to fit his idea of a rapable woman, and then remakes her into the socialized image of the woman who invites rape, thereby limiting the chances of Gwendolen renaming and redefining herself.

Gwendolen thus learns early the sobering lesson that the "bad girl" image is a usurper of female identity. She slowly and painfully recognizes the fact that this image is deeply woven in her family's perception of who she is, beginning with its startling reinforcement by her grandmother, who initially seemed ready to insulate her from its vicious impact. Reading Gwendolen's walk— the way "she always rolled her backside when she moved" —as a signifier of seductive desire, "Granny Naomi herself started calling her a bad girl" (36), revealing at once her complicity in the patriarchal construction of the rape victim and her sexual jealousy of the young woman she calls "June-June." Thus by age eleven, Gwendolen had lost her innocence and her discerning young mind had achieved maturity on two fronts: the importance of a name and the realization that "adults could tell lies and wriggle out of tricky situations, simply because they were respected members of their community" (35).

Gwendolen's adolescent identity crisis intensifies under the seemingly benign paternalism of her father. The larger possibilities of life in England notwithstanding, Winston Brillianton still chokes on his daughter's name, preferring instead to silently savor her remarkable transformation into a blooming woman. He continues to call her "June-June," not to cement the tenuous link between past and present but to conceal his aroused sexual interest in his daughter. In school Gwendolen comes to realize that her identity is not only frozen but is chipped into pieces by the different claims made on her. She is, by turn, "Juney-Juney," "June-June," "Grandolee," and "Grandalew." Sloughing off these commodified selves for the one embodying her birthright constitutes Gwendolen's first act of self-determination in her new environment: "And my name not June-June. My name is Gwendolen, or Gwen. Don't call me no June-June no more" (79).

Gwendolen's act of self-legitimization fails to thwart her father's incestuous desire but it enables her eventual active engagement in her own rescue from the emotional cauldron of incest. For Gwendolen, the process of self-salvation begins with her correct reading of the signs of her incestuous text: her father's sexually provocative playfulness and her mother's distinct discomfort with the social intercourse between father and daughter. The situation is a disturbing throwback to the relationship between her grandmother, Uncle Johnny and herself. The fact that "[a]nger blazed in every word" (87) of the scolding she receives for "laughing with your Daddy" (87) is her clue to be "cautious" and to "tread warily" (89). "[L]ooking at his long-lost daughter with a new eye" (87), Winston sees a woman who could be his wife, a fact proven by Gwendolen's role as "little mother" (118) in the absence of Sonia, the rape act, and his attendant rage for not being "the first" (145).

As she watches her father's sanctimonious demeanor in church the following day, Gwendolen realizes that he is not above contempt and that her recovery from the domestic terrorism to which she has been subjected is entirely in her own hands. She retires into "the shell she had built around herself against in Granville" (146) and there she finds nurturing energy that sustains her through her scandalous pregnancy, her involvement with Emmanuel, her running away from home, her commitment to a mental hospital, her father's suicide, and her mother's eventual discovery of the shameless truth. After setting the record straight with Emmanuel, Gwendolen utters the words that point to a new realm of experience for herself and, possibly, her creator: "I don't think he'll blame himself in the future, when he learns, as I have now done, that nothing is meaningless that is given for the love of another person" (214).

Emecheta's sensitive portrait of Gwendolen may hold the key to her future engagement with the rape victim. Gwendolen's achieved maturity, her ability to surmount a tumultuous passage into adulthood and in the process forge an identity of her own portend well for Emecheta's growing discourse on rape. The inventory of evidence presented in this essay bears all the marks of the author's determination to confront "the absence or gap that is both product and source of textual anxiety, contraction, or censorship"[3] in her narrative representation of rape. Emecheta's novels plot a trajectory that culminates in aggressive opposition to the scourge of women's sexual violation, reconciling ultimately the tensions between nationalism and feminism, acquiescence and protest, silence and voice that mark her effort to write rape. Her skillful negotiation in *The Rape of Shavi* of literal and symbolic rape not only measures the distance she travels from the repressed response to female rape inscribed in her early novels but also pries open the conventions of African rape discourse to admit the woman writer and women's bodies.

NOTES

1. For a male perspective on rape see, for example, Yambo Ouologuem's *Bound to Violence* (New York: Harcourt, Brace, Jovanovich, 1971); Nuruddin Farah's *From a Crooked Rib* (London: Heinemann, 1970); and Ngugi wa Thiong'o's *Devil on the Cross* (Portsmouth, NH: Heinemann, 1982).
2. Florence Stratton discusses in detail the subversive relationship between African male and female writers. See *Contemporary African Literature and the Politics of Gender* (London: Routledge, 1994). Marie Umeh drew my attention to her book after I had written this essay.
3. See *Rape and Representation*, Lynn A. Higgins and Brenda R. Silver, eds. (New York: Columbia University P, 1991).

WORKS CITED

Achebe, Chinua. *Things Fall Apart*. Greenwich, CT: Fawcett Publications, 1959.

Aidoo, Ama Ata. *Changes*. New York: The Feminist Press, 1993.

Anderson, Benedict. *Imagined Communities: Reflections on the Origin and Spread of Nationalism*. London: Verso, 1983.

Armah, Ayi Kwei. *The Beautyful Ones Are Not Yet Born*. London: Heinemann, 1968.

Carby, Hazel. *Reconstructing Womanhood: The Emergence of the Afro-American Woman Novelist.* New York: Oxford University Press, 1987.

Chinweizu, ed. *Voice from Twentieth-Century Africa: Griots and Towncriers.* Boston: Faber and Faber, 1988.

Emecheta, Buchi. *The Bride Price.* New York: George Braziller, 1976.

—-. *Destination Biafra.* London: Allison and Busby Ltd., 1982.

—-. *The Family.* New York: George Braziller, 1989.

—-. *Head Above Water.* London: Fontana, 1986.

—-. *In the Ditch.* London: Barrie and Jenkins, 1972.

—-. *The Joys of Motherhood.* New York: George Braziller, 1979.

—-. *The Rape of Shavi.* New York: George Braziller, 1985.

—-. *Second-Class Citizen.* New York: George Braziller, 1974.

—-. *The Slave Girl.* New York: George Braziller, 1977.

Higgins, Lynn A. and Brenda R. Silver, eds. *Rape and Representation.* New York: Columbia University Press, 1991.

Hove, Chenjerai. *Bones.* London: Heinemann, 1990.

James, Adeola, ed. *In Their Own Voices: African Women Writers Talk.* Studies in African Literature. London: James Currey, 1990.

Kaplan, Louise J. *Female Perversions: The Temptations of Emma Bovary.* New York: Anchor/Doubleday, 1991.

Lees, Sue. Judicial Rape. *Women's Studies International Forum* 16.1 (1993): 11–36.

Ogundipe-Leslie, Molara. "The Female Writer and Her Commitment." *Women in African Literature Today* 15(1987): 5–13.

Shafer, Carolyn M., and Marilyn Frye. "Rape and Respect." In *Women and Values: Readings in Recent Feminist Philosophy.* Ed. Marilyn Pearsall. Belmont, CA: Wadsworth Publishing Co., 1986, 188–96.

Buchi Emecheta, guest speaker celebrating Women's History Month, March, 1991 at John Jay College of Criminal Justice, CUNY.

Desire and The Politics of Control in *The Joys of Motherhood* and *The Family*

Shivaji Sengupta

Desire is a longing which gives life its force. It asserts individuality, changes needs to wants. It is pure energy. In the complex interplay between control, hunger, and anger, desire is the invisible mover. But when I talk of desire in the women of Buchi Emecheta's novels, I am not necessarily talking about desire as Julia Kristeva has discussed it. It is not *jouissance*, the very overflow of desire as it were, carrying with it the notion of fluidity, diffusion, duration. Kristeva's desire is a giving, an expanding, a dispensing of pleasure without concern for end or closure (Kristeva 1980). Kristeva writes about the rich. Emecheta's novels are about poor women who are controlled and exploited by race, colonialism, and sex.

There are two kinds of desire in Buchi Emecheta's novels, *The Joys of Motherhood* (1979) and *The Family* (1990). Nnu Ego,

Gwendolen, and Sonia want to survive. Ona and Adaku want freedom. In both novels Emecheta underscores the importance of the struggle that African women and women of color encounter especially where sexuality and motherhood are concerned. Aware of the exploiting link between sexuality and motherhood, Emecheta's clear message is that being a mother should not be the only reason for women's existence. Making marriage and motherhood the central theme of these two novels, Emecheta shows how women themselves adopt the ideals of motherhood created by men, fall into their traps, and are eventually destroyed.

This paper is about desire and control: about the women of the two novels, the interior and exterior of their struggle for control over their lives. This is not an extraordinary ambition, but it is customarily denied to women of poor and developing countries. In her own life Emecheta has had to battle male-dominated societies to constantly prove herself, to be her own woman. Emecheta's principal female characters toil for the same privileges. Ona refuses to accept wifehood. Nnu Ego lives for motherhood. But neither Ona nor Nnu Ego control their own destiny. Ona's natural instinct is to kick against any confinement. Nnu Ego is more submissive. Both women, despite their different attitudes toward men's control, are eventually destroyed. Ona dies because she realizes that her body was ultimately too frail to contain her free spirit, her father and Agbadi, too powerful. Nnu Ego meets a tragic end because she could not really want anything for herself. Having no personal agenda, not knowing how to negotiate, she died resentful and confused. Only Gwendolen, the protagonist in *The Family*, seemed to have the hunger for finding herself, to gain some control over her life. The complex interaction between hunger, anger, and desire thus becomes critical in any discussion of *The Joys of Motherhood* and *The Family*. I will call it the politics of control.

Think of the two protagonists, Nnu Ego and Gwendolen. Because Gwendolen was a female child, her parents went away to England leaving her behind in Jamaica. As a result, Gwendolen's maturation was stunted. She lacked self-esteem. Nnu Ego was born a victim. Offspring of Agbadi and Ona's lust, she lost her mother when still very young because Ona, a male daughter and therefore nobody's wife, died during her second childbirth. Furthermore, Nnu Ego was a reincarnation of a slave girl whom Agbadi's men killed so that she could accompany his senior wife to her grave. The girl begged for her life and then, struck upon her head with a fatal blow, vowed to return as Agbadi's daughter. Nnu Ego was that daughter. Condemned by her *chi*, her personal god, she would never have happiness and contentment. Nnu Ego wanted to be a mother. Gwendolen wanted her parents' love. Both were violated: Nnu Ego beaten and discarded by her first husband; Gwendolen raped first by a neighbor and then by her own father because all she wanted was affection. Both tried to escape. Nnu Ego attempted suicide after the death of her first child. Gwendolen ran away from her grandmother after the first rape. Each failed and were hauled back to life as it were. In the course of the novels, both get what they want—Nnu Ego babies, Gwendolen her parents—but with cruel twists of fate that constantly make them lose control over their lives. While Nnu Ego represented the male ideal of Nigerian motherhood, living almost entirely for her children, Gwendolen represented the complete effacement of womanhood itself. Until she met her lover, Emmanuel, who was adolescent and white, and became a mother, she was a body without identity. Ironically, if Nnu Ego wanted the "joys of motherhood," for Gwendolen, joy was motherhood, bringing her self-awareness and identity, transforming her from a non-person to woman. In this sense, Emecheta's novels are about searching for one's identity and about the hunger of finding one-self. By contrast, Ona's defining characteristics were anger and passion; Nnu Ego's, resentment.

Hunger comes from being aware of one's own incompleteness; anger is the result of being violated. It comes from injured personal worth, hunger and unfulfillment. In its acute form, hunger is want. Mixed with emotion, it becomes desire. Nnu Ego's hunger was for motherhood. She obtained it at great personal cost. But having fought for something she wanted so desperately, she was dismayed that it amounted to nothing. Ona fought off the powerful Agbadi each time she was transgressed upon, but only as long as her own father was alive. After his death, Ona was not strong enough to look out for herself. Each character suffers extreme transgression. Each deals differently with her anger.

Nnu Ego's anger came from being doomed from her birth, and from not being able to do anything about it. Time and again she has passionate—and hopeless—arguments with her *chi*. From childhood she had heard the stories of her dazzling mother, Ona; she heard that she had neither Ona's beauty nor her brains. Unlike her mother, Nnu Ego grew up to be responsible, took care of her aging father, and accepted timidly the man Agbadi chose to be her husband. Things went downhill from the time she failed to bear a child for her first husband, Amatokwu. Discarded by him, she left without complaint. Without a husband's love she began to slowly shrivel up, until she was married off a second time to Nnaife, a man she did not know and could not respect. She lived with him far away from her village, Ibuza, in the harsh city of Lagos. As much as she hated Nnaife, her second husband, she bore him seven children, three of them sons. Yet Nnaife married again and because they were poor, he slept with his new wife in the same room as Nnu Ego, flaunting his sexual prowess. Nnu Ego was filled with jealousy and hatred but, once again, she steeled her emotions and accepted her 'promotion' to senior wife. Despite achieving motherhood, her hunger for the ordinary dignities of wifehood went unfulfilled. She felt transgressed upon by Nnaife and his new wife. For Nnu Ego nothing was free. Lacking the desire to make anything of her life except achieve motherhood, she was not able to do anything for herself. She felt controlled by men and fate. Aware as she was about her hunger and anger, she ultimately had no real desire except to be alive as someone's wife and mother. Not having a sense of herself as an independent entity, she did not know how to negotiate for herself in a world dominated by men.

Gwendolen was aware of her victimization but she was too afraid to complain. Lacking any sort of moral or intellectual development, Gwendolen was not even capable of being angry at anyone. Fear dominated her. Reduced to living for life's bare necessities, Gwendolen never felt she deserved anything. Whatever she received, the good with the mostly bad, she knew she had to be grateful for. And grateful she was, so that when she was raped by her own father, and made pregnant by him, she suppressed her anger with fear. Gwendolen loved her father who affectionately used to call her June-June. Her rape by him, therefore, was all the more cruel. Still, in the end she was able to negotiate her life through the love and friendship of Emmanuel. Emecheta rescues Gwendolen with Emmanuel's love, and the unfulfilled love Gwendolen had felt for her father was compensated when she had his daughter. Furthermore, she is also able to get some control over her own life. She has her own apartment, a baby, and a friend in Emmanuel.

It may be asked why Emecheta gives Gwendolen what she denies Nnu Ego. The reasons are complex. It has to do with age, location, colonialism, and race. The most obvious is the age. At the end of *The Family*, Gwendolen was still young while by the end of *The Joys of Motherhood* Nnu Ego was a middle-aged woman with nothing to look forward to. But there are other important factors.

We can better appreciate the difference if we compare the condition of Gwendolen with that of her mother, Sonia, a Jamaican woman without an education and living in London. She was past her prime when her husband committed suicide, leaving her with little money and several young children to feed. She thought that her husband had committed suicide because Gwendolen got herself pregnant by a white boy. It was useless being angry at Winston, her dead husband. So she prepared to kill Gwendolen. But looking at her daughter, with her baby girl that looked so much like her husband, she realized that the baby's father was her own husband. She could not kill Gwendolen. Running out into the street howling, she stabbed a garbage bin over and over again. Gwendolen was saved. Sonia was not.

For Nnu Ego, the problem was not only the men in her life, but also poverty and living in the big city of Lagos, where they were but objects of convenience for the British rulers. Thus Nnu Ego did not have the protection of Ona who lived in the village. One of the first points of irritation for Nnu Ego was to see Nnaife slave for the white master and mistress with servility and gratitude. It jarred her conception of manhood. Later, Nnaife also turns out to be financially irresponsible, unable to get a job when his British employers leave. He is picked up without even his knowing it and pushed into military service. Before he or his wife was aware of it, Nnaife is shipped off to India to fight the Germans. In Lagos, the people are simply exploited without the British giving anything back.

In England, when Gwendolen came to live with her parents, it was a different era. Colonialism had given way to post-colonialism. Britain inherited immigrants from the once colonized countries like Jamaica, Nigeria, India, Pakistan, and other Asian countries and by law had to give them the social benefits that she gave her own subjects. Gwendolen was forced to go to school and later, after her nervous breakdown, she was able to get the necessary mental health care. Nnu Ego could not hope for these amenities in Lagos. Sonia was too old to reap these benefits. For them nothing in life is free. They struggle constantly, meeting life head-on as it were, trying to keep their heads above water. It is rather ironic, and not unlike Emecheta's own experience in London, that Gwendolen received better treatment from the British whites than from her own folks. Perhaps this is why she gives Gwendolen a white lover, an adolescent Greek boy, who has not yet formed racial prejudices.

It is apparent from the above discussion that while control is external to the characters, something against which these women had little defense, their struggle was nevertheless to *internalize* that control and take control over their own lives. Ona, Nnu Ego and Sonia were unable to achieve this. Gwendolen was lucky to succeed. Desire, on the other hand, was internal, a cherishing for something that they all harbored. But Gwendolen learned to *externalize* that desire by actively participating in the realization of it. Her decision to make love to Emmanuel and her interest in self-recovery at the mental hospital is proof. Nnu Ego failed to do so. Ona was able to express and externalize her desire but she was overcome with the odds stacked against her. There is thus movement in Buchi Emecheta's characters—a dynamic between the external and the internal. She shows that successful negotiations with life lead to internal control which is, after all, real control. This results in the ability to express desire, to externalize it.

In the rest of this paper I intend to show this movement, or the lack of it, through brief textual readings from the two novels. I intend to show that Emecheta achieves this through a process of signification, i.e., evoking in the reader through plot and images, binary oppositions between the internal and the external, thereby creating a free play of thoughts and images that throw some light on her own literary style. Furthermore, through a study of Emecheta's significations we may also understand the Anglo-Nigerian sensibilities that she has consciously developed throughout her evolution as a writer.

If a powerful symbol of the tension between the internal and external is desire and control, then sex is the energy that sets off the binary opposition. Emecheta shows in these novels that for women of color, sex can be a double-edged sword. On the one hand, it can give pleasure. On the other, in societies where women are oppressed by men, sex can be used as a negotiating tool. Sexuality thus has an important role in Emecheta's novels, not because she supports men's exploitation of women and their use of sex as a way to get some control, but as a process of signification of the complex interplay between desire and control. Emecheta shows Ona, Nnu Ego and Gwendolen in sexual encounters. But in each case, Emecheta describes their sexuality differently. Though they all conceive and become mothers, motherhood itself has different meaning for each. Sex, closely linked with desire, therefore, becomes a controlling factor in their lives.

THE JOYS OF MOTHERHOOD

Let us begin with two portraits, that of Ona and her daughter, Nnu Ego, themselves symbolic of the external and internal. Ona was an outgoing woman, beautiful and brilliant in personality and gait. She dressed flamboyantly, with aggressive suggestions of sexuality. She was her father's only daughter and held complete sway in her household. She tortured the man she loved by denying him control over her life, her only pleasure emanating from seeing Agbadi frustrated. Nnu Ego was an introvert, attractive but not brilliant like her mother. She was also dearly loved by her father but she never tried to control him and dictate her own life. One of the sharpest distinctions between the two women lies in their attitude to sex. Let us read Emecheta's description of Ona:

> One of these mistresses was a very beautiful young woman who managed to combine stubbornness with arrogance. So stubborn was she that she refused to live with Agbadi. Men being what they are, he preferred to spend his free time with her, with this woman who enjoyed humiliating him by refusing to be his wife...She refused to be dazzled with his wealth, his name or his handsomeness. (11)

This was Ona; Ona of the gorgeous waist beads and "mysterious movement," Ona who would "cup her hands to support her breasts," which naked, "swung with health." Always scantily dressed, she gave the impression of being haughty and conservative, "cold as steel...remote." She lived for pleasure and power over her man.

In the following love scene Emecheta shows Ona falling victim to her own snares. Verena Andermatt Conley has written that feminine writing must contain "decipherable libidinal femininity," by which writings by women or about women can be immediately recognized. This can happen either in the depiction of social issues that women can immediately identify with or through a typical woman's point of view. I believe the paragraph describing Ona that has been just quoted is an example of writing that according to Conley, "is said to be feminine." Emecheta explains Agbadi's irrational persistence of Ona even though Ona refuses to be his wife by saying men are what they are. Her description of how Agbadi "tamed" Ona is strangely both masculine and feminine: her description of Agbadi's technique of making love as "masterful" and Ona's craving as "libidinal femininity" (Conley's term). This is how

Emecheta describes Ona and Agbadi's lovemaking. Agbadi was recovering from a near fatal injury he received in one of his hunting expeditions. Emecheta writes:

> Cool night air blew in through the open roof window....He heard a light breathing nearby...Ona was lying there beside him. He watched her bare breasts rising and falling as she breathed...."The heartless bitch. . . I will teach her." He winced as his still sore shoulder protested, but he managed to turn fully on his side and gazed his fill at her....He felt himself burn. Then the anger came to him again as he remembered how many times this young woman had teased and demeaned him sexually. He found himself rolling towards her, giving her nipples gentle lovers' bites, letting his tongue glide down the hollow in the center of her breasts and then back again. He caressed her thigh with his good hand, moving to her small night lappa and fingering her coral waist beads. Ona gasped and opened her eyes. She wanted to scream but Agbadi was faster, more experienced. He slid on his belly, like a trapped animal, but Agbadi was becoming himself again. He was still weak but not weak enough to ignore his desire. He worked on her, breaking down all her resistance. He stroked and explored with his perfect hand, banking heavily on the fact that Ona was a woman, a mature woman who has had him many a time. And he was right. Her struggling and kicking lessened. She started to moan and groan instead, like a woman in labor. He kept on and would not let go, so masterful was he in his art. He knew that he had reduced her to longing and craving for him. He knew he had won. He wanted her completely humiliated in her burning desire. And Ona knew. (19-20)

The conquest is sealed with Ona's total surrender. "Please, I am in pain," she said wanting to be "relieved of the fire inside her." "Yes," comes his confident reply, "I want you to be." (20) Thus Ona is tamed. Extremely passionate lovemaking follows with an intensity that can only be possible when lovers have been separated for a long time. In the grips of lust, Ona shouts and screams in pleasure and in pain, waking up Agbadi's entire household. The intense and wanton love embarrasses Agbadi's senior wife who cannot bear the indignity. Overcome with humiliation and grief, she dies. The power of sex, however, is both killing and life-giving. Agunwa dies; Ona conceives.

We see in the paragraph just quoted a binary opposition between desire and control where both Ona and Agbadi desire and try to control each other. But Emecheta develops several other binary oppositions: Agbadi is both the "trapped animal" and the hunter—he "was becoming himself again." He was weak and not weak. He did not ignore his desire and the effect was that Ona's "struggling and kicking lessened. She started to moan and groan instead."(20) That last word, "instead" suggests a displacement of power. The control has passed from Ona to Agbadi. "Masterful [in] his art," Agbadi "reduces" Ona to "longing and craving." Agbadi wins, completely "humiliating Ona in her burning desire." And finally, as we have seen, the eventful lovemaking results in the ultimate opposition: that of life and death.

Agbadi's triumph was Agunwa's death and Ona's obliteration. She becomes with child but does not want to be Agbadi's wife. When Ona's father dies, she is alone with her baby Nnu Ego and is thus forced to live with Agbadi because she wanted the child's safety. But Agbadi cannot have her for long. Ona dies in her second childbirth. As she lays dying she speaks the truth about their tempestuous relationship: "You see that I am not destined to live with you. But you are stubborn...I am stubborn. Please do not mourn me for long." (28) Her dying wish is a plea for her daughter: "Allow [Nnu Ego] a life of her own...allow her to be a woman." (28)

It is this baby girl, Nnu Ego, that we see as we open the first pages of the book. Nnu Ego is now a woman of twenty-five. We see her in flight. We do not know what the flight is about, only that it is a running away from something. We are conscious of a young woman running blindly:

Nnu Ego backed out of the room, her eyes unfocussed and glazed, looking into vacancy. Her feet were light and she walked as if in a daze, not conscious of using those feet. She collided with the door, moved away from it and across the veranda, on to the green grass that formed part of the servants' quarters. The grass was moist with dew under her bare feet. Her whole body felt the hazy mist in the

air and part of her felt herself brushing against the
white master's washing on the line. This made her
whirl around with a jerk, like a puppet reaching the
end of the string. She now faced the road, having
decided to use her eyes, her front instead of her back.
She ran, her feet lighter still, as if her eyes now that
she was using them gave her extra lightness. She ran
past the master's bungalow, past the side garden, and
shot into the untarred gravel road; her senses were
momentarily stunned by the color of the road which
seemed to be that of blood and water. She hurried on
beyond this short road that led to the big tarred one,
ran like someone pursued, looking behind her only
once to make sure she was not being followed. She
ran as if she would never stop. (7)

Nnu Ego never did stop. Her only son had just died. Stunned into
silence, about the only thing she could do was to run. Her eyes
were "unfocussed... glazed ...looking into vacancy." *Looking* into
vacancy is fraught with irony. With the death of her only child, her
life itself was empty with nothing to fill her up. Since she was driv-
en away from her first husband, Amatokwu's home, she had been
empty until Nnaife impregnated her. Nnu Ego remembered the
pleasure Amatokwu gave her, gliding in easily into her anticipat-
ing body. By contrast, Nnaife's lovemaking was crude and hungry,
intensely passionate with no desire. Nnu Ego only suffered through
it, waiting for him to finish. But it was Nnaife who impregnated
her, not Amatokwu. Becoming a mother, and that too of a son, Nnu
Ego easily forgave her husband and forgot Amatokwu. The son
enveloped her life. And now this! Her life, like her eyes, was suddenly vacant. No one was in. Still she ran, not even conscious of
using her feet, until she was knocked against the door, against the
master's washing line. "This made her whirl around, *like a puppet
reaching the end of its string*." She ran "her feet lighter still," as if her
eyes had given them an extra lightness. The lightness of her feet
rushed her toward the darkness of death. She would soon be there,
under the deep, black water of the river. There she would meet her
chi and she would ask her why she had punished her so. She knew
that her *chi* was a woman, "only a woman would be so thorough in
punishing another. She was now going to her, to talk it over with
her, not on this earth but in the land of the dead"(9).

But Nnu Ego does not die. We catch a fleeting glimpse of the twenty-five year old wife, crazily aware of "the color of the road...blood and water." Blood and water: two words that probably sum up her whole life. The blood was that of the slave girl whose incarnation was Nnu Ego. She had to bear the guilt of her father's murder of the slave girl, and of her mother's lust: "Out damn'd spot! Out I say!" All the perfume of Arabia would not take away the smell of the slave girl's blood. No matter how much she ran toward that still dark water she could not reach her *chi*. Her *chi*, the slave girl, awaits, deep under water. In this flight then we may see the microcosm of Nnu Ego's life and struggle. As we know, she does not die at this point. The running was a running away from everything, especially her failed transaction with Nnaife: sex for babies. She could not keep her motherhood; hence, the flight.

A reading of the passage just quoted reveals Nnu Ego as merely the plaything of fate: part of her brushed against the white master's washing line; *this made her whirl around with a jerk, like a puppet reaching the end of the string.* At every turning point in Nnu Ego's life she is made to "whirl around with a jerk." She was turned out of her first husband's house; married to Nnaife; the death of the baby; attempted suicide; beginning life anew; becoming a mother again; Nnaife's second marriage; more babies; Nnaife's departure for India to fight the "Germans;" the return of Nnaife, and so it goes on. Not one of these events were brought about proactively by Nnu Ego, except for the sexual barter with Nnaife. I am not suggesting that as Nnaife's wife, she was in a position to bargain with sex in the way Ona, her mother, used to do with Agbadi. As his wife, Nnu Ego was supposed to sleep with him. But since Nnu Ego wanted to be a mother desperately, she made a conscious decision to *receive* Nnaife's hypersexuality not only without complaint but also with expectation. Emecheta describes Nnu Ego's first sexual encounter with Nnaife:

> He demanded his marital right as if determined not to give her a chance to change her mind. She had thought she would be allowed to rest on the first night after her arrival before being pounced upon by this hungry man, her new husband. After such an experience, Nnu Ego knew why horrible looking men raped women, because they were aware of their inadequacy. This one worked himself to an animal passion. She was sure he had never seen a woman before. She bore it and relaxed as she had

been told, pretending that the person lying on her was Amatokwu, her first sweetheart of a husband. This man's appetite was insatiable, and by morning she was so weary she cried with relief...She felt humiliated, but what was she to do?....She was used to her long wiry Amatokwu who would glide inside her when she was ready, not this short, fat stocky man, whose body almost crushed hers. What was more, he did not smell healthy either, unlike men in Ibuza who had the healthy smell of burning wood and tobacco. This one smelt all soapy, as if he was over-washed. (44)

As a satisfied Nnaife leaves for work, Emecheta writes: 'O my *chi*,' she prayed as she rolled painfully to her other side of the raffia bed. 'O my dead mother, I will be his faithful wife and put up with his crude ways and ugly appearance...If I should become pregnant...'(45) Dreaming of her baby, Nnu Ego falls asleep.

Thus, Nnu Ego uses consciously the only leverage she has. She accepts Nnaife's sexual enthusiasm in the hope of becoming a mother. The hunger for motherhood creates the desire, not for sex per se, but for using sex for the purpose of barter and negotiations. With the baby, Nnu Ego hopes, she would be restored to the position of respect that her first husband never could give her. Her desire, essentially internal, is still very subdued. But Emecheta never really allows Nnu Ego the luxury of enjoying sex. After her fourth child, Nnaife marries again. The arrival of the new wife signals the end of sex as barter for Nnu Ego. Although she had more children, the rest of her life did not change very much. She was the mother of seven children, three of them boys. But her life ends tragically. Ill and mentally unstable, she dies alone on a street.

The Joys of Motherhood is a post-colonial novel in which the demise of the protagonist highlights exploitation involving gender and race. Through the story of Nnu Ego, a thrice-marginalized woman, we witness the politics of control upon a woman whose ego, hunger, and anger were eventually squashed. She could never externalize her desire. Whatever she bartered for, trying to get a semblance of control in her life, came to naught.

As an Indian-American reader, I find comparisons between *The Joys of Motherhood* and an Indian short story written in Bengali by Mahesweta Devi, called *The Breast Giver*. It is a story about a Bengali wet-nurse—the breast-giver—who works for a wealthy family, nursing its many wives' babies so that the young mothers can keep their figures. In order to stay "wet," however, the wet-nurse had to have numerous children, so many that she literally lost count. In the end the breast-giver has breast cancer and is promptly "retired" by her employers. As she slowly dies in the hospital, conscious of her life ebbing away, she hallucinates about all her children and milk-children being at her side. She dies alone, anonymous. The last rites are performed by government employees.

Both Nnu Ego and the breast-giver nurse rear children, giving their breasts to newborns. Both serve important economic functions, but are exploited to the fullest by relatives and strangers alike. Neither of them have the slightest idea of where each is heading. Their respective stories end with their deaths amidst outsiders.

Writing about Third World novels, Gayatri Chakravorty Spivak observes that the poor people of the Third World nations have not benefitted from the independence of their countries. This is because "the elite culture of nationalism participated and participates with the colonizer in various ways...we witness the ruins of parliamentary democracy and of the nation when bequeathed to the elite of a colonized people"(Spivak, 245). Whatever the progress that nationalists claim to usher in, it does not make much difference to the Nnu Egos and the wet-nurses of these poor nations. Not only do these "national" changes not touch them, in many instances they are absolutely ignorant of the politics engulfing their country. Nnu Ego and Nnaife, for instance, have no idea why Nnaife has to go to India to fight for the British against the "Germans," or even where India is in the first place. I think it is for these reasons that I am persuaded that a uniform, international feminist movement is almost impossible. The likes of Kristeva will find it very difficult to empathize with the Indian breast-giver or with Nnu Ego. But for Buchi Emecheta it is another story. She *has* to try to show in *The Joys of Motherhood* that despite the poverty, Nnu Ego, like Ona, could have tried to exert her personality, to wrest some of the control from the outside and internalize it, to give vent to her desire and externalize it so that the men in her life would at least know what she wanted. Instead, she dies living only for her children. She dies alone on a street when she is no longer needed. To both Nnu Ego and the breast-giver, sex was not something to be enjoyed. It was a social and economic tool, not "the very overflow of desire ...a dispensing of pleasure without concern for end or closure" (Kristeva, 248).

THE FAMILY

Let us look at the circumstances and the manner in which
Gwendolen was raped the first time by her neighbor, Uncle Johnny.
This was an elderly man, about Gwendolen's grandmother's age
who was almost fifty years old when Gwendolen's mother, Sonia,
left for England to join her husband. Johnny was a family friend
who had known Gwendolen from the time she was born. After her
parents' departure, Johnny and Granny often got together in the
evenings to share a bottle (or two) of rum. Gwendolen, sleeping in
the same room, used to hear them talk and drink, thinking about
her parents in England, wondering whether she will ever be sent
for as her mother had promised. Let Emecheta take it from here:

> One such night, she dozed off however, but was
> woken by Uncle Johnny. He was kneeling on the
> bamboo bed. He was touching her face and mouth,
> telling her not to cry, that he was here to take care
> of her. She struggled to get up, but he shushed
> her....The hand Uncle Johnny kept on her mouth
> was firm, but his other hand touched all her body,
> as if Uncle Johnny had four hands instead of two.
> His breath smelt of rum....He put his hand under
> the bed clothes and tickled her with his fingers...and
> shock froze all her emotions. Was this the man with
> the iron grip over her mouth the same Uncle
> Johnny who used to bring her...sweets and lemon-
> ade drinks?...Was this Uncle Johnny who used to
> rub oil on her grazed knee?...who used to call her
> Juney-Juney?...What was the matter with Uncle
> Johnny tonight? She wanted very much to ask him
> what he was doing, but she could not: his hand was
> firmly over her mouth and she could not struggle
> because her body was frozen. Only her eyes roamed
> and it was dark. He was on top of her. She almost
> suffocated, but he soon rolled to one side. 'Your
> Mammy gone na England to join your Daddy. Dem
> no want you dere, but me look after you,
> right?...This our secret, right? Don't tell nobody,
> because they'll say you're a bad gal. You'll do any-
> thing for your Uncle Johnny, not so, Juney-
> Juney?'...His voice was hoarse, his breath came and
> went and the sickly smell of rum escaped every

time he opened his mouth. Gwendolen could listen
no more. She struggled out of his hands and rushed
into the dark backyard. Her inside burned and she
felt sore...'Mammy, why you no take me with
you?'(21-22)

Needless to say, Gwendolen was raped at an age when she knew
little about sexual desire. The dominating feelings in this passage
are fear and confusion, mixed with physical pain and a tremendous sense of a child's insecurity whose parents have left her:
'Mammy, why you no take me to England with you?' Imagine an
eight year old girl waking up, being touched on the face and mouth
by an 'uncle' she has known all her life. She cried and she struggled to get up, only to be gripped in the face with an iron hand.
Uncle Johnny had four hands, touching her all over, the same
Uncle Johnny who has nursed her wounds in the past, giving her
candies, the same Uncle Johnny who was her grandmother's best
friend. The first thing this Uncle Johnny tells the eight-year-old
girl after the rape is that her parents will never again fetch for her,
that she was to tell no one what happened this time or "they'll think
you're a bad gal." (22) Gwendolen's insides burnt with the rape.
Outside, she was numb with fear. But I think what she felt the most
was a terrible sense of isolation: *her parents did not want her.*

Gwendolen had other problems which were exacerbated now
with the rape. Possibly because of insecurity, she was given to bed-
wetting, a source of deep shame to her. It was a secret that the little girl went all out to protect, to the extent that she wouldn't argue
with her peers lest they taunt her about this embarrassing occurrence. After the rape, the bed-wetting increased, exposing her to
her grandmother's wrath and causing intense guilt and shame.
Uncle Johnny continued to visit, drink rum with her grandmother, and continued to take Gwendolen's little body after the old
woman was soused with drink. He also threatened Gwendolen that
he would tell all her friends about her bed-wetting if she told on
him. Thus Gwendolen was confronted with probably the worst
dilemma of her young life: should she tell her grandmother? Apart
from Uncle Johnny's threat, would Granny even believe her,
believe that she was innocent? She doubted very much. Besides,
there was work to do on the farm, from morning to night. Uncle
Johnny was always with them, helping the grandmother who was,
in turn, grateful beyond words to this man. "Gwendolen could find
no time to tell Granny what happened that night. So she pushed it

from her mind...."(23) The rapes continued to happen, night after night. Because of her age, she got no pleasure out of it. But she was learning to give pleasure, hating it all the time.

The second person to rape Gwendolen was her father, Winston. Having finally fulfilled her dream to join her parents in England, Gwendolen came to live with them when she was eleven. For three years she was very happy despite the heavy daily chores she shared with her mother, Sonia, to look after the brothers and maintain their tiny apartment. Then Granny died and Sonia had to return to Jamaica and stayed there for two years.

Her father Winston was a part-time preacher at the Sunday church. There, and in his work, he had made friends with other Africans and Caribbean men. They talked to each other about their customs and cultures. Winston had many erroneous and weird notions about Nigerians. One of them was that Nigerian men married their daughters. His Nigerian friend, Ilochina, emphatically corrected his error, narrating to him legends full of sensations which forbade incest in their culture. Winston, though, still wondered about it.

Meanwhile, Gwendolen had grown to be sixteen years old. Emecheta writes:

> Gwendolen was so playful. She would walk about the house with her flimsy gym slip on and when amused she would lift her leg up and laugh out loud, like a woman teasing a lover. And she was sixteen. Her young bosom taunted him. What could he do? He was not drunk. He just went into her, hoping she would fight him off like any other woman. Because she was like any other woman to him. She was almost grown before she came back into his life. He tried to equate this young and vibrant person with the baby he kissed goodbye years back in Jamaica, but could not. Cheryl was his biological and social daughter. But somehow, Gwendolen was only a biological one and he never really felt socially responsible for her. She looked so much like her mother...She was like another person, yet the type of woman he favored, small, vulnerable, and just like Sonia. And like this other woman he expected her to fight him off. After all women were expected to do that—ward men off....

But Gwendolen remembered Uncle Johnny. He had said to her, 'Every gal done it. Dat's why they're girls.' She remembered too that you got into trouble with the old women, if you should tell them. But she wished her father would not ask her to do this. She could not scream, because though he begged, he covered her mouth with that strong hand of his. It was soon over. (44-45)

It is worth noticing that while the first rape by Uncle Johnny was narrated from the perspective of the little girl, in this one, Emecheta gives us both perspectives. Lacking the common explanation of being drunk, Winston gives the classical male excuse: women should ward men off. He quite forgot that Gwendolen was not a woman yet. Other reasons why he approached his daughter were because she used to walk about in flimsy gym slips, that she was growing up to be a woman; and, significantly, she looked like Sonia, her mother, "the type of woman he favored, small, vulnerable, just like Sonia"(144). The next sentence is indicative of the times he was denied by Sonia. "Like this other woman," he expected to be turned back in his approach. But, Emecheta says, "He was not prepared for the look of resignation on Gwendolen's face"(144). And he was also not prepared for something else: the way Gwendolen let him take her made him aware that she was not a virgin. He did not know that "She had been taught. In this project she was already adept, much older than her age." Furious that his daughter was not a virgin when he took her, he called her a bitch, "wicked gal, devil gal"(145). He came to the swift and convenient conclusion that "The girl was stupid"(144). With cruel irony, Emecheta narrates the events of the morning after:

The following day was a Sunday. It took her a long time to get ready for church. When her father Winston started to preach about the sins of the world, she wondered if her father did not know that what he did to her last night was a grave sin. She looked at him as if in a daze. Something was telling her that this man, though her father whom she loved dearly, was not going to get away with it. The pain was too deep to surface. Uncle Johnny was a stupid old man. But what of her lovely Daddy? To her, he was dead now.... (145-46)

243

Gwendolen's second rape caused a total reversal of her life. Hitherto, she had been coming along nicely, leaving the terrible poverty and rape behind, going to school, learning slowly. Gwendolen went back to the shell she had built around herself against adults in Granville. After the rape she started missing school. "What was the point?" She began to realize that adults were poor, cynical and vicious. The rape created a second—and abnormal—separation and individuation process in her life. She began to realize that she was separate from her Mammy and Daddy. Her mother had left her to danger twice. Her father raped her.

Gwendolen became pregnant. And around the same time she made an acquaintance with Emmanuel, the adolescent Greek boy who became her friend and lover. After the rape, Winston stayed mostly silent which was both intimidating and relieving for Gwendolen. She pretty much did what she wanted, dropped out of school, stayed indoors and tried to hide her condition. Then she met her new friend. Winston saw this and allowed it, even encouraged his daughter to mix with him, hoping that if they got sexually involved, he would be able to blame the pregnancy on Emmanuel. Soon the young adolescent couple made love. This is the only lovemaking scene that Emecheta describes in her two novels that is an unconditional joy to the female partner. Ona, in *The Joys of Motherhood*, enjoyed sex, but also used it to hold power against Agbadi. Nnu Ego enjoyed sex with Amatokwu but Emecheta does not describe their lovemaking and emphasizes the fact that Nnu Ego could not conceive with him. Emecheta's description of Nnaife's making love to Nnu Ego was, to Nnu Ego, more like making war, a rape. In *The Family*, the author has described two rapes. But finally, Gwendolen has been having a good time with someone, Emmanuel. She enjoys going for walks and hanging around cheap restaurants with him. Then one night, opportunity comes. Gwendolen takes him home. Winston is awake but says nothing, for after all, this was an opportunity for him too. Emecheta narrates:

> ...at first [they] simply giggled. They felt triumphant in having cheated the adult world all evening. Gwendolen had seen sex scenes on television. She used to wonder why people seem to like it. From her limited experience, sex was a humiliation in which women had to give in to their men just to make them happy. Her stay in England had taught her she could refuse. With her Daddy she was too

> stunned to say a word. Emmanuel was different. With him it was a play. It was an escape from reality. She pushed to the very back of her mind the knowledge of her pregnancy. They played, they fondled. And the fact that they were mildly drunk made things easier still...'Lawd, white boy. You very good. You perfect. You're loving.' Gwendolen was almost sobbing now. She would have liked him to go on like this, just living like this...Why should life not be this simple? She jolted herself back to reality...Tears were running from her eyes now. (155-6)

"Playing, fondling, very good, perfect, loving," these are some of the things Gwendolen felt with Emmanuel. Emecheta presents this opportunity to her, at first, as an escape from reality. But with the joy of sex for once preceding the "joys" of motherhood in importance (Gwendolen pushed the knowledge of her pregnancy to the back of her mind), other significant things happen. In the ecstasy of making love, other barriers seem to recede: "to send to hell all her worries about education, about race, you brown, you white and me black; and to say 'so what' about her pregnancy"(156). The seeds of Gwendolen's personality and identity had been sown. Emmanuel had brought her love.

As I have argued in the first section of this essay, from here on, including the nervous breakdown, Gwendolen was on her way to recovery. With the help of proper mental care, through love and friendship, and her baby, she would find her self-identity. She would learn to externalize desire by expressing love, by transforming external control of her, and by developing internal control. The first indication came when she refused to have an abortion, refused to give up her baby for adoption. She managed her friendship with Emmanuel with love. Then with the birth of her baby girl, her *father's girl*, Gwendolen's metamorphosis was complete. There was no shame, no guilt. When finally Gwendolen sees her mother after a long absence of running away from her, she is altogether a different woman. Sonia saw "Gwendolen standing there, a grown woman in a white running suit, carrying a tray full of tea-things. She placed the tray on a plain pine table...and ran to her mother"(237). The baby's name, Sonia discovers, is Iyamide meaning 'my mother is here.' Gwendolen had lost her father even before he died. But through him, she discovered her mother.

NOTES

1. The phrase 'politics of control' assumes that control itself is the result of a dynamic between the controller and controlled. Human nature both tries to control and break control by others. Elsewhere, I have called this phenomenon the politics of prohibition. It is my contention that literature teaches us both to exert control over others and to break that control. See my introduction to *A Critical Edition of Dryden's MacFlecknoe* and *Absalom and Achitophel*.
2. I am grateful to my colleague, Ana Maldonado, for asking me this question, a question that cleared up many issues for me while reading these novels.
3. See Verena Andermatt Conley, *Helene Cixous*, pp. 129-161.
4. *The Joys of Motherhood*. All references, cited in the text, are from this edition, unless otherwise stated.
5. See translation by Gayatri Chakravorty Spivak in her *In Other Worlds: Essays in Cultural Politics*, pp. 220-240.
6. *The Family*. All references, cited in the text, are from this edition, unless otherwise stated.

WORKS CITED

Conley, Verena Andermatt. *Helene Cixous: Writing Feminine*. Lincoln: University of Nebraska Press, 1984.

Emecheta, Buchi. *The Family*. New York: George Braziller, 1990.

—. *The Joys of Motherhood*. New York: George Braziller, 1979.

Kristeva, Julia. *Desire in Language*. New York: Columbia University Press, 1980.

Sengupta, Shivaji. *A Critical Edition of John Dryden's MacFlecknoe and Absalom and Achitophel*. New Delhi: Konark Press, 1991.

Spivak, Gayatri Chakravorty. *In Other Worlds: Essays in Cultural Politics*. New York: Routledge, 1987.

PART FOUR
READING EMECHETA—
THE POETIC VOICE(S)

This section, "Reading Emecheta—The Poetic Voice(s)," brings together four papers with varied approaches that reveal the devices and fictive elements on which the novels of Buchi Emecheta hinge. The paper by Ernest N. Emenyonu on "Technique and Language in Buchi Emecheta's *The Bride Price, The Slave Girl* and *The Joys of Motherhood*" is a stylistic study of Emecheta's narrative art. Emenyonu identifies the anthropological posturings of *The Bride Price*; the improved mastery of the novel form in *The Slave Girl*, especially in the use of irony; and the blend of subject matter as well as the technique and language in *The Joys of Motherhood*. This critic insists that in *The Joys of Motherhood*, the novelist's "figurative expressions have also acquired rhythmic and incantatory cadences that reveal in the process an emerging affinity with, and an awareness of the imaginative techniques of the traditional African artists whose language was characterized by its undertones, its subtlety and its direct purposeful appeal to a particular audience." On the other hand, Abioseh M. Porter in his essay, "*Second-Class Citizen*: The Point of Departure for Understanding Buchi Emecheta's Major Fiction," emphasizes that "as a novel of personal development, *Second-Class Citizen* is quite successful in the depiction of Adah's growth from the initial stage of naivete and ignorance to her final stage of self-realization and independence." Porter concludes by asserting that Emecheta's novel loses some of its strength because of the way it is inadequately structured "by the author's blatant intrusion to pour what looks like personal venom into the text." However, he adds that notwithstanding "these minor blemishes, *Second-Class Citizen* can and should be seen as a powerful example of the *Bildungsroman* in African fiction" and that "the novelist's sustained attention to the themes of individual growth, progress, development and the coherence of selfhood—all of which have pervaded her later writings and for which she received genuine and well-deserved critical acclaim—have their roots in this early piece." In effect, the critics of Emecheta's novels appear to accept a basic fact—Emecheta's growth as a novelist.

Similarly, M.J. Daymond in "Buchi Emecheta, Laughter and Silence: Changes in the Concepts of 'Woman,' 'Wife,' and 'Mother'" centers her discussion on the tropes of silence and laughter in *The Joys Of Motherhood* in order to propose that "if silence is a chosen part of a woman's speech, as it is in Nnu Ego's case, then the matter is different, then the subversion of misogynistic practices and the possible opening of a female linguistic range can be achieved by imagining the way a woman's laughter or her silence helps to do this." With Emecheta's protagonist, Nnu Ego, what is achieved should be liberating for all users of language. But the conflicts and contradictions she highlights in both the criticism of Emecheta's novel and in the novel itself illuminate the tensions ever present between creative writing and the reading of it. Nevertheless this paper also assures us that Emecheta has developed in a positive way.

In "Language and Gender Conflict in Buchi Emecheta's *Second-Class Citizen*" by Obododimma Oha, there is a critical extension of that idea of growth as he answers the self-imposed questions on the types of linguistic choices the main characters make, their verbal interactions, the nature of rhetorical display and its relationship to the internal cross-sex discourse, the presuppositions underlying the text and the implications of context for male-female relations. Oha further clarifies the issue of technique and language, although the preceding essay by Abioseh M. Porter provides an appropriate juxtapository view. All the same, the conclusion of Oha that Emecheta (the writer) "is as guilty as Francis (the character) in the offensive and gendered uses of language" means that "she is guilty of the very offense she is criticizing in *Second-Class Citizen*." In sum, the issue of language and gender conflict which he portrays in the study definitely appears cogent. Undoubtedly, these papers portray various ways of reading Buchi Emecheta.

Ezenwa-Ohaeto

*Marie Umeh and Buchi Emecheta at Fairleigh
Dickinson University in 1992.*

Technique and Language in Buchi Emecheta's *The Bride Price, The Slave Girl,* and *The Joys of Motherhood*

Ernest N. Emenyonu

> In the British Museum I'm classified as an English
> writer writing about Africa because of my language
> which they feel is different from other African writ-
> ers. They claim that I write as if English is my first
> language.[1]

The Nigerian novelist Buchi Emecheta, who until recently was little known by Nigerian readers, has become black Africa's most prolific female writer in the second half of the twentieth century. Her
works include books for children, plays for the radio and television, some poetry and nine major novels, *In the Ditch* (1972),
Second-Class Citizen (1974), *The Bride Price* (1976), *The Slave Girl*
(1977), *The Joys of Motherhood* (1979), *Destination Biafra* (1981),
Naira Power (1981), *Double Yoke* (1981) and *The Rape of Shavi* (1983).

Her autobiography, *Head Above Water*, was published in 1986. Recipient of a number of literary awards including the Jock Campbell Award (1987), Emecheta has become a powerful and influential feminine voice not only on the African scene but in the entire Third World. The lot of the African woman is Buchi Emecheta's thematic preoccupation and the picture is nothing to smile about. The educated working-class African woman is not an exception to the subjugation of cruel and derisive social forces. Many of the reflections in Emecheta's novels are of her own life and the lives of people close to and around her. She asserts that the events that found her "in the ditch" and submerged her humiliatingly as a "second-class citizen" are "90% autobiographical."[2] Through the events in her personal life, Emecheta articulates the oppression, predicament, and precariousness of African women, whom she characteristically refers to as "peasant women."

The themes of liberation, feminism, and African womanhood are favorite topics of critics and scholars of Buchi Emecheta's fiction. This paper is a shift from a thematic emphasis to a stylistic study of Emecheta's narrative art, with particular reference to her use of language in three of her novels—*The Bride Price* which launched her career as a writer, *The Slave Girl*, and *The Joys of Motherhood* which many critics agree is, so far, her best novel. In these works, Emecheta's narrative technique is evident in her profuse use of the figurative language, omniscient comments, and irony, which she employs to set the mood and tone of the story as well as to define the theme and characters of the novel. In *The Bride Price*, the awkward handling of language manifests Emecheta's amateurish beginnings. In *The Slave Girl*, Emecheta demonstrates in her language usage the promise of artistic talent whose highest maturity and development are evident in *The Joys of Motherhood*. Language is an important aspect of Emecheta's fiction. She says that her "attitude and language is very English"[3] and believes that much of her international acclaim is because of her "language which they feel is different from other African writers."

Unlike many contemporary African writers, Buchi Emecheta is unequivocal about her audience. According to her, "I write about Africa for the Western world and at the same time Africa for Americans."[4] This emphasis on describing Africa for a Western audience is most evident in *The Bride Price*, her first novel. "When I write," she says, "I look for a problem in a certain society and I write about that problem strictly from a woman's point of view."[5]

The "certain society" that Emecheta writes about in *The Bride*

Price is Ibuza, an Igbo-speaking community of Bendel State in Nigeria, which happens to be Emecheta's home. The major problem she depicts therein is that of a tortured and dehumanized womanhood. The female in the novel is portrayed as an empty shell, pitied by some but mocked by most. Men, a cruel society and a blind culture join in an unholy alliance to despise and abuse the female in their midst. The woman has little chance in her efforts at co-existence with men, who are beasts in Buchi Emecheta's literary perception. Alone, despite the predicament of all her kind, the woman is capable of rational judgement and genuine love. She is guided by her intuition and feminine discretion. But whenever she comes in contact with man, the weaker opposite sex, she is driven to the point of mental and psychological paralysis. A reviewer has pointed out that Emecheta's portrait of men in her fiction is invariably "one-sided and flat." The woman symbolized by the author in her omniscient role "is ultimately innocent, more sinned against that sinning....She is always drawing our attention to other people's failures and weaknesses in life, while her own life is adorned with guilelessness. She is always suffering but never causes pain."[6] Emecheta's male characters, on the other hand, are generally villains, at best caricatures.

Contemporary African writing has often incorporated proverbs, sayings, aphorisms, witticisms, and humorous anecdotes within the mainstream of the narratives. The African color and setting of each work is thus established without recourse to gratuitous cultural delineations which often bore the reader. In *The Bride Price*,[7] this is not the case. In an attempt to establish authentic "Africaness" for the setting of the novel, Emecheta allows several scenes in the course of the narrative to degenerate into anthropological digressions. For instance, in the early pages of the novel, a reference to an auntie as "your little mother," said to a little girl, evokes the following explanation of "big mothers" and "small mothers" in the Igbo polygamous family system:

> To the Ibos and some Yorubas in Nigeria, a natural mother is not a child's only mother. A grandmother may be known as the "big mother" or the "old mother," and one's actual mother may be called "little mother," if her mother or mother-in-law is still alive. The title is extended to all young aunts or elder sisters, in fact to any young female who helps in mothering the child. Ibuza is a town where every-

body knows everybody else, so a child ends up having so many mothers, so many fathers, that in some cases the child may not see much of his true parents. This is much encouraged because not only does the child grow up knowing many people and thinking well of them but also the natal parents' tendency to spoil their off-spring is counteracted. It is very important that a child is the child of the community. (36—37)

Later in the course of the narrative, the author mentions "age groups" while talking about the different social organizations in the town, Ibuza. This draws out another lecture as follows:

Age groups were created at three-year intervals, each one characterized by an important incident. (Children [sic] born at that time grow into adolescence; they will hold meetings, organize dances, in the big market; they might have special dances which will take years of practice for the Christmases of their youth or the Ifejioku yams festivals.) (100)

Shortly after this passage, Emecheta indulges in one of her many literal translations of Igbo words. After a reference to the River Niger "eating children," the author gratuitously adds:

The Ibo people would never say that a victim had drowned but that he or she had been eaten by the river, for underpinning such an event was the belief that every river had a goddess who could do with one or two human sacrifices from time to time. (101)

Similarly, at the mention of akpu in an earlier scene, the author felt obliged to explain the nature of cassava (63). The reference of *Osu* (note the inconsistency in its spelling: it is osu on p. 91, *oshu* on pp. 106 and 107) equally draws out a commentary on cultural taboos.

But if she was forced to live with these people for long, she would soon die, for that was the intention behind all the taboos and customs. Anyone who contravened them was better dead. If you tried to hang on to life, you would gradually be helped towards death by psychological pressures. And when you were dead, people would ask: Did we not say so?

Nobody goes against the laws of the land and survives. (141)

A similar mention of "night games" among boys and girls had also
triggered off this explanation:

Their custom allowed this. Boys would come into the
mothers' hut and play at squeezing a girl's breasts
until they hurt; the girl was supposed to try as much
as possible to ward them off and not be bad-tempered
about it. So long as it was done inside the hut where
an adult was near, and so long as the girl did not let
the boy go too far, it was not frowned on. (97)

These digressions slow down the pace of the narrative and portray
the author as the eager anthropologist anxious to unravel the intricacies of her culture to an alien world.

In this book, too, many of the author's figurative expressions
are trite and flat. Breasts are "as large as huge pumpkins" (38); a
child is "as fat as a plump yam" (112); one of the characters, Okolie
"croaked like a frog with a bad cold" (113). Another character
"padded slowly towards the door, like a duck carrying a ruptured
egg" (129), and Chike's father's neck "seemed to be swelling like
an African snail coming out of its shell" (86). One character's chest
"was heaving up and down like a disturbed sea" (138), while a
female character looked "like a young widow in an old lappa" (154).
Another character "gnashed his teeth like a squirrel cracking nuts."
(95) There are such bland expressions as "the girls' laughter was
like the sound of clear bells on a Christmas morning" (109), "little
sufferer" (164), and "too bright to be earthly" (166). In several other
places in the book the author's narrative method lacks clarity and
originality. This is how Emecheta describes Aku-nna's first glimpse
of the forest near her new home:

The landscape changed slightly after Benin. The soil
was redder, the leaves were that type of deep green
which suggests a tinge of black. The forests became
really dense like mysterious groves. Here you saw
a narrow footpath like a red ribbon winding itself
into the mysterious depths. There you saw a human
figure emerge as it were from a secret green retreat,
carrying on her head a bunch of ripe, blood-coloured
palm fruits. . . . (60)

The images in this passage are stale and trite and do not invigorate the narrative. 'A road like a ribbon,' 'mysterious groves,' 'secret retreats' are dull and over sentimental. Yet occasionally, Emecheta shows exceptional skill as when she says that Chike made love to young Aku-nna "as gently as if she were an egg that might crack at any touch" (161), or when she says, while casting her slur on polygamy, that "there were men who would go about raping virgins of thirteen and fourteen, and still expect the women they married to be as chaste as flower buds" (84).

Emecheta is not very successful either in her use of dialogue in *The Bride Price*. Very often the subject of conversation is incongruous as when Ngbeke informs her young children: "I am the woman who taught your father what a woman tastes like. I disvirgined your father and he disvirgined me. And I gave birth to you" (76). After this it is not surprising when the children want to know from their mother who their father has been making love to—"Has our father not slept with her mother?" (77)— which prompts the author to add a rather later rider that the inquisitive children had forgotten, "that they were not supposed to let their mother know, since such matters were not for women to discuss." This lack of judgement in conversational propriety has its climax in the scene where Ngbeke disparages Aku-nna while still on the subject of sex with Aku-nna's half-brothers:

> I don't see any strength in that girl. Can you see her
> bearing children, that one? Her hips are so narrow,
> and she has not even started to menstruate yet; we
> are not even sure yet that she is a woman. Look at
> your sister— they are of the same age, and she start-
> ed almost a year ago. Had it not been that I asked
> your father to wait until she is fifteen, she could
> have been married off during the last yam festi-
> val...because she was born here, because she is my
> daughter, because I don't put her in frocks and teach
> her to wag her bottom when she walks. . . . (78)

This type of passage portrays the author as either unable to use language befitting certain situations and characters, or unable to develop the right ear for the right type of conversation, or both. In contrast Emecheta is unrivalled in her mastery of language and control of her subject in the passage where she describes with acute sensitivity Aku-nna's first experience of her maturity into womanhood. The inexperienced Aku-nna was on the school premises when the event came upon her, and of all people, it was her adult male teacher who noticed and came to her rescue. Emecheta's handling of the episode makes the complex situation seem natural and simple. This is part of the passage:

> She swirled round quickly, looked and saw that there was blood smeared on a part of the hem of her dress. At first she was frightened, thinking that she had hurt herself. Then common sense took over, and she knew what was happening to her. She had heard about it from her friends so many times, she had seen it happen to many women, she had been told about it often by her mother and she knew the responsibility that went with it. She was now fully grown. She could be married away, she could be kidnapped, a lock of her hair could be cut by any man to make her his wife forever. All at once she was seized by a severe cramp; her feet left [sic] like giving way, small pains like needles shot in her back and she could feel something warm running down her legs. What should she do now. . . ? (92)

The story of *The Bride Price* is told with a feminine touch and with passion, but the author manifests an anticlimactic dialectical ambivalence in her manner of the resolution of the conflict at the end of the story. Aku-nna, the heroine, dies while giving birth because she rebelled against an outdated oppressive tradition. This appears to contradict Emecheta's crusade for women's liberation. Emecheta defends this apparent contradiction by maintaining that "Aku-nna had to die because at sixteen she chose someone other than the one her family wanted her to marry."[8] In a personal way, Emecheta draws a parallel between herself and the fictional Aku-nna and contends that she feels convinced that, like Aku-nna, her own marriage broke up because she did not allow her prospective husband to pay her bride price. Aku-nna's bride price was not paid as custom demanded; therefore she had to die. "If a girl wished to live long and see her children's children, she must accept the husband chosen for her by her people, and the bride price must be paid. If the bride price was not paid she would never survive the birth of her first child. It was a psychological hold over every young girl that would continue to exist, even in the face of modernization until the present day. Why this is so is, as the saying goes, anybody's guess" (168). This is an unsatisfactory ending, for it confirms the traditional superstition that the author knowingly (unlike her fictional heroine) seeks to eradicate. It removes the sense of commitment in Buchi Emecheta's fiction and makes her no more than a reporter who succeeds in narrating the woes of African womanhood, echoing its agonies, exhibiting its wounds, while firmly withholding a balm for its gaping sores. *The Bride Price* becomes a protest that projects no clear sense of alternative direction. Although perception, sensitivity, and an eye for detail are present in *The Bride Price*, it is generally overshadowed by sentimentality.

By the time Emecheta wrote *The Slave Girl*,[9] her mastery of the novel as an art form had improved tremendously. The language is more concise, the imagery clearer and the descriptions more apt. The birth of Ojebeta, the heroine of the novel, is described with passion and sensitivity at the opening pages of the novel:

> So, with Umeadi kneeling on the damp banana leaves in front of her husband's hut, bearing down gently, with Ukabegwu's wife's hands outstretched to catch the baby and the sharp hearth knife between her teeth, a little baby girl yelled her way into this world. (17)

Similarly, Emecheta's descriptions of nature and the environment are more charming and sensual:

> It was still dark when they started on their winding, red-earthed journey to Onitsha. The late night stars had withdrawn from above and were now well hidden behind the tangled foliage of trees and the looming clouds. The grey mist of dawn lay so heavily upon the horizon that it was impossible to see beyond a few yards.
>
> The silence was profound. The night animals had gone into hiding and day ones were still reluctant to start their early morning business. . . . Overhead hung the tangled branches of huge tropical trees, on both sides of them were large leaves, creeping plants and enormous tree-trunks, all entwined together to form this impenetrable dark green grove.
>
> The foot track they were following was like a thin red snake hemmed in by the two sides of this green

> presence so that they could not even see its head,
> because the end was blocked by the meeting of the
> two green walls ahead. (31)

Throughout the novel, Emecheta maintains control of her figurative language. The clichés and sentimentality which prevailed in *The Bride Price* are reduced to the minimum. Only the authorial intrusions persist. Emecheta must still explain to us and insert unneeded opinions instead of allowing the characters and situations to speak for themselves. The last paragraph of the book is an example of the author's propensity for forcing on the reader "enlightening" information.

Emecheta's most effective technique in the depiction of her general theme of oppression and its consequences is irony. In *The Slave Girl* this technique is well realized through juxtapositions of verbal irony, dramatic irony, and ironic contrast. By the end of the story Ojebeta has ironically substituted one form of slavery for another. But the first example of ironic contrast takes place at the end of Chapter 6 and the beginning of Chapter 7. As Ojebeta realizes her predicament she attains dignity:

> Chiago looked helplessly at the little girl who was doing her utmost to cling on to her individuality. She did not yet know that no slave retained any identity: whatever identity they had was forfeited the day money was paid for them. She did not wish to rob this child of the shred of self-respect she still had .... The ghost of a smile crossed Ojebeta's tear-stained face and for a moment illuminated her swollen eyes. She might have lost her identity, but at least she could still hold on to the dream of it. (72)

In Chapter 7, Okolie's loss of dignity contrasts sharply; the irony is that the master and slave dealer lose more than the slave.

Through the first part of the novel, Ojebeta remains an innocent girl, which intensifies the dramatic irony. For instance, when Ojebeta runs to Okolie for protection she is ignorant of his intent; not so the reader:

> He stooped down for her like a man in deep supplication. His otuogwu right out as if it were the wing of a black guiding angel..."Come," he begged again. She could no longer refuse. She ran into the protection of his wide arms. (36)

By the end of the book Ojebeta is still in chains, although no longer innocent. In the last chapter the title's irony is complete.

Like *The Slave Girl*, the title of *The Joys of Motherhood*[10] is also ironical in nature. It is in this novel that Emecheta achieves her best writing. The irony is well conceived and exploited. The author has solved her other weaknesses as a writer and the full effect of the irony in this novel remains unmarred. But these are not the only attributes of the novel. The language in the novel is well controlled and Emecheta is not distracted by her message as in the previous novels. Emecheta's similes and metaphors are devoid of triteness and they appropriately fit characterization.

In *The Joys of Motherhood*, the suffering of the African woman persists and so does Emecheta's pessimism, but she is less ambivalent in her stand on the fate of the African woman caught in the dilemma. Nnu Ego has just given birth to her second set of girl twins. Her husband is not pleased— "All this ballyhoo for two more girls! If one had to have twins, why girls, for Olisa's sake?" (186). To this the author comments:

> Men—all they were interested in were male babies to keep their names going. But did not a woman bear the woman-child who will later bear the sons? "God, when will you create a woman who will be fulfilled in herself, a full human being, not anybody's appendage?"...."After all, I was born alone, and I shall die alone. What have I gained from all this? Yes, I have many children, but what do I feed them on? On my life. I have to work myself to the bone to look after them. I have to give them my all. And if I am lucky enough to die in peace, I even have to give them my soul. They will worship my dead spirit to provide for them: it will be hailed as a good spirit so long as there are plenty of yams and children in the family, but if anything should go wrong, if a young wife does not conceive or there is a famine, my dead spirit will be blamed. When will I be free?"...."Never, not even in death. I am a prisoner of my own flesh and blood. Is it such an enviable position? The men make it look as if we must aspire for children or die. That's why when I lost my first son I wanted to die, because I failed to live up to the standard expected of me by the males in my life, my father and my hus-

260

band—and now I have to include my sons. But who
made the law that we should not hope in our daughters? We women subscribe to that law more than anyone. Until we change all this, it is still a man's world,
which women will always help to build." (186—187)

Although the heroine of *The Joys of Motherhood* dies at the end of
the novel, Emecheta's handling of her situation not only reveals
her maturity in her treatment of her theme, but also manifests her
remarkable growth as a novelist. Nnu Ego's death reinforces the
irony of the fate of woman in the African society. It asks the African
woman to re-examine her role in her suffering, for she is indeed
the author of her own misfortune. The author's appeal to the
African woman is conceived on a much higher plane than appears
to be manifested on the surface. Emecheta seems to be ideologically urging African women to rise, for they have nothing to lose
but their chains. This is the idea that is surreptitiously woven into
the apparently deceptive title, *The Joys of Motherhood*, for in her
present circumstances the African woman has no joys alive or
dead. In "after-death" when she attains a higher place, she is still
beset by problems arising from men's fundamental image of the
woman in their midst and women's unquestioning acceptance of
that image and all that it entails.

Emecheta's style is also much more secure and confident. Her
sentences are shorter. The pace of the narrative is faster and her
mastery of the art of suspense is complete. The digressions into
patronizing explanations of cultural norms are held to a minimum.
Authorial intrusions which weakened the style of *The Bride Price*
and slowed down the pace of the narrative are virtually eliminated. Emecheta's narrative techniques have become sharpened and
impressive. Despite the gloomy atmosphere conveyed by the setting of the story, Emecheta's peculiar type of humor is evident. After
Nnu Ego had been kept "busy" all night on the very first day of her
arrival to join her husband whom she had never known or seen
before, and whose physical appearance was utterly revolting,
Emecheta deflates the tension in part with, "Nnu Ego knew why
horrible-looking men raped women, because they are aware of their
inadequacy" (44). Emecheta's descriptions and presentations of her
characters are more precise and memorable, as is evident in her
introduction of Nnaife. The reader is obliged to share Nnu Ego's disgust and contempt for the man who was to be her husband:

. . .(Nnu Ego) was just falling asleep...when in

> walked a man with a belly like a pregnant cow, wob-
> bling first to this side and then to that. The belly,
> coupled with the fact that he was short, made him
> look like a barrel. His hair, unlike that of men at
> home in Ibuza, was not closely shaved: he left a lot
> of it on his head, like that of a woman mourning for
> her husband. His skin was pale, the skin of some-
> one who had for long time worked in the shade and
> not in the open air. His cheeks were puffy and
> looked as if he had pieces of hot yam inside them,
> and they seemed to have pushed his mouth into a
> smaller size above his weak jaw. And his clothes—
> Nnu Ego had never seen men dressed like that:
> khaki shorts with holes and old loose, white singlet.
> If her husband-to-be was like this, she thought, she
> would go back to her father. Why marrying such a
> jelly of a man would be like living with a middle-
> aged woman! (42)

There is feeling in this passage characterized by its apt and vivid imagery culminating in the irony of the last sentence. One imme-diately gets the classic picture of the unwilling beauty and the enthusiastic and ravaging beast.

Emecheta's figurative expressions have also acquired more authenticity, her prose is dignified, and her voice has acquired rhythmic and incantatory cadences that reveal an emerging affin-ity with, and an awareness of, the imaginative techniques of the traditional African artist, whose language was characterized by its undertones, its subtlety, and its direct purposeful appeal to a par-ticular audience. There are vivid figures of speech. In the evoca-tive passage on the elephant hunt (13—15) it is said that "the animal was so enraged that, uncharacteristically for a big elephant, it chased after him blindly, bellowing like a great locomotive, so that the very ground seemed about to give way at its heavy approach" (13). Ona, the sly mistress of Agbadi who both loved and loathed her man, nervously and anxiously "galloped on the balls of her feet" (14) after the men bearing the unconscious body of her lover. The author says that "for the first time, she realized how attached she was to this man Nwokocha Agbadi, though he was cruel in his imperiousness. His tongue was biting like the edge of a circumci-sion blade" (15). Emecheta's portrait of Agbadi calls to mind Chinua Achebe's portrayal of Okonkwo in *Things Fall Apart*—a man, bold and imperious in posture yet insecure and almost fragile within, a determined and hard man who is not without humor and passion in the deep recesses of his heart. Even Emecheta's sexual imagery is no longer characterized by its crudity and indecorum. Agbadi wakes up in the night while still nursing the injuries of his encounter with the elephant, to notice his half-clothed but defiant mistress lying beside him. Then "he managed to turn fully on to his side and gazed his fill at her. To think that in that proud head, held high even in sleep, and to think that in those breasts, *two beautiful mounds on her chest looking like calabashes turned upside-down* [emphasis mine], there was some tenderness was momentarily incredible to him. He felt himself burn" (19). And when he could no longer restrain himself, "he *slid on his belly like a big black snake* [emphasis mine], he left her abruptly, still unsatiated, and rolled painfully to the other side of the goatskin"(21). Even when Emecheta indulges in translations they are no longer circumlocutory. "They (twins) were identical in appearance but not in character: the one called Kehinde, 'the second to arrive,' was much deeper than Taiwo, 'she who tasted the world first'" (203). Neighbors acknowledged the beauty of Nnaife's newly arrived wife by remarking that "they had sent him a 'Mammy Waater', as very beautiful women were called" (43) and Nnaife had "at first greeted her (Nnu Ego) only shyly with a single word, 'Nnua—Welcome'" (43).

At the end of the novel, the author's creative vision is quite clear. Her solution for the problems of the African woman lies in education. "I am beginning to think that there may be a future for educated women. I saw many young women teaching in schools. It would be really something for a woman to be able to earn some money monthly like a man," Nnu Ego said looking into the distance (189). Perhaps the most critical awareness of the female predicament depicted in the novel is the comment that "parents get only reflected glory from their children nowadays" (213), which the author later amplifies succinctly:

> Nnu Ego had allowed herself to wonder where it was she had gone wrong. She had been brought up to believe that children made a woman. She had children, nine in all, and luckily seven were alive.... Still, how was she to know that by the time her children grew up the values of her country, her people and her tribe would have changed so drastically, to the extent where a woman with many children

> could face a lonely old age, and maybe a miserable
> death all alone, just like a barren woman? She was
> not even certain that worries over her children
> would not send her to her grave before her *chi* was
> ready for her. (219)

Thus in *The Joys of Motherhood*, more than in any of her other novels so far, Buchi Emecheta achieves success in her handling of her theme and language, both of which in the tradition of African narrative art, are characterized by precision, subtlety and a sense of inviolable mission. *The Joys of Motherhood* is not only an ironic commentary on the destinies of African womanhood; it is also a parable on the misplaced values of life in general, in Africa as elsewhere. The irony becomes more biting as the story progresses. Nnu Ego has placed all her hope for joy and success in her children, yet she is continually disappointed. The final irony in the novel is devastating. Directly contrasting with what society and Nnu Ego's own beliefs have promised her, she finds no joy in her grown children. The spoiled boys have become selfish, egotistical men, due in large part to Nnu Ego's attitudes toward her male children. Nnu Ego is given a fancy funeral, but it is too late. While dying, as in her life, she did not have the support or comfort of her children:

> After such wandering on one night, Nnu Ego lay
> down by the roadside, thinking that she had arrived
> home. She died there quietly, with no child to hold
> her hand and no friend to talk to her. She had never
> really made many friends, so busy had she been
> building up her joys as a mother. (224)

Through an examination of imagery, figurative language, omniscient commentary, and irony it is possible to understand the growth of Emecheta as a writer in the three novels *The Bride Price*, *The Slave Girl*, and *The Joys of Motherhood*. Buchi Emecheta presents the plight of the African woman in a culture involved in a clash between traditional society and Western influence. In spite of the author's pessimism as an artist, and despite the stereotyped male characters, these novels exhibit strong artistry which makes Buchi Emecheta one of the best storytellers in modern Africa.

NOTES

1. "Interview with Buchi Emecheta." by Davidson and Marie Umeh, at the University of Calabar, Nigeria, 1980.

2. Jurgen Martini, "Linking Africa and the West: Buchi Emecheta." *Spare Rib* (no date), 15
3. "Interview with Buchi Emecheta."
4. *ibid.*
5. *ibid.*
6. Susan B. Uyoh, reviewing Buchi Emecheta's *Second-Class Citizen*, for *The Gong*, Magazine of the Department of English and Literary Studies, University of Calabar, Nigeria, May, 1981, p. 34.
7. Buchi Emecheta. *The Bride Price*. London: Collins/Fontana, 1976. (All quotations are from this edition and page references will be indicated in brackets within the text.)
8. "Interview with Buchi Emecheta."
9. Buchi Emecheta. *The Slave Girl*. New York: George Braziller, 1977. (All page references are to this edition.)
10. Buchi Emecheta. *The Joys of Motherhood*. London: Heinemann, 1979. (All page references are to this edition.)

Second-Class Citizen: The Point of Departure for Understanding Buchi Emecheta's Major Fiction

Abioseh Michael Porter

It has been said that "of all the women writers in contemporary African literature Buchi Emecheta of Nigeria has been the most sustained and vigorous voice of direct feminist protest."[1] While there is no doubt about the validity of this statement, one thing that is questionable is the persistent attempt by some scholars (Katherine Frank, Eustace Palmer, for example)[2] to read Emecheta's *Second-Class Citizen*[3] only within the feminist protest tradition. It would be nonsense, of course, to suggest that in evaluating the works of a writer such as Emecheta (who in all of her novels deals quite seriously with the role of women in various societies), one can avoid the feminist question. It is something else, however, to imply that this is the only aspect worth examining in her *oeuvre*. In fact, Frank, in her essay, "The Death of the Slave Girl: African Womanhood in the Novels of Buchi Emecheta," demonstrates the danger of focusing almost exclusively on Emecheta's feminist theme by making all kinds of sweeping and erroneous generalizations about the African woman's "bondage" and the Western woman's "freedom" in Emecheta's works. We can also say that because *Second-Class Citizen* has often been seen as a somewhat flawed feminist novel, critics such as Lloyd W. Brown have failed to notice the novel's full generic potential. Brown comments that "the emphasis on individual growth and self-reliance is more fully developed in *Second-Class Citizen*" than in Emecheta's first novel, *In the Ditch*;[4] however, he also consistently deplores the heroine, Adah, in those sections where she is obviously displaying naivete, immaturity, and ignorance—qualities commonly found among protagonists of the novel of personal development. One other critic does not even mention Emecheta in an essay dealing with the female *Bildungsroman* in the Commonwealth.[5]

It is my view, however, that if *Second-Class Citizen* were read as a novel of personal development (*Bildungsroman*), some of the seeming inconsistencies within the text would be more fully understood. Also, a look at this work as a novel dealing with a young African woman's gradual acquisition of knowledge about herself as a potential artist and about the themes of love and marriage and the subject of student life overseas (especially in a hostile environment) will add more weight to the already popular feminist theme in the book. Finally, Emecheta's (albeit lukewarm) acceptance of Dickens—that master creator for apprenticeship novels—as a possible source of influence on the structure of *Second-Class Citizen* can be seen as a further reason for reading the work as a novel of personal development.[6]

Adah, the protagonist of *Second-Class Citizen*, is portrayed as an intelligent, ambitious young girl who has to fight against considerable odds to gain an education in Lagos. As a child, she has to inject herself into the classroom of a friendly neighboring teacher before she is finally enrolled in school. This is so because her parents (especially her mother) have doubts about the wisdom of sending girls to school. Tragedy soon strikes for Adah when her relatively liberal father dies not too long after her registration at school. She then moves into a relative's home where she is kept as a ward-cum-slave. After a life of abject misery and exploitation, and by dint of hard work and proper self-motivation, Adah is able to win a scholarship in the highly competitive secondary school entrance examinations.

As a result of a first-rate performance at the school-leaving examinations, the heroine is able to procure a job as a librarian at the African consulate in Lagos—a job that easily brings her the comforts of middle-class life. During this same period she meets Francis Obi, a young student of accounting whom she agrees to marry because she thinks he will provide some necessary protection, support and, above all, love for her in Lagos. Looking at Adah's salary as a convenient means of financial support, Francis (with his parents' approval) decides to go abroad and continue his studies in Britain. The idea is accepted by Adah because, in part, it provides an avenue for her to fulfill her own childhood dreams of going to study in England.

Francis goes to England and is soon followed by Adah and their three children. But, from the time she arrives in Britain, Adah (like some other protagonists in African novels dealing with student life overseas) begins to notice that the country is far different from the fairyland she had been brought up to conjure. Worse, she realizes that Francis, who had always been dependent on her, has become even more so—and more manipulative—in England. His lifestyle is now characterized by gross antisocial behavior, a feeling of inferiority, laziness, and utter irresponsibility. Adah tries at first to support the family and take care of the home but it also becomes clear to her that Francis's irresponsibility is in direct proportion to his desire to create more children. When Adah confronts him with this obvious domestic problem, Francis becomes defensive and starts brutalizing her. The final clash occurs when, after the birth of their fifth child (at a time when Adah is barely twenty-two), Francis spitefully burns the manuscript of Adah's first novel. *Second-Class Citizen* ends with the heroine seizing independence for herself and her children and with preparations to start a fresh life at last.

As with all works belonging to the apprenticeship novel tradition, Adah's innocence and naivete serve as generic markers in the initial sections of the story. Significantly, *Second-Class Citizen* starts with a reference to Adah's "dream" of going to England. Using rhetoric that clearly emphasizes her innocence, Adah mentions how, with the help of her father, she goes through adolescence with an exaggerated and false conception of Britain. Like her father, she grows up believing that the United Kingdom is synonymous with heaven (8). She makes a "secret vow" quite early to herself that "she would go to this United Kingdom one day" and she wrongly assumes that her arrival in the United Kingdom "would be the pinnacle of her ambition" (17). If there were any doubts about the differences in point of view between the novelist and her young alter ego, statements such as these should erase such doubts.

Adah's problems, however, go deeper than merely being ignorant of the culture of a foreign country. As descriptions of life with
her husband show, she enters into a hastily arranged and ill-con-
ceived marriage without the least idea about the real nature of love,
marriage, and the related notions of individual liberty and mutual
support. This situation is so because Adah has grown up in environments where she has been deprived of learning about or experiencing such concepts, which are so vital for successful marital
relationships. In fact, it is shown that up to the time Adah and Francis
get married she has neither experienced any serious love relationship nor has she ever thought deeply about the implications of marriage. She sincerely believes that all it takes to have a successful
marriage is to be married to a young spouse of modest means.

It is important to consider the true nature of Adah's naivete and
her juvenile interpretations of love, marriage, and "life outside
school" (as the narrator calls it), because without such consideration it becomes quite inviting to blame Emecheta for what looks
like her endorsement of the young Adah's seemingly amoral
manipulation of Francis, especially with regard to their marriage.
Brown, for example, suggests that "the casualness with which Adah
enters and describes her loveless marriage is the more striking
when we remember her own invectives against parents who sell
their daughter into loveless matches for the profit of the bride price,
and even more disconcertingly, neither Adah nor Emecheta seems
aware of or concerned about the apparent inconsistency."[7] One
suspects, however, that in a scene such as this one Brown is asking Emecheta to impose a point of view that would have been totally incongruous with Adah's immaturity at the time of Adah's
wedding. It is only if we assume that the novelist is using the narrator to describe events as they should have been, instead of as
they happened to Adah, that we will agree with the view that Adah
should have been presented at the outset as being less dependent,
less manipulative, and less manipulable.

At the time of their wedding, Adah is shown as a young woman
who, with no home to live in, imagines that a seemingly ambitious
and modest young man like Francis will ultimately provide protection, shelter and, maybe, love for her. It is also implied that it
is Adah's artlessness that makes her equate happiness in marriage
with youth and unhappiness in marriage with old spouses. Indeed,
it is only when we consider Adah's lack of experience at the beginning that most of her subsequent shocks, disappointments, and

eventual independence make sense. Adah's initial naivete explains why this otherwise bright woman has to depend upon her less astute husband and in-laws—people who rely so much on her for financial sustenance—for intellectual and other forms of guidance.

But, although this type of situation continues for the greater part of *Second-Class Citizen*, it becomes obvious that by the end of the novel Adah demonstrates that in order to become both the good writer and independent human being that she hopes to become, she has to free herself from the exploitative relationship between herself and Francis, create her own identity and, in general, try to understand human relationships better. Thus, in the end, Adah asserts her independence in a way which shows that she is now ready to be in complete control of her own and her children's lives. The scene is in the family court in London and Francis, who has been charged with assaulting Adah, resorts to all kinds of mean tricks (including denying paternity of their children) in order to avoid payment of alimony. Here is how the narrator describes Adah's reaction: "Francis said they had never been married. He then asked Adah if she could produce the marriage certificate. Adah could not. She could not even produce her passport and the children's birth certificates. Francis had burnt them all. To him, Adah and the children ceased to exist. Francis told her this in court in low tones and in their language.... Something happened to Adah then. It was like big hope and a kind of energy charging into her, giving her so much strength even though she was physically ill with her fifth child. Then she said very loud and very clear, *"Don't worry sir. The children are mine and that is enough. I shall never let them down as long as I am alive"* (191; my emphasis). The finality in the tone of voice and the determined manner in which Adah decides to formally accept responsibility for the children (which had always been hers anyway) are decidedly different from her behavior in most of the earlier scenes, situations in which she was invariably portrayed as a compliant character. She obviously understands now that she was totally wrong in looking up to Francis as a source of support; she also realizes that if she wants to succeed both in her creative endeavors and in the rearing of her children she has to take full control of her life. From this moment henceforth, one cannot imagine either the narrator saying of Adah (as on previous occasions) that "she simply accepted her role as defined for her by her husband" (104) or Adah herself relying on the unworthy Francis (or any man), as she had previously done.

As a novel of personal development, *Second-Class Citizen* is quite successful in the depiction of Adah's growth from the initial stage of naivete and ignorance to her final stage of self-realization and independence. She starts confronting the well-known tests usually set for all protagonists of apprenticeship novels when, upon her arrival in England—which, as we know, she had always equated with heaven—she is given only a "cold welcome" (39). But Adah's initial introduction to the British weather, landscape, and people is nothing compared to the other forms of initiation she goes through as she continues her stay in England. She has hardly overcome her first real shock over the legendary lack of warmth in England when she is faced with an even greater shock, i.e., learning to live in the hovel which Francis (now referred to as the "new Francis" by the narrator) shows her as their new home in London.

The protagonist gradually learns that coming to England is not and should not necessarily be the pinnacle of one's dream. She comes to know, through her experiences with the children's nanny Trudy, that some British people can be just as dishonest and irresponsible as people anywhere else. Adah becomes aware of the true nature of racism when, together with Francis, she goes house hunting in London. She is also exposed to petty jealously and envy from some of her fellow Nigerians living in London. These characters (who include the landlord and landlady of the Ashdown Street house), out of spite and malice, do all they can to bring Adah down to the inferior level they have partly allowed society to relegate them to. It is thus evident that, because of their hateful attitude toward Adah, these characters (who should otherwise have been helping the young woman) qualify for the roles of "faux-destinateurs" or detractors of the main character. As Susan Suleiman points out in an essay on the structure of the apprenticeship novel, in almost all novels of this type, there is always at least one character who, instead of helping the protagonist, will serve as an impediment to the latter's progress. In addition, there also are other structural categories—"destinateurs" and "adjuvants" on the one hand and "opposants" and "faux-destinateurs" on the other—who, as their names suggest, will also serve either as positive guides or as hindrances to the protagonist.[8]

It is also clear that Francis, Adah's husband, is her leading "opposant" or opponent. But before discussing Francis's role as Adah's chief opponent, I must refer to a basic weakness in Emecheta's writing style—a weakness which, I suspect, makes it difficult for some critics to recognize the artistic distance Emecheta creates between herself and Adah. Again, as Lloyd Brown asserts,

Emecheta's criticisms of African men "are often marred by generalizations that are too shrill and transparently overstated to be altogether convincing."[9] When, for instance, Francis endorses his
father's disapproval of Adah going to study in Britain, the narrator
comments that "Francis was an African through and through. A
much more civilized man would probably have found a better way
of saying this to his wife. But to him, he was the male, and he was
right to tell her what she was going to do" (30). The narrative voice
here certainly seems to be that of the adult (and presumably more
mature) Adah; we therefore cannot understand why she makes
such a stupid remark. In another episode, the narrator tries to convey Francis's unwillingness to support his wife but, as in the previous example, Emecheta succeeds only in conveying the
impression that she endorses racial stereotypes about black men
by suggesting that if only Francis were an Englishman, he would
know how to treat his wife with love and respect (179). Surely,
Emecheta knows that selfishness and inconsideration are not
innate traits of African men, nor are supportive behavior and common decency toward one's spouse peculiar to English men. But,
despite these and other obvious fallacies of hasty and inaccurate
generalizations, it is true that Francis is Adah's leading opponent
in *Second-Class Citizen*.

Using descriptions that inevitably allow Francis to degenerate
into a caricature, Emecheta depicts him (with good reason) as being
one of the most unredeemable villains in African literature. In
scenes that are too numerous to elaborate upon here, Francis is
shown to be self-centered, cruel, narrow-minded, and in fact downright venal. Instead of helping Adah to develop the creative potential she obviously has (and part of which she uses to support him),
Francis only proves himself to be an obstacle on her route toward
self-improvement. Because he is so selfish and greedy, Francis
readily agrees with his parents' decision that Adah should remain
working in Lagos to support him and his parents while he is "studying" in London. When (after outmaneuvering Francis's mother)
Adah finally joins Francis in England, she quickly realizes that if
Francis had been dependent, lazy, and manipulative in Lagos, he
has become even worse overseas. He is correctly shown as an irresponsible parent, spouse, and student. As was mentioned earlier,
he brutalizes Adah, deliberately tries to inject a feeling of inferiority into her and, when all that fails, he tries to deprive her of
what she values most—her children and her potential to become
a writer.

It is also true, however, that toward the end of the story Adah fully recognizes Francis's absolute lack of love for her as well as the need for her own freedom. She is greatly assisted in this regard by another cast of characters who, in different ways, help her on the path toward the knowledge of her self-worth. Several of these characters (such as her boss at the Finchley Road library, Mrs. Konrad, and Mr. Okpara, the Nigerian who repeatedly urges Francis to smarten up) belong to the structural category often referred to as "adjuvants," i.e., those characters who guide the protagonist of a novel of personal development on the right path. But one "adjuvant" who is of particular note is Bill, the bibliophile from Canada. He is the character who not only encourages Adah to read several African and other literary works, but who also literally guides her on the path of becoming a writer. Not surprisingly, the narrator remarks that "Bill was the first real friend [Adah] had outside her family" (167).

The success of *Second-Class Citizen* as a literary work rests largely on Emecheta's evocation of childhood and its concomitant problems. The work is also very good in its depiction of a young woman who not only tries to survive in rather hostile environments (both domestic and elsewhere), but who does in the end acquire her personal independence. But, on balance, this Emecheta novel loses some of its strength because of the way it is inadequately structured. Emecheta demonstrates a pitfall common among writers of the *Bildungsroman* by blatantly intruding to pour what looks like personal venom into the text. Because the narrator consistently depicts Francis as a disappointment to Adah, we are never made to see most of the other characters in full perspective. Some characters who play very important roles (such as Bill and Mr. Okpara) are not developed as they otherwise should have been.

Notwithstanding these minor aesthetic blemishes, *Second-Class Citizen* can and should be seen as a powerful example of the *Bildungsroman* in Africa. This novel does not match Emecheta's later, more sophisticated, and more overtly feminist works such as *The Bride Price* (1976), *The Slave Girl* (1977), and especially *The Joys of Motherhood* (1979). It is also true, however, that the novelist's sustained attention to the themes of individual growth, progress, development, and the coherence of selfhood—all of which have pervaded her later writings and for which she received genuine and well-deserved critical acclaim—have their roots in this early piece. Thus, I must agree, at least partly, with Katherine Frank's assertion that "the best place to approach Emecheta's fiction is with neither her first nor her last book, but with *Second-Class Citizen*."[10]

NOTES

1. Lloyd Welesley Brown, *Women Writers in Black Africa*. Westport, CT: Greenwood Press, 1981, 35.
2. Katherine Frank, "The Death of the Slave Girl: African Womanhood in the Novels of Buchi Emecheta," *World Literature Written in English* 21.2 (1982): 476—97; Eustace Palmer, "The Feminine Point of View: A Study of Buchi Emecheta's *The Joys of Motherhood*," *African Literature Today*. 13 (1982): 54—65.
3. Buchi Emecheta, *Second-Class Citizen*. London: Fontana, 1977. (All page references are to this edition.)
4. Brown, 44-48.
5. Margaret Bucher, "The Female *Bildungsroman* in the Commonwealth Literature," *World Literature Written in English*. 21.2 (1983): 262—65.
6. Buchi Emecheta, "A Nigerian Writer Living in London," *Kunapipi* 4.1 (1982): 115.
7. Brown, 45.
8. Susan Suleiman, "La Structure d'apprentissage," *Poetique* 37 (1979): 24—42.
9. Brown, 36.
10. Frank, 479.

George Braziller, publisher, and Buchi Emecheta at Fairleigh Dickinson University where she received an honorary Doctor of Literature degree in 1992.

Buchi Emecheta, Laughter and Silence: Changes in the Concepts "Woman," "Wife," and "Mother"

M. J. Daymond

In the three *novels—The Bride Price, The Slave Girl* and *The Joys of Motherhood*—in which Buchi Emecheta explores the reality of women's lives in Nigeria in the early decades of this century, each protagonist's story ends in defeat. Although these novels are all written from a post tribal perspective, the flavor of these defeats varies because the protagonists' capacities are progressively enlarged over the three novels. Emecheta's central figure changes from being unaware of the real nature of her struggles and defeat to having a much fuller consciousness of the meaning of what is happening. Thus when the first protagonist, Aku-nna in *The Bride Price,* dies in childbirth having defied her family in marrying Chike, the *osu* (descended from slaves) man of her choice, she is quite unaware that her death will be understood by her community as reinforcing the "superstition" she had "unknowingly set out to eradicate" (168)—

the belief that unless a girl accepts the husband her family chooses and unless the bride price is paid, she will not live to enjoy children. In *The Slave Girl*, Ojebeta finds the strength of will to flee from
slavery and return to her childhood village. Having managed this
degree of choice, she finds that once again she must flee, this time
to Lagos, in order to be able to marry Jacob rather than the illiterate farmer, Adim, who is favored by her uncle. Her story ends when
Jacob repays the price that Ma Palagada had originally given for
Ojebeta when she was sold into slavery. Ojebeta kneels in simple
gratitude to her husband, saying, "Thank you my new owner. Now
I am free in your house. I could not wish for a better master" (190).
Although the ironies of her situation reach Ojebeta's lips, she is still
so immersed in her people's traditions that she does not hear what
he has said. It is left to a wry narrative comment to recognize that
"Ojebeta, now a woman of thirty-five, was changing masters" (190).

In *The Joys of Motherhood* Emecheta gives her protagonist a
much greater capacity to comprehend the ironies in the "joy" of the
title. In Lagos, as Nnu Ego struggles to meet the many new demands
made on her (that she take responsibility for feeding, clothing, housing, and educating her children), her concept of herself as woman,
wife, and mother begins to change. She gains considerable autonomy in her actions, although she cannot always bring her new capacities to full, conscious recognition. This is why, when asked in court
to define the nature of the economic responsibilities she has shoul-
dered, she is capable only of restating the traditional, tribal basis of
her marriage: "Nnaife is the head of our family. He owns me, just
like God in the sky owns us. So even though I pay the fees, yet he
owns me. So in other words he pays" (217). The court erupts in
laughter. Such a sign of the colonizing power's incomprehension
and strange system of justice is galling to Nnu Ego, but it is not here
that her defeat lies. In raising her children in the belief that her
sons must be educated in Western fashion if they are to rise in the
new urban world, Nnu Ego does not see that the education she
struggles to provide will in fact alienate her sons from her. So, in
late middle age, she is left longing for one word of recognition from
her sons who are studying in America and Canada. Finally, she dies
defeated by their neglect. It takes her death to earn Nnu Ego her
sons' attention; they return to give her the "noisiest and most costly second burial Ibuza had ever seen" (224). They clearly do not
recognize their part in her lonely death for they also build "a shrine
...in her name so that her grandchildren could appeal to her should
they be barren" (213) and that they will not provide the direct

rewards she had once expected, this lesson does not seem to extend to her sons' understanding of what they have required of her. Their final tribute, which demands that she sustain the old terms of bountiful maternity, terms which in her own life have been forcibly changed, contains such contradictions that her response is, properly, silence. It is the silence of refusal. By giving this degree of understanding and judgement to her third protagonist, Buchi Emecheta changes her project from a narrative description, made from an external and more knowledgeable perspective on women's real situation (1), to a narrative exploration, made from within, of a woman's consciousness. Thus the sequence culminates in the creation of a woman with the capacity to respond to a new world, to reconceptualise herself in it and to express her judgement on it. This means that the silence with which all three novels end changes from being that of uncomprehending defeat to that of chosen refusal. At the end of *The Bride Price*, Aku-nna's incomprehension and silence, because it is not part of her consciousness, establishes an unbridged gap between reader and character. This gap is narrowed in *The Slave Girl* and virtually closed in *The Joys of Motherhood*. There, silence is not solely a condition to be recognized by the reader but is one that has been incorporated into experience as it is registered by the character herself. At times in this narrative, silence does represent incomprehension, but this changes until finally silence becomes Nnu Ego's chosen response. A refusal to use her traditional power has become Nnu Ego's most appropriate means of self-expression and, besides its coming from her own judgement, it represents the view that the reader is asked to reach.

In this progression, silence changes its narrative functioning from being the element which surrounds the protagonist and which the reader, aided by narrative comment, must interpret, to being an aspect of the protagonist's own language. Nnu Ego is not silenced, but silent. Her silenced forbears can be seen as examples of what Tillie Olsen, in her study of women's creativity calls "the unnatural thwarting of what struggles to come into being, but cannot" (Olsen, 6) and their stories illustrate why Adrienne Rich, echoed since by many feminist scholars, said that the "entire history of women's struggle for self-determination has been muffled in silence over and over" (Rich, 11). But the feminist must come to a different conclusion about Nnu Ego's silence, one that draws in the current debate about women and language.

When Nnu Ego moves from her Ibo village, Ibuza, to Lagos, she has literally to learn a new language, that of the city, which is

Yoruba; but what is crucial in her move is not the new set of sounds but the new concepts operative in urban life that she has to learn. These entail the Western ways that the colonizers have imposed as well as the new meanings the traditional terms have acquired in the changed context. The changes which Nnu Ego has to manage involve changes in belief and attitude, in thought and emotional patterns, and they manifest themselves primarily in language. For this reason, discussion of Nnu Ego's language refers to her whole mind, and the particular examples which illustrate the complexity of the process of change are the shifts that occur in her own under-standing and use of the concepts "woman," "wife," and "mother." It is helpful to see that in her move to Lagos, Nnu Ego is, once again, experiencing entry into what Julia Kristeva calls "the symbolic" (2), a term for social life and its language, the way in which language is an imprisoning as well as an enabling tool. Nnu Ego's first entry into the symbolic was her childhood immersion in tribal ways and, if the difference between it and her later encounter with a new lan-guage in Lagos is schematized, its presentation can be seen to estab-lish the conditions of having a language at all—it shapes as well as expresses our being. By contrast, her learning the concepts she needs for life in Lagos, her second entry, enables the reader to rec-ognize, in addition to the way that the general constraints of lan-guage work, the specific limitations that the androcentricity of language imposes on women. Thus, the second entry supplies what Ruthven asks for: a demonstration that "language is much more of a prison-house for women than it is for men" (1984, 59).

Aku-nna and Ojebeta, Nnu Ego's silenced forbears, show in detail what the first stage of her story also conveys: that however much of a prison-house language may be, it is the means by which men and women constitute themselves in their world and, more importantly, by which they gain reflective access to their experi-ences of that constituted world. In the second stage of her story, as she replaces meanings with new ones, Nnu Ego is facing the specific difficulties of a woman who, traditionally the silent, pas-sive, and obedient user of language, has to work out for herself, rather than simply receive, the man-made concepts of her new world. In her village life, the acquisition of language had been a simpler matter of absorbing the attitudes and cultural expectations which govern the uses of speech; once in Lagos, Nnu Ego, who is left alone to fend for her children for much of the time, has to replace one set of concepts with another. To do this she has to depend on her own resources in identifying, understanding and then using the concepts she needs to survive. Being largely unaided, she is quite clearly developing her own language. Thus each time that her husband returns and challenges her practices, asserting his attitudes and expectations and thereby destroying what Nnu Ego has created, he makes unusually explicit the way in which women are dominated, and even oppressed, by male uses of language. The particular value of this second entry into the symbolic for feminists is that Nnu Ego's interactions with the new language she has to absorb can be seen; they are explicit rather than the speculative reconstruction, which theorists like Kristeva have put forward of how a woman first acquires language.

The Joys of Motherhood is structured so that the stages of Nnu Ego's self-instruction are clearly signposted. The major division is between her tribal life, in which she finds no reason to question the concepts and behavior that her ancestral language has taught her, and her urban life. In this latter section, the narrative also demarcates very clearly the steps by which Nnu Ego comes to awareness of her task, learns to articulate her problems, and then manages to act on her circumstances.

For the pre-urban stage, before Nnu Ego's consciousness can be used by the narration, the questioning slant with which it must be seen is set up by the opening scene—Nnu Ego's attempted suicide in Lagos. As the narrative proceeds to a substantial retrospective presentation of tribal life without explaining what has led to her attempt, the wish for death becomes an enigma through which events in these chapters must be read. In them, Emecheta establishes both the strengths and weaknesses of Nnu Ego's attitudes (from an urban point of view) as they are constituted in the language of tribal custom. A major constituent of these is the position of Ona, Nnu Ego's mother. She is both a spirited beauty, beloved of Agbadi, and the daughter through whom her own father, Obi Umunna, hopes to acquire the male heir he so desperately wants. It is clear that Ona has been allowed to retain her independent status as Agbadi's lover, rather than becoming one of his wives, not because her own wishes are being respected but because her remaining part of her father's household gives him a claim on any offspring. Either way, as wife or lover, Ona is a man's possession and her chief function is to bear male children.

Nnu Ego absorbs the tribal view of womanhood completely, so much so that she is almost destroyed by her own failure to bear children when she marries. When her husband repudiates her, she shares his view of her worthlessness; when she has recovered some of her vitality in her father's household, his decision that she should try marriage again, this time in Lagos, clearly suits her mentality. Thus, by the time the narration catches up with the opening event, the culture which has produced Nnu Ego is known to the reader as a coherent way of life which functions effectively in given circumstances. But the reader also knows from within the picture of that culture, and long before the protagonist herself, the sources of the strains and contradictions that will burden Nnu Ego as she has to learn the language of Lagos.

It is after her first baby's sudden death (the cause of her attempted suicide) that Nnu Ego is called on to make her first conscious effort to understand her plight. This involves her in finding the new features of her language which will loosen the hold over her of her tribal concepts. Previously, once she had borne Nnaife's son, her tribal view of motherhood and the importance of male children had been her means of accepting life in Lagos with her potbellied little laundryman husband. Emecheta does not suggest that the effort by which Nnu Ego begins to find this is one of great and deliberate travail, for she shows the first, crucial break with tradition coming through the easy, shared laughter of two friends as they discuss their husbands:

> "... And I worry that people may think I am mad. Even Nnaife calls me a mad woman sometimes."

> Ato laughed again, this time really startling Nnu Ego who had not heard such laughter for a very long time. "He can talk, that fat fufu dough of a man. If he calls you mad, tell him to look in the mirror!"

> Nnu Ego could not help laughing almost as loudly as her friend. "No, he is a man, and you know men are never ugly."

> "I know," Ato confirmed. She became serious again. "Let him sleep with you. Please don't let your people down." She started to laugh again. "Even if you don't find him a good lover because of his round stomach, you may find him loving. Many men can make love and give babies easily but cannot love."

> "I know, loving and caring are more difficult for our men. But Nnaife is very loving; you see, he copies the white people he works for. He is not bad

in the other way, too... I just did not know him before—no, I don't mean that, I didn't dream I would end up marrying a man like him."

"Neither did I dream of marrying a man who would stay away months at a time. You know something, they say men who work on the ships have mistresses wherever they land."

"Oh!" Nnu Ego exclaimed, covering her mouth. "Your husband would never do a thing like that." (75)

Laughter is the vital paralinguistic act that releases Nnu Ego into her first step towards employing the new concepts her situation demands. The friends' laughter is directed at a male maxim, "men are never ugly," that is characteristic of what Mary Jacobus sees as the reductive, generalized rules by which male dominance is "maximized" and maintained (52). It is also an example of the ways in which members of a "muted group" can achieve communication that is disruptive of reigning orthodoxies while remaining just within the bounds of conventional language. "Muted" is the term which Elaine Showalter (30) takes up to describe how women's way of perceiving the world can, although it is constituted within and by the language of the dominant (male) group, assert itself with some small degree of independence. Following Showalter's suggestions, the laughter with which Nnu Ego invokes the tribal maxim can be seen to come from that small, peripheral area of language that is free from male control, and as being able to create a gap between her and that maxim. Her laughter, inserting a new register of detachment into her language, enables her to look afresh at the customs which have hitherto ruled her life. From the other side of the gap it creates, she can turn to her own, unique experience—"Nnaife is very loving"—for guidance and so begin the process of adaptation. In this crossing over, she is guided by Ato's account of what she has had to learn in marriage to a sailor, but it is also clear that Ato goes too quickly for Nnu Ego who is left "covering her mouth" as though their words are suddenly too powerful and must be checked.

By now, the three concepts which Nnu Ego has to re-examine and which must take on new meaning in her life, those of "woman" (in the sense of an individual unit in society), "wife," and "mother" are entering Nnu Ego's active reconsideration. Emecheta takes care to show that while her protagonist is reconstituting one of these notions, she often has to manage this by clinging for support to the traditional form of the others. The first of these concepts to come under attack during Nnu Ego's fresh start with Nnaife is that of "woman" when she finds that economic responsibility for her family falls entirely on her. When Nnaife goes to Fernando Po for work, Nnu Ego is turned out of their yard because the army requires the buildings. Alone and penniless, having never before handled money, she has to find shelter, as well as food for herself and two children. During the struggles, Ibuza, its ways and its values, remains Nnu Ego's consciously invoked support; but at the same time she is absorbing the new powers taught her by necessity. In particular her economic responsibilities are teaching her self-reliance and the vocabulary associated with it begins to accrue to her. With the narrative observation that, "having made up her mind, she walked with confidence carrying her day's purchases on her head" (109), it is clear that this "confidence" is locatable both as an external observation and as a new element in Nnu Ego's own language about herself. In comparison with an earlier picture of her mother's walk, which is the intuitive blending of person and environment, Nnu Ego's movements begin to speak of the power to separate oneself from one's world so as to act on it. That these powers unexpectedly return immediately strips his wife of all her newly found powers of decision-making.

The first time Nnu Ego consciously registers that tribal attitudes are not going to sustain her in Lagos comes shortly after Nnaife's return. Here Emecheta uses coincidence to draw attention to the processes of change and to establish that Nnu Ego's emergent language will be shaped by a reaction against tribal customs as well as by response to urban demands. On the day that Nnaife gets a permanent job with the Lagos railways, the news of his elder bother's death arrives. This means that Nnaife inherits his wives. Nnaife's becoming the stable breadwinner dislodges Nnu Ego from the economic role within which she has begun to think of herself; the arrival of Adaku, an inherited wife, also dislodges her—this time from the wifely role within which she has always though of herself. As her tribal self is willing to take on the new role of senior wife, Nnu Ego cannot at first understand why Adaku's presence disturbs her so much. Once she realizes that it is because Ibuza traditions do not translate in Lagos, she sees, for the first time, that the old world is preferable to the new.

Nnu Ego, as the daughter of a great chief, is a deeply conservative woman and for some time she finds that the two codes within which she lives are simply antagonistic; they are too contradictory for her to live between them. Deadlock is broken when Adaku rebels against Nnaife and persuades Nnu Ego to join her in refusing to cook for him until he gives them more of his money. Their rebellion fails but it does force Nnu Ego to analyze more vigorously her discontent:

> On her way back to their room it occurred to Nnu Ego that she was a prisoner, imprisoned by her love for her children, imprisoned in her role as the senior wife. She was not even expected to demand more money for her family; that was considered below the standard expected of a woman in her position. It was not fair, she felt, the way men cleverly used a woman's sense of responsibility to actually enslave her.... It seemed that all she had inherited from her agrarian background was the responsibility and none of the booty. Well, even though she had now given in and admitted defeat, she was going to point this out to Nnaife that very evening when she came home from work. With that final decision, confidence sprang inside her like water from below the ground and seemed to wash away her gloomy thoughts with its clear, sparkling gush. (137)

However painful her position, Nnu Ego is no longer suspended between two antipathetic languages; something new is emerging and this time the springing of "confidence" is wholly within her own conscious recognitions.

As Nnaife is, that very day, conscripted into the army and so does not return home to hear his wife's resolve, Emecheta is clearly using coincidence to do more than indicate the tricks that life can play on someone who is battling through to a new epistemological basis. Nnu Ego's analysis is made in solitude and goes unheard; in a larger sense, nothing of the resolution that she achieves is ever heard by anyone. Emecheta seems to be drawing attention to the view that within the second, male language of the city, into which her protagonist is now moving, the private satisfactions of clarity and resolve are all that is in prospect: the give and take of dialogue, which would demand some recognition of the woman's language, is not available. The silence that greets Nnu Ego's recognition of the extent of the change demanded of her has the effect of making her own final silence more than a withdrawal; it becomes her positive indication that she can give (or not give) as good as she gets.

The final break with tribal language is also triggered by Adaku. Because Adaku has used Nnaife's army pay to set herself up in trade during the senior wife's absence, Nnu Ego appeals to the men of the Ibo community in Lagos. They condemn Adaku, using the tribal evaluation that the wife who has borne male children is the superior one and should get the money, but, although the judgement goes in her favor, Nnu Ego cannot concur. While she still shares their belief in the importance of male children, the realities of her urban life (her threadbare clothes, her empty stomach, her urine-stained and bug-ridden bed) as well as certain sisterly sympathies for Adaku do not allow her to ally herself with the tribal verdict.

Nnu Ego's understanding of "wife" and of "woman" has now undergone profound change, but the challenge to her sense of "mother" is still to come. Her goal throughout has been to ensure that her sons should be well-educated, but she has been unable to see that in exposing them to an alien world she would risk losing them. Therefore her sons' choices, to study abroad rather than to take well-paid local jobs, come as a painful shock to her. She seems at first to succeed in accommodating herself to their decision for she is able to say of the new basis on which she must relate to her sons that "parents only get reflected glory from their children nowadays" (213), but in Nnu Ego's subsequent lonely death, Emecheta indicates that the sons' neglect is a betrayal of the concept of motherhood as Nnu Ego still really understands it, and that betrayal kills her. That her sons have also not really understood the change they have been demanding of her is evident in their building a shrine to tribal motherhood in memory of her. As their gesture denies Nnu Ego's efforts to come to terms with contemporary, urban motherhood, she is left with only one way of making the importance of her endeavors felt—the silence of refusal.

This woman's final silence joins her earlier laughter as being an example of the small but vital way in which her being can be expressed within—but not on the terms set by—male language. The space created by this silence at the end of the novel words rather like the reading to Isak Dinesen's short story "The Blank Page" proposed by Susan Gubar (1982). The story involves the display of the wedding sheets of Portuguese princesses and tells how, in the framed, named, and dated collection of linen, only one sheet is unmarked by the required shedding of virginal blood. Gubar suggests that this blank sheet is to be read as a "mysterious but potent act of resistance" which is powerful by virtue of its raising so many unanswerable questions: "the blank page contains stories in no story, just as silence contains all potential sound and white contains all colour" (89). This is a claim that will work if an intention can be attributed to absence. Elaine Showalter comments on the dangers in women's remaining silenced (21) but if silence is a chosen part of a woman's speech, as it is in Nnu Ego's case, then the matter is different; then the subversion of male language can be seen to occur.

Identifying the ways in which the subversion of the limitations imposed by a male language may occur in women's lives is not an easy project for any woman writing, let alone for an African woman. Introducing a collection of writing by African women, Charlotte Bruner says that writing itself, in as much as it is to break with a non-individualized cultural code and to "speak out as an individual and as a woman" (xiii), demands something exceptional of an African woman; Buchi Emecheta herself corroborates this view in an interview with Itala Vivan:

> In a society where there is no social security, and where every boy or girl must belong to someone or something, there is no place for feminism, for individualism or for independence. Therefore I say that those of us in Africa, if we are feminist, [we] must be ultrafeminist, because our job is so much harder. (77)

The problem facing writers who take up the "ultrafeminist...job" is, as Mary Jacobus puts it, to speak "both for and as a woman (rather than 'like' a woman)" (15). What has been identified here in Emecheta's writing is how her novel, by depicting a second entry into the symbolic, can expose both the imposition and the subversion of androcentric concepts. Whether or not it is possible or even desirable to get beyond such subversion and achieve a distinctively female language, let alone the *ecriture feminine* envisaged by Helene Cixous and Luce Irigaray, is a matter which they, by proposing such an idea, have made it possible to debate but not yet to resolve. The possibility of creating an inevitable link between biology and writing which seems to haunt such debates and which might only serve to render women's writing forever marginal, may be avoided by the suggestion made by Mary Ellman (1986) that the desired female qualities should be looked for in the writing, not in the writer. As her quirky examples of Norman Mailer and Mary McCarthy indicate, this would leave it open for women or men to achieve the desired release of hitherto circum-scribed capacities. Ellman identifies one characteristic of such writing as the disruption of authority and sees it as a liberating rather than a simply embattled force in writing. Thus, if the sub-version of misogynistic practices and the possible opening of a female linguistic range can be achieved by imagining the way a woman's laughter or her silence helps to do this, as happens with Emecheta's protagonist, then what is achieved should be liberating for all users of language.

NOTES

1. The conditions of women in Nigerian society are discussed by Brown (1981) and Umeh (1980).
2. The dialectical relationship of "the symbolic" to the prelinguistic phase, "le semiotic" as Kristeva terms it, is discussed in Toril Moi (1985) and in K.K. Ruthven (1984). Their works also introduce the ideas of Helene Cixous and Luce Irigaray.

WORKS CITED

Brown, Lloyd W. *Women Writers in Black Africa*. Westport, Connecticut: Greenwood P, 1981

Bruner, Charlotte H. *Unwinding Threads*. London: Heinemann, 1983.

Dinesen, Izak. *Last Tales*. Harmondsworth: Penguin, 1983.

Ellman, Mary. "Thinking About Women."In Mary Eagleton ed., *Feminist Literary Theory: A Reader*. Oxford: Basil Blackwell, 1986.

Emecheta, Buchi. *The Bride Price*. London: Fontana, 1978.

—. *The Slave Girl*. London: Fontana, 1979.

—. *The Joys of Motherhood*. London: Heinemann, 1980.

Gubar, Susan. "The Blank Page." Ed. Elizabeth Abel. *Writing and Sexual Difference*. Brighton: Harvester P, 1982.

Jacobus, Mary. "The Difference of View." Ed. Mary Jacobus. *Women Writing and Writing About Women*. London: Croom Helm, 1979.

—. "The Question of Language: Men of Maxims and *The Mill on the Floss.*" Ed. Elizabeth Abel. *Writing and Sexual Difference*. Brighton: Harvester P, 1982.

Kristeva, Julia. *La Revolution du Langage Poetique*. Paris: Seuil, 1974.

Moi, Toril. *Sexual/Textual Politics*. London: Methuen, 1985.

Olsen, Tillie. *Silences*. London: Virago P, 1980.

Rich, Adrienne. *On Lies, Secrets, and Silence*. London: Virago P, 1980.

Ruthven, K.K. *Feminist Literary Studies: An Introduction*. Cambridge: CUP, 1984.

Showalter, Elaine. "Feminist Criticism in the Wilderness." Ed. Elizabeth Abel. *Writing and Sexual Difference*. Brighton: Harvester P, 1982.

Umeh, Marie. "African Women in Transition in the Novels of Buchi Emecheta." *Présence Africaine*. 116 (1980): 190–201.

Vivan, Itala. *Tessere per un mosaico Africano*. Verona: Morelli, 1984. Quotation translated by Linda Palazzo.

Language and Gender Conflict in Buchi Emecheta's *Second-Class Citizen*

Obododimma Oha

Contemporary scholarship on gender conflict, among other things, focuses on the relationship between language and gender. Among the different orientations in the study of this relationship are (a) the investigation of the differences between male and female linguistic productions, and (b) the investigation of the elements that suggest the deployment of language in waging "gender war."

The first orientation mentioned above assumes that the sex or gender of the user of language, whether speaker or writer, determines the pattern of language he or she produces; that is to suggest that "genderlect" exists. Philips, for instance, has tried to show variable syntactic and discourse differences of male-female courtroom discourse. Also, Bodine discusses sex-conditioned preferences made in the choices of linguistic forms.[1] The main point, however, as Sally McConnell-Ginet in "Language and Gender" has rightly stated, is that:

> ... focus on gender as just involving properties of individual linguistic agents can obscure important insight into how gender affects language production. For example, there might be no connection at all between the agent's sex or gender and patterns of language produced but significant interaction between forms produced and sex or gender of the audience....

> ... Production patterns might show systematic dependence on the sex/gender relation between agents and their audience....(79)

The language-difference orientation, as McConnell-Ginet rightly argues, tends to give the impression that it is only the sex/gender of the agent that determines linguistic production, whereas there are other contextual factors that even more significantly obligate the agent's verbal behavior. A writer, for instance, does not just use certain discourse strategies because he is male, but because there are pragmatic objectives, audience dispositions, etc., to be satisfied.

One danger in the language-difference approach is that it (indirectly) promotes gender stereotyping. Once it is accepted that men are fond of using particular linguistic forms, then a woman who uses such forms would be seen as "crossing," or trying to speak or write "as a man." Granted that, as Bruner and Kelso state, "there are two separate universes of discourse, one for men and another for women" (241), men and women nevertheless are not eternally occupants of any Whorfian prisons! In cross-sex verbal interactions, universals must be spoken/written.

What is rather very crucial is how both sexes could exploit the resources of language in promoting gender-specific interests. In this respect, quite a lot of interesting studies have been done, particularly on how men attempt to maintain their dominance over women through the choices they make in language, and through the imposition of male-referential terms on our so-called "universal" language. I will just mention a few of these studies here. West and Zimmermann have revealed that men, in their conversations with women, try to demonstrate their being in control through such impolite actions as interruptions (which are violations of turn-taking speaking rules). Such interruptions, in fact, seem to be prompted also by the man's assumption that he is superior, and that by allowing the woman to talk freely, he would be granting equality to her and, by so doing, threatening his own position. But it does not mean that only men interrupt women in discourse. The violation occurs both ways, and does suggest gender conflict and mutual aggression.

The political dimensions and sex-power implications of linguistic choices have been well studied by Sally McConnell-Ginet and O'Barr & Atkins. In my paper on male rest room graffiti, I have also tried to analyze the mechanisms of meaning used by male graffitists in their attempt to deploy language as a "weapon" for attacking, conquering, and subjecting women.

The use of language in fighting against women has been noted in Germaine Greer's seminal work, *The Female Eunuch* (279), particularly men's tendency of degrading and derogating women. In the same vein, Faust makes the following observation on man's inclination towards abusing women:

> ... Man's ingenuity knows no bounds when he wishes to insult *woman* and force her to see herself as he sees her (or as he wishes to think he sees her) ... he knows the power of language. He knows that language can control not only behavior, but thought itself. (97)

In their same-sex discourse, as Caroline Cole has shown, women also try to console themselves and consolidate their gender base. Even though they do not attack men directly, their protective approach, to me, is also a part of the gender warfare. Defense, obviously, is an important way of preventing defeat.

The investigation of the deployment of language in gender conflict, therefore, is challenging and useful, and could be extended to data from prose fiction. It would also be worthwhile to approach the novels of Buchi Emecheta from such a discourse and analytical standpoint. Emecheta's *Second-Class Citizen* (henceforth, *SCC*), which the present study focuses on, is a feminist text produced by a woman for the consumption of both sexes. The approach therefore, on the one hand, could help us understand more about the nature of (fictionalized) male-female conflict and what could be learnt from such conflicts for the (re-)ordering of actual human society.

On the other hand, the study complements other theoretical approaches to Emecheta's writings, as there are always many different ways of perceiving the same object. Extant studies on Emecheta's writings generally examine her themes and literary techniques. Marie Umeh, for instance, studies Emecheta's "campaign" for female emancipation through the love story of *Double Yoke* which, she observes, is told in "the blues mode." Also, Chimalum Nwankwo studies Emecheta's social vision and makes the very provocative observation that:

> Figuratively speaking, the bloody battle which women are waging to show how evil men are is a tragic waste of energy. There is more hurt and loss than profit in such futile exercises. (4)

The battle-axe Nwankwo waves in his essay is not my concern here. I am rather interested in the important observation made by Carole Boyce Davies on areas that need attention in the study of feminist and non-feminist African writings:

> A number of areas remain uncovered: Language, symbolic structure and how these are revealed in the works of male and female African writers is a relatively unexplored area. (17)

The questions this paper attempts to answer, therefore, are as follows: what types of linguistic choices do the main characters (who happen to be male and female, or husband and wife) in *SCC* make in their verbal interactions and what implications do such choices have for personal and gender faces? Also, at the narrational level (or the level of implied narrator-audience discourse, which could signify novelist-reader discourse), what is the nature of rhetorical display? What is the relationship of such rhetoric to internal cross-sex discourse involving characters? All together, what are the presuppositions underlying *SCC* as a female-created text, and what are the implications of content (as an expression of attitude) for male-female relations?

THE DATA

Before I tackle the questions outlined above, let me first of all provide an overview of the data: the gender conflict situation presented by Emecheta and the linguistic productions to be analyzed. Emecheta, in *SCC*, tells the story of the sufferings of Adah in the hands of her husband, Francis. To say "in the hands of her husband," in fact, is to be euphemistic; the story is clearly that of a man's enslavement of a woman in the name of marriage.

But Adah's problems begin from the fact that she is born into a patriarchal culture, a culture that prefers a male child to the

292

female, a culture in which proper formal education is given to the male and not to the female, a culture in which a woman is punished mercilessly when she offends, or is believed to have offended, and a culture in which the female child is a commodity for sale to the highest bidder. Emecheta presents this patriarchal culture as a background and partial factor for the behaviors of the agents involved in the gender conflict in the novel. Francis may have grown with full acquisition of beliefs and assumptions about his (male) supremacy, as a given in his culture. Adah, also, has obviously grown with bitterness about female deprivation (for instance, her father's and mother's disapproval of her going to school); dehumanization (for instance, the brutal beating she receives from male agents both at school and from her cousin at home); and commercialization (the high bride price charged on her head by those who didn't want to train a female).

Thus when Adah joins her husband, Francis, in London, we begin to see a rupture of socialization and psychological dispositions that stand in opposition. Adah, as the female "slave," has to toil to feed her "master" and also endure his uncontrollable sexual aggression. The master-slave relationship also makes it almost impossible for Adah's voice to be heard in the home, since voice and power are synonymous to a male chauvinist like Francis. Above all, as in the slave tradition, Adah once in a while receives a series of beatings from her "master."

This relationship between Adah and Francis, as presented in *SCC*, could be summarized as follows:

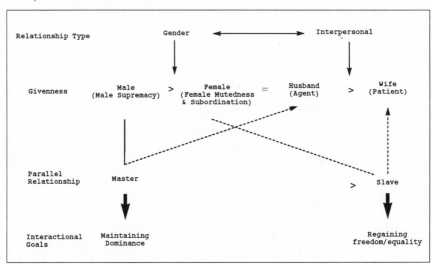

It is against the background of this genderized conflict that I examine the nature of language used by both Francis and Adah in addressing and/or referring to each other. In other words, I will base the analysis on Direct Speech (DS), in which Emecheta presents the actual words used by the characters with reporting tag or clause; Free Direct Speech (FDS), in which these actual words of the characters are presented without the reporting clause or tag; Indirect Speech (IS), or reported speech, in which the words of the narrator and those of the characters are mixed, with a transmutation of words—from present tense to past tense and first and second persons to the third person; and Free Indirect Speech (FIS), which is an IS without the reporting clause provided by the narrator. Since the novel also very distinctly makes the use of the stream-of-consciousness technique in which the narrator presents the thoughts of the character (verbalized and unverbalized), I will also in my analysis recognize and draw evidence from Direct Thought (DT), in which the verb used in reporting clause or tag merely refers to thought or mental function; Free Direct Thought (FDT), in which the supposedly verbalized thoughts are reported as direct, with present tense and first person pronouns, but with no reporting tag or clause, as in FDS; Indirect Thought (IT), which, like IS, shows a presentation of thought with a blend of the narrator's words and those of the characters; and Free Indirect Thought (FIT), in which the reporting clause is absent in the presentation of characters' thoughts, but with the transmutation pattern of the IS.[2] The considerations of both speech and thought would provide us with a fuller view of perspectives between Adah and Francis, and also help us in our discussion of the nature of the rhetorical display in the implied narrator-audience discourse and the gender implications of the suggested narrational sympathy in the FIS and the FIT.

WARRING IN WORDS: ADAH VS FRANCIS

Language could be used in (re)building as well as demolishing interpersonal and intergroup relationships. In the relationship between Adah and Francis, which signifies gender relationship, the tendency to deploy language in demolishing (or undermining) a relationship is higher than that of (re)building it. And, more specifically and personally, Francis (a male) has the greater inclination towards the genderized and negative function of language than Adah (a female). A few samples from *SCC* would suffice here:

(1)She told Francis about *The Bride Price* in the evening. But he replied that he would rather watch *The Saint* on the television which they had hired. Adah pleaded, and wailed at him that it was good, that her friends at the library said so. He should please read it. She said that Bill thought it should be typed out, because it was good.

Then Francis said, "*You keep forgetting that you are a woman* and that you are black. *The white man can barely tolerate us men, to say nothing of brainless females like you who could think of nothing except how to breast-feed her baby.*"

"That may be so," cried Adah, "but people have read it. And they say it is good. Just read it, I want your opinion. Don't you know what it means to us if in the future I could be a writer?"

Francis laughed, "What ever was he going to hear next? *A woman writer in his own house*, in a white man's country?" (184).

(2)"Why did you not tell your wife that your father had tails, Pa Noble?" Adah blurted out. She felt sick. Why must Pa Noble descend so low? Just to be married to this woman?

Mr. Noble simply laughed, or rather croaked, "*Iyawo, you are very, very young and inexperienced. I hope you'll learn very soon?*"

"*She's only a woman*," Francis said by way of an apology. (102, emphasis mine)

In (1) and (2) above, Francis uses face-threatening language in interactions with Adah. He derogates and depersonalizes Adah on the basis of the fact that she is "a woman." His perception and use of the word "woman" (you keep forgetting that you are a *woman* ...) is not just the ordinary denotative sense of

$$
\begin{bmatrix}
+ & \text{Human} \\
- & \text{Male} \\
\pm & \text{Adult}
\end{bmatrix}
$$

as could be componentially represented, but of sexist connotations:

$$
\begin{bmatrix}
+ & \text{Weak} \\
+ & \text{Subordinate} \\
- & \text{Rational} \\
- & \text{Trustworthy} \\
- & \text{Competent} \\
+ & \text{Childish}
\end{bmatrix}
$$

These prejudiced attitudinal meanings are expressed also in the DS (2): "she's only a woman." The presupposition in this statement is that Adah cannot say something acceptable (as wise) because she is "a woman" and a woman is not gifted with wisdom. The argument embedded in the presupposition is illogical because the presupposition contains a false premise, very much like what Arthur Schopenhauer would say of women:

> Women are suited to being the nurses and teachers of our earliest childhood precisely because they themselves are childish, silly and short-sighted, in a word big children, their whole lives long: a kind of intermediate stage between the child and the man, who is the actual human being, 'man.'(81)

The assertion, "she's only a woman," as a follow-up to Pa Noble's statements in (2), also seems to suggest the following:
a) Adah could be excused for her inexperience because she's only a woman and women are never experienced, never learn;
b) Adah's audacity in questioning Pa Noble's attitude and action could be accounted for by her sex and its (stereotypical) features. Francis hopes Pa Noble would be able to recover his meaning (the assumption) on the basis of the presupposition that he shares knowledge and/or male presuppositions about the woman with him.

The use of the presupposition by Francis is thus a matter of taken-for-grantedness. As McConnell-Ginet in "Language and Gender" rightly says:

> . . . in order to mean, agents presuppose, take things for granted, and . . . what can be taken for granted depends on what has been (often and audibly) expressed and can be assumed to be readily accessible . . . . To devise reasonable strategies for being

understood, agents must take account of what their audience is likely to take for granted—not necessarily to believe, but to treat as the 'unmarked' opinion. (92)

The idea of female depravity, to Francis, is unmarked, and is such that Pa Noble should know already. And for Adah to process the assertions, "You keep forgetting that you are a woman" and "she's only a woman," as insulting and face-threatening, she also has to refer to cultural stereotyping of the woman. Again, in this regard, McConnell-Ginet further explains:

To understand 'you think like a woman' as an insult a hearer need only recognize the general accessibility of devolution of woman's thinking; she need not accept it. On the other hand, a speaker who means to insult through uttering 'you think like a woman' and succeeds in so doing may (perhaps mistakenly) take his success to signal his hearer's agreement with his negative appraisal he depends on. (91-92)

But Adah does not overtly show her perception of the statements as insulting and Francis may still understand her silence or the hedging ("that may be so,") as in (1) agreement, and may intensify his derogation of her.

In fact, to Francis, as seen in (1) and (2), women are "brainless" and can only breast-feed babies. Thus in the FIT in (1) "A woman writer in his own house. . . ?" There is a presupposition of the woman's mental disadvantage, such that Adah daring to write is a waste of time and energy. Also in the reported laughter preceding the FIT in (1) there is a paralinguistic communication of disdain, and the laughter, as a response to Adah's preceding request and rhetorical question, clearly suggests scorn. Laughter in other situations could mean support and satisfaction, but in some situations amusement and derision meant to embarrass. The latter cases, which are uncharitable, are positioned as an attack on the aspiring "*woman writer in his own house.*" Both the laughter and the use of the decivilizing word "brainless" pose a threat to what Lim and Bowers (420) refer to as "competence face," the desire by an interactant in discourse that his or her abilities be recognized and respected.

Also in the same FIT in (1) above, Adah, as a wife, is alienated. Adah is perceived not as house-owner or as co-house-owner, but as a squatter. Note the use of the possessive "his" (not "her" or "our") and the modifying element "own." The FIT is an expression of the male-oriented cultural view of the world which Francis must have acquired. The acquisition of cultural thought or world-views interacts or co-occurs with language acquisition. Language acquisition is a mental process and in that process, what is captured by the mind is not only knowledge of grammatical rules but also content or meanings. It is not that language determines thought (or that thought determines language), as the strong form of the Whorfian hypothesis might suggest, but the culture—or *Weltanschauung*—"predisposes" meanings expressed in language.[3] It is from this standpoint, probably, that Geoffrey Leech states:

> The Sapir-Whorf position on language diversity is alliance with the empiricist view of language acquisition, since the exposure of children to different cultural environments, in which they learn different languages, can explain how they come to learn different conceptualizations of experience. (28)

Growing up in a culture or subculture that espouses male-dominance would therefore mean a psychological, behavioral and linguistic training for the expression of such dominance. The patriarchal system in which Francis grew up of course teaches that the house inhabited by a man and his wife belongs to the man, even if he has not built it. So, even though Francis is a tenant in London, he *thinks* that the house is "his own," not "her own" or "our own." To say "our own" would mean to include Adah, to make her "an insider" (instead of her being "an outsider") and to empower her. Such a thought, as explained in Wales' *A Dictionary of Stylistics*, is indeed *linguistic*, since thought is often described as "inner speech" (128). Thus the assertion and the ". . . inner speech. . ." on Francis' mind in (1) not only threatens Adah's "sex" and competence face, but also her "fellowship face" (the desire to be seen as a member of an in-group, or an insider) (Lim and Bowers 420). It distances her (+ DISTANCE).

Adah, on her own part, also uses face-threatening language in addressing Francis, but not at random, and also without (overt) sexist undertones like those of the latter. It is only in some of her DTs, FDTs and FITs, in which we have narrational/authorial presence, that sexist language occurs; see samples (5) and (6) below. In samples (3) and (4) below, her language is impolite, but apparently justified by her husband's misconduct and annoying utterances:

(3)Adah was still talking. She was going to Trudy. She was going to get the truth from her, if it killed her.

"God help you," Francis said. "This is not home, you know. You can be jailed for accusing her falsely. You will be in trouble if you go and fight a woman in her own home, you know. After all, she is keeping Titi for us."

"Yes, I know she is keeping Titi so that you can pretend to go and see her at eleven o'clock every night. Last night you left at eleven, and you did not come back until I was ready for work. . . . Seeing Titi!" An uncomfortable pause followed, during which Adah seemed to be weighing up her freedom. After all, she earned the money in the family.

She continued in a strange threatening way: "If she does not give me a good answer, I shall bring Titi home with me and I am not leaving this house to work for you until the kids are admitted into the nursery or you agree to look after them. I don't care what your friends say. I am going to Trudy. She has something to tell me."

"You're just like your mother after all. That quarrelsome troublemaker! People say women grow up to be like their mothers. But unfortunately for you, you're not as tall and menacing as she was. You're small, and I'm sure Trudy will teach you a lesson or two." (70—71)

(4)"You could have tried, Francis. Look at your friend, Mr. Eke—when he knew that his wife was coming with their daughter, he made sure he moved away from this lot," she said aloud.

"Sorry, but I was too busy. It's not bad, you can keep to yourself, you don't have to mix with them. You have your children to look after, you don't have to see them!"

"You make it all sound so easy—I don't have to see

them. You forget I have young children, and they will bring me into contact with the neighbors. You should have thought of that before. Have you no shame at all or have you lost your sense of shame in this God-forsaken country? Oh, I wish I had not come. I wish I had been warned. I wish. . . ." (42)

The FDS in (3)—"Yes I know. . . . Seeing Titi!" carries an implication of Francis' adulterous relation with Trudy. The implication is indeed strategic for, on the surface level, Adah could be said to have *avoided* performing a face-threatening act (FTA) of *accusing*. But at the level of pragmatic meaning, the FTA could be inferred. It is therefore left for Francis, the addressee, to derive the FTA but not to hold Adah responsible for (directly) accusing him. In other words, it is only Francis that has accused himself if he says that Adah has accused him! It is not surprising then that Francis says nothing to follow-up Adah's utterance of the indirect accusation and only waits for Adah to perform a bald act of threatening before he replies with an FTA that diverts attention and shields him completely from the you-say-so indirect accusation.

The act of accusing indirectly is tactful also because it adequately protects Adah even though it is contextually possible for Francis to recover the implicated meaning.[4] The FTA performed by Adah is therefore not as "bald" (without redress for face) as the FTA's performed by Francis against her. The absence (or scarcity) of mitigating elements and non-avoidance of FTA in utterances marks Francis out as one who is inclined toward using language to "do things" against the other, as one who is very unwilling to accommodate the other. Such an inclination is certainly egoistic and power-oriented, i.e., it produces the configuration (+ P)ower (+ D)istance.

The analysis has also shown that Francis uses language not only to subjugate Adah as a person, but also to pursue the interests of gender, i.e., to subjugate the woman. This use of language as a weapon for oppressing the female Other is a significant aspect of gender conflict addressed by the Emecheta rhetoric in *SCC*.

THE GENDER-ORIENTED RHETORIC

Wayne C. Booth makes a point which, I believe, is fundamental to the conceptualization of fiction as a rhetorical display:

. . . The author cannot choose to avoid rhetoric; he

can only choose the kind of rhetoric he will employ.
He cannot choose whether or not to affect his readers' evaluation, by his choice of narrative manner;
he can only choose whether to do it well or poorly.
(149)

Buchi Emecheta, in *SCC*, presents the "gender-oriented"
rhetoric about the oppression of the woman (the Patient) by the
man (the Agent). The rhetoric, naturally, is presented in such a
way that the sympathy of the implied audience would be for the
patient. In other words, the "implied narrator" (Booth 157), through
the narrative, attempts to influence the audience's feelings and
judgement. The rhetoric would, therefore, inevitably require the
creation and use of resources necessary for argumentation and persuasion.

SCC could thus be understood as making an argument (and also
playing on the reader's feelings at the same time) on the issue of
gender. Understood in the Toulminian sense, an argument in
rhetoric proceeds from Data (or Evidence/Proof) to Claim (or
Conclusion) through Warrant, which may also have a Backing. The
Claim (C) may have a Rebuttal (R), which refers to reservations or
exceptions to the (C), and a Qualifier (Q), which presents the
degree of force attached to the (C). The Evidence (E) in *SCC* com-
prises the linguistic productions, actions and postures by Francis
(the male Agent) which are against Adah (the female Patient).

What rather seems more crucial is the way Emecheta has tried
to put her gender-oriented argumentation and postures across, and
within the constraints of the genre. In the first place, the nature of
the narrative and the narration require attention.

The narrative is a display in indirectness posture. There is the
fictive or implied narrator who is not involved in the actions in the
story and who narrates from the omniscient point of view, knowing every thought and action of Adah and Francis. With such
"knowledge" of the Agent and the Patient, the implied narrator is
able to supply us with the thoughts and actual utterances of the
Agent and the Patient that have gender implications.

But what is the relationship between this implied narrator and
the novelist? This question calls for reference to the debate on the
(mode of the) presence of the author in his or her writing. Roland
Barthes in "The Death of the Author" in this regard would shock
us with the modernist argument that "the text is . . . made and read
in such a way that at all its levels the author is absent" (147), the

301

consequences being the impossibility of interpretation of a text:

> Once the Author is removed, the claim to decipher
> a text becomes quite futile. To give a text an Author
> is to impose a limit on that text, to furnish it with a
> final signified, to close the writing. (Barthes, 147)

Barthes' view, which would appeal to deconstructionists like Derrida and De Man, seems to obscure the rhetorical and/or discoursal conceptualization of fiction—the fact that an individual language user is interacting with another. Even though an author of fiction may not want to reveal his or her presence in the text (for reasons I shall give shortly), it is possible to discern his or her "God-presence." Booth rightly contends that:

> The author is present in every speech given by any
> character who has had conferred upon him, in what-
> ever manner, the badge of reliability. Once we know
> that God is God in Job, once we know that Monna
> speaks only truth in "The Falcon," the authors speak
> whenever God and Monna speak. (18)

The strategy adopted by Emecheta in *SCC* is that of speaking through an implied narrator who shows sympathy for the female Patient (I shall show the evidences of such sympathy later). And, it is not only that there is indirectness of source, there is also the indirectness of the mode—the narrative form which, as I have stated above, merely *suggests* the author's argument and judgement. By maintaining an indirectness posture, the author is being tactful.[5]

To be direct is to quickly reveal the pragmatic objective of the communication, and, in fact, to betray artistic communication, as I have observed in "The Role of Face in Wole Soyinka's *From Zia With Love*." The indirectness of source and mode is an avoidance of threat to "autonomy face" of the reader, the desire by an interactant in discourse that he or she be left undisturbed or not imposed upon (Lim & Bowers, 420). Thus, even though the author suggests a claim through the implied narrator, the reader is free to proclaim the claim invalid, to interpret the implied argument differently, or to fault the Evidence. It is this "freedom" of the reader, I believe, that has been over-emphasized by Roland Barthes in his assertion:

> . . . A text is made of multiple writings, drawn from

many cultures and entering into mutual relations
of dialogue, parody, contestation; but there is one
place where this multiplicity is focussed and that
place is the reader, not as was hitherto said, the
author. The reader is the space on which all the quotations that make up a writing are inscribed without any one of them being lost; a text's unity lies not
in its origin but in its destination. Yet this destination cannot any longer be personal: the reader is
without history, biography, psychology; he is simply that *someone* who also holds together in a single
field all the traces by which the written text is constituted. (148)

Within the narration itself, however, this avoidance strategy fails.
The narrator (an author) eventually interferes with the reader's
judgement by blending her thoughts with those of the female
Patient, Adah, and by making comments which are prejudicial to
the face wants of the Male Agent. The following exemplify such
intrusions:

(5)Adah was now standing by the sink and felt like
laughing at Francis, standing there all flushed. *How
like animals we all look when we are consumed by our
basic desires, thought Adah, standing there by the sink,
like a wicked temptress luring her male to destruction.
All that Francis needed to be taken for a gorilla was
simply to bend his knees.* . . .

Then Francis went on, pleading like a fool, 'Oh, yes,
we'll go tomorrow. Is that all you wanted? Have I
refused anything you said? Are you not like my
mother to me in this country? Have I ever refused
your command?'

Adah has to laugh here. Her command, indeed! *How
funny men can be*!

She heard the church bell chiming seven o'clock,
when *Francis rolled on his side, like an exhausted
drunk.* (95)

(6)It was Francis who followed the nurse, listening
to all the talk. *Of course he heard only the sweet words,
he did not see that the baby's shawl was not new. That*

> *it was off-white and not soft. Men are so blind.* (137,
> emphases mine)

In (5), the narrator's thoughts and voice merge with the
thoughts of the female Patient. It is not only the female Patient
that mentally (re)constructs the male Agent as debased and ani-
malistic, the narrator also identifies with the Patient in such conceptualization. Just as we would have in any other rhetoric of
conflict—for instance, war rhetoric—the "enemy" is presented in
decivilizing and derogatory terms which could alienate him from
the audience.[6] The vilification strategy in conflict rhetoric is an
attempt to make the audience follow the speaker or writer in hating the "enemy." As Sam Keen has said,

> In all propaganda, the face of the enemy is designed
> to provide a focus for our hatred. He is the other.
> The outsider, the alien. He is not human. If we can
> only kill him, we will be rid of all within and with-
> out ourselves that is evil. (16)

By identifying with the Patient and vilifying the Agent, as a representative of "men," Emecheta makes the conflict between Adah
and Francis a case of "Us" versus "Them," not necessarily Adah versus Francis. The generalizations ("How funny men can be!" and
"Men are so blind") in (5) and (6) presuppose that binary distinction in which we find the author and the patient included in the
same gender camp as patients. It also presupposes (falsely too) the
culpability and wrongness of *all men* as a result of the culpability
and wrongness of only one man. It is obvious that the author-narrator has sneaked into view to counter the anti-woman rhetoric
used by Francis in his interactions with Adah. In other words, at
the narrational level, the author comes to the aid of the supposedly helpless female patient. The engendering of rhetoric in *SCC*,
in fact, seems to presuppose the primordial antagonistic demarca-
tions group consciousness generates. As Keen further says:

> The corporate identity of most peoples depends on
> dividing the world into a basic antagonism:
>
> > Us versus them
> > Insiders versus Outsiders
> > The tribe versus the enemy. (17)

Thus, men versus women. The humiliation of one woman becomes
the humiliation of all women by all men!

The faulty generalization in the narration indeed weakens the rhetoric of the novel. It is not only that it does not follow from evidence(s) provided, but it also subverts the narrative as a mode of indirect argumentation. Also, as cross-sex discourse, the narrative appears to distance Men (+ D) and to promote difference.

In spite of the problems of faulty generalization in the narrative, the use of parallel case makes the implied argument on gender conflict stronger. The deprivation Adah suffers as a woman is juxtaposed with the deprivation blacks suffer in England. There is thus the "silent" proposition that gender deprivation is parallel to racial deprivation: in other words, that deprivation or oppression is bad, no matter the axis on which it occurs, whether on the axis of race or on the axis of sex/gender. Male oppression of the female is a destruction of creativity (as seen in Francis' mindless burning of Adah's manuscript) and also to work, life, and the concept of "home" (as seen in Francis' disruptive sexual tendencies and physical assault on Adah).

Generally, therefore, the gender-orientation of rhetoric in SCC is an attempt to re-order social relations to the advantage of the woman. It is a counter-rhetoric that Emecheta presents, a response which merely intensifies conflict at the macro level through linguistic productions that threaten the fellowship face wants of the man. On the contrary, her rhetoric, which shows sympathy for the female Patient, does the face work of promoting female solidarity.

CONCLUSION

The paper upholds the view that participants in discourse (could) use their linguistic productions in pursuing the interests of gender and in generating gender conflict.

Buchi Emecheta not only shows this function of language in connection with the gender conflict in the verbal interactions between Adah and Francis, but also in the process uses the rhetoric of her narration in waging gender war. In other words, SCC, as a response in the discourse on conflict between Man and Woman in society, reveals that language is an important issue to which scholarship on gender should pay more attention, not just on descriptive criteria but also as a contribution to conflict resolution. The resolution of conflict, as I have pointed out in "Language and Conflict Resolution," urgently requires linguistic disarmament. Obviously, Emecheta is as guilty as Francis is in the offensive and genderized uses of language. In other words, she is guilty of the very offense (verbally ruining inter-sex relationship) which she is also criticizing in *SCC*. Writers of fiction, and indeed of all other genres, need to be conscious of the repercussions of their rhetoric or face at the levels of gender, creed, race, and ethnicity.

NOTES

1. For further investigation of this orientation, See Edward M. Bruner's and Jane Paige Kelso's essay, "Gender Differences in Graffiti: A Semiotic Perspective."
2. I am using the concepts of DS, FDS, FIS, IS, DT, FDT and FIT in the senses presented in Katie Wales' *A Dictionary of Stylistics*.
3. Edward Sapir's assertion that "we see and hear and otherwise experience very largely as we do because the language habits of our community *predispose* certain choices of interpretation" (emphasis mine) opens up a more acceptable and less rigid form of the hypothesis. For Whorf's position on the relationship between language and thought, see his essay, "The Relation of Habitual Thought and Behavior to Language."
4. A parallel discussion of this claim could be found in the essay, "What Men and Women are Said to Be: Social Representation and Language" by Kruse, Weimer and Wagner.
5. Seen from the standpoint of Grice's co-operative principle, the use of indirectness by Adah in (3) is a violation of the Maxim of Relation ("Be relevant"). The violation is deliberate; so we assume that Adah is still co-operating at a deeper level, inviting Francis to seek and recover meaning at such level.
6. The use of decivilizing and derogatory terms, as I have observed in my study of war rhetoric, characterizes anti-enemy rhetoric, and could be found in other discourses of conflict, especially those we often configure as "war," for instance, "gender war" or "war of the sexes."

WORKS CITED

Barthes, Roland. "The Death of the Author." *Image—Music—Text*. Trans. Stephen Heath. Glasgow: Fontana/Collins, 1979.

Bodine, A. "Sex Differentiation in Language." *Language and Sex: Difference and Dominance*. Eds. B. Thorne and N. Henley. Rowley: Newbury House, 1975.

Booth, Wayne C. *The Rhetoric of Fiction*. Chicago: University of Chicago P, 1975.

Bruner, Edward M. and Jane Paige Kelso. "Gender Differences in Graffiti: A Semiotic Perspective." *The Voices and Words of Women and Men*. Ed. Cheris Kramar. New York: Pergamon P, 1980. 239—252.

Cole, Caroline M. "Oh Wise Women of the Stalls." *Discourse and Society* 2.4 (1991): 401—411.

Davies, Carole Boyce. "Feminist Consciousness and African Literary

Criticism." *Ngambika: Studies of Women in African Literature.* Eds. Carole Boyce Davies and Anne Adams Graves. New Jersey: Africa World P, 1986. 1—23.

Emecheta, Buchi. *Second-Class Citizen.* London: Fontana, 1988.

Faust, Jean. "Words That Oppress." *Women Speaking* (April, 1970): 90—108.

Greer, Germaine. *The Female Eunuch.* New York: McGraw-Hill, 1970.

Grice, H. P. "Logic and Conversation." *Syntax and Semantics, Vol.3: Speech Acts.* Eds. P. Cole and J. L. Morgan. New York: Academic P, 1975. 41—58.

Keen, Sam. *Faces of the Enemy: Reflections of the Hostile Imagination.* San Francisco: Harper and Row, 1986.

Kruse, Lenelis, Ernst Weimer and Franc Wagner. "What Men and Women are Said to Be: Social Representation and Language." *Speakers: The Role of the Listener.* Eds. Carl F. Graumann and Theo Herrmann. Clevendon /Philadelphia: Multilingual Matters, 1989. 85—104.

Leech, Geoffrey. *Semantics: The Study of Meaning.* New York: Penguin, 1981.

Lim, Tae-Seop and John Waite Bowers. "Facework: Solidarity, Approbation, and Tact." *Human Communication Research.* 17.3 (1991): 415—450.

McConnell-Ginet,Sally. "Address Forms in Sexual Politics." *Women's Language and Style.* Eds. D. R. Butturf, and E. J. Epstein. Akron: University of Akron P, 1978.

——. Review of *Language, Sex and Gender: Does 'La Difference' Make a Difference?* Eds. J. Orsanu, M. K. Slatter and L. L. Adler, and *Sexist Language: A Modern Philosophical Analysis.* Ed. M.Vetterling-Braggin. *Language* 59 (1983): 373—391.

——. "The Origins of Sexist Language in Discourse". *Discourses in Reading and Linguistics.* Eds. Sheila J. White and Virginia Teller. New York: Annals of the New York Academy of Sciences, 1984.

——. "Language and Gender." *Linguistics: The Cambridge Survey, Vol. IV, Language: The Socio-Cultural Context.* Ed. Frederick J. Newmeyer. Cambridge: Cambridge University P, 1990. 75—99.

Nwankwo, Chimalum. "Emecheta's Social Vision: Fantasy on Reality?" *Ufahamu* XVII.1 (Fall 1988): 35—44.

O'Barr, W. and B.K. Atkins. "Women's Language" or "Powerless Language"? *Women and Language in Literature and Society.* Eds. Sally McConnell-Ginet, R. A. Borker and N. Furman. New York: Praeger, 1980.

Oha, Obododimma. "Language as a Weapon of Gender War in Male Restroom Graffiti." Paper Presented at a Conference of West African Association of Commonwealth Literature and Language Studies, Owerri. (April, 1994).

——. "The Role of Face in Wole Soyinka's *From Zia With Love:* A View From Discourse Pragmatics." *Ase* 2.2 (1994).

——. *Language in War Situation: A Stylistic Study of the War Speeches of Yakubu Gowon and Emeka Ojukwu.* Unpublished Ph.D. Thesis. Ibadan: University of Ibadan, 1994.

——. "Language and Conflict Resolution." *ASUU—University of Calabar Newsletter* 1.1 (August, 1994).

Philips, S. U. "Sex Differences and Language." *Annual Review of Anthropology*

9 (1980): 523—544.

——. "The Interaction of Variable Syntax and Discourse Structure in Gender-Differentiated Speech in the Courtroom." Paper presented at NEH Conference on Sex Differences in Language, University of Arizona, 1983.

Sapir, Edward. *Selected Writings in Language, Culture and Personality.* Ed. D.G. Mandelbaum. Berkeley: University of California P, 1949.

Schopenhauer, Arthur. *Essays and Aphorisms.* New York: Penguin, 1978.

Toulmin, Stephen Edelston. *The Uses of Argument.* Cambridge: Cambridge UP, 1958.

Umeh, Marie. "Reintegration With the Lost Self: A Study of Buchi Emecheta's *Double Yoke." Ngambika: Studies of Women in African Literature.* Eds. Carole Boyce Davies and Anne Adams Graves. New Jersey: Africa World P, 1986. 173—180.

Wales, Katie. *A Dictionary of Stylistics.* Harlow: Longman, 1990.

West, C. and D. Zimmermann. "Small Insults: A Study of Interruptions in Cross-Sex Conversations Between Unacquainted Persons." *Language, Gender and Society.* Eds. B. Thorne, Cheris Kramarae and N. Henley. Rowley: Newbury House, 1983.

Whorf, Benjamin Lee. "The Relation of Habitual Thought and Behavior to Language." *Language, Thought and Reality: Selected Writing of Benjamin Lee Whorf.* Ed. John B. Carroll. Massachusetts: The M. I. T. P., 1978. 134—159.

PART FIVE
(RE)CONSTRUCTING
GENDER RELATIONS

A reading of Buchi Emecheta informs us of the ways fiction, particularly women's writing, plays a part in the process of constructing subjectivity to create a world in which women can live complete lives, a world that affords women opportunities for freedom, creativity, cultivation of the intellect, work, self-expression, political action, friendship, intimacy, and love on the same terms as men. The papers in this section examine the (re)construction of gender relations in the novels of Buchi Emecheta. However, through widening critical perspectives the critics explore the implications of those gender relations for both the society and the fictive characters in the selected novels. In the essay, "They Were There, Too: Women and the Civil War(s) in *Destination Biafra*," Abioseh M. Porter argues that Emecheta's fictional discussion of the historical prelude to the war and the manner in which she challenges some of the fundamental assumptions about women—especially during war—are generally so complex and insightful that the reader remains undeterred by whatever flaws the novel may possess. The major achievement of Emecheta, according to Porter, is in her presentation of female characters who transcend the traditional and stereotypical roles often reserved for them and that as "the war progresses, the atrocities and injustices women suffer provide them with greater impetus to take action aimed at ending the war on both the political as well as sexual levels." Nevertheless, Porter's reading of the political and cultural implications in the novel possess its own problematics, for he insists that "the point is not that specific incidents (of atrocities) like those recorded in the novel may not or indeed could not have happened. Rather the point is that the accounts seem too lopsided." But that is the reality of wars; atrocities are lopsided as a result of the possession of superior arms and also as a consequence of the battles taking place in localities inhabited by a particular ethnic group. Nevertheless, he accepts the (re)evaluation of the contributions of women to the war in the novel as part of the necessary examination of gender relations.

John C. Hawley's essay, "Coming To Terms: Buchi Emecheta's *Kehinde* and the Birth of a 'Nation,'" focuses on the issue of nationhood at the core of *Destination Biafra* and also on the invariable theme of "the Nigerian woman caught between two worlds." Hawley posits that Emecheta "delights in defamiliarizing the terrain, hijacking the expectations of readers who prefer clear borders and moral rites of passage." Of course that assertion reopens the debate initiated by Chinweizu *et al.* in *Towards the Decolonization of African Literature* on the question of the Eurocentric or Afrocentric imagination of writers from Africa. Nevertheless Hawley is convinced that the choice of Kehinde as a character is a decision that "has been a long time coming in Emecheta's fiction, the result of an internal argument that has listened to two voices for years and struggled to heal the breach."

Ezenwa-Ohaeto examines in his essay, "Tropes of Survival: Protest and Affirmation in Emecheta's autobiography, *Head Above Water*," the basis for Emecheta's dogged persistence in transforming gender relations in an Igbo society. Considering the pervasive trope of survival in *Head Above Water*, Ezenwa-Ohaeto highlights the tension between protest and affirmation in the life of Buchi Emecheta which inevitably seeps into her fiction, for he states that "the idea of survival gradually permeates her life as she grows, absorbing the traditions and cultures of the various locations in which she lived." Nevertheless, the critic insists that protest positively nurtures Buchi Emecheta into an individual whose desire to survive is capable of surmounting all odds. He argues that the constant interrogation of her intentions and the doubts cast on her aspirations create the feeling of protest that ultimately leads Buchi Emecheta to affirmatively seek to achieve her aims. The positive development of the protagonist's life is shown to derive much energy from the affirmative support of other people—individuals and groups. All the same Ezenwa-Ohaeto's identification of instances of characters responding negatively to the issue of survival magnifies Emecheta's vision as encompassing intercontinental communities and societies. The conclusion is that the key to Emecheta's creativity lies in this autobiography and that there is a blend of personal development and socio-historical movements within the period in which *Head Above Water* is set.

Christine Sizemore's essay, "The London Novels of Buchi Emecheta" scrutinizes the characters of Ada, Gwendolen, and Kehinde not only in terms of the imperatives of an alien culture but more interestingly as emigrants deployed as fictive voices standing in a "liminal space between cultures where they search for a secure place for themselves and their families and freedom within the city." Sizemore rightly points out that these London novels show a coming together in London of women's voices from African and Afro-Caribbean cultures and provides some hope that racism and abuse can be overcome. In addition, the critic, in representing *Kehinde* as the return of the novelist to the terrain of the diasporic and the post-colonial, asserts that Emecheta and the character have joined the diaspora, and that "they have become immigrants, true Londoners, feminist denizens of the cosmopolis."

Contrastive to Abioseh M. Porter's essay and a relevant examination of gender relations in the same novel is J.O.J. Nwachukwu-Agbada's essay, "Buchi Emecheta: Politics, War and Feminism in *Destination Biafra*" in which he states as follows: "Emecheta is so concerned about the treatment inflicted by both Nigerian and Biafran soldiers on her Western Igbo people during that war that she seems to have forgotten to condemn war as prominent writers over the ages usually do. The author is more concerned with the circumstances of her people." This critic believes that the contradictions he highlights in the essay deepen the artistic cleavages in the novel for he emphasizes that the image of Debbie Ogedemgbe "is that of a character who leaps from one difficulty to another in a quixotic succession." Nwachukwu-Agbada's conclusion is cogent for he insists that "Emecheta's greatest achievement in the work is her insistence that although more men might have died from the actual fight, women were largely its practical casualties" and that the story shows "how women battled to save themselves and

311

their families in a time of national emergency."

John C. Hawley's view appears to be that supported and extended by Pauline Ada Uwakweh's essay, "To Ground the Wandering Muse: A Critique of Buchi Emecheta's Feminism" which demonstrates that the new female protagonist Kehinde, falls short of Emecheta's vision in *Destination Biafra*. Through the three angles of Kehinde's marriage, motherhood, and rebellion, Uwakweh claims that Kehinde is driven by the problems of unemployment, self-imagined humiliation, and the trauma of dependence. She also asserts that Kehinde's claim to "motherhood is artistically consistent with her actual role as mother" but that her rebellion is a mere "sexual revolt." Her conclusion significantly calls for an artistic consideration of women's roles as nurturers and preservers and that "the African female's pursuit of independence cannot compromise the significance of children to the African world view."

Clearly these papers highlight the way in which Emecheta has (re)constructed gender relations and the varied perspectives here, even in their dissonance, highlight that essential aspect.

Ezenwa-Ohaeto

They Were There, Too:
Women and the Civil War(s)
in *Destination Biafra*

Abioseh M. Porter

In the world of contemporary African literary history, the progress
made by female authors is now acknowledged as being quite
remarkable. Charlotte Bruner, in a survey of African women
authors written in 1985, not only views the 80s as the decade of
African and African Diaspora women writers but also suggests,
among other things, that "[p]erhaps the fact that women now may
actively engage in war, and the fact that wars no longer spare civilian populations,..." has led to a situation where "Women today can
write authoritatively, authentically about almost any subject. What
they write is important, for today and for tomorrow."[1] It is also ironic, however, that some of the most celebrated attempts to discuss
works dealing with the Nigeria-Biafra civil war—one of the pre-
dominant themes of modern African literature—have either
ignored or underestimated the literary efforts of female writers.
The prominent absence of a novel such as Buchi Emecheta's

Destination Biafra from most critical discussions of the war novel in Africa clearly seems to negate some of the high hopes Bruner has for women authors, especially those writing nontraditional genres of fiction. Whereas pages and pages have been written on the civil war, including essays on some of the most trivial poems by male authors, most critics discussing works dealing with the tragic events of 1967–1970 often fail to include *Destination Biafra*,[2] even though this novel unmistakably adds several new thematic dimensions to the genre in Africa, as Marie Umeh bluntly puts it:

> African women writers have not been treated as major contributors to the general output of war literature. In postwar writing in Nigeria, women writers are conspicuous by their absence.... One does not get the impression that post-war writing comprises any other than the male sex.[3]

To get to some of the specific contributions Emecheta makes to the genre of war writing in African literature, we must begin by looking at the subjects that have generally been covered by some of her male counterparts writing about that same war. Most male authors writing about the Nigeria-Biafra war often discuss events as they take place either during or immediately after the war. Thus topics such as the military reasons (including tactical and strategic maneuvers and battlefield scenarios) for Biafra's loss of the war, the consequences of the war on the ordinary folks who had made tremendous sacrifices for their nation and received nothing but contempt and insults as reward, and the behavior of those individuals who used the war as an opportunity to empower and enrich themselves form the core of works by authors such as Eddie Iroh, S.O. Mezu, and Cyprian Ekwensi—to name a few.

Emecheta, on the other hand, makes some distinct contributions by attempting to answer, in fictional form at least, some other important questions about the war: "What were the historical reasons for the Nigeria-Biafra civil war?" "Indeed, what caused that upheaval?" "What were the roles of women during that conflict?" "What is the future role of women in postwar Nigeria?" True, some of these questions have been raised by various writers, but what makes *Destination Biafra* such a powerful work is Emecheta's unconventional and compelling description of the probable causes of the war and the role of women during that war. And so, in spite of some of Emecheta's cartoon-like portrayal of the atrocities and consequences of the war itself (where we often see her biases leading her to create some highly implausible, idealized, and even preposterous situations and characters), Emecheta's fictional discussion of the historical prelude to the war and the manner in which she challenges some of the fundamental assumptions about women—especially during war—are generally so complex and insightful that the reader remains undeterred by whatever flaws the novel may possess.

A major point that is made throughout *Destination Biafra* is that the political legacy that was bequeathed to Nigerians by the British after independence was not only bound to fail but also had the potential of leading to inevitable chaos. For the novel's narrator and some of the British authorities (and, we suspect, for Emecheta herself), the kind of "democracy" by "proportional representation" that the British decided to leave Nigerians with had very little to do with genuine democratic principles. It was based primarily (if not solely) on ensuring governance by what they considered to be the feudalistic, politically naive, and less radical Hausas (who also happened to be the largest ethnic or regional group in Nigeria). It was assumed by the British authorities that if they could get the more ambitious and more radical Ibos and Yorubas out of real political control (at least on the federal level), British economic interests would be safeguarded. This is why at the beginning of the novel, Governor MacDonald, the last Governor of pre-independence Nigeria, is shown to be extremely worried and upset by the refusal of the Sardauna of Sokoto—the traditional ruler of the North—"to leave his palace to come and live with the 'Kaferis'—non-believers—in the South [read: Lagos]" (3). For the British in this novel, the criteria for selecting Nigerian successors to the colonial administration never include attributes such as capability, dedication, ability, or loyalty to one's country. All that really matters is the assurance that British economic interests are secured. No surprise then that MacDonald concludes a discussion with some of his friends by saying "the thing is to back the Hausas with everything we have" (9). It is also why these same friends, the former Governor, Sir Fergus Grey, and especially his son Alan (a military training officer with the Nigerian government and an embodiment of the cold war) are so desperate to ensure that Nigeria does not fall into the 'wrong' Nigerian hands. Alan, the stereotypical "friend of Africa," and a lover of the pre-independence Nigerian finance minister's daughter, Debbie Ogedemgbe, provides what seems the rationale for the British position:

> These vast areas are full of oil, pure crude oil, which
> is untouched and still needs thorough prospecting.
> Now we are to hand it over to these people, who've
> had all these minerals since Adam and had not
> known what to do with them. Now they are begin-
> ning to be aware of their monetary value. And after
> independence they may sign it all over to the
> Soviets for all we know. (6)

It seems quite logical, then, that even after the Sardauna refuses
to become Prime Minister of Nigeria, the British authorities (especially Governor MacDonald and Alan Grey) do their very best—
including having the Governor make a premature announcement
of victory by the British-supported Hausa candidate in the general elections—to have a Hausa, Nguru Kano elected as Prime
Minister while an Ibo is named President, a largely ceremonial
post. Emecheta thus makes the point that some of the manipulation by external forces which became so flagrant during the civil
war—and which are written about quite extensively by her male
compatriots—actually had their genesis at some earlier periods.

The novelist is, of course, aware that the civil war did not take
place only because of British (or foreign) instigation and interference. She also demonstrates how some of the causes of this war
were directly attributable to the actions of some of the Nigerian
politicians themselves. She points out that, in addition to the British
manipulation of events, there were Nigerian politicians who used
tribalism as perhaps the only way of convincing their constituents
to vote for them: "They [the Tetekus and Ogedemgbes] were from
the same minority tribe, and people knew that if all went well for
the Ogedemgbes in the general election their relations and tribesmen would not be forgotten." (16) We are also told that during the
electioneering campaign, one candidate, "to the accompaniment
of talking drums, told his constituents that if they voted for a person from another tribe they would be selling their own soul to the
devil: If you offend a man from your own tribe you can beg him
through the gods of the family. But if you offend a man who does
not even understand your language, how can you tell which is his
god?" (16) Emecheta, perhaps with some exaggeration, suggests
that such appeals for group identification and group loyalty as well
as the kind of ethnic 'solidarity' that encourages voters to vote only
for members of their own ethnic group (regardless of qualifications
and ability) were partly responsible for the subsequent breakdown

of the country's political structures.

In several episodes, Emecheta indicates how, in spite of partially idealistic and partially pragmatic efforts at genuine national reconciliation by a few Nigerian politicians (the Ibo, Dr. Ozimba, and the Hausa Alhaji Malinki, for example), almost all of the elections were conducted on a purely tribal basis. The crass and unprogressive nature of tribalism is shown most forcefully in the famous Bakodaya episodes in Northern Nigeria, where several northern [read: Hausa] candidates get an average of no less than 400,000 votes each while their non-northern opponents receive bakodaya or absolutely nothing.

The writer also points to the unstatesmanlike, even childish, behavior of two of the older politicians, Chief Oluremi Odusomu and Chief Durosaro. When Odumosu, who had given up his position as leader of the Yoruba-dominated Action Group party to contest in the federal elections, is appointed leader of the relatively powerless federal opposition party, he engages in a very bitter and, ultimately, infantile struggle with his former deputy and friend, Durosaro, to regain the position of leader of the more powerful regional Action Group. Emecheta's description of the "squabbles" between the two chiefs leaves no doubt that their actions contributed quite directly to the initial wave of killings in the Western region:

> At home, the Ogedemgbes switched on the television, and it was then that they heard what at the time sounded comical and childish, as the squabbles of the two Western chiefs were reported. But then the horrific news started to come. Over thirty people had been killed...thugs had been employed by both sides and innocent people were being killed in the streets...many market places had been emptied as rival thugs looked for their opponents.

> "Honestly, could not Chief Odumosu have given in gracefully? Whose fault was it that he didn't become a minister in the Federal House? And after all, five years isn't forever!" Stella Ogedemgbe spat in anger. "All those innocent people killed for nothing," observed Debbie mournfully.

> "That's politics, my dear. I only hope our Prime Minister acts in time to stop more atrocities...."

317

> "Power, just greed for power," his wife started again,
> her anger mounting. (48–49)

Emecheta uses passages such as this one to make one of her major points: a good number of politicians in post-independence Nigeria were interested only in gaining power by all means and not in genuinely serving their country and compatriots. This, she suggests, was a major contributing factor toward the war. It certainly was not the sole factor, however. She points to the indecisiveness of the Prime Minister, Nguru Kano, as another reason for the political turmoil. Instead of Kano taking effective and preventive action against potentially dangerous rabble rousers, he "was going up and down, consulting first of all with the now redundant governor-general and then, on MacDonald's advice, his master the Sardauna in the North" (56). This vacillation is in fact what provokes one of the ringleaders of the first coup and first military Head of State, Brigadier Onyemere, to comment that "I wish we had a Prime Minister who would act quickly. It's all very well for him to be dignified, but we need someone quick-thinking to deal with this kind of situation. Let's hope it will be the last" (56). As it turns out, Onyemere's fears are not completely unfounded, for very soon people begin to demonstrate and riot in various cities—actions which finally force the Prime Minister to declare a state of emergency in the riot-torn Western region. In the meantime, however, the Ibos in Northern Nigeria, reeling from the "majority ethnic group takes it all" approach of the last elections, increasingly feel betrayed and insecure while those in the East become more and more resentful and apprehensive because of suggestions by the federal government that they should be prepared to share revenues from the newly discovered oil in their region with the rest of the country. They regard such a suggestion as unfair because "During the cocoa and timber days of the West, they reasoned, all the money went to the Yorubas there; and the revenue from the groundnuts went to the North. So why should the East now be deprived of oil revenue?" (59)

According to Emecheta, then, the causes of the war were multifarious and complex. They included but were not limited to the imposition of an ineffective and nominally independent administration by a greedy, foreign power (Britain), the desperate desire for and manipulation of power by local politicians who were interested only in the trappings of government and the material advantages that come with it, tribal and regional chauvinism, and, of course, political corruption and economic exploitation (both internal and external). But while the novelist goes back to the pre-independence period to provide us with some context and perspective for the later behavior of some of the actors in the novel, it is in her narration of events just before and, especially, after the first coup that we see even more forceful reasons for the war. We learn that while Northerners, including particularly the revered Sardauna and the Prime Minister, Nguru Kano, are either killed or literally led to their deaths and while a non-Ibo like the Federal Minister of Finance, Samuel Ogedemgbe, is summarily executed during the coup, "not a single top Ibo politician had been killed" (66). To make matters worse, the Ibos living in Northern Nigeria arrogantly and recklessly start rejoicing in celebration of the coup. With inconceivable stupidity and lack of sensitivity, "The banners, placards and slogans thrust up where Ibos lived in Hausaland jeered at the death of the Sardauna" (69). We also read of Ibo-inspired, provocative graffiti and placards mocking the death of the Sardauna, "the anointed King's son" (70).

With almost no exceptions, the situation after the first coup is described as being rife with mutual suspicion, insecurity, and fear not only among people in society at large but even among the military officers themselves. Initially, the officers try to establish control by appointing Brigadier Onyemere, the most senior officer, as Head of State and by selecting some other senior officers (Abosi, Saka Momoh, etc.) as commissioners of the different regions. Onyemere does his best to reduce the tensions and inter-ethnic and inter-religious rivalry that seemed to prevail in the country. He apologizes to the Northerners for the suffering and losses they had incurred during the first coup and he also tries to appease the other angry factions. When, in response to a statement by Alan Grey, he says "But I want to make them [the people] understand that the old politicians will not even smell the lucrative posts they had before. I want to hand power back to the people" (74), readers, like the narrator, feel that he is genuine about it. But all this lasts for only a short time; after a triumphant visit to the North, Onyemere and the Yoruba Commissioner for the Western region, Oladapo, are murdered during a counter coup and very soon events in the country make it degenerate into tribal killing fields.

It is at this stage that Emecheta introduces another new and major theme into this novel, indeed the Nigerian war novel: the role(s) of women in the war. How important, then, is Emecheta's characterization of Debbie Ogedemgbe and the other women in *Destination Biafra?* To answer this question, we must remember that though this novel is not, as Katherine Frank suggests, "probably the only war novel within recent memory written by a woman,"[4] it certainly is the first African novel that backs up Margaret Higonnet's thesis that civil wars, which take place on 'home' territory, have more potential than other wars to transform women's expectations.

That women are present and at times play active roles in other Nigerian war novels is not in doubt, as we can see in a work such as Eddie Iroh's *Toads of War*. Where Emecheta is different from other chroniclers of the civil war, however, is in her presentation of female characters who transcend the traditional and stereotypical roles often reserved for them. Her major female characters in this work—Debbie Ogedemgbe, Dorothy, and Mrs. Uzoma Madako—are presented as people (most of them ordinary folks) who are forced by personal experience, idealism, or the suffering of others to become active participants in the struggle for genuine freedom.

When we first meet Debbie Ogedemgbe, we are impressed by her thoughtful and somewhat progressive ideas. No doubt, she comes from an extremely privileged background: her corrupt and fabulously wealthy father is the finance minister in the first post-independence government in Nigeria, and she had lived a good portion of her life in England. But it is clear from the moment she is introduced that, her Oxford education notwithstanding, she is not satisfied with and cannot accept the status quo. Of course, her background and social class have not prepared her for or even provided her with revolutionary credentials, so Emecheta depicts her initially in an ambivalent manner. On the one hand, Debbie almost seems ready to accept the stereotypical role that her parents and society expect of her while, on the other hand, her own instincts push her toward revolutionary and liberating idealism. So, during the Abosis' wedding reception, for example, we are told that "she charmed everyone, playing the dutiful daughter of Samuel Ogedemgbe" (44); very soon after (and during the same reception), though, we are informed again that "If her [Debbie's]parents thought they could advertise her like a fatted cow, they had another thing coming. She would never agree to a marriage like theirs, in which the two partners were never equal....So she did not want that; her own ideas of independence in marriage had no place in their set-up. She wanted to do something more than child breeding and rearing and being a good passive wife to a man whose ego she must boost all her days..."(45). And although the reader is not sure whether Emecheta's portrayal of Debbie is unwittingly or deliberately done, the ambivalence does have a certain appropriateness. It makes Debbie's originally naive even if ultimately well-intentioned entry into the world of military (and sexual) warfare seem more credible.

When Debbie decides to enlist in the Nigerian army, she seems to have done it out of both an idealistic and a childlike motivation. The selfish and self-destructive behavior of the two Western (or Yoruba) leading politicians honestly alarm her, and she declares "defiantly" to her parents that she is going to sign up in the army. But then we also read that:

> She had thought of going to join Abosi and the others in Ibadan, not only because that was where the action at the moment was but also because there her father's strong moneyed tentacles would be less able to prevent them from accepting her....For her, joining the army was not a matter of going into action to shoot. She would be trained in military familiarization, but what she really hoped to achieve was to be a lecturer in one of the military academies. (57–58)

One feels that, her protestations notwithstanding, Debbie initially views the army as some kind of adventurous "proving ground" where she finally can prove herself and establish her own individuality and personhood. This is why she adopts an uncharacteristically and ridiculously heartless and macho pose the first time she is left in charge of twenty soldiers. The barking of orders, the yelling at the top of her voice, the reckless trigger-pulling response to a harmless gesture like laughter from her victims all point to an insecure wish to prove that she can bully and intimidate just like men. And one might argue that in an environment where the supposedly reasonable Onyemere can conclude that, if Debbie "can be a useful tool I don't see why we should not use her and others like her" (69), it is perhaps understandable that she behaves in this way.

An even more consequential point, however, is that although Debbie's incentive for entering the army and her initial performance there may not have been particularly impressive, Emecheta allows her to develop into a more mature individual with greater potential for leadership (on both the military and civilian levels) than almost all of the men who had previously been in charge. She begins to show signs of maturity by asserting quite firmly to her British lover,

Alan Grey, that Britain, with its "divide and rule" policy has been partly responsible for the sad state of affairs in Nigeria. She also expresses the dilemma in which at least some Nigerians would have found themselves during the war when she tells her mother: "Trouble is, I want to continue as a Nigerian soldier and at the same time still feel like helping Abosi [and the Ibos]" (114). It is this desire to be of assistance to a people who, for whatever reasons, seem cornered by the majority of their compatriots, as well as her goal of being loyal to a country that she wants to remain united and undivided, that induce her to agree with the ubiquitous Alan Grey and Saka Momoh, the second military Head of State, to serve as a peace ambassador between Momoh and the secessionist-minded Abosi. In the words of the narrator, "[Debbie] was neither Ibo nor Yoruba, nor was she a Hausa, but a Nigerian" (126).

Debbie's mission to the East turns out to be a true voyage of discovery. During this journey, she is able to learn more and more, and often in very painful ways, about the different kinds of wars (civil, sexual) that are going on among her fellow citizens, the warring factions and the motivators behind them; and, above all, about her relationship to herself and to others. So, as she travels to Benin in the Mid West with her mother and their driver, Ignatius, she, her mother and another woman are raped and she also witnesses first-hand, the murder of Ignatius and the woman's husband by bandits-cum-provincial militia posing as "patriotic" Nigerians. This, however, marks just the beginning of Debbie's harrowing experiences. In Sapele, she beholds the havoc wreaked on other women by some soldiers and she and others are subjected to intense tribal hatred by various 'nationalists'. When, in the company of some fleeing Ibos, she leaves Benin for the Eastern region, Debbie experiences first-hand what most ordinary, unarmed civilians undergo on a routine basis during the war: women (including the very old) are stripped, beaten, and violated (leading to pregnant women having premature deliveries), while unarmed men are shot for no other reason than belonging to a particular ethnic group.

It is during this period of extreme suffering that Debbie becomes friends and a fellow sufferer with some of the other characters—dispossessed women and children such as Mrs. Madako, Mrs. Uzoma, Dorothy, and children such as the boys, Boniface and Ngbechi—with whom, in normal circumstances, she never would have crossed paths. Emecheta uses Debbie and these characters to register her major proposition that women, especially, and children contributed and suffered much more during the civil war than they have generally been recognized for.

At first, almost all of the women treat Debbie with suspicion—what with her incongruously sharp British accent and mannerisms and "unAfrican" ways—but gradually she earns their respect and confidence. Their mutual suffering, and the regard and love they show for each other,—in sharp contrast to the dangerous competition that reigns among the men and which in part precipitated the war—helps to bring about feelings of trust. Inspired by the wisdom and generosity of these other (mostly economically disadvantaged) women—the relatively less educated Mrs. Madako, for example, explains the class and sex dimension of warfare to Debbie while Dorothy, the young nursing and starving mother decides to breast-feed the orphan baby, "Biafra," after the latter loses his mother—and sensitized by the suffering of the most vulnerable in society, including children, Debbie is transformed from being the streotypical young Nigerian "princess" to a genuine heroine. Indeed, it seems as if Emecheta uses Debbie to answer a rhetorical question Debbie asks herself: "When the history of the civil war was written, would the part played by her and women like Babs, Uzoma and the nuns in Biafra be mentioned at all?" (195).

From what we read in most of the civil war novels, the answer is negative, but Emecheta is also suggesting that this should not be the case, for not only did the women suffer as severely as the men did, but (as we see exemplified in Debbie and others) they also show the potential and ability to succeed where the men failed. As the war progresses, the atrocities and injustices the women suffer provide them with greater impetus to take action aimed at ending the war on both the political as well as sexual levels. This is perhaps Emecheta's greatest contribution to the genre of war fiction in African writing. Although she indicates throughout the novel that society, under the direction of men, has not been properly governed, it is when we get to the chapter, appropriately captioned "Women's War," that Emecheta becomes quite specific about the contribution of women during that war. By the time we get to this chapter, Debbie and her small band of dispossessed—ordinary women and children—have literally formed a small, but progressive and relatively more mature army of their own. After several tragic events (including the symbolic death of the eponymous baby "Biafra"), the women are spurred on to act more courageously and in better ways. They demonstrate that, important as their men may be, the women need to be less dependent on the men and should be prepared to fight not only for their own survival but also for that which is right. This, for example, is the way Debbie and others react when Ngbechi, a young boy in their group, is martyred by a thoughtless, gung-ho federal soldier:

> Debbie, Dorothy and Uzoma left the children in their care and ran up to the soldiers, screaming: "Go on, shoot all of us! Shoot us too, please shoot us!"

> Debbie did not realize what came over her. She jumped on top of the bewildered officer and began to wrestle with him. She was badly torn and beaten before she became too exhausted to cry any more. (221)

At first glance, this might seem like a rash, even risky, act. What it emphasizes, however, is the women's refusal to tolerate this kind of bullying perpetrated mostly against women, the poor, the weak, and children. The war becomes intolerable to Debbie and the other women because, as they continue on this journey of discovery and pain, they learn that the real (and perhaps only) sufferers in this war of "freedom" are the most vulnerable people in society. The "sons of the rich" escape: "Luckily, the two women's sons listened to their mothers, and left Biafra along with the list of goods and bags of Biafran money. They wrote to their fathers soon afterwards to say that they were safe, and Dr. Eze and Dr. Ozimba both shook their heads and remarked, "These women, what they can do" (228). But while the sons of the rich "leaders" are cowardly hiding in distant places, their fathers (embodied in Drs. Eze and Ozimba respectively) send four Biafran soldiers on a clandestine mission aimed at launching biological warfare against the federal forces. It seems rightful, therefore, that because most of the women—including even those who would otherwise have been sympathetic to the Biafran cause—now know what they know, they respond to the Biafran soldiers in this way:

> One woman stepped boldly forward and said, "Biafra, Biafra, what is Biafra? You killed our man from this part, Nwokolo; the Nigerian soldiers came and killed what your soldiers left. We are Ibuza people, but we now live in the bush, thanks to your Abosi and your Biafra. Our town is now a ghost town. Go there and see Hausa soldiers killing and roasting cows. They shoot anything in sight, and kill

anyone who gave shelter to your people. And when we needed you, where were you? Where was your Abosi when our girls were being raped in the market places and our grandmothers shot? Please go back to your Biafra. You call us Hausa Ibos, don't you? You call us fools because we fought your wars for you, and you are well protected in your place, claiming the glory? Please go away before you bring us bad luck."

"Your soldiers? You have your own soldiers?" asked the leading Biafran soldier.

"Yes, we became tired of being in the middle. Your Biafran soldiers killed our men and raped our girls, because you accused us of harboring enemy soldiers, then Nigerian soldiers would accuse us of the same thing even though we were innocent. There was nobody to protect us, so we formed our own militia." (230-231)

The women manifest their frustration and anger in this way because they realize that they (with the children) have perhaps borne the brunt of this fraternal butchery. It is no surprise then that at this stage Debbie is with this militia rather than with either of the fighting armies.

After many more painful ordeals (including experiencing the very corruption for which the former civilian rulers were supposed to have been ousted), Debbie finally makes it to Abosi in the East. She is able, after some serious persuasion, to convince Abosi that because she is from a minority ethnic group and a Nigerian, above all, she has been neutral in the war and would therefore like to go to Britain to "stir the consciences of people over there....I'll tell them, I'll tell the world that you are not fighting only over oil but what you've just told me, the right to live" (240).

The novel then draws to a close with a most bizarre series of events. First, after Debbie's stint in Britain, trying to call world attention to the plight of Biafrans, she inexplicably becomes an agent for the federal side and gets involved in an attempt to kill Abosi as the latter, having refused to agree to her suggestion to surrender, escapes from the country. Next, Debbie refuses to accept Alan Grey's invitation to "leave this Godforsaken country" (258) and we read the announcement of her decision to help rebuild her country and publish her war memoirs. More importantly, though, we read finally that:

> After all, [Grey's] mission was complete. Nigeria had been successfully handed over to the approved leader, Saka Momoh. The fact that he came from a minority tribe, and had an ample supply of guns and bombs, would stabilize his position. Nigeria badly needed that stability to allow foreign investors to come in and suck out the oil. Nigeria would need the money, too, to repay the debts she owed the "friendly nations" for their generosity in supplying her with arms, during the time when one tribe was fighting against the other. (259)

In short, Emecheta finishes *Destination Biafra* by reiterating most of the basic issues she has discussed throughout the novel. Through Debbie, she makes one last point about the role of the new woman in Africa; her final jab at the 'approved leader,' Saka Momoh, and his foreign patrons is to emphasize the fact again that foreign powers care only for profit and that ultimately it is the ordinary Africans who come out as losers. Alan Grey's eventual departure for his homeland is indeed the very last reminder of this point: "Alan Grey boarded the plane, leaving the Nigerians to go on killing each other if they so desired" (259).

A work expressing indignation and bitterness at both the causes of the civil war and the affliction and undue punishment brought upon a good number of ordinary Nigerians and Biafrans (especially women and children), *Destination Biafra* could easily have degenerated into a tragic tale evoking nothing but pathos. Emecheta, in the main, avoids that by distilling her personal concerns—true freedom for women, for example—with her political interests in quite convincing ways. But as even a thoroughly empathetic Emecheta critic like Katherine Frank acknowledges, *Destination Biafra* has some very serious weaknesses. To quote Frank, "we can say that though Emecheta's heart is in the right place, the book [*Destination Biafra*] as a whole languishes in a shadowy region between manifesto and fiction."[5] Consequently, we are left with a heroine who, again to quote Frank, "is a flat, unchanging figure—something even of a puppet at times...[who] does not grow or develop."[6]

Another major flaw of the novel can be found in Emecheta's demonizing of characters who are non-Ibo (and especially Hausa or Yoruba). Although Debbie's goal and efforts are to work for a united and progressive Nigeria; although the narrator often professes the need for national unity; and, finally, although Emecheta has done well in fusing events from recent Nigerian history with purely imaginative incidents, the novel is still too heavily weighted against non-Ibos. Granted, there are a few instances when Ibos actually are portrayed quite negatively: the incidents involving the Ibuza women's rebellion against the four Ibo soldiers and the surreptitious dispatch of sons of rich Ibo families to safe havens abroad while their less privileged brothers and sisters are wantonly killed in Biafran battlefields are two such instances. On the whole, however, the novel's rhetoric is decidedly pro-Ibo and, at times, dangerously anti-Hausa or anti-Yoruba.

In countless instances, Emecheta's Hausa characters seem to justify Alan Grey's stereotyping of them as a "people... comparatively ignorant and happy in their ignorance" (6); the Yoruba characters, again by their actions, seem to embody the jaundiced view of them expressed by a Hausa teacher in the North: "All you know is mouth-mouth and so much show off!" (14). The Ibos, *au contraire*, are usually the symbols of intelligence, savoir-faire, and decency. For example, while the Hausas do not seem to understand what elections are all about and would be pleased to vote only as they are instructed by the Sardauna, and while the Yoruba-dominated Action Group is using stupid measures (such as throwing printed campaign material to a predominantly illiterate Hausa electorate), the Ibos develop some sophisticated, workable, and positive strategies. They try to forge an alliance with a dominant Northern party in the North and select a Northerner, Alhaji Manliki, as their "eye" in the region; they also choose a song that reflects the need for true freedom for all Nigerians as their campaign song.

After the first post-independence elections, we learn that Chief Odumosu "called on Governor MacDonald to resign and go back to his country. Many supported this motion, but the Ibos under Dr. Ozimba, though the most offended, were more cautious. It was decided that the governor should be given a chance to say his piece on why it was that he had nominated Alhaji Nguru Kano before the final result was heard" (30). This passage is important because it typifies Emecheta's basic attitude toward her Ibo and non-Ibo characters in the novel. For the most part, the non-Ibo characters are presented as greedy, hungry, power-grabbers, buffoons, and insecure and ignorant political pretenders, while the Ibos and their supporters in general are praised and even admired for their intelligence and consideration.

As I indicated previously, the two Yoruba chiefs (Odumosu and Durosaro) are held partly accountable for the breakdown of the country's political structure; the country's first Prime Minister, Nguru Kano (who happens to be a Northerner) is shown as being so ineffectual that soldiers (for whom he is the commander-in-chief) decide to quell street riots in Ibadan without even seeking his permission. On the other hand, when the military officers decide to seize power and forge a new nation because they feel the civilian politicians have failed the existing one, it is the Ibo, Abosi, who articulates the most persuasive argument for founding the new nation, Biafra:

> I would rather say our destination is 'Biafra,' since as far as I am concerned we're not yet independent. We sent away one set of masters, without realizing that they had left their stooges behind. Even the matches we use in our kitchens come from abroad. I think this country needs a military respite, and so to Biafra we will go. *Destination Biafra!* (60)

Abosi's lucidity and idealism here are very much in consonance with that reserved for most Ibo characters in the novel.

My interpretation of this section is meant to accentuate the intensely 'tribal' nature of the work. Whatever else may have happened during the civil war, it is doubtful whether the villainy of non-Ibos was as great and especially as one-sided as Emecheta makes it out to be. A "military soldier [who] looked like a Northerner" forces captured Ibo soldiers to eat their excrement (82); after the killing of Brigadier Onyemere, the idealistic first military head of government, the Hausas (who had come to see him as a genuine leader of all Nigerians) take their revenge on non-Northerners whose tribesmen, they feel, had killed Onyemere for being too good to the Northerners. The language Emecheta uses to describe the Hausa reaction is instructive:

> The Hausas were at first sorry for the demise of the man who only a few days previously had almost been successful in consoling them for their loss. Less than forty-eight hours after the announcement, the radicals again started up their cries about a holy war. They carried clubs and machetes, tore down from their own areas into the Sabon Garri ["strangers

quarters"] shouting, "Death to the Kaferi infidels!"
At the Barclays Bank, they hacked humans to death
and those who tried to escape were clubbed and battered to death. "Down with all Ibo infidels! Down
with the enemy!" they screamed, and the bank
workers stared horrified. Anybody who did not have
a tribal mark on his face was regarded as Ibo. (87)

In addition to the mindless savagery of the Hausas in the North,
we read of that of the Yorubas in the West and South. According to
an Ibo woman whose chemist (pharmacist) husband had gone out
to help a dying Yoruba child in Lagos, this is what happened on the
night he was killed:

"We had heard rumors that our people were being
molested, but we did not believe them... Most
responsible Ibo men started sleeping outside their
houses. My husband did the same. But on the night
they took him away a Yoruba child, one of our neigh-
bours, was ill and called around nine o'clock for a
bottle of dysentery tablets. My husband was a
chemist and we owned our own shop. As he was
locking up, I heard the heavy footsteps of soldiers.
I thought they were just passing but they banged on
our house and forced me to open up. They asked
where my husband was, and I told them that I did
not know. My husband was from outside, but he was
more worried for us. I wish he had not come in. Of
course they grabbed him, and he promised to give
them everything. They threatened to kill me and
our two babies. My husband ordered me to do what
they said. As he said so, one of the soldiers landed
the butt of his heavy gun on his back. He called for
help as they started to drag him out of the
house....We all heard the firing, and I disobeyed him
and ran out...." (96-97)

The point is not that specific incidents like this may not (or indeed
could not) have happened. Rather, the point is that the accounts
seem too lopsided. Whereas Emecheta may be right in including
some of these scenes to give readers some reasons for the civil war,
her descriptions make it seem that the villainous Hausa and
Yorubas, for a long time, had only been interested in the annihila-

tion of Ibos. Her rhetoric often suggests most of these characters'
utter contempt for non-Ibo leaders. Before war is declared, Abosi
(representing the East) and Saka Momoh (the federal government)
meet in Ghana with the aim of reconciling whatever differences
they may have:

> Their host, Ankrah, was very hopeful and it showed
> in his welcome. He greeted the two leaders togeth-
> er, referring to them as brothers. Abosi was relaxed
> but watchful. Momoh was jumpy and apprehensive,
> like a schoolboy who had neglected to do his home-
> work; if he failed at this important meeting, in
> which so many Nigerians put so much hope, he
> could not foretell what would happen. He had
> brought fewer advisers than Abosi and gave the
> impression that he was going to make all the deci-
> sions by himself. It was clear that he trusted no one.
> (100)

Later on, Momoh is depicted as being downright obtuse, not being
able to understand even the meaning of 'autonomy' or the full ram-
ifications of the negotiations with Abosi. He is also shown as being
a powerless, even if a power-hungry, pawn in the hands of foreign
masters while Abosi (even though occasionally castigated for his
arrogance and sexism) is repeatedly depicted as a brilliant and idealistic strategist. And although Biafran soldiers, just like their federal counterparts, rape, plunder and pillage, they never truly come
close to the ferocious federal beasts created by Emecheta. Here is
a brief exchange among some federal troops:

> "But whatever they [Biafran soldiers] use, we are
> here to clean up after Colonel Lawal, to purge the
> country of the Yanmiri bastards. Do I make myself
> clear? Any questions?"
>
> "Sir, what do you do if the people surrender?" asked
> a soldier obviously new to the art of killing, looking
> rather sick.
>
> "Surrender? Let me tell you once again: the only
> good Ibo is a dead one! One minute they will sur-
> render, the next minute the very person you have
> just been merciful to will stick his knife into your
> unsuspecting back. Anything that moves must be

shot and anything that doesn't move must be shot
too, to make sure that it can never move again. (204)

It may well be that Emecheta wants us to see things primarily from
the Biafran point of view, but after a while it becomes all too pre-
dictable. The evil actions of federal soldiers become monotonous.
They wantonly shoot women and children and, even though
Debbie wants Abosi to pay in the end by trying to shoot him and
his plane down, the reader is left with the impression that the only
real victims were Ibos. Emecheta's narrative technique is perhaps
another reason why her bias is so evident. She hardly ever tries to
distance herself from the divisive and even stupid stereotypes
mouthed by some of her characters. She also has a tendency to
preach instead of allowing the characters to act out whatever dilem-
mas or situations they may find themselves in. There are too many
passages which read like the following excerpt:

> But Chief Odumosu, too, had debts to pay. His peo-
> ple were used to his squandering money to impress
> and also to help some of the underprivileged in his
> extended family—it had to be so, since there was no
> state welfare money to take care of them. That was
> one of the tragedies at this time in Nigeria. If a man
> became an MP, it was his duty to see to the well-
> being of his extended family; he must show his
> wealth by helping this ageing farmer, that clever boy
> born of poor parents, make sure that his village had
> the best amenities, the largest buildings and all the
> paraphernalia of modern living. Of course, no gov-
> ernment minister was paid enough to be able to
> afford this, and so as not to lose face they would go
> behind the scenes for their percentage. (49)

With all this said, one must still acknowledge that Emecheta's place
in the development of the African war novel is most assured because,
in spite of all that is flawed and idiosyncratic about the work,
Destination Biafra makes some specific and very important contributions to the genre. This novel provides some of the most convincing probable reasons for the war; it helps us (re)evaluate the
contributions of women to that war, and it emphasizes the potential
of women as credible and serious leaders in a new Africa. In sum,
then, Emecheta extends the work done by her male counterparts by
rendering in a deeper and more subtle manner some of the issues

of the civil war previously ignored by other writers. "Without [this] female voice, no complete picture of the Nigerian Civil War (1967—1970) will be recorded in Nigerian literary history."[7]

Notes

1. Charlotte Bruner, "A Decade for Women Writers," in Stephen Arnold, Ed. *African Literary Studies: The Present State/L'Etat présent* (Washington, D.C.: Three Continents P, 1985): 227.

2. Buchi Emecheta, *Destination Biafra* (London: Fontana, 1982). All references (cited, by page number, in the text) are to this edition.

3. Marie Umeh, "The Poetics of Thwarted Sensitivity." in Ernest Emenyonu, Ed. *Calabar Studies in African Literature: Critical Theory and African Literature* (Ibadan: Heinemann, 1987), 194. There now exists a solid body of secondary literature on the Nigeria-Biafra Civil War as we can see, for example, in Craig McLuckie's "Preliminary Checklist of Primary and Secondary Sources on Nigerian Civil War/Biafran War Literature," *Research in African Literatures* 18, 4 (1987): 510—527, and in his *Nigerian Civil War Literature: Seeking an "Imagined Community"* (Lewiston, NY: Mellen, 1990). The importance of Umeh's essay for a reading of *Destination Biafra* becomes obvious, however, when one looks at the wealth of detail it presents even when viewed in the context of the small company to which the article belongs, i. e., the very small number of articles that have paid serious scholarly attention to *Destination Biafra*. Some other writers who have discussed Emecheta's novel with some seriousness include: Katherine Frank, "Women Without Men: The Feminist Novel in Africa," *African Literature Today* 15 (1987): 14—34; Jane Bryce, "Conflict and Contradiction in Women's Writing on the Nigerian Civil War," *African Languages and Cultures* 4, 1 (1991): 29—42; and Chimalum Nwankwo, "Emecheta's Social Vision: Fantasy or Reality?" *Ufahamu: Journal of the African Activist Association,* 17, 1 (1988): 35—44. It is also interesting to note that *Destination Biafra* is curiously absent even in feminist essays that could have accommodated some discussion of that work; for example, Susan Andrade, "Rewriting History, Motherhood, and Rebellion: Naming an African Women's History Literary Tradition," *Research in African Literatures,* 12, 3. (1989): 559—574; and Nancy T. Bazin, "Venturing into Feminist Consciousness: Two Protagonists from the Fiction of Buchi Emecheta," *Sage,* ll, 1 (Spring, 1985): 32—36. Moreover, Chidi Amuta, who more than most critics tries to provide a good historical context for the war, completely ignores Emecheta—the author who has attempted most thoroughly to cover that aspect of the war in fiction—in his rather hyperbolic "The Nigerian Civil War and the Evolution of Nigerian Literature," *Canadian Journal of African Studies,* 17, 1 (1983): 85—99.

4. Frank, 25.

5. *Ibid.* 28.

6. *Ibid.* 27.

7. Umeh, 194.

Coming To Terms:
Buchi Emecheta's *Kehinde*
And The Birth of A 'Nation'

John C. Hawley

> Aunt Nnebogo had no child of her own, and she
> wanted to protect me. She even gave me a Christian
> name: Jacobina, after Jacob, who fought and won
> the battle against his brother Esau in the Bible. Aunt
> Nnebogo loved the Bible stories, which reminded
> her of our moonlight stories. She told me that story
> so many times that, for a while, I thought it was the
> story of my own birth.
> — Buchi Emecheta, *Kehinde*

The point of *Kehinde*, of course, is that this is *not* the story of her
own birth. *Her* Esau must *not* go down in defeat, but must be
embraced—or, in the terms Emecheta has chosen, consumed—or
else Jacobina will not be whole. Buchi Emecheta's portrayal of a
woman who must reach this decision for herself in defiance of the
narrative that others would impose upon her life, results in a para-

ble that suggests the novelist's own struggle throughout her writing career to find a "story" that adequately conveys her (ongoing) birth.

As each of her books is added to a steadily expanding list, Buchi Emecheta's created world reverberates with echoes and whispers. The reader is happy to see characters re-emerging, their qualities under a new lighting scheme and their social status subtly shifting. And it has been true, as Bruce King notes, that Emecheta "seems continually to write her autobiography, or that of her mother, or to imagine alternative lives; . . . her attitudes change on most topics as if no position were right. Her prose shifts from line to line in register and idiom from British to Nigerian and through various social levels" (King 201). More clearly than most novelists, Emecheta's fictive world is comfortably familiar (uncomfortable though the characters' lives may be), and easily fits Otto Heim's description of much crosscultural writing as "dialectical": such writing typically "take[s] into account that a text cannot be fully described as a cultural object, nor is it solely the product of a discourse that writes back to the center from a peripheral position. Instead, the text engages writer and reader in a communicative process where meaning is produced and negotiated; interpretation and critical theory remain provisional and pragmatic" (Heim 140). Theme and variation are played out in an imagined world that demands a reader's engagement; but Emecheta's central topic, the Nigerian woman caught between two worlds, rarely varies. She recognizes its intransigence; she knows the need to revisit it until her "saying" of the words, like some incantation, effects a change not only in the reader, but somehow in society as well.

Emecheta nicely embodies both her persistent theme and her trademark writing technique in *Kehinde*, most notably in the book's principal symbol: a supposedly dead twin who is forever lost and forever present, speaking in crucial moments and eliciting a courage from her living sister that seems to come from nowhere. One speaker in this dialogue "is" Kehinde, and the other is like a guardian angel, a superego; in effect, Kehinde communes with her own soul. The process that Emecheta has hit upon in this novel serves as a clever vehicle for an interior debate that Bernd Schulte has described as typical in certain contemporary novels:

> 'Intercultural writing' takes place in a historical situation which confronts the countries of the former colonies with the problems of finding 'national iden-

334

tities' somewhere between tradition and modernity—in a sort of socio-cultural moratorium.
Orientation and identity formation seem to be
staged within processes of intercultural oscillation.
Thus, on a structural level, authors of 'new' literatures in English often develop patterns of motiva-
tional dispositions and they conceptualize their
protagonists by fictionalizing such processes within the framework of *distance* and *participation*. The
writers' own attitudes towards Indian, African or
other traditions turn out to be part of their biographies and a literary principle at the same time, as
is demonstrated by their autobiographical as well as
fictional works. (Schulte 35)

In this world of increasing "creolization" (see Hannerz 1987) the
technique works brilliantly for Emecheta's readers. They recognize that this struggle between "distance" and "participation" is at
the heart of Kehinde's difficulties. But within the story casual
passersby, usually Westernized Nigerian women, overhear only
one half of the conversation; they feel embarrassment for this
apparently disoriented woman and they implicitly demand that
such unorthodox communing cease. After all, they would say, one
should speak in society (especially British society) with one voice,
presenting a single face to meet the faces that we meet. If one
shares the internal dichotomy implied by Kehinde's mumbling,
that is one's private concern, and all the more reason to keep this
poor woman "whole"—or quiet.

These social controls in the novel ramify in Emecheta's public
life. Critics, Western or African, "overhear" portions of her interi-
or conversation bubbling to the surface in one book or another, and
some, like Chinweizu, express an embarrassment for the author,
or anger. Such critics seem to hear half of what is said, and are con-
founded by hearing snatches of the "response," as well. But her
publication history demonstrates her discomfort with univocal declarations, by anyone, of whom she must be one. She circles the
topic once again, her "taiwo" serves as her Muse, and her incantation wants *all* her accumulated voices to speak the words. Thus,
though the public has a sense of *déja vu* with each new novel, the
geography is a bit upsetting. Emecheta delights in defamiliarizing
the terrain, and hijacking the expectations of readers who prefer
clean borders and moral rites of passage.

Her public sees conjoined in Buchi Emecheta a dual conundrum: what sort of Nigerian is she, and what sort of feminist? Her books seem to argue these points as though each were a contending voice demanding her attention. She rather pointedly dedicates *The Family* (1989), for example, "to that woman in the Diaspora who refused to sever her umbilical cord with Africa." In effect, she dedicates the book to herself, defiantly celebrating both her independence from and life-giving connection to Nigeria—and glorying in the "intercultural oscillation" to which Schulte refers. Beyond that, she seems to speak here for all migrant women throughout the world who have taken root in the West but have maintained their "twin" identity in their homeland. These are women who refuse to sever their connection with the nation of origin; they will not be denied by those who might otherwise disown them. In *Kehinde*, however, the protagonist yearns to go back to Nigeria to rejoin her husband, but is literally left in London with a broken connection—"staring blankly at the mouthpiece" (63). With Emecheta, this is very much a woman's issue, subject as women are to univocal declarations in the country of origin based on their sex and to univocal declarations in their new countries based on their nationality.

Emecheta herself questions her Nigerian identity. "By now," she tells Feroza Jussawalla in 1992, "I think my writing isn't English or African as much as more international, more universal. . . . I try to write for the world" (Jussawalla 85). Such expatriate notions lead the interviewer to observe that African writing in English, or French, for that matter, is "indebted to the European forms and languages in which it is expressed," but Jussawalla argues that this in itself does not make the literature "eurocentric" (as Chinweizu would see it) as much as it makes it "multicultural, combining aspects of African and European culture in a complex mix and synthesis" (9). An "afrocentric" criticism, in Jussawalla's view, would prefer a "uniculturally African mode of cultural expression. But to be truly afrocentric, one should go back to writing in African languages" (9).

Keeping in mind the "national" question at the heart of *Kehinde*'s domestic problems, two corollaries of Jussawalla's argument are relevant. We might first ask whether Emecheta's novels are "typically" English, or whether they fall somewhere "between" Great Britain and Nigeria in their psychological and spiritual milieu. This is partially a question of language and partially a question of topic. In a 1986 interview the author noted that she and her publisher are seeing some changes, at least in the reading public's perception of the novelist: "Writing coming from Nigeria, from Africa" she tells Adeola James, "sounds quite stilted. After reading the first page you tell yourself you are plodding. . . . But with some of my books you can't tell that easily any more because, I think, using the language every day and staying in the culture [Great Britain, one assumes] my Africanness is, in a way, being diluted. My paperback publisher, Collins, has now stopped putting my books in the African section" (James 39). This is just the sort of data that critics like Chinweizu would find most reprehensible. On the other hand, Emecheta also notes that "one publisher wrote to me and said that he will publish my book if I can change my name to Edith Smith or something like that. But I didn't give in" (James 43). "My attitude and language is very English," she remarks, but she nonetheless wants to be classed as an African writer—if for no other reason than to "help bring Nigerian writing up to standard" (Umeh & Umeh 21). She refuses to sever her umbilical cord with Africa, but some Africans wish she would.

The second corollary that arises from Jussawalla's position is an implied comparison between the choice of Emecheta and writers like her, and the choice of the relatively few, like Ngugi wa Thiong'o, who establish themselves in the "language of the colonizer" and then choose to return to an African language, from which their works are quickly translated into English or French. This is a complicated issue and has to do as much with the economics and politics of publishing houses as with an author's choice of audience. It is clear that Emecheta admires Ngugi's decision, at least on one level, and she tells an interviewer that "if I decide to settle here in Nigeria, I will begin to write plays, like James Ngugi, in the vernacular, and have them staged in the market places where women can see the irony of their lives" (Umeh & Umeh 22). Yet, in the same interview she notes that she feels very alienated from the working classes in Nigeria (so would they want to be shown the "irony" of their lives?), and she elsewhere notes that she can write Yoruba but not Igbo (James 37). African critics would draw further ammunition, perhaps, from her admission that "I started speaking the English language when I was fourteen. So I can never really fill those fourteen years in which I had another mode of expressing myself" (Jussawalla 99). These early years, a significant emotional source for many writers, would be a serious lacuna if, in fact, Emecheta really has little means of their recovery. If this is based on the imposition of the colonizer's language, the argument could reasonably be made that, however admirable her creative output, the British Empire has nonetheless crimped her style.

It is clear, therefore, that a good deal is lost to an individual writer who chooses to (or has to, if an indigenous language is not available, or a representatively large indigenous audience is not probable) write in the colonizer's language. The political stakes are raised if such writers do their work in the colonizer's home base, as so many do. Emecheta is interestingly dualistic on this point: "working from Nigeria," she suggests, "is difficult because creative people cannot find exposure for their work. Anything produced abroad, Nigerians think it's excellent" (Umeh & Umeh 20). But in her description of her children, who are now more fully acculturated to Great Britain, Emecheta suggests the *dual* voice that continues to ramify in her own mind and in her novels. [My children], she notes, "speak English and understand Igbo. But for them, English is their emotional language. My son is a writer now, but English is his language too. You know that he is somebody whose English is his first language. His style is completely different from mine. And he explores and plays with the language more than I do. . . . My emotional language is Igbo. I also speak Yoruba. As this is the first language I spoke as a child, it will always be my emotional language" (Jussawalla 97-98). It is important, therefore, to understand what she means above when she describes much African writing as stilted. She is condemning those overly colonized writers who write a formal English that no one, even in England, speaks today. Instead, she praises writers like Amos Tutuola and Cyprian Ekwensi who generate a "Nigerian English" (89), one that is living and, as an added benefit, also more accessible to common people within Nigeria.

Thus, Emecheta is quite aware of the consequences of the choices she makes by straddling both worlds and belonging to neither. She is never fully English. But, by Chinweizu's standards, she is not a fully African writer, either. The criticism of his school, which might be described as localism, is "the belief in using critical criteria derived from the region or locale to understand and judge the literature of that region. Such an approach inevitably stresses the Africanness of African literature in English, the Indianness of Indian literature in English, the ways in which the new literary expression reflects the culture that existed before the arrival of the colonial powers" (Jussawalla 10). But the fact that many Africans don't follow Chinweizu shows there is more to it and them. Yet, "If Chinweizu's version of localism is incomplete because it insists on the relevance of only the local context or originating culture of these writers, other more theoretical approaches may well err in the other direction, insisting only on the nomadic, international, 'deterritorialized' elements of their work" (Jussawalla 21). It is true, as Bruce King observes, that the new internationalism "differs from Commonwealth, Third World or ethnic writing in that [the internationalists] write about their native lands or the immigrant experience from within the mainstream of British literature" and that they share, in varying degrees, a "confusion as to where real life is to be found" (King 191, 193, 194). It is also true that Emecheta writes fiction that fits Schmidt-Grözinger's definition of "progressive"—in immigrant literature. She writes, there are three modes of orientation:

1. The retrospective mode, in which the individual retreats into a partly self-imposed isolation and defines himself through his origins
2. The conformist mode, in which the individual adapts himself completely to the norms of the new country, even to the extent of denying his heritage, and
3. The progressive mode, in which the individual critically assesses his past and present situation and acts according to the conclusions he draws in order to improve his situation (Schmidt-Grözinger 112).

Kehinde, and most of Emecheta's female protagonists fit this third category. But, having said this, it must also be agreed that these characters are not rootless—rather, they are doubly rooted. They do not live *between* countries, but instead attempt to form a psychic bridge across the metaphysical space separating them.

Kehinde, I would argue, is Emecheta's boldest statement of her preference for this "dual" citizenship, and her clearest recognition that others will do whatever they can to make such complexity impossible. What is required is a coming to terms with oneself and reaching a level of comfort with one's own multiple "voices." The novel is a keening for some part of herself for whose death she feels partially responsible, but this sense of loss is accompanied by a bold decision to go forth into a new multicultural world that offers few moral guidelines. This natural ambivalence, running through so many of her novels, builds in this one on ironic Yoruba understanding of the relationship between the *taiwo* (the firstborn) and the Kehinde (the one who comes after). In the world's eyes, the firstborn *taiwo* would have seniority and be given the greater respect, but for the Yoruba she is seen as having been sent into the world as the *kehinde's* servant and scout—one who reports back with news of the world's welcome or its threat. The poignancy of Emecheta's use of the symbol is, therefore, more of a challenge than may at first meet the eye: *her kehinde-protagonist* chooses to step into this brave new world with *no* guide. Kehinde has, so her neighbors tell her, "eaten" Taiwo in the womb—and she now carries the twin's spirit, her *"chi,"* within her. There is more to her "individualism," therefore, than may meet the eurocentric eye.

This brings us to the second aspect of Emecheta's conundrum: her feminism. Susan Andrade makes a most interesting intervention into the argument over whether or not feminism is possible in an African context. She refers to the dispute on this issue between Katherine Frank and Carol Boyce Davies, and denies the implicit assumption underlying the debate, which seems to be that feminism is necessarily a metaphor for individualism (Andrade 93). Andrade's argument is broader, and is based upon the historical intertextuality between Flora Nwapa's *Efuru* and Emecheta's *The Joys of Motherhood*. We are looking at the symbolic structure of *Kehinde* as a "conversation" between the protagonist's two halves, seeing this framework as metonymic of Emecheta's recurring questions. Andrade's use of Bakhtin's theories in her argument can be suggestive of the direction our reasoning may wish to go:

> Through the women's failed cooking strike, *The Joys of Motherhood* problematizes *Efuru's* assumption that tradition is the only appropriate avenue to power. . . . *The Joys of Motherhood* dialogizes *Efuru's* easy success and blind adherence to Igbo tradition by separating the discourse of tradition from that of power and locating them in rival characters, privileging the latter over the former. . . . The discourse of tradition is represented by Nnu Ego (who bears the children Efuru desires), that of rebellion by Adaku (who controls her destiny and achieves Efuru's economic independence). (Andrade 103–4)

Some might accuse Kehinde of putting herself above everyone else in her decision to leave her husband in Nigeria and return, again, to London. Certainly, her husband's family sees it this way! Her son, too, scandalized not by his father's polygamy but by his mother's affair with Michael Gibson, threatens to maintain "Nigeria's" hold on his mother by taking (unsuccessful) steps to gain legal possession of the London home. Kehinde's friend, Moriammo, is forbidden by her Muslim husband from visiting such a brazen and disobedient wife. Indeed, Emecheta so stacks the deck in her protagonist's favor, in the eyes of most readers, that one reasonably wonders what she is so worried about: does she fear her readers are likely to take sides against Kehinde? This is an indication that Emecheta has a larger audience in mind than Europeans or Americans. She seems intent on demonstrating that Kehinde has been painted into a corner, and she holds up before the reader as many different "types" of women's responses as possible, and she shows each to be inadequate.

On the other hand, some may feel uncomfortable with Emecheta's portrayal of Kehinde's abortion as the token of her servitude. Told of her latest pregnancy on the eve of his decision to return in glory to Nigeria, Kehinde's husband insists on an abortion. Before this reaction, she had "related to Albert as to a friend, a compatriot, a confidant" (6); afterward, "she felt like a boat adrift on a stormy night. . . . She was alone, in spite of what they said about marriage being two people in one. . . . She glanced at Albert as if he were a new person, his profile clear against the window of the car. He had nothing to offer her"(33). Upset by her disturbing news, he had swerved dangerously in traffic and become unwittingly ironic: "A police siren tore into his thoughts, and set him wondering whether it was right to drive at such high speed. They could end up killing an innocent somebody" (7). He, like most of Emecheta's male characters, is too literal: he sees those he endangers on the sidewalk who pass before his eyes, but he cannot see the fetus, he cannot see his wife, and he cannot see Taiwo, who has begun to reassert her presence and claim her rightful role in Kehinde's life. "Albert could not help her. How could he? . . . It could not mean the same to him that the child she had just flushed away was her father coming back. Albert's imagination could not carry him that far" (33). The world of these spirits—the world to which he is purportedly soon returning—is more present to his wife in London than it will ever be to him in Lagos. In fact, he has no intention of returning to the Nigeria of the spirits—there are, Emecheta suggests, many Nigerians—and some of those who have traveled to foreign shores carry within them a Nigeria far more central to Igbo or Yoruba consciousness than do those who trumpet nationalism at home, accumulate money, and lose their souls.

Emecheta's feminism, therefore, like her (inter)nationalism, is typically nuanced and regularly debated by her critics. She further complicates the question in her choice of a University professor as

Albert's new Nigerian wife, whom he quickly impregnates. As an educated woman with the means for economic independence, such a woman might be assumed to be a most likely candidate for full autonomy, a role model that a right-thinking "new" novelist might want to show to the world as the possible future open to her countrywomen. But Rike is like a repentant Nko, the student in *Double Yoke* (1983). Far from denigrating education for women, Emecheta seems to suggest that this, alone, will not bring greater self-awareness or freedom to Nigerian women. An Nko, in the earlier novel, may sacrifice much to get her degree, but once that has been attained, a Rike must go further to find a place in Nigerian society: she must become docile and "polygamous."

In this case, however, the spotlight is really on Kehinde, who rejects Rike's accommodation to custom and thereupon *cannot* find a "feminist"—that is, a self-respecting—way to live in her homeland. As Marie Umeh predicted in her discussion of *Double Yoke*,

> The African woman more so than the African man, is caught in a bind. In order to be liberated and fulfilled as a woman she must renounce her African identity because of the inherent sexism of many traditional African societies. Or, if she wishes to cherish and affirm her 'Africanness' she must renounce her claims to feminine independence and self-determination. Either way she stands to lose; either way she finds herself diminished, impoverished. It is Emecheta's growing awareness of the futility of attempting to resolve this dilemma that accounts for the growing bitterness that engulfs Nko. (Umeh 175)

In *Kehinde* Nko's earlier bitterness is muffled by Rike's cooptation by the system; the bitterness has, in a sense, come home to roost, since Kehinde, as Emecheta's spokesperson, is its unintended target. As she notes, women such as Rike are often the unfortunate agents for maintaining the status quo: woman against woman in subservience to the man. This raises questions about the logic of Elinor Flewellen's possibly too rosy view of the polygamy that Kehinde would contest: "The Western view of polygamy," she writes, "seldom considers a fact that seems uncontestable: polygamy has made it necessary for the African woman to be self-sufficient. Whether single or married, polygamous or monogamous, the modern African woman, especially the younger and more educated, believes in doing something about her own situation" (Flewellen 17). Certainly, Rike has "done something about her own situation"; but in the process she has totally disrupted Kehinde's life, offered no resistance to a system that favors men in such a lopsided way, and ends up worried that her husband's "situation" is not, in the final analysis, "her own": he is, after all, about to take yet another wife. If this is the "self-sufficiency" that Nigeria offers its women, Kehinde is fortunate to be able to rely on a taiwo to show her to the door.

In 1986 Emecheta put the problem this way: "As I am beginning to say in some of my later novels, half of the problem rests with the women. They are so busy bitching about one another, the men say the women are acting just as is expected. But when you deal with foreign women, say you go to a place like Norway, or even here in England, all you have to do is give a talk and they appreciate you and express solidarity with you. But it isn't so in our own country" (James 36). But this is a lesson that Emecheta teaches her protagonist painfully, like a mother allowing her daughter to make necessary mistakes and trusting her to come to the same conclusions that she herself has. She opens her story with Kehinde's rejection of Mary Elikwu as "a fallen woman who had no sense of decorum" (*Kehinde* 38), but in not many pages has Kehinde view herself in much the same light: "The world was suddenly much more complicated than it had seemed hitherto. She was now a fallen woman. . ." (61). Mary Elikwu is a woman who leaves her sadistic husband and takes her six children with her—in other words, a victim who chooses to change her life, and to do so in a most responsible way. Now, having led Kehinde through various types of sexual degradation, in both Lagos and London, Emecheta has her hero recognize that women "in their ignorance pass judgment on their sisters" (132). Kehinde ultimately admires Mary Elikwu's freedom to make decisions and to work for change, in opposition to whatever false and limiting definitions the world around her may impose.

It is this emphasis on Mary's will, on her decisive acts of intervention and affirmation, that typifies the thrust of Emecheta's feminism. But she recognizes the attractions of the alternative choice and reminds Kehinde of its charms. When her protagonist returns to Nigeria she notices how big and important her husband appears ("Women knew the country did this to their men. There was no doubt about it, Albert was thoroughly at home" [66]), and she recognizes the charms of the harem ("It was a long time since she had had the luxury of being looked after. She had arrived keyed up and combative, ready to justify herself, but slipped effortlessly back into her old submissive role" [66]). But the world of her subconscious, speaking to her in dreams as it speaks to her through Taiwo, will have none of this "old submissive role." She dreams of her childhood, and her abandonment, and she recalls, "I did not miss my father. He had so many people to love that I felt insignificant" (83). Scandalous or not, Kehinde ultimately chooses significance over acceptance.

In an ironic twist on Ibsen's *Doll's House*, where the newly liberated woman ominously slams the door behind her and sets out into the world, Emecheta brings her own hero fullcircle. Early in the story Kehinde remarks to her husband "Now you earn enough money, own a house" to which Albert replies, "*We* own a house." As the narrator notes, "he was not unaware of the legal status of a wife here in Britain." (4) It is only much later in the novel that a significant change in perception takes place in Kehinde and prompts an act worthy of Ibsen: "The For Sale sign flapped forlornly in the wind. Something propelled her back outside, and with unexpected strength she wrenched it from the ground. 'This house is not for sale,' she declared. 'This house is mine'" (Kehinde 108)—from "you" to "we" to "I." Having rid herself of her husband and all he has come to represent for her, Kehinde's "seizure" of her property is a liberating act of possession, a laying claim to an identity. It is also, significantly, a positioning of Emecheta's spokesperson on *London* land. Tearing down the For Sale sign, therefore, ends the tentative emigrant status that would not let Kehinde—or Emecheta—settle. Her liberating act as a woman is also her liberating act as a Nigerian—one who chooses to redefine the possibilities of nationality for women such as herself.

This interesting nexus between national identity and feminist self-consciousness illuminates a final thread that runs through Emecheta's work and leads to this symbolic claim to property. In her discussion of *Adah's Story* (1983), Schmidt-Grözinger remarks that this is an "account of the protagonist's continual attempts to gain liberty through self-determination" (Schmidt-Grözinger 116). Most of Emecheta's readers would agree, no doubt, that the same description might be offered of almost all her novels. But in this particular novel the protagonist's struggle is compared to that of a "young nation seeking independence" (*Adah* 209). This explicit politicization of the personal suggests the sort of resolution that Emecheta has found for herself, and for several of her characters, regarding questions of personal choice and national obligation.

She has, for example, remarked that there is, in general, too much Nigerian literature about the effects of colonialism: "We forget that some of us have been independent for more than two decades. It is about time we started writing about ourselves now." (James 39) She instinctively builds upon a condition that one critic describes as true for most emerging nations: "Like all other writers, the Nigerians stand at that distance from their own culture which follows from turning it into the object of their attention. They are also distant from that long ago Nigeria, when it was still itself, not yet altered or even alterated from itself by the impact and legacy of colonial appropriation" (Gohrbandt 116). Standing at such a distance, there is inevitably a romanticizing of that past age of innocence; Emecheta herself perhaps shares in that yearning for a simpler time, as in her provocative response to the question, what can African women gain from the Western world's liberation movement?: "They can gain what they had before the colonial power came into Nigeria. Women can become independent within their families (Umeh & Umeh 23)." Perhaps readers will know how to interpret this if they consider Kehinde's situation at the novel's end: her independence "within" her family is in defiance of her son, and on a separate continent from her husband.

But her comments reflect her personal attack on what might be called a neocolonialism of the subject. As Schmidt-Grözinger observed in her discussion of *Adah's Story*, in London Adah is threatened with the worst of both worlds: her husband has adjusted to the new culture by interiorizing Britain's disdain for the African, but at the same time he insists on imposing Nigerian social standards on his wife. As Schmidt-Grözinger sees it, "Adah's decision to leave Francis is not only a challenge to his male authority, but at the same time a challenge to the continuity of African socialization even abroad (Schmidt-Grözinger 116)." Adah—like Kehinde and so many of Emecheta's protagonists—implicitly strikes a blow against the neocolonialization that would crush her burgeoning "national" identity as a self-defining entity.

We have seen, though, that Emecheta is far from naive in her observation of the welcome that England is prepared to offer to these new "nations," these new satellites who jar themselves free from older and narrower orbits. Like Schmidt-Grözinger, Abioseh Porter implies an interesting connection between the personal and the national searches for independence in his discussion of *Second-Class Citizen* (1975), though I believe the protagonist's epiphany in that early novel more clearly suggests Emecheta's own blunt experience of racial prejudice in England. As Porter argues, *Second-Class Citizen* can be read as an apprenticeship novel in which Adah has a dream of going to England; she comes to see the dream as an illusion (Porter 125; see also Martini). In this novel, her disillusionment with England coincides with her disillusionment with Francis (*Second-Class Citizen* 39) . He, in fact, claims that they had never been married (much as former colonizing powers may sometimes choose to claim?) and, as Porter puts it, Adah "obviously understands now that she was totally wrong in looking up to Francis as a source of support. (Porter 126)" It would be too strong to say that Emecheta suggests in this analogy that commonwealth women are "totally wrong" to look up to Great Britain as a source of support in their struggle to define a new identity—she clearly admires the freedom that England offers to women such as herself—but the implication seems clear: any support is inadequate, because unreliable. One must muster one's resources and strike out into foreign territory.

As with the "repetition" of Nko in the character of Rike, in *Kehinde* there are other echoes of earlier novels. Porter notes that, in *Second-Class Citizen*, "When (after outmaneuvering Francis's mother) Adah finally joins Francis in England, she quickly realizes that if Francis had been dependent, lazy, and manipulative in Lagos, he becomes even worse overseas" (Porter 128). *Kehinde* echoes these sentiments, to a point, but makes several interesting adjustments. In the latter novel it is to Nigeria that the protagonist finally (and against her husband's will) returns, and it is his sisters who "protect" him from his willful wife. Furthermore, whereas in the earlier novel the husband was lazy in Lagos and simply became worse in London, in *Kehinde* Albert is a hard worker with a responsible job in London, but ultimately becomes unemployed once he returns to Nigeria. This may suggest a growing intolerance toward Nigerian intransigence. In any case, it fits Emecheta's broader pattern of call and response—*taiwo* and *Kehinde*—running through her novels as they rehearse much the same scene. Her accumulated protest seems clear: this writer has considered the options and has not made her choices lightly.

Emecheta's tone in *Kehinde* suggests that she has reached a certain level of comfort in her resolution of this dual attraction to two cultures. It is important to note that, just before her protagonist removes the For Sale sign, she has a significant visitation:

Inside the narrow hallway, the smell of the London

terrace house welcomed her like a lost child. Before she could suppress it, a voice inside her sang out, 'Home, sweet home!' Taiwo, who had not spoken to her since she had gone to Nigeria, was back. Kehinde rebuked the voice: 'This is not my home. Nigeria is my home.' As she said it, she knew she was deceiving herself, and Taiwo would not let her get away with it. 'We make our own choices as we go along,' came the voice. 'This is yours. There's nothing to be ashamed of in that.' (108)

It is a decision that has been a long time coming in Emecheta's fiction, the result of an internal argument that has listened to two voices for years and struggled to heal the breach. This is the centering epiphany of the novel. It only remains for Emecheta to accommodate Kehinde to her rich complexity: "She had stopped protesting that all her thoughts were hers alone, and started accepting Taiwo's voice as a permanent part of her consciousness" (135). Readers who are fond of this novelist and aware of the many women writers who share her struggle cannot help but sense the note of triumph in this novel's closing lines: "'Now we are one,' the living Kehinde said to the spirit of her long dead Taiwo" (141). It is intriguing to imagine the effect this obvious resolution will have on Buchi Emecheta's future fiction.

WORKS CITED

Andrade, Susan Z. "Rewriting History, Motherhood, and Rebellion: Naming an African Woman's Literary Tradition," *Research in African Literatures* 20,1 (Spring 1990):91—110.

Davies, Carole Boyce and Anne Adams Graves, eds. *Ngambika: Studies of Women in African Literature*. Trenton: Africa World P, 1986.

Emecheta, Buchi. *Second-Class Citizen*. New York: Braziller, 1975.

—. *Adah's Story*. London: Allison & Busby, 1983.

—. *The Family*. New York: George Braziller, 1990.

—. *Kehinde*. Oxford: Heinemann, 1994.

Flewellen, Elinor C. "Assertiveness vs. Submissiveness in Selected Works by African Women Writers," *Ba Shiru: A Journal of African Languages and Literature* 12,2 (1985): 3—18.

Frank, Katherine. "Feminist Criticism and the African Novel," *African Literature Today* 14 (1984):34—47.

Gohrbandt, Detlev. "Narratives of Africa from Without and Within: The Problem of Understanding Others." *Mediating Cultures Probleme des Kulturtransfers: Perspektiven fur Forschung und Lehre*, ed. Norbert H. Platz, 102—107, Essen: Die Blane Eule, 1991.

Hannerz, Ulf. "The World in Creolization," *Africa* 57,4 (1987):546—59.

Heim, Otto and Anne Zimmerman, "Report on the Workshop: Cultural Mediation—Mediating Concepts of Culture." *Mediating Cultures Probleme des Kulturtransfers: Perspektiven fur Forschung und Lehre,* ed. Norbert H. Platz, 139-44. *Essen: Die Blaue Eule,* 1991

James, Adeola, ed. *In Their Own Voices: African Women Writers Talk.* London: Heinemann, 1990.

Jussawalla, Feroza and Reed Way Dasenbrock. *Interviews with Writers of the Post-Colonial World.* Jackson and London: Univ. Press of Mississippi, 1992.

King, Bruce. "The New Internationalism: Shiva Naipaul, Salman Rushdie, Buchi Emecheta and Kazuo Ishiguro." *The British and Irish Novel Since 1960,* ed. James Acheson, New York: St. Martin's Press, 1991. 192—211.

Martini, Jürgen. "Linking Africa and the West: Buchi Emecheta." *Festschrift zum 60. Geburtstag von Carl F. Hoffmann,* ed., Franz Rottland, Hamburg: Helmut Buske Verlag, 1986. 223—233.

Platz, Norbert H., ed. *Mediating Cultures Probleme des Kulturtransfers: Perspektiven fur Foschung und Lehre.* Essen: Die Blaue Eule, 1991.

Porter, Abioseh Michael. "*Second-Class Citizen*: The Point of Departure for Understanding Buchi Emecheta's Major Fiction," *The International Fiction Review* 15,2 (Summer 1988):123—129.

Schmidt-Grözinger, Dagmar. "Problems of the Immigrant in Commonwealth Literature: Kamala Markandaya, *The Nowhere Man,* Buchi Emecheta, *Adah's Story.*" *Tensions Between North and South: Studies in Modern Commonwealth Literature and Culture,* ed., Edith Merke, Würzburg: Königshausen and Neumann, 1990, 112—117.

Schulte, Bernd. "Cultural Transfer and Cultural Transformation: Attempts at Exploring Dimensions of 'Interculturalism' in the New Literatures in English." *Mediating Cultures Probleme des Kulturtransfers: Perpektiven fur Forschung und Lehre,* ed. Norbert H. Platz, 29—39. Essen: Die Blaue Eule, 1991

Umeh, Davidson and Marie Umeh. "An Interview with Buchi Emecheta." *Ba Shiru: A Journal of African Languages and Literature* 12,2 (1985):19—25.

Umeh, Marie. "African Women in Transition in the Novels of Buchi Emecheta," *Présence Africaine* 116,4 (1980):190—201.

—. "Reintegration with the Lost Self: A Study of Buchi Emecheta's *Double Yoke.*" *Ngambika: Studies of Women in African Literature,* eds., Carol Boyce Davies & Anne Adams Graves, Trenton, NJ: Africa World P, 1986, 173-80.

Tropes of Survival: Protest and Affirmation in Buchi Emecheta's Autobiography, *Head Above Water*

Ezenwa-Ohaeto

Survival as a fundamental issue in human interactions involves protest and affirmation. The individual motivated to survive often protests against all forms of subjugation and oppression and in the process there is an affirmation for self-fulfillment and self-actualization. Although all individuals in one aspect of life or the other are confronted with the need to survive, it is often in the affairs of disadvantaged peoples—especially women in societies with numerous social restrictions—that it becomes a primary objective. Buchi Emecheta in her autobiography, *Head Above Water*, fashions this issue of survival as a trope on which she hinges the story of her life. Though it could be argued that this creative trope is inevitable, the pattern of the narrator's life and the linkages between the characters and events illustrate the importance of the trope.

Furthermore, that trope is woven into the novel in the form of a chain which leads from event to event and also as a circle which widens and engulfs those events. One critic points out that "an autobiography may perhaps then be compared to a pond. There is a thin plop called birth followed by widening ripples which stretch out in every lateral direction. The author's orientation and skill are best seen in the angle from which he looks at the ripples and the point at which he elects to confine the process" (Fraser 87). It is from the angle and perspective of survival that Emecheta looks at the ripples of her life for the metaphor in "keeping one's head above water" implicated in the title that reiterates her survival. Thus the novelist delineates the thread of survival not only through the skein of her life but also through the inevitable intersections with her cultural traditions. In the process survival, becomes an inherited trait, for even in her somewhat ambivalent praise of her mother the trope of survival is distinct as she describes:

> "My mother, that slave girl who had the courage to
> free herself and return to her people in Ibusa, and
> still stooped and allowed the culture of her people
> to reenslave her, and then permitted Christianity to
> tighten the knot of enslavement." (3)

But this enslavement which Emecheta perceives as the ultimate cultural bond is not total, for within its bars, a woman could still protest and affirm her individuality, albeit, only with great determination. The birth of Buchi Emecheta, which is woven into the story through the storytelling session of Nwakwaluzo, the Big Mother, reiterates that determination to survive as the storyteller says: "My brother Nwabuike saw in the child's determination to live, the fighting spirit of our mother, Agbogo. And he too was determined to make his daughter live" (10). That baby daughter survived and Buchi Emecheta lives to tell the story through an internalization of that survival instinct.

The circumstances of her birth highlight the prevalence of survival and the subsequent events that affect Buchi Emecheta grow out of a resistance perception of those circumstances. Nwakwaluzo describes her entrance into the world with a hint of ironic humor: "What trouble did she not cause as she ran out of her mother's belly in seven months when other children stayed nine?" In addition she says that basic medical facilities were scarce in the locality in which

she was born while her size is described thus: "She was a little bigger than the biggest rat you've ever seen, all head."(10) The fact
that the baby is a girl adds to the sense of disappointment indicating that quite early in her life, Buchi Emecheta commences generating ambivalent feelings in her acquaintances. However, that
feeling is shortlived, as the next child born to her parents is a male
and his arrival is attributed to the elder Buchi. The narrator writes:
"I was forgiven for being born premature with a big head and small
body and for being a girl, because I must have recommended my
parents highly to the children living beneath the earth for Olisa to
send my mother my brother, who arrived with no fuss, who stayed
the whole nine months in her belly, and who appeared roaring his
way into the world. And they did not need to tuck him up with
rags" (11). In effect the attitudes reflected in the reception of Buchi
and her brother Adolphus Chisingali illustrate the primacy and origin of the protest which permeates the later life of Buchi, for it is
a protest to survive. She commences her life with that instinctive
reaction even as she is named—"Who is my God" (Onyebuchim)
or as Emecheta puts it "Are you my God?"—while the brother is
called, "God has ordered my promotion" (Chisingali). Those initial
attitudes, rather than depressing the girl, inculcate in her the will
to survive through the articulation of distinct protests that affirm
that will. Thus the idea of survival gradually permeates her life as
she grows, absorbing the traditions and cultures of the various locations in which she lives. It is perhaps this internalized survival
instinct that is often woven into the fiction Emecheta writes that
has informed such comments as the one by Marie Linton-Umeh
that "through her characters she challenges some of the assumptions of traditional Igbo society which frustrate the gifted woman
from the realization of herself as an entity" (Linton-Umeh 177),
and the contrary one by Afam Ebeogu that "much as the author
tries to paint men as crude primitives who would never give
women a chance, the humanist in her often subtly challenges the
inadequacies of the author's autobiographical inclinations" (Ebeogu
86). Nevertheless it has been remarked elsewhere that in her novels there is "an emphasis on the sense of womanhood and its liberation from the shackles of societal limitations" (Ezenwa—Ohaeto
22). The sense of liberation functions as an appendage to survival
in *Head Above Water*.

In the home as well as in public, survival is a palpable issue in
the autobiography. She learns to use her teeth as a weapon, as the
novel indicates: "Even at School in Lagos I was the greatest biter

amongst my friends. It usually worked, rendering my opponent helpless in no time, especially if I dug my teeth into the really painful parts of his body. My brother's back until this day carries the bumps and criss-cross marks of my teeth" (14). This incident illustrates that in the onerous task of survival, the protagonist is willing to make maximum use of certain natural weapons in subduing obstacles. But despite the use of that defensive weapon (the teeth), the protagonist obviously does not cherish violence for there is an exploration of other forms of resistance to injustice. In one instance the narrator recollects: "One thing that still surprises me about the discipline of my early school days was our maturity in human relations," though she "was not confident enough to take any kind of criticism well." (21) All the same it is also in that school environment with its institutionalized routes for development that an obstacle to development and self-fulfillment occurs. In a literature class, the protagonist in a reply to a question on a possible profession after the secondary school education answers: "I would like to be a writer." (23) The teacher Miss Humble is shocked and she orders: "Go out, out and straight to the chapel. Go there and pray for God's forgiveness." (23) The young girl departs but not to the chapel since it is not clear what sin has been committed. That refusal to succumb to an order that would have oppressed her objective in life is the first significant conscious protest and it certainly illustrates an affirmative act for survival. The debate that proceeds in the mind of the protagonist is an interrogation of different perceptions of reality that conflict with each other. Emecheta's protest at that unnecessary oppressive act is also a moral interrogation of the association of authority with wisdom, for she ruminates on Miss Humble's voice ringing in her ears as "the voice of authority. The voice one had been taught to associate with correctness. The voice one had never questioned. The voice that simply had to be obeyed." (24) It is significant that at the time that this voice is asserting its authority, the protagonist suddenly hears, "the voice of (her) *Chi*, little and at first insecure (which) started to filter in" asking her, "What are you going to tell God, ehh? What, Florence, are you going to tell him, when you go inside there to ask his forgiveness?" (24) That debate illuminates the moral dimensions of that incident as well as the symbolic nature of the protagonist's refusal to be humiliated while harboring an innocent perception of her future. Its symbolic effects are also related to the erroneous association of academic authority with moral authority, which is what generates the protest element in

Buchi Emecheta's reaction. Moreover, the conscious establishment of this protest at the level of an impressionable secondary school stage in a colonial society requires a strength of character that is not common, and it is that consciousness which positively transforms the later life of the protagonist. Thus its symbolic projection is that there is the need to develop an attitude that engages authorities in an interrogatory appraisal in spite of the ostensible importance of their secular roles. That act, in addition, emphasizes the importance of survival even when an environment possesses outward signs of disciplined organization and it metaphorically reflects the constant pressures on a growing mind.

An early marriage does not emasculate the survival instinct, in spite of the fact that the husband Sylvester Onwordi, according to the author, possesses "a dangerously weak mind" (27). The perseverance of the young Buchi enables her to proceed to England to join the husband. The labor to procure the travel money is motivated by the desire to fulfill a dream, and the journey to England is in fulfillment of that dream. As usual, dreams differ from reality, and the experience in England turns out different from the expectations for she confesses: "England gave me a cold welcome." Thus a trying period in her life begins. The little impediments in her early life now metamorphosize into larger obstacles. Survival for the individual is difficult enough, but when it is added to the survival of a marriage and the survival of a family it becomes magnified. The act of unfaithfulness which makes Buchi lose the respect that she has for Sylvester is not purely a result of the culture shock in London, because it occurs at a time that the man does not possess a reason for his callous act. She narrates:

> The day I brought Christy home from hospital I caught Sylvester sleeping with a white woman friend. I telephoned him for hours from the hospital to ask him to come and collect us, but he ignored my calls, so I packed my new baby and arrived on a Sunny May Day. The sunshine disappeared as I went upstairs and saw why my husband could not come for us. (32)

This emotional obstacle in the life of Buchi Emecheta occurs at a time when there is the need for her to be in possession of a peaceful, well ordered home. Thus the behavior of Sylvester is not only immoral but also inhuman for he denies the wife the necessary emotional stability.

Interestingly, a neighbor of Buchi Emecheta, known as Mrs. Ola, in whom she confides concerning her decision to separate from Sylvester, only perceives the incident in terms of an unpleasant experience that has been ordained by fate. The protagonist adds that Mrs. Ola "was able to recount all that she had gone through" in her marriage and "her experiences were such that they almost made me forget my woes." (32) In addition the excuse that such acts of unfaithfulness are prevalent, meaning that Buchi should condone it, is unreasonable because it conceives a marital relationship as a union of unequal partners in which the female partner tolerates even inhuman treatment. Emecheta's assertion that "if a husband was going to be unfaithful, he should have the decency to do it outside and not on his wife's bed and especially not on the day that she was bringing home their new baby" (33) is equally an indication of negative tolerance that contradicts the matrimonial injunctions. Perhaps it is an ironic assertion because unfaithfulness from either the male or female partner destroys the moral basis of the union. In addition, the husband refuses to work, insisting that "he came to England to study, not to work for me to stay at home simply to wash nappies, knit jumpers and indulge in my lazy dreams" (34). In a bid to show part of her individuality, she writes a novel *The Bride Price*. Unfortunately Sylvester after reading the book burns it and it is this act that leads to a breakdown of the marriage. It was a terrible act and the destruction of her manuscript parallels the destruction of an "offspring," for Emecheta regards the work as her "brain child." Thus that unnecessary but willful act is an equivalent of murder since the creation of a work of art is like the production of a baby, absorbing the energies, thoughts, and parts of the life of the writer. Emecheta finds accommodations elsewhere, but Sylvester, in order to escape responsibility denies his paternity in court, claiming that he never married her. The curse she delivers, though it has a superstitious connotation, is the consequence of desperation and frustration. It is really at this point that Emecheta's battle to survive commences and a critic's observation that her fiction is marred by "her preoccupation" to protest "on too many fronts: welfarism, racism and sexism" (Ogunyemi 67) is clearly the consequence of her own real life experience.

Similarly, the circumstances surrounding the birth of Buchi Emecheta's fifth child also establish the survival instinct in her. It is not only the fact that as a single parent she bears the pregnancy for nine months and delivers safely, but also she courageously accomplishes the associated tribulations. The narration of the circumstances of the delivery confirms her courage:

> They said Alice had arrived eight days earlier than expected and they had not prepared for this emergency. It was no use explaining to them that after eight and a half months, babies could arrive at any time. It was not their fault, I kept saying. It was the fault of my *Chi*, who landed me with Sylvester, of all men. Never mind I'd survive. (41)

It is interesting that the lament ends on an optimistic note that portrays the determination to survive in spite of the unpleasantness of the experience undergone. In effect Buchi Emecheta reiterates quite often the idea encapsulated in the Igbo aphorism that "when one says yes, the personal god or *chi* affirms." It is that affirmation in support of the protagonist's positive determination that widens the scope of this autobiography into a metaphoric depiction of reality. The metaphor of protest that is linked with affirmation clearly establishes an intrinsic human attitude to survival in the midst of mundane obstacles. *Head Above Water* also makes that metaphorization indelible in the mind of the reader through the interplay of despair and hope. That interplay is part of life, but the change of environment or acquaintances or jobs is expected to minimize its unwholesome effects on the individual.

However, in new houses and new environments there are new acquaintances and new tribulations. Neighbors are sometimes disconcerting and her protest proceeds beyond the small circle of a marital partner to a wider circle of people with varied mannerisms. In all those encounters it is the will of the protagonist to survive that emerges, especially in the determination to be a writer. It is obviously this element of determination that encourages Carole Boyce Davies to assert that "the act of autobiographical writing itself, for the African woman writer, therefore, fulfills a range of personal requirements" and that it allows her "to order, to make sense of painful experience, to articulate herself, to write her *self*" and "above all to create" (Davies 207). The scope of opposition to Emecheta's aspiration to be a writer is wide: the husband Sylvester considers it unattainable; Miss Humble regards it as a sin; and Carole the social worker is convinced that writing "does not necessarily make you rich enough to buy a house." But it is this constant interrogation of her intentions and doubts cast on her aspirations that create the feeling of protest that leads Buchi

Emecheta affirmatively to seek to achieve her aims as this statement reveals:

> Sometimes it is very good to meet people like
> Carole, Miss Humble and Sylvester. Such people
> were particularly good for me and my *Chi*, because
> one way to set my mind on achieving something
> was for another person to tell me that I could not do
> it. I would then put all my thoughts into it, I would
> pray for it and go out for it, in search of the miracle.
> (49)

That the miracle eventually materializes for the female writer,
albeit only after a period of uncertainties and perplexities including the acquisition of a sociology degree, is not without its own
related impediments: the protagonist recalls that she "was made to
understand that it would be a formidable task," which she thinks
"was an unnecessary attempt to scare me off by the Head of
Studies, Mr. Ashton." But she agrees later that "sociology was proving impossible for me to understand." In addition she feels that
"studying with eighteen and nineteen-year olds, who seemed to
have no cares in the world while I had a full house to look after,
did nothing to alleviate my perilous position." (53) Ultimately, what
these issues highlight is that the size of the problem or obstacle,
rather than oppressing the protagonist, makes her devoted, dedicated, and determined.

The writing career embarked on at about the same time progresses in a flurry of protests: a friend who types the manuscript
charges eight pounds and Buchi protests; however, at the end she
"paid the money, but lost a friend." (63) The tribulations persist
and finally the book *In the Ditch* is published, marking the accomplishment of one issue of survival. That event also marks a positive dimension to the life that has revolved around protests. In the
words of a protagonist: "I had come a long way, and only people
who have set their hearts on achieving something and eventually
getting it will realize how one feels at a time like this" (74). The
success is not only inspiring but also therapeutic. In addition, an
obvious implication of the success is not just to reiterate its pleasure but also to highlight the cumulative effects of affirmative
determined efforts.

That determination is partly mingled with notions of survival
against all forms of oppression and subjugation. In the matter of
the mock reconciliation between Buchi and Sylvester, it is the sur-

vival streak that galvanizes her to insist on a separate but fulfilling existence. Thus her resistance, albeit mild, in giving "him an uncomfortable push with (the) elbow" is part of the protest and a sign of determination to exist on equal terms, although she says: "The depth of my rebellion surprised me and so did the intensity of my sense of self-preservation." (93) That self-preservation is not without obstacles, such as the insensitivity of the narrator's female "friends" who are keen that she re-enter the life of matrimony, which Buchi later realizes is envy, for "the facts that I got myself published and was reading for a degree were too much for some of my female friends." (96) Interestingly, by contrast, the female companions working with Buchi for a Sociology degree are sensitive and understanding. It is their combined efforts, paralleling the need for female unity in other spheres of life, that elicit a success that is not dampened even by the side effects of the sleepless nights and the drugs she takes "to make (her) learn how to go back to sleep" (103). The consequence is the tendency for the narrator's legs to collapse at unexpected moments, but as usual she applies her antidote to obstacles: "I simply willed it away and somehow it went" (107). That ability to "will sickness away" is clearly related to the cultivation of an affirmative perspective on life. It also illustrates the manner in which survival becomes an icon, practicalized and projected on the canvas of harsh realities.

In effect, *Head Above Water*, in as much as it is the story of a self narrated by that self, portrays metaphorically how the harshness of life could be tempered and manipulated towards affirmative ends. Thus impediments in her writing career—unlike her first novel, *In the Ditch* (e.g., when *Second-Class Citizen* fails to excite the publishers) are overcome by pushing the issue of survival to the fore and learning to exist with opposition, thereby fulfilling what one critic characterizes as "faith in a positive reality that may lie on the other side of the limits of expression or even experience." (James, 116) That other side of experience emanates from the acceptance of the job of a social worker at the Seventies Club, which is also part of the desire to extend the instinct of survival to other members of her race. The dimensions of the reality of the Seventies Club are both wide and worrisome, for the members "were free to vent their grievances on the workers, and the Committee was to tell the workers the limit of their power in such situations or simply to ignore the members' complaints, as the case might be" (132). It was therefore left to people like Buchi Emecheta to "keep (the) dissatisfied youth in check" (133). The consequence of this attempt to channel the feelings of frustration and dissatisfaction into useful occupations through feminine mildness almost yields tragic results. But Emecheta accepts her responsibilities based on altruistic considerations of an envisaged help to the community; which is an intrinsic element of her cultural roots that are still vibrant in spite of the existence in a foreign land. The determination is encapsulated in the statement: "seeing people of my race reduced to banging tables and shouting at each other instead of talking overpowered my other instincts. I must accept the job. I must improve the lot of these young people. I must help." (139) That view is as selfless as it is trying, but Buchi Emecheta in the narration of this incident stresses the importance of widening the horizon of survival beyond the self to the group and to the race. The narrator illustrates that quite often the benefits of a survival instinct are only felt when the individual is conscious of its clearsighted application in the affairs of associates and acquaintances. In a way, that knowledge is significantly emphasized by the matrimonial interactions of the narrator, for it is the lack of a mutual survival instinct that causes the breakdown of Emecheta's marriage: her persistent efforts to make Sylvester develop a survival instinct and reorder his priorities in life fails, because he is incapable of cultivating or appreciating the benefits of that instinct. However, an element of controversy resides here because the perspective of Sylvester to life may be different and there is also the awareness that in autobiographies, "disagreeable facts are sometimes glossed over or repressed, truth may be distorted for the sake of convenience or harmony and the occlusions of time may obscure as much as they reveal" (Cuddon 63). Nevertheless the assessments of the facts justify the author's perception of Sylvester, while an assessment of the other man, Chidi, who comes into Buchi's life indicates a more positive force and perhaps more emotional links than the novelist presents.

All the same, Emecheta is put under extreme pressure in the Seventies Club, where the young black boys take drugs and smoke all kinds of dangerous weeds. The protagonist, trained in sociology, is interested in making the lives of the unfortunate blacks better and success-oriented. The fervent desire of the protagonist is to "help the members of the Seventies in my noble aims" (141), and those noble aims revolve around the conviction that the young black boys "could still lead useful lives even if they had spent a great part of their lives so far in remand homes or approved schools." (142) A prominent feature of that noble aim is the maternal instinct of the protagonist, which enables her to perceive the human elements necessary for the performance of her duties. She treats the boys as human beings, striving to inculcate in them the spirit of self-determination. However, the experiences they have undergone prove an insurmountable impediment, because the society and the Committee of the Seventies Club are structured in a manner that does not accord attention to the racial necessities of the youngsters. In addition, their background and their concept of the English society in which they find themselves are identified by the novelist as the major generators of their antisocial behavior in spite of their physical endowments. Emecheta sincerely takes this responsibility with a commitment that is positively enviable.

But the obstacles are enormous, for it requires not only a change of attitude on the part of the deprived, disadvantaged youths, but also a mental reorientation. Part of the task of the narrator is to convince the committee of the Seventies Club to put into practice ideas that would achieve that reorientation, but "the members of the committee who were mostly volunteers were not always in the mood to be burdened with our tales of woe." (150). The protagonist persists and, rather than succumb to the defeat of ineffectual activity of cosmetic social work, decides to "write about them and let the world know that some black youngsters went through that phase in the mid-1970s" (157). In a way the writing and publicity which the narrator decides to give to the sociological issue is a way of exorcising her sense of defeat in the club, for publicity is guaranteed to arouse public awareness towards the need for creating in the minds of the youngsters positive notions of survival.

Nevertheless, it has been established in varied human endeavors that quite often it is difficult to achieve success in spite of efforts made. The protagonist Emecheta becomes the target of violent attention from the problem youngsters, which makes her resign. This resignation at the same time haunts the protagonist as a sign of failure. It is part of the candor of the writer that she does not gloss over such incidents perceived as failures in as much as it is also part of the structure of autobiographies and biographies to concentrate "either on deeds, feats, merits and creative accomplishments, or on the structure of the hero's destiny in life, his happiness, and so on" (Bakhtin 17). The manner in which the events in her life occur, in pairs of negative and positive forms, makes it possible for an event that reiterates her success to be placed after that incident in order to provide a pleasant perspective. That event is the decision of Allison and Busby to publish

Second-Class Citizen, which serves as an appropriate antidote to the feeling of despair. Emecheta shows in *Head Above Water* that survival depends on those instances of affirmative support, like the response of the publishers and the invitation to set up another youth center to be known as "Dashiki." The Dashiki experiment not only differs from the Seventies Club in terms of orientation but also in terms of incorporating a survival motive as one of its hidden tenets. The author describes it thus:

> Dashiki was different. The atmosphere was like this,
> "Yes, we all know that you had a rotten time in the
> past, your parents have rejected you, the school you
> have been shuffled through has declared you une-
> ducable—now we want you to forget all that. Turn
> over a new leaf and let us start all over again." (165)

The narrator adds: "That was exactly what I was determined to do" (166). That determination, which has become a personal objective to survive, has absorbed an institutionalized concept of survival. This synthesis affects the participants at the Dashiki Youth Center for the general desire for a useful transformation of their personal lives enables the boys to relocate their focus in life as well as develop worthwhile ambitions and realize that the obstacles can always be overcome. In addition to the boys who desire to survive, the founder of the Dashiki Center also expects the Center to survive. It is thus not surprising that Buchi Emecheta finds the development at the Center highly fulfilling, thereby illustrating the values of survival constructed within that trope in the novel as beneficial to human existence. These accomplishments in the midst of the social realities of performing parental roles make the issue of survival paramount for the author narrates: "The lone parent is the bread-winner, the mother, the father, the Counsellor, the Comforter. I knew I had to shoulder the burden. It was one's cross, which one simply has to carry" (167). The nature of the burden becomes symbolic when the protagonist discovers that the constraints of survival could transcend race, for at the "Dashiki Center" there is an impediment to its development emanating from members of the same deprived black race. The novelist writes: "I hate unpleasantness, especially when we blacks do it to ourselves," and she reveals that the committee, made up of supposed friends that Vince, the founder of Dashiki, establishes "wrote to the Council to stop the grant and not only that, they also wrote to most of the boroughs from which we used to get our small funding, to ask them to stop sending money for the boys in our care" (175). This deplorable deed is used by the protagonist to illustrate that a similar racial background does not provide protection from antagonism.

It is more reprehensible when it is considered that the tradition which originally produced these antagonistic people was extolled for its communal values. Such values Emecheta had explored and analyzed in her two teenage novels, *The Wrestling Match* and *The Moonlight Bride*. She makes that communal perspective significant when she states in *Head Above Water*: "I had realized that what makes all of us human is belonging to a group. And if one belongs to a group, one should try and abide by its laws. If one could not abide by the group's law; then one was an outsider, a radical someone different who had found a way of living and being happy outside the group" (166). Nevertheless, the idea which Emecheta stresses in that reference to laws and obedience is that such laws should not be fashioned according to gender or material possessions. Thus, she is constantly comparing what she considers the traditional concept of interpersonal relationships with what she considers to be the accepted norms of the society in which she finds herself. In the process her exploration of her feelings and motives parallels an anatomy of the general feelings and motives of human beings in the wider society. The ideas that emerge from those explorations become parabolic in their connotative implications for multiracial societies.

It is significant that the narrator makes a distinction between negative and positive survival. At the Quintin Kynaston School where she works as a "Supply Teacher," she meets an Indian known as Mrs. Patel, another "Supply Teacher." They are part of an exploited group of teachers who could be dropped at the end of term despite their performance of all the duties of regular teachers. However, in order to be confirmed as a regular teacher Mrs. Patel, stops associating with Buchi Emecheta. She is frank to confess that "she wanted to be an established teacher and she would rather be seen getting on with the white teachers. She was sure that white teachers got upset when they saw her sitting with Emecheta and another black teacher and talking even though they all spoke in English" (179). The ambition of Patel to survive is natural, but her subsequent desire to survive at the expense of Emecheta is abhorrent, for she "would call" any misdemeanor on the part of Emecheta "to the attention of the Head of Social Studies" whenever she "had done anything wrong" (179), like rushing to do her shopping whenever she had finished teaching for the day. It is not surprising that Mrs. Patel fails to get a regular teaching post, for her brand of survival is detrimental to communal interactions and her experience magnifies the idea that a positive ambition should not be established on a negative attitude to survival. Another instance of the depiction of the negative angles to the issue of survival is demonstrated through the experience of Jake, Buchi's son, at the Tottenham School, where he complains that the pupils "are allowed to bang into (their) teachers" and also that a big boy says to him that "the best way to survive (there) is never to give in to no teacher because all "blacks should stick together" (227). But what that big boy is asking for is a union of disobedient pupils which is against the academic values associated with education. This negative manifestation of the notion of survival is perceived by the narrator as damaging to the mind, especially impressionable, young minds. It is this view of survival that makes Buchi withdraw her son from that school, for it confirms the result of unsupervised education in local schools. In effect she is illustrating through those two incidents that a degeneration of the issues of survival leads to a moral devastation of the individual and the character.

In addition the narrator illustrates that antagonism and ignorance coexist and that often the elimination of ignorance obliterates antagonism. At the ceremony of the "International Women's League," in which Buchi Emecheta is invited to give a speech, her performance turns the occasion into an illumination of that ignorance. She writes: "I told those women everything I felt, and they applauded me for my sincerity and assured me that steps would be taken to bring the black and white women together. In my blind and stupid way, I did hit on the truth" (190). That sincerity and ability to tell the truth are part of the writer's protest tradition and they add impetus to the effort to survive. Another distinct characteristic which the incident highlights is the view that "historical gender differences in the roles, classes, social positions and life models of women and men alone contribute to women's discovery of their designation as cultural other," with the result that "for each woman writing, her own gender status and her female models" contribute to "a concept of self and a quality of writing voice that are distinctively of woman" (Watson, 180—181). It is this quality that in *Head Above Water* becomes symbolic of the intricate patterns of contemporary lives and social interactions.

All the same, there is also an indication in *Head Above Water* that protest takes several forms, sometimes in the nature of hints that are subtle, especially for an individual who has acquired recognition as a writer. After an unpleasant holiday the narrator says:

> I thought I would write about it, and told one social
> worker so. I didn't know whether I could have done
> it, because it was the year I was thinking of repeat-
> ing my Part One in Sociology, and bad holidays were
> the least of my troubles. But after the revealing
> descriptions in *In the Ditch*, I only had to say, "I think
> I may write about it" for people to take me serious-
> ly. In short, the council returned all the money I
> paid, with a letter of apology. (195)

The experience illustrates another form of protest and another avenue for survival, since it indicates the fear of the written word in antagonists. That fear results from the perception that "we know that even when the writer uses the classic construct "I" that there is still little difference between autobiography and fiction in the sense that both are created versions of the world, shaped and ordered, and merely employing different forms" (Fido 331−2). But the written words have other benefits too for in 1975 "just two weeks before Christmas, the letter and first deposit for the *Granada Crown Court* play, 'Juju Landlord,' came and Emecheta 'felt so rich'" (208). However, it is not only the remuneration that emphasizes the survival perspectives of that play because the opportunity which provides for the black actors and actresses in London becomes fulfilling and the narrator records: "One thing really made me happy: that I was in a position to bring happiness to so many black artists" (213). That opportunity which Emecheta creates for others is what she protests to acquire in her own case, as in the issue of buying a house when she persists until she finds an opportunity. The joy in that accomplishment catalyses her children into action as they convince the student helpers to pack their property to the new house. Although it is unplanned and most of the items had not been nearly arranged, the feeling of joy made the family go "to bed without unpacking or undressing" and the author feels that "it was mad, but nice" (222). Such accomplishments and joys are sharpened, as the writer climbs the ladder of success, by the little disasters and disappointments.

Ultimately the recognition which Buchi Emecheta elicits is a recognition of not only herself but also a recognition of her ideas, especially the idea that a woman can survive in the face of great odds emanating from the husband, the children, the acquaintances, the colleagues at work, the publishers, and a host of incidental human beings that are encountered in the course of living one's life. To every challenge the reaction of the protagonist is to make of it a rung on the ladder of survival which takes her beyond the current stage onto another one. Thus her encounter with the publisher George Braziller, who hints that the "age of Africa in literature had gone" is countered by her statement that she is "going to write a sage" (205) and that her books about Africa would encompass various periods and subjects. In encompassing those subjects that are reflected in her novels , The Bride Price, In the Ditch, The Slave Girl, and The Joys of Motherhood, Emecheta makes a statement on her attitude towards life, towards society and towards human beings. It is the statement that survival is primary and must be fashioned in order to derive maximum positive benefits and also that disasters are not restrictive if the individual sensibly deflects their effects in order to pursue other enriching objectives in life.

It is this mixture of pain and suffering, protest and affirmation, and sorrow and joy that provide the tension in the life of Buchi Emecheta which Head Above Water illustrates. It is also in this autobiography that the answer to the dynamics of the creative works resides. Thus the observation that "there are great omissions in Emecheta's vision which threaten her art with the badge of fantasy, omissions which reduce many of the works to private crusades waged for the vicarious revenge for private hurt" (Nwankwo 40) finds confirmation in the autobiography. But that does not imply that the feelings are suspect because, as Head Above Water indicates, success does not create a cocoon from the prevalent survival issues facing the protagonist and her children.

However, the protagonist needs different strategies to help the children survive. When the first daughter, Chiedu, reacts peevishly by marching "upstairs [and packing] her things and left" (237), the narrator realizes that experience often yields an avenue for knowledge which occurs after several weeks as the daughter returns contrite. Furthermore, Emecheta discovers that writing and survival have become synthesized, which is ultimately the metaphor of Head Above Water. She survives by turning the deep sorrow of the daughter's temporary rejection into a therapeutic writing session as she "banged away the whole of Christmas, the whole January 1977, and by the end of that month, almost six weeks after Chiedu left, The Joys of Motherhood was finished" (238). The purgation of emotions, comprehensively encapsulated in the creation of a novel, establishes the affirmation of hope in her life.

It is in this act, in which the sorrowful spirit becomes the protest spirit and which leads to the survival spirit, that Emecheta's *Head Above Water* makes telling use of the trope of survival. In the end, it is an act of survival simply to tell stories like that of the big mother Nwakwaluzo, the "only difference" being that "instead of using the moonlight and her own emotional language as tools," Emecheta has "to use electricity, a typewriter and a language that belonged to those who once colonized the country of [her] birth" (242).

The autobiography of Buchi Emecheta clearly establishes that protest could be positively channeled to achieve self-fulfillment. Although there are instances of silence in the novel and there are also contradictions in the narration, *Head Above Water* magnifies the trope of survival through the widening of its metamorphic and symbolic dimensions. In the selection and depiction of incidents, the facts establish the nature and importance of experience to the refinement of values and the struggle to fulfill a destiny. In conclusion, the blend of her personal development and the sociohistorical movements within the period in which the autobiography is set makes the literary shape of survival a trope worthy of critical appreciation in *Head Above Water.*

ACKNOWLEDGEMENT

The author is grateful to the Alexander von Humboldt Foundation for funding and the University of Mainz, Germany for the use of its facilities.

WORKS CITED

Bakhtin, M.M. "The *Bildunsgroman* and its Significance in the History of Realism (Towards a Historical Topology of the Novel)." *Speech Genres and Other Late Essays.* Austin: Univ. of Texas Press, 1986.

Cuddon, J.A. "Autobiography," *A Dictionary of Literary Terms*, London: Andre Deutsch, 1979. 63–67.

Davies, Carole Boyce. "Private Selves and Public Spaces: Autobiography and the African Woman Writer." *Neo-Helicon* 17,2 (1990):183–210.

Ebeogu, Afam. "Enter the Iconoclast: Buchi Emecheta and the Igbo Culture." *Commonwealth: Essays and Studies.* 7,2 (1985): 83–94.

Emecheta, Buchi. *Head Above Water: An Autobiography.* London: Fontana, 1986.

Ezenwa-Ohaeto. "Emechta's Teenage Fiction: The Individual and Communal Values in *The Wrestling Match* and *The Moonlight Bride*." *Commonwealth: Essays and Studies.* 13,1 (1990):22–27.

Fido, Elaine Savory. "Mother/Lands: Self and Separation in the Work of Buchi Emecheta, Bessie Head and Jean Rhys." *Motherlands: Black Women's*

Writing from Africa, the Caribbean and the South Asia. London: The Women's Press, 1991. 330–349.

Fraser, Robert, "Dimension of Personality: Elements of the Autobiographical Mode." Ed. Doireann MacDermott. *Autobiographical And Biographical Writing in the Commonwealth*, Barcelona: University of Barcelona and Editorial AUSA, 1984. 83–87.

James, Louis. "Wole Soyinka's *Aké*: Autobiography and the Limits of Experience," Ed. Doireann MacDermott. In *Autobiographical And Biographical Writing in the Commonwealth*, Barcelona: University of Barcelona and Editorial AUSA, 1984. 91–121.

Linton-Umeh, Marie. "Reintegration with the Lost Self: A Study of Buchi Emecheta's *Double Yoke*." In Carole Boyce Davies and Anne Adams Graves, eds. *Ngambika: Studies of Women in African Literature*. Trenton, New Jersey: Africa World P, 1986. 173–180.

Nwankwo, Chimalum. "Emecheta's Social Vision: Fantasy or Reality?" *Ufahamu*. 17,1 (1988):35–43.

Ogunyemi, Chikwenye Oknojo. "Buchi Emecheta: The Shaping of a Self." *Komparatistische Hefte*. 8 (1983):65–77.

Watson, Julie. "Shadowed Presence: Modern Women Writer's Autobiographies and the Other." Ed. James Olney. In *Studies in Autobiography*. New York and Oxford: Oxford University P, 1988. 180–189.

The London Novels of Buchi Emecheta

Christine W. Sizemore

Buchi Emecheta has published four London novels. The first two
novels that she wrote, *In the Ditch*, (1972) and *Second-Class Citizen*
(1974) are highly autobiographical and are set in the London of the
1960s. They were jointly republished as *Adah's Story* in 1983.
Recently, after writing five novels and several nonfiction works set
in Nigeria, Emecheta has returned to the London setting in *The
Family* whose British title is *Gwendolen* (1989) and *Kehinde* (1994).
In all four of these novels, Emecheta speaks from that space which
Homi Bhabha calls "the liminality of the national culture" (Bhabha,
304)[1] and thus provides a new kind of voice that opens up the tradition of the London novel.[2] The urban novel has always been characterized by multi-voicedness; indeed Mikhail Bakhtin uses the
urban novels of Dickens and Dostoyevsky to illustrate his concept
of "heteroglossia,"[3] but unlike the American city novel, ethnic
diversity is only recently being recognized as a part of the British
tradition. In her 1983 novel, *Londoners*, Maureen Duffy argues that
these new ethnic voices are the "true Londoners,"[4]the ones who
can portray the multicultural reality of the contemporary "cos-

mopolis." Her white, working-class narrator says:

> I've become as much a stranger as Jemal or Wolfgang, more because they don't expect to be at home in my native city. They are the true Londoners, denizens of cosmopolis. (23) Frank's ancestors were Phoenician traders, migrants from the island city of Tyre, Paul's were Scots from Celtic Ireland, Jemal's North West Indian, Suli's Sinbad's sailors and mine were mongrel, polymorph; . . . I can hear the songs they sing. (223)[5]

Buchi Emecheta's Adah, Gwendolen, and Kehinde are "true Londoners" precisely because they do "not expect to be at home" there. London, for them especially, is "a contested cultural territory where the people must be thought in a double-time" (Bhabha 297). Emecheta's London novels chart the progression of her Nigerian-British and Caribbean-British heroines in opening up a space for themselves and establishing a place for themselves, a new home. Geographer Yi-Fu Tuan says that "place is security, space is freedom" (Tuan 3). Emecheta's characters must search for both in their new city.

Helen Tiffin argues that postcolonial writers from places like

> India . . . the African countries, [and] the nations of the South Pacific . . . are able to challenge European perspectives with their own metaphysical systems. In areas like the Caribbean, or for non-indigenous peoples of Canada, Australia and New Zealand, there are no such formulated systems which may be recuperated to challenge the imported or imposed European one . . . . (Tiffin 173)

Black African writers, in Tiffin's view, have an advantage over white Canadian or Australian writers because they have a "metaphysics" or culture of their own to juxtapose against the British one. An emigrant writer like Emecheta, however, is in a different situation, a liminal situation, because from the perspective of England she sees problems for women within patriarchal Nigerian culture but from the perspective of her homeland she sees the problems for blacks within racist British culture. Emecheta's Nigerian characters are especially aware of the liminality of their space because they are emigrants, not immigrants. In her autobiography, Emecheta distinguishes between the Caribbeans who came to

London for jobs[6] and the Africans who came to London to "work their way through college. Most of them hoped to go home after their studies" (*Head Above Water* 140).[7] Immigrants who voluntarily leave their own country[8] are apt to be less ambiguous about their new country's culture than emigrants who think that they might return to their "homeland" some day. Emecheta's Nigerian characters, Adah and Kehinde, are emigrants. Because of her youth, Emecheta's Caribbean character, Gwendolen, has no choice but to join her family when summoned. They all three stand in a liminal space between cultures where they search for a secure place for themselves and their families and freedom within the city.

One of the cultural perspectives that is most ambiguous for Emecheta is that of feminism. The distrust that some African women feel for feminism is revealed in the vehemence of African critic Chikwenye Ogunyemi in her comments on Emecheta's novels. In a 1985 article, Ogunyemi says that Emecheta's first two novels are "deeply groitaled in the British and Irish feminism in which she was nurtured" (Ogunyemi 66). Ogunyemi castigates Emecheta for feminizing African males, for turning away from her African identity, and for being narcissistic (67). It is not surprising that in spite of her focus on female characters Emecheta too is wary of the term "feminist." In a 1984 interview Emecheta said emphatically: "My novels are not feminist; they are a part of the corpus of African literature" (Ravell-Pinto 50). Cynthia Ward summarizes Emecheta's dilemma: "Success in speaking unequivocally in the service of feminism produces a voice that serves neocolonialism; speaking for anticolonialism produces a voice that serves patriarchy" (Ward 86). Emecheta relents somewhat and acknowledges her ambivalence when in a 1980 interview and at a 1986 conference she describes herself as "a feminist with a small 'f'" (Umeh 23; Emecheta 175). In her 1986 speech Emecheta seems much more comfortable with the term when she characterizes "feminism" as not just being against marriage (Umeh & Umeh, 23), but as embracing a particular literary perspective:

> I write about the little happenings of everyday life.
> . . . I see things through an African woman's eyes. I
> chronicle the little happenings in the lives of the
> African women I know. I did not know that by doing
> so I was going to be called a feminist. But if I am
> now a feminist then I am a feminist with a small 'f.'
> (Emecheta 1988, 175)

The focus on "the little happenings of everyday life" is not only feminist but also, according to Bhabha, a characteristic of writing from a liminal perspective: "The scraps, patches, and rags of daily life must be repeatedly turned into the signs of a national culture" (Bhabha 297). When these "scraps, patches and rags of daily life" are those of an emigrant African woman, a feminist with a small 'f', the national culture is remade into a blend of multicultural voices that expand the tradition of the urban novel.

Emecheta says that her first two London novels, *In The Ditch* and *Second-Class Citizen*, are "over fifty percent" autobiographical (*Head Above Water* 58). Like Adah, Emecheta followed her husband, Sylvester Onwordi, to London in 1962 with their two young children. In London Emecheta worked at the North Finchley Library and soon had three more children. She left Sylvester in 1966 and eventually she had to move to public housing. In *Head Above Water*, Emecheta explains her relationship to her character:

> Because the truths were too horrible and because I suspected that some cynics might not believe me, I decided to use the fictitious African name of Adah, meaning 'daughter'. . . . using the fictitious name Adah instead of Buchi gave the book a kind of distance, and the distance gave the book the impression of being written by an observer. I was writing about myself as if I was outside me . . . . (58)

Although Emecheta criticizes herself for this stance in her autobiography, it allowed her the objectivity and distance to begin writing about herself and her marriage.

Although *Second-Class Citizen* was written after *In The Ditch*, it actually begins the story of Adah's arrival in London and her search for a safe place for her family. Adah comes to London from Nigeria to be with her husband, Francis Obi, who is "studying" for an advanced degree. Adah must cope not only with the difficulties of English life, but also with the sexism of her husband. Francis does not believe in birth control, but he also expects his well-educated wife to work to support him:

> Francis was from another culture. There was a conflict going on in his head. What was the point of marrying an educated woman? Why had his parents been asked to pay a big price if all she was going to do was to come to England and start modelling her

life on that of English women, not wanting to work,
just sitting there doing nothing but washing the
babies' nappies? (163)

Adah carries what Emecheta describes in the title of one of her
African novels as "a double yoke;" she is expected to be a traditional
wife, subservient to her husband, but also to be educated and modern, working to support the family. Adah has no trouble getting a
good job at a library because of her education and experience, but
she has a very hard time with her additional pregnancies and child-
care because she no longer has the support of the extended African
family. Adah can live with the fact that her husband is not successful in his academic work and that he involves himself with various English girls and is jealous of her success, but she hates the
inadequate housing and worries about the care of her children.
There are no places in the nurseries and the English woman who
acts as a "daily minder" for the children has a dirty house. It is not
until Adah's son gets meningitis that a social worker finds a place
for Adah's children at a nursery.

Although Adah goes to work every day, there is very little
description of her public life. The public "space" of the city and
even the freedom to work are less important to Adah than the security of a "place" both for herself and her children. Adah is the same
age as several of the other women working at the library, but they
discuss only fashion and boyfriends whereas Adah has by then
three children and problems with her husband who "did not believe
in friendship" (95). Adah has a family but no community, no
friends. The novel takes place primarily in the two sets of rooms
that they rent from other Nigerians, the places of day care for the
children, and the hospital where Adah has a caesarian delivery.

The novel's "voices" are Adah's own. Her modern working identity is in dialogue with her identity as a traditional wife. Elizabeth
Meese applies a feminist viewpoint to Bakhtin's concept of voices
by pointing to the "simultaneous traces of complicity and disruption in women's texts"(Meese 120). These voices can be heard in
Second-Class Citizen. Chapters entitled "Role Acceptance," "Learning
the Rules," and "Applying the Rules," suggest complicity with traditional roles, but Adah disrupts such roles when she begins to
assert herself against Francis. When after the caesarian birth of
their fourth child Francis takes for his own use the money given
to Adah by her colleagues at the library, Adah realizes that she "was
dealing not with the husband of her dreams, but with an

enemy"(122). When Francis calls in his landlord and the other tenants to shame Adah after he learns that she has gotten a cervical
cap for birth control, she decides that her marriage is "finished"
(147). Soon after Francis attempts to silence her by burning the
manuscript of her first novel (Sylvester Onwordi burnt the first
version of *The Bride Price*), she leaves him. At the divorce court
Francis says that he is willing for the four children to be sent out
for adoption. Adah, pregnant now with her fifth child, rallies and
says to the judge that she will care for her children. This novel ends
with her divorce. Although the multiplicity of voices is not as evident in this novel as in some of Emecheta's other novels, different
voices can be heard in Adah's own attempts to bear the double yoke
of African womanhood and to find her identity and a place for her
family in London.

Emecheta describes her other autobiographical London novel,
In The Ditch, as a "documentary novel of the daily happenings of
my life when I was living in the place officially known as 'Montagu
Tibbles' off Prince of Wales Road in North London. By the time I
moved in there, however, the block of flats was locally known as
'Pussy Cat Mansions'" (*Head Above Water* 66). This novel was initially serialized in the socialist paper, *The New Statesman*. Although
In The Ditch has the objectivity resulting both from Emecheta's
degree in sociology and from the distance created by using the name
"Adah" for her protagonist, Emecheta incorporates her own African
communal values in this novel as well as British feminist ones. It
describes a community of women, both English and African, working together to create a place for themselves and their children. In
this novel Adah, free of Francis' sexism if not of poverty, has a clearer identity of her own and portrays a much more complex microcosm of London life.[9] "The Ditch" is "Pussy Cat Mansions," which
is Council (welfare) housing. There, in spite of the rundown conditions, Adah finds a community of women. Although the concrete
steps up to her flat stink of urine, the light bulbs in the stairway are
often out and the cupboards are full of mildew, Adah is much hap-
pier than she was when she was living with Francis or alone in a
room rented from a fellow Nigerian. The welfare mothers of Pussy
Cat Mansion welcome her into their midst:

> The little group talked, gossiped and laughed; all
> were happy. They found joy in communal sorrow.
> . . . Adah stopped being homesick. She was begin-
> ning to feel like a human being again with a defi-

> nite role to perform—even though the role was in
> no other place but in the ditch. It was always nice
> and warm in the ditch. (61)

Adah finds that the problems of poverty bring women together and create an interracial community whose values are more like the ones she has known in Africa. Her neighbor, "Whoopey," teaches Adah how to complain to the authorities about problem dogs:

> The other clerks had now stopped work and simply
> stared at the two white women with a black one
> sandwiched in between like a good sponge cake.
> Differences in culture, colour, backgrounds and God
> knows what else had all been submerged in the face
> of greater enemies—poverty and helplessness. (71)

Marie Umeh comments on the feminism in this novel: "What makes this novel appealing to a wider cross-section of people is Emecheta's sympathy toward women's rights. All the female inhabitants of Pussy-Cat Mansions are oppressed victims" (Umeh 1980, 192). This sympathy enables Emecheta to combine British feminist analysis of the oppression of women with African values of women working together to form a community. Whoopey's mother, Mrs. Cox, serves as the advisor for all the young mothers: "Mrs. Cox became the 'Mum' for everybody. Sometimes more than a mum and more of a working-class Wise Woman. . . . Mrs. Cox also reminded Adah of most African matrons. . . . [who] have that sense of mutual help that is ingrained in people who have known a communal rather than an individualistic way of life" (65). The younger women have that communal sense of life as well. When Adah is sick with the flu, Whoopey comes in to help. When Adah learns that seventy-year-old Mr. Jada's young English wife has left him again, Adah joins another mother in going up to help him put the six young children to bed.

Adah and all of the other families are finally moved out of "the Ditch." Adah likes her clean new flat near Regent's Park, but she goes back to "the Crescent" near her old neighborhood to shop. There she enjoys the multicultural variety of a London market. Now that Adah has achieved the security of a physical place in which to live and a socially secure place within a community of women, she can enjoy the public spaces of London:

> Saturday was always busy at the Crescent. There
> were many Indian shops selling African food, and

this drew large numbers of Africans. . . . The market was once in the centre of a poor working-class
area. But modern housing estates had sprung up
round it like mushrooms; people got mixed, the rich
and the poor, and there was no knowing which was
which.

The noise, clatter and bustle was like that of birds
in an aviary. . . . . Children with chocolately mouths
and fingers followed the trails of mums with shopping trolleys loaded to overflowing with 'bargain'
foodstuffs. Africans, Pakistanis and West Indians
shopped side by side with the successful Jews,
Americans and English from Highgate, Hampstead,
Swiss Cottage and other equally expensive places.
(131–32)

Adah glories in the freedom she can now experience in the variety of multicultural London life. Because of her involvement in a
community of women Adah is able to achieve both place and space
in London.

After concentrating on African settings for fifteen years,
Emecheta returns to a London setting in *The Family* (British title—
Gwendolen), in which Emecheta concentrates on the pathology of
the patriarchal family. Although Emecheta said in a talk at John
Jay College in March of 1991[10] that this novel is based on an actual story she was told by a Caribbean girl while on a visit to Sussex
College, she also is able to achieve some distance in her analysis
of sexual abuse and incest in the patriarchal family by making the
family Jamaican and by blaming the sexual abuse and incest on
the effects of slavery that robbed the men of their African heritage
and values. Emecheta's ambivalence about African patriarchy is
split in this novel between the "bad" Jamaican abusers who have
lost their culture and the "good" Nigerians who maintain their culture even in exile.

In *The Family*, Jamaica has created abusers because of the lingering effects of the slave culture and because of the extreme
poverty that drives black Jamaicans to emigrate. The narrator
explains why Gwendolen's parents, Winston and Sonia Brillianton,
emigrate to London:

If they had stayed in Jamaica . . . the best accommodation he [Winston] could afford, on the odd jobs

he was doing, would have been one of those bar-
rack-like shacks in a cheap shanty district. If one
was white in Jamaica, one could coast along, if one
was brown, life could still have a meaning, but if
one was black and uneducated, life was a steady
downward pull to Hades. (86)

Winston is able to get a good job in London as a construction worker, but their daughter Gwendolen is left behind, insufficiently protected by her elderly grandmother, whose "friend" Johnny sexually
abuses her. Finally after three more children are born, the
Brilliantons send for Gwendolen to help with the children. She is
thrilled to be with her family again and feels protected by her
strong silent father, but the mere fact of being united with her family does not necessarily provide Gwendolen with a safe place.
Winston has a hard time acknowledging her as his daughter. When
she first arrives, he "was surprised and uneasy at the antics of this
little girl, who was his daughter, and whom he was beginning to
realize he had to work hard and wake up fatherly feelings
towards"(49). Winston doesn't abuse his daughter, however, until
his wife Sonia goes back to Jamaica to see her mother who she
thinks is dying. Unfortunately this departure is based on the
Brillianton's ignorance of African culture. Neither parent can read
so they get their Nigerian landlord to read a telegram for them that
tells of Sonia's mother's death. The landlord, relying on Nigerian
codes of politeness says "Your mother-in-law is very sick. Your wife
must go home and see her" (116). Winston misunderstands his
Nigerian landlord's politeness in saying that his mother-in-law in
Jamaica was sick rather than dead and makes arrangements for
his wife to return to Jamaica. The narrator explains: "If Mr
Brillianton had been a Nigerian, he would have guessed straight
away that his mother-in-law had died. But the man had had that
part of his cultural heritage taken away from him by slavery (116)
. . . . the gulf which was made by slavery that separated brother
from brother was still too wide and too deep to be crossed by a single narrow bridge made of the wooden plank of the English language" (120). When Sonia is detained in Jamaica for two years by
the shock of losing her mother and the loss of a stillborn baby,
Winston commits incest with Gwendolen: "She was like any other
woman to him. She was almost grown before she came back into
his life. He tried to equate this young and vibrant person with the
baby he kissed goodbye years back in Jamaica, but could not" (144).

Although Ogunyemi says that Emecheta "deals mainly with the black woman as victim of black patriarchy" and ignores the complexities and oppression that black men face (67), in this novel, Emecheta ties the incest to Winston's isolation and loss of culture as a result of poverty and the residue of slavery.

Winston, the abuser, is contrasted in the novel with a Nigerian wise man who has managed to retain his culture. On his construction job, Winston becomes friends with a Nigerian man, Mr. Ilochina. When Winston asks Mr. Ilochina whether in Africa a man can marry his daughter, Mr. Ilochina is aghast: "What have those culture killers done to a nice brother like this?" (142) Like the narrator, Mr. Ilochina feels that the slave passage of Winston's ancestors had taken away Winston's heritage. Mr. Ilochina tells Winston that "a father who had any sexual urge towards his daughter had offended the Earth" (143) and if not killed by the women of the community would be killed by an earth force like thunder and lightning. Winston is ashamed but continues the incest until Gwendolen becomes pregnant.

Neither her mother nor English culture can protect Gwendolen from this abuse. When Sonia returns and is shocked at Gwendolen's pregnancy, Winston implies that she was impregnated by her Greek boyfriend. Gwendolen is unable to confide in her mother because for them too that "closeness between African mother and daughter had been lost during the slave passage." (170) Gwendolen is as isolated in her family of origin as Adah was in her marriage. The educational system, which served Adah's children well, does not help Gwendolen. Because she could neither read nor write and spoke Jamaican English when she arrived in England at age twelve, she was soon the victim of racist assumptions that she was slow. The narrator comments bitterly: "Those who made society's laws are still a long way from knowing that Gwendolen's inability to speak or understand one brand of the English language did not automatically condemn her to be an imbecile. But to keep a school like hers running smoothly with less friction for all concerned, it was easier for her to be regarded as one" (74). England provides Winston Brillianton with a job, but it does not replace the African culture that he lost nor does it provide Gwendolen with protection from abuse. Families alone can provide neither the safety of a secure place nor freedom from racism. It is not surprising that Gwendolen runs away.

There is, however, the hint of a place for Gwendolen in a potential community of women of the African diaspora. In contrast to

In The Ditch, white women are not present in this novel. There is not a movement away from integration to separation because Gwendolen does have a supportive white boyfriend, but the most important community is among black women. Gwendolen meets her mother's Nigerian friend, Gladys Odowis, when Gwendolen first comes to London. When Gladys' Nigerian husband beats her, Gladys flees with her children to Sonia Brillianton. Although "Sonia could not understand her BBC Nigerian English at the best of times. . . . [Gladys'] husband Tunde did not dream of looking for his well—educated wife and their two children at the house of their 'Illiterate West Indian daily minder and her equally bungling husband'" (61). (Here Emecheta does criticize a Nigerian man for beating his wife, although the contrast between the Jamaican abuser and the Nigerian wise man, Mr. Ilochina, remains dominant.) The two women are friends although Gwendolen is primarily aware of their differences: "Her mother and Mrs. Odowis had several things in common, they were both black women, and they both had young children, yet they were so different. She wondered why this was so" (98). In spite of these differences, when Sonia finally returns from Jamaica after two years, it is Gladys to whom she goes when Sonia cannot find her family because they have moved to a council flat.

Gwendolen too finds support from several African women after she runs away. When she is put briefly in a mental hospital after she becomes incoherent in a police station, she is befriended by a Ghanian nurse, Ama, who takes care of her and visits her when Gwendolen is released and given a flat of her own. It is Ama who gives Gwendolen the name of her baby: Iyamide. The "name is not a Ghanaian one. It is a Yoruba one. It is 'Iyamide.' My mother, my female friend, my female saviour, my anything-nice-you-can-think-of-in-a-woman's-form, is here" (210). Mrs. Odowis is the one who brings about Gwendolen's reconciliation with her mother. When Winston is killed in a construction accident, which represents the earth force Mr. Ilochina had warned him of, Gladys Odowis insists that Sonia go see Gwendolen and her grandchild. When Sonia sees Iyamide, she realizes that she is Winston's child and forgives Gwendolen. Sonia admires Gwendolen's new found independence and mothering abilities. Gwendolen has a place of her own and the beginning of a supportive community. The novel ends perhaps too optimistically for an incest victim,[11] but it does show a coming together in London of women's voices from African and Afro-Caribbean cultures and provides some hope that a resilient young woman like Gwendolen can overcome the legacies of racism and abuse. In spite of the tremendous costs portrayed in this novel, the potential for community among women survives.

In *Kehinde*, Emecheta confronts African patriarchy directly in her portrayal of Kehinde Okolo's life in both London and Nigeria. The novel opens with a description of the London life of Albert and Kehinde Okolo and their two children, Joshua and Bimpe. Albert and Kehinde have lived in London for eighteen years. They arrived in 1960 when jobs were easy for foreigners to get. Although she was only eighteen when she arrived in London, Kehinde was able to get a good job in a bank since she had worked in a bank in Lagos. Albert works as a storekeeper and although Kehinde earns more money, he is comfortable in his job. They own a terrace house in East London and rent out the upstairs rooms. They retain their Nigerian culture, however, eating Nigerian food and speaking to each other in Igbo. They consider themselves temporary emigrants, assuming that "they would return eventually and build their own house in Ibusa, their home village" (41). Although she enjoys the freedom of a well-paying job and can "talk to her husband less formally than women like her sister, Ifeyinwa, who were in more traditional [polygamous] marriages" (6), Kehinde thinks of herself as a traditional Nigerian wife: "The Igbo woman in her knew how far to go. She could tell Albert what she liked, but would not malign his relatives. Not to his face, at any rate" (22). Kehinde is contemptuous of a fellow Nigerian woman, Mary Elikwu, who left her husband because he beat her: "To Kehinde she was a fallen woman who had no sense of decorum. . . . a woman who refused to work at her marriage" (38—39). Kehinde is happy in her marriage and happy in London. She has a secure place in her joint ownership of the house, her supportive family, and a good friend at the bank (a Muslim Nigerian woman named Moriammo), as well as the freedom of a well-paying job and the status of being a married woman.

Albert, however, is anxious to go home, and this desire reveals him as a traditional African patriarch. His sisters urge him to return to Nigeria and take his place as head of the family. Albert played to perfection the role of the Igbo family man in London. But he was far from satisfied with its restrictions. . . . he needed room to breathe. As Kehinde was perfectly well aware, behind the veneer of westernisation, the traditional Igbo man was alive and strong, awaiting an opportunity to reclaim his birthright (35).

Albert reveals the selfishness in his desire to return home when he forces Kehinde to have an abortion so that she will not miss her promotion at the bank and thus be able to pay for their passage home. Both as a Roman Catholic and as a Nigerian Albert knows abortion is wrong, but he rationalizes "we are in a strange land, where you do things contrary to your culture"(15). Albert does not fully realize, however, exactly how contrary to his culture the abortion is. After the abortion Kehinde has a dream in which Taiwo, her *chi*, her personal spirit who is also the spirit of her twin who died in the womb, comes to tell her that the baby that she aborted was the spirit of their father who was returning to protect Kehinde. Kehinde is devastated and feels estranged from Albert: "Albert could not help her. How could he? She was alone . . . . He had nothing to offer her"(33). Albert returns to Nigeria and before long the children follow him to go to boarding school. Kehinde stays behind to sell their house.

Although Kehinde still has her job and the house and a new friendly Caribbean tenant named Michael Gibson, she feels estranged from the London Nigerian community: "Without Albert, she was a half-person" (59). Her *chi* urges her to go to Albert lest he get a girlfriend. Even Moriammo urges her to go to Nigeria and enjoy her status as a "rich, been-to madam" (47, 52). Kehinde quits her job and leaves her house in the care of her tenants, but she does not realize that her place in Nigeria has been usurped by Albert's older sisters and his second wife.

In interviews Emecheta is sanguine about polygamy. In 1984 she explained: "In a polygamous society every woman has a husband whom she shares with a number of other women. This gives her more freedom in some respects: she has the opportunity of pursuing a career as well as having children. . . . The children belong to an extended family with a number of mothers, and the women, after the initial jealousy, share a kind of sisterhood" (Ravell-Pinto 51). In 1986 she continues the defense, saying: "People think that polygamy is oppression, and it is in certain cases. But I realize, now that I have visited Nigeria often, that some women now make polygamy work for them" (Emecheta 176). In her novels, however, Emecheta concentrates on the jealousy and not on the sisterhood of polygamy. This is true to a certain extent in *The Joys of Motherhood* and even more so in *Kehinde*. Kehinde has always been aware of the sufferings of her older sister Ifeyinwa in a polygamous marriage, and she had thought that Albert agreed with her because he had seen the sufferings of his own father's two wives. When she arrives in Nigeria, however, Kehinde finds that the place allotted to a senior wife, even a "been-to madam," is a lot different than she had imagined. She is ushered into a small bedroom with a single bed, not the double bed which she had helped pay for and had sent to Nigeria. When Kehinde calls to Albert to ask about her room, Ifeyinwa reminds her that it rude to call a husband by his given name. Kehinde must now call him "Joshua's father" or "our husband" to acknowledge the role of his new wife, Rike. When Kehinde gets in the front seat of the car beside Albert to go visit her children at school, she is reprimanded by Albert's older sister:

> 'I say, I am coming with you. What is wrong with you? . . . who do you think you are? Don't you see your mate, Rike? Don't you see her sitting at the back with her maid and baby. When we, the relatives of the head of the family are here, we take the place of honour by our Albert. . . .' Kehinde almost died of shame . . . . Only young brides with poor training made such mistakes. (88)

Kehinde cannot get a job in Nigeria because she has no degree and she is no match for the sophisticated Rike, who has a doctorate and teaches at a university, or for her husband's powerful sisters. Even her children are happy at school and no longer need her. In the land of her birth Kehinde is forced because of gender to inhabit a smaller and more liminal space than she had in London: "The Africa of her dreams had been one of parties and endless celebrations, in which she, too, would enjoy the status and respects of a been-to. Instead, she found herself once more relegated to the margins" (97). Even Rike is not protected from marginal status. Ifeyinwa gets revenge upon Rike for her treatment of Kehinde by being the one to tell Rike that Albert has taken a third wife, an even younger Fulani woman from the north.

Kehinde is nostalgic for the space and freedom and even the weather of London:

> . . . this was October, autumn in England. The wind would be blowing, leaves browning and falling. In a few weeks, the cherry tree in her back garden would be naked of leaves, its dark branches twisted like old bones. On a day like this, after the Friday shopping, her feet would be stretched in front of her gas fire, while she watched her favourite serials on television until she was tired and until her eyes ached. Autumn in England.

Her eyes misted. . . . She even felt nostalgia for the
wet stinking body-smell of the underground. (96)

Kehinde writes to Moriammo of her predicament, and Moriammo
sends her a plane ticket to London. Even the damp cold autumn
weather of London seems inviting. Bhabha comments on the relationship of English weather to its multicultural inhabitants:

The English weather . . . invoke[s] . . . the most
changeable and immanent signs of national difference. It encourages memories of the 'deep' nation
crafted in chalk and limestone; the quilted downs;
the moors menaced by the wind; . . . The English
weather also revives memories of its daemonic double: the heat and dust of India; the dark emptiness
of Africa . . . the tropical chaos that was deemed
despotic and ungovernable and therefore worthy of
the civilizing mission. These imaginative geogra-
phies that spanned countries and empires are
changing; those imagined communities that played
on the unisonant boundaries of the nation are
singing with different voices. If I began with the
scattering of the people across countries, I want to
end with their gathering in the city. The return of
the diasporic; the postcolonial. (319)

Kehinde represents the return of the diasporic, the postcolonial.
Fortunately Kehinde never sold her London house. In spite of the
difficulty of getting a new job, Kehinde finds that in order to gain
freedom in London she is willing to give up her old "homeland"
and even embrace English weather.

Emecheta comments in several interviews about the freedom
of European women in comparison to African women. She said to
the Umehs in 1980: "The comparative ease with which the women
in Europe move around became clear. One can live alone; one can
have children. The women in Britain have much more freedom
than Nigerian women. It is when you're out of your country that
you can see the faults in your society" (Umeh & Umeh 1985, 22).
Ten years later Emecheta does not see much improvement in the
status of Nigerian women: "In Nigeria women are riddled with
hypocrisy, you learn to say what you don't feel. . . . I find I don't
fit in there any more" (James 38).

Like Emecheta herself, Kehinde learns that marriage and

homeland are not the only "places" for women. She discovers that there is room in the city of London for the diasporic and the post-colonial to achieve both place and space. Although Kehinde can not get her job in banking back and has to start working as a maid in a hotel to survive, she eventually gets a degree in sociology and a job in social services. She starts an affair with her Caribbean tenant, Michael Gibson. In London Kehinde finds a home, an education, a career, and a lover. Even her son Joshua has to learn that his mother owns the house, and that being male gives him no rights over it in England. Kehinde has found in London a place from which to speak, and she can join her Caribbean lover, in what Paul Gilroy calls the culture of the "Black Atlantic," a culture of the African diaspora that creates a space for black men and women not just in Africa, or even America, but all around the Atlantic. In *Kehinde*, a woman can find security and independence, not just in a community of women friends, but within the city at large.

Although Emecheta never stinted her criticism of British racism even in her early London novels, she has become increasingly vocal in her criticisms of patriarchy, especially African patriarchy. Her earlier novels implied that the problems African women faced in London were a result of individuals like Francis in *Second-Class Citizen*, or of the structure of white patriarchy that relegated women to poverty and welfare housing in *In The Ditch*, or a result of the loss of culture because of the history of slavery in *The Family*. Now, in *Kehinde*, Emecheta faces the problems of Nigerian patriarchy directly. As a woman Kehinde finds greater freedom of space and a more secure place in London than in Lagos. Both Kehinde and Emecheta have joined the diaspora. They have become immigrants, true Londoners, feminist denizens of cosmopolis. The scraps and patches and little happenings of their daily lives create the songs of the new urban novel.

NOTES

1.   Bhabha's concept of writing that comes from "the liminality of national culture" is similar to Gilles Deleuze and Félix Guattari's concept of "minor literature," the primary characteristic of which is "deterritorialization": "A minor literature doesn't come from a minor language; it is rather that which a minority constructs within a major language. But the first characteristic of minor literature in any case is that in it language is affected with a high coefficient of deterritorialization" (Deleuze and Guattari 16). Carol Boyce Davies applies the concept of "deterritorialization" to African women's literature (253-254, 260) and argues for the polyvocal nature of African women's writing.

2. Emecheta's first two London novels were included as part of a 1986 exhibit on the London novel, *20,000 Streets under the Sky: the London Novel 1896-1985*, at the Royal Festival Hall.
3. See: M. M. Bakhtin, *The Dialogic Imagination: Four Essays*, ed. Michael Holquist, trans. Caryl Emerson and Michael Holquist, (Austin: Univ. of Texas Press, 1981), especially pp. 301—331; and Mikhail Bakhtin, *Problems of Dostoyevsky's Poetics*, ed. and trans. Caryl Emerson (Minneapolis: Univ. of Minnesota Press, 1984).
4. Although only about 5% of the people living in the United Kingdom are people of color, a 1981 census says that 14.3% of the greater London area is Black or Asian (Fothergill and Vincent 88, 14-15)
5. See my book, *A Female Vision of the City: London in the Novels of Five British Women* (Knoxville: Univ. of Tenn Press, 1989) for a full discussion of Duffy's novel.
6. These characters are portrayed in the London novels of Samuel Selvon, an Afro-Indian novelist from Trinidad. Selvon's novels, *The Lonley Londoners* (1956), which Emecheta mentions in her 1965 autobiography, *The Housing Lark*, and, *Moses Ascending* (1975) are much less ambiguous about British culture than are Emecheta's novels, but the pervasive sexism in the Selvon novels reveals some of the hidden costs of immigration.
7. My student, Omnika Simmons, experienced this same kind of division during her junior year in Britain in 1993. She writes about the different cultures of the African diaspora that she experienced in Britain in her 1994 Spelman senior honors thesis, "Fragmented Realities in Writings from Black Women in Britain: Home, Community and Gender in Selected Works by Joan Riley, Buchi Emecheta and Michelle Cliff" (3-8).
8. In "Black Matter(s)" Toni Morrison describes some of the motivations of voluntary immigrants coming to America. They include not only escape from poverty or oppression in the Old World but also a "flight from license"—from a too permissive society, or a search for adventure, or, "of course," the acquiring of "cash." (258—59).
9. Abioseh Michael Porter joins Lloyd Wellesley Brown in saying that *In The Ditch* is not as good a novel as *Second-Class Citizen*. Porter shows how *Second-Class Citizen* follows the traditional western *Bildungsroman* form that focuses on the developing individual.(Porter 123) *In The Ditch*, however, is not less developed but rather formed around the more communal values of the neighborhood rather than the strictly Western masculine ones of the *Bildungsroman*.
10. I am grateful to Marie Umeh for sharing the videotape of this talk with our NEH seminar led by Susan Gubar on "Feminism and Modernism" at Indiana University in the summer of 1991.
11. See Judith Herman and Lisa Hirschman, "Father-Daughter Incest" for a description of the continuing problems that most incest victims have (Herman & Hirschman 1983).

WORKS CITED

Bakhtin, Mikhail. *The Dialogic Imagination: Four Essays*, ed. Michael

Holquist, trans. Caryl Emerson and Michael Holquist. Austin: Univ. of Texas P, 1981.

—. *Problems of Dostoyevsky's Poetics*, ed. and trans. Caryl Emerson. Minneapolis: Univ. of Minnesota P, 1984.

Bhabha, Homi K. "DissemiNation: time, narrative, and the margins of the Modern Nation," *Nation and Narration*, Ed. Homi K. Bhabha. London: Routledge, 1990.

Brown, Lloyd Wellesley. *Women Writers in Black Africa*. Westport, Conn.: Greenwood P, 1981.

Davies, Carol Boyce. "Writing Off Marginality, Minoring and Effacement," *Women's Studies: International Forum*. 14,1 (1991):249—263.

Duffy, Maureen. *Londoners*. London: Methuen, 1983.

—. "Foreword." *20,000 Streets Under the Sky: The London Novel 1896-1985*. Catalogue of an Exhibition at the Bookspace, Royal Festival Hall, London, Feb. 17-March 12, 1986. London: The Bookspace, 1986:7—8.

Deleuze, Gilles and Félix Guatarri. *Kafka: Toward a Minor Literature*. Trans. Dana Polan. Minneapolis: Univ. of Minn. P, 1986.

Emecheta, Buchi. *Double Yoke*. New York: Braziller, 1983.

—. *Head Above Water: An Autobiography*. Oxford: Heinemann, 1986.

—. *The Family*. New York: Braziller, 1989.

—. "Feminism with a small 'f'!" *Criticism and Ideology: Second African Writer's Conference*, Stockholm 1986, Ed. Kirsten Holst Peterson. Uppsala, Sweden: Scandinavian Institute of African Studies, 1988: 173—85.

—. *In the Ditch*, rev. ed. 1972. Oxford: Heinemann, 1994.

—. *The Joys of Motherhood*. New York: Braziller, 1979.

—. *Kehinde*. Oxford: Heinemann, 1994.

—. *Second-Class Citizen*. New York: Braziller, 1974.

Fothergill, Stephen and Jill Vincent. *The State of the Nation*. London: Heinemann, 1985.

Gilroy, Paul. *The Black Atlantic: Modernity and Double Consciousness*. Cambridge, Mass.: Harvard Univ. P, 1993.

Herman, Judith and Lisa Hirschman. "Father-Daughter Incest." *The Signs Reader: Women, Gender and Scholarship*. Ed. Elizabeth Abel and Emily K. Abel, Chicago: Univ, of Chicago P, 1983. 257—278.

James, Adeola. "Buchi Emecheta." *In Their Own Voices*. Oxford: Heinemann, 1990:34—45.

Meese, Elizabeth. *Crossing the Double Cross: the Practice of Feminist Criticism* . Chapel Hill: Univ. of North Carolina P, 1986.

Morrison, Toni. "Black Matter(s)." In *Falling into Theory: Conflicting Views of Reading Literature*. Ed. David H. Richter. Boston: St. Martin's P, 1994. 256—268.

Ogunyemi, Chikwenye Okonjo. "Womanism: The Dynamics of the Contemporary Black Female Novel in English." *Signs* 11,1 (1985):63—80.

Porter, Abioseh Michael. "*Second-Class Citizen*: The Point of Departure for Understanding Buchi Emecheta's Major Fiction." *The International Fiction Review* 15,2 (1988):123—129.

Ravell-Pinto, Thelma. "Buchi Emecheta at Spelman College." *Sage* 2,1 (Spring 1985):50—51.

Simmons, Omnika. "Fragmented Realities in Writings from Black Women in Britain: Home, Community and Gender in Selected Works by Joan Riley, Buchi Emecheta and Michelle Cliff." Honors senior thesis, Spelman College, 1994.

Sizemore, Christine Wick. *A Female Vision of the City: London in Novels of Five British Women.* Knoxville: Univ. of Tenn. P, 1989.

Tiffin, Helen. "Post-Colonialism, Post-Modernism and the Rehabilitation of Post-Colonial History." *Journal of Commonwealth Literature* 23,1 (1988):169—181.

Tuan, Yi-Fu. *Space and Place: The Perspective of Experience.* Minneapolis: Univ. of Minn. P, 1977.

Umeh, Davidson and Marie. "Interview with Buchi Emecheta." *Ba Shiru: A Journal of African Languages and Literature* (1985): 19—25.

Umeh, Marie. "African Women in Transition in the Novels of Buchi Emecheta." *Présence Africaine: Revue Culturelle de Monde Noir* 116,4 (1980):190—201.

Ward, Cynthia. "What They Told Buchi Emecheta: Oral Subjectivity and the Joys of 'Otherhood.'" *PMLA* 105,1 (Jan. 1990):83—97.

Buchi Emecheta in front of her North London home, 1994.

Buchi Emecheta:
Politics, War and Feminism
in *Destination Biafra*

J.O.J. Nwachukwu-Agbada

Buchi Emecheta's usual literary terrain is the gruesome domestic experience of female characters, and the way in which these characters try to turn the tables against the second-class and slavish status to which they are subjected either by their husbands or some male monster. Emecheta borrowed her thunder from Flora Nwapa, the first female Nigerian novelist of international English expression, whose literary career was directed at revising and reversing the image of the female, at showing that she enjoys some dignity and that she can be economically independent. The Nwapa vintage is usually a portrayal of men as morally debased economic parasites while her women are elegant and gifted. It is this idiom which Buchi Emecheta, Nwapa's "literary 'daughter'... got hold of and extended to nauseating proportions" (Nnolim 16). Earlier in 1985, Afam Ebeogu, worried by Emecheta's literary radicalism, drew attention to her icon-breaking incursions into certain Igbo cultural practices and accused her of misreading and misrepresenting the Igbo cultural reality to satisfy her mythic ends (Ebeogu 82-93).

However, in *Destination Biafra* her concerns and fictive strategy enjoy an enlarged field of discourse. For the first time she shows interest in her country's pre-war politics and its fallout, the thirty-month Civil War. While she is engaged, her feminist temper remains unassuaged and unmitigated. The author's short biodata and her foreword to *Destination Biafra* indicate that she has been an outsider to the Nigerian political experience, especially as she is said to have left the country in 1962, "since when she has lived in North London with her five children." Although her long sojourn abroad does not disqualify her from discussing her country's politics and period of tension, it does affect the quality of verisimilitude borne by her novel. Chinweizu comments as follows: "*Destinatation Biafra* does not convey the feel of the experience that was Biafra. All it does is leave one wondering why it falls so devastatingly below the quality of Buchi Emecheta's previous works" (Chinweizu 228). However, she is saved from the argument as to whether or not her work is a reliable artistic document on the Nigerian political crisis of the 1960s by her admission in the preliminary pages of the novel that she had to depend so much on her friends and relations who witnessed the Nigerian debacle. Yet her artistic depiction of the historicity of the genesis of the postindependence Nigerian political setbacks cannot be dismissed outrightly as inaccurate.

The shuffling of the names of the key figures in the first phase of the Nigerian political life does not prevent us from identifying her subjects. Although she warns in "Note to the Reader" that "no character in this book is intended to represent any actual person," she equally reminds us that this "does not mean that people like them could never have existed or will never exist."

But, in the end, every prominent pre-war political actor is identified with a new name. Dr. Ozimba is the great Zik of Africa whose verbal theatricals attract "Zimm Zimm" from his audience. The Sarduana's identity is unhidden in the text. Saka Momoh is Yakubu Gowon, "one of those recommended to be sent to Sanhurst for training" (*Destination* 9). Mallam Nguru Kano is the first prime minister of Nigeria, a surrogate of the Sarduana. Chief Odumosu is Chief Awolowo, whose Action Group Party took the country by storm when it employed a jet plane to use its thick smoke to write "Vote AG" in the clouds of Northern Nigeria. Giles Murray, one of the outgoing colonial figures, remark to another, Alan Grey, the following: "What a waste! Most Hausas can't read. Look at what it says in the clouds: 'Vote A.G.'"(13). Awolowo's bitter rival, the late Samuel Akintola, is in the novel referred to as Chief Durosaro while the first Nigerian Minister of Finance, F.S. Okotieboh, is here known as Samuel Ogedemgbe. The latter's daughter—Debbie Ogedemgbe—is the story's heroine and Emecheta's quintessential female liberator, her *l'enfant terrible*. But we shall return to her later.

A rehash of the political experience of the country, which Emecheta revisits for artistic reasons, is not necessary here. However, the bold political statements which her text embodies are certainly of interest. The first is that Nigeria is a country whose real power base lies outside its geographical boundaries. MacDonald, Sir Fergus, Sergeant Giles Murray, Alan Grey, to name only a few, work at cross-purposes to the genuine interests of Nigeria. Of all the ethnic components of the country, they consider the Hausa as the ethnic group which could most easily protect British interests in postcolonial Nigeria. MacDonald, the outgoing British Governor of Nigeria, is nervous over the poor quality of the election campaign of the Northern party and confides in Captain Alan Grey, his countryman, thus:

> I only hope the Hausas turn out to vote for their own
> men. If not, we'll have a great deal of explaining to
> do. All I know is that a Hausa man must be Prime
> Minister. That is the only way to maintain peace in
> this place. (17)

It is the British anxiety over who should control the saddle after their exit that makes Macdonald hurriedly nominate Mallam Nguru Kano "to be the first Prime Minister of Nigeria" (22) when "we have only forty results out of a hundred and ninety from the North" (22). Earlier the Sarduana declined going down to Lagos in the south to assume the leadership of the country: "He did not wish to come down to the South, but was sending his 'right eye' down to be his presence in the South" (23). Meanwhile the great Dr. Ozimba who virtually fought the British single-handedly and forced them to grant independence is not considered for the prime ministerial position because "the British thought that the only slight opposition they would face would be from the Ibo party led by Dr. Ozimba" (10).

Consequently, the author seems to be saying that the British are at the foundation of Nigeria's political problems. The role they play in the reversal and abandonment of the Aburi Accord between Saka Momoh (Yakubu Gowon) and Chijioke Abosi (Odumegwu Ojukwu) is typical of British meddlesomeness in Nigerian political problems. The neat phrase for British political wiles in Nigeria is "divide et impera," which Chapter 8 of *Destination Biafra* celebrates. At a time when every Nigerian thought Aburi would restore faith in their country, it is the British who seem to have felt otherwise, as evidenced by the quality of the advice they give to Saka Momoh, now the head of state after the death in a *coup d'etat* of Brigadier Onyemere. Debbie retorts, crying as follows: "Alan, what happened at Aburi? What part did you play in changing Momoh's mind? Alan!" (113)

The third political assertion made by the author is that Brigadier Onyemere (Aguiyi Ironsi) is a political neophyte, who equates his acceptance in certain private circles as a gentleman with his acceptance at an ethnic cosmos as a leader of a troubled nation where there had been frayed nerves. By neglecting his own security and thinking that honesty is enough to keep a leader in the saddle, Onyemere is accused of being politically naive. His death in the hands of Saka Momoh and his men is not mourned in the text nor does it attract any ire, even from his ethnic group, as he is essentially a political dreamer.

Fourthly, Abosi's secessionist attempt is justified by the author, but Abosi is berated for insisting on facing the enemy on the battlefield when he has little or no arms, when he has no outlet to any ocean corridor. Moreover, Biafra remains a poorly knit, hurriedly established entity. It is an ideologically barren enclave. The face-off between Abosi and Colonel John Nwokolo (Nzeogwu)—the hero of the first *coup d'etat*—and the fate of Western Igbo people in the crossfire between Nigeria and Biafra are among the factors which weakened the unity of the Igbo, who form the bulk of Biafra. In particular, the killing of Western Igbo people on accusation of sabotage by Eastern Igbo soldiers is a source of angst to the author, for the former turn out to be "neither the animal of the land nor of the sky" as it is said in Igbo. They are targets for both Nigerian and Biafran soldiers alike, a fact which makes them head-and-tail losers. It is important to point out that Emecheta is of Western Igbo stock. She has used her privileged position as a writer of some consequence to draw attention to the plight of her people during a senseless war. The truth anyway is that it was not her own group alone which faced the scourge of Biafra or Nigerian soldiers once any of the sides was losing ground. Even among the Eastern Igbo group, many communities were victims of Biafran army reprisals for one mishap or the other. Emecheta could have enriched her art if she had approached her subject not from the premise that the Western Igbo were regarded as inferior Igbo and thereby easily abandoned and dispensed with, but from the angle of a psychological search into reasons that in a war situation brothers merely separated by a river could turn into saboteurs, oppressors, and victims as the case may be.

I think Emecheta is so concerned about the treatment inflicted by both Nigerian and Biafran soldiers on her Western Igbo people during that war that she seems to have forgotten to condemn war as prominent writers through the ages have done. The author is more concerned with the circumstances of her people: that they became the common enemy of both sides in the war. Cries a Western Igbo woman as she meets Biafran soldiers: "... the Nigerian soldiers came and killed what your soldiers left... And when we needed you where were you... You call us Hausa Ibos, don't you? Please go away before you bring us bad luck" (230). In the hands of Federal troops, they are raped and slaughtered, and their houses burnt down. Their kith in the East are all too willing to abandon them when it is felt that they are not interested in the Biafran cause. The loss of ground to the Federal troops by the Biafrans is marked by the shooting of Colonel John Kwokolo (the Nzeogwu figure) who is blamed for the sudden misfortunes in the war-front. This disappointment is equally expressed in the treatment meted out to the Western Igbo. Says Dr. Eze as follows: "We'll have to leave them to their fate. We can't afford to worry about them now. Those of them who wish to cross the river into the East are welcomed to do so" (182). Abosi's reply, when Ozimba angrily questions the lack of seriousness with which their predicament is being handled, is symptomatic of a house divided among itself: "We'll solve their problems after the war is over... Biafra stands for freedom, freedom for the persecuted Easterners, most of whom are Ibos. Yes, let's leave it like that" (183). And like that it was left.

The truth is that the civil war on the Biafran side was fought on continuously shifting grounds. The loss of land occupied by Biafrans meant that on each occasion they were more concerned with protecting areas yet to be attacked. Once any part of it was captured by the Federal forces, the Biafran soldiers retreated and got fortified in areas nearest to such a part. There was no question of mounting attacks which could retrieve lost ground. If, as Emecheta points out, there was not really much in terms of arms for the Biafrans, one wonders what the author expected losing soldiers in battle to have done for the inhabitants of a lost land. As it has been pointed out, Emecheta seems to have done little to condemn war except the "mission impossible" on which she sends Debbie: a mission meant to bring Saka Momoh (Yakubu Gowon) and Chijioke Abosi (Odumegwu Ojukwu) together. Thus Emecheta creates a major role for her favorite female character—a device for which early notable male African writers have been chastised.

Feminism in African fiction is an intrusive voice which calls our attention to the "failures" of male African writers with respect to the portrayal of women in their works. It is a voice that regularly accuses us of having left certain things undone. Often the female African writer was forced to wield her pen with the impulse to revise and re-portray female characters in a new light. Emecheta has been involved with this revisionist impulse since the days of her novel, *In The Ditch* (1972).

Debbie Ogedemgbe is the author's *"la femme terrible,"* her notion of the modern woman. She is the iconoclast, questioning prevalent ideas and doing things differently. Her only known boyfriend is a white male, Alan Grey. Oxford-trained, she smokes and refuses to marry in spite of her beauty and elegance: "She gave Babs a cigarette and started to cough as she smoked, which made Mrs. Ogedemgbe wring her hands" (108). Her mother is so disgusted with her behavior and that of Babs, her friend, that she blasts out as follows: "We all want freedom for women, but I doubt if we are ready for this type of freedom where young women smoke and carry guns instead of looking after husbands and nursing babies" (108). Emecheta arms her heroine with a gun by making her enlist in the army. However, both her gun and her army uniform are of no consequence when she faces rapists who are supposed to be fellow Nigerian soldiers: "She felt her legs being pulled this way and that, and at times she could hear her mother's protesting cries. But eventually, amid all the degradation that was being inflicted on her, Debbie lost consciousness" (134).

Her mission to bring the message of peace from Momoh to Abosi reminds one of the Igbo myth of how death became the lot of living beings on earth. According to the myth, to find a solution to the scourge of death, men and animals hold a meeting. And on the directives of a diviner, they send the dog and the chameleon on a trip to God—the dog is to tell Him that living beings desire to die and return to life, and the chameleon to relay to Him the opposite view. The dog is chosen to handle the real desire of living beings because of its association with speed and smartness. Unfortunately, the dog arrives late, having spent much of the time going after food crumbs and excrement. Before then the chameleon, known for its slowness, had arrived and delivered its message, which was acceptable to God. In like manner, it seems to me that Debbie is ill-equipped for the role of the myth-

ical dove, the wielder of the olive branch. First, in spite of her brava-
do, she knows that she needs the help of a man: "Mama, we have to
start packing," Debbie began, and then gave a short, nervous laugh:
"But I think we shall need a man with us... I'll ask our driver Ignatius
to get ready" (119). Ignatius gets killed on the way largely because he
is a male. The women are merely raped but the men are killed. Why
the author bemoans the rapes more than the deaths is not explained
anywhere in *Destination Biafra*: "Over two thousand Ibo men died
along the Benin-Asaba road on Operation Mosquito. But as they say,
that was war"(177). Again "nearly all the five hundred or so women
hiding here in the bush had lost someone dear" (231). Men are being
taken away to be slaughtered and when Debbie is mistakenly ordered
to move, she cries out, "But I am a woman." The author comments
as follows: "The women had so far been left alone in a chilling suspense, so why start molesting them now?" (173) Secondly, Debbie is
not Igbo; she does not hear a word of Igbo. What kind of mission does
the author expect her to engage in? Consequently, she faces a lot of
problems on the way. An old nun asks her: "Look, you're not Ibo,
what are you doing here?" (217)—to which she has no real answer.
By making her Oxford-trained and a fluent and masterly speaker of
English, Emecheta exposes her errand-girl to much hardship.

Debbie eventually gets to Abosi because the author wants her to
get to him. Otherwise there is no logical reason why Debbie should
have reached Abosi in a hostile and crude war. Like the mythical
errand-going dog, she is late. So much damage has been done. The
war is even ending. Debbie is aware of her lateness: "Now I think
my mission has come too late. Many people have died and still hun-
dreds die each day, and yet it continues... this war, I mean" (239).
Abosi apologies with his tongue in his cheek: "But I am sorry if you've
risked your life for nothing" (239). When Abosi refers to her as "little you," her impulsive response is to attribute her disdainful treatment by the Biafran leader to her sex: "Tell me, if I were a man...
would you have dismissed my mission?" (239) Just as Debbie thinks
that being a soldier will make her strong, so does she think that getting to Abosi is what matters. It is naive of her to expect Abosi to take
her message of peace seriously even as her English boyfriend supplies arms and mercenaries to Momoh. Her inability to sense such
a contradiction in her mission is part of the reason that she is ill-
equipped as a favorite heroine given such a herculean task.

In the only major assignment given to her by her creator, Debbie
is a failure. Her failure has to do with her antecedents: she is an intellectual who is somewhat elevated above the common run of women.

Why she needed such an education from Oxford to lead other women is not clear in the text. She is the daughter of a very wealthy politician—a situation which also means that in class relations, she is distinctly alien to the folk. The author's notion of empowerment is defeated when Debbie's gun is taken away from her by a man's trickster antic. Why she needed to have enlisted in the army to salvage the country is bizarre. In the end the author does not allow her to get fulfilled within the Nigerian army, hence her rape by fellow Nigerian soldiers may be symbolic of her failure in the soldierly career. Her image is that of a character who leaps from one difficulty to another in a quixotic succession. Perhaps Debbie is the author's mental projection of how the future African woman could possibly be. So be it. But the author will need to equip such female characters, not necessarily by giving them Oxford or Cambridge education, but by preparing them to play their roles within a realistic possibility devoid of the melodramatic in which we need to willingly suspend our disbelief before the story can make sense to us.

In conclusion, the novel is Emecheta's boldest attempt to transcend the domestic scenario. Although her interpretation of the Nigerian political crisis may lack the class perspective, the major issues raised by her historicism remain accurate. She has no overt philosophical statement about the war, but invariably she fires our imagination to inquire why two brothers separated by a body of water—the eastern and western Igbo—could so easily suspect each other. Her viewpoint seems to be anchored in the fact that, in connection with the Nigerian civil war, her western Igbo people are double losers, having neither satisfied their eastern Igbo brethren nor those Nigerians on the Federal side. Emecheta's greatest achievement in the work is her insistence that although more men might have died from the actual fight, women were largely its practical casualties. Here, it is no longer "girls at war" but "women at war." The story is no longer about how girls freely exchanged relief materials with their sex, but how women battled to save themselves and their families in a time of national emergency.

WORKS CITED

Chinweizu. "Time of Trouble." *Times Literary Supplement*. February 26, 1982.

Ebeogu, Afam. "Enter the Iconoclast: Buchi Emecheta and the Igbo Culture." *Commonwealth* 7,2 (1985):83—93.

Emecheta, Buchi. *Destination Biafra*. London: Fontana, 1983. (originally published 1982)

Nnolim, Charles E. "Trends in the Nigerian Novel." *Matatu* 2,1 (1987):7—22.

To Ground The Wandering Muse: A Critique Of Buchi Emecheta's Feminism

Pauline Ada Uwakweh

> I write about the little happenings of everyday life.
> Being a woman, and African born, I see things
> through an African woman's eyes. I chronicle the
> little happenings in the lives of the African women
> I know. I did not know that by doing so I was going
> to be called a feminist. But if I am now a feminist
> then I am an African feminist with a small 'f'.[1]

Kehinde (1994), Buchi Emecheta's recently published novel, is
another landmark in her prolific literary career. In terms of subject matter, Emecheta's depiction of female independence is indicative of her ideological commitment to feminism. Emecheta
maintains that her residence in Europe has made her more perceptive to the disadvantages African women face. She states, "It is
when you're out of your country that you can see the faults in your

society."[2] Without a doubt, her career as a writer is geared toward exposing the social inequities facing African women. This primary objective places her in the forefront of African feminism. Emecheta has, however, rejected the feminist label.[3] Nevertheless, it is in *Destination Biafra* (1982), a novel faulted by critics, that she attains the height of her feminism. In this novel, Emecheta creates her first model of the African New Woman.[4] Debbie Ogedemgbe is not only Western educated, but she also expresses an identity crisis about her status as a true African woman. Through her nationalist and feminist struggles, she overcomes her identity crisis by embracing her African cultural ideals. She achieves the position of a model of the African new woman on two levels: vowing to "mother" orphans of the Nigerian civil war, and vowing to write/tell the story of the war. Thus, Debbie affirms the traditional role of African women as nurturers, oral artists, and preservers of history.[5] Significantly, Debbie's role debunks the myth of obligatory marriage as a prescription for female self-fulfillment. In accordance with African feminist tenets, Debbie's feminism does not exclude children. Citing Filomena Steady's position on African feminism, Carole Boyce Davies (1986) outlines its features as including "female autonomy and cooperation; an emphasis on nature over culture; the centrality of children, multiple mothering and kinship," (Davies 1986, 6). Debbie's vow to "mother" the orphans is in itself an acknowledgement of the centrality of children in African culture. This role defines her African female identity, her recognition of women's roles as nurturers and preservers. More importantly, it also makes her a veritable symbol of Emecheta's African New Woman.

It is necessary to evaluate Emecheta's latest female protagonist, Kehinde, in this light, and to determine the extent to which she is a valid representative of the African New Woman. As I have indicated here, female autonomy that embraces African cultural ideals is of utmost importance in defining this New Woman. In view of this, this paper argues that the new female protagonist, Kehinde, falls short of Emecheta's vision in *Destination Biafra*.

Kehinde is culturally ambiguous and her identity crisis is evident in three areas of her experience: her marriage, her motherhood, and the nature of her rebellion. Her portrayal raises a crucial question: Can the message of African feminism be projected through a culturally ambiguous protagonist? The character of Kehinde fails to integrate successfully the author's own African feminist aspirations, and I am inclined to attribute her protagonist's identity crisis to Emecheta's own feminist ambivalence. Emecheta seems to be torn by her allegiance to African culture and her ideological commitment to feminism. In contrast to her clearly articulated vision of the African New Woman in *Destination Biafra*, Kehinde's feminist struggle is marked by cultural alienation rather than integration. She is alienated from family, children, and the benefits of extended kinship. She achieves her independence at the expense of her children. In fact, it is unclear where her children stand in relation to her new life. Consequently, Kehinde's credibility as a true African female suffers.

KEHINDE IN MARRIAGE

The marriage institution is a site of feminist struggle.[6] Emecheta opens with this scenario and leads us through Kehinde's final rebellion. Her sexual revolt is comparable to Amaka's in Flora Nwapa's *One is Enough* (1982). But unlike Amaka, Kehinde is already assertive in marriage as her story unfolds; she has achieved a degree of equality with her husband in their sixteen years of marriage. She talks to her husband, Albert, less formally and relates to him as "a friend, a compatriot, a confidant." These are the very qualities that Debbie Ogedemgbe saw lacking in her parents' marriage, causing her to reject the submergence that the marriage institution imposes on the African female. Artistically, Kehinde's initial assertiveness erodes the significance or import of her rebellion at the end of the novel. Furthermore, her cultural ambiguity projects her identity crisis. The warning signs of this crisis are exhibited at the outset. In a heated argument between Albert and Kehinde over the need for an abortion, she asserts categorically, "my dreams about home are confused. I haven't a clear vision what I'm supposed to be looking for there" (*Kehinde*, 22).

As a professional worker in a bank, Kehinde earns more than her husband, Albert. Her position in the bank had enabled them to get a mortgage for their house. Her financial advantage over her husband, therefore, entitles her to the legal ownership of their house. On one hand, Emecheta presents Kehinde as "traditional," since by Nigerian standards "a good wife was not supposed to remind her husband of such things. When Kehinde said 'your house,' she was playing the role of the good Nigerian woman" (Kehinde, 4). Albert conversely says "our house" so as not to upset Kehinde. On the other hand, she underlines the fact that this is a "game" that husband and wife play without thinking after sixteen years of marriage.

Being a traditional Nigerian male at heart, Albert regrets the restrictions of their marital relationship. He pines for male freedom in a Nigerian environment, a luxury he could not afford in Britain. Albert regrets the erosion of male authority and rights that residence in Britain has imposed on his marriage. When he gives in to his sisters' demands to come home, it is not just because "he pined for sunshine, freedom, easy friendship, warmth;" it is also because he wants to build his own house, to be someone by Nigerian standards, something he feels he has not accomplished in Britain. This bespeaks a basic insecurity in his relationship with his wife, Kehinde, focused on his lack of claim over the house on London Terrace. Kehinde's professional and legal status as wife in Britain also appears to threaten his male ego.

As a result of his wife's unplanned pregnancy, Albert selfishly persuades her to get an abortion. This is primarily to ensure his homecoming plans and his wife's promotion. He rejects tradition where it suits his purpose by arguing that "this is not the right time for another one. I know abortion is wrong but we are in a strange land, where you do things contrary to your culture" (*Kehinde*, 15). As Kehinde's righteous anger suggests, she too dislikes the idea of an abortion, but she does not take steps to stop it commensurate with her assertiveness in the marriage. Rather, Kehinde chooses an alternative—but un-African—route, when she makes her consent to the abortion conditional upon having her tubes tied as she can no longer rely on her husband's sense of precaution. Despite the inner voice that tries to dissuade her from undergoing the abortion, she carries out her plans. Both husband and wife regret the abortion, thus reinforcing the African traditional preference for male offspring. For example, when she asks her husband, "If you had known it was a boy, Albert, would you have made me abort it?" it is obvious that she too regrets the action mainly because the fetus turned out to be the spirit of her dead father. She says to Moriammo, "The child I just flushed away was my father's *chi*, visiting me again. But I refused to allow him to stay in my body. It was a manchild" (*Kehinde*, 32). In this critical situation, Albert is unable to comfort his wife. He seems oblivious of her pain and offers nothing except his regret on the loss of a manchild.

If Kehinde accepts the abortion plan as a condition for marital peace, she is wrong. She perceives her action as a concession that entitles her to greater devotion from her husband. She fails to heed the inner voice, which is also the voice of her *chi* and her dead twin sister, Taiwo. Whereas the abortion may have ensured her promotion, it proves otherwise for her marriage. It is surprising that she becomes more amenable to her inner urging to go home to Nigeria when her fears about Albert's infidelity become strongly insistent. No sooner has Albert settled in Nigeria than he saddles himself with another wife, thus putting Kehinde into an unwanted and unasked for position as senior wife.

In marriage, to say that the female's search for independence is directly linked to her subjugation is stating the obvious. Interestingly enough, Kehinde's experience within the patriarchal institution of polygamy reflects Emecheta's ambivalence on this issue. There is a peculiarly Western oriented individualism to Kehinde's struggle which contrasts with Emecheta's dramatization of the African communal lifestyle inherent in this institution. As Boyce Davies notes, the "African feminist author Buchi Emecheta was soundly attacked for daring to suggest that polygamy worked in many ways to women's benefits" (Davies 1986, 9); she admits, however, "that Emecheta, who has written several novels which show polygamy in a negative light would not have come to her position casually" (Davies 1986, 20). In Buchi Emecheta's (1988) article, "Feminism with a small 'f,'" the author herself states:

> In many cases polygamy can be liberating to the woman, rather than inhibiting her, especially if she is educated. ... Polygamy encourages her to value herself as a person and look outside her family for friends. It gives her freedom from having to worry to be sure that he is in a good mood and that he is washed, and clean and ready for the wife, because the wife has now become so sophisticated herself that she has no time for a dirty, moody husband. And this in a strange way, makes them enjoy each other. (Emecheta 1988, 179)

If *Kehinde* is meant to illustrate the positive aspects of polygamy, Emecheta's depiction of the protagonist reveals a tension between her feminism and her allegiance to African culture. Kehinde's experience in polygamy appears to expose a traditional institution which devalues and humiliates women. Simultaneously, Emecheta delineates its positive aspects in terms of extended kinship and sharing of the responsibilities of child care.

Having taken the trouble to get home, Kehinde does not wait

to assess the possibilities of her new marital situation or to resolve the problem of her unemployment. She is driven more by the humiliation and the trauma of being a dependent senior wife without status, the lack of attention from Albert, and her unfulfilled dreams of a celebrated "been-to" madam. There is neither the squabble common among co-wives in a polygamous marriage nor any strong suggestions that Rike's behavior is anathema to Kehinde. Exhibition of jealousy in this polygamous relationship is on Kehinde's part alone because she sees herself as older, less attractive, and dependent. As a result, she feels cheated, unrecognized, and undervalued in her new position. Kehinde sees herself more and more as an outcast, a situation that deepens her alienation from family and the benefits of extended kinship. When her inability to find employment further erodes her self-confidence as a senior wife, Kehinde strikes out alone, taking the first opportunity that presents itself.

Her letter to Moriammo is a painful *cri de coeur*, a plea for release from the humiliation of her financial dependence on a husband who has betrayed their love. A female critic rightly points out that "the single most compelling factor of female subjugation was her economic dependence on the male, and the social demands that made a woman give all her earnings to the home because her identity lies there."[7]

> He gave me the first housekeeping money in over eighteen years of marriage, and I had to take it. When I refused to kneel to take it, his sisters levied a fine of one cock. Paying the fine took half the housekeeping. It's a man's world here. No wonder so many of them like to come home, despite their successes abroad. Honestly, if not for the children, I would have come back long ago. But now, I have no money for the fare back. (*Kehinde*, 94)

Emecheta's position on polygamy is unclear. She gives some hints about her views through Kehinde's daughter, Bimpe. However, she does not dramatize this convincingly to make her own intentions clear, which doubtless would have provided a new perspective on this much-criticized African institution and blazed a new trail for African women writers. Bimpe's detailed letter to her "special mum," Kehinde, states the case succinctly:

> Mum, I must tell you about Dad's wife, Rike. She is

not bad, you know.....I know it was painful for you, what Dad did. Joshua and I were shocked at first, but we soon learnt that it is very common here. And Rike is not bad at all. She prays for all of us all the time. And we are family, Mum. I love all the members of my family. *I have many mothers*, but you will always come first, not just because you carried me for nine months before I was born, but because you are a special person. (*Kehinde*, 121-122, emphasis mine)

In Kehinde's absence, it is Rike, Albert's second wife, who fulfills the responsibilities of mothering. She accepts Joshua and Bimpe as her children, thus warranting Bimpe's statement, "She is not bad, you know...And we are family, Mum...I have many mothers" (122).

Kehinde appears to be a "traditional" female who believes that a woman's proper place is in marriage, beside her husband. Yet Kehinde shows no convincing reasons for abandoning the same institution for which she had derided Mary Elikwu, other than reasons of humiliation and betrayal. Kehinde's attempts at reconciliation with Mary Elikwu are born of guilt rather than admiration for the latter's status as "single" mother. Kehinde may, therefore, be charged with over-reaction to a situation which she could have explored for its benefits. Ironically, it is Rike's educational qualification and her independence that are instrumental in Kehinde's decision to further her own education.

Raising children is no longer enough. The saving grace for us women is the big 'E' of education. This girl, Rike, doesn't even have to live with us because her education has made her independent. *Yet, she is content to be an African wife in an Igbo culture. How come we in England did not see all this.* (*Kehinde*, 95; emphasis mine)

KEHINDE'S MOTHERHOOD

Kehinde's claim to motherhood is artistically inconsistent with her actual role as mother. She fails the first test of motherhood by agreeing to Albert's abortion plan. There is, therefore, no convincing basis for Kehinde's claim to motherhood. Emecheta distances

Kehinde from this claim by the absence of genuine consideration for her children's welfare. This artistic ploy or irony invalidates her significant statement, "Claiming my right does not make me less of a mother, not less of woman. If anything it makes me more human" (*Kehinde*, 141). As character, Kehinde leaves the reader only with the impression of a self-centered woman.

Again, Kehinde indicates in her letter to Moriammo that it is due to her children that she is unable to return to Britain. Yet, in this woman about to abandon her children to the care of an unworthy husband and father and his "untrustworthy" junior wife, there is no deep psychological turmoil that characterizes the African woman's attachment to her children. In fact, her children seem to receive secondary consideration. Her brief visit to them at the boarding school confirms that she only came to inform them, to let them know that they are free to join her when the going gets rough. This calls into question her self-acclaimed status as mother. Bimpe, her daughter, sees her mother's action as reneging on her duty as "the backbone of the family." It is important to note that Kehinde cannot validly claim her children as an excuse for her one-year stay in Nigeria, given her feelings about the polygamous arrangement. She is simply seeking financial assistance from Moriammo for her "escape" back to Britain. Her action not only makes her "less" of a mother, it leaves her isolated at the end of the novel when her son, Joshua, slams the door in her face. Kehinde may not be the self-sacrificing mother that Nnu Ego represents in *The Joys of Motherhood* (1979), but she definitely shares the latter's final isolation from family and children.

Emecheta's ideological feminist stance apparently resides in her protagonist's ability to shape her own destiny. By her action, Kehinde joins the cast of rebellious females in African fiction written by women. Interestingly enough, Kehinde strongly maintains that her action indicates pragmatism rather than heartlessness. Her existence separate from family and children leaves one wondering if Emecheta's feminist disposition is not more Western than African, as some African critics have argued. Chikwenye Ogunyemi (1983), for example, argues that Emecheta's feminism "needs further grounding in the Nigerian indigenous cultural milieu to make the impact of her writing felt by those who can effect a change of heart and attitude... the African woman and the African man."[8]

KEHINDE'S REBELLION

The house on London Terrace is definitely central to the novel, and Kehinde's claim over the house is not in dispute. What is questionable, however, is Emecheta's artistic use of the house as symbol of the protagonist's revolt and independence. The security that property ownership gives Kehinde quickly makes up for her ill-treatment in Nigeria. Kehinde's feeling of security is succinctly captured in this short exchange:

> The smell of the London Terrace house welcomed her like a lost child. Before she could suppress it, a voice inside her sang out, 'Home, sweet home!' Taiwo, who had not spoken to her since she had gone to Nigeria, was back. Kehinde rebuked the voice: 'This is not my home.' As she said it, *she knew she was deceiving herself*, and Taiwo would not let her get away with it. 'We make our own choices as we go along,' came the voice. 'This is yours. There's nothing to be ashamed of in it.' (*Kehinde*, 108; emphasis mine)

By British legal standards, Kehinde's claim over the house is unquestionable. Even Albert, her husband, does not dispute this. As symbol, the house fails to carry the weight of Kehinde's rebellion. Re-asserting her rights of ownership to a house that is already hers seems needless and artistically contrived. Nevertheless, the argument between mother and son over property rights enhances Emecheta's feminist stance. While Joshua argues that his mother be true to her role as wife and mother by relinquishing the right of ownership to him, Kehinde maintains firmly that her right to independent existence and control over the house on London Terrace cannot be compromised. In answer to Joshua's "I thought you were supposed to live for your children," Kehinde counters, "I did when you were young. My whole life was wound around your needs, but now you're a grown man! Mothers are people too, you know" (*Kehinde*, 139). It is ironical, yet true to life, that this showdown over property rights should be between mother and son, rather than between husband and wife. This is perhaps Emecheta's reminder to future generations of African males of the validity of a mother's/woman's rights to property ownership. Emecheta succeeds in making this point, but she fails to portray convincingly the bases of Kehinde's claim to motherhood, the sensitivity of a mother toward her children, and their right to moral guidance.

Emecheta's belief in the concept of family is very strong. Yet in her protagonist, Kehinde, she does not delineate that belief or give her cogent reasons for leaving the marriage.

> In my books I write about families because I still believe in families. I write about women who try very hard to hold their family together until it becomes absolutely impossible. I have no sympathy for a woman who deserts her children, neither do I have sympathy for a woman who insists on staying in a marriage with a brute of a man, simply to be respectable. (Emecheta 1988, 175)

Albert does not seem to be such a 'brute' as to warrant his wife's desertion. It is a mother like Mary Elikwu, who leaves an abusive marriage with her children, who win our admiration. She combines the demands of family, education, and her responsibilities as a social worker, a "spokesperson for the 'milk for our babies' campaign." She is, perhaps, the ideal symbol of the modern woman and mother. Emecheta herself asserts:

> ...It is our work to bring the next generation into the world, nurture them until they are grown old enough to fly from the nest and then start their own life. It is hard. It could be boring and could sometimes in some places be a thankless job. But is it a mean job? (Emecheta 1988, 179)

The dominant aspect of Kehinde's rebellion is her sexual revolt. In depicting Kehinde's rebellion, Emecheta falls victim to this literary cliche, thus affirming Katherine Frank's assertion that "the feminist literary imagination in Africa has yet to delineate fully the new life of the African New Woman."[9] Must female independence be attained at the cost of family, and children?

This form of rebellion poses a problem, as some concerned African female critics have noted. Must female independence be tagged with immorality? Helen Chukwuma explains the inclination among African female writers toward this form of revolt as "a streak of extremism as to be expected when one is desperate to be heard."[10] She calls for a reevaluation of this negative image of the independent female and for the need for African women novelists to "seek better forms of revolt than sexual" (141). Kehinde's individualism, her cultural alienation, indeed jeopardizes Emecheta's vision of the African New Woman. If we admire Kehinde's self-ful-filling act, it is not her ability to keep a male companion and enjoy her sexuality without "hurting anybody;" it is her educational suc-cess—obtaining a university degree in three years— that we admire. And yet, to our frustration, Emecheta fails to explore the benefits of her protagonist's newly acquired degree.

In conclusion, there is a need for African female novelists to project positive alternatives of female independence. Female rebel-lion that tends toward sexual expression needs to be reviewed to enhance the African sense of moral order. The importance of rec-onciling African feminist objectives with character portrayal can-not be overemphasized. African female emancipation must reckon with women's roles as nurturers and preservers to ensure a sense of ethical and moral stability. In addition, the African female's pur-suit of independence cannot compromise the significance of chil-dren in the African world view. It is necessary for African female writers to explore these two crucial issues in the lives of African women.

NOTES

1. Buchi Emecheta, "Feminism with a small 'f!'," *Criticism and Ideology*, Ed. Kirsten Petersen (Stockholm, Sweden: Uppsala, Scandinavian Institute of African Studies, 1988), p.175.
2. See Davidson Umeh & Marie Umeh, "An Interview with Buchi Emecheta," *Ba Shiru* 12.2 (1985): 22.
3. See Emecheta's article, "Feminism with a small 'f!'," (1988), p.175. See also Molara Ogundipe-Leslie's "The Female Writer and Her Commitment," *African Literature Today* 15 (1987): 11. She attributes the African female writers' rejection of the feminist label to "male ridicule, aggression and backlash (which) have resulted in making women apolo-getic and have given the term 'feminist' a bad name."
4. It is important for the African New Woman to combine her feminist aspi-rations with her African identity. To attain this she must overcome her identity crisis or cultural ambiguity. See for example, Katherine Frank's point in her article, "Women Without Men: The Feminist Novel in Africa," *African Literature Today*. 15 (1987): 17.
5. This argument was made by me in an earlier paper, "Female Choices: The Militant Option in Buchi Emecheta's *Destination Biafra* and Alice Walker's *Meridian*." Paper presented at the African Literature Association Conference, March 20-24, 1991.
6. See, for example, Helen Chukwuma,"Voices and Choices: The Feminist Dilemma in Four African Novels," *Calabar Studies in African Literature: Literature and the Black Aesthetics*, Eds. Ernest Emenyonu et al. (Ibadan, Nigeria: Heinemann, 1990), p.133. See also Paulina Palmer, *Contemporary*

Women's Fiction: Narrative Practice and Feminist Theory (Jackson, Mississippi: Univ. Press of Mississippi, 1989), p.43. Other sites acknowledged by radical feminist critics and theorists include the family, sexual relations, the labor market, the media, the medical profession, and clinical psychology.
7. Helen Chukwuma, "Voices and Choices," p.132.
8. Chikwenye Ogunyemi, "Buchi Emecheta: The Shaping of a Self," *Komparatistische Hefte* 8 (1983): 75.
9. See Katherine Frank, "Women Without Men," p.32.
10. See Helen Chukwuma, "Voices and Choices," p.141.

Works Cited

Chukwuma, Helen. "Voices and Choices: The Feminist Dilemma in Four African Novels." *Calabar Studies in African Literature: Literature and the Black Aesthetics*, Eds. Ernest Emenyonu et al., Ibadan, Nigeria: Heinemann, 1990. 131—142.

Davies, Carole B. "Feminist Consciousness and African Literary Criticism." *Ngambika: Studies of Women in African Literature*. Eds. Carole B. Davies & Anne Adams Graves, Trenton, New Jersey: Africa World P, 1986. 1—23.

Emecheta, Buchi. *Kehinde*. Portsmouth, N.H.: Heinemann Educational Publishers, 1994.

—. *Destination Biafra*. Portsmouth N.H.: Heinemann Educational Publishers, 1982.

—. *The Joys of Motherhood*. Portsmouth, N.H.: Heinemann Educational Publishers, 1979.

—. "Feminism with a Small 'f'!" *Criticism and Ideology*, Ed. Kirsten Petersen, Stockholm, Sweden: Uppsala, Scandinavian Institute of African Studies, 1988. 173—185.

Frank, Katherine. "Women Without Men: The Feminist Novel in Africa." *African Literature Today* 15 (14—34): 1987.

Nwapa, Flora. *One is Enough*. Enugu, Nigeria: Tana, 1982.

Ogundipe-Leslie, Molara. "The Female Writer and Her Commitment." *African Literature Today* 15 (5—13): 1987.

Ogunyemi, Chikwenye. "Buchi Emecheta: The Shaping of a Self." *Komparatistische Hefte* 8 (1983): 65—77.

Palmer, Paulina. *Contemporary Women's Fiction: Narrative Practice and Feminist Theory*. Jackson, Miss.: Univ. Press of Mississippi, 1989.

Umeh, Davidson & Marie Umeh. "An Interview with Buchi Emecheta." *Ba Shiru* 12.2 (1985): 19—25.

PART SIX
AFRICAN PEDAGOGY IN
EMECHETA'S FICTION FOR
CHILDREN AND ADOLESCENTS

Writing children's literature is a very delicate task. For it to be meaningful to very young and adolescent readers, it must satisfy certain basic pedagogical necessities. Since the child is a growing synthesis of the father and mother of every human being, books meant for the child should assist, in a subtle manner, in making him/her develop along the path of potential responsible parents.

Thus, children and adolescent fiction should inculcate moral and spiritual values such as love, devotion to duty and the acquisition of a high sense of responsibility in the minds of its readers. Children's books, according to Mabel Segun, a prolific Nigerian writer for children, "should entertain, stretch the imagination, help a child to identify with others and make him/her understand the world in which he/she lives. They should teach him/her good behavior, condemn vices, such as disobedience, greed, jealousy, pride, laziness and deceit" (7).

Naiwu Osahon, another prolific writer for children, gives a far reaching pedagogical essence of children and adolescent literature.

He states explicitly that children's books are designed "to instill pride in our rich history, create self-knowledge and confidence, and help in developing logic and reasoning; aiding self as well as adult aided study; teaching spelling; assisting word study and dictionary use; highlighting little-known words to improve vocabulary; ensuring broad, well-rounded knowledge of science and the arts; making reading visually entertaining, compelling and fun; sharpening wits and triggering curiosity and yet learning a sweet, positive myth for the child to revel in" (Preface). In other words, literature for young people is meant to guide the child's journey through the complex realities of our world where there is a constant and fierce battle between the forces of good and evil, kindness and cruelty, hatred and love, selfishness and selfless devotion, truth and falsehood.

The pedagogical parameters outlined above are found in Emecheta's children's books which are mainly but *not* exclusively targeted toward children and adolescents. Julie Agbasiere, in "Toward A Cultural Symbiosis: Buchi Emecheta's Children's Books," examines the pedagogical relevance for children in Emecheta's *Titch the Cat, Nowhere To Play, The Moonlight Bride* and *The Wrestling Match*. In these stories, children are portrayed as having a very high feeling of reciprocal love for one another in spite of occasional bickering which is not unusual among children.

Agbasiere's analyses in these books highlight the social and cultural environments created by adults as very significant and determining factors in the growth and development of children. When they are properly brought up, African children respect the elders and are usually not prone to negative cultural prejudices when they are with their playmates from other countries.

Jacqueline Brice-Finch, in "The Magic of Motherhood: Buchi Emecheta and the Caribbean *Bildungsroman*," demonstrates the effects of the absence of basic elements of African pedagogy in the development of the child. In her discussion of *The Family*, Brice-Finch paints the stark and unenviable realities of an abandoned child who endures "hunger, neglect and abuse," as a result of irresponsible parents who pretend to live their own lives as if their offspring are inanimate objects who don't need care, love and direction. Gwendolen, the abandoned child in *The Family*, becomes a wreck, a social misfit, and a tool for indecent sexual assaults because her parents fail in their duties to the child. It is only through the help, guidance and protection of an extended family of friends that Gwendolen survives a bout with madness as a result of her rape by and alienation from family members.

Parents without a strong sense of cultural values eventually mislead their children. This is the poignant message prevailing in Emecheta's adolescent books, *Naira Power* and *A Kind of Marriage*. Tunde Fatunde, in "Conflicting Social Values in *Naira Power* and *A Kind of Marriage*," explains how corruption, stealing and deception in high places have completely destroyed the moral fabrics of Nigerian children. Too many of them therefore end up as drug pushers, smugglers and cheats. The children become successful failures. Even when one of them shows encouraging signs of honesty and hard work, he is destroyed by a compatriot who has imbibed the wrong social values created by adults. As one lays a bed, says an universal adage, that is the way one sleeps on it. Some parents in these two novels failed to inculcate basic African pedagogical values of honesty and hard work in their children. In this way parents unconsciously prepare their children, in one way or another, for untimely death.

In her typical revisionist thrust, Emecheta's children and adolescent fiction contain the struggle between positive pedagogical values and negative social influences. This is the dilemma confronting children growing up in a complex world full of cruelties and uncertainties. The main objective of our creative writers' books is to get children and adolescents to acknowledge the existence of these realities and in the process imbibe the positive values while rejecting the negative influences. This is the essence of Emecheta's children's and adolescent fiction.

Tunde Fatunde

WORKS CITED

Osahon, Naiwu. *The Hawk and The Eagle*. Lagos: Obobo, 1981.

Segun, Mabel D. "The Children's Writer and Her Art." Keynote Speaker's Address at the 3rd. Annual Enugu Book Fair. Enugu, Nigeria. January 25, 1988.

Toward A Cultural Symbiosis: A Study of Buchi Emecheta's Children's Books

Julie Agbasiere

The kite shall perch and the eagle shall perch;
whichever says to the other, "Don't perch," may
its wings break.[1]

— *Igbo Proverb*

The call for cultural relevance of reading materials meant for the education of the African child has consistently been made by educators, scholars and critics. The consensus is that books used in schools should have an African background and reflect the realities of the child's environment. Literary critics maintain that the two major criteria that have been used for evaluating children's books are socializing relevance and familiarity of the subject matter (Gundu 221, and Ogu 85). It is on the basis of these criteria that Emenyonu condemns the literature books by British authors used in Nigerian schools during the colonial era. He finds them inappropriate, saying that the folk tales, for instance, "did not have the cosmic, magical or supernatural dimensions that featured in most local folk tales. Their codes of ethics, too, were too sophisticated for the usual morality of the African trickster tale" (48). In the same vein, Achebe points out the negative influences which reading western authors are bound to have on the child during his/her formative years. The child is exposed to inheriting "all kinds of nefarious ideas about race, about color and so on" (Chinweizu 23). To these two criteria, Nana Wilson-Tagoe adds that "the type of story, the act of narration, the nature of characterization, the quality of dialogue and the general language of narration, are important to the fundamental development of the African child" (20-21).

The publication of Cyprian Ekwensi's *Ikoro the Wrestler and Other Igbo Tales* (1957) and, subsequently, *The Drummer Boy* (1960) marks a departure from the Western tradition. With these (and others that followed[2]), Ekwensi presents the child audience with literature books that have an African background and reflect the socio-cultural realities of the people. Ashimole comments as follows:

> Ekwensi's children's literature may therefore be said to have initiated a deliberate attempt to give the Nigerian child cultural identification in her reading. Fortified by the dominant literary movement of reasserting cultural roots to counteract Western propaganda, Ekwensi did for the Nigerian child what Achebe and Aluko were doing for adults—reasserting the lost cultural identity. (92)

Many writers have been producing books to promote this cultural revolution. Folk tales have been put in print, and in some cases they have been used to comment on contemporary historical events. Achebe's *How the Leopard Got its Claw* (1972) reflects the Nigerian civil war of 1967–1970. The majority of the writers produce realistic fiction with themes taken from the socio-political, economic and cultural life of the people. The stories portray the child in various life situations such as the home, in Kola Onadipe's *Call me Michael* (1981); the school, in Anezi Okoro's *One Week One Trouble* (1972); and adventure, in Chinua Achebe's *Chike and the River* (1966). Some of them also write fantasies such as Flora Nwapa's *Mammywater* (1979). Fantasy stories are given a scientific tinge with Naiwo Osahon's *Madam Universe Sent Man* (1981). In fact, there has been a rapid increase in the production of children's books during the past three decades, and at present, as Acholonu observes there is a "mad rush to turn out children's books for the primary and junior secondary schools" (243).

Buchi Emecheta, in the tradition of writing for children, has published four books: *Titch the Cat* (1979), *Nowhere to Play* (1980), *The Moonlight Bride* (1980) and *The Wrestling Match* (1980). She is unlike most other writers in two respects. First, she does not translate oral folk tales to reflect the African cultural past but rather sets two of her books, *The Moonlight Bride* and *The Wrestling Match*, in the African past. Second, she sets the other two, *Titch the Cat* and *Nowhere to Play*[3] in a Western environment and writes what may be termed Westernized African fiction. These two books are based on stories told by Emecheta's own children: *Titch the Cat* by her eleven year old daughter, Alice, and *Nowhere to Play* by the twelve year old daughter Christy. Thus, Emecheta portrays both African and Western cultures, and shows the integration of the African child in the two cultures.

Buchi Emecheta's first junior novel, *Titch the Cat*, portrays an African family comprising Amanda, Steve, Dan, May and June, with their Mum and cousin, Ofunne, all living in a house in Crouch End in North London. It is the story of a tiny kitten which June obtains from her friend, Julie Brown and, with her mother's permission, keeps as a pet. By the time she is six months old, Titch has had many adventures including scratching Mum who consequently drops her on the floor, having a fight with another cat, hunting mice and birds just for fun, getting lost and locked up in the cellar, catching an infection and biting the veterinarian who tries to give her an injection.

Like other growing children, June and her brothers and sisters are lively and have the bickering which does not degenerate into ill feelings or animosity. Titch adds warmth to the family and brings the children closer to one another. They learn and practice the virtues of caring, sharing, helping, giving and loving. Titch turns out to be psychedelic and peculiar to the London milieu. As June affirms, "Titch was one of those pampered cats that fed entirely on tinned cat food and milk" (48). It does not eat mice.

By exploiting a theme prevalent in the Western society where the children are living, Emecheta shows the level of the African child's integration in a foreign milieu. She shows that the child can adapt and get involved in the preoccupations, preferences and tastes of the immediate community, but she points out that inasmuch as the child has to adapt to his/her milieu, she/he should maintain a link with his/her African roots. In this regard, she makes the children obedient and respectful, calling their mother by no other name than "Mum." She introduces "Ofunne[4] from Nigeria" (9) as an enhanced African presence in the house.

In *Nowhere to Play*, Buchi Emecheta portrays the African child again in a Western society but this time at grips with the problems of having no safe place to play, and the resulting problems of relating to adults, especially outside the home. The children are May, June, Dan, Ricky, Jane and Michael, aged between six and twelve years, spending their long vacation with no organized activities to keep them occupied. The story is set in London, in Regent Park, where there are huge apartment buildings but no provisions for outdoor recreational facilities for the children. As the children go from place to place in search of where to play, they get into trouble with the adults. They are chased from the Green, expelled from the Crown Bushes, driven away as they play "knocking dollies out of bed" and, finally, frightened from the church.

The children in this story are of different nationalities: African (Dan and his sisters), Irish (Moya and Ricky), and others not specified (Michael and Jane). In this book, Emecheta shows the African child as living in peace and harmony, and cooperating with children from other cultures. The child is aware of the differences but is not inhibited by them. Emecheta gets all the children to participate in the same adventures, face the same perils and derive some fun from the adventures. She shows that it is only as children that people can live and work together harmoniously and with much understanding, sympathy, love, tenderness and comradeship. This is a point that Osahon makes in *Right-On Miss Moon* (1981). According to Fatunde, the author is trying "to show that children whose minds have not yet been polluted by adults' racial or ethnic poisons could live in harmony while recognizing their different cultural background" (165).

In his/her relationship with adults outside the home, the African child behaves like the people around him/her and through whom she/he is socialized in the first instance. She/He shares in the other children's problem of finding a safe place to play. Together they cautiously try to circumvent the adult's prohibitions in order to satisfy their basic needs. The elders appear unsympathetic to the needs of the children as they try to protect their privacy and tranquillity. The children do not impudently confront the elders nor do they show that they are obliged to obey without question. This confirms the Kitzingers' opinion that "in childhood, the person is supposed to be reasonably obedient and to comply with the wishes of the parents at least most of the time" (73). Emecheta is saying in this book that children are the same everywhere: lively, boisterous, fun loving with unbiased minds. As Bruner concludes, they "are healthy, lively and lovable. Their adventures bring a chuckle not a grimace" (135).

With *The Moonlight Bride* and *The Wrestling Match*, Emecheta attempts to recreate "in the reader's mind a whole traditional way of life" (Taiwo 28). She depicts the child as having virtually completed his/her early childhood socialization process. Whereas the former portrays the child as she/he rehearses the values internalized, the latter shows him/her as questioning the received values. She thus shows a progression in the stages of development of the African child from childhood to adulthood.

The story of *The Moonlight Bride* is set in Odanta and begins with Ogoli and Ngbeke agreeing to make clay pots and lamps as wedding presents for a bride arriving into their cluster of homesteads on a moonlit Eke night. The bridegroom turns out to be the deformed, lazy and never-do-well Chiyei, and the bride is Echi, the albino, fondly nicknamed Alatiriki. The two are married and have children.

In this book, Emecheta postulates that a child brought up in the traditional society imbibes the virtues of bravery, loyalty, obedience to and respect for elders, humility, communalism and good neighborliness. The child's behaviors are most of the time rooted in the traditions of the people. Thus Ogoli and Ngbeke, on their own volition, embark on making lamps and pots to welcome their new bride just as the elders and young men make their own contributions, they too join with the others in the marriage celebrations. Theirs is the period of consolidation and they accept, practice and restate the lessons they have been taught. Ogoli initiates activities and Ngbeke judges people's actions and points out discrepancies and injustices such as blaming mothers for the wrong steps deliberately taken by children and asserting that an older person is necessarily wiser. Through Ogoli, the author keeps Ngbeke's critical spirit in check. When the latter objects to Chiyei's being a prospective suitor, Ogoli silences her by saying, "you just have to accept the person chosen for you by your people. And look, Ngbeke, you must be loyal to the people of your clan" (29). Thus the children know the societal expectations of them.

The author indicates that in traditional society, everybody has a place and accepts his/her position on the social ladder. This is the secret of the stability which is apparently synonymous with traditional village life. In Odanta, the head and oldest member of the community is Obi Ibekwe followed by Obi Okonitsha. In the family, the husband is the head and the senior wife occupies a place of honor among the co-wives. The boys get preference over the girls, and all the children have their specific roles to play in the society. Children are affected by the social status of their parents and their position in the line of siblings. Ogoli is doted upon as the youngest child of the senior wife of Obi Ibekwe. Ngbeke is not so favored. But this consideration does not prevent the children from relating well among themselves.

Emecheta uses the marriage institution to underscore communalism, cohesiveness, patriotism, the leadership role of the elders, and respect for and submission of youth to the elders. The marriage of Chiyei and Echi is at the insistence of the elders; the couple complies and is the better off for it. When Chiyei is insulted by his future brother-in-law, everybody in Odanta rallies to his support. Echi proves to be an exemplary wife and through her, the author gives the moral of the story:

> Alatiriki of a wife had the best sense of humor in all our umunna[5], and she taught us it matters little the color or superficial beauty of any person, the most important thing is the beauty of the heart. And our wife Echi, or Alatiriki, had that. (77)

Ngbeke and Ogoli are thus well grounded in the ethics of the community. Ngbeke recounts all that they are taught as constituting bad manners for children. These include being angry with one's relatives, not greeting people whom one passes on the road, hating and harboring malice, asking the elders many questions, arguing with them and looking them straight in the eye when talking with them.

The narrator of *The Moonlight Bride* is the twelve-year-old Ngbeke. Her choice is apt for she describes the people and events from the point of view of a child. This book is bound to interest young children because they can identify with Ogoli and Ngbeke. Their world is uncomplicated, happy and stable. This reflects the authors' conception of childhood as a period when the child unobtrusively imbibes positive values and eschews negative ones. It is possible that, according to Agbasiere, Emecheta believes that "Happy childhood ensures the necessary psychological strength that enables the child to take in his stride the values of the society

416

even where it hurts"(130).

From "acquiescent childhood" (Kitzinger 74), the child moves into late adolescence and life becomes rough. The child is beset with many problems of which Agwu gives the highlights — "discovering sex roles, developing relationships with people of their own age, achieving an easy relationship with members of the opposite sex, accepting their bodies, changing their relationship with parents, working for pay, finding a vocation and becoming aware of their values" (212). *The Wrestling Match* is the story of coming of age of the Umu aya Biafra age grade: that is, the children born during the Nigerian civil war of 1967-70. The protagonist, Okei, and the boys who have had some education refuse to go and work in the farms and become a problem to the elders. The latter contrive to get them engaged in a wrestling contest and use up their stormy energy.

Unlike Odanta in *The Moonlight Bride*, Igbuno is a society undergoing some cultural changes. The mention of schools, hospitals, torch lamps, motor cars and new modes of dressing are indicative of cultural fertilization and permissiveness. The boys who have some education look down on the illiterate ones, the farmers' boys, who work on the farms with their parents. However, they all work as a team in conformity with the societal dictum that a member of an age grade should never be cut off from the rest of the group. Okei and his age mates condemn farm work, the major economic activity of the community for being a waste of time and energy. They jettison folk tales which they consider useless in their present circumstance, and resent the elders' undue interference in their lives. They are virtually asking for autonomy.

The boys show a favorable disposition towards the new culture. Thus, when the Igbuno boys decide to wrestle with their counterparts in Akpei, Okei and Nduka prepare, using modern European wrestling as a model. The farmers' boys raise an objection, "This is like a white man's wrestling, you two dancing about each other as if you are playing hide and seek. It is beautiful to watch, it is amusing. But it will not do for those Akpei people" (52). Okei thereafter changes his style and tactics and adopts the traditional mode. The author organizes the story in such a way that the new values and ideas do not edge out the traditional ways of life. Thus, Okei appears for the wrestling contest with a combination of the traditional and the modern: "He only wore a plain pair of shorts and a pair of colorful plimsolls to match. But on top of this, he had several charms slung round his neck" (67).

Buchi Emecheta has said that she is using *The Wrestling Match* "to show young people that in any war or friendly fight that goes sour, nobody wins" ("The Nigerian Writer...." 121). Apart from this message, she is also teaching the child to respect and obey the elders. The latter act out the saying that "the adult has always felt and still feels duty bound to teach the young" (Agwu 212). For the child to grow into a responsible adult and a leader she/he has to accept the elders' leadership role, and humbly learn from the elders. As Elechi Amadi maintains, " ...young people eventually become elders, and it is important that they should learn to be humble and respectful before they have the chance to rule" (55). Okei undergoes a transformation. Shedding his rude, disdainful and uncompromising behavior, Okei becomes humble and caring, and cultivates his uncle's friendship. As the proverb goes, "... a child who washes his hands eats with elders." Thus Okei "was no longer ordered to go and eat with women, so Nne Ojo could not complain about his nasty eating manner. Once he started to eat with the elders, he began to behave himself" (60).

In this book, the author shows the resilience of the traditional society in absorbing the changes occasioned by the cultural contact. She appears to be saying that it is in the nature of late adolescents to be unruly and critical of adults but that they eventually toe the line of adults, out of conviction, and become more mature. She acknowledges that society is changing and advocates cultural symbiosis with the child taking what is best in the two cultures.

The study of Buchi Emecheta's children's books has shown that the African child integrates well into the Western milieu and the traditional environment where there is no conflict of ideas and values. Both the authentic traditional society and the Western one project a dominant culture, thereby becoming a melting pot for the children living within its confines. Africa's colonial experience results in a disorganization of the traditional system of values. Emecheta proposes that there should be some level of harmony between the two cultures.

In these books, Emecheta puts aside feminist investigation.[6] As the flag-bearer of feminism in the African letters, one would have liked to find at least in one or two of her junior novels full-fledged feminist characters who ferret innovative ideas and values in order to achieve a balanced attitude towards womanhood. Such characters can influence even adult readers who, as Nzewi claims, "consciously and subliminally internalize ideas, opinions, standards, social and moral values expressed in books they read" (71). If the feminist concerns are started early from childhood and positive feminist child-characters created, it will go a long way toward boosting the image of womanhood in the contemporary novel and averting the trauma that adult characters and the family have been experiencing. Hoffman's assertion becomes pertinent here: "... any writer or artist can move things on a bit by creating new images and stimulating new ideas. It is not one's job to endorse the *status quo*" (49). Buchi Emecheta is equal to this task, and we await more children's books where both females and males act out androgynous roles.

NOTES

1. With people becoming more tolerant and broad-minded, a variant of this proverb has come into use: "The kite shall perch and the eagle shall perch; whichever says to the other 'don't perch,' let it show it where to perch."
2. Cyprian Ekwensi is a prolific writer. He situates most of his children's books in the city, thereby opening the child-readers' eyes to the negative values and corrupting influences prevalent in our towns. Crime, violence, cheating and robbery abound in these works.
3. By setting these two books in London, Emecheta is repeating the pattern she adopts in her adult novel. The first two, *In the Ditch* (1972) and *Second-Class Citizen* (1974), are set in the London metropolis. Similarly, considering the chronological order of events in the stories, *Nowhere to Play* should precede *Titch the Cat* just as *Second-Class Citizen* should have preceded *In the Ditch*.
4. Dan and his brothers and sisters all answer to Western Christian names. Ofunne is an authentic African name and contrasts sharply with the other names.
5. This is an Igbo word which means kindred or clan.
6. This situation is of great concern to feminist critics.
7. Ashimole is at a loss charging female writers of male chauvinism! ("Nigerian Children's Literature ..." 79); Marie Umeh charges Emecheta of being "in favor of the status quo" and not establishing "the 'female imagination' in Children's literature" (7).

WORKS CITED

Acholonu, Catherine O. "Writing and Publishing for Children: Nigerian Children's Literature: A Critique." *Literature and The Black Aesthetic.* Gen. Ed. Ernest N. Emenyonu. Ibadan: Heinemann, 1990. 233 - 245.

Agbasiere, Julie. "Social Integration of the Child in Buchi Emecheta's Novels." *Children and Literature in Africa.* Gen. Ed. Ernest N. Emenyonu. Ibadan: Heinemann, 1992. 127 - 137.

Agwu, Sunday A. "Adolescent Literature in Nigeria: A Study of Macmillan Publishers' Pacesetter Series." *Literature and The Black Aesthetic.* Gen. Ed. Ernest N. Emenyonu. Ibadan: Heinemann, 1990. 209 - 219.

Amadi, Elechi. *Ethics in Nigerian Culture*. Ibadan: Heinemann, 1982.

Ashimole, Elizabeth O. "Nigerian Children's Literature and the Challenge of Social Change." *Children and Literature in Africa*. Gen. Ed. Ernest N. Emenyonu. Ibadan: Heinemann, 1992. 70 - 81.

——. "Beyond Ekwensi: Trends in Nigerian Children's Literature," *Current Trends in Literature and Language Studies in West Africa*. Eds. Ernest N. Emenyonu and Charles E. Nnolim. Ibadan: Kraft Books Ltd., 1994. 91 - 100.

Brunner, Charlotte. "The Other Audience: Children and the Example of Buchi Emecheta. *African Studies Review*. 29.3 (1986): 129 - 139.

Chinweizu. "Interview with Chinua Achebe." *Okike*. 20 (1981): 19-32.

Emecheta, Buchi. *Titch the Cat*. London: Allison and Busby, 1979.

——. *Nowhere to Play*. London: Allison and Busby, 1980.

——. *The Moonlight Bride*. Ibadan: Oxford University Press, 1980.

——. *The Wrestling Match*. Ibadan: Oxford University Press, 1980.

——. "A Nigerian Writer Living in London." *KUNAPIPI*. 4.1 (1982): 114 - 123.

Emenyonu, Ernest. *Cyprian Ekwensi*. London: Evans, 1974.

Fatunde, Tunde. "African Pedagogy in Osahon's Stories for Children." *Children and Literature in Africa*. Gen. Ed. Ernest N. Emenyonu. Ibadan: Heinemann, 1992. 159 - 173.

Gundu. G.A. "Content and Narrative Forms in the Nigerian Child's Literature: The Case of the Tiv Child's Written Literature." *Literature and The Black Aesthetic*. Gen. Ed. Ernest N. Emenyonu. Ibadan: Heinemann, 1990. 220 - 232.

Hoffman, Mary. "New Writing on Contemporary Themes." *How to Write and Illustrate Children's Books and Get Them Published*. Consultant Eds. Treld Pelkey Bicknell and Felicity Trotman. Macdonald Orbis, 1988. 44 - 53.

Kitzinger, Shelia and Celia, Kitzinger. *Talking with Children about Things that Matter*. London: Pandora, 1989.

Nzewi, Esther N. "Children's Literature: Identification Process and Value Internalization." *Current Trends in Literature and Language Studies in West Africa*. Eds. Ernest N. Emenyonu and Charles E. Nnolim. Ibadan: Kraft Books Ltd., 1994. 71 - 81.

Ogu, J. N. "Creativity and Children's Literature." *Children and Literature in Africa*. Gen. Ed. Ernest N. Emenyonu. Ibadan: Heinemann, 1992. 82 - 87.

Taiwo, Oladele. *Culture and the Nigerian Novel*. London: Macmillan Education Ltd., 1976.

Umeh, Marie. "Children's Literature in Nigeria: Revolutionary Omissions" in *MATATU: Zeitschrift für Afrikanische Kultur and Gesellschaft*. (Forthcoming).

Wilson - Tagoe, Nana. "Children's Literature in Africa: Theoretical and Critical Issues." *Children and Literature in Africa*. Gen. Ed. Ernest N. Emenyonu. Ibadan: Heinemann, 1992. 18 - 23.

The Magic of Motherhood: Buchi Emecheta and the Caribbean *Bildungsroman*

Jacqueline Brice-Finch

There has been scant attention paid to Buchi Emecheta's eleventh novel, *Gwendolen* (1989), reprinted as *The Family* (1990). The book is the latest of Emecheta's works focused on the maturation process which the girl-child of the African diaspora undergoes. This theme is first explored in such novels as *Second-Class Citizen* (1975) and *The Bride Price* (1976) in which the protagonist is a Nigerian girl-child. *Titch the Cat* (1979) and *Nowhere to Play* (1979), set in England, depict children of African descent born abroad. During a telephone interview, the author explained that *Gwendolen* is the first of a series of her novels that will bear the name of a woman. The second is *Kehinde* (1994).

In the reviews of *Gwendolen* by Carole Boyce Davies, Reginald McKnight and Caryl Phillips, these critics frame their remarks around the surprise that Emecheta, a Nigerian novelist, has written a book about a Caribbean family. Davies notes that "Emecheta is clearly speaking against an essentialized, romanticized Caribbean identity" (20). McKnight places the novel amid the African American and African works which discuss "the problems that plague the African diaspora—rootlessness, 'hue prejudice,' self-hatred and perhaps even some of the sexual violence that nearly destroys Gwendolen—are the direct result of slavery and colonialism" (30). Phillips concludes that the novel is "an ambitious story of West Indian migration that has been told before, but never from the point of view of the African 'mother country' as opposed to the Caribbean 'moder kontry'" (B4).

It is precisely Emecheta's perspective, the African viewpoint, that makes this novel a valuable addition to the canon, particularly to the Caribbean *Bildungsroman*. The heroine of *Gwendolen* is Gwendolen Brillianton, known only as June-June until she emigrates from Granville, Jamaica, to England at the age of twelve. She differs substantially from other West Indian girl children depicted in the canon. For the most part, the Caribbean child is nurtured by family and community. Conflicts arise usually during adolescence. However, Gwendolen's suffering begins when she is only five. She endures hunger, neglect and abuse once her parents leave for England. Her guardian, Granny Naomi, cannot raise Gwendolen properly, burdened by the losing struggle to feed herself and granddaughter on the sporadic income that their labor on a distant bee farm and the produce from their garden provide.

Gwendolen cannot attend a proper school because her parents do not send adequate support. They cease sending any money once they have additional children abroad. Thus, Gwendolen leaves for England at age twelve essentially illiterate and lacking social graces, having had only meager tutelage from a Sunday School teacher, Miss Peters. The prognosis given this student is not hopeful:

> Miss Peters did not need to be a wizard to know that Gwendolen might be a shy and sensitive child, who was not interested in the intricacies of multiplication tables and the ABC. She did her best, though. She taught Gwendolen the catechism and some church hymns and Gwendolen began to recognize some words in the songs. For months on end, she practiced how to write 'Jesus Christ Our Lord'. (26)

In contrast, Merle Hodge offers in *Crick Crack Monkey* (1970) a wholesome, if unconventional, childhood for children, born in Trinidad, whose parent emigrates. When their mother dies and

422

their father leaves for England, two aunts war over who could be the better guardian for Cynthia, nicknamed "Tee," and her brother Toddan. Understanding that education is the *sine qua non* for success in life, the aunts are aggressive about the quality of education for their charges. Tantie battles to get Tee in the best possibly schools while Aunt Beatrice finally gains custody of the girl in order that Tee may benefit from attending high school in the city. By the time Tee leave her island to join her Dad, not only has she successful negotiated the transition from village to city life but also has become an intelligent, poised adolescent.

Emecheta's handling of emerging female sexuality also contrasts markedly with that of her Caribbean counterparts. In one of the early twentieth century novels, *Banana Bottom* (1933), Claude McKay rather clumsily describes the rape of Bita Plant by a man aptly called Crazy Bow. In the aftermath the man is speedily incarcerated and local reaction summarized in a ditty composed shortly after the incident. Bita, spared pregnancy, is whisked off for education abroad at the expense of white benefactors. Upon her return home some ten years later, no stigma of illicit behavior clings to the young lady Bita has become. Crazy Bow, the male, is solely responsible for the rape; the child/woman is not faulted.

In another romantic rendition of coming of age in the Caribbean, the aforementioned *Crick Crack Monkey*, Cynthia's initial guardian is her raucous aunt Tantie, who has many lovers. The various "uncles" frequent the woman's home and interact with the young children. They function only as fun-loving relatives. Men in the Hodge novel are weak, even henpecked. There is no hint of sexual impropriety toward the precocious children.

Like Bita of the McKay novel, ten year old Gwendolen is raped in the first few pages of *Gwendolen*, not by a madman, though, but by an elder, a trusted family friend. "Uncle" Johnny had been her grandfather's best friend, and, following her grandfather's death, become Naomi's lover and helpmate. After carousing one night with Naomi, this family friend forces himself on the sleeping child. He cruelly reminds Gwendolen of her parents' desertion and his kindness to her over the years. Initially shocked at his behavior, Gwendolen submits before running outside. There she poignantly asks, "Mammy, why you no take me with you" (22) before reasoning that to awaken her grandmother to report the assault would just add to the girl's punishment.

Keeping the sexual abuse a secret becomes increasingly difficult for Gwendolen. When she begins to have bouts of bedwetting, she feels humiliated by her inability to control herself and by having to carry the soiled bedclothes around the yard as punishment. In desperation, Gwendolen goes to her paternal grandmother in Kingston, seeking love and comfort. While Granny Elinor, a very light-skinned woman, is happy to see her, Gwendolen is rejected, the child suspects, simply because of her dark skin. She concludes that "She would go back to Granny Naomi. She would tell her everything" (31).

At first, the Granville community responds appropriately to the news of Johnny's criminal behavior. Granny Naomi has to be restrained from attempting to do the man bodily harm, and others shun him as a pariah. Although Granny Naomi refuses to see her friend/lover, in time she and the others subsequently change toward Gwendolen, suspecting her of complicity. The narrator opines that, as a result, "Gwendolen had lost her innocence. So adults could tell lies and wriggle out of tricky situations, simply because they were respected members of their community" (35). Gwendolen learns sadly that there is no adult in Jamaica who cares about her welfare.

Healthy intergenerational ties between grandmother and granddaughter are depicted in other Caribbean novels. One of the main conflicts of *Harriet's Daughter* (1988) by Marlene Nourbese Philip's novel is a child's longing to return to a loving grandma in the Caribbean. Like Gwendolen, Zulma too feels abandoned by family as she struggles with homesickness for Tobago while coping with life in Toronto. Yet Zulma is supported in her distress by the protagonist, Margaret. The climax occurs when a neighbor, the elderly Mrs. B, convinces the girls' parents that both should go to Tobago. Another example is the grandmother in *Crick Crack Monkey*, who, like Naomi, lives in a rural area. However, Ma's home in Pointe d'Espoir is lush land, bountiful in spiritual, as well as physical, nurture for all of her grandchildren, whether they live in the city or country.

When Gwendolen finally gets to join her parents two years after her rape, she discovers that she is alienated from her nuclear family as well. Gwendolen does not have the typical West Indian introduction to the "Moder Kontry" (11). She comes expecting to be welcomed into her family, a family she has hardly known. She has never met her three siblings—her brothers (Ronald and Marcus) and the infant Cheryl, all born in England. Initially Gwendolen feels enveloped in the "warm womb of the family" (52). However, Gwendolen is to be denied the opportunity to assume the role solely of older sister and to pursue the education denied her in Jamaica that is compulsory and free in England. Emecheta subverts the text by having Gwen function as a maid to her own family, not the stereotypical white employer. Sonia has told her best friend, Gladys Odowis, "If June-June here, she for help with the pikneys...When June-June come Ah go a work...When June-June come, life easy for me, you know...." (61-62). Her mom Sonia wants Gwendolen to be the family child minder and maid, "to be under her" (91) in the execution of domestic chores.

The father/daughter relationship from the start is dysfunctional. When he picks Gwendolen up from the airport, Winston Brillianton "was surprised and uneasy at the antics of this little girl, who was his daughter, and whom he was beginning to realize he had to work hard and wake up fatherly feelings toward" (49). When she says his name upon being awakened once they arrive by taxi to their flat, "The word 'Daddy' sounded so reassuring to her that it felt like she had just acquired a new toy" (50). He later rationalizes that his younger daughter Cheryl was "his biological and social daughter. But somehow Gwendolen was only a biological one and he never really felt socially responsible for her" (144). That Gwendolen is a mirror image of Sonia in physicality and personality is what attracts Winston.

Gwendolen's relationship with Sonia is blighted for the same reason. Her mother becomes jealous of the relationship which develops between father and daughter. When Sonia arrives home from work one evening a year after Gwendolen has joined her family, the mother is stunned by the tone of Winston's laughter. She begins to cry and feel inadequate. Gwendolen is not unaware of her mother's insecurity. Within days of her arrival, Gwendolen is attempting to ingratiate herself with her mother. The child says, "Me no like school" (63) to support her mother's indifference to Gwen's education.

Mother-daughter rivalry occurs in other Caribbean novels about the maturation of females. Jamaica Kincaid's *Annie John* (1983) focuses on the tension between a mother and daughter. When her mother notices that Annie has reached puberty, she becomes cold toward the child to whom she had been almost smotheringly close. No longer is Annie allowed to dress like her mother, accompany her on errands, or participate in a mutual toilette, which includes a shared bath. The mother even allows Annie to catch her parents making love, as if to mark her husband as hers alone, not a male to be shared with the girl/woman Annie is becoming.

In *No Telephone to Heaven* (1987) by Michelle Cliff, Kitty Savage decides to return to Jamaica with her younger, brown-skinned daughter, leaving her husband and older daughter Clare in New York. The woman is tired of the racism in the United States and thinks that Clare, being very light-skinned as is her father, will follow in Boy's footsteps and pass for white. This abandonment by her mother haunts Clare in much the same way as the rape affects Gwendolen.

Because she receives little help from her community following the sexual abuse by Uncle Johnny, Gwendolen has not recovered from that experience by the time she emigrates to England. Thus, when her father commits incest with her, she is resigned to her plight. She does not seek out an elder female to report her father for the same reason.

An African tale of incest becomes the framework for the novel at this point. When Sonia goes on an extended absence to care for her sick mother in Jamaica, Winston acts out his attraction for Gwendolen. Plagued with guilt, the dad seeks counsel surreptitiously from an African co-worker. Winston asks the man, "But do you marry your daughters?" (142). Azu Ilochina, quickly grasping the import of the question, recalls the story of a man who raped his daughter and was executed by the women of the village, who "pounded him into pulp with their cooking utensils." An African who sins against the Earth, Ilochina intones, "If he is not discovered, he will surely be killed by an Earth force like thunder, you know, natural electricity, drowning, just an Earth force" (144). Months later, Ilochina visits Sonia to report that Winston had died that morning after a gas explosion caused him to fall into a vat of tar. He tells the uncomprehending wife, "Gas and electricity are Earth forces we call Ani. They have their way of meting out vengeance" (200).

Though Sonia is assumed not to know the African exemplum, she does carry out the symbolic execution of her husband at the novel's end. She has become maddened by the small insurance settlement she receives and the shame of having her purchases taken on credit repossessed. Deciding that Gwendolen is responsible for the humiliation Sonia feels, the mother reasons that "the wrath of God had descended on her family" (235) and grabs a kitchen knife with which to kill her daughter. When Sonia goes to Gwen's flat and sees the baby, the grandmother instantly sees the resemblance to Winston and is physically transfixed by her epiphany.

Now, Sonia instinctively knows on whom God's wrath must

descend. After she leaves the flat, she stabs the kitchen knife repeatedly into the refuse of a rubbish bin "as if she was stabbing a snake that had bitten her" (238). Emecheta describes this scene as being "like a ritual," the exorcism of Winston Brillianton from Sonia's life.

Another convention with which Emecheta laces the novel is a potpourri of African aphorisms. The African characters function as the chorus in this modern tale. Embraced by her Mom at the London flat, Gwendolen "felt as rich as her African ancestors who firmly believed that it was always better to have people rather than money" (52). It is a Nigerian neighbor who is critical of the Brilliantons' actions in regard to Gwendolen's lack of schooling and heavy family responsibilities. Yet Grace Odonis will not allow Gwendolen to speak ill of her mother's taste in decor, believing "It was a thing not done in her culture. You stand by your family, no matter what" (97). Ilochina, an Ibo coworker, is puzzled when Winston questions the idea of having many children to raise. Ilochina explains that "'Ubakanma and onye nwe madu ka onye nwe ego'—a person who is rich in relations is greater than he who is rich in material wealth" (104). After giving birth to Iyamide, Gwendolen recalls that a Ghanaian nurse remarked that "babies are a woman's greatest achievement" (183). Finally, to comfort the bereaved Sonia, Ilochina assures her that Winston will have a proper funeral in spite of the incest:

> Don't worry, Mrs Brillianton. You buy everything
> here, even beautiful funerals. This is not like African
> people. In my town, our people will not bury your
> husband, I'm sorry to say. But here in England,
> money buys honour. (199)

Once again Emecheta is subverting the text, for these African beliefs the Brillianton family and the Caribbean society Emecheta creates, in general, fail to practice.

It is the Caribbean *Weltanschauung* that Emecheta portrays which Davies questions. Davies remarks,

> Emecheta will perhaps be faulted for depicting the
> Caribbean as the site of great backwardness by those
> who hold a more developed view of the region. The
> way that illiteracy is posed here for the family may
> be a valid social statement, but it is not representa-
> tive of Caribbean experience. Emecheta has a super-

> ficial knowledge of Caribbean Creole, and at times
> uses the West African pidgin versions.... Emecheta
> seems to see little of value in Caribbean cultures,
> unless they respond to African teachings. (20-21)

However, Emecheta does satirize the prejudices that Africans and West Indians exhibit toward each other. Emecheta cleverly introduces the mutual biases by focusing first on language issues. June-June learns from a stewardess on the plane to England as a twelve year old that her legal name is Gwendolen, a name she has difficulty pronouncing. Her parents cannot pronounce her name properly either, for Sonia introduces Gwendolen to the landlord as "Grandalee." After the man asks Sonia if his pronunciation of the name, "Grandalew," is correct, Sonia snaps, "Me no know, man" (57). Even her brothers had never heard the name. It is as if pet names are for island children only, for Ronald, Marcus and Cheryl are always addressed thus. In contrast, Gwen reflects that everyone in Granville called her June-June, even her paternal grandmother Granny Elinor and Miss Peters, her teacher—both adults of a higher station and caste than the Granville villagers.

The landlord's name is also unpronounceable to Sonia, who calls Mr. Aliyu "Mr. Aula." He, in turn, displays his exasperation when blacks mispronounce his name, having reasoned that whites simply can't be bothered to make the effort. The narrator affirms that Aliyu "had learned to regard it as one of the dehumanizing processes of existence you have to go through in a country that is not your own" (57). Sonia cannot get the name of Winston's coworker right either. Ilochina is "Mr Mechima or whatever his name was. Those African People they have so many long names" (196). The Africans are disdainful of Caribbean accents also. Aliyu "thought that because he was studying engineering at a local polytechnic he could not be bothered with 'West Indians' who spoke funny" (115).

Speech patterns also are examined. To the newly arrived Gwendolen, the voice of the Nigerian landlord "reminded her of the voice of a man chewing coconut and talking at the same time" (57). Sonia, on the other hand, describes another Nigerian, Ilochina, as having "a posh African voice" (197).

Ilochina comments on the transformation that occurred to the African spirit during the middle passage. He concludes, "Stupid African," (126) after hearing the love story of Winston's grandfather, Keke Kwekwu Tijani, who "followed his sweetheart Adaora," (125) his grandmother, into slavery. Yet, when Ilochina asks

Winston if he would imitate his grandfather, Winston responds, "Don't be 'tupid, man. Me a Christian, nuh. Dem days people not Christians. Dem be uncivilized African Muslims. Nuh Ah know better" (126). Ironically the men's sensibility seems identical, though based on different ideologies.

This culture clash between Caribbean and African has tragic results when Sonia's mother, Naomi, dies. When a telegram is sent containing this information, Mr. Aliyu, the Nigerian landlord who knows that Winston cannot read, takes the notice to the Brillianton flat. Aliyu tells Winston only that his mother-in-law is very ill. The narrator explains that

> Being originally from one of those African kingdoms to whose people understatement was equivalent to good manners, he referred to the fact that Granny Naomi had died as "some news." As Mr Brillianton "could not find his glasses" Mr. Aliyu's position was intricate. Should he be like an Englishman and tell the family what had actually happened? But he could remember quite vividly stories from his early moonlight nights in his village in Ijeba land; stories in which bearers of bad news could be killed. In his own culture it was quite correct to say that Granny Naomi had not died, but was very ill. If Mr Brillianton had been a Nigerian, he would have guessed straight away that his mother-in-law had died. But the man had had that part of his cultural heritage taken away from him by slavery. (115-116)

The Brillianton family pays for Aliyu's delicacy in delivering the bad news. Winston does not intuit that Naomi has died and punches Aliyu when he finds out the truth, causing Aliyu's head to bleed and him to twist his ankle in trying to flee. The landlord, incensed at Winston, has the family evicted. Luckily, Ilochina counsels Winston regarding the acquisition of a council flat. This new housing is a welcome improvement, being larger and better suited for the large family than the basement flat in Aliyu's Victorian house. Sonia spends so much money buying medicine for her "sick" mother that she can afford only a one-way ticket to Jamaica. When she learns on her arrival in Granville that her mother is not sick but dead, Sonia has a nervous breakdown and bears a stillborn child.

Gwendolen becomes vulnerable to her dad with her mother away. Her luck changes with the advent of Emmanuel. This Greek not only befriends her but also becomes her first consensual lover and teaches her to read. Emmanuel remain steadfast through Gwendolen's breakdown following her mother's return and after he knows that he is not the father of Gwendolen's baby.

There is consensus among the West Indians and Africans about several customs. Both Africans and West Indians love to dress up for church. Winston and Ilochina agree that Nigerians and Jamaicans eat monkey. Ilochina adds an African proverb, "We say monkeys have ugly faces but delicious meat" (124). In their conversations, Sonia and Grace discuss wife-beating and the fact that "We black women, we never travel light" (164).

The thematic climax occurs with the naming of Gwendolen's baby. Initially, Ama, a Ghanaian nurse who cares for Gwendolen after her breakdown, is reluctant to supply African names for the newborn. She is offended when Gwendolen asks about a Ghanaian name for a girl child who looks like her grandfather. Ama retorts, "Why Ghana? You're not a Ghanaian. And you can't give her the name of your father. You can give her the name of his mother, if she looks like her" (209).

Knowing that this black baby in no way resembles her fair-skinned Granny Elinor, Gwendolen then asks for a name "that will show that this baby is my friend, my mother, my sister, my hope, all in one" (210). Not only is the Yoruba name Iyamide easily pronounceable to Gwendolen, but also, more importantly, her grandmother Sonia can say the word Iyamide easily.

Emecheta can't resist one last swat at this issue. Sonia grouses, "That no Christian name. You give the baby uncivilized African voodoo name" (237). After Gwendolen, Gladys Odowis and Emmanuel all laugh at Sonia's plaint, Gladys does voice a mild retort about people who pronounce "Gwendolen" as "Granada." She muses on "when these Caribbeans would stop calling Africans uncivilized as if they were civilized themselves! Whatever that word meant" (237). The addition of the final clause softens this comment by her reflection on the connotation of "civilized."

Gwendolen ends on a positive note. Gwendolen Brillianton has matured into a self-sufficient mother. Understanding the symbolism of her daughter Iyamide's name, Gwendolen affirms that "everything I ever wanted, warmth, security, comfort, is all here in a female form" (237). Child-bearing for her has been a liberating experience. Following her breakdown, Gwendolen is taken to an asylum where she, for the first time, is cosseted and protected from painful reality. No demands are made on her that she must obey, for attempts to get her to name the father of her baby fail. Gwendolen decides that she will "educate herself and get a good job" (182). Last pictured in a white running suit in her lovely council flat, Gwendolen Brillianton is a new Africana—a woman poised to celebrate the magic of motherhood.

NOTES

1. In a telephone conversation with the author, Emecheta stated that she entitled the novel *Gwendolen* and prefers this title to the Braziller title *The Family*, for two reasons: the novel is the young girl's story, and her parents cannot pronounce properly their older daughter's name.
2. Beryl Gilroy's *Boy Sandwich* (1989) portrays the loving relationship between a grandson and his grandparents.
3. Kincaid's novel *Lucy* (1990) is a sequel to *Annie John* and further illumines the mother/daughter clash. It culminates after Lucy's refusal to read her mother's letters results in the daughter's not knowing, until much too late to attend the funeral, that her father has died.
4. Government housing in this Emecheta novel is a marked contrast to the "Pussy Cat Mansions" for immigrants in earlier Emecheta novels.

WORKS CITED

Cliff, Michelle. *No Telephone to Heaven*. New York: Dutton, 1987.

Davies, Carole Boyce. "You Big 'Oman Nuh, June-June." *Belles Lettres*. (Fall 1990), 20-21.

Emecheta, Buchi. *Gwendolen*. London: Collins, 1989; rpt. *The Family*. New York: George Braziller, 1990.

—.*Kehinde*. London: Heinemann, 1994.

—.*Nowhere to Play*. London: Allison & Busby, 1979.

—. *Second-Class Citizen*. London: Allison & Busby; New York: George Braziller, 1975.

—.Telephone interview. 18 September 1994.

—. *The Bride Price*. London: Allison & Busby; New York: George Braziller, 1976.

—. *Titch the Cat*. With Alice Onwordi. London: Allison & Busby, 1979.

Gilroy, Beryl. *Boy Sandwich*. London: Heinemann, 1989.

Hodge, Merle. *Crick Crack Monkey*. London: Andre Deutsch; London: Heinemann, 1970.

Kincaid, Jamaica. *Annie John*. New York: Farrar, Straus & Giroux, 1983.

—.*Lucy*. New York: Farrar, Straus & Giroux, 1990.

McKay, Claude. *Banana Bottom*. New York: Harper & Row, 1933.

McKnight, Reginald. "Lost in the Moder Kontry." *The New York Times Book Review* (April 29, 1990), 30.

Philip, Marlene Nourbese. *Harriet's Daughter*. London: Heinemann, 1988.

Phillips, Caryl. "Survival with the British: West Indian Woman's Search for Identity." *The Washington Post* (February 22, 1990), B4.

Conflicting Social Values In Buchi Emecheta's *Naira Power* and *A Kind of Marriage*

Tunde Fatunde

Money can buy you everything. Everything...
because his parents had more children than they
could ever afford, and their father rejected them,
and they lived in a society where naira could buy
anything, even a good name. If such a person was
faced with a business in which he could make several thousand naira in one night, would you regard
him as insane to snap up that opportunity to make
such a fortune?

— Buchi Emecheta, *Naira Power*

Let us not deceive ourselves. A country that allows
its leaders to revel with impunity and reckless aban-

don in the worst forms of corruption and misrule
cannot hope to be blessed with the grace of light.

— Obafemi Awolowo, *My March Towards Prison*

Naira Power (NP) and *A Kind of Marriage* (AKM) were written and
published in the 80s when Emecheta's country, Nigeria, witnessed
an unprecedented growth in material wealth occasioned by foreign exchange proceeds from the sale of crude oil to the developed
industrialized countries of Europe and North America. This period was popularly known as the era of oil-boom, as exemplified in
Festus Iyayi's novel *The Contract* (1982) and Tunde Fatunde's play
No More Oil-Boom (1985). Many Nigerian creative writers, including Buchi Emecheta, focused sharply on the far reaching consequences of this mismanaged material boom on the complex social
values of their fellow countrymen and women.

And with specific reference to the two above-mentioned novels of Emecheta, one should note that the conflicting social values
raised within the novels are historically determined. Therefore,
these values should be analyzed strictly within the historical context of their birth, growth and dynamics. All social values are created by human beings for the purpose of historically determined
useful aims and objectives (Lucien Goldmann, 338).

These values are in turn fashioned out, teleguided and eventually imposed as an assemblage of dominant philosophies upon the
society by the historically determined ruling elite. They are subtly
inculcated in the mind of the citizen through various social institutions like the family, schools, churches, mosques and the mass
media. To the average citizen, the values are made to look and sound
indispensable, eternal, unchangeable and a-historical. In other
words, the ruling elite presents these values as a way of life.

The major thrust in Emecheta's *Naira Power* and *A Kind of
Marriage* is to reveal the extent to which the social values in Nigeria,
during her oil-boom era, did contribute towards the corruption and
eventual destruction of the youth. Broadly, there were two diametrically opposed values: the parental values on the one hand
and the social values on the other hand.

The parental values, as one would expect, were geared towards
bringing up the youth along the path of educational success which
was generally perceived by the youth as the gateway towards material and social prosperity. Fundamental to these parental aspirations was the secret hope, in the mind of the parents, that as the

youth grew up and became successful in their various professions, attained through formal education, the youth should and could cater reciprocally to their aging parents.

However, the larger social values ran counter to those of the parents. Corruption, injustice and stealing became practices, subtly secreted, like poisoned bile, into the society by the ruling elite. Like all poisoned biles, they threatened the vision of individual parents in connection with their social goals for the youth. Thus, the latter were pulled in diametrically opposed directions between the major dominant social values exemplified by corruption and the values of the parents, whose massive investment in formal education was, in principle, meant to produce a mature, honest, and decent, incorruptible youth. Here lay the dilemma of the young ones who were caught in the web of very dynamic but complex conflicting social values.

As a literary medium for gauging the strength and weakness of these divergent values, Emecheta created, among others, four young boys: Ramonu and Latifu in *Naira Power*; Osita and Afam in *A Kind of Marriage*. Their parents who belonged to different socio-professional milieux, clearly considered as their responsibility and policy the task of making them acquire formal education, by sending them to school. The importance of schooling was graphically demonstrated by Emecheta when she made one of her characters, Amina inform the readers about the kind of values placed upon formal education within Ramonu's immediate parental environment: "Ramonu at this time was sixteen. He was not doing well at school, and the Alhaji was always going at him for wasting his money. He kept threatening to remove him from school. This used to frighten Kudi, it used to frighten every mother, because you know what education is to us. *It is one's lifeline.* Each time, he made his threat, the two frightened wives would give their husband more of love meat which they were now both preparing" (*NP* 63-64). The anxiety of Latifu's father over his son's future career was amply shown when his father asked him the following pertinent question: "What are you going to do when you leave school? You have been going to that school for a long time now, you must have an idea what you intend doing" (*NP* 72).

Osita and Afam were young boys whose father, Charles, an educated Permanent Secretary in a federal establishment, made it a duty to send them to a very good and expensive school in Lagos. While Charles was, indeed, satisfied with Osita's brilliant performance at the university (*AKM* 80), he was, at the same time highly traumatized by the inability of Afam to complete his formal education. Consequently, Afam became a permanent nuisance and a liability to Charles (*AKM* 110-116).

Parents could only succeed when the larger society played positive and complimentary roles in shaping and fulfilling the aspirations of the young ones. In other words, the theory and practice of the dominant social ethos determined the progress or regression of the youth. In both novels, the social values during the oil-boom era did corrupt, ruin and destroy the four young boys.

In the descriptions of Lagos given by the story teller Amina and analyzed by the University Professor, Auntie Bintu, one could decipher the fact that the oil proceeds from the oil-boom have been largely mismanaged. The only lucrative and thriving successful industry created by the ruling but irresponsible Nigerian elite was corruption. The latter as the dominant but unwritten social philosophy became rampant to such an extent that "...big thieves who can swindle the government of millions of naira are respected and honored, pickpockets are not" (*NP* 34). Consequently, according to Amina, "Everybody does it, cheating here and there" (*NP* 32). And in the light of widespread corruption, which basically signified the use of foul and dishonest means to enrich one's self, one could only agree with Auntie Bintu who exclaimed in obvious frustration about the suffocating influence of corruption: "Ah yes, you must be ready to bribe your way openly here, or perish" (*NP* 6). And Amina strongly supported her observation: "Money can buy you everything, even justice. Everything...Money speaks here" (*NP* 10). It was, therefore, not surprising to Amina who remarked that "Many thieves who are handed over to the police were so rich that they could pay their way through the courts anyway, and escape sentence as a result" (*NP* 13).

Moreover, it is instructive to note that corruption became a flourishing enterprise through the nebulous and undefined popular medium called "business": "Business comes in different shades and colors doesn't it? When people say they are in business, you seldom go out of your way to ask what type of business they actually do, because here so many people caught in shady dealings usually describe themselves as businessmen" (*NP* 84). Lawmakers were the greatest lawbreakers and promoters of corruption:

> For instance, you know that the government says no smuggling, and anybody who smuggles and brings in foreign goods will be sent to jail. But

Auntie, you remember the day we came for you at the airport. You remember that many of the Senators returned in the same plane. You saw all the goods they brought in. You saw that all the airport officials were saying, 'yessir, yessir' and nobody searched them. You saw one of them carrying a bale of lace openly flouting the law they made for ordinary people like us. Well, how then can we blame people like Ramonu if they refuse to work and clear the rubbish that is choking the life out of the streets of Lagos. So if we can be out of work and able to make it in 'business,' one is respected and dubbed clever. (*NP* 30)

Given the strong, polluting, pervading, persuasive and dominant social value dubbed "business," which was just a glorified name for lucrative corruption, it was therefore not surprising that all the four young men created by Emecheta with the obvious exception of Osita, who became a brilliant but short-lived medical doctor, were goaded into "business." Closely related to and intertwined with business is stealing. Latifu, Amina's senior brother temporarily dropped out of school and joined the flourishing "business" venture of Ramonu, a young boy who turned out to be a smuggler and a narcotic drug merchant (*AKM* 89). Amina says the following: "I have heard my brother say to my father, education is not everything, but money speaks the universal language, Ramonu had all the naira power a woman could ever want in this world" (*NP* 81). Latifu's father warned his son about his close association with Ramonu: "Do you want to go to jail to bring that ill luck into this house, Latifu?" (*NP* 80). Until he was mistakenly caught, lynched and burnt alive by angry football fans, who initially thought he stole the money of a football spectator, "Ramonu had so great a belief in the power of his ill-gotten money that he did not see any reason why he could not get what he wanted" (*NP* 79).

The attractive and corrosive influence of business over formal education in the choice of career made by Afam, a primary school drop-out, was obvious. Afam chose business. This led to very revealing and sharp differences between Afam and his father Charles: "Look Afam, I have recently been to see your brother in the UK. He is now qualified as a doctor. You'll have no right to blame anyone in the future but yourself. We sent you to the same school but you refused to work hard. Don't go round in the future saying that

Osita did not help you, when you refused to help yourself" (86). And in the same breath Afam angrily retorted: "Oh, for God's sake. I am fed up with hearing of Osita's achievement. Doctors now don't get much money anyway. I will be rich. It's your son Osita who will come and beg money from me and not me from him. He spat and stalked away" (*AKM* 86).

And Amina, the story teller, provided extensively the reason for Afam's inordinate ambition—he was simply bought over by the need to enrich himself through the shortest route:

> We should not blame Afam for thinking it is easy to get rich quick without having to work hard. He had apparently seen men and women who had never gone to school riding around in big cars and living well. So when Charles warned him about his future, he could boast and say, 'You do not have to be a doctor or even to be educated to be rich'. Yes, it is the word 'rich' that you keep hearing, not education. If you are highly educated in this place and have no money to back it up, you are not respected. (*AKM* 88)

Afam, strongly convinced that his father's penchant for formal education was inferior to the dominant social vogue called "business," made up his mind that he was going to be a very successful businessman, famous and rich:

> All he could see was that people who did not go to school at all got all contracts from government ministries so what about him—he at least had spent several years in private schools. He did not see any obstacle and he day-dreamt a good deal. He stopped going to farm. Now he did not make any pretence about it. If people should say 'Afam why aren't you in the fields helping your grandfather's workers?' he would snap, 'Because I am created for bigger things.' (*AKM* 91)

Persuaded that it was more honorable to engage in dubious business activities, Afam tried to obtain a loan from a bank by using his father's name. The attempt failed. He abandoned farming and tried to make a living as a proprietor of a beer parlor at Ibusa, his hometown. The venture collapsed. There once more, from the omnipresent voice and eyes of Amina, the ubiquitous story teller in both novels, Afam decided to quit Ibusa and settle down in Lagos as a business man. Amina's words are as follows: "You cannot blame the youth. When you see people who do not work riding around in big cars showing off their wealth, they too want to acquire luxuries like that, so they run into cities looking for contracts" (*AKM* 92).

Afam could not get someone to give him the much-needed initial capital to start his own private venture. He angrily fell out with his father who advised him to go back and resume farming at Ibusa. As a last resort, he organized a robbery operation against his senior brother, Osita. During the midnight raid into Osita's house, he gave the following instructions: "Take everything he wears, take it all, but don't harm him, no don't kill my brother, no, no, don't kill my brother: I only need some money for the business" (*AKM* 118). However, Osita was killed in the operation:

> Apparently when Afam saw that his friends had killed his brother, he got mad and started to attack them just like an enraged animal. The friends were frightened, because they knew that if they were caught, they would hang. And the only way to be sure of not being found out was to silence Afam. One hammer blow finished him just outside the door leading to Osita's lovely flat. (*AKM* 119)

It is evident that Emecheta's heroes were successful failures. As tragic heroes, they died very young. They were consumed by the corrupting booby-traps planted in their path by the dominant philosophy of trying to get rich at all costs. The youth were destroyed by the Gandhian adage of politics without principle, pleasure without conscience, wealth without work, knowledge without character and business without morality.

The strength of the two novels resided in the abundant intratextual empirical evidence demonstrated descriptively: the tragic evolution of these young and energetic heroes who, unfortunately, met their untimely death. Emecheta efficiently handled in descriptive terms the growth and complex dynamic of her heroes. Events leading to the death of Ramonu, Osita and Afam were convincing. These young boys were not congenitally designed to be unenviable individuals. They were simply victims of historically determined social vices. Their tragic end was not a product of their polygamous parental background. One can only feel angry, through Emecheta's descriptive language in the two novels, at the Nigerian corrupt elite, especially during the oil-boom period, because of its reckless and wasteful pattern of the country's human (the youth) and material (crude oil) resources.

However, despite Emecheta's successful handling of the intra-textual descriptive evidence of how the larger society destroyed the youth, she failed at the time, within the two novels, to provide profound theoretical insight into the origin and dynamics of these corrupting values. One must quickly add here that one is not challenging her inalienable right, as a creative writer, to make use of her creative qualities as she deems it right. The issue at stake, here, is as follows: leaning upon some extra-literary and indeed literary principle to which Emecheta whole-heartedly subscribes, one would have expected her, through well-known literary techniques, to elucidate to readers the reasons and "possible resolutions" of these serious corrupting values which have destroyed and are still destroying Nigerian youth. What are these extra-literary and literary principles?

Emecheta strongly and explicitly subscribes to a kind of realist and didactic form of literature. She is perfectly entitled to her views and method of work. She says as follows:

> I write from a sociological perspective. And that is because sociologically you learn to look at society from different angles and you put that in your work. It makes your work not just fiction but informative fiction. This is worthy in eleven American universities, most of my books are used in sociology departments. Some professors use them for literature while others use them for all sorts of things— Yes, I do that because sociology is my discipline—So you don't go and write fiction just for people to enjoy themselves. You write with a message. (*ANA Review* 6)

Adhering strictly to her self-proclaimed extra-literary principles, to which once again she has an inalienable right, Emecheta proceeded by creating Auntie Bintu, a University Professor (*AKM* 20) who was also a writer of books (*AKM* 70). In both novels, there was a structural division of labor, from the viewpoint of narrative techniques, between Amina and Auntie Bintu. While Amina told the stories, Auntie Bintu analyzed them. Thus, the reader gets firsthand testimony of major events in the society through Amina. And simultaneously, Auntie Bintu, a literary intellectual mirror-image and embodiment of Buchi Emecheta, analyzed for the reader the theoretical and philosophical significance of Amina's stories. Emecheta successfully handled, through Amina, the tragic and destructive education of Nigerian youth. However, the author poorly handled from an artistic standpoint, Auntie Bintu. The latter did not measure up to the standard expected of a university professor and "a writer of books." Auntie Bintu failed to provide profound theoretical and philosophical insight into reasons for the failure of the youth. This is a serious artistic and aesthetic deficiency in both novels. How?

The reasons adduced by Auntie Bintu for the tragic failure of Nigerian youth, in both novels, are disappointingly superficial. She trivialized and, in the process, minimized the trauma Nigerians were going through in the midst of material abundance when she says: "Well, we are now independent, are we not? And we are an old nation, even though we may be experiencing some minor hiccups, but they will smooth over. Nonetheless, we are now a nation to reckon with, so that has gone a long way in helping to alter the image of the black person" (*AKM* 107). Amina justified every event which took place as the direct and invisible handiwork of an extrasensory body called Allah, i.e. the Islamic monotheist God. The misfortune of all these young boys in the two novels was directly traceable to "the will of Allah" (*NP* 27). One cannot fault Amina's level of reasoning because she was nurtured and cultured strictly within a conservative Islamic milieu. And she could not rise above such a culture since she did not, unlike Auntie Bintu, go through the walls of a university where she could have either reaffirmed or rejected such an Islamic world view as a philosophical means to analyze the conflicting values of her society.

Here again, Auntie Bintu's response to Amina's superficial Islamic world view was disappointing and unconvincing:

> I know that sometimes we put the blame for all that happens to us on Allah or, simply, fate. When someone dies suddenly due to careless driving or some accident which the living think could have been prevented, we simply say it had to happen so. These explanations console the bereaved, who otherwise could start blaming themselves for all that had happened to their departed loved ones. Well, this may be the case, but my own reading and experience of many unnecessary deaths do make me skeptical— but after the early age of ten or so, every child

441

should know, or at least guess, the rights and wrongs of society. Ramonu should have known that he was asking for trouble and that though big thieves who can swindle the government of millions of naira are respected and honored, pickpockets are not. (*NP* 34)

The above statement was the longest statement of a theoretical and philosophical view given expression by Auntie Bintu—the literary and intellectual embodiment of Buchi Emecheta. This viewpoint barely scratched the surface in trying to provide reasons for the conflicting values of the Nigerian society and their effects on young boys. Auntie Bintu doubted the metaphysical explanations put forward by Amina. However, she failed to provide an alternative explanation. This situation is not acceptable because, as a University Professor and a writer of books, Auntie Bintu should not have created a theoretical void at the very moment she was not satisfied with Amina's metaphysical world view. This void represents a serious literary deficiency in this work by Buchi Emecheta.

Moreover, Auntie Bintu pontificated that every child who has attained the age of ten should at least have a guessing knowledge of the rights and wrongs of society. Here again one is faced with a very sweeping "theoretical" statement which cannot be found in any book in children's psychology. It is only an adult like Auntie Bintu, through a combination of formal education and years of personal experience, who is capable of guessing and knowing the rights and wrongs of society.

Another literary and theoretical pitfall in Emecheta's handling of Auntie Bintu can be found in the categorical statement that was entirely responsible for Ramonu's misfortune. The author who strongly and correctly believes in the intellectual capacity of a woman professor such as Auntie Bintu should have corrected the wrong theoretical premise for Ramonu's misfortune. Sociologists and philosophers are broadly in agreement on at least one issue: man is a social being. His success or failure is a complex combination of both his own actions and that of the society in which he lives. He may be largely responsible for his lot. However, the society has a minimum role to play in relation to his destiny. In other words, man is a product of his environment. Consequently, Romanu's tragic failure is like the failure and death of Osita and Afam and should not be placed entirely on the shoulders of these young boys. They were victims of the historically determined values of their society.

WORKS CITED

Awofinfa, Mike. "I won't say I am a Feminist: Conversation with Buchi Emecheta." *ANA Review* (1990): 6.

Emecheta, Buchi. *A Kind of Marriage*. London. Macmillian Pacesetters, 1986. (References to this novel are indicated by *AKM*.)

—-. *Naira Power*. London. Macmillian Pacesetters, 1982. (References to this novel are indicated by *NP*.)

Goldmann, Lucien. *Pour Une Sociologie Du Roman*. Gallimard, Paris. 1964.

PART SEVEN
A CONVERSATION WITH
DR. BUCHI EMECHETA

OLADIPO JOSEPH OGUNDELE

JULY 22, 1994

This interview was conducted in the serene atmosphere of Dr. Buchi Emecheta's beautiful home in North London. Friday, July 22, 1994, turned out to be a very sunny and airy day. I arrived at the door of 144 Cranley Gardens late in the afternoon with lots of thoughts and questions on my mind. Dr. Emecheta and I were not strangers; I had met her several times during her visits to the United States. In fact, three years earlier, she was the keynote speaker at the Women's History Month Lecture Series in March, 1991, when I was a student resident at John Jay College of Criminal Justice, CUNY.

I was welcomed by a smiling and younger-looking Emecheta. I thought she looked very good and undoubtedly very happy. She had just celebrated her fiftieth birthday the previous day. She had some of her family and friends over on her birthday because I clearly remember hearing musical songs and happy voices in the background, when I had called her that day to confirm our appointment for the next day.

As I stepped into the living room, I could not help but notice how elegantly it was decorated. The furnishings were simple yet very elegant. A bookshelf with all her published books were standing at the side of the room. I observed that most of the books were translated into other languages such as German and Italian, to mention only two. Dr. Emecheta was wearing a two piece Nigerian dress.

Throughout the interview, the acclaimed author maintained a friendly posture and she exhibited a clear understanding and mastery of the subject matter. However, I detected much anxiety in her tone of voice when she responded to the question on Alice Walker's views on clitoridectomy. Like Audre Lorde in her essay, "An Open Letter to Mary Daly," she resented the sensationalistic and insensitive nature of North American feminists toward issues within feminist politics. The interview lasted about two hours.

Ogundele:Dr. Buchi Emecheta, award-winning novelist, essayist, playwright, publisher, author of children's books, editor, single parent, and writer of nineteen published books, how does it feel to be successful?

Emecheta:Well, I think I take my success as part of my daily bread. Writing is something that I have been wanting to do for a long time and the fact that I am fairly successful is one of the graces of God.

Ogundele:What are the rewards and difficulties of being the most significant African female writer today?

Emecheta:The reward is that you are being read by few Africans and mostly by people from other parts of the world. The repercussion is that you sort of feel isolated because we don't have many African women who are actually writing full time. Most of them are engaged in other things apart from writing or teaching.

Ogundele:Is there a particular difficulty for a woman alone to raise five children and write creatively?

Emecheta:Yes, there are so many difficulties apart from feeding and looking after the children. There is the physical and mental difficulties of not knowing what to expect from day to day. Then you have to think creatively about your work and all this requires a lot of energy and mental priorities.

Ogundele:How and where do you establish your priorities?

Emecheta:Well, I don't have priorities as such. I would say that I write my books for the world to read. But at the moment and for a very long time, I have concentrated on the African situation. I was born in Nigeria and I grew up there. So, in most of my books I go back to Africa. But I write about Africa for the whole world.

Ogundele:What do you believe is distinctive about your diction? What makes it good? Why are you considered the most popular female writer of Africa?

Emecheta:Well, I don't know about the diction. I just write the way I speak. Being considered the most popular female writer in Africa is because I have written a lot. Moreover, Britain is a country where you can afford to say, "I want to write." And you start writing. After some time, your books become fairly popular and people get to know them.

Ogundele:Which persons/writers and what books are responsible for your creativity? Your literary imagination?

Emecheta:Well, we were brought up with the old colonial English system where you are encouraged to read as widely as possible. As a child, my reading was Catholic. I read everything I could lay my hands on. So it is very difficult to be able to pin point and say that this is the person who actually helped me. But I know that my style is more like story telling. My style is ballad like. The way I recount things that happen comes from the way we speak in our part of Nigeria.

Ogundele:Who (which author) is doing work now that you respect?

Emecheta:Do you mean in Africa or in the world?

Ogundele:Generally.

Emecheta:Here in England we get to read and review several books every week and that gives you the general view of the people. I like women writers as well as African writers but things are not what they used to be. I actually don't know what is happening. Years ago, we had people like Chinua Achebe and Wole Soyinka. But for the past three years we have not seen anything cogent from African writers. Maybe it is because of the situation in Africa. The danger now is Southern Africa. Now that Apartheid has been eradicated, one wonders what will happen in the post-Apartheid era since all their writers have been writing about it. I think there is going to be a period while people diversify their energy literally. For now, there is really nothing coming out of Africa. Here in London, we have a few good writers like Ben Okri. He has written a couple of good books and he won the Booker Prize. But his style of writing tends to border more on sensational issues. I think he is

447

a good writer.

Ogundele:How do you see your growth and development as a successful writer?

Emecheta:Well, my growth is quite natural. After writing a book, you write another and you keep writing and writing. But what I think helps me mostly is the fact that I go to Nigeria at least twice a year. Nigeria is a land full of stories. Every time I am there, I always come in contact with something new. I returned a few months ago and I am already digesting my experiences there to see how I can fit them into another story.

Ogundele:Can you tell us something about how you handle the process of writing? What is it like to have characters whose actions you cannot always predict? Do you tell your characters what to do? For example, is Nnu Ego's life dictated by you?

Emecheta: Well, you have a vague idea of what the story is going to be about and as I said, you have the message or the topic of the novel. What I do is to look back into the African situation. You can use the same book to kill two birds at the same time because you are telling the world and Africa about where you live. And to be able to do that, it is essential for me to go home. I don't tell my characters what to do. Nnu Ego in *The Joys of Motherhood* is about population control. You have a vague idea that you want to use this woman to depict the fact that having so many children does not mean that you are going to be rich in your old age. Once you stay with a work for a very long time, the character just takes off from there; but you have to plan everything you want to do from the beginning. You cannot predict the creative side. It depends on what happens from day to day.

Ogundele:Do you like/love all you characters? Which ones do you identify with? Nnu Ego? Adaku? Orisha-Debbie? Kehinde? And why?

Emecheta:Well, I don't agree with some of them. And you don't have to like your characters. If there is a character that I like in all my books, it is Debbie Ogedemgbe in *Destination Biafra*. I think that she is still my best character and the one that I would like to identify with. Unfortunately, I can never be like her. In *Destination Biafra*, she was a woman who could handle guns and she protected all those women and trekked on the long journey from Agbor to Ibuza in the Asaba area. I am frightened of guns. I can't even kill a chicken. I admire women like Debbie who also have a western education.

Ogundele:Naming is an important preoccupation in your novels,

The Bride Price, The Joys of Motherhood, and *Kehinde*, to name only three. Would you discuss its significance?

Emecheta:In Nigeria and African situations, especially in our own culture, we just don't give people names. Our names have to identify with something. For example, Nnu Ego, a beautiful woman, means twenty bags of cowries or ten million pounds in the western world. When a child is beautiful, we say Nnu Ego. Adaku means the child of wealth. Then you find out in the book that she has nothing. Then again, Gwendolen Brillianton is a name that sounds Victorian. You would assume that it is somebody coming out of the Victorian high ball. The satire in the book is that Mr. Brillianton, someone with such a dauntless name, stutters and can't even express himself. I always choose my characters' names carefully. The latest one 'Kehinde' is one of the twins in the novel of the same name. And of course, you find out how the other twin Taiwo, the first born, is affecting her life. I needed to establish a reason why some women hear voices from unknown sources. These voices can affect our lives but we learn to live with them.

Ogundele:How do you conceive your function as a writer? Do you have a mission in mind?

Emecheta:Apart from telling stories, I don't have a particular mission. I like to tell the world our part of the story while using the voices of women. Women in our area are silenced a lot. Even amongst writers, you will notice that there is a bias towards male writers. For instance, I have produced more books than most male writers. But you hear more about the male writers. My hope is that in the future, people will start reading more books by female writers and realize that African women do have voices.

Ogundele:What is your favorite novel and why?

Emecheta:The one I like is one that is not very popular and that is *The Rape of Shavi*. *The Rape of Shavi* is an allegory about how our area became raped by Europe. And after raping it, they put nothing there. The book is not very popular because of its stringent nature. It is very much against the west. If I was from a very literally strong country like the Caribbean, the book would be more popular. The book should have been read by everyone in Nigeria. But of course, our country is very weak literally and you are not recognized if you are just a literary star unless you are rich or a drug dealer. It is only then you have a name. In Nigeria, writing is not regarded as a good profession.

Ogundele:Are there any autobiographical elements in your writing outside of *In the Ditch, Second-Class Citizen*, and *Head Above*

Water?

Emecheta:No, most of the episodes I have used usually come from what I have seen or experienced or what somebody or someone who experienced it told me. Like I said, when I want to write about something, I usually go back home and sort of revitalize the Africanness or Nigerianess in me. In my latest book, *Kehinde*, most of the episodes are things that I have seen myself like the scene near Festac where a policeman was dozing on duty. You experience these things and use them to structure your book. I don't sit down and say I am going to write a book and this or that has to be there. You sort of have those experiences recorded in your memory like a reservoir and they just come out when you want to use them.

Ogundele:Can you describe the physical and mental evolution of Adah from her role in your first book *In the Ditch* to her portrayal in *Second-Class Citizen?*

Emecheta:Those are very autobiographical books. *In the Ditch* was serialized in the *New Statesman*. These were articles I wrote about to describe the way I used to live at that time. When I decided to turn it into a book, I changed the name of the main character from Buchi to Adah. I changed a lot of the sequences in order to form it into documentary novels.

Ogundele:Do you have some advice for women or men who would like to write?

Emecheta:Well, it is difficult to advise people. If you are convinced that you want to be a writer, especially if you are black, you just have to stick it out. There are no short cuts and you have to read as much as possible which unfortunately most of our people don't do.

Ogundele:Flora Nwapa Nwakuche has died. What do you feel was her contribution to the world of literature?

Emecheta:Well, it was a very sad story and I am still recovering from the shock because people know us together as sisters. Wherever we went, people referred to her as my big sister. She was the first woman to be published in the whole of Africa outside by Heinemann a long time ago. The sad thing is that at one time in her career, she went into politics and she never quite achieved the same standards again. She was just coming out again and trying to establish herself in places like America and then death struck. It is very unfortunate because she was very young looking and her mother is still alive.

Ogundele:What impact did Flora Nwapa have on you as a writer?

Emecheta:Well, I heard of her name several years ago when we were in school. I never thought that we were going to meet some-day as equals. I remember she came to my home when *The Joys of Motherhood* was published and wanted to know who wrote the book. I was very flattered. As a person, she struck me as a very nice and humble woman. She had passed the peak of her career by the time I met her although I didn't know it then. Looking at it later, it was very sad because she really had no time to settle down. That taught me a lesson. Writing is something that requires com-plete commitment. If you flutter you just lose yourself by the way. As I said it is very unfortunate that she died so early.

Ogundele:What was your reaction to Toni Morrison winning the 1993 Nobel Prize for Literature?

Emecheta:Oh, I just love Toni. I have always liked Toni Morrison. We met here several times when she came to launch her book *Song of Solomon*. I remember that there were only five of us who came to the launching despite the fact that it was advertised. She was not well known here. We even had dinner together after the launch-ing. She is a nice woman. I have said over the years that she was an unsung heroine. She did not have the right connection which would have brought her name up very early. I am very glad that she is now being recognized. Her early books like *Sula* and *The Bluest Eye* were unbeatable. I taught *Sula* at the University of Calabar. I am very glad that eventually she is being recognized and awarded this great prize.

Ogundele:What do you feel are the links between African and African-American female writers and their thematic concerns?

Emecheta:We have lots of links. For instance, *Their Eyes Were Watching God* is one of the first African-American books that I read and I quite like the language. But of course, Toni Morrison is my champion. I have always liked her work. The link is that theirs is the next stage. We deal with the Pan African situation that we expe-rienced while theirs are the interpretations over generations. They get their secondary ideas from Africans who have lived in the States for a very long time or through books written by Africans. But when you look at it, we are all talking about the same thing in order for people to hear our voices. Some people like Alice Walker through their exuberance or enthusiasm try to put Africans down without knowing it. Luckily, we don't experience that type of attitude from the majority of African-American writers. As far as I am concerned, we are all doing the same thing but they use the digested African-American language which I find very interesting indeed.

Ogundele: Would you like to mention a few of the differences that you find interesting among Africans and African-Americans as far as literature is concerned?

Emecheta: The main difference as I said is their language. The way they use the English language is innovative. They tend to mix it with Creole or other language experiences. They have given American English new life. There is a lot of poetic rhythm in it. In Toni Morrison's *Beloved,* for example, *abiku,* that is someone born to die, comes out of Nigeria. Since hers was translated, you have to go through it several times before you realize what she is talking about. If you now compare *abiku* to my own *ogbanje,* which is the Igbo name for *abiku* in the novel, *The Slave Girl,* you will find out that mine is the raw thing. *Ogbanje* means someone who comes several times, someone who is born again and again. In her own case, it has been diluted with slavery and yet she used it to produce a marvelous book.

Ogundele: Now that South Africans have a new government and President Nelson Mandela as its leader, has your expectations of South African writers changed?

Emecheta: It will have to change especially in regards to the subject. Years ago people asked Chinua Achebe why he has not been writing like he used to and he said that before independence, he was writing for Nigerian independence by mocking and complaining about British domination. After independence, he found out that he had to start writing about his own colleagues who were now in government. This was very difficult because he had to write about their corruption and domination of the country. South Africa is going to be like that. Post-Apartheid writing is going to be another type of writing entirely. I pray that because of their long struggle, such a beautiful country will not degenerate to the level of Nigeria in terms of corruption. You know the name Nigeria is synonymous with the term corruption. I am sure that their long fight for independence will color their writing. I think we still have to wait and see.

Ogundele: Do your female characters have a special role to play in your novels?

Emecheta:I use the voices of women to talk about corruption and the inadequacies of so many things because women have been silenced for so long. I make most of them the protagonists in my books. It is only in a few of my books like *Double Yoke, The Rape of Shavi* and parts of *Destination Biafra* that I used male voices. Like I said, we have been silenced for so long.

Ogundele: What about your male characters, do they possess particular strengths or weaknesses? For example, Nnaife in *The Joys of Motherhood*?

Emecheta: No, they don't possess any type of weakness. I describe Nigerian males as we see them but once they are read outside the culture people realize how weak they are. But our men don't realize that they are weak because they hide behind the women and at the same time, they put the women down by not acknowledging the type of addition the women make to our daily living. By so doing, their weaknesses don't show in real life until you put them down on paper then they become visible. When you see these characters in black and white you will realize that our men need to reeducate themselves or reexamine their actions because it is overflowing from individual families to our government. You can see their weaknesses in the way they run our government. The funniest thing about it is that every body is talking about it and there is nothing they can do to change it.

Ogundele: In *The Joys of Motherhood*, your most dynamic character Ona dies. Why? Nnu Ego also dies a premature death at 45 years of age. Why?

Emecheta: Well, Ona died because she had to give birth to Nnu Ego because Ona is Nnu Ego's mother so she did not live to see her daughter grow into womanhood. The immorality that surrounded the way in which she gave birth was not right. The man she married was going against her father's wishes. It was against the culture; that was why she had to die the way she did. The subject of the book is population control. Having so many children does not make you a better human being. Nnu Ego's children left her to go to different places to study. It does not mean that they did not love her. What the western type of civilization demanded was not the type of civilization demanded earlier on.

Ogundele: Nnu Ego does not answer prayers for children? Why? What are you trying to tell us?

Emecheta: Well, even in death when something favorable happens men are given the credit. In the west, every hurricane or catastrophe is named after a woman. So even after Nnu Ego's death people still prayed to her spirit to give them children. People said that she did not give children because she died unhappy. These people knew in their hearts that she was neglected in her old age. Instead of accepting their guilt they blamed her for not answering their prayers for children in her area. The effect was that young women did not have children in that area.

Ogundele:In your opinion, have the last three decades been important for the growth of Black Literature? In which ways?

Emecheta:Yes, because it brought out people like Wole Soyinka and Toni Morrison who won the Nobel Prize. I remember that when Wole Soyinka won the Nobel Prize it made headlines because people did not know that Black people can write. For instance, in Italy it was a big deal because they believed that Black people could not write or even read. Many male African-American writers don't even understand Toni Morrison when she speaks and writes the type of language I talked about. So the last three decades did a lot and I hope it continues.

Ogundele:In Nigeria, is incest and rape a power play? How can we transform the society? What is your opinion about rape in Africa and the African diaspora in general?

Emecheta:Well, rape is something that is a taboo in our area of Nigeria and the fact that our people don't talk about it doesn't mean that it doesn't happen. Here in the west, when Africans and Caribbeans come out of that tight family situation, it becomes more rampant and people talk more about it. When people leave their culture as I said in my novel, *Gwendolen*, it happens, because that man has left his culture.

Ogundele:In Alice Walker's novel, *Possessing The Secret of Joy*, she argues extensively against clitoridectomy and says that it should be eradicated because it stunts female growth and mutilates female children. Did you treat female circumcision in any of your books? If not, why? What are your views on female genital mutilation?

Emecheta:Well, I did not treat it in any of my books because in our area it is not all that important. I was in Nigeria for three months and I saw only boys being circumcised. Like I said when people have left Africa for a long time, they get excited over irrelevant things. Reading some of her books, you would think that as soon as you get to Africa, every girl is snatched and circumcised. That is the type of picture she is painting and we are very offended about it here in London because it is not that important. Why can't she focus her attention on other issues like the millions of people dying in Rwanda or the Albanians who sell their children. You see, Africa is so vulnerable. So she wants to write about something sensational to bring Africans down. In *The Color Purple*, she talked about how bush we are and we swallowed it and now she is following it up with this. We are not proud of her. Female circumcision in Africa is dying. Alice Walker lives in California where women mutilate their breasts and reshape their lips everyday. If she wants to save humanity let her write about that. In Africa, female circumcision is no longer relevant culturally. We had it done to us years ago. I personally don't welcome her intervention and there is a group of us who are very angry about it. We can do without her denigration. Our people have realized that female circumcision is no longer relevant. For example, why circumcise a girl who could end up marrying a white man? I used to like her work but I changed my opinion when she delved into this topic. She parades herself all over talking down on African old women and reducing us to nothing. You know we respect our old women. She talked down to them and that is unforgivable. That's why I stick to Toni Morrison.

Ogundele:Comparatively, what do your characters, Kehinde, Gwendolen and Adah have in common? As women from the Black World residing in London, what is the significance of their gender?

Emecheta:Well, the significance is how they coped with the changes from one culture to the other and survived. For instance, Kehinde came here, went back, and then returned after a long stay. It shows the spirit of Black women toward survival. They survive despite all odds. Most of these women have a western education but their color hinders their opportunities and advancement in society. Because of the situation in most African countries, many prefer to stay here and survive at all costs. These women depict the black woman survivor just like their ancestors survived slavery to bring up all those illustrious black people in America. These women are trying to make the best of a bad situation.

Ogundele:Does your strong opposition to abortion in *Kehinde* come from your spiritual background or the fact that a woman should have full and total control over her body?

Emecheta:Well, coming from Africa where life is sacred and where we believe in the reincarnation of our ancestors, I said in *Kehinde* that after remaining in the womb for a certain time, the *chi* of a child is already formed. The child has a life. That is why I am not for abortion on demand. I think that it should be left to the woman. She should have a chance to make that decision. I personally won't abort or encourage any of my children to abort a child unless there is physical illness or danger to the life of the mother. Abortion should not be used as a form of contraception. In *Kehinde*, her husband forced her to have an abortion against her will, only for her to find out on her arrival back home that his new wife was having babies. That is the dilemma a woman faces. In a situation like that, he should have allowed her to make the decision herself.

455

Ogundele:What is your personal opinion about interracial marriages? In your book *Destination Biafra*, Debbie Ogedemgbe did not go through with her earlier intention to marry Captain Alan Grey. Why?

Emecheta:Well, *Destination Biafra* was set from 1967 to 1970 when the Nigerian Civil War was going on. At that time, white people still regarded black women as lower in class and it was also post independence for most African countries so the whites still felt an aura of superiority over Africans. At that time, it was very dicey. A black woman had to be over qualified before she is noticed by the white man. I remember that an African-American female writer (name withheld) once said, "If I am not this good, I won't be married to a white man." She felt superior because she was married to a white man. But now things are changing. As you can see in the novel, *Gwendolen*, children born here no longer consider the color of the skin an important factor. Even in present day Europe, people are also paying less attention to one's skin color. But in our generation, it used to be a big deal. At that time there was a big question mark but not anymore.

Ogundele:Finally, are you working on another book? What is your next book going to be about? Do you have a title?

Emecheta:I am resting at the moment. The weather now is so beautiful in England that I don't even remember where my typewriter is. I have just returned from Nigeria where I did the celebration of my mother's life. I explored the spirituality of Christianity which I found has done a lot of harm to our African religion and culture. My next book will revolve around that topic. I will explore deeply the African spiritual life. I have not yet decided on a topic for the book. I have bits and pieces of ideas but I haven't taken the time to put them together. Maybe I will start writing in autumn or winter but at the moment, I am enjoying the good weather.

Ogundele: Thank you very much Dr. Emecheta.

Chronology

1944   July 21: Born Florence Onyebuchi Emecheta in Lagos, Nigeria to Jeremy and Alice Ogbanje (Okwuekwu) Emecheta. Both from Ibusa, Nigeria, Delta State.

1951   Attends Ladilak School in Yaba, Lagos.

1953   Attends Reagan Memorial Baptist School in Yaba, Lagos.

1954   Attends Methodist Girls Secondary School in Yaba, Lagos.

1960   Marries Sylvester Onwordi.

1960   Her daughter, Chiedu, is born.

1961   Her son, Ikechukwu, is born.

1962   Leaves Nigeria to join her husband in London in February. Her second son, Chukwuemeka, is born in December.

1964   Her second daughter, Obiajulu, is born.

1966   Her third daughter, Chiago, is born.

1966   Separates from her husband, Sylvester Onwordi.

1972   Publishes *In the Ditch*.

1974   Receives her Bachelor of Science in sociology from London University.

1975 Publishes *Second-Class Citizen;* receives the Daughter of Mark Twain Award for this work. Publishes plays: *A Kind of Marriage* for the BBC, London, and *Juju Landlord* for Granada Commercial TV in England.

1976 Publishes *The Bride Price.* Receives her Masters degree in philosophy from London University.

1977 Publishes *The Slave Girl.*

1978 Receives the New Statesman/Jock Campbell Award for *The Slave Girl.* Receives the Sunrise Award for the Best Black Writer in the World, also for *The Slave Girl.*

1979 Publishes *The Joys of Motherhood, Titch the Cat,* and *Nowhere to Play. The Joys of Motherhood* is Book of the Month selection.

1980 Publishes *The Moonlight Bride* and *The Wrestling Match.* Receives Best British Writer's Award for *The Joys of Motherhood.*

1981 Publishes *Our Own Freedom* with Maggie Murray. Fellow at the University of Calabar in Calabar, Nigeria.

1982 Publishes *Destination Biafra, Naira Power,* and *Double Yoke* Appointed to serve the Home Secretary on Race and Immigration. Appointed to serve on the Arts Council of Great Britain. Establishes a publishing company, namely, Ogwugwu Afor.

1983 Publishes *Adah's Story* and *The Rape of Shavi.*

1984 Her eldest daughter, Chiedu, dies.

1985 *Double Yoke* is made into a movie in Holland.

1985 Lecturer of Creative Writing at London University.

1986 Publishes *Family Bargain,* a children's book for the BBC.

1986-to date Fellow at London University.

1986   Publishes the novel, *A Kind of Marriage,* and her autobiography, *Head Above Water.* Her husband, Sylvester Onwordi, and her brother Adolphus, die.

1989   Publishes *Gwendolen* in London.

1990   Becomes a member of PEN (Poets, Essayists, and Novelists). Publishes *The Family* (aka *Gwendolen*) in the United States.

1992   Receives Doctor of Literature degree from Fairleigh Dickinson University in Madison, New Jersey.

1994   Publishes *Kehinde.*

BIBLIOGRAPHY

Brenda F. Berrian

AUTOBIOGRAPHY

Head Above Water. London: Fontana, 1986.

NOVELS

In the Ditch. London: Barrie & Jenkins, 1972; New York: Shocken, 1980.

Second-Class Citizen. London: Allison & Busby; New York: George Braziller, 1975.

The Bride Price. London: Allison & Busby; New York: George Braziller, 1976.

The Slave Girl. London: Allison & Busby; New York: George Braziller, 1977.

The Joys of Motherhood. London: Allison & Busby; New York: George Braziller, 1979.

Destination Biafra. London: Allison & Busby; New York: George Braziller, 1982.

Adah's Story (In the Ditch and Second-Class Citizen). London: Allison & Busby, 1983.

Double Yoke. London: Ogwugwu Afor Co. Ltd., 1982; rpt. New York: George Braziller, 1983.

The Rape of Shavi. London: Ogwugwu Afor, 1983; New York: George Braziller, 1985.

Gwendolen. London: Collins, 1989; rpt. *The Family*. New York: George Braziller, 1990.

Kehinde. London: Heinemann, 1994.

CHILDREN'S LITERATURE

Titch the Cat. With Alice Onwordi. London: Allison & Busby, 1979.

Nowhere to Play. London: Allison & Busby, 1979.

JUVENILE LITERATURE

Naira Power. London: Macmillan, 1982.

The Moonlight Bride. London: Oxford UP, 1980; rpt. New York: George Braziller, 1983.

The Wrestling Match. Oxford: Oxford UP, 1980; New York: George Braziller, 1983.

A Kind of Marriage. London: Macmillan, 1986.

PERFORMED PLAYS

"A Kind of Marriage," Performed for B.B.C. Radio and Television

"The Juju Landlord," Performed for B.B.C. Radio

"Tanya, a Black Woman," Performed for B.B.C. Radio

"Family Bargain," Performed for B.B.C., 1987.

ESSAYS: AUTOBIOGRAPHICAL

"Baptism by Socialization-*In the Ditch*-1," *New Statesman* 8 Jan. 1971: 43-44.

"Down to the Dole House-*In the Ditch*-2," *New Statesman* 15 Jan. 1971: 77-78.

"The Ministry's Visiting Day-*In the Ditch*-3," *New Statesman* 22 Jan. 1971: 110.

"Out of the Ditch and into Print," *West Africa* 3 Apr. 1978: 669-72.

"An African View in Church of England," *West Africa* 24 Apr. 1978: 805-6.

"The Human Race Decides to March through London," *West Africa* 19 June 1978: 1177-80.

"A Time Bomb," *West Africa* 30 Oct. 1978: 2139-40.

"Through West African Eyes," *CMS Magazine* Oct.-Dec. 1978: 18-19.

"Give Us This Day and Our Daily Bread," *West Africa* 4 Dec. 1978: 2410-11. "Christmas Is for All," *West Africa* 25 Dec. 1978: 2590-91.

"A Writer's Day," *New Fiction* 20 (1979): 3.

"Another Fear of Flying," *West Africa* 25 June 1979: 119-20.

"Darry and a Bouquet of Flowers," *West Africa* 9 July 1979: 1215-16.

"Language Difficulties," *West Africa* 16 July 1979: 1267-68.

"A Question of Dollars," *West Africa* 30 July 1979: 1367-68.

"US Longing for Roasted Yams," *West Africa* 27 Aug. 1979: 1560-62.

"US Police Convince Me I Am Lost," *West Africa* 24 Sept. 1979: 1761-62.

"What the Carol Singers Are Missing," *West Africa* 24-31 Dec. 1979: 2385-86.

"A Week of Ghana," *West Africa* 13 Oct. 1980: 2015-16.

"Head Above Water," *Kunapipi* 3.1 (1981): 81-90.

"That First Novel," *Kunapipi* 3. 2 (1981): 115-23.

"Calabar Contrasts and Complaints," *West Africa* 12 Jan. 1981: 71-72.

"Lagos Provides a Warm Welcome," *West Africa* 19 Jan. 1981: 110-11, 113.

"African Woman," *Root* Aug. 1981: 22-25, 30.

"Simpler than Sociology," *West Africa* 10 Aug. 1981: 1813-14.

"Nigeria: Experiencing a Cultural Lag," *West Africa* 2 Nov. 1981: 2582-83.

"A Nigerian Writer Living in London," *Kunapipi* 4. 1 (1982): 114-23.

"Women of Pittsburgh," *Root* Feb. 1982: 14-15, 25.

"Black and a Woman," *New Society* July 1984.

OTHER ESSAYS

"Introduction and Comments," *Our Own Freedom*. With Maggie Murray. London: Sheba Feminist Press, 1981.

"Mixed Marriage," *African Weekly Review* 1. 17 (1968): 13.

"Buchi's Social Column—Marriage Does It Pay?" *African Weekly Review*, 20 Oct. 1967: 12.

"Should Husbands Control a Wife's Salary?" *African Weekly Review* 1. 3 (1967): 8.

"Review of Peter Fryer's Staying Power: This History of Black People in Britain," *New Society* 24 May 1984: 323.

"Nigeria—the Woman as a Writer," *Realities* (Spring 1985): 1, 22-24.

"African Women Step Out," *New African* 1 Nov. 1985: 7-8.

"Education: US," *Women: A World Report*. New York: Oxford UP, 1985: 205-18.

"Feminism with a Small 'f'!" *Criticism and Ideology*. Second African Writers Conference, Stockholm 1986. Ed. Kirsten Holst Peterson. Uppsala, Sweden: Scandinavian Institute of African Studies, 1988: 173-85.

EXTRACTS FROM NOVELS

"A Man Needs Many Wives," *Daughters of Africa: An International Anthology of Words and Writings by Women of African Descent: From the Ancient Egyptian to the Present*. Ed. Margaret Busby. New York: Ballantine Books, 1994. 656-666.

"A Man Needs Many Wives," *Unwinding Threads: Writing by Women in Africa*. Ed. Charlotte Bruner. London: Heinemann, 1983. 44-61.

"The Wrestling Match," *African American Literature: Voices in a Tradition*. Ed. William L. Andrews et als. New York: Holt, Rinehart and Winston, 1992. 885-941.

INTERVIEWS

Anon. "Two Faces of Emancipation," *Africa Woman* 2 (Jan. 1976): 48-49.

Anon. "Matchet's Diary: Buchi Emecheta," *West Africa* 6 Feb. 1978: 238-39.

Anon. *West Africa* 3 Apr. 1978: 671.

"It's Me Who's Changed," *Opzij* (Amsterdam) Sept. 1981.

Baker, Jo. "Buchi Emecheta," *Happy Home* March 1982: 4-5, 10-11.

Boss, Joyce. "Women and Empowerment: Interview with Buchi Emecheta," *Ufahamu: Journal of the African Activist Association* 16. 2 (1988): 93-100.

Bryce, Jane. "Feminism with a Small 'f'," *The Leveller* 30 Oct. 1981: 15.

—."Interview with Buchi Emecheta," *Marxism Today* May 1983: 34-35.

Davies, Wendy. "Two Nigerian Women Writers," *Centerpoint* 3.9 (1981).

Ezeigbo, Theodora Akachi. "Conversation With Buchi Emecheta," *The Independent*. Sept-Oct, 1993: 19-25.

Fraser, Gerald. "A Writer Who Seeks To Reconcile 2 Worlds," *The New York Times*, 2 June 1990.

James, Adeola. "Buchi Emecheta," *In Their Own Voices: African Women Writers Talk*. London: James Currey, 1990: 35-46.

Jussawalla, Feroza. "Interview with Buchi Emecheta," *Interviews with Writers of the Post-Colonial World*. Eds. Feroza Jussawalla and Reed Way Dasenbrock. Jackson and London: University of Mississippi Press, 1992: 82-91.

Kenall, Ena. "A Room of My Own: Buchi Emecheta," *Observer* 25 Mar. 1984: 46-47.

Obadina, Tunde. "A Worshipper from Afar," *Punch* (Nigeria) 17 May 1979.

Ravell-Pinto, Thelma. "Buchi Emecheta at Spelman College," *Sage* 2. 1 (1985): 50-51.

Umeh, Davidson and Marie. "An Interview with Buchi Emecheta," *Ba Shiru* 12. 2 (1985): 19-25.

Wilson, Judith. "Buchi Emecheta: Africa from a Woman's View," *Essence* Feb. 1980: 12, 14.

BROADCAST LITERATURE

"The Extraordinary People Show: Buchi Emecheta," B.B.C. Television Show, London, 1981.

"In the Light of Experience: Buchi Emecheta," B.B.C. Television Show, London, 1983.

CRITICISM OF EMECHETA'S WORK

Acholonu, Catherine. "Buchi Emecheta," *Perspectives on Nigerian Literature: 1700 to the Present*. Vol.II. Ed. Yemi Ogunbiyi. Lagos: Guardian Books, 1988. 216-222.

Agbasiere, Julie. "Social Integration of the Child in Buchi Emecheta's Novels," *Calabar Studies in African Literature Children and Literature in Africa*. Eds. Chidi Ikonné and Emelia Oko. Ibadan: Heinemann, 1992. 127-137.

Allan, Tuzyline J. "Feminist and Womanist Aesthetics: A Comparative Study," *Dissertations Abstracts International* (*DAI*) 51. 10 (1991): 3403A.

—. *Womanist and Feminist Aesthetics: A Comparative Review*. Ohio: Ohio University Press, 1995.

Amuta, Chidi. "The Nigeria Civil War and the Evolution of Nigerian Literature," *Canadian Journal of African Studies* 17. 1 (1983): 90-103.

Andrade, Susan Z. "Rewriting History, Motherhood, and Rebellion: Naming an African Woman's Literary Tradition," *Research in African Literatures* 21. 1 (1990): 91-110.

Asanbe, Joseph. "The Place of the Individual in the Novels of Chinua Achebe, T.M. Aluko, Flora Nwapa and Wole Soyinka," *Dissertation Abstracts International (DAI)* 40 (1980): 5447A.

Barthelemy, Anthony. "Western Time, African Lives: Time in the Novels of Buchi Emecheta," *Callaloo* 12. 3 (1989): 559-74.

Bazin, Nancy Topping. "Venturing into Feminist Consciousness: Two Protagonists from the Fiction of Buchi Emecheta and Bessie Head," *Sage* 2. 1 (Spring 1985): 32-36; rpt. *The Tragic Life: Bessie Head and Literature in Southern Africa*. Ed. Cecil Abrahams. Trenton, N.J.: Africa World Press, 1990. 45-58.

—. "Weight of Custom, Signs of Change: Feminism in the Literature of African Women," *World Literature Written in English* 25. 2 (1985): 183-97.

—. "Feminist Perspectives in African Fiction: Buchi Emecheta and Bessie Head," *Black Scholar* 17. 2 (1986): 34-40.

Birch, Eva Lennox. "Autobiography: The Art of Self-Definition," *Black Women's Writing*. Ed. Gina Wisker. London: Macmillan, 1993. 127-45.

Brown, Lloyd W. *Women Writers in Black Africa*. Westport, CT: Greenwood Press, 1981. 35-60.

Bruner, Charlotte. "The Other Audience: Children and the Example of Buchi Emecheta," *African Studies Review* 29.3 (1986): 129-40.

Bruner, Charlotte and David. "Buchi Emecheta and Maryse Conde: Contemporary Writing from Africa and the Caribbean," *World Literature Today* 59. 1 (1985): 9-13.

Bryce, Jane. "Conflict and Contradiction in Women's Writing on the Nigerian Civil War," *African Languages and Cultures* 4.1 (1991): 29-42.

Chinwezu. "Time of Troubles," *Times Literary Supplement* (London) 26 Feb. 1982: 228.

Christian, Barbara. "An Angle of Seeing: Motherhood in Buchi Emecheta's *The Joys of Motherhood* and Alice Walker's *Meridian*," Black Feminist Criticism. New York: Pergamon Press, 1985. 211-52.

Chukwuma, Helen. "Nigerian Female Authors, 1970 to the Present," *Matatu* (Germany) 1. 2 (1987): 23-42.

—. "Posivitism and the Female Crisis: The Novels of Buchi Emecheta," *Nigerian Female Writers: A Critical Perspective*.

Eds. Henrietta Otukunefor and Obiageli Nwodo. Ikeja, Lagos: Malthouse Press, 1989. 2-18.

—. "Voices and Choices: The Feminist Dilemma in Four African Novels," *Calabar Studies in African Literature: Literature and Black Aesthetics*. Ed. Ernest N. Emenyonu. Ibadan: Heinemann, 1990. 131-142.

Cosslett, Tess. "Childbirth on the National Health: Issues of Class, Race, and Gender Identity in Two Post-War British Novels," *Women's Studies* 19. 1 (1991): 99-119.

Coulon, Virginia. "Women at War: Nigerian Women Writers and the Civil War," *Commonwealth Essays and Studies* 13. 1 (1990): 1-12.

Crichton, Sarah. "Buchi Emecheta," *Publisher's Weekly* 11 June 1979: 10-11.

Dailly, Christophe. "*Second-Class Citizen* and *The Bride Price* de Buchi Emecheta (Review)," *Revue de litterature et d'esthetique negro-africaines* 2 (1979): 145-46.

Davies, Carole Boyce. "Motherhood in Male and Female Igbo Novels: Achebe, Emecheta, Nwapa and Nzekwu," *Ngambika: Studies of Women in African Literature*. Eds. Carole Boyce Davies and Anne Adams Graves. Trenton, NJ: Africa World Press, 1986. 241- 56.

—. "Writing Off Marginality, Minoring and Effacement," *Women's Studies International Forum*, 14. 4 (1991): 249-263.

—. "Private Selves and Public Spaces: Autobiography and the African Woman Writer," *Neohelicon* 17. 2 (1992): 183-210.

Davies, Wendy. "*Destination Biafra:* Mission Not Quite Accomplished," *Africa Now*. Mar. 1982: 75.

Davis, Christina. "Mother and Writer: Means of Empowerment in the Works of Buchi Emecheta," *Commonwealth Essays and Studies* 13. 1 (1990): 13-21.

Daymond, M.J. "Buchi Emecheta, Laughter and Silence: Changes in the Concepts of 'Woman,' 'Wife,' and 'Mother'," *Journal of Literary Studies* 4.1 (1988): 64-73.

Ebeogu, Afam. "Enter the Iconoclast: Buchi Emecheta and the Igbo Culture," *Commonwealth Essays and Studies* 7.2 (1985): 83-94.

Emenyonu, Ernest N. "Technique and Language in Buchi Emecheta's *The Bride Price, The Slave Girl* and *The Joys of Motherhood*," *Journal of Commonwealth Literature* 23. 1 (1988): 130-41.

Ezeigbo, Theodora Akachi. "Traditional Women's Institutions in

Igbo Society: Implications for the Igbo Female Writer,"
African Languages and Cultures (England) 3. 2 (1990): 149-65.

—. "Reflecting the Times: Radicalism in Recent Female-Oriented
Fiction in Nigeria," *Calabar Studies in African Literature:
Literature and Black Aesthetics.* Ed. Ernest N. Emenyonu.
Ibadan: Heinemann, 1990. 143-157.

Fido, Elaine Savory. "Mother/lands: Self and Separation in the
Works of Buchi Emecheta, Bessie Head and Jean Rhys,"
*Motherlands: Black Women's Writing from Africa, the Carib-
bean, and South Asia.* Ed. Susheila Nasta. London: The
Women's Press, 1991. 330-49.

Flewellen, Elinor C. "Assertiveness vs. Submissiveness in
Selected Works by African Women Writers," *Ba Shiru* 12. 2
(1985): 3-18.

Frank, Katherine. "The Death of the Slave Girl: African
Womanhood in the Novels of Buchi Emecheta," *World
Literature Written in English* 21. 3 (1982): 426-29.

—. "Feminist Criticism and the African Novel," *African Literature
Today* 14 (1984): 34-48.

—. "Women Without Men: The Feminist Novel in Africa," *African
Literature Today*, 15 (1987): 14-34.

Gleichmann, Gabi. "Ljuspunkter? Pa en gra melerad o? Om 'brit-
tiskt' och 'exotiskt' i litteraturen," *Bonniers Litterara Magasin*
(Sweden) 57. 3 (1988): 171-78.

Gover, Daniel. "Agbala and Nneka: Gender and Tragedy in
African Literature," *The Literary Griot*, 3. 2 (1991): 17-27.

Haraway, Donna Jeanne. "Reading Buchi Emecheta: Contests for
'Women's Experience' in Women's Studies," *Simians, Cyborgs,
and Women: The Re-invention of Nature.* London: Free
Association, 1990. 109-24.

Holloway, Karla F. C. *Moorings and Metaphors: Figures of Culture
and Gender in Black Women's Literature.* New Brunswick:
Rutgers University Press, 1992.

Iesué, Renata. "Romance and Reality: Popular Writing by
Nigerian Women," *Commonwealth Essays and Studies* 13. 1
(1990): 28-37.

Kandji, Diouf. "Des calvaires de la femme africaine dans la creation romanesque de Buchi Emecheta, Flora Nwapa, Ngugi
wa Thiong'o et Ahmadou Kourouma," *Bridges: A Senegalese
Journal of English Studies* 4 (1992): 113-133.

Katrak, Ketu H. "Womanhood/Motherhood: Variations on a
Theme in Selected Novels by Buchi Emecheta," *Journal of*

Commonwealth Literature 22. 1 (1987): 159-70.

Kemp, Yakini. "Romantic Love and the Individual in Novels by Mariama Bâ, Buchi Emecheta, and Bessie Head," *Obsidian* II 3.3 (1988): 1-16.

Kenyon, Olga. "Buchi Emecheta and the Black Immigrant Experience in Britain," *Writing Women: Contemporary Women Novelists*. London: Pluto Press, 1991. 113-33.

Kerridge, Roy. "More White Mischief," *Times Literary Supplement* 3 Feb. 1984: 116.

King, Bruce. "The New Internationalism: Shiva Naipaul, Salman Rushie, Buchi Emecheta, Timothy Mo and Kazuo Ishiguro," *The British and Irish Novel Since 1960*. Ed. James Acheson. New York: St. Martin's Press, 1991. 192-211.

Lauer, Margaret Read. "Buchi Emecheta's *The Bride Price* (Review), *World Literature Written in English* 16 (1977): 308-10.

Lazarus, Neil. "Africa," *Longman Anthology of World Literature by Women, 1875-1975*. Ed. Marian Arkin and Barbara Scholler. New York: Longman, 1989. 1061-72.

Levitov, Betty. "Social Theory and Literary Sources in the Novels of Buchi Emecheta," *Dissertations Abstracts International (DAI)* 44. 8 (1984): 2471A.

Lewis, Desiree. "Myths of Motherhood and Power: The Construction of 'Black Woman' in Literature," *English in Africa* (South Africa) 19. 1 (1992): 35-51.

Lindfors, Bernth. "Big Shots and Little Shots of the Anglophone African Literature Canon," *Commonwealth Essays and Studies* 14. 2 (1992): 89-97.

—. "The Famous Author's Reputation Test," *Kriteria: A Nigerian Journal of Literary Research*. 1.1 (1988): 25-33.

Little, Kenneth. *The Sociology of the Urban Woman's Image in African Literature*. London: Macmillan, 1980. 40-43, 113-14, 151, 156-57.

Lyonga, Pauline Nalova. "Uhamiri or a Feminist Approach to African Literature: An Analysis of Selected Texts by Women in Oral and Written Literature," *Dissertations Abstracts International (DAI)* 46. 7 (1986): 1940A.

McKnight, Reginald. "Lost in the Moder Country (Review)," *New York Times Book Review* 29 Apr. 1990: 30.

Martini, Jürgen. "Linking Africa and the West: Buchi Emecheta," *Festschrift zum 60. Geburtsatg von Carl Hoffman*. Ed. Franz Rottland. Hamburg: Buske, 1986. 223-33.

Newman, Judie. "The Untold Story and the Retold Story: Intertextuality in Post-Colonial Women's Writing," in *Motherlands: Black Women's Writing from Africa, the Caribbean and South Asia*. Ed. Susheila Nasta. London: The Women's Press, 1991. 24-42.

Ngcobo, Lauretta. "Introduction," *Let It Be Told: Black Women Writers in Britain*. London: Virago, 1987. 1-34.

Niven, Alistair. "The Family in Modern African Literature," *Ariel* 12. 3 (1981): 81-91.

Nkosi, Lewis. "Women in Literature," *Africa Woman* 6 (1976): 36-37.

Nnaemeka, Obioma. "Feminist Protest in Buchi Emecheta's Novels," *International Third World Studies Journal and Review*. 1.1(1989): 1-10.

—. "Feminisms, Rebellious Women, and Cultural Boundaries: Rereading Flora Nwapa and Her Compatriots." *Research in African Literatures*. 26.2 (Summer, 1995): 81-114.

—. "From Orality to Writing: African Women Writers and the (Re)Inscription of Womanhood," *Research in African Literatures*. 25 (1994): 137-157.

Nwankwo, Chimalum. "Emecheta's Social Vision: Fantasy or Reality?" *Ufahamu* 17. 1 (1988): 35-44.

Nwoga, Donatus Ibe. *The Supreme God as Stranger in Igbo Religious Thought*. Abiazu, Mbaise, Imo State: Hawk Press, 1984. 65.

Ogundipe-Leslie, Molara. "The Female Writer and Her Commitment," *African Literature Today* 15 (1987): 5-13.

—. *Re-Creating Ourselves: African Women & Critical Transformations*. Trenton, NJ: Africa World P, 1994.

Ogunyemi, Chikwenye. "Buchi Emecheta: The Shaping of a Self," *Komparatistische Hefte* 8 (1983): 65-77.

—. "Womanism: The Dynamics of the Contemporary Black Female Novel in English," *Signs: Journal of Women in Culture and Society* 11. 1 (1985): 63-80; Rpt. *Revising the Word and the World: Essays in Feminist Literary Criticism*. Eds. VèVè Clark Ruth-Ellen B. Joeres & Madelon Sprengnether. Chicago: University of Chicago Press, 1993.

Ohaeto, Ezenwa. "Replacing Myth with Myth: The Feminist Streak in Buchi Emecheta's *Double Yoke*," *Critical Theory and African Literature*. Ed. Ernest N. Emenyonu. Nigeria: Heinemann, Calabar Studies in African Literature, 1987. 214-24.

—. "Emecheta's Teenage Fiction: The Individual and Communal

Values in *The Wrestling Match* and *The Moonlight Bride*," *Commonwealth Essays and Studies* 13. 1 (1990): 22-27.

Ojo-Ade, Femi. "Female Writers, Male Critics," *African Literature Today* 13 (1983): 158-79.

—. "Women and the Nigerian Civil War: Buchi Emecheta and Flora Nwapa," *Etudes Germano-Africaines* 6 (1988): 75-86.

—. "Of Culture, Commitment, and Construction: Reflections on African Literature," *Transition: An International Review* 53 (1991): 4-24.

Oko, Emelia. "The Female Estate: A Study of Buchi Emecheta's Novels." Paper presented at the Literary Society of Nigeria Conference. University of Benin, February, 1984. 1-32.

Oku, Julia Inyang Essien. "Courtesans and Earthmothers: A Feminist Reading of Cyprian Ekwensi's *Jagua Nana's Daughter* and Buchi Emecheta's *The Joys of Motherhood*," *Critical Theory and African Literature*. Ed. Ernest N. Emenyonu. Nigeria: Heinemann, Calabar Studies in African Literature, 1987. 225-33.

Onwuhara, Kate C. "The Tension of Two Cultures: Ambivalence in Buchi Emecheta's Feminism," *Critical Theory and African Literature*. Ed. Ernest N. Emenyonu. Heinemann, Calabar Studies in African Literature, 1987. 207-13.

Otokunefor, Helen and Obiageli Nwodo, eds. *Nigerian Female Writers: A Critical Perspective*. Lagos: Malthouse, 1989.

Oyovbaire, Sam. "Who Is Lagging?" *West Africa*, 16 Nov. 1981: 2717-18.

Palmer, Eustace. "The Feminine Point of View: A Study of Buchi Emecheta's *The Joys of Motherhood*," *African Literature Today* 13 (1982): 38-55.

—. "A Powerful Female Voice in the African Novel: Introducing the Novels of Buchi Emecheta," *New Literature Review* 11 (1982): 21-33.

Perry, Alistair. "Buchi Emecheta—The Feminist Book Fair," *West Africa* 18 June 1984: 1263.

Peterson, Kirsten Holst. "Unpopular Opinions: Some African Women Writers," *Kunapipi* 7. 2-3 (1985): 107-20; rpt. *A Double Colonization: Colonial and Post-Colonial Women's Writing*. Ed. Kirsten Holst Peterson and Anna Rutherford. Mundelstrup, Denmark: Dangaroo Press, 1986. 10-22.

—. "Four Days in Sweden," *West Africa* 9 June 1986: 1212.

—. "Unorthodox Fictions about African Women." The Edward A. Clark Center for Australian Studies, Univ. of Texas at Austin,

International Literature in English: Essays on the Major Writers.
Ed. Robert L. Ross. New York: Garland, 1991. 283-92.

—. "Buchi Emecheta," *Twentieth-Century Caribbean and Black
African Writers First Series,* DLB 117. Ed. Bernth Lindfors and
Reinhard Sander. Detroit: Gale Research, 1992. 159-66.

Phillips, Caryl. "Survival with the British (Review)," *Book World*
22 Feb. 1990: B4.

Phillips, Maggie. "Engaging Dreams: Alternative Perspectives on
Flora Nwapa, Buchi Emecheta, Ama Ata Aidoo, Bessie Head
and Tsitsi Dangarembga's Writing." *Research in African
Literatures.* 25 (1994): 89-103.

Porter, Abioseh M. *"Second-Class Citizen*: The Point of Departure
for Understanding Buchi Emecheta's Major Fiction,"
International Fiction Review (Canada) 15. 2 (1988): 123-29.

Ross, Jacob. "Editorial, Don't Put Flowers On My Grave; Give Me
the Flowers Now," *Black Arts in London* 103. 1-3 (1988): 2.

Sample, Maxine J. Cornish. "The Representation of Space in
Selected Works by Bessie Head, Buchi Emecheta, and Flora
Nwapa," *Dissertations Abstracts International (DAI)* 51. 5
(1990): 1611A.

Sarr, Ndiawar. "The Female Protagonist as Part of a Traditional
Generation in *The Joys of Motherhood,*" *Bridges* (Senegal) 5
(1993): 25-34.

Schipper, Mineke. "Women and Literature in Africa," *Unheard
Words.* Ed. Mineke Schipper. London: Allison & Busby, 1984.
22-58.

Schmidt-Grözinger, Dagmar. "Problems of the Immigrant in
Commonwealth Literature: Kamala Markandaya, *The
Nowhere Man* and Buchi Emecheta, *Adah's Story,*" *Tensions
Between North and South: Studies in Modern Commonwealth
Literature and Culture.* Ed. Edith Metke. Würzburg:
Konigshausen and Neumann, 1990. 112-117.

Slomski, Genevieve. "Dialogue in the Discourse: A Study of
Revolt in Selected Fiction by African Women," *Dissertation
Abstracts International (DAI)* 47. 5 (1986): 1721A.

Solberg, Rolf. "The Woman of Black Africa, Buchi Emecheta: The
Woman's Voice in the New Nigerian Novel," *English Studies*
64. 3 (1983): 247-62.

Sougou, Omar. "The Experience of an African Woman in Britain:
A Reading of Buchi Emecheta's *Second-Class Citizen,*" *Crisis
and Creativity in the New Literatures in English.* Ed. Geoffrey
V. Davis and Hena Maes-Jelinek. Amsterdam: Rodopi, 1990.

511-22.

Stevens, Andrew. "Ripe for Promotion," *Sunday Times Magazine* (London), 13 Feb. 1983: 30-33.

Stratton, Florence. "The Shallow Grave: Archetypes of Female Experience in African Fiction," *Research in African Literatures* 19. 2 (1988): 143-69.

—. "Their New Sister: Buchi Emecheta and the Contemporary African Literary Tradition," *Contemporary African Literature and the Politics of Gender*. London: Routledge, 1994. 108-131.

Strummer, Peter. "Die Rassenfrage im Zeitgenossischen England: Realitat und narrative Reflexion," *Anglistik & Englischunterricht* (Germany), 16 (1982): 9-30.

—. "Buchi Emecheta und die Erfahrung der schwarzen Frau," *Drama in Commonwealth*. Ed. Gerhard Stilz Gunter. Tubingen: Narr, 1983. 91-102.

Taiwo, Oladele. "Culture, Tradition and Change in Buchi Emecheta's Novels," *Medium and Message* 1 (1981): 122-42.

—. *Female Novelists of Modern Africa*. London: Macmillan, 1984. 100-27.

Tapping, Craig. "Irish Feminism and African Tradition: A Reading of Buchi Emecheta's Novels," *Medium and Message* (Calabar) 1 (1981): 178-96.

Tax, Meredith. "Follow the Leader: Buchi Emecheta's Text Education," *Village Voice Literary Supplement* 85 (May 1990): 25.

Topouzis, Daphne. "Buchi Emecheta: An African Story-Teller," *Africa Today* 35.2 (1990): 67-70.

Ugwu, F.I. "Changing Images of Womanhood in Modern West African Fiction as Portrayed by Cheikh Hamidou Kane, Sembène Ousmane, and Buchi Emecheta," B.A. Thesis, University of Nigeria, Nsukka, 1980-81.

Umeh, Marie Linton. "African Women in Transition in the Novels of Buchi Emecheta," *Présence Africaine* 116 (1980): 190-201.

—. "*The Joys of Motherhood*: Myth or Reality?" *Colby Library Quarterly* 18.1 (1982): 39-46.

—. "Women and Social Realism in the Novels of Buchi Emecheta," *Dissertation Abstracts International (DAI)* 42. 11 (1982): 4825A.

—. "Reintegration with the Lost Self: A Study of Buchi Emecheta's *Double Yoke*," *Ngambika: Studies of Women in African Literature*. Eds. Carole Boyce Davies and Anne Adams Graves. Trenton, NJ: Africa World P, 1986. 173-80.

—. "A Comparative Study of the Idea of Motherhood in Two Third

World Novels," *CLA Journal* 31. 1 (1987): 31-43.

—. "The Poetics of Thwarted Sensitivity," *Critical Theory and African Literature*. Ed. Ernest N. Emenyonu. Calabar Studies in African Literature. Ibadan: Heinemann, 1987. 194-206.

Uyoh, Susan B. "Review of *Second-Class Citizen*," *The Gong Magazine* (Nigeria), May 1980, 34.

Walker, Alice. "A Writer Because Of, Not in Spite of Her Children," *MS* 4. 7 (Jan. 1976): 40.

Ward, Cynthia. "What They Told Buchi Emecheta: Oral Subjectivity and the Joys of 'Otherhood,'" *PMLA* 105 (1990): 83-97.

BIBLIOGRAPHICAL REFERENCES

Berrian, Brenda F. "Bibliographies of Nine Female African Writers," *Research in African Literatures* 12 (1981): 214-36.

—. comp. *Bibliography of African Women Writers and Journalists*. Washington, D.C.: Three Continents Press, 1985. 2, 6, 14, 19, 46, 55, 86, 97-98, 113, 120, 133, 160-64, 178, 183-84, 210, 218, 220, 221, 223, 231, 245, 246, 255.

—. "An Update: Bibliography of Twelve African Women Writers," *Research in African Literatures* 19. 2 (1988): 214-18.

Creque-Harris, Leah. "Literature of the Diaspora by Women of Color," *Sage* 3. 2 (1986): 61-64.

Mayes, Janis A., Debra Boyd-Buggs and Carole Boyce Davies, comps. "Studies of African Literatures and Oratures: An Annual Annotated Bibliography," *Callaloo* 10. 4 (1986): 761-820.

Mayes, Janis A. *et al.*, comps. "Studies of African Literatures and Oratures: An Annual Annotated Bibliography, 1987," *Callaloo* 11. 4 (1988): 846-903.

Zell, Hans, Carol Bundy and Virginia Coulon, comps. *A New Reader's Guide to African Literature*. New York: Africana, 1983. 150-51, 384.

CONTRIBUTORS

Julie Agbasiere is a Senior Lecturer in French at Nnamdi Azikiwe University in Awka, Nigeria. She is the author of several articles on African literature in books and journals including *Présence Francophone and Children and Literature in Africa*.

Tuzyline Jita Allan teaches in the Department of English at Baruch College of the City University of New York. She is the author of *Womanist and Feminist Aesthetics: A Comparative Review* and co-editor of *Literature Around the Globe*. Her literary criticism includes articles on Virginia Woolf, Alice Walker, Ama Ata Aidoo and Nella Larsen. She is currently working on a book-length study of gender and African nationalism.

Susan Arndt is a doctoral candidate at Humboldt University in Berlin, Germany where she also teaches African literatures. She has presented papers on African literatures at various conferences and published essays in scholarly journals globally.

Nancy Topping Bazin is a Professor of English at Old Dominion University in Virginia. Her books include *Virginia Woolf and the Androgynous Vision* (1973) and *Conversation With Nadine Gordimer* (1990). Her critical essays appear in scholarly journals, such as *The Black Scholar, Sage* and *World Literature Written in English*.

Brenda F. Berrian is an Associate Professor and Chair of the Department of Africana Studies at the University of Pittsburgh. She is the editor of *Bibliography of African Women Writers and Journalists* (1985) and *Bibliography of Women Writers from the Caribbean* (1989). Her articles on African-American, African and Caribbean writers appear in scholarly books and journals across the globe.

Rebecca A. Boostrom held positions as a Foreign Expert at Dalian Marine University, Dalian, China; Xian Foreign Languages Institute, Xian, China; and Qingdao University of Oceanography, Qingdao, China in the 1980s. Since 1987, she has been in the Graduate School at Indiana University, Bloomington, studying English literature, economics and business law. She received her B.S. degree in English literature from St. Louis University and her M.A. degree in English literature from Kansas State University.

Jacqueline Brice-Finch teaches Caribbean and African-American Literature at James Madison University in Virginia. She edited the special June, 1992, *MAWA Review* issue on papers presented at the 1991 "African Americans in Europe Conference," held in Paris. She also has biocritical essays on Caribbean and African American women in the *Dictionary of Literary Biography, Notable Black American Women,* and *The Oxford Companion to African American Literature.* Her articles have appeared in scholarly journals such as, *Caribbean Quarterly, Studies in the Literary Imagination, The Literary Griot and World Literature Today.* Her poems appear in *Crossing the Boundaries: Black Women's Writing,* edited by Carole Boyce Davies and Molara Ogundipe-Leslie.

Margaret Busby was born in Ghana, West Africa and was educated in England. On graduating from London University she co-founded the publishing company, *Allison and Busby* of which she was Editorial Director for twenty years (1967-87). She has written articles and reviews for numerous publications and was a contributor to the anthology, *Colours of a New Day: Writing for South Africa.* She is the editor of *Daughters of Africa: An International Anthology of Writing by Women of African Descent from the Ancient Egyptian to the Present* (1992).

Margaret J. Daymond teaches in the English Department at the University of Natal in Durban, South Africa, specializing in women's writing and feminist theory. She is an editor of the journal, *Current Writing: Text and Reception in Southern Africa* and is editing a feminist selection from this journal for Garland Publishing Inc. Recently, she has edited and written Introductions to Bessie Head's hitherto unpublished novella, *The Cardinals,* and Frances Colenso's *My Chief and I,* which first appeared in 1880 under the pseudonym Atherton Wylde. She has also published numerous articles on Southern African Writers in critical anthologies and in journals in Europe, North America and South Africa.

Ernest N. Emenyonu is the Provost of Alvan Ikoku College of Education in Owerri, Nigeria. His published books include *The Rise of the Igbo Novel* (1978), *The Essential Ekwensi* (1987), and *Uzo Remembers His Father* (1992). He is the founding editor of the *Calabar Studies in African Literature*. His critical essays have appeared in scholarly journals, such as *The Journal of Commonwealth Literature* and *African Literature Today*.

Theodora Akachi Ezeigbo is a Senior Lecturer in the Department of English at the University of Lagos in Lagos, Nigeria. Her published articles have appeared in journals and books, such as *African Languages and Cultures, LARES* and *Literature and Black Aesthetics*. She is also author of *Fact and Fiction in the Literature of the Nigerian Civil War*, two collections of short stories, *Rhythms of Life* (1992) and *Echoes in the Mind* (1994), and a children's book, *The Prize* (1994).

Ezenwa-Ohaeto is a Humboldt Research Fellow and Visiting Professor at the University of Mainz in Germany. His published books are *Songs of a Traveller* (1986), *I wan bi president* (1988), *Bullets for Buntings* (1989), and *Pieces of Madness* (1994). His critical essays have appeared in scholarly journals and books throughout the world.

Tunde Fatunde is a Senior Lecturer in Francophone Studies at the Lagos State University, Lagos, Nigeria. A sociologist of literature, he has staged and published plays in Nigerian pidgin English namely: *No More Oil-Boom, No Food No Country, Oga Na Tief-Man*, and *Water No Get Enemy*. His latest play in French is titled *Calebasse Cassée*. He is the author of several articles in journals and books.

John C. Hawley is an Associate Professor in the Department of English at Santa Clara University in Santa Clara, California. He is the editor of *Reform and Counterreform: Dialectics of the Word in Western Christianity Since Luther* (1994) and *Cross-Addressing: Discourse on the Border* (1995). He has published critical essays in *Research in African Literatures*.

J. O. J. Nwachukwu-Agbada teaches at Abia State University in Uturu, Nigeria. His first novel, *God's Big Toe*, was published in 1987.

A novelist, short story writer and poet, he is also a critical essayist. He has published short stories, poems and articles in academic journals in Africa, England, America, Germany, Canada and France.

Oladipo Joseph Ogundele attends John Jay College of Criminal Justice of the City University of New York. An avid student activist, he is listed in *Who's Who Among Students in American Colleges and Universities.* He is currently working on a book, *Traditional African Names and Their Origins.*

Obododimma Oha is currently a lecturer in the Department of English and Literary Studies at the University of Calabar, in Calabar, Nigeria. His research areas include language in politics, gender semantics and meaning in natural and literary discourses. He is also a playwright and a poet, with publications in literary journals and anthologies both in Nigeria and in the United States.

Abioseh Michael Porter, a native of Sierra Leone, West Africa, is an Associate Professor of Humanities at Drexel University in Philadelphia. His published articles and reviews appear in journals and books such as, *Research in African Literatures, International Fiction Review, ARIEL: A Review of International English Literature, World Literature Written in English,* and *Design and Intent in African Literatures.*

Shivaji Sengupta is Vice-President of Academic Policy at Boricua College and a Professor of English. He has published many articles on literary criticism and theory in American, British and Indian journals. He has published *A Critical Edition of John Dryden's MacFlecknoe* (1985) and *Absalom and Achitophel* (1991). Professor Sengupta has also published a book of poems, *Jonaki* (1980).

Christine W. Sizemore is a Professor of English at Spelman College, Atlanta, Georgia. She is author of *A Female Vision of the City: London in the Novels of Five British Women.* She has also written articles on twentieth-century novelists in such journals as *Modern Fiction Studies, Journal of Modern Literature, Frontiers,* and *The Doris Lessing Newsletter.* Recently she contributed an article on Virginia Woolf and Doris Lessing to *Breaking the Mold,* edited by Ruth Saxton and Jean Tobin.

478

Tom Spencer-Walters is an Associate Professor of Pan-African Literature at California State University. At present, he is a Visiting Professor of African Literature and Resident Director for the California State University International Program in Harare, Zimbabwe. He is author of *Shared Visions* and the editor of *Kapu-Sens: A Literary Review*. His scholarly articles and review essays appear in various literary journals.

Florence Stratton taught literature at Njala University College in Sierre Leone for nineteen years. Her book, *Contemporary African Literature and the Politics of Gender* was published in 1994 by Routledge. Her scholarly articles have appeared in *Research in African Literatures*. Currently, she is teaching at the University of Regina, Canada.

Marie Umeh teaches literatures of the Black World in the Department of English at John Jay College of Criminal Justice, CUNY, New York. She has published articles in journals and books, such as *Présence Africaine, The Colby Library Quarterly, Research in African Literatures, Calabar Studies in African Literature, Perspectives on Nigerian Literature, Sturdy Black Bridges: Visions of Women in Literature* and *Ngambika: Studies of Women in African Literature.*

Pauline Onwubiko Uwakweh is a doctoral candidate in the Department of African-American Studies at Temple University in Philadelphia. Formerly she taught in the Department of English and Literary Studies at the University of Calabar in Nigeria. She is the author of the novel, *Running for Cover* (1988), based on the Nigerian Civil War.

Index